TRANSLATOR AND SENIOR EDITOR:
Rabbi Israel V. Berman

MANAGING EDITOR:
Baruch Goldberg

EDITOR:
Rabbi David Strauss

ASSOCIATE EDITORS:
Rabbi Mendel Shapiro
Rabbi Moshe Sober

CONTRIBUTING EDITORS:
Rabbi Ḥayyim Ya'akov Bulka
Dr. Jeffrey M. Green
Rabbi Yair Kahn

COPY EDITORS:
Gershon Gale
Alec Israel
Michael Plotkin

BOOK DESIGNER:
Ben Gasner

GRAPHIC ARTIST:
Michael Etkin

TECHNICAL STAFF:
Moshe Greenvald
Meir Hanegbi
Chana Lawrence

Random House Staff

PRODUCTION MANAGER:
Linda Kaye

ART DIRECTOR:
Bernard Klein

CHIEF COPY EDITOR:
Mitchell Ivers

The Talmud
The Steinsaltz Edition

Volume III

Tractate Bava Metzia

Part III

VOLUME III
TRACTATE BAVA METZIA
PART III

RANDOM HOUSE
NEW YORK

THE TALMUD

תלמוד בבלי

THE STEINSALTZ EDITION

Commentary by Rabbi Adin Steinsaltz

 Published in the United States by Random House, Inc., New York, and simultaneously in Canada by Random House of Canada Limited, Toronto.

This work was originally published in Hebrew by The Israel Institute for Talmudic Publications, Jerusalem.

Library of Congress Cataloging-in-Publication Data

Talmud. English.
The Talmud : the Steinsaltz edition / the Talmud with commentary by
Adin Steinsaltz
p. cm.
ISBN 0-394-58234-9 (v. III)
I. Talmud—Commentaries I. Steinsaltz, Adin. II. Title.
BM499.5.E4 1989 296.1'250521—dc20 89-42911

Manufactured in the United States of America
98765432
First American Edition

This volume is dedicated in loving memory
of our fathers

שמואל לייב הכהן קען

Samuel Ralbe Kan

and

אליעזר ב"ר אברהם חיים שייקין

Lawrence Leo Shaykin

by their children

Norah and *Leonard Shaykin*

The Steinsaltz Talmud in English

The English edition of the Steinsaltz Talmud is a translation and adaptation of the Hebrew edition. It includes most of the additions and improvements that characterize the Hebrew version, but it has been adapted and expanded especially for the English reader. This edition has been designed to meet the needs of advanced students capable of studying from standard Talmud editions, as well as of beginners, who know little or no Hebrew and have had no prior training in studying the Talmud.

The overall structure of the page is similar to that of the traditional pages in the standard printed editions. The text is placed in the center of the page, and alongside it are the main auxiliary commentaries. At the bottom of the page and in the margins are additions and supplements.

The original Hebrew-Aramaic text, which is framed in the center of each page, is exactly the same as that in the traditional Talmud (although material that was removed by non-Jewish censors has been restored on the basis of manuscripts and old printed editions). The main innovation is that this Hebrew-Aramaic text has been completely vocalized and punctuated, and all the terms usually abbreviated have been fully spelled out. In order to retain the connection with the page numbers of the standard editions, these are indicated at the head of every page.

We have placed a *Literal Translation* on the right-hand side of the page, and its punctuation has been introduced into the Talmud text, further helping the student to orientate himself. The *Literal Translation* is intended to help the student to learn the meaning of specific Hebrew and Aramaic words. By comparing the original text with this translation, the reader develops an understanding of the Talmudic text and can follow the words and sentences in the original. Occasionally, however, it has not been possible to present an exact literal translation of the original text, because it is so different in structure from English. Therefore we have added certain auxiliary words, which are indicated in square brackets. In other cases it would make no sense to offer a literal translation of a Talmudic idiom, so we have provided a close English equivalent of the original meaning, while a note, marked "lit.," explaining the literal meaning of the words, appears in parentheses. Our purpose in presenting this literal translation was to give the student an appreciation of the terse and enigmatic nature of the Talmud itself, before the arguments are opened up by interpretation.

Nevertheless, no one can study the Talmud without the assistance of commentaries. The main aid to understanding the Talmud provided by this edition is the *Translation and Commentary,* appearing on the left side of the page. This is Rabbi Adin Steinsaltz's highly regarded Hebrew interpretation of the Talmud, translated into English, adapted and expanded.

This commentary is not merely an explanation of difficult passages. It is an integrated exposition of the entire text. It includes a full translation of the Talmud text, combined with explanatory remarks. Where the translation in the commentary reflects the literal translation, it has been set off in bold type. It has also been given the same reference numbers that are found both in the original text and in the literal translation. Moreover, each section of the commentary begins with a few words of the Hebrew-Aramaic text. These reference numbers and paragraph headings allow the reader to move from one part of the page to another with ease.

There are some slight variations between the literal translation and the words in bold face appearing in the *Translation and Commentary.* These variations are meant to enhance understanding, for a juxtaposition of the literal translation and the sometimes freer translation in the commentary will give the reader a firmer grasp of the meaning.

The expanded *Translation and Commentary* in the left-hand column is intended to provide a conceptual understanding of the arguments of the Talmud, their form, content, context, and significance. The commentary also brings out the logic of the questions asked by the Sages and the assumptions they made.

Rashi's traditional commentary has been included in the right-hand column, under the *Literal Translation.* We have left this commentary in the traditional "Rashi script," but all quotations of the Talmud text appear in standard square type, the abbreviated expressions have all been printed in full, and Rashi's commentary is fully punctuated.

Since the *Translation and Commentary* cannot remain cogent and still encompass all the complex issues that arise in the Talmudic discussion, we have included a number of other features, which are also found in Rabbi Steinsaltz's Hebrew edition.

At the bottom of the page, under the *Translation and Commentary,* is the *Notes* section, containing additional material on issues raised in the text. These notes deepen understanding of the Talmud in various ways. Some provide a deeper and more profound analysis of the issues discussed in the text, with regard to individual points and to the development of the entire discussion. Others explain Halakhic concepts and the terms of Talmudic discourse.

The *Notes* contain brief summaries of the opinions of many of the major commentators on the Talmud, from the period after the completion of the Talmud to the present. Frequently the *Notes* offer interpretations different from that presented in the commentary, illustrating the richness and depth of Rabbinic thought.

The *Halakhah* section appears below the *Notes.* This provides references to the authoritative legal decisions reached over the centuries by the Rabbis in their discussions of the matters dealt with in the Talmud. It explains what reasons led to these Halakhic decisions and the close connection between the Halakhah today and the Talmud and its various interpreters. It should be noted that the summary of the Halakhah presented here is not meant to serve as a reference source for actual religious practice but to introduce the reader to Halakhic conclusions drawn from the Talmudic text.

English commentary and expanded translation of the text, making it readable and comprehensible

Hebrew/Aramaic text of the Talmud, fully vocalized, and punctuated

Literal translation of the Talmud text into English

REALIA

קַלְתָּהּ **Her basket**. The source of this word is the Greek κάλαθος, kalathos, and it means a basket with a narrow base.

Illustration from a Greek drawing depicting such a basket of fruit.

CONCEPTS

פֵּאָה ***Pe'ah*. One of the presents left for the poor** (מַתְּנוֹת עֲנִיִּים). The Torah forbids harvesting "the corners of your field," so that the produce left standing may be harvested and kept by the poor (Leviticus 19:9).

The Torah did not specify a minimum amount of produce to be left as *pe'ah*. But the Sages stipulated that it must be at least one-sixtieth of the crop.

Pe'ah is set aside only from crops that ripen at one time and are harvested at one time. The poor are allowed to use their own initiative to reap the *pe'ah* left in the fields. But the owner of an orchard must see to it that each of the poor gets a fixed share of the *pe'ah* from places that are difficult to reach. The poor come to collect *pe'ah* three times a day. The laws of *pe'ah* are discussed in detail in tractate *Pe'ah*.

Marginal notes provide essential background information

TRANSLATION AND COMMENTARY

[1]**and her husband threw her a bill of divorce into her lap or into her basket**, which she was carrying on her head, [2]would you say **here, too,** that **she would not be divorced**? Surely we know that the law is that she *is* divorced in such a case, as the Mishnah (*Gittin* 77a) states explicitly!

אָמַר לֵיהּ [3]Rav Ashi **said** in reply to Ravina: The woman's **basket is** considered to be **at rest, and it is she who walks beneath it**. Thus the basket is considered to be a "stationary courtyard," and the woman acquires whatever is thrown into it.

MISHNAH הָיָה רוֹכֵב [4]**If a person was riding on an animal and he saw an ownerless object** lying on the ground, **and he said to another person** standing nearby, **"Give** that object **to me,"** [5]if **the other person took** the ownerless object **and said, "I have acquired it for myself,"** [6]he has **acquired it** by lifting it up, even though he was not the first to see it, and the rider has no claim to it. [7]But **if, after he gave** the object **to** the rider, the person who picked it up **said, "I acquired** the object **first,"** [8]**he** in fact **said nothing**. His words are of no effect, and the rider may keep it. Since the person walking showed no intention of acquiring the object when he originally picked it up, he is not now believed when he claims that he acquired it first. Indeed, even if we maintain that when a person picks up an ownerless object on behalf of someone else, the latter does *not* acquire it automatically, here, by *giving* the object to the rider, he makes a gift of it to the rider.

GEMARA תְּנַן הָתָם [9]**We have learned elsewhere** in a Mishnah in tractate *Pe'ah* (4:9): **"Someone who gathered *pe'ah*** — produce which by Torah law [Leviticus 23:22] is left unharvested in the corner of a field by the owner of the field, to be gleaned by the poor — **and said, 'Behold, this *pe'ah*** which I have gleaned **is** intended **for so-and-so the poor man,'** [10]**Rabbi Eliezer says:** The person who gathered the *pe'ah* **has acquired it**

בִּרְשׁוּת הָרַבִּים [1]וְזָרַק לָהּ גֵּט לְתוֹךְ חֵיקָהּ אוֹ לְתוֹךְ קַלְתָּהּ — [2]הָכָא נַמִי דְּלָא מִגָּרְשָׁה?
[3]אֲמַר לֵיהּ: קַלְתָּהּ מֵינָח נַיְיחָא, וְאִיהִי דְּקָא מְסַגְּיָא מִתּוּתָהּ.

מִשְׁנָה [4]הָיָה רוֹכֵב עַל גַּבֵּי בְהֵמָה וְרָאָה אֶת הַמְּצִיאָה, וְאָמַר לַחֲבֵירוֹ "תְּנָה לִי", [5]נְטָלָהּ וְאָמַר, "אֲנִי זָכִיתִי בָּהּ", [6]זָכָה בָּהּ. [7]אִם, מִשֶּׁנְּתָנָהּ לוֹ, אָמַר, "אֲנִי זָכִיתִי בָּהּ תְּחִלָּה", [8]לֹא אָמַר כְּלוּם.

גְּמָרָא [9]תְּנַן הָתָם: "מִי שֶׁלִּיקֵּט אֶת הַפֵּאָה וְאָמַר, 'הֲרֵי זוֹ לִפְלוֹנִי עָנִי', [10]רַבִּי אֱלִיעֶזֶר

LITERAL TRANSLATION

in a public thoroughfare [1]and [her husband] threw her a bill of divorce into her lap or into her basket, [2]here, too, would she not be divorced?

[3]He said to him: Her basket is at rest, and it is she who walks beneath it.

MISHNAH [4][If a person] was riding on an animal and he saw a found object, and he said to another person, "Give it to me," [5][and the other person] took it and said, "I have acquired it," [6]he has acquired it. [7]If, after he gave it to him, he said, "I acquired it first," [8]he said nothing.

GEMARA [9]We have learned there: "Someone who gathered *pe'ah* and said, 'Behold this is for so-and-so the poor man,' [10]Rabbi Eliezer says:

RASHI

קלתה — סל שעל ראשה, שנותנת בה כלי מלאכתה וטווי שלה. **הכי נמי דלא הוי גיטא** — והאנן תנן במסכת גיטין (עז,א): זרק לה גיטה לתוך חיקה או לתוך קלתה — הרי זו מגורשת!

משנה לא אמר כלום — דאפילו אמרינן המגביה מציאה לחבירו לא קנה חבירו, כיון דיהבה ליה — קנייה ממה נפשך. אי קנייה קמא דלא מתכוין להקנות לחבירו — הא יהבה ניהליה במתנה. ואי לא קנייה קמא משום דלא היה מתכוין לקנות — הויא ליה הפקר עד דמטא לידיה דהאי, וקנייה האי במאי דעקרה מידיה דקמא לשם קנייה.

גמרא מי שליקט את הפאה — אדם בעלמא שאינו בעל שדה. דאי בבעל שדה — לא אמר רבי אליעזר זכה. דליכא למימר "מגו דזכי לנפשיה", דאפילו הוא עני מוזהר הוא שלא ללקט פאה משדה שלו, כדאמר בשחיטת חולין (קלא,ב): "לא תלקט לעני" — להזהיר עני על שלו.

Hebrew commentary of Rashi, the classic explanation that accompanies all editions of the Talmud

Numbers link the three main sections of the page and allow readers to refer rapidly from one to the other

NOTES

מִי שֶׁלִּיקֵּט אֶת הַפֵּאָה **If a person gathered *pe'ah*.** According to *Rashi*, the Mishnah must be referring to someone other than the owner of the field. By Torah law the owner of a field is required to separate part of his field as *pe'ah*, even if he himself is poor, and he may not take the *pe'ah* for himself. Therefore the "since" (מגו) argument

Notes highlight points of interest in the text and expand the discussion by quoting other classical commentaries

HALAKHAH

קַלְתָּהּ **A woman's basket.** "If a man throws a bill of divorce into a container that his wife is holding, she thereby acquires the bill of divorce and the divorce takes effect." (*Shulḥan Arukh, Even HaEzer* 139:10.)

הַמְלַקֵּט פֵּאָה עֲבוּר אַחֵר **A person who gathered *pe'ah* for someone else.** "If a poor person, who is himself entitled to collect *pe'ah*, gathered *pe'ah* for another poor person, and said, 'This *pe'ah* is for X, the poor person,' he acquires the *pe'ah* on behalf of that other poor person. But if the person who collected the *peah* was wealthy, he does not acquire the *pe'ah* on behalf of the poor person. He must give it instead to the first poor person who appears in the field," following the opinion of the Sages, as explained by Rabbi Yehoshua ben Levi. (*Rambam, Sefer Zeraim, Hilkhot Mattenot Aniyyim* 2:19.)

On the outer margin of the page, factual information clarifying the meaning of the Talmudic discussion is presented. Entries under the heading *Language* explain unusual terms, often borrowed from Greek, Latin, or Persian. *Sages* gives brief biographies of the major figures whose opinions are presented in the Talmud. *Terminology* explains the terms used in the Talmudic discussion. *Concepts* gives information about fundamental Halakhic principles. *Background* provides historical, geographical, and other information needed to understand the text. *Realia* explains the artifacts mentioned in the text. These notes are sometimes accompanied by illustrations.

The best way of studying the Talmud is the way in which the Talmud itself evolved – a combination of frontal teaching and continuous interaction between teacher and pupil, and between pupils themselves.

This edition is meant for a broad spectrum of users, from those who have considerable prior background and who know how to study the Talmud from any standard edition to those who have never studied the Talmud and do not even know Hebrew.

The division of the page into various sections is designed to enable students of every kind to derive the greatest possible benefit from it.

For those who know how to study the Talmud, the book is intended to be a written Gemara lesson, so that, either alone, with partners, or in groups, they can have the sense of studying with a teacher who explains the difficult passages and deepens their understanding both of the development of the dialectic and also of the various approaches that have been taken by the Rabbis over the centuries in interpreting the material. A student of this kind can start with the Hebrew-Aramaic text, examine Rashi's commentary, and pass on from there to the expanded commentary. Afterwards the student can turn to the Notes section. Study of the *Halakhah* section will clarify the conclusions reached in the course of establishing the Halakhah, and the other items in the margins will be helpful whenever the need arises to clarify a concept or a word or to understand the background of the discussion.

For those who do not possess sufficient knowledge to be able to use a standard edition of the Talmud, but who know how to read Hebrew, a different method is proposed. Such students can begin by reading the Hebrew-Aramaic text and comparing it immediately to the *Literal Translation*. They can then move over to the *Translation and Commentary*, which refers both to the original text and to the *Literal Translation*. Such students would also do well to read through the *Notes* and choose those that explain matters at greater length. They will benefit, too, from the terms explained in the side margins.

The beginner who does not know Hebrew well enough to grapple with the original can start with the *Translation and Commentary*. The inclusion of a translation within the commentary permits the student to ignore the *Literal Translation*, since the commentary includes both the Talmudic text and an interpretation of it. The beginner can also benefit from the *Notes*, and it is important for him to go over the marginal notes on the concepts to improve his awareness of the juridical background and the methods of study characteristic of this text.

Apart from its use as study material, this book can also be useful to those well versed in the Talmud, as a source of additional knowledge in various areas, both for understanding the historical and archeological background and also for an explanation of words and concepts. The general reader, too, who might not plan to study the book from beginning to end, can find a great deal of interesting material in it regarding both the spiritual world of Judaism, practical Jewish law, and the life and customs of the Jewish people during the thousand years (500 B.C.E.–500 C.E.) of the Talmudic period.

THE TALMUD

THE STEINSALTZ EDITION

VOLUME III

TRACTATE BAVA METZIA

PART III

Introduction to Chapter Four

הַזָּהָב

"And if you sell something to your neighbor, or buy something from your neighbor's hand, do not oppress one another" (Leviticus 25:14).

"And you shall not oppress one another, but you shall fear your God, for I am the Lord your God" (Leviticus 25:17).

"You shall neither vex a stranger nor oppress him, for you were strangers in the land of Egypt" (Exodus 22:20).

"And if a stranger sojourns with you in your land, you shall not vex him" (Leviticus 19:33).

The two principal themes of this chapter are the rules governing the acquisition of movable property, and the laws of *ona'ah* (which concern financial and verbal wrongdoing). One of the general questions arising in connection with the laws of acquisition is how and when acquisition takes place — i.e., at precisely what point does the transfer of ownership take effect when property is purchased? Does the buyer gain title to the property as soon as he pays for his purchase, or only after he takes physical possession of the merchandise? If monetary payment cannot effect a sale, does it have any legal validity? And is a verbal agreement between the buyer and the seller in any way binding? The chapter opens with the specific issue of the rules governing an exchange of coins, and deals with a fundamental problem: How is money defined? Is "money" an absolute concept, which invariably refers to a particular means of acquisition, or is it a relative notion, the definition of which changes with the circumstances? This question has ramifications with regard to the laws of acquisition and of *ona'ah*, as well as to the laws of interest (discussed in the next chapter).

The laws of *ona'ah* fall into two categories: (1) Monetary wrongdoing, whether because the seller overcharged or the buyer underpaid. (2) Verbal wrongdoing, i.e., taunting other people and hurting their feelings.

Numerous questions arise in connection with the Torah's prohibition against financial wrongdoing: Precisely what is considered overcharging? Does the prohibition apply only if one overcharges a fixed sum (or by a fixed percentage), or even in a case of minimal overcharging? What legal remedies exist when one overcharges or underpays? Is fraud in business an offense punishable in court, or is it merely subject to civil litigation? And is a sale entailing fraud valid, or void? Must the party who was defrauded be reimbursed, and if so, to what extent? Does the prohibition against *ona'ah* apply equally to all people and transactions, or not?

Verbal oppression is also examined. Precisely what is considered verbal wrongdoing? Are there cases where this is permitted, and if so, what are they? Does this prohibition apply equally to all people?

These general issues, along with their specific applications, are dealt with in this chapter.

TRANSLATION AND COMMENTARY

MISHNAH According to the Halakhah, mere agreement between two parties to transfer ownership of an item of property does not by itself finalize the transaction, and either party can cancel the agreement. For the agreement to become legally enforceable, a formal act of acquisition must be performed. The act of acquisition — there are several kinds, depending on the circumstances — is called the *kinyan* (קִנְיָן). Only after the *kinyan* has been performed does the object of the transaction become the legal property of the buyer. After that point, neither party can cancel the agreement. Our Mishnah and Gemara discuss the application of three modes of acquisition to the purchase of movable property: money, i.e., paying for the article; *meshikhah* (מְשִׁיכָה), drawing the article into the physical possession of the buyer; and *ḥalifin* (חֲלִיפִין), the exchange or barter of one article for another.

The point of departure for understanding our Mishnah is that payment of money is not a valid mode of acquisition for movable property. Even after payment has been made, the seller remains the owner of the property, and both he and the buyer may still withdraw from the sale. The sale takes legal effect only when the buyer performs a valid *kinyan* such as *meshikhah,* taking hold of the merchandise and drawing it into his possession. Once *meshikah* has been performed, the merchandise is acquired and the ownership of it passes from the seller to the buyer. Neither party may then retract, and the buyer owes the seller the price of the merchandise.

The same principles also apply to buying and selling coins. In Mishnaic and Talmudic times, coins made of different metals — gold, silver and copper — circulated side by side. The less valuable coins were more suitable for daily use, whereas the more valuable coins were more suitable for saving and transport. Hence, coins of different metals were frequently bought and sold. Since *meshikhah* must be performed on the merchandise being bought, and not on the money used as payment, a question arises with regard to the buying and selling of coins: Which of the two coins is considered the merchandise upon which the *meshikhah* must be performed, and which is considered the money, the payment of which does not finalize the transaction?

הַזָּהָב קוֹנֶה אֶת הַכֶּסֶף [1]The Mishnah begins: **Gold acquires silver.** When gold coins are exchanged for silver coins, the gold coins are considered the merchandise and the silver coins are considered the money offered as the purchase price for the gold. Accordingly, the party who seeks to acquire the gold coins is regarded as the buyer in this transaction, and the sale takes effect when he performs *meshikhah* and draws the gold coins into his possession. After that time, neither party can retract, and the buyer of the gold coins is obligated to give the other party the silver coins as payment. [2]**But silver does not acquire gold.** If the party who seeks to acquire the gold gives the other party the silver coins first, his action does not effect the sale, because the silver is considered the purchase money, and the payment of money does not effect a sale. Both parties may therefore still withdraw from the transaction.

LITERAL TRANSLATION

MISHNAH [1]Gold acquires silver, [2]but silver does not acquire gold.

הַזָּהָב

[1]קוֹנֶה אֶת הַכֶּסֶף, [2]וְהַכֶּסֶף אֵינוֹ קוֹנֶה אֶת הַזָּהָב.

RASHI

משנה הזהב קונה את הכסף – הלוקח דינרי זהב טבועים בדינרי כסף, ונתן לו דינרי זהב – משיכת הזהב קונה את הכסף לבעל הזהב, ונתחייב לו זה משקיבל דינרי זהב לתת לו דינרי הכסף, ואינו יכול לחזור בו. אבל הכסף אינו קונה את הזהב, שאם נתן לו דינרי הכסף תחילה – לא קנה, ויכולין שניהם לחזור. דמטבע כסף הוי מעות משום דחריפי לינתן בהוצאה, ודינר זהב אינו אלא כשאר מטלטלין. ופירות ומעות אינן קונות עד שימשוך המטלטלין. אבל משיכת המטלטלין – קונה, ואין אחד מהם יכול לחזור בו. ובגמרא מפרש טעמא, איכא דיליף משיכה מן התורה, ואיכא דמוקי לה בתקנתא דרבנן.

NOTES

הַזָּהָב קוֹנֶה אֶת הַכֶּסֶף **Gold acquires silver.** When one kind of money is exchanged for another, how do we determine which is the commodity and which is the means of payment? The Halakhah developed rules for determining this. For example, if a person wishes to purchase foreign currency, the law is that the more current and usable currency is considered to be the money, whereas the other currency is the commodity. In other words, the local currency has the status of money, and the foreign currency has the status of merchandise. Thus, handing over the local currency is *not* an act of acquisition, as the foreign currency is merchandise, and the rule is that movable property can acquire money, but money cannot acquire movable property.

In Talmudic times, the value of a coin had a strong connection to its metallic content. This meant that the

HALAKHAH

הַזָּהָב קוֹנֶה אֶת הַכֶּסֶף **Gold acquires silver.** "All types of coins (no matter what metal they were coined from) are considered money in relation to other types of merchandise. However, gold coins are considered merchandise vis-à-vis

CONCEPTS

קִנְיָן **Acquisition, mode of acquisition.** A formal procedure to render an agreement legally binding. Usually *kinyan* refers to a mode of acquisition. After the act of *kinyan* has taken place, the object is legally the property of the buyer. Neither party can then withdraw from the agreement, regardless of any change in market values, or any unanticipated change in the article itself. Even if the object were to be destroyed while still in the possession of the seller, the buyer would not be entitled to get his money back. Depending on the nature of the object, various modes of acquisition confer ownership, such as *meshikhah* (מְשִׁיכָה) — pulling the article; *mesirah* (מְסִירָה) — transfer; *ḥazakah* (חֲזָקָה) — performing an act of taking possession; *hagbahah* (הַגְבָּהָה) — lifting the article; and *ḥalifin* (חֲלִיפִין) — exchange or barter. On occasion, more than one action may be involved in the acquisition of an object. For example, money may be paid and the object may then be picked up. The Sages discussed the question of which act is the legal *kinyan.* In general, the payment of money is not a valid *kinyan* for acquiring movable property. The word *kinyan* may also refer to taking possession of abandoned property, or to the precise moment when a forbidden action such as theft or robbery is said to have taken place. The term *kinyan* also applies to the conclusion and ratification of an action not directly connected to purchase and sale, such as performing a *kinyan* to confirm one's acceptance of responsibility with regard to a future action.

BACKGROUND

קִנְיָן **Acquisition, mode of acquisition.** The term קִנְיָן is derived from the Hebrew root קנה, meaning to purchase or acquire. In Halakhic literature, the term refers to specific formal procedures that render a sales agreement legally enforceable, or that conclude and ratify legal undertakings not directly connected to purchase and sale. In its legal sense, the term קִנְיָן is not

¹הַנְּחֹשֶׁת קוֹנָה אֶת הַכֶּסֶף, ²וְהַכֶּסֶף אֵינוֹ קוֹנֶה אֶת הַנְּחֹשֶׁת. ³מָעוֹת הָרָעוֹת קוֹנוֹת אֶת הַיָּפוֹת, ⁴וְהַיָּפוֹת אֵינָן קוֹנוֹת אֶת הָרָעוֹת. ⁵אֲסִימוֹן קוֹנֶה אֶת הַמַּטְבֵּעַ,

LITERAL TRANSLATION

¹Copper acquires silver, ²but silver does not acquire copper.

³Bad coins acquire good [coins], ⁴but good [coins] do not acquire bad [coins].

⁵An *asimon* acquires a coin,

RASHI

הנחושת — פרוטות של נחושת. **קונה את הכסף** — דינרי של כסף או כל מטבע של כסף, כולן טעם אחד להם: מי שטבעו חשוב לטבוע — הוי מעות ואינו קונה, ומי שאין טבעו חשוב וחריף — הוי כפירות, ומשיכתן הוא קיום דבר. **מעות הרעות** — שנפסלו. **אסימון** — שאין עליו צורה, *פלדו״ן בלעז, זוזים עגולין ומוכנים לצור עליהם את הצורה בחותם שקורין **קוי״ן.

TRANSLATION AND COMMENTARY

הַנְּחֹשֶׁת קוֹנָה אֶת הַכֶּסֶף ¹Similarly, **copper acquires silver.** When copper coins are exchanged for silver ones, the copper coins are considered the merchandise. When the party who seeks to acquire the copper coins draws them into his possession, the sale takes effect and he becomes obligated to give the other party the silver coins as payment. ²**But silver does not acquire copper.** If the party who seeks to acquire the copper coins gives the other party the silver coins first, his action does not effect the sale, because the silver is considered the money used as payment, and the payment of money does not effect a sale. Both parties may therefore still withdraw from the transaction.

מָעוֹת הָרָעוֹת קוֹנוֹת אֶת הַיָּפוֹת ³Similarly, **bad coins acquire good coins.** Coins which have been invalidated by the government, or which have become worn through use, or which are not widely accepted in a particular place, are considered the merchandise when they are exchanged for good coins. When the party who seeks to acquire the bad coins draws them into his possession, the sale takes effect and he must give the other party the good currency as payment. ⁴**But good coins do not acquire bad coins.** In a transaction involving the exchange of good coins for bad coins, the good coins are considered the purchase money; and their payment does not by itself effect the sale. Even after the good coins are delivered as payment, both parties may still withdraw from the transaction.

אֲסִימוֹן קוֹנֶה אֶת הַמַּטְבֵּעַ ⁵**An *asimon* acquires a minted coin.** Round pieces of unminted metal, called *asimonim* in Hebrew, are considered merchandise when exchanged for minted coins. When the party who seeks to acquire the unminted coins draws them into his possession, the sale takes effect and he must give

NOTES

relative values of coins fluctuated with changes in the price of metals, and it also meant that certain types of coins were more practical for day-to-day use, and others for saving. For example, a coin made of a soft metal like gold wears down with constant use, and a coin made of a metal subject to corrosion like copper would be likely to deteriorate if buried in the ground. Thus, the question arose: When exchanging coins made of different metals, which is classified as the money and which as the commodity? The answer to this question is the topic of our Mishnah.

As explained in the commentary, silver does not acquire gold because silver in relation to gold is regarded as money. For reasons explained by the Gemara (below, 47b), the payment of money is *not* a valid act of acquisition in the purchase of movable property. To effect such a purchase, a separate act of acquisition — *kinyan* (קִנְיָן) — must be performed. Conversely, once an effective act of acquisition has been performed, the transaction is legally finalized, even if no money has yet changed hands.

Small movable objects are usually acquired by picking them up and physically taking possession of them — an act called *meshikhah* (מְשִׁיכָה) — "pulling" or "drawing towards oneself" — in Talmudic literature. Hence, the moment the buyer picks up the purchased article, the transaction is finalized, even if money has not yet changed hands.

In addition to finalizing the purchase, the act of drawing the merchandise also finalizes any terms of sale that are part of the transaction. Thus, for example, even if no money has yet been paid, changes may not be made in the purchase price or conditions of payment.

In summary, the act of *meshikhah* on a purchased object is an act of acquisition that transfers ownership of the object. By contrast, the act of payment is not an act of acquisition at all. This is what the Mishnah means when it says that movable objects acquire coins, but coins do not acquire movable objects.

אֲסִימוֹן **An *asimon*.** Our description of *asimon* in the commentary follows *Rashi,* who explains that the *asimon* is an unstamped piece of metal in the shape of a coin.

Because the values of Talmudic coins were closely tied to

HALAKHAH

silver coins. Hence, if a person draws gold coins into his possession, in payment for which he has promised silver, he is obliged to pay either new or old silver coins, in accordance with whatever was agreed upon. However, if he gives silver coins as payment for gold coins, he does not acquire the gold coins until he draws them into his possession." (*Shulḥan Arukh, Ḥoshen Mishpat* 203:4.)

הַנְּחֹשֶׁת קוֹנָה אֶת הַכֶּסֶף **Copper acquires silver.** "Copper coins are considered merchandise in relation to silver coins. Therefore by drawing the copper coins into his possession, the buyer obligates himself to give the agreed amount of silver coins in exchange." (Ibid., 203:5.)

מָעוֹת הָרָעוֹת וּמָעוֹת הַיָּפוֹת **Bad coins and good coins.** "Bad coins, i.e., coins that have been canceled by the

related to the payment of money.

The student is cautioned against the confusion that may ensue if the term קִנְיָן — or acquisition — is understood in our Mishnah in its colloquial rather than its legal sense. The rule "gold acquires silver" does not mean that gold may serve as payment for silver, but rather that the performance of an act of acquisition on gold coins legally finalizes a transaction involving the exchange of gold and silver coins, and obligates the buyer to pay for the gold.

מָעוֹת הָרָעוֹת **Bad coins.** This expression refers to coinage which, for various reasons, people are unwilling to use, or which they attempt to exchange for other types of money.

Essentially there are three kinds of bad coinage: (1) Coins which are in principle valid, but which have been worn smooth through use. Because the value of a coin depended on its metallic content, worn coins were worth less than newly minted ones. Nevertheless, not everyone took care to avoid accepting slightly worn coins, and generally it was possible to use them. Naturally, however, after a coin became worn beyond a certain point, it was no longer worth its nominal value (see below, 51b, for a detailed discussion of this issue). (2) Coins which are intrinsically valuable but whose use has been prohibited by the government for political or economic reasons (מַטְבֵּעַ שֶׁפְּסָלַתּוּ מַלְכוּת). (3) Legal tender which has been devalued by the authorities, so that citizens do not wish to accept it at its nominal value (מַטְבֵּעַ שֶׁפְּסָלַתּוּ מְדִינָה). Regarding the latter two categories, see below, 46b.

LANGUAGE

אֲסִימוֹן **Asimon.** The source of this word is the Greek ἄσημον, *asimon*, meaning a coin on which no legend has been inscribed.

LANGUAGE (RASHI)

פלדו״ן* From the Old French *fladon*, "a round piece of uncoined metal."

קוי״ן** From the Old French *coinz*, a die used for minting coins.

וְהַמַּטְבֵּעַ אֵינוֹ קוֹנֶה אֶת אֲסִימוֹן.[1]
מִטַּלְטְלִין קוֹנִין אֶת הַמַּטְבֵּעַ,[2]
מַטְבֵּעַ אֵינוֹ קוֹנֶה אֶת הַמִּטַּלְטְלִין.[3]
זֶה הַכְּלָל: כָּל הַמִּטַּלְטְלִים קוֹנִין זֶה אֶת זֶה.[4]
כֵּיצַד?[5] מָשַׁךְ הֵימֶנּוּ פֵּירוֹת וְלֹא נָתַן לוֹ מָעוֹת,[6] אֵינוֹ יָכוֹל לַחֲזוֹר בּוֹ.[7] נָתַן לוֹ מָעוֹת וְלֹא מָשַׁךְ הֵימֶנּוּ פֵּירוֹת,[8] יָכוֹל לַחֲזוֹר בּוֹ.[9]

LITERAL TRANSLATION

[1] but a coin does not acquire an *asimon*.

[2] Movable goods acquire coin, [3] [but] coin does not acquire movable goods.

[4] This is the rule: All movable goods acquire each other.

[5] How so? [6] [If] he [the buyer] drew produce (lit., "fruit") from him [the seller] but did not give him money, [7] he cannot retract. [8] [If] he gave him money but did not draw produce from him, [9] he can retract.

RASHI

כל המטלטלין קונין זה את זה – בין בתורת חליפין, שהחליף אלו באלו, כיון שמשך האחד – קנה חבירו את שלו. בין בתורת דמים: בכמה תתן לי את שלך? – בכך וכך. וזה חוזר ואומר לו: בכמה תתן לי שלך? בכך וכך. ונתרצו, ומשך האחד – נתקיימו הדברים. והאי "כל" – לאתויי אפילו כיס מלא מעות בכיס מלא מעות, כדריש לקיש בגמרא. **יכול לחזור בו** – זה וזה.

TRANSLATION AND COMMENTARY

the other party the minted coins as payment. [1] **But a minted coin does not acquire an *asimon*.** In a transaction involving the exchange of minted coins for unminted ones, the minted coins are considered the purchase money; their payment does not by itself effect the sale. Even after the minted coins are delivered as payment for the unminted coins, both parties may still withdraw from the transaction.

מִטַּלְטְלִין קוֹנִין אֶת הַמַּטְבֵּעַ [2] **Movable goods acquire coins,** [3] **but coins do not acquire movable goods.** In a transaction involving the use of money in the purchase of movable property, the movable property is considered the merchandise. By drawing the movable property into his possession, the buyer effects the sale and becomes obliged to pay the seller. Payment of the money without *meshikhah* of the movable property is not in itself sufficient to effect the sale.

זֶה הַכְּלָל [4] The preceding cases all illustrate the same principle: *meshikhah* performed on the merchandise effects the sale and obligates the buyer to pay for his purchase. The Mishnah now introduces a second mode of acquisition and states: **This is the rule. All** kinds of **movable property acquire each other**, whether by means of *meshikhah* or by means of the mode of acquisition known as *ḥalifin* (barter, or exchanging one article for another). When two parties agree to exchange goods by means of *ḥalifin*, once one of the parties draws into his possession the article he seeks to acquire, the second party automatically acquires full ownership of the other item.

כֵּיצַד [5] The Mishnah now explains the practical applications of these principles. **How so?** [6] **If the buyer has drawn** the seller's **merchandise** into his possession (or in the case of an exchange of coins, if he has drawn the coin which is considered the merchandise) **but has not** yet **given the seller** the purchase **money,** [7] **neither he** nor the seller **can retract.** The sale was effected by the act of *meshikhah,* and the buyer must now pay the seller the full purchase price. [8] However, **if** the buyer **has given** the seller the purchase **money but has not** yet **drawn the merchandise from him,** [9] both the buyer and the seller **can retract.** Since payment of money does not effect a sale, both parties may withdraw from the transaction. But although payment by itself does not create a legally enforceable sale, once payment has been made the parties are under a moral obligation to complete their transaction. Thus, if after payment has been made one of the parties seeks to withdraw from

NOTES

their metallic content, even an unminted coin could be used as a substitute for a coin, although it was not legal tender (*Ramban*, explaining *Rashi*). It is possible that a piece of metal with some imprint other than that of a coin would also fall into this category (*Tosafot*, explaining *Rashi*). *Meiri* suggests that the *asimon* may have been a mold for minting coins in which the letters were inset rather than raised.

However, many Rishonim explain that the *asimon* is a properly stamped coin that has been damaged.

כָּל הַמִּטַּלְטְלִים קוֹנִין זֶה אֶת זֶה All movable goods acquire each other. This clause introduces a new mode of acquisition known as *ḥalifin* (חֲלִיפִין), meaning barter or

HALAKHAH

government or have been forbidden to be used in a particular locality, or coins that will not be accepted as legal tender in that particular locality are considered merchandise in relation to good coins," following the Mishnah and *Rambam*. According to *Rema* (quoting *Tosafot* and *Rosh*), even coins that have ceased to circulate widely are to be treated like merchandise. (Ibid., 203:8.)

הַמִּטַּלְטְלִים קוֹנִין זֶה אֶת זֶה Movable goods acquire each other. "All movable goods may be used to acquire other movables through *ḥalifin* (barter). Thus, once one party to the transaction draws one of the items into his possession, the other immediately acquires the item offered in exchange for it." (Ibid., 203:1.)

אֵינוֹ יָכוֹל לַחֲזוֹר בּוֹ He cannot retract. "Movable goods are

CONCEPTS

מִטַּלְטְלִין Movable property. This differs Halakhically from immovable property, i.e., real estate, in many ways. Certain modes of acquisition are effective only with regard to movable property (e.g., pulling or lifting the item being purchased), but not with regard to real estate. Similarly, the modes of acquisition effective with regard to real estate are generally ineffective with regard to מִטַּלְטְלִין. In a lawsuit, the litigants cannot be required to take an oath unless the property in dispute is movable. According to Talmudic law, movable property may not be collected in payment for debts against a borrower's will, although a Geonic ruling based on certain Talmudic precedents permitted collecting payment from the heirs of the borrower even from movable property. The laws dealing with overcharging (אוֹנָאָה) apply only to movable property. With regard to certain laws, the Halakhic status of documents and slaves is the same as that of land, even though they are in fact movable objects. This is so because of special Biblical rulings, or because of the nature of the Halakhot under discussion.

מְשִׁיכָה Pulling. One of the modes of acquiring movable property. Specifically, the purchaser of an object too heavy to be lifted, or the recipient if the object is a gift, must pull it in the presence of the seller (or donor) in order to acquire it. According to the Halakhah, the transfer of ownership of movable property is not effected through the transfer of money that usually accompanies *meshikhah*, but only through the actual, physical transfer of the object.

חֲלִיפִין Barter, exchange. A legal act of acquisition formalizing the transfer of ownership of an article. Once two parties agree on the barter of one article for another, the acquisition by one party of one of the articles through a recognized mode of acquisition (for example, by *meshikhah*) automatically causes the second article to become the legal property of the other party. This principle is also the basis for the transfer of ownership by means of קִנְיָן

LITERAL TRANSLATION

[1]But they said: He who punished the men of the generation of the flood and the generation of the dispersion, [2]He will punish him who does not stand by his word.

[3]Rabbi Shimon says: Whoever has the money in his hand has the upper hand.

GEMARA [4]Rabbi taught Rabbi Shimon his son: "Gold acquires silver." [5]He said to him: My teacher, you taught us in your youth: "Silver acquires gold," [6]and will you retract and teach us in your old age: "Gold acquires silver"?!

[1]אֲבָל אָמְרוּ: מִי שֶׁפָּרַע מֵאַנְשֵׁי דוֹר הַמַּבּוּל וּמִדּוֹר הַפַּלָּגָה, [2]הוּא עָתִיד לְהִפָּרַע מִמִּי שֶׁאֵינוֹ עוֹמֵד בְּדִבּוּרוֹ.

[3]רַבִּי שִׁמְעוֹן אוֹמֵר: כָּל שֶׁהַכֶּסֶף בְּיָדוֹ יָדוֹ עַל הָעֶלְיוֹנָה.

גמרא [4]מַתְנֵי לֵיהּ רַבִּי לְרַבִּי שִׁמְעוֹן בְּרֵיהּ: ״הַזָּהָב קוֹנֶה אֶת הַכֶּסֶף״. [5]אָמַר לוֹ: רַבִּי, שָׁנִיתָ לָנוּ בְּיַלְדוּתֶיךָ: ״הַכֶּסֶף קוֹנֶה אֶת הַזָּהָב״, [6]וְתַחֲזוֹר וְתִשְׁנֶה לָנוּ בְּזִקְנוּתֶיךָ: ״הַזָּהָב קוֹנֶה אֶת הַכֶּסֶף״?!

RASHI

כל שהכסף בידו כו׳ — פליג אדרבנן, דאמרי: נתן לו מעות יכול לחזור בו אפילו לוקח, ואתא רבי שמעון למימר: מוכר שהכל בידו — הוא דיכול לחזור בו, אבל לוקח — אין יכול לחזור בו. ובגמרא מפרש טעמא.

TRANSLATION AND COMMENTARY

the transaction, the other party may demand that the court exert moral pressure on the reneging party by pronouncing a curse upon him. [1]The Sages **said: God, who punished the generation of the flood** (the contemporaries of Noah; see Genesis 5:5-13) **and the generation of the dispersion** (the builders of the tower of Babel; see Genesis 11:1-9), [2]**will punish anyone who does not stand by his word.**

רַבִּי שִׁמְעוֹן אוֹמֵר [3]**Rabbi Shimon** disagrees with the first view presented in the Mishnah — that both parties may withdraw from a transaction even after payment is made — and **says: Whoever has the money in his hand** (i.e., the seller who has received payment) **has the upper hand** and may retract. The buyer, however, may not retract once he has paid, even if he has not yet drawn the goods into his possession.

GEMARA מַתְנֵי לֵיהּ רַבִּי [4]Rabbi Yehudah HaNasi **taught Rabbi Shimon, his son,** as follows: **"Gold acquires silver,"** as is stated at the beginning of our Mishnah. [5]His son **said to him: My master, you taught us in your youth: "Silver acquires gold."** [6]Why, then, **do you now retract** your earlier opinion **and teach us in your old age** the reverse: **"Gold acquires silver"?!**

סוּדָר — a symbolic form of barter that extends the principle of *ḥalifin* to many legal acts of acquisition. There are differing views in the Talmud as to whether money and other things can be acquired by means of *ḥalifin*.

SAGES

רַבִּי שִׁמְעוֹן **Rabbi Shimon.** Where the name Rabbi Shimon occurs without a patronymic in Tannaitic literature, it usually refers to Rabbi Shimon bar Yoḥai, one of the greatest Tannaim of the generation preceding the completion of the Mishnah. Rabbi Shimon was a close disciple of Rabbi Akiva, and regarded himself as following in his teacher's path. Rabbi Akiva thought very highly of his disciple, saying of him, "It is sufficient for you that I and your Creator know your power." Rabbi Shimon was a master of both Halakhah and Aggadah, and his teachings are quoted frequently throughout the Talmud. Although the Halakhah does not always follow his rulings (especially against Rabbi Yose and Rabbi Yehudah), nevertheless in many important areas of Halakhah his opinion prevails. Rabbi Shimon used a particular method of Halakhic Midrash called "seeking the reason for the verse" — drawing Halakhic conclusions from the Bible on the basis of the spirit and purpose of particular passages.

Rabbi Shimon was sent to Rome as an emissary of the Jews, though he was deeply hostile to the Romans. Because he did not conceal his feelings about them, he was sentenced to death and forced to remain in hiding for many years.

His character was ascetic, and he tended to be stringent in his rulings. He was famous in his generation as a righteous man and as a miracle worker, and there are many famous stories about the numerous wonders he performed.

The Sifrei — a collection of Halakhic Midrashim on Numbers and Deuteronomy — was produced in his academy. He is also the central figure in the principal book of Kabbalah, the *Zohar,* and was regarded with extraordinary veneration in his own time

NOTES

exchange. Unlike *meshikhah* mentioned previously in the Mishnah, where the act of drawing the merchandise into the buyer's possession creates the obligation to pay, in the case of *ḥalifin*, when either party to the exchange acquires one of the articles being exchanged, the second article automatically becomes the legal property of the other party. The regulations concerning *ḥalifin* are discussed at length in the Gemara below.

The words זֶה הַכְּלָל — "this is the general principle" — are missing in certain manuscripts, and seem to have appeared in the texts used by some Rishonim. In fact, as we have explained it, this clause is not a general principle governing the regulations listed previously in the Mishnah, but an introduction to what follows.

אֲבָל אָמְרוּ מִי שֶׁפָּרַע **But they said: He who punished....** People who broke their word in the course of business dealings were the object of great Rabbinic disapproval. The extent of this disapproval depended on the stage a transaction had reached before one party decided to withdraw. If a transaction was at the stage where the parties had exchanged promises but neither had begun performance, the Rabbis expressed their disapproval by the statement that "the Sages are displeased" by a person who reneged on a promise because of price fluctuations. More serious was the case where a seller reneged on an agreement after payment had already been made. In that case, the Rabbis maintained that a promise that has already led to payment of money, though still not legally enforceable, must never be violated by an honest man except under the most extreme circumstances. In order to strengthen the moral imperative to complete a transaction after payment, and to prevent an unscrupulous party from exploiting the fact that the transaction is not yet legally enforceable, the Sages pronounced a curse upon anyone who reneged on a transaction after payment.

שָׁנִיתָ לָנוּ בְּיַלְדוּתֶיךָ **You taught us in your youth.** In his youth, Rabbi Yehudah HaNasi was of the opinion that, in an exchange of gold and silver coins, the gold coins were the money and the silver coins were the merchandise. Later, however, he changed his opinion and ruled that it was silver that was the money and gold the merchandise.

It is clear from our Gemara that his son, Rabbi Shimon, was uneasy about his father's change of mind, but the Gemara does not say why. *Maharshal* suggests that Rabbi Shimon may have been trying to determine whether his father had really changed his mind, or whether the new version was the result of elderly forgetfulness. At all events, the conclusion of our Gemara is that Rabbi Yehudah

HALAKHAH

acquired by the buyer drawing them into his possession. Indeed, by so doing he finalizes the transaction even if he has not yet paid any money, and neither party can retract. However, if the buyer has paid but has not yet drawn the merchandise into his possession, either party may retract, although the person who retracts at this point is subject to the imprecation of 'He who punished,'" following the Mishnah. (*Shulḥan Arukh, Ḥoshen Mishpat* 198:1, 204:1.)

TRANSLATION AND COMMENTARY

בְּיַלְדוּתֵיהּ מַאי סָבַר [1]The Gemara does not record Rabbi Yehudah HaNasi's response, but continues with an analysis of his two conflicting statements, asking: **What did** Rabbi Yehudah HaNasi **maintain in his youth and what did he maintain in his old age?** What was the basis of his original view, and what was the reason for his subsequent change of opinion?

בְּיַלְדוּתֵיהּ סָבַר [2]The Gemara explains: Rabbi Yehudah HaNasi based both his earlier and his later rulings on the same principle — that by drawing the merchandise into his possession a buyer consummates the sale and becomes obligated to pay the purchase price to the seller. The two rulings differ as to the criterion by which to determine which of two kinds of coinage — gold or silver — is considered the money in relation to the other, and which is considered the merchandise. **In his youth,** Rabbi Yehudah HaNasi **maintained that** relative value is the determining factor, and therefore **gold, which is** more **valuable** than silver, **is** considered **money** in relation to silver, [3]and **silver, which is not** as **valuable** as gold, **is** considered **merchandise** in relation to gold. [4]On the basis of the rule set forth in our Mishnah that **merchandise acquires money,** silver acquires gold. [5]But **in his old age he maintained** that the criterion for determining the relationship between different kinds of coinage is the ease with which they each pass in the marketplace as legal tender. [6]Therefore **silver,** [44B] **which circulates easily, is** considered **money**

[1]בְּיַלְדוּתֵיהּ מַאי סָבַר, וּבְזִקְנוּתֵיהּ מַאי סָבַר? [2]בְּיַלְדוּתֵיהּ סָבַר: דַּהֲבָא, דַּחֲשִׁיב, הָוֵי טִבְעָא; [3]כַּסְפָּא, דְּלָא חֲשִׁיב, הָוֵי פֵּירָא, [4]וְקָנֵי לֵיהּ פֵּירָא לְטִבְעָא. [5]בְּזִקְנוּתֵיהּ סָבַר: [6]כַּסְפָּא [44B] דְּחָרִיף, הָוֵי טִבְעָא.

LITERAL TRANSLATION

[1]In his youth what did he maintain, and in his old age what did he maintain?

[2]In his youth he maintained: Gold, which is valuable, is money; [3]silver, which is not valuable, is merchandise (lit., "fruit"), [4]and merchandise acquires money. [5]In his old age he maintained: [6]Silver, [44B] which is current, is money.

RASHI

גמרא דחריף — יוצא בהוצאה ועובר לסוחר.

NOTES

HaNasi's change of mind was well considered, and that we follow his later opinion and view gold as the merchandise.

In the parallel passage in the Jerusalem Talmud, the story of Rabbi Yehudah HaNasi's change of heart is described in detail: Originally he wrote: "Silver acquires gold." Later, when he was a very old man, he asked his son to change the text of the Mishnah to read: "Gold acquires silver," as it appears in our texts, but his son refused, arguing that the earlier ruling was better founded. The Jerusalem Talmud concludes that the son's view prevailed, and the text of the Mishnah found in the Jerusalem Talmud reads: "Silver acquires gold." This also affected the name of the chapter. In our texts it is called הַזָּהָב — "Gold" — whereas in the Jerusalem Talmud it is called הַכֶּסֶף — "Silver."

Ra'avad and other Rishonim note that the Mishnah listed the metals and types of coins in a particular order. In the Jerusalem Talmud there is a generalization: The lower the item is on the Mishnah's list, the more it is to be considered merchandise; if two items on the list are exchanged for one another, the lower one always acquires the higher.

כֶּסֶף וְזָהָב **Silver and gold.** This issue, regarding which Rabbi Yehudah HaNasi changed his mind, and about which the Babylonian and Jerusalem Talmuds disagree, is closely connected to a problem which became extremely important in modern economics, especially during the nineteenth century — the issue of whether money is to be based on the gold or on the silver standard. The conclusion reached in the Babylonian Talmud, which was also the path taken by the Halakhah, was that monetary value is to be linked to the silver standard, which thus became the basis for determining the value of minted coins of metals such as gold or copper. Fluctuations in the market were therefore defined as rises and falls in the price — expressed in silver — of gold, copper and other types of coins and commodities.

These definitions are used to determine all the assessments and measurements within the Halakhah which involve any sort of monetary value (such as the money used in betrothal, marriage contracts, the redemption of firstborn sons, and many other matters).

The worldwide changes in money and banking which have taken place following the introduction of paper money, the abandonment of precious metals as a monetary standard, and the introduction of new and unclear standards of monetary value which are dependent on the economies of industrial nations have not yet been sufficiently explored by Halakhic experts.

דַּהֲבָא דַּחֲשִׁיב **Gold which is valuable.** *Ritva* asks: Why is the fact that gold is more precious than silver relevant? The exchange is based on equivalent value, not weight!

Shittah Mekubbetzet answers that the distinction is subjective: People cherish money more highly than commodities of equal value, and similarly they cherish gold more highly than silver; therefore, in an exchange of gold for silver, gold should be considered the money and silver the commodity.

Ritva, in the name of his teacher, offers a different explanation: Even though the value of a coin was based on its metallic content, officially stamped gold coins were valued at a premium, with the premium on a stamped gold coin being greater than they on a stamped silver coin; hence the value of the gold coin was more the result of its being a coin and less the result of its being a more precious metal. Therefore, in an exchange of gold coins for silver ones, the gold coins should be the money and the silver coins the commodity.

and in following generations. Among his major students was Rabbi Yehudah HaNasi, the editor of the Mishnah. Rabbi Shimon's son, Rabbi Elazar the son of Rabbi Shimon, was also a famous Sage.

SAGES

רַבִּי שִׁמְעוֹן בֶּן רַבִּי **Rabbi Shimon, the son of Rabbi Yehudah HaNasi.** Rabbi Yehudah HaNasi's youngest son, Rabbi Shimon, was also his closest disciple. Exchanges between father and son are mentioned several times in the Talmud. This son of Rabbi Yehudah HaNasi became one of the most important Sages of his generation, and Rabbi Yehudah HaNasi's other disciples — even those who were older than Rabbi Shimon — were his students. He was a particularly close friend of Rabbi Hiyya, who was his partner in the silk trade. He discussed Halakhic issues with the other Sages of his generation, and his name is mentioned once in the Mishnah. Because he was Rabbi Yehudah HaNasi's youngest son, he did not assume his position as Nasi, president of the Sanhedrin, but his father did appoint him to take over the important position of "Hakham" in his yeshivah after his death. This was the third most important position in the Sanhedrin.

BACKGROUND

רַבִּי שָׁנִיתָ לָנוּ **My teacher, you taught us.** Since the son addresses his father as "my teacher," we may assume that they were not at home but rather in the House of Study, where it was fitting for him to use the honorific title belonging to the head of the yeshivah rather than the personal appellation of "father," which is suitable for private and intimate occasions.

חָרִיף **Current.** The primary meaning of this word is "sharp," both in the physical sense of a blade being sharp and also in the metaphorical sense of someone's wits being sharp. The meaning was then extended to the quality of swiftness, for a sharp blade cuts quickly, and a sharp mind thinks quickly. Money is

"sharp" when it circulates quickly and widely.
Since the value of coins depends on the amount of precious metal they contain, silver coins are worth much less than gold coins of the same weight, and less valuable coins circulate far more rapidly and widely than coins of higher value.

SAGES

רַב אַשִׁי **Rav Ashi.** A Babylonian Amora of the sixth generation. Head of the Sura Yeshivah and editor of the Babylonian Talmud. See *Bava Metzia*, Part II, pp. 22-23.

TRANSLATION AND COMMENTARY

in relation to gold, [1]but **gold which does not circulate** as **easily** as silver **is**, despite its greater value, **considered merchandise** in relation to silver. [2]Thus, in accordance with the rule that **merchandise acquires money,** the Mishnah correctly states that "gold acquires silver."

אָמַר רַב אַשִׁי [3]Having explained the basis for both rulings of Rabbi Yehudah HaNasi, the Gemara now argues that the Mishnah should read as Rabbi Yehudah HaNasi had taught in his youth — that silver acquires gold — for only that reading is consistent with the next clause of the Mishnah. **Rav Ashi said:** The ruling given by Rabbi Yehudah HaNasi **in his youth stands to reason,** [4]**for** the Mishnah **teaches** in the next clause: **"Copper acquires silver,"** and unless we assume that silver is considered merchandise in relation to gold, as Rabbi Yehudah HaNasi taught in his youth, this clause is rendered superfluous. [5]Rav Ashi argues as follows: The statement of the Mishnah that "copper acquires silver" is **appropriate if you say that** the first clause of the Mishnah reads: "Silver acquires gold," thereby implying that **silver in relation to gold is** considered **merchandise.** [6]**This is why** the Mishnah **teaches** the next clause: **"Copper acquires silver"** — [7]to teach us that **even though** silver **is** considered **merchandise in relation to gold,** because it is less valuable than gold, [8]**it is** nevertheless considered **money in relation to copper,** because silver is more valuable than copper. Thus the clause "copper acquires silver" teaches us a rule that we would not otherwise have known: That silver is regarded as merchandise in relation to gold and as money in relation to copper. [9]**But if you say that** the first clause of the Mishnah should read: "Gold acquires silver," as Rabbi Yehudah HaNasi taught in his old age, thereby implying **silver in relation to gold is** considered **money** because it circulates more easily than gold, then why is it necessary for the Mishnah to add the clause that "copper acquires silver"? [10]**Now, if in relation to gold,** [11]**which is more valuable** than silver,

LITERAL TRANSLATION

[1]Gold, which is not current, is merchandise, [2]and merchandise acquires money.

[3]Rav Ashi said: As in his youth stands to reason, [4]for it teaches: "Copper acquires silver." [5]Granted if you say [that] silver in relation to gold is merchandise, [6]this is [why] it teaches: "Copper acquires silver"; [7]for even though in relation to gold it is considered merchandise, [8]in relation to copper it is money. [9]But if you say [that] silver in relation to gold is money, [10]now, [if] in relation to gold, [11]which is more valuable than it,

[1]דַּהֲבָא, דְּלָא חָרִיף, הָוֵי פֵּירָא, [2]וְקָנֵי לֵיהּ פֵּירָא לְטִבְעָא.

[3]אֲמַר רַב אַשִׁי: כְּיַלְדוּתֵיהּ מִסְתַּבְּרָא, [4]מִדְּקָתָנֵי: "הַנְּחֹשֶׁת קוֹנָה אֶת הַכֶּסֶף". [5]אִי אָמְרַתְּ בִּשְׁלָמָא כַּסְפָּא לְגַבֵּי דַּהֲבָא פֵּירָא הָוֵי, [6]הַיְינוּ דְּקָא תָּנֵי: "הַנְּחֹשֶׁת קוֹנָה אֶת הַכֶּסֶף"; [7]דְּאַף עַל פִּי דִּלְגַבֵּי דַּהֲבָא פֵּירָא הָוְיָא, [8]לְגַבֵּי נְחֹשֶׁת טִבְעָא הָוֵי. [9]אֶלָּא אִי אָמְרַתְּ כַּסְפָּא לְגַבֵּי דַּהֲבָא טִבְעָא הָוֵי, [10]הָשְׁתָּא, לְגַבֵּי דַּהֲבָא, [11]דַּחֲשִׁיב מִינֵּיהּ,

RASHI

כילדותיה מסתברא — דודאי כן קיבלה מרבו רבי מאיר, שסתם משנה שלו, מדאתנייה בהדה "הנחשת קונה את הכסף". **אי אמרת בשלמא** — הכסף קונה את הזהב אתנייה. **היינו דאצטריך למתנייה הכסף אינו קונה את הנחשת** — דאף על גב דלגבי דהבא הוי פירא, לגבי נחשת, דלא חשיב — הוי טבעא. **אלא אי אמרת כו'** — "והזהב קונה את הכסף" אתנייה, למה לי לאתנויי תו "הנחשת קונה את הכסף"?

NOTES

דַּהֲבָא דְּלָא חָרִיף הָוֵי פֵּירָא **Gold, which is not current, is merchandise.** According to Rabbi Yehudah HaNasi's later opinion, gold coins are considered merchandise in relation to silver. The Gemara discusses the ramifications of this ruling in several areas: the acquisition of coins, when gold is exchanged for silver; the loan of gold coins; and the redemption of second-tithe coins, when silver coins are exchanged for gold. In all three areas, the issue is the status of gold coins in relation to silver. *Rav Hai Gaon* (*Sefer Mikkaḥ U'Mimkar*, and cited by many Rishonim) extends this ruling and argues that since gold is not considered money in relation to silver, it ought not be treated as money at all, even in relation to ordinary movable goods. He concludes that although money cannot be acquired by means of exchange (*ḥalifin*; see below, 46a), gold coins may be acquired in this manner, for they are not considered money. Most Rishonim (*Rif, Ramban, Rosh*) reject *Rav Hai Gaon*'s ruling, and adduce numerous proofs from our Gemara and related passages which indicate that at issue here is only the status of gold in relation to silver and other currencies, but not the status of gold in relation to ordinary movable goods.

כְּיַלְדוּתֵיהּ מִסְתַּבְּרָא **As in his youth stands to reason.** *Rashi* adds that this opinion follows Rabbi Meir, whose viewpoint was of great authority. *Ḥokhmat Manoaḥ* explains that this attribution is significant because it shows general support for the opinion, or more specifically because Rabbi Meir was Rabbi Yehudah HaNasi's teacher, and the rule is that in a dispute between a teacher and a disciple, the Halakhah follows the teacher. As noted above, the Jerusalem Talmud describes the argument between Rabbi Yehudah HaNasi and his son in detail, and reports that his son preferred the earlier opinion because it was delivered when Rabbi Yehudah HaNasi was at the height of his powers. *Ritva* understands *Rashi* to mean that Rabbi Yehudah HaNasi was consistently committed to following Rabbi Meir's opinion on this point, but changed his mind as to what Rabbi Meir in fact maintained.

TRANSLATION AND COMMENTARY

[1]**you say** that silver is considered **money** [2]because it circulates more easily than gold, **is it necessary** to add that silver is considered money **in relation to copper,** given that silver is both more **valuable and circulates more easily** than copper? Thus, if our Mishnah reads as Rabbi Yehudah HaNasi taught in his old age — that "gold acquires silver" — the rule that copper acquires silver seems self-evident, and its inclusion in the Mishnah is superfluous.

אִיצְטְרִיךְ [3]The Gemara, however, rejects Rav Ashi's argument. Even if the first clause of the Mishnah reads: "Gold acquires silver," as Rabbi Yehudah HaNasi taught in his old age, it is still necessary to mention that copper acquires silver. **It might have occurred to you to say** [4]that **copper coins, in places where they circulate, circulate more easily than silver,** [5]and **so you might say** that copper is considered **money** in relation to silver. [6]**Hence it** was necessary for the Mishnah to **tell us** that copper acquires silver. [7]**Since there are places where** copper coins **do not circulate** at all, [8]**they are** always considered **merchandise** in relation to silver coins; silver coins — which circulate everywhere — are considered money.

וְאַף רַבִּי חִיָּיא סָבַר [9]The Gemara relates the following incident to prove that **Rabbi Ḥiyya, too, maintained that gold is** considered **money**, and not a commodity, in accordance with Rabbi Yehudah HaNasi's early ruling: [10]**Rav** once **borrowed** gold **dinarim from Rabbi Ḥiyya's daughter.**

[1]אָמְרַתְּ טִבְעָא הָוֵי, [2]לְגַבֵּי נְחשֶׁת, דְּאִיהוּ חֲשִׁיב וְאִיהוּ חָרִיף, מִבָּעֲיָא?! [3]אִיצְטְרִיךְ, סָלְקָא דַּעְתָּךְ אָמִינָא: [4]הָנֵי פְּרִיטֵי, בְּאַתְרָא דְּסָגְיֵי, אִינְהוּ חֲרִיפֵי טְפֵי מִכַּסְפָּא, [5]אֵימָא טִבְעָא הָוֵי. [6]קָא מַשְׁמַע לָן: [7]כֵּיוָן דְּאִיכָּא דּוּכְתָּא דְּלָא סַגִּי בֵּיהּ, [8]פֵּירָא הָוֵי. [9]וְאַף רַבִּי חִיָּיא סָבַר דַּהֲבָא טִבְעָא הָוֵי. [10]דְּרַב אוֹזִיף דִּינָרֵי מִבְּרַתֵּיהּ דְּרַבִּי חִיָּיא.

LITERAL TRANSLATION

[1]you say it is money, [2]in relation to copper, where it is [more] valuable and it is current, is it necessary [to teach this]?

[3]It is necessary, [for] you might have thought to say: [4]These [copper] coins, in the place where they circulate, are more current than silver, [5][so you might] say they are money. [6][Hence] it tells us: [7]Since there is a place in which they do not circulate, [8]they are merchandise.

[9]And Rabbi Ḥiyya, too, maintains [that] gold is money. [10]For Rav borrowed dinarim from Rabbi Ḥiyya's daughter.

RASHI

אוזיף דינרי – לוה זהובים.

NOTES

הָנֵי פְּרִיטֵי These copper coins. The Mishnah discusses an exchange of gold and silver coins, as well as an exchange of copper and silver coins, but does not rule on an exchange of gold and copper coins. Some Rishonim (*Rosh*, in the name of *Tosafot; Ritva*) maintain that in such an exchange, "gold acquires copper," i.e., copper is viewed as money in relation to gold. Copper is considered merchandise in relation to silver only because there are places where copper is not accepted at all, whereas silver is universally accepted. But in relation to gold, which is not widely accepted anywhere, copper should certainly be considered money, despite gold's greater value. Others (*Rosh, Ramban*) argue that in such an exchange, "copper acquires gold," i.e., gold is considered money in relation to copper. Gold is considered merchandise in relation to silver only because silver's wide acceptance is coupled with its relatively high value, which together outweigh gold's greater value in determining which is to be considered the money. But in relation to copper, which has little value, gold should certainly be considered money, despite copper's greater acceptability.

דַּהֲבָא טִבְעָא Gold is money. Our Gemara focuses on whether gold coins are to be considered money or merchandise in relation to silver coins. The more general issue of the status of gold coins with respect to other merchandise is not raised explicitly in the Gemara, but is discussed by the Rishonim. Most Rishonim follow *Rif*, who rules that even after Rabbi Yehudah HaNasi changed his mind and maintained that gold coins should be regarded as merchandise in relation to silver coins, he did not deny that gold coins generally remained money; it was only in relation to silver coins that they became a commodity. *Ba'al HaMa'or* disagrees, arguing that in the absence of any evidence one way or the other we must assume that a gold coin is always treated as a commodity.

דְּרַב אוֹזִיף דִּינָרֵי For Rav borrowed gold dinarim. To understand the story of Rav's loan, it is important to review some of the regulations surrounding the Torah's prohibition against taking interest.

The Torah prohibits lending money, produce, land or any other property for interest (Exodus 22:24, Leviticus 25:35-38, Deuteronomy 23:20-21). It is, of course, permitted to borrow and return commodities, provided no greater value is returned than was originally borrowed. However, there is a Rabbinic prohibition called "a *se'ah* for a *se'ah*," against borrowing and returning commodities by volume or weight rather than by value. The reasoning behind this prohibition is as follows: Since market prices fluctuate, if the borrower were to return the same quantity he borrowed, the lender might receive a commodity more valuable than the one he lent, and this would be a form of interest.

Hence the Gemara objects to Rav's loan. For if gold is a commodity, borrowing gold dinarim when gold is inexpensive and returning the same number of gold dinarim after its price has risen would be a violation of "a *se'ah* for a *se'ah*."

דְּרַב אוֹזִיף דִּינָרֵי For Rav borrowed gold dinarim. *Tosafot* asks: The Gemara concludes that Rabbi Ḥiyya's ruling was based on the principle that it is permitted to borrow a *se'ah* and pay a *se'ah* if the borrower already has some of the borrowed commodity in his possession, and is borrowing "until my son comes" or "until I find my key." This principle

SAGES

רַב וְרַבִּי חִיָּיא Rav and Rabbi Ḥiyya. Rabbi Ḥiyya was Rav's teacher as well as his maternal and paternal uncle. Rav's father was Rabbi Ḥiyya's older brother (they had the same father, but different mothers), making Rabbi Ḥiyya Rav's uncle on his father's side. However, Rav's father also married Rabbi Ḥiyya's half-sister (from a different father), making Rabbi Ḥiyya Rav's uncle on his mother's side as well. Personal relations between uncle and nephew were extremely close. Rabbi Ḥiyya was Rav's principal teacher as well as his employer or partner in business.

BACKGROUND

בְּאַתְרָא דְּסָגְיֵי In the place where they circulate. As noted, the value of silver coins was determined by the amount of silver they contained. For that reason, silver coins were used everywhere. In contrast, the value of copper coins was not determined by the amount of metal they contained, but by the denomination minted on them, and that value depended solely on the conventions of the state in which they were minted. Moreover, since silver coins were small in size but high in value, money changers were willing to exchange them — even if they could not be used in commerce in a foreign country — because the possibility existed of transferring them to their country of origin and exchanging them there. However, copper coins, which were large in size and low in value, were not worth the money changer's while to exchange, so they were of no use in places where they were not legal tender.

BACKGROUND

טָבִין וּתְקִילִין Good and full weight. This is a proverbial expression for money which is legal tender. The precise meaning of the expression is that the coins are "good" in that they are minted with all the proper legal symbols, and "full weight" in that their weight conforms to their nominal value; they have not been worn down through use, in which case their value would be reduced.

CONCEPTS

סְאָה בִּסְאָה A *se'ah* for a *se'ah*. The Torah (Leviticus 25:36-37) explicitly prohibits borrowing and lending for interest, whether in money or kind. The main principles of the laws of interest are explained at length in the fifth chapter of this tractate. The primary definition of interest is that the borrower pays back more than he borrowed. Usually a loan for interest is based on an agreement between the parties. However, interest was also forbidden in instances where the parties had not initially intended to engage in a transaction involving interest. One example of unintended payment of interest is when someone borrows a specific quantity of a commodity and obligates himself to return exactly the same amount of that commodity. In that case, if the price of the commodity rises before the borrower returns the loan, he will in fact be returning something worth more than when he borrowed it, and this amounts to interest. To avoid situations of this kind, it was forbidden for a borrower to be obligated to return a specific quantity of a commodity. Instead, the monetary value of the loan was determined at the time it was made, so when the borrower repaid the loan he had to return a quantity worth the amount originally determined.

[1] לְסוֹף אִיַּיקּוּר דִּינָרֵי. [2] אֲתָא לְקַמֵּיהּ דְּרַבִּי חִיָּיא. [3] אֲמַר לֵיהּ: ״זִיל, שַׁלֵּים לָהּ טָבִין וּתְקִילִין״. [4] אִי אָמְרַתְּ בִּשְׁלָמָא דַּהֲבָא טִבְעָא הָוֵי, שַׁפִּיר. [5] אֶלָּא אִי אָמְרַתְּ פֵּירָא הָוֵי, [6] הֲוָה לֵיהּ סְאָה בִּסְאָה [7] וְאָסוּר!

[8] רַב דִּינָרֵי הָווּ לֵיהּ, [9] וְכֵיוָן דְּהָווּ לֵיהּ דִּינָרֵי, נַעֲשָׂה כְּאוֹמֵר לָהּ:

LITERAL TRANSLATION

[1] Ultimately the dinarim appreciated. [2] He came before Rabbi Ḥiyya. [3] He said to him: "Go, pay her good and full weight [dinarim]."

[4] Granted if you say gold is money, it is well. [5] But if you say it is merchandise, [6] it is [like] a *se'ah* for a *se'ah* [7] and is forbidden!

[8] Rav had dinarim, [9] and since he had dinarim, it is as if he said to her:

RASHI

אתא לקמיה דרבי חייא — חושש היה משום רבית. **אי אמרת בשלמא דהבא טבעא הוי** — ואין היוקר והזול תלוי בהן, אלא הזול תלוי במעות, דמעות הכסף הם שהוזל להנתן הרבה בדינר, וזה — מטבע הלוה, ומטבע יקבל. **הוה ליה סאה בסאה** — שהיוקר והזול תלוי בפירות. **ואסור** — דתנן לקמן (עה,א): לא יאמר אדם לחבירו ״הלויני כור חטין ואני נותן לך בגורן״ — שמא יוקרו ויבא לידי רבית. **דינרי הוו ליה** — כשלוה את אלו, וגבי סאה בסאה תנן: ״אבל אומר לו הלויני עד שיבא בני או עד שאמצא המפתח״, שאלו שבידו נקנין למלוה וברשותו הוקרו, דרבית סאה בסאה דרבנן, ובכי האי גונא לא גזור.

TRANSLATION AND COMMENTARY

[1] **Ultimately,** by the time the loan became due, **the dinarim** had **appreciated** in value in relation to silver, and were worth more silver coins than at the time of the loan. [2] Rav **came before Rabbi Ḥiyya** and asked what he should do. He was concerned that if he repaid the same number of gold dinarim he had borrowed, he would be paying back a greater sum of money than he had borrowed, and might thus violate the prohibition against paying interest. [3] Rabbi Ḥiyya **said to him: "Go** and **pay her good, full-weight** gold **dinarim,** equal in weight and number to those you borrowed." Rabbi Ḥiyya maintained that Rav's concern that full repayment might result in violation of the prohibition against interest was groundless.

אִי אָמְרַתְּ בִּשְׁלָמָא [4] The Gemara now explains why this incident proves that Rabbi Ḥiyya was of the opinion that gold is considered money in relation to silver. **Granted if you say** that **gold is** considered **money** in relation to silver, then the ruling of Rabbi Ḥiyya is **well** founded. For if gold coins are considered money in relation to silver coins, they remain fixed in value, neither appreciating nor depreciating. A change in the relative values of gold and silver is thus a change in the price of *silver*, for silver is the merchandise whose price fluctuates. Therefore the loan may be repaid at its nominal value in gold even though the gold coins are now equal in value to a greater number of silver coins than at the time of the loan. If the matter is viewed in this way, Rav was ordered to return no more money than he actually borrowed. [5] **But if you say that** gold **is** considered **merchandise** in relation to silver, [6] Rav's loan should be considered **like** a loan of **a *se'ah*** (a measure of volume) of produce which is to be repaid **with a *se'ah*** of produce. [7] Such a loan is Rabbinically **prohibited** because the value of a *se'ah* of produce may rise between the time of the loan and the time of repayment. This increase amounts to prohibited interest, because in monetary terms the borrower is returning a more valuable *se'ah* than he originally borrowed. Similarly, if you say that gold is considered merchandise — equivalent to the *se'ah* of produce in the above case — then if at the time of repayment gold coins are equal in value to more silver coins than they were at the time of borrowing, the gold should be viewed as having appreciated. Repaying the same number of coins as those borrowed would thus constitute a violation of the laws of interest, because in monetary terms the borrower is returning more than he received. Since Rabbi Ḥiyya allowed Rav to repay his loan with gold dinarim, he must have been of the opinion that gold is considered as money having a fixed value, and not as merchandise, the value of which can fluctuate.

רַב דִּינָרֵי הָווּ לֵיהּ [8] The Gemara now rejects this proof that Rabbi Ḥiyya considered gold as money in relation to silver. Even if Rabbi Ḥiyya considered gold to be merchandise, and therefore judged Rav's loan to be in the same category as a loan of a *se'ah* for a *se'ah*, there would still be no violation of the laws of interest in Rav's case. For **Rav had** gold **dinarim** in his possession elsewhere, [9] **and since he had** these other gold **dinarim,**

NOTES

is stated expressly in a Mishnah (below, 75a), and Rav was surely as aware of it as Rabbi Ḥiyya. Why then did Rav need to ask Rabbi Ḥiyya if the transaction was permitted?

Tosafot answers that the rule of "until I find..." is disputed by Hillel. Hence, Rav wished to be reassured that the Halakhah indeed follows the anonymous Tanna who formulated the rule, and that the "until-I-find" argument is acceptable. *Rashba* adds that when Rav first borrowed the gold coins, he was convinced that the Halakhah followed the anonymous Tanna, but when doubts arose in his mind he went to Rabbi Ḥiyya to resolve them.

In the version of this story found in the Jerusalem Talmud, it was Rabbi Ḥiyya's daughter, and not Rav, who came to her father to be reassured that her transaction with Rav was acceptable.

TRANSLATION AND COMMENTARY

it is considered **as if he said to** Rabbi Ḥiyya's daughter: [1] **"Lend me** a measure of wheat **until my son comes," or:** "Lend me a measure of wheat **until I find the key** and gain access to the produce in my possession." Such a short-term loan is permitted despite the prohibition concerning the loan of a *se'ah* for a *se'ah*, because the produce (or the gold dinarim in our case) in the borrower's possession is considered as having already been transferred to the lender at the time of the loan. Any subsequent rise in value occurs when the produce is already considered to be in the lender's possession, and consequently there is no violation of the laws prohibiting interest.

אֲמַר רָבָא [2] **Rava said**: The following **Tanna** also **maintains that gold is** considered **money** in relation to silver, as did Rabbi Yehudah HaNasi in his youth. [3] **For it has been taught** in a Baraita: **"The perutah** — a copper coin **of which** the Sages **speak** in various contexts in Rabbinic literature — **is** equal to **one-eighth of an Italian isar."**

לְמַאי נָפְקָא מִינָּהּ [4] Before continuing the quotation from this Baraita, the Gemara examines its first sentence and asks: **What is the practical significance** of this statement? [5] The Gemara answers: It is relevant **for the betrothal of a woman.** According to the Halakhah, a man can betroth a woman by giving her a perutah or an object of equivalent value. The Baraita informs us of the value of a perutah, and teaches us that a woman can be betrothed with no less than the equivalent of one-eighth of an Italian isar.

אִיסָּר אֶחָד [6] The quotation from the Baraita now continues: **"An isar is** equal to **one twenty-fourth of a silver dinar."**

לְמַאי נָפְקָא מִינָּהּ [7] The Gemara again interrupts and asks: **What is the practical significance** of this statement? [8] It answers: It is relevant **for buying and selling.** According to the Halakhah, movable goods may not be sold for more than their market value or bought for less than their market value. A sale which violates these rules — known as the rules of *ona'ah* (אוֹנָאָה) or "overreaching" — is regarded as an "overreaching" or fraudulent

[1] "הַלְוֵינִי עַד שֶׁיָּבֹא בְּנִי", אוֹ "עַד שֶׁאֶמְצָא מַפְתֵּחַ". [2] אֲמַר רָבָא: הַאי תַּנָּא סָבַר דַּהֲבָא טִבְעָא הָוֵי. [3] דְּתַנְיָא: "פְּרוּטָה שֶׁאָמְרוּ — אֶחָד מִשְּׁמוֹנָה בְּאִיסָּר הָאִיטַלְקִי". [4] לְמַאי נָפְקָא מִינָּהּ? [5] לְקִדּוּשֵׁי אִשָּׁה. [6] "אִיסָּר — אֶחָד מֵעֶשְׂרִים וְאַרְבָּעָה בְּדִינַר שֶׁל כֶּסֶף". [7] לְמַאי נָפְקָא מִינָּהּ? [8] לְמִקָּח וּמִמְכָּר.

LITERAL TRANSLATION

[1] "Lend me until my son comes," or "until I find the key."

[2] Rava said: This Tanna maintains [that] gold is money. [3] For it has been taught: "The perutah of which they spoke is one-eighth of an Italian isar."

[4] What difference does it make (lit., "what comes out of it")?

[5] For betrothal of a woman.

[6] "An isar is one twenty-fourth of a silver dinar."

[7] What difference does it make?

[8] For buying and selling.

RASHI

לקדושי אשה — שאמרו חכמים בפרוטה, הודיעך כמה היא פרוטה. **למקח וממכר** — מכר לו דינר ביותר מעשרים וארבע איסרין, כל מה שהעלה יתר על כן — נתאנה לוקח, ואם יש אונאה שתות — יחזיר אונאה.

NOTES

אֶחָד מִשְּׁמוֹנָה בְּאִיסָּר הָאִיטַלְקִי One-eighth of an Italian isar. *Rashba* asks: The Gemara proves that gold coins are money from the fact that the Tanna links the value of a silver coin to that of a gold coin. But surely, by the same argument, the silver coins could be money, as the Tanna links the value of the copper perutah to a silver coin, and not to a gold one.

Rashba answers that all three coins are money when taken by themselves. The Gemara is interested here in their relative status. Thus the Baraita teaches that if the relative prices of gold and silver fluctuate, the sum needed to redeem the firstborn is linked to the value of gold. Hence it follows that when gold coins are exchanged for silver ones, it is the gold coins that are the money and the silver the commodity. But there is no doubt that when silver coins are exchanged for copper coins, it is the silver that is the money. Hence it is possible for the Baraita to link the value of copper to that of silver.

לְמִקָּח וּמִמְכָּר For buying and selling. Our commentary reflects *Rabbenu Ḥananel* and most Rishonim, who agree that the isar was a copper coin (see Tosefta *Bava Metzia*

HALAKHAH

פְּרוּטָה, אִיסָּר, דִּינָר Perutah, isar, dinar. "The perutah mentioned in Rabbinic literature is equal to one-eighth of an Italian isar, which in turn is equal to one twenty-fourth of a silver dinar. A perutah is worth half a barley grain's weight of pure silver, and the values of the different types of currency mentioned in Rabbinic literature are calculated accordingly in every generation." (*Rambam, Sefer Zemanim, Hilkhot Shekalim* 1:3; ibid., *Sefer Mishpatim, Hilkhot To'en VeNit'an* 3:1.)

פְּרוּטָה לְקִדּוּשֵׁי אִשָּׁה A perutah for betrothal. "To betroth a woman by means of money, one must give her at least a perutah or an object worth a perutah." (*Shulḥan Arukh, Even HaEzer* 31:1.)

REALIA

אִיסָּר הָאִיטַלְקִי Italian isar.

LANGUAGE

אִיסָּר Isar. This word is derived from the Latin *assarius*, which is the name of a Roman coin.

BACKGROUND

הַלְוֵינִי עַד שֶׁיָּבֹא בְּנִי Lend me until my son comes. Since the prohibition against lending a specific quantity of produce against the return of the same amount (סְאָה בִּסְאָה) derives solely from concern that interest may become a consideration, the Sages decreed that this prohibition applies only when the loan is for a long period. But if the loan is only for a short time, and the borrower knows he can immediately return what he has borrowed since he needs it only until his son brings him some of his own, or until he finds his key and can enter his house to return the produce to the lender, it is permitted.

לְקִדּוּשֵׁי אִשָּׁה For betrothal of a woman. At the beginning of tractate *Kiddushin* the Sages determined that when a betrothal is effected by means of money, the minimum amount that may be used is a perutah. If for the purpose of betrothal a man gives a woman a coin or an object worth less than a perutah, the betrothal is invalid.

לְמִקָּח וּמִמְכָּר For buying and selling. This determination is significant in defining the true value of the Roman isar, for if an exchange is not transacted at that rate, it entails error or fraud. This explanation would also apply to determining the value of a perutah or a dinar. However, in those cases the Gemara preferred to find a reason in the area of ritual law, beyond the obvious and simple reason why the Sages had to determine the value of coins.

פְּרוּטָה Perutah. The perutah was the smallest coin in

[1]"A silver dinar is one twenty-fifth of a gold dinar." [2]What difference does it make? [3]For the redemption of the [firstborn] son.

[4]Granted if you say it is considered money, [5]the Tanna is calculating by something which is fixed. [6]But if you say it is merchandise, [7]does the Tanna calculate by something that appreciates and depreciates?!

[1]״דִּינָר שֶׁל כֶּסֶף אֶחָד מֵעֶשְׂרִים וַחֲמִשָּׁה בְּדִינָר שֶׁל זָהָב״. [2]לְמַאי נָפְקָא מִינָּהּ? [3]לְפִדְיוֹן הַבֵּן.

[4]אִי אָמְרַתְּ בִּשְׁלָמָא טִבְעָא הָוֵי, [5]מְשַׁעֵר תַּנָּא בְּמִידֵּי דְּקִיץ. [6]אֶלָּא אִי אָמְרַתְּ פֵּירָא הָוֵי, [7]מְשַׁעֵר תַּנָּא בְּמִידֵּי דְּאוֹקִיר וְזִיל?!

sale, and can be voided in whole or in part, depending on the discrepancy between the price paid and the fair market value. Our Baraita teaches us that if a dinar is sold for more than twenty-four isarim, the laws of *ona'ah* — defrauding by overcharging — begin to apply.

דִּינָר שֶׁל כֶּסֶף [1]The Baraita now concludes: **"A silver dinar is equal to one twenty-fifth of a gold dinar."**

לְמַאי נָפְקָא מִינָּהּ [2]The Gemara once again asks: **What is the practical significance** of this statement? [3]It answers: It is relevant **for the redemption of a firstborn son.** The Torah (Numbers 18:16) requires a father to redeem his firstborn son by giving five silver shekels to a priest. One Biblical shekel is equal in value to four silver dinarim current in the days of the Mishnah, and hence the redemption of a firstborn son requires twenty silver dinarim. The Baraita's statement that one gold dinar is equal to twenty-five silver dinarim is significant with regard to the redemption of a firstborn son, since it shows that the redemption requires four-fifths of a gold dinar. Thus if the father gives the priest a golden dinar, the priest must give him back five silver dinarim.

אִי אָמְרַתְּ בִּשְׁלָמָא [4]Having quoted the Baraita and the explanations in connection with it given by the Gemara, Rava now argues that the Tanna of this Baraita must be of the opinion that gold is considered money in relation to silver: Only **if you say** that gold **is** considered **money** does it make sense to state the obligation to redeem a firstborn son in terms of gold. [5]Clearly, **the Tanna calculated** that obligation in terms of a currency **which is** considered **constant.** For if gold is considered money in relation to silver, then the redemption of the firstborn always requires four-fifths of a gold dinar, no matter what the rate of exchange is between gold and silver. **But if you say** that gold **is** considered **merchandise** in relation to silver, why does the Tanna state the obligation to redeem a firstborn in terms of gold? [6]**Would the Tanna calculate** that obligation in terms of **something that appreciates and depreciates**? For if gold is considered merchandise, then the amount required for the redemption will not always be four-fifths of a gold dinar, but rather twenty silver dinarim or the

RASHI

לפדיון הבן — שהוא חמשה שקלים, ושקל דאורייתא הוא סלע, והסלע ארבעה דינרי כסף שהם עשרים דינר, ואם נתן לו אבי הבן דינר זהב — מחזיר לו הכהן חמשה דינרי כסף. **אי אמרת בשלמא דהבא טבעא הוי** — ואין היוקר והזול תלוי בו. **משער תנא במידי דקיץ** — שיער תנא פדיון הבן במטבע הקצוב, שאפילו בזמן שאינו נמכר יותר מעשרים דינרי כסף — יחזיר לו הכהן חמשה דינרים, שהזהב תמיד דמיו קצובין עשרים וחמשה דינרים, שהוא המטבע, והכסף הוי פירא לגביה והמעות הן שהוקרו, ואם נמכר בשלשים — לא יחזיר לו הכהן אלא חמישית שבדמיו, שדמיו לעולם קצובין וארבעה חומשי דמיו הן פדיון הבן.

NOTES

3:7). Thus the Baraita teaches us that if the isar is mentioned in a contract, its value is set at one twenty-fourth of a silver dinar, regardless of fluctuations in the relative values of silver and copper.

Rashi, however, is of the opinion that the isar was itself a silver coin like the dinar (see below, 55a). Accordingly, when the Gemara referred to the practical differences "for buying and selling," it could not have been referring to fluctuations in the relative price of metals. Rather, the Gemara meant that when silver dinarim are exchanged for silver isarim, they must be exchanged at the rate of one dinar to twenty-four isarim, and that anything else constitutes *ona'ah* — overreaching or fraud — and is subject to the laws of *ona'ah* discussed later in the chapter (from 49b).

לְפִדְיוֹן הַבֵּן For the redemption of the firstborn son. The Rishonim ask: The Torah (Numbers 18:16) expressly determines the sum required to redeem the firstborn — five shekels of *silver* (five sela'im in Talmudic terminology). How then can there be any doubt as to which metal is intended?

Rosh answers that this Baraita follows Rabbi Yehudah HaNasi's youthful opinion, according to which the coins

HALAKHAH

חֲמִשָּׁה סְלָעִים לְפִדְיוֹן הַבֵּן Five sela'im for redeeming the firstborn son. "It is a commandment of the Torah that all firstborn sons (except those born by Caesarean section) be redeemed from a priest. This positive commandment applies to a woman's firstborn son, provided she is not the daughter of a priest or Levite, or that the father of the child is not a priest or Levite. The redemption money is five sela'im, which are worth 120 ma'aot of pure silver." (*Shulḥan Arukh, Yoreh De'ah* 305:1.)

circulation among the Jews in antiquity. For Halakhic purposes the Sages decreed that the perutah has a certain absolute value, which is that of approximately half a gram of silver. But the term is sometimes used broadly to designate any copper coin of low value. Thus coins known as "perutot" may have been worth more or less than the Halakhically determined value of a perutah.

TERMINOLOGY

לְמַאי נָפְקָא מִינָּהּ What difference does it make? I.e., what practical consequences does it have? This expression is used when a problem raised or a statement quoted by the Gemara seems merely academic.

שְׁמַע מִינָּהּ Hear from this, learn from this, conclude from this. (1) At the beginning of an argument, this expression means: "Draw the following Halakhic conclusion" from the previous statement. (2) At the end of an argument, this expression is used to confirm that the previous conclusion or explanation is indeed correct.

CONCEPTS

פִּדְיוֹן הַבֵּן The redemption of the firstborn. The Torah requires that all firstborn sons be redeemed from a priest (Exodus 13:12-13). This positive commandment applies to a woman's firstborn son, provided she is not the daughter of a priest or Levite or that the father of the child is not a priest or Levite. Only children born by natural birth are redeemed; those born by Caesarean section are excluded.

TRANSLATION AND COMMENTARY

equivalent in gold, however much that happens to be. [1]If the father always gives the priest four-fifths of a gold dinar, **there will be times when the priest will be required to return money** — when the gold dinar has appreciated. [2]**And there will** also **be times when** the father **will have to add** money to give **to the priest** — if the gold dinar has depreciated. [3]**Rather, conclude from here** that the Tanna is of the opinion that gold **is money**, and therefore the redemption of the firstborn son always requires four-fifths of a gold dinar. [4]The Gemara accepts Rava's argument and says: Indeed, it is correct to **draw this conclusion from** the Baraita quoted.

תְּנַן הָתָם [5]The Gemara now considers the status of gold and silver coins for the redemption of second-tithe produce. Before agricultural produce could be consumed by its owners, terumah — the priestly dues — and first tithe (for the Levites) had to be set aside. An additional tithe was then separated from what remained. In the first, second, fourth and fifth years of the Sabbatical cycle, this tithe is known as *ma'aser sheni* (מַעֲשֵׂר שֵׁנִי) — the second tithe. The second tithe had to be taken up to Jerusalem to be eaten there by its owners. If it was too difficult to take the produce itself to Jerusalem, it could be redeemed for an equivalent sum of money. This redemption money was then taken to Jerusalem, where it was spent on food. **We have learned elsewhere** in a Mishnah (*Ma'aser Sheni* 2:7) the following difference of opinion concerning second-tithe redemption money: [6]"**Bet Shammai say : A person may not exchange** silver **sela'im** of second-tithe money **for gold dinarim**. If second-tithe produce has been redeemed with silver sela'im, those sela'im may not thereafter be exchanged for gold dinarim in order to make it easier to transport the money to Jerusalem. [7]**But Bet Hillel permit** this exchange.

רַבִּי יוֹחָנָן וְרֵישׁ לָקִישׁ [8]**Rabbi Yoḥanan and Resh Lakish disagreed** in their understanding of the dispute between Bet Shammai and Bet Hillel. [9]**One said** that **the difference of opinion** specifically **concerns** the exchange of **sela'im for dinarim**, i.e., whether silver coins received from the redemption of second-tithe produce may be further exchanged for gold coins. According to Torah law, the second tithe can be redeemed only by money, but not by other commodities. Hence the importance of determining the relationship between gold and silver coinage. [10]**Bet Shammai maintain** that **silver is money, and gold is considered merchandise** in relation to silver, [11]**and** since **we are not permitted to redeem** second-tithe **money with** coins that are viewed as

LITERAL TRANSLATION

[1]Sometimes the priest will return [money] to him, [2]and sometimes he will add [money] for the priest! [3]Rather, conclude from this: It is money. [4]Conclude from it.

[5]We have learned elsewhere: [6]"Bet Shammai say: A person may not exchange sela'im for gold dinarim. [7]But Bet Hillel permit."

[8]Rabbi Yoḥanan and Resh Lakish [disagree]. [9]One says: The difference of opinion concerns sela'im for dinarim. [10]For Bet Shammai maintain: Silver is money and gold is merchandise, [11]and we may not redeem money with merchandise.

[1]זִימְנִין דִּמְהֲדַר לֵיהּ כָּהֲנָא, [2]וְזִימְנִין דְּמוֹסִיף לֵיהּ אִיהוּ לְכָהֲנָא! [3]אֶלָּא, שְׁמַע מִינָּהּ: טִבְעָא הָוֵי. [4]שְׁמַע מִינָּהּ.

[5]תְּנַן הָתָם: [6]"בֵּית שַׁמַּאי אוֹמְרִים: לֹא יַעֲשֶׂה אָדָם סְלָעִין דִּינָרֵי זָהָב. [7]וּבֵית הִלֵּל מַתִּירִין". [8]רַבִּי יוֹחָנָן וְרֵישׁ לָקִישׁ. [9]חַד אֲמַר: מַחֲלוֹקֶת בִּסְלָעִים עַל דִּינָרִין. [10]דְּבֵית שַׁמַּאי סָבְרִי: כַּסְפָּא טִבְעָא וְדַהֲבָא פֵּירָא, [11]וְטִבְעָא אַפֵּירָא לָא מְחַלְּלִינַן.

RASHI

תנן התם – במסכת מעשר שני. לא יעשה אדם סלעין דינרי זהב – מי שיש לו סלעין כסף מעשר שני לא יחליפם בדינר זהב להקל המשוי מעליו. טבעא אפירא לא מחללינן – דרחמנא אמר "וצרת הכסף".

TERMINOLOGY

תְּנַן הָתָם We have learned elsewhere. A term used to introduce a quotation from a Mishnah not at present under discussion (usually from another tractate or another chapter of the tractate being studied), but which has a bearing on the present discussion.

BACKGROUND

פִּדְיוֹן מַעֲשֵׂר שֵׁנִי The redemption of the second tithe. The Torah (Deuteronomy 14:25) says that if it is difficult to bring the second tithe itself to Jerusalem, one may redeem (מְחַלְּלִים) it with money (minted coins only, not paper money, bullion or any other commodity), and then the produce itself is no longer consecrated. The money, however, takes on the sanctity of the second tithe, and must be brought up to Jerusalem, where it must be used to buy food and drink. The money then loses its sanctity, and the purchased food becomes consecrated as though it itself was second-tithe produce, and must be eaten in Jerusalem. When the owner is the one who redeems the tithed produce, he must add a fifth (חוֹמֶשׁ) to its price. The language of the Torah implies that redemption of the second tithe involves the exchange of produce for money. The questions here and in the rest of this passage concern changes in this procedure: Can produce be exchanged for other produce, money for other money, or money for produce?

SAGES

רַבִּי יוֹחָנָן Rabbi Yoḥanan (ben Nappaḥa). The most important Palestinian Amora of the second generation. See *Bava Metzia*, Part I, pp. 19-20.

רֵישׁ לָקִישׁ Resh Lakish. Otherwise known as Rabbi Shimon ben Lakish, Resh Lakish was a leading Palestinian Amora of the second generation, a student, colleague and brother-in-law of Rabbi Yoḥanan. See *Bava Metzia*, Part II, pp. 12-13.

NOTES

were listed in the order of their importance. The most important coin always determines the value of the less important. Therefore, when the Torah said five shekels, it must have meant four-fifths of a gold dinar, and may have cited the figure in silver in order to employ whole numbers rather than fractions.

מַחֲלוֹקֶת בֵּית שַׁמַּאי וּבֵית הִלֵּל בְּעִנְיַן מַעֲשֵׂר שֵׁנִי The dispute between Bet Shammai and Bet Hillel concerning second tithe. The Gemara explains that the dispute between Bet Shammai and Bet Hillel revolves around the question of the relationship between gold and silver. According to Bet Shammai, silver is considered money and gold is considered merchandise, and since second-tithe money may not be redeemed with a coin considered to be merchandise, second-tithe sela'im may not be exchanged for gold dinarim. According to Bet Hillel, silver is considered merchandise and

HALAKHAH

סְלָעִין וְדִינָרֵי זָהָב בְּמַעֲשֵׂר Sela'im and gold dinarim as tithe-money. "One may exchange silver coins of second-tithe redemption money for gold dinarim," following Bet Hillel. (*Rambam, Sefer Zeraim, Hilkhot Ma'aser Sheni* 5:13.)

חִלּוּל מָעוֹת מַעֲשֵׂר עַל פֵּירוֹת Redeeming tithe-money with

¹וּבֵית הִלֵּל סָבְרִי: כַּסְפָּא פֵּירָא
וְדַהֲבָא טִבְעָא, ²וּפֵירָא אַטִּבְעָא
מְחַלְּלִינַן. ³אֲבָל פֵּירוֹת עַל
דִּינָרִין, דִּבְרֵי הַכֹּל מְחַלְּלִינַן.
⁴מַאי טַעְמָא?
⁵מִידֵּי דַּהֲוָה אַכֶּסֶף, לְבֵית הִלֵּל.
⁶כֶּסֶף, לְבֵית הִלֵּל, אַף עַל גַּב
דְּכַסְפָּא לְגַבֵּי דַּהֲבָא פֵּירָא הָוֵי,

LITERAL TRANSLATION

[1] But Bet Hillel maintain: Silver is merchandise and gold is money, [2] and we may redeem merchandise with money. [3] But according to everyone, we may redeem produce with dinarim.

[4] What is the reason?

[5] Just as is [the case] with silver, according to Bet Hillel. [6] Silver, according to Bet Hillel, even though silver in relation to gold is merchandise,

TRANSLATION AND COMMENTARY

merchandise, second-tithe silver sela'im may not be further exchanged for gold dinarim. [1] **But Bet Hillel maintain** that **silver is** considered **merchandise** in relation to gold, [2] **and gold is money.** Since **we are permitted to redeem** second-tithe coins that are considered **merchandise with** other coins that are viewed as **money**, second-tithe sela'im may be exchanged for dinarim. [3] **But according to everyone** — both Bet Shammai and Bet Hillel — **we are permitted to redeem** second-tithe **produce** itself **with** gold **dinarim**, as gold coins are considered money in relation to second-tithe produce even according to Bet Shammai.

מַאי טַעְמָא [4] Concerning this last statement the Gemara asks: **What is the reason** that Bet Shammai would agree here that gold coins are considered money in relation to second-tithe produce? Why not say that if gold dinarim are not considered money in relation to silver sela'im, they may not be used for redeeming second-tithe produce at all?

מִידֵּי דַּהֲוָה [5] The Gemara answers: Bet Shammai's position about gold may be understood **just as** we understand **the case** of **silver according to Bet Hillel.** [6] **According to Bet Hillel, even though silver is** considered

RASHI

אבל פירות — ראשונים של מעשר שני.
דברי הכל מחללינן — על דינרי זהב, דאפילו לבית שמאי דאמרי פירא הוא לגבי כספא, מודו דלגבי פירא טבעא הוא.
מידי דהוה אכסף לבית הלל — זהב לבית שמאי אנו למדין מכסף לבית הלל, כדמפרש ואזיל.

NOTES

gold is considered money, and since second-tithe money may be redeemed with other coins that are considered money, second-tithe silver sela'im may be exchanged for gold dinarim. Although the Gemara does not say so explicitly, most Rishonim understand that the dispute between Bet Shammai and Bet Hillel parallels the two opinions held at different times by Rabbi Yehudah HaNasi. Bet Hillel maintain that gold is considered money, as Rabbi Yehudah HaNasi maintained in his youth, whereas Bet Shammai maintain that silver is considered money, as he maintained in his later years. Thus, it would follow that in his final opinion, Rabbi Yehudah HaNasi accepted the position of Bet Shammai against that of Bet Hillel, although Bet Hillel's position is almost always accepted as normative.

A number of Rishonim note that the dispute between Bet Shammai and Bet Hillel as recorded in the Mishnah can only be understood according to Rabbi Yehudah HaNasi's early position, and that he is following the view of Bet Hillel that gold is considered money. According to Rabbi Yehudah HaNasi's later opinion, the dispute between Bet Shammai and Bet Hillel should be revised accordingly, so that it is Bet Hillel who say that sela'im may not be exchanged for gold dinarim because silver is considered money and gold is considered merchandise, and it is Bet Shammai who forbid such an exchange. (*Rosh, Ramban.*)

Ba'al HaMa'or has a different interpretation entirely, according to which the dispute between Bet Shammai and Bet Hillel is not connected to the two opinions of Rabbi Yehudah HaNasi. According to *Ba'al HaMa'or*, both Bet Shammai and Bet Hillel agree with Rabbi Yehudah HaNasi's later opinion that silver is considered money in relation to gold. The dispute only concerns the issue of second-tithe money. According to Bet Hillel, the Torah's repetition of the word "money" (כֶּסֶף) in the verse relating to tithe redemption (Deuteronomy 14:25) expands the concept of money to include gold as well. Even though with regard to acquisition, currency is the determining factor in deciding which coin is money in relation to the other, with regard to tithe redemption the determining factor is value. And since gold is more highly valued than silver, silver sela'im may be exchanged for gold dinarim. According to Bet Shammai, the same criteria used for acquisition apply to tithe redemption, and therefore sela'im may not be exchanged for dinarim.

מִידֵּי דַּהֲוָה אַכֶּסֶף, לְבֵית הִלֵּל Just as is the case with silver according to Bet Hillel. Even though Bet Hillel consider silver a less effective currency than gold, they still permit second-tithe produce to be redeemed with silver coins. This is clear because the dispute between Bet Hillel and Bet Shammai concerns redeeming silver coins with gold coins, showing that silver coins had originally been used to redeem the second-tithe produce. By the same token, Rabbi Yoḥanan argues that Bet Shammai should allow produce to be redeemed directly with gold coins even though they consider gold a less effective currency than silver.

The Aḥaronim ask: How can Rabbi Yoḥanan compare the positions of Bet Shammai and Bet Hillel? When the Torah commands us to redeem the second tithe for money, it uses

HALAKHAH

produce. "Money which has been used to redeem second-tithe produce may not thereafter be redeemed with other produce. However, if one did redeem tithe-money with produce, the produce must be taken to Jerusalem and eaten there." (*Rambam, Sefer Zeraim, Hilkhot Ma'aser Sheni* 4:6.)

TRANSLATION AND COMMENTARY

merchandise in relation to gold, [1]nevertheless **in relation to** second-tithe **produce** itself, **it is** considered **money,** and may certainly be used for the initial redemption of second-tithe produce. [2]So **too** it stands to reason that **according to Bet Shammai,** [3]**even though gold is** considered **merchandise in relation to silver,** [4]nevertheless **in relation to** second-tithe **produce** itself **it is** considered **money.** Bet Shammai therefore agree with Bet Hillel that second-tithe produce may initially be redeemed with gold dinarim, and the difference of opinion between Bet Shammai and Bet Hillel is limited to the issue of the subsequent exchange of silver sela'im for gold dinarim.

וְחַד אָמַר [5]Thus far the Gemara has suggested that Bet Hillel and Bet Shammai agree that gold coins can be used directly to redeem second-tithe produce. **But the other** Sage (Rabbi Yoḥanan or Resh Lakish) **said: The difference of opinion also concerns** the redemption of second-tithe **produce** directly **with** gold **dinarim.** According to Bet Shammai, the produce may not be redeemed with gold dinarim under any circumstances, because gold coins are not considered money, even in relation to produce.

וּלְמַאן דְּאָמַר [6]The Gemara now asks: **According to the opinion** just expressed — **that the difference of opinion** between Bet Shammai and Bet Hillel **also concerns** the issue of **redeeming produce with** gold **dinarim** — it is difficult to understand why the focus of the dispute is the reexchange of silver coins for gold ones: [7]**Rather than** stating that the **disagreement** between Bet Shammai and Bet Hillel was **about** exchanging silver **sela'im for** gold **dinarim,** [8]**let** the Mishnah state that they **disagree about** redeeming second-tithe **produce with** gold **dinarim.** If Bet Shammai and Bet Hillel do in fact disagree as to whether gold can be used to redeem second-tithe produce, the Mishnah should surely have focused its attention on this fundamental disagreement. The absence of an explicit statement to this effect in the Mishnah indicates that it is everyone's opinion that gold *can* redeem second-tithe produce. Furthermore, had it been stated in the Mishnah that Bet Shammai are of the opinion that second-tithe produce may not be redeemed with gold because gold is not considered money for the purposes of second-tithe redemption, we could have inferred on our own that silver sela'im may not be exchanged for gold dinarim.

[1]לְגַבֵּי פֵּירָא טִבְעָא הָוֵי. [2]זָהָב נַמִי, לְבֵית שַׁמַּאי, [3]אַף עַל גַּב דְּדַהֲבָא לְגַבֵּי כַּסְפָּא פֵּירָא הָוֵי, [4]לְגַבֵּי פֵּירָא טִבְעָא הָוֵי.

[5]וְחַד אָמַר: אַף בְּפֵירוֹת עַל דִּינָרִין מַחֲלוֹקֶת.

[6]וּלְמַאן דְּאָמַר אַף בְּפֵירוֹת עַל דִּינָרִין מַחֲלוֹקֶת, [7]אַדְּמִיפַּלְגֵי בְּסְלָעִין עַל דִּינָרִין, [8]לִפְלוֹג בְּפֵירוֹת עַל דִּינָרִין!

LITERAL TRANSLATION

[1]in relation to produce it is money. [2]Gold, too, according to Bet Shammai, [3]even though gold in relation to silver is merchandise, [4]in relation to produce it is money.

[5]And [the other] one says: The difference of opinion also concerns produce for dinarim.

[6]And according to the one who says [that] the difference of opinion also concerns produce for dinarim, [7]rather than disagreeing about sela'im for dinarim, [8]let them disagree about produce for dinarim!

RASHI

לגבי פירא טבעא הוי – כדקתני "סלעין", אלמא: תחילת הפירות נתחללו על הכסף, ומודו בית הלל דקדשו במעשר. **אף בפירות על דינרין מחלוקת** – שמאי והלל, דלבית שמאי פירא הוא ואין מחללין. **לפלגו בפירות על דינרין** – ולימרו בית שמאי "אין מחללין", ואנא ידענא דכל שכן סלעין על דינרין וכו׳, דכיון דדהבא לגבי פירא פירא הוא – כל שכן לגבי כספא.

TERMINOLOGY

אַדְּמִיפַּלְגֵי בְּ... לִפְלוֹג בְּ Rather than differing about X, let them differ about Y! This term introduces an objection to a previously suggested interpretation of a difference of opinion between Tannaim. Such an objection is usually expressed as follows: "Rather than their differing about case X, it would have been more reasonable for these Tannaim to disagree about case Y, and in this way the subject would be better clarified."

NOTES

the word כֶּסֶף, which literally means "silver." Hence it is obvious that the Torah allowed silver coins to be used for this purpose. Now, according to Bet Hillel, gold coins are even better than silver coins. Hence, since the Torah permitted silver coins, it follows that either metal may be used. But according to Bet Shammai, silver coins are better than gold, and the Torah mentioned only silver. From where, then, did Bet Shammai derive the idea that gold may also be used to redeem second-tithe produce?

Torat Ḥayyim explains that the etymology of the word כֶּסֶף should be ignored, and the word should be translated not as "silver" but as "money." Thus the Torah is teaching us nothing about which coin to use, and both Bet Shammai and Bet Hillel derive their respective opinions from logical arguments alone. These lead to the conclusion that second-tithe produce may be redeemed by gold.

וְחַד אָמַר: אַף בְּפֵירוֹת עַל דִּינָרִין מַחֲלוֹקֶת And the other one says: The difference of opinion also concerns produce for dinarim. According to this opinion, Bet Shammai maintain that silver sela'im may not be redeemed with gold dinarim, and that even second-tithe produce itself may not be redeemed with gold coins. *Rif* understands that according to this opinion, gold is considered merchandise absolutely, even in relation to ordinary movable goods, but he rejects the ruling of *Rav Hai Gaon,* who accepted such a position in practice. *Rif* rejected *Rav Hai Gaon*'s ruling on the grounds that this is only the position of Bet Shammai, and only according to Resh Lakish, and only according to the first two versions of the dispute between Resh Lakish and Rabbi Yoḥanan, and therefore not normative.

Ramban interprets Bet Shammai's position as applying only to the redemption of second tithe. Second-tithe money must ultimately be used for the purchase of food in Jerusalem, and gold coins must be exchanged for smaller

TERMINOLOGY

תִּסְתַּיֵּים Conclude. Sometimes the Talmud notes that there was a controversy between two Sages concerning a certain issue, but it is not clear which Sage took what position. In such cases, the Talmud's initial attempt to attribute the views correctly is often introduced by the expression תִּסְתַּיֵּים דְּרַבִּי פְּלוֹנִי הוּא דְּאָמַר — "Conclude that it was Rabbi X who said... [and that Rabbi B holds the other view]." If this suggestion is confirmed later in the discussion, the Talmud may close the discussion with the remark תִּסְתַּיֵּים — "Conclude [that the suggested identification was indeed correct]."

TRANSLATION AND COMMENTARY

אִי אִיפְּלוּג בְּפֵירוֹת עַל דִּינָרִין [1]The Gemara answers: The disagreement between Bet Shammai and Bet Hillel was stated with regard to exchanging sela'im for dinarim in order to clarify the position of Bet Hillel and to avoid a possible misunderstanding. For **if the disagreement had been stated** only **with regard to** redeeming second-tithe **produce with** gold **dinarim,** [2]**I might have said** that the disagreement was limited and only **applies to** the issue of redeeming second-tithe **produce with** gold **dinarim.** I would have assumed that Bet Hillel are of the opinion that second-tithe produce may be redeemed with gold dinarim, because gold coins are considered money in relation to produce, and that Bet Shammai disagree. [3]**But in the case of** exchanging silver **sela'im for** gold **dinarim,** I would have assumed that **Bet Hillel concede to Bet Shammai that gold is** considered **merchandise in relation to silver,** [4]**and** that since second-tithe redemption money may not be exchanged for coins considered merchandise in relation to second-tithe redemption money, **we are not permitted to redeem** silver sela'im with gold dinarim. [5]**Therefore,** to avoid this erroneous deduction, the Mishnah **teaches us** that, unlike Bet Shammai, Bet Hillel are of the opinion that sela'im may be redeemed with dinarim because gold is considered money in relation to silver.

תִּסְתַּיֵּים [6]The Gemara stated above that Rabbi Yoḥanan and Resh Lakish disagreed in their understanding of the difference of opinion between Bet Shammai and Bet Hillel recorded in the Mishnah from tractate *Ma'aser Sheni.* But the Gemara did not specify which of the viewpoints ("one said... the other said...") was that of Rabbi Yoḥanan and which was that of Resh Lakish. The Gemara now addresses this issue: **Conclude that it is Rabbi Yoḥanan who said** that Bet Shammai are of the opinion that **we may not redeem** even second-tithe produce for gold dinarim. [7]For Rabbi Yoḥanan said: [45A] **It is forbidden** by Rabbinic decree **to borrow dinarim** if the loan is to be repaid **with** other **dinarim,** in case they appreciate during the period of the loan. Such a loan would be included in the prohibition against lending a *se'ah* of produce when the loan is to be repaid with a similar *se'ah* of produce. As noted above, this was prohibited by the Rabbis because the value of the produce might

[1]אִי אִיפְּלוּג בְּפֵירוֹת עַל דִּינָרִין, [2]הֲוָה אָמִינָא: הָנֵי מִילֵּי בְּפֵירוֹת עַל דִּינָרִין, [3]אֲבָל בִּסְלָעִין עַל דִּינָרִין, מוֹדוּ לְהֶן בֵּית הִלֵּל לְבֵית שַׁמַּאי דְּדַהֲבָא לְגַבֵּי כַּסְפָּא פֵּירָא הָוֵי, [4]וְלָא מְחַלְּלִינַן. [5]קָא מַשְׁמַע לָן. [6]תִּסְתַּיֵּים דְּרַבִּי יוֹחָנָן הוּא דְּאָמַר "אֵין מְחַלְּלִין". [7]דְּאָמַר רַבִּי יוֹחָנָן: [45A] אָסוּר לִלְווֹת דִּינָר בְּדִינָר.

LITERAL TRANSLATION

[1]If they had disagreed about produce for dinarim, [2]I might have said: This applies (lit., "these words") to produce for dinarim, [3]but in [the case of] sela'im for dinarim, Bet Hillel concede to Bet Shammai that gold in relation to silver is merchandise, [4]and we may not redeem [with it]. [5][Therefore] it tells us [that this is not so].

[6]Conclude that it is Rabbi Yoḥanan who said: "We may not redeem." [7]For Rabbi Yoḥanan said: [45A] It is forbidden to borrow a dinar for a dinar.

RASHI

הוה אמינא – דלא איפלוג בית הלל עלייהו אלא בפירות, אבל בסלעין – אימא מודי להו דאין מחללין על דינרים. **תסתיים דרבי יוחנן [הוא] דאמר** – לבית שמאי אין מחללין אפילו פירות על דינרין, דשמעינן לרבי יוחנן דאיכא למאן דאמר דהבא פירא הוי, ואפילו לגבי נפשיה. **אסור ללות דינר בדינר** – שמא יוקירו ויבא לידי רבית, ובדינר זהב קאמר, כדמפרש ואזיל.

NOTES

silver coins before they are so used. Since in that future transaction, the gold will be considered merchandise — because gold is merchandise in relation to silver — redeeming produce with gold is considered as redeeming with merchandise. But no conclusion may be drawn from here that gold is considered merchandise in absolute terms.

Rambam's interpretation clarifies the dissimilarity between gold and silver. Even according to the opinion that silver is considered merchandise in relation to gold, second-tithe produce may certainly be redeemed with silver coins. For silver coins are money, and the fact that silver is merchandise in relation to gold is irrelevant, since there will be no need to convert the silver into any other currency before it is used to purchase food. Similarly, copper coins may be used to redeem second-tithe produce even though copper is merchandise in relation to silver (and according to some opinions, even in relation to gold), because copper too can be spent without converting it into a different currency. The fact that upon arrival in Jerusalem the gold coins will have to be converted into silver or copper coins leads us to inquire into the status of gold in the context of second-tithe redemption.

אָסוּר לִלְווֹת דִּינָר בְּדִינָר It is forbidden to borrow a dinar for a dinar. The Gemara's conclusion is: According to the opinion that gold is merchandise relative to silver and may not be used to redeem second-tithe silver coins, gold coins

HALAKHAH

אָסוּר לִלְווֹת דִּינָר בְּדִינָר It is forbidden to borrow a dinar for a dinar. "It is forbidden by Rabbinic decree to borrow objects with the intention of repaying the loan with other objects of equal value, lest such objects appreciate in the interim, in which case the borrower will be violating the prohibition against paying interest, since the object he is

TRANSLATION AND COMMENTARY

rise between the time of the loan and the time of repayment, and the increase in value is a form of interest on the loan, which is prohibited. Similarly, Rabbi Yoḥanan forbids lending dinarim if the loan is to be repaid with other dinarim, lest they appreciate during the period of the loan. If such appreciation were to take place, the borrower would have to return dinarim worth more at the time of repayment than at the time of the loan.

דִּינָר דְּמַאי [1]The Gemara asks: To **what sort of dinarim** is Rabbi Yoḥanan referring? [2]**If we say** that he forbids borrowing **silver dinarim** if the loan is to be repaid **with** other **silver dinarim**, [3]**is there anyone who says that** silver **is not** considered **money** even **in relation to itself?** Such a loan should be permitted, because silver is certainly considered money, and the prohibition against borrowing objects when the loan is to be repaid with similar objects applies only to merchandise, the value of which fluctuates, and not to currency, the value of which is constant. [4]**Rather, it is obvious that** Rabbi Yoḥanan's ruling **means** that it is forbidden to borrow **gold dinarim** if the loan is to be repaid **with** other **gold dinarim**.

[1]דִּינָר דְּמַאי? [2]אִילֵימָא: דִּינָר שֶׁל כֶּסֶף בְּדִינָר שֶׁל כֶּסֶף, [3]לְגַבֵּי נַפְשֵׁיהּ מִי אִיכָּא לְמַאן דְּאָמַר לָאו טִבְעָא הָוֵי? [4]אֶלָּא, פְּשִׁיטָא: דִּינָר שֶׁל זָהָב בְּדִינָר שֶׁל זָהָב.

LITERAL TRANSLATION

[1]A dinar of what? [2]If we say: A dinar of silver for a dinar of silver, [3]in relation to itself is there anyone who says [that] it is not money? [4]Rather, it is obvious [that it means]: A dinar of gold for a dinar of gold.

REALIA

דִּינָרֵי זָהָב וְכֶסֶף **Gold and silver dinarim.**

A gold *dinarius* (*aureus*) of the Emperor Nero.

A silver *dinarius* of the Emperor Vespasian.

NOTES

are subject to the "*se'ah*-for-a-*se'ah*" prohibition, and may not be lent and returned freely, even though gold coins are money relative to produce and may be used to redeem the second-tithe produce itself. For although gold coins are money for the purpose of redeeming second-tithe produce, nevertheless "since they are considered merchandise for the purpose of buying and selling, they are also considered merchandise for the purpose of loans."

Rishonim ask: Why should the applicability of the "*se'ah*-for-a-*se'ah*" prohibition depend on gold's status as merchandise relative to silver in the redemption of second-tithe coins, and not on its status as money for the purpose of redeeming second-tithe produce?

Ramban argues that because of the severity of the prohibition against usury, the Rabbis apply the "*se'ah*-for-a-*se'ah*" prohibition whenever a price fluctuation may be perceived to be a profit, even if objectively it is not. Thus the application of "a *se'ah* for a *se'ah*" to a loan of a gold dinar depends on whether it is viewed as a loan of a gold dinar or as a loan of 25 silver dinarim. Because of its great value, a gold coin must be converted into silver before it can be spent. Hence, a loan of gold dinarim may be perceived as a loan of the silver dinarim into which it will be converted, and is therefore subject to the "*se'ah*-for-a-*se'ah*" laws.

A similar argument applies to redeeming second tithe. Using gold coins to redeem the produce depends only on the absolute status of gold, and is permitted. But using gold coins to redeem silver coins is forbidden, since it will in any case be necessary to convert the gold coins back to silver before they can be used, and if the price fluctuates, the result may be a drop in the value of the second-tithe money. Therefore the question of the applicability of the "*se'ah*-for-a-*se'ah*" prohibition to a gold coin depends on whether we are permitted to use it to redeem second-tithe silver coins, and not on whether we are permitted to use it to redeem the second-tithe produce.

דִּינָר שֶׁל כֶּסֶף בְּדִינָר שֶׁל כֶּסֶף **A dinar of silver for a dinar of silver.** The Gemara's conclusion is that, according to Rabbi Yehudah HaNasi's later ruling that gold is merchandise relative to silver, gold coins are subject to the "*se'ah*-for-a-*se'ah*" prohibition. However, silver coins are never subject to that prohibition even according to Rabbi Yehudah HaNasi's earlier opinion that silver is merchandise relative to gold. The Gemara does not specifically refer to lending copper coins, but it does say that even Bet Shammai, who do not permit second-tithe money to be redeemed with gold coins, would permit it to be redeemed with copper coins. From this the Rishonim infer that even if the "*se'ah*-for-a-*se'ah*" prohibition applies to gold coins, it does not apply to copper.

The Rishonim were troubled by the dissimilarity in the "*se'ah*-for-a-*se'ah*" law regarding the different metals. They ask: Why should gold coins be the only ones subject to the "*se'ah*-for-a-*se'ah*" prohibition? Since gold coins may not be borrowed, according to Rabbi Yehudah HaNasi's later opinion, because they are regarded as merchandise, why should it be permitted to borrow silver coins according to Rabbi Yehudah HaNasi's earlier opinion? And why should it be permitted to borrow copper coins, even though everyone agrees that copper is merchandise relative to silver?

Ramban accounts for gold's anomalous status in accordance with his explanation that the laws of usury depend on the participants' subjective perception of the loan (see previous note). A loan of gold coins is in practice perceived to be a loan of silver coins, since the gold coins must be converted into silver coins before they can be spent. Hence gold is subject to "a *se'ah* for a *se'ah*. But silver or

HALAKHAH

returning is worth more than the object originally borrowed. This prohibition also applies to borrowing gold coins with the intention of repaying the loan with other gold coins. But it is permitted to borrow silver coins or other merchandise on such terms, if the object's monetary value is assessed at the time of the loan." (*Shulḥan Arukh, Yoreh De'ah* 162:1.) *Rema* writes that, in his time, gold coins were treated like silver coins (since they were considered currency and not produce), and his view is accepted. (Aḥaronim on this section of the *Shulḥan Arukh*.)

[1]וּלְמַאן? [2]אִי לְבֵית הִלֵּל, הָא אָמְרִי טִבְעָא הָוֵי! [3]אֶלָּא, לָאו לְבֵית שַׁמַּאי, [4]וּשְׁמַע מִינָּהּ רַבִּי יוֹחָנָן הוּא דַּאֲמַר אֵין מְחַלְּלִינַן! [5]לָא! לְעוֹלָם אֵימָא לָךְ: [6]רַבִּי יוֹחָנָן הוּא דַּאֲמַר מְחַלְּלִינַן. [7]וְשָׁאנֵי הַלְוָאָה. [8]כֵּיוָן דִּלְעִנְיַן מִקָּח וּמִמְכָּר שַׁוְיוּהוּ רַבָּנַן כִּי פֵּירָא, [9]דְּאָמְרִינַן אִיהוּ נִיהוּ דְּאוֹקִיר וְזִיל, [10]לְגַבֵּי הַלְוָאָה נַמִי פֵּירָא הָוֵי.

LITERAL TRANSLATION

[1]And according to whom? [2]If according to Bet Hillel, surely they say it is money! [3]Rather, is it not according to Bet Shammai, [4]and conclude from here [that] it is Rabbi Yoḥanan who said [that] we may not redeem! [5]No! In fact I can say to you [6][that] it is Rabbi Yoḥanan who said [that] we may redeem. [7]But a loan is different. [8]Since for the subject of buying and selling the Rabbis considered it [gold] as merchandise, [9]for we say that it is *it* that appreciates and depreciates, [10]with regard to a loan, too, it is merchandise.

TRANSLATION AND COMMENTARY

וּלְמַאן [1]The Gemara now asks: **According to whom** — Bet Hillel or Bet Shammai — does Rabbi Yoḥanan forbid such a loan of gold dinarim? [2]**If** you say that he is ruling **according to** Bet Hillel, **surely they say that,** in relation to silver, gold **is** considered **money,** for they rule that silver sela'im of second-tithe money may be exchanged for gold dinarim. If they view gold as money with regard to second tithe, they must also view it as money with regard to loans. [3]**Rather, is it not** clear that Rabbi Yoḥanan's ruling is **in accordance with** the viewpoint of **Bet Shammai**, who maintain that gold is considered merchandise in relation to silver, for they rule that silver sela'im of second-tithe money may not be exchanged for gold dinarim. [4]**And** thus we may **infer from here that it is Rabbi Yoḥanan who said that** according to Bet Shammai **we may** not **redeem** second-tithe produce with gold **dinarim.** Since Rabbi Yoḥanan prohibits borrowing gold dinarim if the loan is to be repaid with other gold dinarim — in accordance with the viewpoint of Bet Shammai — we may infer that it is Rabbi Yoḥanan who maintains that, according to Bet Shammai, such coins are considered merchandise in all circumstances, and not only in relation to silver. For this reason, gold coins may not be used to redeem second-tithe produce.

לָא לְעוֹלָם אֵימָא לָךְ [5]The Gemara rejects this conclusion, saying: **No! In fact I can say to you** [6]**that it is Rabbi Yoḥanan who says** that even Bet Shammai agree that **we may redeem** second-tithe produce with gold dinarim. [7]**But** even though gold coins are considered money with regard to redemption, **loans are different.** The criteria used to define "money" and "merchandise" with regard to loans differ from those that apply to the redemption of second tithe. [8]The Gemara goes on to explain: **Since,** by using the expression "gold acquires silver" in our Mishnah, **the Rabbis considered gold as merchandise with regard to buying and selling** — [9]**for we say** that when the prices of gold and silver fluctuate in relation to each other, **it is** the gold **that appreciates and depreciates,** whereas the value of the silver remains constant — [10]therefore gold **is considered merchandise with regard to loans as well.** Hence Rabbi Yoḥanan rules that it is forbidden to borrow gold dinarim if the loan is to be repaid with other gold dinarim, because if gold appreciates in value during the period of the loan, the borrower will return dinarim that are worth more than those he received, and this would be considered interest. Nevertheless, Rabbi Yoḥanan might say that, even according to Bet Shammai, gold coins are suitable for second-tithe redemption.

RASHI

לעולם אימא לך רבי יוחנן הוא דאמר דברי הכל מחללינן — לגבי פירא טבעא הוי. **כיון דלענין מקח וממכר שויוהו רבנן כי פירא** — כדתנן (בבא מציעא מד,א): הזהב קונה את הכסף.

NOTES

copper coins can easily be spent without being converted. Hence they are not subject to this prohibition.

Other Rishonim accept the Gemara's statement that the "*se'ah*-for-a-*se'ah*" prohibition should apply whenever a coin is considered merchandise relative to another coin. As to the question why the "*se'ah*-for-a-*se'ah*" prohibition does not apply to a loan of silver coins according to Rabbi Yehudah HaNasi's earlier opinion, *Rosh* points out that even according to this opinion, most business is carried out using silver coins. Hence it is clear that loans of silver are permitted. *Ra'avad* adds that the Torah always refers to money as silver. Moreover, when the Torah commands us to lend money to a poor man, it says: "If you lend silver to my people...you may not impose usury upon him," and it would be perverse to classify a loan of silver as inherently usurious when the Torah specifically commands us to make such loans.

In response to the question why it should be permitted to lend copper coins, *Rashba* suggests that the Rabbis imposed the "*se'ah*-for-a-*se'ah*" prohibition only on those coins that circulate least freely. Thus gold — which is merchandise relative to all other coins — is subject to this prohibition, while copper — which is merchandise relative to silver but money relative to gold — is not subject to it.

[1]הָכִי נַמִי מִסְתַּבְּרָא. [2]דְּכִי אֲתָא רָבִין אָמַר רַבִּי יוֹחָנָן: [3]אַף עַל פִּי שֶׁאָמְרוּ אָסוּר לִלְווֹת דִּינָר בְּדִינָר, [4]אֲבָל מְחַלְּלִין מַעֲשֵׂר שֵׁנִי עָלָיו. [5]שְׁמַע מִינָּהּ.

[6]תָּא שְׁמַע: ״הַפּוֹרֵט סֶלַע מִמְּעוֹת מַעֲשֵׂר שֵׁנִי, [7]בֵּית שַׁמַּאי אוֹמְרִים: בְּכָל הַסֶּלַע, מָעוֹת. [8]וּבֵית הִלֵּל אוֹמְרִים: בְּשֶׁקֶל, כֶּסֶף; [9]בְּשֶׁקֶל, מָעוֹת״.

LITERAL TRANSLATION

[1]This also stands to reason. [2]For when Ravin came, he said in the name of Rabbi Yoḥanan: [3]Although they said [that] it is forbidden to borrow a dinar for a dinar, [4]nevertheless we may redeem second tithe with it. [5]Conclude from it.

[6]Come [and] hear: "Someone who changes a sela of second-tithe coins, [7]Bet Shammai say: For the entire sela, coins. [8]But Bet Hillel say: For a shekel, silver; [9]for a shekel, coins."

TRANSLATION AND COMMENTARY

הָכִי נַמִי מִסְתַּבְּרָא [1]The Gemara now brings confirmation that **it stands to reason** that it was Rabbi Yoḥanan who maintained that Bet Shammai agree that second-tithe produce may be redeemed with gold, and that he distinguished between second-tithe redemption and loans: [2]**For when Ravin came** from Eretz Israel to Babylonia, **he said in the name of Rabbi Yoḥanan:** [3]**Although** the Sages **said that it is forbidden to borrow** gold **dinarim** if the loan is to be repaid **with** other gold **dinarim,** [4]**nevertheless we may redeem second-tithe** produce **with them.** [5]Thus we can **conclude from** the ruling reported by Ravin that Rabbi Yoḥanan indeed maintains that gold is considered merchandise with regard to loans, but money for the purpose of redeeming second tithe. Since it has already been shown that Rabbi Yoḥanan's ruling must have been issued in accordance with the viewpoint of Bet Shammai, we may also conclude that it was Rabbi Yoḥanan who maintained that even according to Bet Shammai, second-tithe produce may be redeemed with gold coins, whereas according to Resh Lakish gold coins may not be used for such redemption.

תָּא שְׁמַע [6]Having established the respective viewpoints of Rabbi Yoḥanan and Resh Lakish in relation to the difference of opinion between Bet Shammai and Bet Hillel, the Gemara now returns to the question of whether or not second-tithe produce may be redeemed with gold: **Come and hear** what we have learned in the following Mishnah (*Ma'aser Sheni* 2:8): "If **someone** wishes to **change a sela's** worth **of second-tithe** copper **coins** for a single silver sela to make it easier to transport the money to Jerusalem, [7]**Bet** Shammai say: He may exchange **the entire sela's** worth of copper **coins** for a single silver sela. [8]**But Bet Hillel say:** He may change **a shekel's** (half a sela's) worth of copper coins **for** a single **silver** shekel, [9]but the other **shekel's** worth of copper coins he may not change. They must remain in the form of copper **coins,** so that he will have small change available to spend in Jerusalem."

RASHI

הכי נמי מסתברא – דרבי יוחנן הוא דאמר מחללין. **הפורט סלע ממעות מעשר שני** – מי שיש לו מעות נחשת של מעשר שני, ובא לפורטן בסלע כסף להעלות לירושלים מפני משאוי הדרך. **בית שמאי אומרים בכל הסלע מעות** – אם בא לפורטן יפרוט כולן, ויתן מעות בשביל כל הסלע. **ובית הלל אומרים לא יפרוט** – אלא חציין, שהפרוטות יוצאות בירושלים, וכשיבא שם יהא צריך לפרוטות מיד לקנות צרכי סעודה, ואם ירוצו הכל אצל שולחני לפרוט – יוקירו הפרוטות, ונמצא מעשר שני נפסד, לפיכך ישאו פרוטות עמהן להוציא במקצת, לכשיכלו יפרוט הכסף שבידו מעט מעט.

NOTES

הַפּוֹרֵט סֶלַע מִמְּעוֹת מַעֲשֵׂר שֵׁנִי **Someone who changes a sela of second-tithe coins.** Our commentary follows *Rashi*, who explains that in this Mishnah (*Ma'aser Sheni* 2:8), the farmer is changing his copper coins into silver ones, so that he can carry them more easily to Jerusalem. But this explanation does not fit the wording of the Mishnah, since the Mishnah uses the word הַפּוֹרֵט, which usually means exchanging larger, more valuable coins for smaller, less valuable ones, whereas here the farmer is exchanging his copper coins for more valuable ones. Nevertheless, the word הַפּוֹרֵט is sometimes used in this way. For example, the Gemara (above, 38a) quotes a Baraita that uses this word to describe a charity collector changing the small coins he has collected into more valuable coins (*Ritva*).

בֵּית שַׁמַּאי אוֹמְרִים: בְּכָל הַסֶּלַע, מָעוֹת **Bet Shammai say: For the entire sela, coins.** Our commentary follows *Rashi*, who explains that in this Mishnah, Bet Shammai *permit* the farmer to change the coins in any way that is convenient to him, whereas Bet Hillel insist that he may only convert half of the copper coins to silver; the rest he must leave as copper so that he will have small change available to spend in Jerusalem without having to pay a money changer to change it back. *Tosafot* objects to this explanation, as this Mishnah appears also in tractate *Eduyyot* (1:9), where the differences of opinion between Bet Shammai and Bet Hillel are categorized, and it is not listed among the cases where Bet Hillel took a strict view while Bet Shammai were lenient, as it should have been according to *Rashi*. *Tosafot* therefore explains that, according to Bet Shammai, the farmer *is required* to change all his copper coins to silver, as it is

HALAKHAH

הַפּוֹרֵט סֶלַע מִמְּעוֹת מַעֲשֵׂר שֵׁנִי **Someone who changes a sela of second-tithe coins.** "If someone wishes to change a silver sela of second-tithe money for copper coins, or a sela's worth of copper coins for a silver sela, whether inside

TERMINOLOGY

הָכִי נַמִי מִסְתַּבְּרָא **This also stands to reason,** i.e., indeed, what has just been stated makes sense (because...). Arguments introduced by this expression are usually considered conclusive.

כִּי אֲתָא רַבִּי פְּלוֹנִי **When Rabbi X came [he said]....** This expression introduces a tradition or a new law quoted by a particular scholar when he came to the Academy, usually when he came to Babylonia from Eretz Israel.

REALIA

סֶלַע **Sela.**

The word סֶלַע, which means "rock" or "stone" in Hebrew, refers to a coin, a usage which is probably connected to use of the word סֶלַע as a unit of weight (cf. the British use of the word "stone," which, however, refers to a much heavier weight). A סֶלַע, the largest silver coin in circulation, was worth four dinars. This sum was a full day's wages for a simple laborer.

SAGES

רָבִין **Ravin.** This is Rabbi Avin, an Amora of the third and fourth generations. He was born in Babylonia and immigrated to Eretz Israel. Ravin was one of Rabbi Yoḥanan's younger students, and also studied under Rabbi Yoḥanan's great disciples. He was apparently a merchant by profession and acted as an "Emissary of Zion," taking the Torah of Eretz Israel to Babylonia. Ravin was known to have transmitted the rulings of Rabbi Yoḥanan and his other teachers with great precision. The Talmud frequently mentions that Ravin's arrival in Babylonia followed that of another emissary, Rav Dimi, and that Ravin's ruling generally determined the Halakhah. The greatest of the Babylonian Sages also respected the teachings he transmitted, though they did not always consider him a great Sage in his own right. His teachings are also found frequently in the Jerusalem Talmud, where he is called Rabbi Boon.

Two Sages bearing the name Ravin (Rabbi Avin) are mentioned in the Talmud. The first Rabbi Avin (discussed here) was the father of the second, and died before the latter's birth.

TERMINOLOGY

לִישָּׁנָא אַחֲרִינָא Another version. This phrase introduces a variant of teachings presented previously. Rather than citing a different version of a statement by an individual Sage, it generally introduces a whole discussion reported earlier in an entirely different fashion, and which will now be restated in accordance with the alternative version. According to the Geonic principles of Halakhic ruling, the Halakhah generally follows this second version of the discussion.

מַחֲלוֹקֶת בְּ... אֲבָל בְּ... דִּבְרֵי הַכֹּל... The difference of opinion concerns [the case of X], but in [the case of Y] all agree that.... This formula is used by the Gemara to limit a Tannaitic controversy to a particular case (or group of cases). At first sight, the disagreement between the Tanaim seems extreme. The Amoraim, however, explain that the disagreement is much more narrow.

LITERAL TRANSLATION

[1]Now, according to Bet Shammai, with regard to [copper] coins we may redeem, [2]with regard to gold is it necessary [to teach this]?!

[3]Copper coins are different. [4]In a place where they circulate, they are current.

[5]Another version: [Some] say this: [6]Rabbi Yoḥanan and Resh Lakish [disagree]. [7]One says: The difference of opinion is about sela'im for dinarim. [8]For Bet Shammai maintain:

[1]הָשְׁתָּא, לְבֵית שַׁמַּאי, לְגַבֵּי פְּרִיטֵי מְחַלְּלִינַן, [2]לְגַבֵּי דַּהֲבָא מִיבָּעֲיָא?!

[3]שָׁאנֵי פְּרִיטֵי. [4]בְּאַתְרָא דְּסַגְיָין, חֲרִיפֵי.

[5]לִישָּׁנָא אַחֲרִינָא אָמְרִי לָהּ: [6]רַבִּי יוֹחָנָן וְרֵישׁ לָקִישׁ. [7]חַד אֲמַר: מַחֲלוֹקֶת בִּסְלָעִין עַל דִּינָרִים. [8]דְּבֵית שַׁמַּאי סָבְרִי:

RASHI

השתא לבית שמאי כו׳ — דמדקתני ״ממעות מעשר שני״ — שמע מינה: חילל פירות על הפרוטות. **לגבי דהבא מיבעיא** — דמחללין פירות, ותיובתא דמאן דאמר ״אף בפירות על דינרין מחלוקת״.

TRANSLATION AND COMMENTARY

הָשְׁתָּא לְבֵית שַׁמַּאי [1]The Gemara now attempts to prove from this Mishnah that, even according to Bet Shammai, second-tithe produce may be redeemed with gold. It argues as follows: **Now,** if **according to Bet Shammai we are permitted to redeem second**-tithe produce **with copper coins** — for the Mishnah's discussion of changing copper coins for other coins assumes that the copper ones had previously been used to redeem second-tithe produce — [2]**is it necessary** to inform us that we are permitted to redeem second-tithe produce **with gold?** Surely gold has a better claim to be regarded as money, for gold is much more valuable than copper. Thus it would appear that even according to Bet Shammai, gold may be used to redeem second-tithe produce, so this Mishnah seems to contradict Resh Lakish, who maintains that, according to Bet Shammai, second-tithe produce may not be redeemed with gold coins.

שָׁאנֵי פְּרִיטֵי [3]The Gemara rejects this line of reasoning: **Copper coins are different,** [4]for **in places where they circulate, they circulate** more **easily** than gold. Since in those places where copper coins circulate, they are more widely accepted as legal tender than gold, it is reasonable to argue that copper would be considered money with regard to tithe redemption, but gold would not. This Mishnah thus offers no proof that second-tithe produce may be redeemed with gold coins.

לִישָּׁנָא אַחֲרִינָא [5]According to the explanations offered above by Rabbi Yoḥanan and Resh Lakish, Bet Shammai and Bet Hillel disagree about the relationship between gold and silver — i.e., which is considered money in relation to the other. But **some report a different version** of the dispute between Rabbi Yoḥanan and Resh Lakish, according to which Bet Shammai and Bet Hillel disagree about an entirely different matter: As stated in the Mishnah from tractate *Ma'aser Sheni* (2:7) quoted above (44b), it is not permitted, according to Bet Shammai, to exchange silver sela'im of second-tithe money for gold dinarim, while according to Bet Hillel this is permitted. [6]**Rabbi Yoḥanan and Resh Lakish disagreed** in their understanding of this dispute. [7]**One said** that **the difference of opinion** specifically **concerns** the exchange of one set of second-tithe coins for another, such as **sela'im for dinarim.** [8]**Bet Shammai maintain** that when the Torah (Deuteronomy 14:25) stated regarding the redemption of second-tithe produce, "You shall turn it into money and you shall

NOTES

forbidden to use copper coins for second-tithe redemption for any length of time because they corrode quickly.

According to *Rashi*'s interpretation, this Mishnah is quite different from the following Mishnah in *Ma'aser Sheni* (2:9), quoted by the Gemara below, which deals with changing silver coins into copper coins in Jerusalem. Even though the two Mishnayot use almost identical language, the first deals with changing copper coins into silver coins for convenience in transportation, whereas the following one deals with changing silver coins into copper coins for use in Jerusalem.

To avoid the discrepancy in the use of the word הַפּוֹרֵט, *Rambam* and *Meiri* explain that, in the first Mishnah as well, the farmer is changing his silver coins into copper coins so that he will have small coins to spend in Jerusalem. According to this interpretation, there is no difference between the laws taught by the two Mishnayot. Both deal with changing silver coins into copper ones for use in Jerusalem. The reason both Mishnayot were needed is to emphasize that Bet Hillel forbid the changing of the entire silver sela even in Jerusalem, while Bet Shammai permit it even outside Jerusalem.

HALAKHAH

or outside Jerusalem, he should not change all the silver tithe-money into copper coins or all the copper tithe-money into silver coins. Rather, half of the sela should be in the form of silver coins, and the other half in the form of copper coins," following Bet Hillel. (*Rambam, Sefer Zeraim, Hilkhot Ma'aser Sheni* 5:14.)

TRANSLATION AND COMMENTARY

bind up **the money,**" it was **referring to "first" money and not "second" money.** In other words, once money has been used to redeem second-tithe produce, this "first" money may not be exchanged for other money. The money to be bound up and brought to Jerusalem must be the same money used to redeem the second-tithe produce. For this reason, dinarim may not be exchanged for sela'im, nor sela'im for sela'im. [1]But **Bet Hillel maintain** that the repetition of the word **"money"** in the verse **amplifies** the application of the law contained in the verse, [2]**and** extends it to **include** other money, **even "second" money.** Since the Torah has already stated "you shall turn it into money (בַּכָּסֶף)," it could have continued "and you shall bind *it* up." It did not need to repeat the word "money" (הַכֶּסֶף) in the second clause. Bet Hillel understand that this repetition of the word means that even "second money" — i.e., money exchanged for the initial tithe-money — must be brought to Jerusalem, and this implies that tithe-money can be exchanged for other money. [3]**But according to** everyone — both Bet Shammai and Bet Hillel — **we are permitted to redeem** second-tithe **produce with** gold **dinarim,** [4]**for they are still** in the category of **"first" money,** and produce may be redeemed with any type of currency, even gold. This is the way one of the Sages — Rabbi Yoḥanan or Resh Lakish — explained the difference of opinion between Bet Shammai and Bet Hillel.

וְחַד אָמַר [5]**But the other** Sage **said: The difference of opinion** between Bet Shammai and Bet Hillel **also concerns** redeeming second-tithe **produce** directly **with dinarim.** According to this interpretation of the difference of opinion, Bet Shammai may agree that it is permitted to exchange "first" money for other money. But silver sela'im may not be exchanged for gold dinarim because gold coins are not considered money, but merchandise. Accordingly, even second-tithe produce itself may not be redeemed with gold dinarim.

וּלְמַאן דְּאָמַר [6]The Gemara now objects to this version of the disagreement between Rabbi Yoḥanan and Resh Lakish in interpreting the dispute between Bet Shammai and Bet Hillel: **According to** the first opinion expressed above — which **says that the difference of opinion** between Bet Shammai and Bet Hillel specifically **concerns** the exchange of **sela'im for dinarim,** and claims that Bet Shammai and Bet Hillel disagree only about whether "first" money can be exchanged for "second" money, but not about the relationship between gold and silver — why was the exchange of sela'im for dinarim specified? If this interpretation of the difference of opinion is correct, [7]**rather than** stating that the **disagreement** between Bet Shammai and Bet Hillel was **about** exchanging silver **sela'im for** gold **dinarim,** [8]**let** the Mishnah state that they **disagree about** exchanging **sela'im for sela'im,** for that case too constitutes "second" money! Since the Mishnah specifies sela'im and dinarim, this implies that the dispute goes beyond the issue of "first" and "second" money, and that Bet Shammai and Bet Hillel disagree about the relationship between gold and silver.

"הַכֶּסֶף" כֶּסֶף רִאשׁוֹן, וְלֹא כֶּסֶף שֵׁנִי. [1]וּבֵית הִלֵּל סָבְרִי: "הַכֶּסֶף... כֶּסֶף" רִיבָּה, [2]וַאֲפִילּוּ כֶּסֶף שֵׁנִי. [3]אֲבָל פֵּירוֹת עַל דִּינָרִין דִּבְרֵי הַכֹּל מְחַלְּלִינַן, [4]דְּאַכַּתִּי כֶּסֶף רִאשׁוֹן הוּא.

[5]וְחַד אֲמַר: אַף בְּפֵירוֹת עַל דִּינָרִין נַמִי מַחֲלוֹקֶת.

[6]וּלְמַאן דְּאָמַר: סְלָעִין עַל דִּינָרִין מַחֲלוֹקֶת, [7]אַדְּמִיפַּלְגֵי בִּסְלָעִין עַל דִּינָרִין, [8]לִפְלְגִי בִּסְלָעִין עַל סְלָעִין!

LITERAL TRANSLATION

"The money" [means] first money, and not second money. [1]But Bet Hillel maintain: "The money... money" amplifies, [2]and [includes] even second money. [3]But according to everyone, we may redeem produce with dinarim, [4]for it is still first money.

[5]And [the other] one says: The difference of opinion is also about produce for dinarim.

[6]And according to the one who says [that] the difference of opinion [is about] sela'im for dinarim, [7]rather than disagreeing about sela'im for dinarim, [8]let them disagree about sela'im for sela'im!

RASHI

הכסף – "וצרת הכסף והלכת" (דברים יד). כסף ראשון – שחללת הפירות עליהם אתה צריך לצור בידך ולהוליך, ולא שתחלל אותו כסף על כסף אחר. הכסף כסף ריבה – "כסף" יתירא כתיב בפרשה. אף בפירות על דינרין מחלוקת – וטעמא דבית שמאי משום דדהבא פירא הוא, ולא מתחלל עליה מעשר. ולמאן דאמר בסלעין על דינרין – דוקא פליגי, וטעמא דבית שמאי משום כסף שני הוי, ולא משום דדהבא פירא הוא. אדמיפלגי בסלעין על דינרין – שיש לטעות ולומר טעמא משום דדהבא חשיב ליה פירא הוא – ניפלגו בסלעין על סלעין, ששניהם של כסף.

BACKGROUND

"הַכֶּסֶף... כֶּסֶף" רִיבָּה "The money... money" amplifies. Bet Shammai argue that since the Torah did not say just "money" (כֶּסֶף) but rather "the money" (הַכֶּסֶף), it was referring specifically to the money mentioned earlier — the money received for the tithed produce — which may not be exchanged for other money. However, according to Bet Hillel, since in the same context it was said "and you shall turn it into money and you shall bind up the money in your hand" (Deuteronomy 14:25), the second mention of the word "money" is meant to expand the meaning of the word, and to say that it need not be exactly the same money that was received for the produce, but can be any money brought in its place.

HALAKHAH

כֶּסֶף רִאשׁוֹן וְלֹא כֶּסֶף שֵׁנִי First money and not second money. "Money that has been used to redeem second tithe may not be redeemed again with other money (whether silver with silver, silver with copper, or copper with silver). However, if one did redeem such tithe-money with other money, the redemption takes effect; the first tithe-money loses its sanctity, and the second money is brought to Jerusalem. Nevertheless, it would appear permissible (see *Rashi*) to redeem tithe money with other coins if the latter circulate more easily than the tithe-money itself." (Ibid., 4:5.)

[1]אִי אִפְלְגִי בִּסְלָעִין עַל סְלָעִין, [2]הֲוָה אָמִינָא: הָנֵי מִילֵּי בִּסְלָעִין עַל סְלָעִין, [3]אֲבָל בִּסְלָעִין עַל דִּינָרִין, [4]מוֹדוּ לְהוּ בֵּית הִלֵּל לְבֵית שַׁמַּאי דְּדַהֲבָא לְגַבֵּי כַּסְפָּא פֵּירָא הָוֵי, [5]וְלָא מְחַלְּלִינַן. [6]קָא מַשְׁמַע לָן.

[7]תָּא שְׁמַע: ״הַפּוֹרֵט סֶלַע שֶׁל מַעֲשֵׂר שֵׁנִי בִּירוּשָׁלַיִם, [8]בֵּית שַׁמַּאי אוֹמְרִים: בְּכָל הַסֶּלַע, מָעוֹת. [9]וּבֵית הִלֵּל אוֹמְרִים: בְּשֶׁקֶל, כֶּסֶף; בְּשֶׁקֶל, מָעוֹת״.

LITERAL TRANSLATION

[1]If they had disagreed about sela'im for sela'im, [2]I might have said: This applies to sela'im for sela'im, [3]but [in the case of] sela'im for dinarim, [4]Bet Hillel concede to Bet Shammai that gold in relation to silver is merchandise, [5]and we may not redeem [with it]. [6][Therefore] it tells us [that this is not so].

[7]Come [and] hear: "Someone who changes a sela of second tithe in Jerusalem, [8]Bet Shammai say: For the entire sela, coins. [9]But Bet Hillel say: For a shekel, silver; for a shekel, coins."

TRANSLATION AND COMMENTARY

אִי אִפְלְגִי [1]The Gemara rejects this reasoning: The basic difference of opinion between Bet Hillel and Bet Shammai is indeed with respect to the issue of "first" and "second" money. The Gemara chose to state this disagreement in connection with the exchange of silver sela'im for gold dinarim in order to avoid a possible misunderstanding of the position of Bet Hillel. **If** the Mishnah had stated that Bet Shammai and Bet Hillel **disagree about** exchanging **sela'im for sela'im,** [2]**I might have said** that their disagreement was limited and **applies** only **to** the issue of exchanging **sela'im for sela'im**, and that the reason Bet Hillel permit this exchange is that, unlike Bet Shammai, they allow "first" money to be exchanged for "second" money. [3]**But in the case of** exchanging silver **sela'im** for gold **dinarim,** [4]I would have assumed that **Bet Hillel concede to Bet Shammai that** this is not permissible because **gold is** considered **merchandise in relation to silver,** [5]**and we are not permitted to redeem** second-tithe coins with merchandise. [6]To avoid this erroneous deduction, the Mishnah **therefore teaches us that this is not so,** and that the dispute between Bet Shammai and Bet Hillel applies even to the redemption of silver sela'im with gold dinarim. Bet Shammai prohibit any exchange that involves "second" money, whereas Bet Hillel permit such an exchange even if silver is exchanged for gold.

תָּא שְׁמַע [7]The Gemara now attempts to prove that the dispute between Bet Shammai and Bet Hillel cannot be about the issue of "first money and not second money," for there is a Mishnah which implies that even Bet Shammai agree that "first" money may be exchanged for "second" money: **Come and hear** what we have learned in the following Mishnah (*Ma'aser Sheni* 2:9): "If **someone** wishes to **change a** silver **sela of second-tithe** money **in Jerusalem** for copper coins of smaller denominations, in order to have small change with which to purchase food to eat in Jerusalem in fulfillment of his obligation with regard to second-tithe money, [8]**Bet Shammai say:** He may **exchange the entire** silver **sela for** copper **coins.** [9]**But Bet Hillel say:** He may change only half of the sela for copper coins, because he will possibly not spend the entire sela during his present stay in Jerusalem, and the remaining copper coins may corrode by the time he returns for his next visit. Therefore he may exchange the sela for **one shekel of silver and one shekel's** worth of copper **coins.** After he has spent all his small change, he may then convert the rest of the silver into copper coins."

RASHI

הוה אמינא – בסלעין על סלעין הוא דפליג בית הלל עלייהו, דלית להו כסף ראשון ולא כסף שני. **אבל בסלעין על דינרין אימא מודו להו** – דלא מיתחלי, משום דדהבא פירא הוא, קא משמע לן. הכי גרסינן: **הפורט סלע של מעשר שני בירושלים** – שהיה מחליף סלעים שבידו ונוטל פרוטות להוציאם לצרכי סעודות מעשר. **בית שמאי אומרים** – אם בא להחליף כל הסלעין שבידו במעות – יחליף. **ובית הלל אומרים לא יחליף אלא חציין** – שמא לא ישהה בעיר עד שיוציא את כולן, ויפקיד בעיר עד רגל אחר והפרוטות מתעפשות, ואם יחזור ויחליפם בסלעין – נמצא שולחני נפסד.

NOTES

הַפּוֹרֵט סֶלַע שֶׁל מַעֲשֵׂר שֵׁנִי בִּירוּשָׁלַיִם **Someone who changes a sela of second tithe in Jerusalem.** Our commentary follows *Rashi*, who explains that, in this Mishnah as well, Bet Shammai permit the farmer to change the coins in any way convenient to him, whereas Bet Hillel insist that he may only convert half of the silver to copper coins, and must leave the rest as silver until the first half is spent.

The reason for Bet Hillel's prohibition is that the farmer might not spend all his copper coins on this visit, and we fear that the coins left over will corrode if stored for a long period. Changing the copper coins back to silver is not an adequate solution because money changers charge a premium for such reconversion. Thus, storing or reconverting the leftover copper coins will diminish their value and the sanctity vested in them. Hence Bet Hillel ordered the farmer to convert only half his money at a time.

Rosh points out that *Rashi*'s explanation finds support in the Jerusalem Talmud, but most Rishonim object to *Rashi*'s explanation of this Mishnah for the same reason they objected to his explanation of the previous Mishnah dealing with changing second-tithe money outside Jerusalem (see note above).

LITERAL TRANSLATION

[1] Now, we may redeem silver for [copper] coins, [2] and we do not say "first money but not second money." [3] With regard to gold, which is more valuable than it, [4] shall we say "first money and not second money"?

[5] Rava said: Are you raising an objection from Jerusalem? [6] Jerusalem is different, as it is written with regard to it: [7] "And you shall bestow the money on whatever your soul desires, on cattle or on sheep."

[8] Come [and] hear: "Someone who exchanges a sela of second-tithe coins, [9] Bet Shammai say: For the entire sela, coins. [10] But Bet Hillel say: For a shekel, silver; for a shekel, coins."

[11] Rather, according to everyone, "the money... money" amplifies, [12] and [includes] even second money.

[1] הָשְׁתָּא, כַּסְפָּא לְגַבֵּי פְּרִיטֵי מְחַלְּלִינַן, [2] וְלָא אָמְרִינַן "כֶּסֶף רִאשׁוֹן וְלֹא כֶּסֶף שֵׁנִי". [3] לְגַבֵּי דַּהֲבָא, דַּחֲשִׁיב מִינֵּיהּ, [4] מִי אָמְרִינַן "כֶּסֶף רִאשׁוֹן וְלֹא כֶּסֶף שֵׁנִי"?

[5] אֲמַר רָבָא: יְרוּשָׁלַיִם קָמוֹתְבַתְּ? [6] שָׁאנֵי יְרוּשָׁלַיִם, דִּכְתִיב בֵּיהּ: [7] "וְנָתַתָּה הַכֶּסֶף בְּכֹל אֲשֶׁר תְּאַוֶּה נַפְשְׁךָ, בַּבָּקָר וּבַצֹּאן".

[8] תָּא שְׁמַע: "הַפּוֹרֵט סֶלַע מִמְּעוֹת מַעֲשֵׂר שֵׁנִי, [9] בֵּית שַׁמַּאי אוֹמְרִים: בְּכָל הַסֶּלַע, מָעוֹת. [10] וּבֵית הִלֵּל אוֹמְרִים: בְּשֶׁקֶל, כֶּסֶף; בְּשֶׁקֶל, מָעוֹת".

[12] אֶלָּא, דְּכוּלֵּי עָלְמָא, "הַכֶּסֶף... כֶּסֶף" רִיבָּה, [13] וַאֲפִילּוּ כֶּסֶף שֵׁנִי.

RASHI

תא שמע — מההיא קמייתא דלא מיירי בירושלים, דמחליף פרוטות ונוטל סלע.

TRANSLATION AND COMMENTARY

הָשְׁתָּא [1] **Now,** argues the Gemara, if according to Bet Shammai **we are permitted to redeem silver with copper coins,** as stated in the Mishnah just quoted, [2] **and we do not say** that the Torah limits the redemption of second tithe to **"first money but not second money,"** [3] **then with regard to gold, which is more valuable than** silver, [4] **how can we say** that according to Bet Shammai second tithe may only be redeemed with **"first money and not second money"?** If Bet Shammai agree that silver can be exchanged for copper, they should certainly agree that silver can be exchanged for gold.

אֲמַר רָבָא [5] **Rava** rejects this argument, and **says: Are you raising an objection from** the exchange of money in **Jerusalem**, arguing that just as silver can be exchanged for copper in Jerusalem, so too it should be permitted to exchange silver for gold outside Jerusalem? [6] The laws applying to second-tithe redemption in **Jerusalem are different, as it is written** (Deuteronomy 14:26) **with regard to** Jerusalem: [7] **"And you shall bestow the money on whatever your soul desires, on cattle or on sheep."** Second-tithe money must be spent in Jerusalem on food. Bet Shammai would therefore agree that, in Jerusalem, silver coins may be exchanged for copper ones because this facilitates the purchase of food. Outside Jerusalem, however, Bet Shammai may rule that the redemption of second tithe is limited to "first money and not second money," and therefore it is not permitted to exchange silver sela'im for gold dinarim.

תָּא שְׁמַע [8] The Gemara now again cites the Mishnah quoted above to prove that Bet Shammai and Bet Hillel do not disagree about the issue of "first money and not second money," and that even Bet Shammai agree that "first" money may be exchanged for "second" money: **Come and hear** what we have learned in the Mishnah quoted earlier from tractate *Ma'aser Sheni* (2:8): "If, outside Jerusalem, **someone** wishes to **change a sela's** worth of **second-tithe** copper **coins** for a single silver sela in order to make it easier to transport the money to Jerusalem, [9] **Bet Shammai say:** He may change **the entire sela's** worth of **coins** for a single silver sela. **But** [10] **Bet Hillel say:** He may exchange only **a shekel's** worth of copper coins **for** a single **silver** shekel; [11] the other **shekel's** worth of copper coins he may not change. They must remain in the form of copper **coins,** so that he will have small change available to spend in Jerusalem." This Mishnah proves conclusively that even according to Bet Shammai it is permitted to exchange "first" money for other money even outside Jerusalem!

אֶלָּא [12] **Rather,** we must reject our earlier interpretation that the dispute between Bet Shammai and Bet Hillel is limited to the issue of "first" and "second" money, and instead we must explain that **according to everyone** — even Bet Shammai — the repetition of the word **"money"** in the verse **amplifies** the application of the law contained in the verse, [13] **and** extends it to **include** other money, **even "second" money**. Consequently, if Bet Shammai nevertheless maintain that it is not permitted to exchange silver sela'im for gold dinarim, it must be because they disagree concerning the relative status of these coins.

BACKGROUND

שָׁאנֵי יְרוּשָׁלַיִם Jerusalem is different. Special laws applied to money received for second tithes, since it had a degree of sanctity. It was forbidden to use it for any purpose outside Jerusalem because the second tithe could be eaten only in Jerusalem, and one had no right to use it anywhere else. However, once the money reached Jerusalem, it was not permitted to leave it in monetary form, but, as commanded by the Torah, to use it to buy food to be eaten specifically in Jerusalem. Hence, rather than being a kind of deposit in its owner's hand, this money was particularly meant to be spent.

NOTES

שָׁאנֵי יְרוּשָׁלַיִם Jerusalem is different. The Gemara implies that in Jerusalem it is permitted to convert second-tithe money into coins of smaller denominations in order to satisfy the Torah's command that second-tithe money be used to buy food. The Rishonim ask: Perhaps the Torah permitted only the purchase of food with the second-tithe

LITERAL TRANSLATION

[1]But if it was stated that Rabbi Yoḥanan and Rabbi Shimon ben Lakish [disagreed], it was stated thus: [2]One says: The difference of opinion concerns sela'im for dinarim. [3]For Bet Shammai maintain: We enact a preventive measure [45B] lest he delay his pilgrimages. [4]For sometimes the zuzim do not amount to a dinar, and he does not bring [them] up. [5]But Bet Hillel maintain: We do not enact a preventive measure, lest he delay his pilgrimages. [6]For even if they do not amount to a dinar, he surely brings them up. [7]But according to everyone, we may redeem produce with dinarim. [8]For since it rots, he will not delay it.
[9]And [the other] one says: The difference of opinion also concerns produce for dinarim.

[1]אֶלָּא אִי אִיתְּמַר דְּרַבִּי יוֹחָנָן וְרַבִּי שִׁמְעוֹן בֶּן לָקִישׁ, הָכִי אִיתְּמַר: [2]חַד אֲמַר: מַחֲלוֹקֶת בִּסְלָעִין עַל דִּינָרִין. [3]דְּבֵית שַׁמַּאי סָבְרִי: גָּזְרִינַן [45B] שֶׁמָּא יַשְׁהֶה עֲלִיּוֹתָיו. [4]דְּזִימְנִין דְּלָא מְלוּ זוּזֵי בְּדִינָרָא, וְלָא מַסֵּיק. [5]וּבֵית הִלֵּל סָבְרִי: לָא גָּזְרִינַן, שֶׁמָּא יַשְׁהֶה עֲלִיּוֹתָיו. [6]דְּכִי לָא מְלוּ נַמִי בְּדִינָרָא, אַסּוּקֵי מַסֵּיק לְהוּ. [7]אֲבָל בְּפֵירוֹת עַל דִּינָרִין דִּבְרֵי הַכֹּל מְחַלְּלִינַן. [8]דְּכֵיוָן דְּמִרְקְבִי, לָא מַשְׁהֵי לְהוּ.
[9]וְחַד אֲמַר: אֲפִילּוּ בְּפֵירוֹת עַל דִּינָרִין נַמִי מַחֲלוֹקֶת.

RASHI

שמא ישהה עליותיו — עד שיספיק להיות לו סלעין מעשר עד שיגיעו לדמי דינר זהב בשנה שניה, שימכור מעשרות שנה הבאה. **אסוקי מסיק להו** — שאין משאן כבד, שמעט הן. **אפילו בפירות על דינרין מחלוקת** — דפירי נמי אתי לשהויי.

TRANSLATION AND COMMENTARY

אֶלָּא [1]The Gemara now suggests an amended version of the difference of opinion between Rabbi Yoḥanan and Resh Lakish: **If it was stated that Rabbi Yoḥanan and Resh Lakish disagreed, it was stated** in the following form: [2]**One** of them **said** that **the difference of opinion** between Bet Shammai and Bet Hillel on the subject of the redemption of second tithe specifically **concerns** the exchange of silver **sela'im for** gold **dinarim.** [3]**Bet Shammai maintain** that even though by Torah law second-tithe coins may be exchanged for coins of any other type, the Rabbis **enacted a preventive measure** [45B] forbidding the redemption of silver sela'im for gold dinarim, **lest** the owner of the tithe money **delay his pilgrimage** to Jerusalem while waiting to accumulate a gold dinar's worth of second-tithe money. [4]**For sometimes the zuzim** (silver coins) of second-tithe money in the owner's possession **do not amount to a** full gold **dinar, and** as a result **he will not bring** those coins he already has to Jerusalem. Since he would prefer to carry fewer coins with him, he may postpone his pilgrimage until he has a full gold dinar's worth of smaller silver coins, which he can then exchange for a single gold coin to bring to Jerusalem. [5]**But Bet Hillel maintain: We do not enact a preventive measure** based on the fear that the owner may **delay his pilgrimage.** [6]**For even if** the silver coins of second-tithe redemption money in his possession **do not amount to a** full gold **dinar, he will** surely **bring** the money — in silver coins — to Jerusalem in any event, since silver coins do not constitute a heavy burden. [7]**But according to everyone** — both Bet Shammai and Bet Hillel — **we are permitted to redeem** second-tithe **produce with** gold **dinarim,** for second-tithe produce may be redeemed with any type of coin, even gold. With regard to second-tithe produce itself, the Rabbis had no reason to enact a preventive measure forbidding the use of gold to redeem the produce, [8]because **since** the produce is liable to **rot,** the owner **will not delay** his pilgrimage to Jerusalem until he has a full gold dinar's worth. This is the way one of the Sages — Rabbi Yoḥanan or Resh Lakish — explained the difference of opinion between Bet Shammai and Bet Hillel.

וְחַד אֲמַר [9]**But the other** Sage **said** that **the difference of opinion** between Bet Shammai and Bet Hillel **also concerns** redeeming actual second-tithe **produce with** gold **dinarim.** According to this second explanation, Bet Shammai are of the opinion that even in such a case the Rabbis enacted a preventive measure forbidding redemption of second-tithe produce with gold, because a person may delay his pilgrimage to Jerusalem until he has a full gold dinar's worth of produce (which he can then redeem with a single dinar to be brought to Jerusalem), even though there is a risk that the delay may cause the fruit to spoil.

CONCEPTS

שָׁלֹשׁ רְגָלִים **The three Pilgrim Festivals.** Pesaḥ, Shavuot and Sukkot. On these three Festivals, Jewish men were obligated to appear in the Temple (Deuteronomy 16:16). All sacrifices previously pledged to the Temple were also brought on these Festivals, so as not to violate the prohibition against delaying sacrifices one had pledged.

BACKGROUND

שֶׁמָּא יַשְׁהֶה עֲלִיּוֹתָיו **Lest he delay his pilgrimages.** If a person had a small field, the quantity of his second tithe was proportionally small, and he received only a few silver dinarim for it. Since the money that a person received for the tithe was likely to be in the form of silver dinarim and copper perutot, which were not always easy to carry in one's hand, and there was reason to fear that they might be stolen on the way to Jerusalem, a person might be tempted to wait until the money reached the value of a whole gold dinar. In such a case, however, he might have to wait a considerable time, and before then he might not take the trouble to go up to Jerusalem.

NOTES

money, and prohibited its conversion into other coins?

Tosafot answers that since the purpose of changing the silver coins into copper coins is to enable the purchase of food in Jerusalem, permission for the exchange is implicit in the Torah's command to spend the money on food.

וְחַד אֲמַר אֲפִילּוּ בְּפֵירוֹת עַל דִּינָרִין נַמִי מַחֲלוֹקֶת **And the other one says: The difference of opinion also concerns produce for dinarim.** In this version, the Gemara does not explain the reasoning behind the opinion (previously shown by the Gemara to be that of Resh Lakish), which maintains that Bet Shammai forbid redeeming produce with gold dinarim. Our commentary follows *Rashi*, who explains that in this version, Resh Lakish basically agrees with Rabbi Yoḥanan's reasoning that the difference of opinion between

[1] בִּשְׁלָמָא לְהַךְ לִישָּׁנָא, דְּאָמְרַתְּ דִּמְדְּאוֹרַיְיתָא מִשְׁרָא שָׁרֵי, [2] וְרַבָּנַן הוּא דְּגָזְרוּ בֵּיהּ, [3] הַיְינוּ דְּקָתָנֵי: ״יַעֲשֶׂה״ וְ״וְלֹא יַעֲשֶׂה״. [4] אֶלָּא לְהַךְ לִישָּׁנָא, [5] דְּאָמְרַתְּ דִּמְדְּאוֹרַיְיתָא פְּלִיגִי, [6] ״מְחַלְּלִינַן״ וְ״לָא מְחַלְּלִינַן״ מִבָּעֵי לֵיהּ.

LITERAL TRANSLATION

[1] Granted according to that version, in which you say that by the Torah it is permitted, [2] and it was the Rabbis who enacted a preventive measure against it, [3] this is why it teaches: "He may [exchange"] (lit., "do") and "he may not [exchange]."

[4] But according to that version, [5] in which you say that they disagree regarding Torah law, [6] it should have [said]: "We can redeem," and "we cannot redeem."

TRANSLATION AND COMMENTARY

בִּשְׁלָמָא לְהַךְ לִישָּׁנָא [1] The Gemara now seeks to show that this version of the difference of opinion between Rabbi Yoḥanan and Resh Lakish is the correct one: **According to this version** of the dispute, **in which you say that by Torah** law **it is permitted** to exchange second-tithe silver sela'im for gold dinarim, [2] **and** that **it was the Rabbis who enacted a preventive measure against** this exchange in order to discourage farmers from delaying their pilgrimage to Jerusalem, the wording of the first Mishnah quoted from tractate *Ma'aser Sheni* (2:7) is appropriate. [3] **This is why that Mishnah stated** that Bet Hillel are of the opinion that the farmer **"may exchange"** sela'im for dinarim **and** Bet Shammai are of the opinion that the farmer **"may not exchange"** sela'im for dinarim. The Mishnah's presentation of the difference of opinion between Bet Shammai and Bet Hillel focuses on the immediate, practical issue of whether farmers may or may not exchange silver sela'im of second-tithe money for gold dinarim. By leaving aside the underlying issue of whether such an exchange succeeds in transferring second-tithe sanctity from the sela'im to the dinarim, the Mishnah implies that all authorities agree that redemption of second-tithe silver sela'im with gold dinarim is in principle valid — i.e., that second-tithe sanctity can be transferred from silver sela'im to gold dinarim. Thus the language of the Mishnah leads to the conclusion that such an exchange is permitted by Torah law, and is only forbidden by Rabbinic law as a preventive measure.

אֶלָּא לְהַךְ לִישָּׁנָא [4] **But according to the other versions** of Rabbi Yoḥanan's and Resh Lakish's interpretation of the difference of opinion between Bet Shammai and Bet Hillel, [5] **in which you say** that Bet Shammai and Bet Hillel **disagree** as **to** whether the exchange of silver sela'im of second-tithe money for gold dinarim is effective **by Torah law,** [6] the Mishnah **should have** said: **"We can *redeem*," and "we cannot *redeem*."** This wording would imply that Bet Shammai and Bet Hillel disagree regarding the validity of the redemption, and not regarding the secondary issue of whether such redemption is advisable from the practical point of view.

RASHI

היינו דקתני לא יעשה — ולא קתני לשון חלול, דקסבר יש חלול, אבל חכמים החמירו עליו. **ואין מחללין מבעי ליה** — הכי איבעי ליה למיתני: בית שמאי אומרים אין סלעים מעשר שני מתחללין על דינרי זהב, אי משום כסף שני, אי משום דהכא פירא הוא דהוי איסור דאורייתא, ולא מיתפסי בקדושת מעשר.

NOTES

Bet Hillel and Bet Shammai concerns the necessity for a Rabbinic prohibition against converting second-tithe silver coins into gold dinarim to prevent the farmer from being tempted to delay his pilgrimage. Resh Lakish, however, goes further than Rabbi Yoḥanan, and argues that this prohibition applies even to using gold dinarim to redeem second-tithe produce. For while it is true that produce does not keep indefinitely, the farmer may still be tempted to put off redeeming it.

Some Rishonim, however, suggest another possible explanation, according to which the difference between the three versions of the dispute between Bet Hillel and Bet Shammai only concerns Rabbi Yoḥanan's explanation of Bet Shammai: In the first version, Rabbi Yoḥanan explained that Bet Shammai maintain that gold is merchandise relative to silver. In the second version, he explained that Bet Shammai maintain that the Torah does not allow "first money" to be redeemed with other money. In the amended second version he explained that Bet Shammai imposed a Rabbinic prohibition against redeeming silver coins with gold coins, lest the farmer delay his pilgrimage. In all three versions, however, Resh Lakish explains Bet Shammai's position in the same way: Gold coins are merchandise relative to silver, and it is forbidden to use them to redeem silver coins or even second-tithe produce.

According to this explanation, Bet Hillel's position is also the same in all three versions. According to both Rabbi Yoḥanan and Resh Lakish, the position of Bet Hillel is that gold is considered even more current than silver, and there is no prohibition — neither Biblical nor Rabbinic — against redeeming "first coins" with other coins of any denomnomination.

According to this explanation, Bet Hillel support Rabbi Yehudah HaNasi's earlier opinion, and only Bet Shammai (according to Resh Lakish) disagree. This explanation, while somewhat more straightforward than *Rashi*'s, presents considerable difficulties to the Rishonim in the light of the tradition that the Halakhah follows Rabbi Yehudah HaNasi's later opinion — that gold is merchandise relative to silver (see *Ritva*, *Rashba*).

מְחַלְּלִינַן מִבָּעֵי לֵיהּ It should have said: "We may redeem it." Our explanation follows *Rashi*, who explains that the Gemara's inference is from the fact that the Mishnah chose the general word לַעֲשׂוֹת — "to do" — rather than the

[1]קַשְׁיָא. [2]אִיתְּמַר: רַב וְלֵוִי. [3]חַד אָמַר: מַטְבֵּעַ נַעֲשֶׂה חֲלִיפִין. [4]וְחַד אָמַר: אֵין מַטְבֵּעַ נַעֲשֶׂה חֲלִיפִין. [5]אָמַר רַב פַּפָּא: מַאי טַעְמָא דְּמַאן דְּאָמַר: אֵין מַטְבֵּעַ נַעֲשֶׂה חֲלִיפִין?

LITERAL TRANSLATION

[1]It is difficult.

[2]It was stated: Rav and Levi [disagree]. [3]One says: Coin can be used for *ḥalifin*. [4]And [the other] one says: Coin cannot be used for *ḥalifin*.

[5]Rav Pappa said: What is the reason of the one who said: Coin cannot be used for *ḥalifin*?

TRANSLATION AND COMMENTARY

קַשְׁיָא [1]Accordingly, the Gemara concludes: The first two versions of the difference of opinion between Rabbi Yoḥanan and Resh Lakish **are difficult** to accept on the basis of the wording of the Mishnah; it is the third version — according to which Bet Shammai and Bet Hillel disagree about the necessity of enacting a Rabbinic preventive measure — which appears to be correct.

אִיתְּמַר [2]The Gemara now introduces an entirely new topic of discussion, dealing with some of the requirements of the mode of acquisition known as *ḥalifin*, meaning "barter" or "exchange." If two parties wish to exchange property, it is not necessary that each of the parties perform *meshikhah* on the object he wishes to acquire. Once the two parties agree on the exchange of one article for another, the acquisition by one party of one of the articles by means of a valid act of acquisition such as *meshikhah* automatically causes the other article to be acquired by the other party. **It was stated** that **Rav and Levi disagreed** about this question: [3]**One** of them **said: Coins can be used for *ḥalifin*.** The Mishnah (above, 44a) ruled that the payment of money is not a valid mode of acquisition for movable property. Even after the buyer has paid for his goods, both parties may still retract until a valid *kinyan* such as *meshikhah* is performed on the merchandise. But this ruling applies only if the money was given as *payment* for merchandise, i.e., where the agreement reached was that the buyer would pay a certain sum of money for specific merchandise, without specifying which particular coins would be used for the payment. But if the two parties agree to exchange specific coins for specific merchandise, then as soon as one of the parties acquires the specified coins through *meshikhah* or some other valid *kinyan*, the other party automatically acquires the merchandise through *ḥalifin*. [4]**But the other** Sage — Rav or Levi — **said:** Unlike other movable property, **coins cannot be used for *ḥalifin*.**

אָמַר רַב פַּפָּא [5]**Rav Pappa said: What is the reasoning of the** authority **who said** that **coins cannot** be used for ***ḥalifin*?** Why should specifically designated coins be treated like other movables which can effect *ḥalifin*? Rav Pappa answers: Only property which has intrinsic value can be used to effect *ḥalifin*, whereas property whose value is not intrinsic cannot effect *ḥalifin*. Ordinary movables, for example, have intrinsic value, whereas a promissory note does not. Its value lies in the fact that it can be used to collect a debt. Thus ordinary

RASHI

מטבע נעשה חליפין — הבא להחליף מטבע בדבר אחר שלא בתורת מקח וממכר אלא בתורת קנין, כדרך שקונין בסודר, שהקונה נותן סודר למקנה והוא מקנה לו הקרקע או המטלטלין במשיכה שהוא מושך הסודר, כדכתיב (רות ד) "שלף איש נעלו ונתן לרעהו", אף מטבע שאף על פי ששנינו "נתן לו מעות ולא משך הימנו פירות יכול לחזור בו" — הני מילי כשנתנו בתורת דמים, כדרך מקח וממכר, אבל אם נתן בתורת חליפין, כיון שמשך זה את המעות — נקנה לו החפץ שלו בכל מקום שהוא. **אין מטבע נעשה חליפין** — כדמפרש רב פפא. **מאי טעמא דמאן דאמר כו׳** — הא ליכא למימר דאית ליה דרב נחמן, דאמר לקמן (מז,א) אין קונין אלא בכלי, ד"נעלו" כתיב, דאם כן — אדמפלגי במטבע, ליפלגו בכל דבר שאינו כלי, אלא על כרחך סבירא ליה דכל המטלטלים נעשין חליפין לקנות את שכנגדו, ובמטבע לחודיה פליגי.

NOTES

word לְחַלֵּל — "to redeem." This suggests that the issue in the Mishnah is the farmer's behavior, not the redemption process itself.

Other Rishonim have a different reading, in which the Gemara's question is מִתְחַלְּלִין מִיבְּעֵי לֵיהּ — "It should have said: 'It is redeemed.'" According to this reading, the Gemara's question is based on the Mishnah's use of the active voice (lit., "the farmer will not do"), which by Talmudic convention indicates that the prohibited action is improper but valid. If the Mishnah had wished to suggest that the redemption was null and void, it should have used the passive voice and said: "The coin is not redeemed." (*Tosafot, Sukkah* 40b.)

HALAKHAH

אֵין מַטְבֵּעַ נַעֲשֶׂה חֲלִיפִין Coin cannot be used for *ḥalifin*. "All movable goods can acquire one another through *ḥalifin*, except for coins, which can neither acquire nor be acquired through *ḥalifin*," following the Gemara's conclusion. (*Shulḥan Arukh, Ḥoshen Mishpat* 203:1.)

TERMINOLOGY

קַשְׁיָא It is difficult. When this term appears at the conclusion of a *sugya*, the Gemara is stating that the difficulty mentioned previously remains unresolved.

SAGES

רַב Rav. The greatest of the first generation of Babylonian Amoraim. See *Bava Metzia*, Part II, pp. 242-3.

לֵוִי Levi. A Palestinian Sage of the transitional generation between the Tannaitic and Amoraic periods. See *Bava Metzia*, Part II, p. 319.

רַב פַּפָּא Rav Pappa. A Babylonian Amora of the fifth generation. See *Bava Metzia* Part I, p. 131.

BACKGROUND

חֲלִיפִין Exchange. The term *ḥalifin*, meaning barter or exchange, refers to two distinct but related modes of acquisition. In its literal sense, *ḥalifin* denotes acquisition by barter. If, for example, A agrees to barter his ox for B's cow, the moment A takes physical possession of B's cow, B acquires ownership of A's ox, even if the ox remains in A's possession. It is not necessary that both A and B perform *meshikhah* on the property they are to acquire. In Jewish law, *ḥalifin* is frequently employed in a derivative sense as a legal term referring to acquisition by way of "symbolic" barter. Where two parties wish to transfer ownership of an item, the transaction may be effected by the seller's taking "symbolic" delivery of a utensil owned by the purchaser. Because symbolic *ḥalifin* is usually carried out by the seller's taking possession of a kerchief belonging to the purchaser, *ḥalifin* is frequently referred to as *kinyan sudar*, or "acquisition by means of a kerchief." Delivery of the kerchief is regarded as "symbolic" because the value of the kerchief is unrelated to the value of the property for which it is exchanged, and the seller generally returns the kerchief to the purchaser after the transaction has taken place.

TRANSLATION AND COMMENTARY

movables can effect *ḥalifin*, whereas a promissory note cannot. [1]Coins are similar to promissory notes, **because** when a person receives money, **his thoughts** concerning its value **are** not on the metallic content of the coin but **on the legend** imprinted on it, which by government regulation gives the coin value as legal tender. [2]But that value as legal tender is extrinsic to the coin, since the **legend** on the coin **is liable to be canceled** by the government. Hence coins may not be used to effect *ḥalifin*.

תְּנַן [3]The Gemara now raises an objection to the view that coins cannot be used for *ḥalifin*: **We have learned** in our Mishnah: **"Gold acquires silver."** [4]Does **it not** mean that when the one party draws the gold coin into his possession, the other party simultaneously acquires the silver coins **by means of *ḥalifin***? [5]**And** may we not **conclude from here that coins can be used for *ḥalifin***?

לֹא [6]The Gemara replies: **No!** The silver is not acquired simultaneously with the gold because coins cannot effect *ḥalifin*. Rather, it is only the recipient of the gold who acquires ownership through his act of *meshikhah*, at which time he becomes obligated to deliver the silver to the other party **as payment.** In other words, our Mishnah describes a case where silver coins are offered as payment for the purchase of gold coins. It does not deal with a situation where specific silver coins are offered in exchange for gold coins.

אִי הָכִי [7]The Gemara objects to this understanding of the Mishnah: **If so,** if the Mishnah is referring to a case where silver is offered as payment for gold, and not as barter for gold, the Mishnah is not phrased correctly. **Rather than saying: "gold acquires silver,"** which implies that an act of *meshikhah* on the gold coins by one party causes the other party simultaneously to acquire ownership of the specific silver coins given in exchange, [8]**it should have said:** "Gold **creates an obligation**," i.e., the *meshikhah* performed on the gold does not actually transfer ownership of the silver coins, but only obligates the recipient of the gold to fulfill his undertaking to pay for it with silver.

[1]מִשּׁוּם דְּדַעְתֵּיהּ אַצּוּרְתָא, [2]וְצוּרְתָא עֲבִידָא דְּבָטְלָא. [3]תְּנַן: ״הַזָּהָב קוֹנֶה אֶת הַכֶּסֶף״. [4]מַאי לָאו בַּחֲלִיפִין, [5]וּשְׁמַע מִינָּהּ מַטְבֵּעַ נַעֲשֶׂה חֲלִיפִין? [6]לֹא, בְּדָמִים. [7]אִי הָכִי, ״הַזָּהָב קוֹנֶה אֶת הַכֶּסֶף״, [8]״מְחַיֵּיב״ מִבָּעֵי לֵיהּ.

LITERAL TRANSLATION

[1]Because his mind is on the legend (lit., "form"), [2]and the legend is liable to be canceled.

[3]We have learned: "Gold acquires silver." [4]Is it not by means of *ḥalifin*, [5]and conclude from it [that] coins can be used for *ḥalifin*?

[6]No, as payment.

[7]If so, [rather than saying] "Gold acquires silver," [8]it should have [said]: "[Gold] obligates."

RASHI

משום דדעתיה אצורתא — דעתו של מקנה את החפץ ונוטל המטבע בחליפין אינו סומך אלא על הצורה שבו, שאין המטבע חשוב אלא על ידי צורה שבו, **וצורתא עבידא דבטלה** — שהמלך פוסלה וגוזר לצור צורה אחרת, הלכך הוה ליה כדבר שאינו מסוים ושלם, ולקמן (שם) ממעטים דבר שאינו מסוים מדכתיב ״נעל״. **הזהב** — דינרי זהב, דהוי ליה מטבע. **הזהב קונה** — משמע מעכשיו הכסף קנוי לו בכל מקום שהוא שם, ואין לשון הזהב נופל אלא בדבר שהוא בעין והחליף זה בזה, ואי בתורת דמים, שמושך הימנו דינר זהב בעשרים וחמשה דינר כסף — אין כאן כסף קנוי, אלא המושך הזהב נתחייב לו מעות במשיכה זו, והכי איבעי ליה למיתני: הזהב מחייב את הכסף, וגורם למושך לחייבו כסף.

In view of its formal, ceremonial nature, *kinyan sudar* is regarded as the quintessential mode of acquisition under Jewish law, and is frequently used to solemnize legal transactions that are unrelated to the transfer of property, much as the modern handshake may sometimes have formal significance (*Arukh HaShulḥan*). This aspect of *ḥalifin* assumed greater significance as society moved from a barter to a money economy, and as commerce increased in sophistication to include transactions beyond the sale of land and goods.

TERMINOLOGY

תְּנַן We have learned. A term used to introduce a quotation from a Mishnah, either in support of an argument or as the basis for an objection.

NOTES

וְצוּרְתָא עֲבִידָא דְּבָטְלָא And the legend is liable to be canceled. Our commentary follows *Ramban* and most Rishonim (*Rashba, Ran*), who agree that the reason a coin cannot be used for *ḥalifin* is that the person receiving it does not think of it as a piece of metal but rather as money, the value of which is primarily symbolic. Hence a coin is actually a sort of promissory note which represents the existence of a debt, and such a financial instrument cannot be used in a *ḥalifin* exchange.

Rashi suggests a different explanation. The Gemara (below, 47a) rules that only a discrete, clearly defined object may be used for *ḥalifin*. Having made the psychological observation that the recipient of a coin sees its value in the coin's capacity to serve as negotiable currency, Rav Pappa draws the conclusion that coins cannot satisfy this requirement. Since the legitimacy of a coin as legal tender is subject to revocable governmental regulation, a coin cannot be described as a discrete, clearly defined object of intrinsic value.

A third explanation is offered by *Meiri* and *Sefer HaḤinnukh*. They explain that since the value of a coin depends primarily on its legend, the person receiving it will feel somewhat uncertain about its worth, as the legend can be canceled at any time. Hence he may perform the exchange with reservations, thereby secretly denying the finality of the transaction.

HALAKHAH

הַזָּהָב קוֹנֶה אֶת הַכֶּסֶף Gold acquires silver. "Gold coins are considered merchandise in relation to silver. Hence if a person uses silver coins to buy gold coins, as soon as the buyer draws the gold into his possession he becomes obligated to give the seller silver as payment." (Ibid., 203:4.)

TRANSLATION AND COMMENTARY

תְּנֵי הַזָּהָב מְחַיֵּיב [1]The Gemara answers: **Interpret** the Mishnah as follows: **Gold creates an obligation** to pay silver. The term "acquires" as used in the Mishnah may be understood as meaning "creates an obligation," and need not necessarily refer to the consummation of a sale and the actual transfer of ownership of the silver.

הָכִי נַמִי מִסְתַּבְּרָא [2]The Gemara adduces support for this interpretation of the Mishnah: **This** explanation, according to which our Mishnah does not refer to acquisition by means of *ḥalifin*, **also stands to reason.** [3]**For the latter clause** of this part of the Mishnah **states: "Silver does not acquire gold."** [4]**Granted if you say** that the Mishnah's statement that "gold acquires silver" means that an act of *meshikhah* performed on the gold creates an obligation of **payment** of silver, then the following clause that "silver does not acquire gold" is understandable. [5]For when gold and silver are exchanged, **this is why we say** that the **gold is** considered the **merchandise** being purchased **and** the **silver is** considered the **money** used as payment. [6]Given the rule that **money cannot acquire merchandise**, payment of the silver does not transfer ownership of the gold. [7]**But if you say** that the Mishnah's statement that "gold acquires silver" means that the transaction was effected **through *ḥalifin*, then** there should be no difference between gold and silver, and [8]**each one**, both gold and silver, **should** be able to **acquire the other!** In the exchange of specific gold coins for specific silver coins, both types of coin should be regarded as merchandise, so *meshikhah* performed on either one should cause the other to be acquired at the same time. Since the Mishnah explicitly teaches that silver does *not* acquire gold, we may conclude that coins cannot effect *ḥalifin*.

וְעוֹד [9]The Gemara now cites additional support for this interpretation of the Mishnah by quoting a Baraita that describes the exchange of gold and silver from two points of view. The Gemara first examines that part of the Baraita which describes the transaction from the point of view of the person selling the silver: **Moreover,** says the Gemara, **it has been taught** in the following Baraita, which elaborates on the ruling found in our Mishnah: [10]**"Silver does not acquire gold.** [11]**How so? If someone sells** another person **twenty-five silver dinarim for one gold dinar,** [12]**even if** the buyer of the silver **has drawn the silver into his possession,** the seller of the silver **does not acquire** the gold **until he draws the gold into his possession."** [13]The Gemara explains: **Granted if you say** that this Baraita refers to the acquisition of merchandise through *meshikhah* and the obligation of **payment** thereby created, **this explains why** the seller of the silver **does not acquire** the gold until he actually draws it into his possession. Since the silver is considered the money in this transaction, *meshikhah* performed

[1]תְּנֵי: ״הַזָּהָב מְחַיֵּיב״.
[2]הָכִי נַמִי מִסְתַּבְּרָא, [3]מִדְּקָתָנֵי סֵיפָא: ״הַכֶּסֶף אֵינוֹ קוֹנֶה אֶת הַזָּהָב״. [4]אִי אָמְרַתְּ בִּשְׁלָמָא ״בְּדָמִים״, [5]הַיְינוּ דְּאָמְרִינַן דַּהֲבָא פֵּירָא וְכַסְפָּא טִבְעָא, [6]וְטִבְעָא פֵּירָא לָא קָנֵי. [7]אֶלָּא אִי אָמְרַתְּ ״בַּחֲלִיפִין״, [8]תַּרְוַיְיהוּ לִקְנוּ אַהֲדָדֵי!
[9]וְעוֹד, תַּנְיָא: [10]״הַכֶּסֶף אֵינוֹ קוֹנֶה אֶת הַזָּהָב. [11]כֵּיצַד? מָכַר לוֹ עֶשְׂרִים וַחֲמִשָּׁה דִּינָר שֶׁל כֶּסֶף בְּדִינָר שֶׁל זָהָב, [12]אַף עַל פִּי שֶׁמָּשַׁךְ אֶת הַכֶּסֶף, לֹא קָנָה עַד שֶׁיִּמְשׁוֹךְ אֶת הַזָּהָב״. [13]אִי אָמְרַתְּ בִּשְׁלָמָא ״בְּדָמִים״, מִשּׁוּם הָכִי לָא קָנֵי.

LITERAL TRANSLATION

[1]Teach: "Gold obligates."

[2]So, too, it stands to reason, [3]since the latter clause teaches: "Silver does not acquire gold." [4]Granted if you say "through payment," [5]this is why we say gold is merchandise and silver is money, [6]and money cannot acquire merchandise. [7]But if you say "through *ḥalifin*," [8]let both of them acquire each other!

[9]And moreover, it has been taught: [10]"Silver does not acquire gold. [11]How so? [If] he sold him twenty-five dinarim of silver for a dinar of gold, [12]although he has drawn the silver, he has not acquired [the gold] until he draws the gold." [13]Granted if you say "through payment," because of this he does not acquire.

RASHI

הכי נמי מסתברא — דבתורת דמים, ולא בתורת חליפין, דתשמע מינה מטבע נעשה חליפין. **וטבעא פירא לא קני** — אי משום דמשיכת ממכר מפורשת מן התורה כדלקמן (מז,ב) אי משום דתיקנוה רבנן, שמא יאמר לו נשרפו חטיך בעלייה. **תרווייהו לקנו** — דכיון דמטבע נעשה חליפין, מה לי של כסף מה לי של זהב. **ועוד תניא כו׳** — דשמעינן מינה דלאו בחליפין עסקינן.

NOTES

תְּנֵי הַזָּהָב מְחַיֵּיב Teach: Gold obligates. Our commentary follows *Rosh*, who explains that the Gemara is not amending the text of the Mishnah, as the word תְּנֵי would seem to imply. Rather, it is explaining that the word קוֹנֶה, which means "it acquires," can also mean "it creates an obligation."

TRANSLATION AND COMMENTARY

on the silver cannot effect the transfer of ownership of the gold. [1]**But if you say** that the Baraita refers to a transfer of ownership effected **through *ḥalifin*,** the one who is to receive the gold **should acquire** it through *ḥalifin* as soon as the other party draws the silver into his possession. If both types of coin are regarded as merchandise — as they should be in a case of *ḥalifin* — it should make no difference on which coin the *meshikhah* is first performed.

אֶלָּא מַאי [2]The Gemara rejects this proof: If you say that the Baraita does not refer to *ḥalifin*, **to what then** does it refer? Can we really understand the Baraita as referring to the creation of an obligation of **payment?** [3]**If so,** an objection arises from the previous clause of the Baraita, which views the transaction from the point of view of the person selling the gold. **Consider the first clause** of the Baraita, says the Gemara, in which it is stated: **"Gold acquires silver.** [4]**How so? If someone sells** another person **a gold dinar for twenty-five silver dinarim,** [5]**once** the recipient of the gold **has drawn the gold into his possession, the silver is acquired** by the other party **wherever it is."** [6]The Gemara explains: **Granted if you say** that the Baraita refers to acquisition **through *ḥalifin*,** [7]**this is why it states: "The silver is acquired wherever it is,"** for indeed *ḥalifin* automatically transfers ownership of the silver coins to their purchaser no matter where they are located. [8]**But if you say** that the Baraita refers to the creation of an obligation of **payment,** then **rather than stating** that by the act of *meshikhah* on the gold **"the silver is acquired wherever it is,"** [9]the Baraita **should have stated** that as a result of the act of *meshikhah* on the gold "the buyer **is obligated"** to pay the silver. For even if we interpret the term "acquires" as referring to the creation of an obligation to pay — as we did in the Mishnah itself — the words "wherever it is" are inappropriate. An obligation to pay does not obligate the purchaser to pay with specific coins, as implied by the phrase "wherever it is." He is merely required to pay the amount agreed upon, without regard to the source of the funds. But until the amount agreed upon is handed over to the seller, it remains the property of the buyer. Thus the Baraita is difficult to understand whether we explain that it refers to the creation of an obligation of payment or that it refers to actual acquisition through *ḥalifin*. The two claims of the Baraita imply contradictory interpretations of the same transaction.

אָמַר רַב אַשִׁי [10]The Gemara answers: **Rav Ashi said: In fact,** we can explain the Baraita as referring to the creation of an obligation of **payment.** [11]**And what** does the Baraita mean when it uses the phrase **"wherever it is"?** [12]It means: **"as it is," "as one party told the other."** [13]For example, if one person **said to** another: "I

[1]אֶלָּא אִי אָמְרַתְּ ״בַּחֲלִיפִין״, נִקְנֵי!
[2]אֶלָּא מַאי? ״בְּדָמִים״? [3]אִי הָכִי, אֵימָא רֵישָׁא: ״הַזָּהָב קוֹנֶה אֶת הַכֶּסֶף. [4]כֵּיצַד? מָכַר לוֹ דִּינָר שֶׁל זָהָב בְּעֶשְׂרִים וַחֲמִשָּׁה דִּינָר שֶׁל כֶּסֶף, [5]כֵּיוָן שֶׁמָּשַׁךְ אֶת הַזָּהָב, נִקְנֶה כֶּסֶף בְּכָל מָקוֹם שֶׁהוּא״. [6]אִי אָמְרַתְּ בִּשְׁלָמָא ״בַּחֲלִיפִין״, [7]הַיְינוּ דְּקָתָנֵי: ״נִקְנֶה כֶּסֶף בְּכָל מָקוֹם שֶׁהוּא״. [8]אֶלָּא אִי אָמְרַתְּ ״בְּדָמִים״, הַאי ״נִקְנֶה כֶּסֶף בְּכָל מָקוֹם שֶׁהוּא״, [9]״נִתְחַיֵּיב גַּבְרָא״ מִיבָּעֵי לֵיהּ!
[10]אָמַר רַב אַשִׁי: לְעוֹלָם ״בְּדָמִים״. [11]וּמַאי ״בְּכָל מָקוֹם שֶׁהוּא״? [12]״כְּמוֹת שֶׁהוּא״, ״כְּדַאֲמַר לֵיהּ״. [13]אִי אֲמַר לֵיהּ,

LITERAL TRANSLATION

[1]But if you say "through *ḥalifin*," let him acquire!

[2]What then? "Through payment"? [3]If so, say the first clause: "Gold acquires silver. [4]How so? [If] he sold him a dinar of gold for twenty-five dinarim of silver, [5]once he has drawn the gold, the silver is acquired wherever it is." [6]Granted if you say "through *ḥalifin*," [7]this is why it teaches: "The silver is acquired wherever it is." [8]But if you say "through payment," [rather than saying] "the silver is acquired wherever it is," [9]it should have [said]: "The man is obligated"!

[10]Rav Ashi said: In fact [it means] "as payment." [11]And what is "wherever it is"? [12]"As it is," "as he said to him." [13]If he said to him,

RASHI

אלא אי אמרת — קונה, ואינו קונה דקאמר בחליפין קאמר. **ליקני** — דהא תנא רישא ״הזהב קונה את הכסף״ דאשמועינן בה מטבע נעשה חליפין. **כמות שהוא** — כמו שהתנה עמו.

NOTES

כְּדַאֲמַר לֵיהּ As he said to him. The Gemara explains that the payment of money must be in the agreed form; the buyer cannot substitute some other coin of equal or even greater value. *Ritva* adds that it follows that the buyer certainly cannot pay in a currency other than the one stipulated. Thus, if the contract stipulated foreign currency,

HALAKHAH

כְּמוֹת שֶׁהוּא As it is. "Someone who undertakes to pay silver dinarim in exchange for merchandise must pay whatever kind he specified (e.g., old dinarim or new dinarim)." (*Shulḥan Arukh, Ḥoshen Mishpat* 203:4.)

BACKGROUND

מֵאַרְנָקִי יְשָׁנָה From an old wallet. New coins occasionally arouse suspicion in the mind of the recipient, who may not be certain that they are genuine. By contrast, coins that have seen use arouse confidence in the mind of the recipient that he is receiving something in which other people have already placed their trust.

SAGES

רַב נַחְמָן Rav Naḥman. A Babylonian Amora of the second and third generations. See *Bava Metzia,* Part I, p. 61.

TRANSLATION AND COMMENTARY

will give you new coins from a new wallet," [1]**he cannot give him old coins from an old wallet, even though they are better,** i.e., they are of proven value. [2]**What is the reason** that stipulations must be honored even when the alternative is superior? If old coins are superior to new ones, let him pay with old coins! [3]The reason the original stipulation must be honored is **because** the one who is to receive the coins **can say to** the one giving them to him: "Even though older coins are generally preferred, **I need** the coins in order **to store them.** I personally prefer new coins, which will retain their luster, whereas old coins are apt to become tarnished over time." Both clauses of the Baraita can therefore be understood as referring not to *ḥalifin,* but to the creation of an obligation of payment, teaching that payment must be made exactly as stipulated.

אָמַר רַב פַּפָּא [4]Until now the Gemara has been discussing whether or not coins can effect *ḥalifin* — i.e., whether performing *meshikhah* on coins transfers ownership of the article being acquired in exchange for the coins. Now the Gemara turns to the question of whether coins may be acquired through *ḥalifin,* i.e., whether a *ḥalifin* exchange of coins for merchandise can be made, in which the performance of *meshikhah* by the buyer of the merchandise causes the coins to become the property of the seller immediately. **Rav Pappa said: Even according to** the authority **who said** that **coins cannot be used for *ḥalifin,*** [5]**even though they cannot effect *ḥalifin,* they can be acquired through *ḥalifin,*** [6]**just like produce** can be acquired through *ḥalifin* **according to Rav Naḥman.** [7]The Gemara now explains: In the case of **produce, according to Rav Naḥman,**

"מֵאַרְנָקִי חֲדָשָׁה יָהֲבֵינָא לָךְ", [1]לָא מָצֵי יָהֵיב לֵיהּ מֵאַרְנָקִי יְשָׁנָה, אַף עַל גַּב דַּעֲדִיפִי מִינַּיְיהוּ. [2]מַאי טַעְמָא? [3]דְּאָמַר לֵיהּ: "לְיַשְׁנַן קָא בָּעֵינָא לְהוּ". [4]אֲמַר רַב פַּפָּא: אֲפִילוּ לְמַאן דְּאָמַר: "אֵין מַטְבֵּעַ נַעֲשֶׂה חֲלִיפִין", [5]מִיעֲבַד הוּא דְּלָא עָבֵיד חֲלִיפִין, אִקְנוּיֵי מִיקְנוּ בַּחֲלִיפִין, [6]מִידֵּי דַּהֲוָה אַפֵּירָא לְרַב נַחְמָן. [7]פֵּירָא לְרַב נַחְמָן,

LITERAL TRANSLATION

"I will give you [new coins] from a new wallet," [1]he cannot give him [old coins] from an old wallet, even though they are better than them. [2]What is the reason? [3]For he can say to him: "I need them to store them."

[4]Rav Pappa said: Even according to him who said: "Coin cannot be used for *ḥalifin,*" [5][even though] it cannot effect *ḥalifin,* it can be acquired through *ḥalifin,* [6]just like produce according to Rav Naḥman. [7]Produce according to Rav Naḥman,

RASHI

מארנקי חדשה — של מטבע, סלעין חדשים. **לישנן בעינא** — צריך אני להניחן זמן מרובה, וחדשים נוחים לי שלא ישחירו יותר מלאי. **אפילו למאן דאמר אין מטבע נעשה חליפין** — לקנות את שכנגדו. **אקנויי מיקנו בחליפין** — קנין סודר או מטלטלין שכנגדו קונה אותו בחליפין, מכיון שמשך בעל המטבע החליפין משכנגדו — נקנה המטבע לבעל הסודר. **מידי דהוה אפירות** — לרב נחמן כל דבר שאינו כלי קרוי פירא לגבי חליפין. ופליגי רב ששת ורב נחמן לקמן (מז,א) במשנתין, דאמר רב נחמן, "נעל" דוקא כתיב, שיהא כלי ולא שום דבר שאינו כלי עושה חליפין, ומודה הוא שכל דבר שכנגד הכלי נקנה בחליפי הכלי, דכתיב (רות ד) "לקיים כל דבר", אלמא אף על גב דפירי לא עבדי חליפין לקנות שכנגדו — נקנה הוא בחליפין של כלי, מכיון שמשך בעל הפירות את הכלי, נקנו פירות לבעל הכלי.

NOTES

for example, the money must be paid in foreign currency, and it is not sufficient to pay the equivalent in local currency, as the seller might have personal reasons for wanting foreign currency.

In this context, *Ritva* points out that the general rule in the payment of ordinary debts is that "any type of movable property — even straw — is considered choice property" (see *Bava Kamma* 7a/b). In other words, the debtor, at his own discretion, may repay his creditor with cash or with any movable property equal in value to the debt. Since all movable property is readily convertible into cash, the creditor cannot insist on receiving cash or land, nor can he refuse to accept movable property, or otherwise stipulate in what coin the debt should be paid — a rule that appears to conflict with the Gemara's ruling here. This rule does not apply in the case of a debt arising out of the sale of property, where the seller may demand payment in cash, even cash of a special type, as it is obvious that the seller did not sell his property merely in order to receive other property that he will have to sell yet again. A similar rule applies to a hired laborer; his wages must be paid in cash, and the employer cannot give him some other property of equal value, as he could if this were an ordinary debt.

Ran adds that the same rule applies to a barter sale. If the sale price was a bushel of wheat, the buyer cannot substitute something else of the same value.

אַף עַל גַּב דַּעֲדִיפִי מִינַּיְיהוּ Even though they are better than them. Our translation follows *Rashi*'s reading, also found in *Rabbenu Ḥananel.* According to this reading, old coins are generally better for use, but new coins are better for storage.

Other Rishonim (*Ran, Meiri*) have the opposite reading: If he said, "I will give you old coins," he cannot give him new coins, even though new coins are better, because he can say, "I need them to store them." According to this reading, new coins are usually preferred, but old coins have an advantage for storage, as new coins are likely to corrode with time, whereas old coins already have a patina of corrosion and are unlikely to corrode further.

[1]לָאו אַף עַל גַּב דְּאִינְהוּ לָא עָבְדִי חֲלִיפִין, [2]אִקְנוּיֵי מִקְנוּ בַּחֲלִיפִין. [3]טִבְעָא נַמִי לָא שְׁנָא. [4]מֵיתִיבֵי: [5]״הָיָה עוֹמֵד בַּגּוֹרֶן וְאֵין בְּיָדוֹ מָעוֹת, [6]אוֹמֵר לַחֲבֵירוֹ: ׳הֲרֵי פֵּירוֹת הַלָּלוּ נְתוּנִים לְךָ בְּמַתָּנָה׳, [46A] [7]וְחוֹזֵר וְאוֹמֵר: ׳הֲרֵי הֵן מְחוּלָּלִין עַל מָעוֹת שֶׁיֵּשׁ לִי בַּבַּיִת׳״.

LITERAL TRANSLATION

[1]although it cannot effect *ḥalifin*, [2]it can be acquired through *ḥalifin*. [3]Coin, too, is no different.

[4]They raised an objection: [5]"[If] he was standing in a granary and he has no money in his hand, [6]he may say to his fellow: 'This produce is given to you as a gift,' [46A] [7]and he may then say: 'It is redeemed with money that I have at home.'"

TRANSLATION AND COMMENTARY

[1]**although it cannot effect *ḥalifin*,** [2]**it can be acquired through *ḥalifin*.** According to Rav Naḥman (see below, 47a), *ḥalifin* can only be effected by means of a utensil, but not by means of produce. *Ḥalifin* as a mode of acquisition is derived from the Biblical verse (Ruth 4:7): "Now this was the manner in former time in Israel concerning redeeming and concerning exchanging to confirm all things: a man pulled off his shoe and gave it to his neighbor, and this was the manner of attesting in Israel." Rav Naḥman derives from the word "his shoe" (נַעֲלוֹ) that *ḥalifin* can be effected only by means of something similar to a shoe, i.e., a utensil, but not by means of produce. However, the words "to confirm all things" (לְקַיֵּם כָּל־דָּבָר) inform us that everything — including produce that cannot effect *ḥalifin* — can be acquired through *ḥalifin*. [3]**Coins, too, are no different;** they, too, can be acquired by *ḥalifin*, even though they cannot effect *ḥalifin*.

מֵיתִיבֵי [4]The Sages **raised an objection** to Rav Pappa's ruling that coins can be acquired by *ḥalifin* from a Mishnah (*Ma'aser Sheni* 4:5). Second-tithe produce may be redeemed by exchanging it for money equal in value to the produce. However, if a farmer redeems his own second-tithe produce, he is required to add one-fifth to the redemption money (Leviticus 27:31). On the other hand, if a farmer redeems his second-tithe produce by selling it to someone else, the extra fifth need not be added. Now, if the farmer wishes to avoid paying the extra fifth, he can do so by giving money to a friend and then accepting the money back in payment for the produce. The friend then returns the produce to him as a gift. In this way the farmer has redeemed his produce with his own money without paying the extra fifth. Now, in the case of an ordinary redemption or sale, there is no need for the money to be on hand. But in the case described above, it is essential for the farmer to first give his friend the money, and the best way is to hand it to him directly. [5]The Mishnah now to be quoted deals with a situation where no money is available: **"If** the farmer **was standing in the granary and he had no money in his hand,** [6]**he can say to his friend: 'This produce is given to you as a gift,'** and give him the produce instead of the money. [46A] [7]Once he has given the produce to his friend, **he may then** turn to him and **say**: 'The second-tithe produce, which now belongs to you, **is** hereby **redeemed with money that I have at home.'"** In this way the farmer may redeem his second-tithe

RASHI

ואין בידו מעות — ורוצה לחלל מעשר שלו והערים בפדיונו לחלל על ידי מקח וממכר שמוכרו לאיש אחר, כדי שלא יתחייב חומש, דכתיב (ויקרא כז) "אם גאל יגאל איש ממעשרו חמישיתו יוסף ממעשרו" ולא הלוקח מעשר שני של אחרים. **אומר לחבירו** — שהוא אוהבו, ויודע בו שאינו עושה אלא להיפטר מן החומש. **הרי פירות הללו** — של מעשר שני. **נתונים לך במתנה** — ומכיון שקנאן זה במתנה נעשה הראשון נכרי אצלם, ויוכל לפדותם בלא חומש. **וחוזר ואמר** — הרי פירות של מעשר שני שלך יהיו מחוללין על מעות שיש לי בבית, ויקנה המעשר הזה את המעות ויצא לחולין.

NOTES

הֲרֵי פֵּירוֹת הַלָּלוּ נְתוּנִים לְךָ This produce is given to you. Our commentary follows *Rashi,* who explains that the farmer is actually giving his friend the second-tithe produce. The Rishonim object: In tractate *Kiddushin* (54b), the Gemara explains that there is a Tannaitic dispute as to whether second-tithe produce is considered the property of the farmer or the property of God (which the farmer is commanded to eat). According to Rabbi Meir, who is of the opinion that second-tithe produce is the property of God, it is impossible for a farmer to give it away, as God has only given it, as it were, to the farmer to consume in accordance with the Halakhah. How, then, can the farmer give the produce to his friend?

Rambam, in his commentary on the Mishnah (*Ma'aser Sheni* 4:5), gives two explanations. Either this Mishnah was written in accordance with the viewpoint of Rabbi Yehudah, who maintains that second-tithe produce is the property of the farmer (presumably this is the explanation followed by *Rashi*), or the farmer in this Mishnah did not give his friend the second-tithe produce itself, but rather the untithed produce from which the friend then separated the second tithe.

הַעֲרָמָה בְּפִדְיוֹן מַעֲשֵׂר Avoiding payment of the additional fifth when redeeming second tithe. The Torah says

HALAKHAH

הַעֲרָמָה בְּפִדְיוֹן מַעֲשֵׂר Avoiding payment of the additional fifth when redeeming second tithe. "It is permissible for a farmer to circumvent the law that he must add one-fifth to the price of redeeming his second-tithe produce, for

[1] טַעְמָא דְּאֵין בְּיָדוֹ מָעוֹת. [2] הָא אִם יֵשׁ בְּיָדוֹ מָעוֹת, [3] לִיקְנֵי לְהוּ לְאִידָךְ בִּמְשִׁיכָה, [4] וּפָרֵיק, דְּהָכִי עָדִיף, [5] דַּהֲוָה לֵיהּ נָכְרִי.

[6] וְאִי אָמְרַתְּ מַטְבֵּעַ נִקְנֶה

LITERAL TRANSLATION

[1] The reason is that he does not have money in his hand. [2] But if he does have money in his hand, [3] he should transfer it to the other [person] by means of *meshikhah,* [4] and he may redeem, as this is preferable, [5] since he is a stranger.

[6] But if you say coin can be acquired

TRANSLATION AND COMMENTARY

produce and yet avoid paying the additional fifth, because his friend was the legal owner of the produce at the time it was redeemed.

טַעְמָא דְּאֵין בְּיָדוֹ מָעוֹת [1] The Gemara now explains how this Mishnah contradicts the ruling of Rav Pappa that coins can be acquired by means of *ḥalifin:* **The reason** for the Mishnah's ruling **is that** the owner of the produce **did not have money with him** at the time. That is why he had to go to the trouble of giving the produce to his friend and then buying it back. [2] **But if** the farmer **did have money with him,** [3] **he should have transferred** the money **to the other person by means of** ***meshikhah*** — by having him draw the money into his possession — [4] **and** then **the other person could redeem the produce** by buying it from him. The Rabbis recognized two variations of this legal device that was used to avoid payment of the additional fifth when redeeming second-tithe produce. In the first case, the farmer gives the second-tithe produce to his friend as a present, and then, when the produce is no longer his legal property, he proceeds to redeem it. In the second case, the farmer gives money to his friend, and the friend redeems the farmer's second-tithe produce with this money. Both variations are effective ways of avoiding payment of the additional fifth that the Torah imposes on a person who redeems his own second-tithe produce. [5] Nevertheless, the Rabbis regarded the second variation — in which the farmer transfers money to his friend — **as preferable, because the person** redeeming the produce — the farmer's friend — is in this case considered **a** true **"stranger"** in relation to the produce, since he is not its owner. The Gemara assumes that it is better to implement the legal fiction by having the second-tithe produce redeemed by a true "stranger" who has never owned it, rather than have the farmer redeem it after transferring ownership of it to his friend. The second procedure, which involves transferring the second-tithe produce itself, is too obvious a method of avoidance, and is only permitted in a case where the owner of the produce does not have money readily available to give to his friend.

וְאִי אָמְרַתְּ [6] The Gemara now argues as follows: The Mishnah seems to assume that if the owner of the second-tithe produce does not have money with him, he must give the other person the produce because he has no way of transferring money to the other person except by physically handing it to him. **But if you say** that **coins can be acquired through** ***ḥalifin,*** then there *is* a way of transferring ownership of money even if it

RASHI

טעמא דאין בידו מעות — דמדקתני "ואין בידו מעות", שמע מינה דאם היה בידו מעות שם בגורן — לא היה אומר לו התנא לעשות כן, אלא המעות הללו היה מוסר לחבירו, ומקנה אותם לו במשיכה. **ופריק** — וחבירו זה פודה את המעשר. **דהכי עדיף** — שאינה נראית ערמה כל כך להיפטר מן החומש. **דהוה ליה** — חבירו נוכרא לגבי מעשר, וקרינן ביה: "ממעשרו" פרט של אחרים.

NOTES

(Leviticus 27:31): "And if a man redeems his tithes, he shall add a fifth thereto." As the verse implies, the additional fifth must be paid only when the produce is redeemed by its owner or his agent. If the owner wishes to redeem his second-tithe produce without paying the additional fifth, he can "give" his second-tithe produce to a friend and, while the produce is no longer legally owned by him, he can redeem it. After the redemption, the friend gives the produce back to its original owner. In this case, the produce has not been redeemed by its legal owner, so the requirement of the additional fifth is not imposed. This Halakhah is unique in that the sale of the produce, which is undertaken with the sole purpose of avoiding the obligation to pay an additional fifth, is not only legally valid but actually recommended! The Sages advised farmers to take advantage of this method rather than pay the additional fifth as the Torah commands (*Ma'aser Sheni* 4:4).

The Jerusalem Talmud bases the Sages' acceptance of this legal device on the verse "for the Lord your God will bless you" (Deuteronomy 14:24), which was stated in connection with the redemption of second-tithe produce. *Pnei Moshe* explains that the "blessing" to which the Torah refers is the possibility of avoiding paying the fifth by arranging a fictitious sale or gift of the produce to someone else.

HALAKHAH

example by donating his produce to another person before second tithe has been removed (since it is forbidden to give others second tithe — *Kesef Mishneh*) and declaring: 'This produce is hereby redeemed with money I have at home.'" (*Rambam, Sefer Zeraim, Hilkhot Ma'aser Sheni* 5:10.)

TRANSLATION AND COMMENTARY

is currently found elsewhere. [1]**Let** the owner of the produce **transfer the money** he has at home **to the other person by means of a kerchief.** The other person can give the farmer a kerchief or some other article, and can thereby acquire the money through *kinyan sudar* — the symbolic version of *ḥalifin* in which two articles of unequal value are exchanged. [2]The other person can then use the money so transferred to buy the produce and so **redeem** it. In this way a farmer can avoid paying the additional fifth. But since the Mishnah does not suggest such a procedure, we may infer that coins cannot be acquired through *ḥalifin*, and thus the viewpoint of Rav Pappa is refuted.

דְּלֵית לֵיהּ סוּדָר [3]The Gemara rejects this argument: The Mishnah may be referring to a particular case **where neither** the farmer nor his friend **has a kerchief.** But if one of them has a kerchief or a similar article, the money can be transferred by means of *ḥalifin,* and this would indeed be the preferred procedure to avoid payment of the additional fifth.

וְנַקְנִינְהוּ נִהֲלֵיהּ אַגַּב קַרְקַע [4]The Gemara raises a further question with regard to this Mishnah: **But** even if we say that money cannot be acquired by means of *ḥalifin,* there is another way that the owner of the second-tithe produce can transfer the money to the other person, even though he does not have the money with him. **Let him transfer** the money he has at home **to** the other person **by way of land,** since all movable property, including money, can be sold or given to someone by including it in a sale or gift of land. When a person buys or is given a piece of real estate, it is possible to stipulate that certain items of movable property are included in the sale or gift. As soon as the buyer or recipient takes possession of the land, he also acquires the movable property, and needs no further act of acquisition. There are no limitations on the size or the value of the land and the movable property involved in this transaction, nor does the movable property have to be physically *on* the land at the time of the transaction. Thus the farmer could give his friend a piece of land and include the money in the transaction, thereby effectively transferring ownership of the money without physically handing it over.

בַּחֲלִיפִין, [1]נִיקְנוּ לֵיהּ מָעוֹת לְהֵיאַךְ אַגַּב סוּדָר, [2]וְלִפְרוֹק!
[3]דְּלֵית לֵיהּ סוּדָר.
[4]וְנַקְנִינְהוּ נִהֲלֵיהּ אַגַּב קַרְקַע!

LITERAL TRANSLATION

through *ḥalifin,* [1]let him transfer the coins to the other [person] by means of a kerchief, [2]and let him redeem!

[3]Where he has no kerchief.

[4]But let him transfer them to him by way of land!

RASHI

נקנינהו נהליה אגב קרקע — יתן לו זה בעל מעשר קרקע בחזקה, ועמהן המעות, ומשיחזיק זה בקרקע — יהיו המעות קנויות לו בכל מקום שהן, דתנן (קדושין כו,א): נכסים שאין להן אחריות נקנין עם נכסים שיש להן אחריות בכסף בשטר ובחזקה, וחבירו זה יאמר: הרי פירות הללו מחוללין על מעות שיש לי בביתך. דהכי עדיף, דהוה ליה נוכראה. והך קושיא לרב פפא לא מקשינן, אלא אתמוהי קא מתמה אמתניתין.

NOTES

דְּלֵית לֵיהּ סוּדָר Where he has no kerchief. Technically, it is the friend who needs a kerchief, as the Halakhah is that a *ḥalifin* exchange is carried out by giving a kerchief for the object being acquired (in this case the money), and it is the friend who is acquiring the money. However, the Mishnah must be referring to a case where neither party has a kerchief (or any other appropriate article). For if the farmer had a kerchief, it would be a simple matter for him to give it to his friend so that his friend could give it back to him in exchange for the money (*Tosefot Rosh, Maharam*).

וְנַקְנִינְהוּ נִהֲלֵיהּ But let him transfer them to him. The Gemara assumes that in the case described in the Mishnah, the farmer has no valid way of transferring his money to his friend without handing it over. Thus it follows that *ḥalifin* cannot be a valid way of transferring money. *Tosafot* asks: The law in monetary cases is that an admission is equal to a hundred witnesses, and cannot be refuted by any amount of evidence from other sources. In practice this means that if a donor admits that his property belongs to someone else, that property is considered to belong to that other person, even if no act of acquisition has been performed. In this way an admission can be regarded as a kind of transfer of ownership. Why then does the farmer not simply admit that the money in his house belongs to his friend? Then his friend can use the money to redeem the farmer's second tithe, and the farmer does not have to pay the additional fifth! (A similar question can be asked about the story of Rav Pappa, a few lines later in the Gemara: Why did Rav Pappa not simply admit that the money belonged to Rav Shmuel bar Aha, instead of giving it to him together with the threshold of his house?)

Meiri explains that the rule that admission equals a hundred witnesses applies only to monetary cases, but here we have a case with ramifications in ritual law. It is as if God Himself must be convinced that the money belongs to the friend in order to exempt the farmer from paying the fifth, and the rule that evidence from other sources cannot refute an admission does not apply in such a situation.

Ritva suggests that an admission is in effect a transfer of ownership only if the property is already in the recipient's possession when the owner admits that it is his. In such a case, the ownership is transferred without a further act of acquisition. But in our case, the money is not in the possession of the friend; it is in the home of the farmer. Hence an admission cannot serve here as a substitute for a proper transfer of ownership.

Alternatively, *Ritva* suggests that when a person admits

LANGUAGE

סוּדָר Kerchief. The source of the word is the Greek σουδάριον, *sudarion,* and the Latin *sudarium,* meaning towel or napkin. In Rabbinic literature it means a piece of cloth that could be used in many ways — as a kerchief or a head-covering. Married Sages often used it for the latter purpose, and it indicated their special status.

CONCEPTS

קִנְיַן סוּדָר *Kinyan sudar,* the transfer of ownership by means of a kerchief. An extension of the principle of חֲלִיפִין — barter. When one article is exchanged for another, the formal acquisition of one automatically transfers ownership of the second. Since there is no requirement for the objects exchanged in this way to be of equal value, the symbolic transfer of a handkerchief or some other small article from one party to another formalizes any agreement made between them. Normally in the case of *kinyan sudar,* the seller simply takes the buyer's handkerchief in his hand and then returns it.

BACKGROUND

אַגַּב קַרְקַע By way of land. Movable property may be acquired together with land by means of an act of acquisition performed specifically with regard to the land. When a piece of land is sold or given as a gift through an appropriate act of acquisition, an unlimited quantity of movables may be sold or given as a gift together with the land, even if they are not actually on the land at the time of the transaction, and even if they are not in any way connected to the land. *Kinyan agav* (קִנְיַן אַגַּב) is a convenient way of transferring movables that are not in the same place as the buyer and the seller. The size of the piece of land that serves as the basis for the transfer of the movables can be minimal and symbolic. The procedure requires that the seller say to the buyer: "Together with the land, acquire the merchandise."

TRANSLATION AND COMMENTARY

דְּלֵית לֵיהּ קַרְקַע [1]The Gemara replies: The Mishnah refers to a particular case **where** the owner of the produce **has no land** by means of which to transfer the money. But if he has land, the money can be transferred together with the land, and this would be the preferred procedure to avoid payment of the additional fifth, for then the second-tithe produce is redeemed by somebody who has never owned it.

וְהָא עוֹמֵד בְּגוֹרֶן קָתָנֵי [2]The Gemara objects: **But** how can you say that the Mishnah refers to a case where the owner of the produce has no land? Surely the Mishnah specifically **states** that the farmer **"was standing in** a **granary,"** and presumably the granary belongs to him!

בְּגוֹרֶן שֶׁאֵינוֹ שֶׁלּוֹ [3]The Gemara answers: The Mishnah is referring to a case where the farmer is standing **in a granary that is not his.**

וְאִיכְפַּל תַּנָּא לְאַשְׁמוּעִינַן [4]The Gemara now asks in astonishment: But did **the Tanna** who taught this Mishnah **go to the trouble of teaching us about a naked person,** [5]**who has nothing** — neither a kerchief (nor any other item) nor land?! It seems unreasonable to interpret the Mishnah as referring only to such an exceptional case. Hence we must conclude that this interpretation is too unlikely to be correct. [6]**Rather,** it seems more reasonable to assume that the Mishnah is referring only to a case where the owner of the produce has no land, and therefore the money cannot be transferred along with land. But he *does* have a kerchief, and despite this fact the Mishnah does not suggest that the owner of the produce transfer the money to his friend through *ḥalifin*. **May we not conclude from this** that **coins cannot be acquired through *ḥalifin*?** This would be the reason for the farmer being forced to give the produce to his friend as a present; he cannot transfer the money he has at home to his friend by means of *ḥalifin*. [7]The Gemara summarizes: Indeed, **conclude from here** that coins cannot be acquired through *ḥalifin*.

וְאַף רַב פַּפָּא הֲדַר בֵּיהּ [8]The Gemara adds: **And Rav Pappa, too, retracted** his opinion that coins can be acquired through *ḥalifin*, **as we may infer from the** following **case**: [9]**Rav Pappa had twelve thousand dinarim** deposited with a bailee **in Bei Ḥozai,** [10]and **he transferred them to** his agent, **Rav Shmuel bar Aḥa,**

[1]דְּלֵית לֵיהּ קַרְקַע. [2]וְהָא ״עוֹמֵד בְּגוֹרֶן״ קָתָנֵי! [3]בְּגוֹרֶן שֶׁאֵינוֹ שֶׁלּוֹ. [4]וְאִיכְפַּל תַּנָּא לְאַשְׁמוּעִינַן גַּבְרָא עַרְטִילַאי, [5]דְּלֵית לֵיהּ וְלָא כְּלוּם? [6]אֶלָּא לָאו שְׁמַע מִינָּהּ: אֵין מַטְבֵּעַ נִקְנֶה בַּחֲלִיפִין. [7]שְׁמַע מִינָּהּ.

[8]וְאַף רַב פַּפָּא הֲדַר בֵּיהּ, [9]כִּי הָא דְּרַב פַּפָּא הֲווֹ לֵיהּ תְּרֵיסַר אַלְפֵי דִּינָרֵי בֵּי חוֹזָאֵי. [10]אַקְנִינְהוּ

LITERAL TRANSLATION

[1]Where he has no land.

[2]But surely it teaches: "[He was] standing in a granary"!

[3]In a granary that is not his.

[4]But did the Tanna go to the trouble of teaching us [about] a naked man [5]who has nothing?

[6]Rather, may [we] not conclude from this: Coin cannot be acquired through *ḥalifin*. [7]Conclude from this.

[8]And Rav Pappa, too, retracted, as [we may infer] from this [case] [9]where Rav Pappa had twelve thousand dinarim in Bei Ḥozai. [10]He transferred them

RASHI

איכפל תנא כו׳ – נתעסק התנא וטרח להורות לנו הלכה בדבר שאינו מצוי, שיהיה אדם עומד בגורן ערום? אלא לאו שמע מינה בגורן שאינו שלו, אבל סודר יש לו, ואפילו הכי – הפירות צריך ליתן לו במתנה, שאין המעות נקנין בחליפין. **ואף רב פפא הדר ביה** – ממאי דאמר מטבע נקנית בחליפין.

TERMINOLOGY

וְאִיכְפַּל תַּנָּא But did the Tanna go to the trouble? This expression appears in several places in the Talmud. It means that the Gemara considers it unreasonable for a Mishnah to describe a Halakhah in general terms when it refers to a very specific and unusual situation.

BACKGROUND

בֵּי חוֹזָאֵי Bei Ḥozai. During the Talmudic period the Persian kingdom was ruled by the Sassanid dynasty and was divided into large units similar to independent states. Bei Ḥozai refers to an area near the Persian Gulf, far from the center of Jewish settlement in Babylonia. This area is known to this day as Khuzistan — the Persian form of the name Bei Ḥozai.

NOTES

that his property belongs to someone else, the property itself is not transferred. Rather, the owner assumes a legally enforceable obligation to give the property to the recipient. In effect, it is a debt. Thus, if the farmer were to admit that the money in his house belongs to his friend, he would owe his friend a debt, but his friend would still not have any money in his possession with which to redeem the second-tithe produce.

דְּלֵית לֵיהּ קַרְקַע **Where he has no land.** *Ritva* asks: The Mishnah is dealing specifically with a case where the farmer is redeeming the tithes from his own produce. But if he has no land, where did he grow the produce?

Ritva answers that the farmer in this Mishnah is a sharecropper who grew the produce on someone else's land and received part of the crop as his share. Thus he has no land, but has produce that he himself grew. Alternatively, the farmer may already have sold the land on which the crops were grown.

Some Rishonim, however, do not understand the Gemara to be saying that the farmer has no land at all. Rather, it is sufficient to say that the farmer has no share in the granary in which he is standing. For even if the farmer has land somewhere else, and wishes to transfer movable property together with it, he must still find a Halakhically acceptable way of transferring the land itself. But since the farmer and his friend have no money and no kerchief, the only practical way to transfer the land is through חֲזָקָה, thus allowing the recipient to physically take possession of it, and that can only be done with the land at hand — the granary — and not with land the farmer owns somewhere else (*Ritva* in *Shittah Mekubbetzet*; see also *Rashi*).

לְרַב שְׁמוּאֵל בַּר אַחָא אַגַּב אַסֵּיפָא דְּבֵיתֵיהּ. [1]כִּי אֲתָא, נְפַק לְאַפֵּיהּ עַד תָּוָוךְ.

[2]וְכֵן אָמַר עוּלָּא: אֵין מַטְבֵּעַ נַעֲשֶׂה חֲלִיפִין. [3]וְכֵן אָמַר רַבִּי אַסִּי: אֵין מַטְבֵּעַ נַעֲשֶׂה חֲלִיפִין. [4]וְכֵן אָמַר רַבָּה בַּר בַּר חָנָה אָמַר רַבִּי יוֹחָנָן: אֵין מַטְבֵּעַ נַעֲשֶׂה חֲלִיפִין.

[5]אֵיתִיבֵיהּ רַבִּי אַבָּא לְעוּלָּא: [6]״הֲרֵי שֶׁהָיוּ חַמָּרָיו וּפוֹעֲלָיו תּוֹבְעִין אוֹתוֹ בַּשּׁוּק, [7]וְאָמַר לַשּׁוּלְחָנִי: ׳תֵּן לִי בְּדִינָר מָעוֹת

LITERAL TRANSLATION

to Rav Shmuel bar Aḥa by way of the threshold of his house. [1]When he came, he went out to him as far as Tavakh.

[2]And similarly Ulla said: Coin cannot be used for *ḥalifin.* [3]And similarly Rabbi Assi said: Coin cannot be used for *ḥalifin.* [4]And similarly Rabbah bar Bar Ḥanah said in the name of Rabbi Yoḥanan: Coin cannot be used for *ḥalifin.*

[5]Rabbi Abba raised an objection to Ulla: [6]"If someone's ass drivers or workers were claiming [wages] from him in the market, [7]and he said to a money changer: 'Give me coins for a dinar

RASHI

ואקנינהו לרב שמואל — שהיה הולך לשם, כדי שיביאם לו, שאילו לא הקנה לו — לא היה נותנם לו מי שהפקדון אצלו, שאם יאבדו בדרך — יחזור רב פפא ויתבעם לו. **אגב אסיפא דביתיה** — מפתן ביתו. אלמא: מדאצטריך ליה לקנויינהו אגב קרקע — שמע מינה אין מטבע נקנה בחליפין. **עד תווך** — שם מקום. **וכן אמר עולא** — האי "וכן" — לעיל קאי אפלוגתא דרב ולוי. **תובעין אותו** — מעות שכרם ומזונותיהם. **תן לי בדינר מעות** — תן לי פרוטות בשוה דינר. והדינר אין עתה בידי, אבל אני אעלה לך עד יום פלוני יפה דינר וטריסית, קא סלקא דעתך דינר יפה היוצא בהוצאה קאמר, וטריסית מעה קטנה.

TRANSLATION AND COMMENTARY

along with the threshold of his house. In other words, Rav Pappa effected the transfer of his money to the agent by linking that transfer to the transfer of a piece of real estate. Had Rav Pappa not transferred ownership of the money to his agent, the bailee might not have been willing to hand over the money to the agent, since the bailee is responsible for the money until it reaches its rightful owner. If the agent lost the money, the bailee would have to reimburse the owner. Therefore Rav Pappa applied the principle that movable property can be transferred together with real estate, and gave Rav Shmuel bar Aḥa a part of his house together with the twelve thousand dinarim. Since Rav Pappa used this method of transferring the money, the Gemara concludes that, in his opinion, coins cannot be acquired through *ḥalifin*. Otherwise, Rav Pappa would presumably have transferred the coins to the agent through *ḥalifin*. [1]The Gemara notes in passing: **When** Rav Shmuel bar Aḥa **came** back with the money, Rav Pappa was so relieved and glad that he **went out to** the town of **Tavakh to** welcome **him.**

וְכֵן אָמַר עוּלָּא [2]The Gemara now returns to the subject of disagreement between Rav and Levi above, citing the views of several other Amoraim, all of whom are of the opinion that coins cannot effect *ḥalifin:* **Similarly, Ulla said: Coins cannot effect *ḥalifin*.** [3]**Similarly, Rav Assi said: Coins cannot effect *ḥalifin*.** [4]**Similarly, Rabbah bar Bar Ḥanah said in the name of Rabbi Yoḥanan: Coins cannot effect *ḥalifin*.**

אֵיתִיבֵיהּ רַבִּי אַבָּא לְעוּלָּא [5]**Rabbi Abba raised an objection to Ulla,** who maintained that coins cannot effect *ḥalifin*, from the following Baraita (found with minor textual variants in Tosefta, *Bava Metzia* 4:9): [6]**"If someone's ass drivers or workers were claiming wages from him** while they were standing **in the marketplace,** [7]**and,** not having any money with him, the employer **said to a** nearby **money changer: 'Give me a dinar's** worth

NOTES

אַגַּב אַסֵּיפָא דְּבֵיתֵיהּ **By way of the threshold of his house.** Our translation follows *Rashi* here. In *Bava Kamma* (104b), *Rashi* quotes an alternative explanation, according to which this expression means the end of his house, i.e., a corner.

עַד תָּוָוךְ **As far as Tavakh.** Our commentary follows *Rashi*. In *Bava Kamma* (104b), *Rashi* adds that Rav Pappa was so pleased at the recovery of his property that he went to Tavakh to meet his agent. *Rashbam* (*Bava Batra* 150b) quotes an opinion that the word תָּוָוךְ means "halfway." *Rabbenu Ḥananel* explains that Rav Pappa had a practical reason for meeting the agent: He wished to claim his money before the agent could be tempted to keep it for himself. Most Rishonim, however, reject this explanation.

HALAKHAH

כֵּיצַד מַקְנֶה מַטְבֵּעַ **Transferring the ownership of coins.** "The ownership of coins cannot be transferred through *ḥalifin*. Therefore, if a person wishes to transfer coins to someone else, he must transfer them together with land, i.e., by selling, donating or renting out land together with the coins. This law applies only if the coins are intact, e.g., if they have been deposited with someone else, who admits that they belong to the owner," following the Gemara's conclusion and the story about Rav Pappa. (*Shulḥan Arukh, Ḥoshen Mishpat* 203:1,3,9.)

BACKGROUND

אַגַּב אַסֵּיפָא דְּבֵיתֵיהּ **By way of the threshold of his house.** Rav Pappa could have limited himself to appointing Rav Shmuel bar Aḥa as his agent. However, as *Rashi* explains, in this case if the money were lost along the way, the debtor would have had to pay it again. Moreover, money was occasionally lost unavoidably — when it was stolen by highwaymen, for example — in which case the man in Bei Ḥozai could not even have sued Rav Shmuel bar Aḥa for the sum he had lost. Consequently the debtor would have been unenthusiastic about entrusting the money to an agent, since he could not be certain that by doing so he would be discharging his debt. By transferring the debt to Rav Shmuel bar Aḥa, Rav Pappa not only gave him full power of attorney to collect the money, but also gave assurance to the debtor that he would be discharging his debt.

SAGES

רַב שְׁמוּאֵל בַּר אַחָא **Rav Shmuel bar Aḥa.** A Babylonian Sage of the fifth generation, Rav Shmuel bar Aḥa is not mentioned frequently in the Talmud. He was apparently a disciple of Rav Pappa, for we find him asking Rav Pappa questions about the Halakhah. Because he was loyal to Rav Pappa, he was entrusted with a mission involving great responsibility, bringing an extremely large sum of money over a long distance.

רַבִּי אַסִּי **Rabbi Assi.** A leading Amora of the third generation. See *Bava Metzia,* Part II, p. 340.

רַבָּה בַּר בַּר חָנָה **Rabbah bar Bar Ḥanah.** An Amora of the third generation. See *Bava Metzia,* Part I, p. 222.

עוּלָּא **Ulla.** A Palestinian Amora of the second and third generations, Ulla was the most important of those scholars who transmitted information and Halakhic rulings from Eretz Israel to the Diaspora. His full name seems to have been Ulla the son of Yishmael. Ulla was one of the

וַאֲפַרְנְסֵם, 1 וַאֲנִי אַעֲלֶה לְךָ יָפֶה דִּינָר וּטְרֵיסִית מִמָּעוֹת שֶׁיֵּשׁ לִי בְּבֵיתִי׳, 2 אִם יֵשׁ לוֹ מָעוֹת, מוּתָּר, 3 וְאִם לָאו, אָסוּר״.

4 וְאִי סָלְקָא דַּעְתָּךְ אֵין מַטְבֵּעַ נַעֲשֶׂה חֲלִיפִין, 5 הָוְיָא לֵיהּ הַלְוָאָה, וְאָסוּר!

6 אִשְׁתִּיק.

LITERAL TRANSLATION

and I will pay (lit., "support") them, [1] and I will repay (lit., "bring up to") you a dinar and a tressis's worth of money that I have at home,' [2] if he has the money, it is permitted, [3] but if not, it is prohibited."

[4] But if it should enter your mind [that] coin cannot be used for *ḥalifin*, [5] this is [considered] a loan, and it is forbidden!

[6] He was silent.

TRANSLATION AND COMMENTARY

of small **coins, so that I can use** them to **pay** my workers, [1] **and** later **I will repay you a dinar and a tressis's** (a small coin) **worth of money that I have at home,'** the question arises whether returning the dinar and tressis's worth of money would violate the laws prohibiting the payment of interest. [2] The Baraita rules: **"If** at the time he makes this arrangement with the money changer, the employer already **has the money** (the dinar and the tressis) available at home, the transaction **is permitted**, as the extra tressis is not considered interest. Since the money is available to be repaid immediately, there is no extension of credit and hence no prohibition of interest. [3] **But if** the employer does **not** have the necessary money at home, the transaction is considered a loan and **is forbidden** because when the employer gives the money changer the extra tressis, he will be paying interest."

וְאִי סָלְקָא דַּעְתָּךְ [4] The Gemara now explains how this Baraita contradicts Ulla's ruling: The Baraita ruled that if at the time the employer received the money from the money changer, he had money at home with which to repay the money changer, the laws forbidding interest would in no way have been violated, even though the employer will later give the money changer more money than he received from him. The transaction would be permitted because the prohibition of interest applies only to loans. Since the employer has money at home, the transaction is considered an exchange of the money changer's money for that of the employer, effected by means of *ḥalifin*. When the employer takes the money from the money changer, the money changer simultaneously acquires the money that is in the employer's house. This ruling is understandable if in fact coins can effect *ḥalifin*; **but if it should enter your mind that coins cannot effect *ḥalifin*,** as Ulla and the other Amoraim maintain, then even if the employer has the money at home, [5] the transaction should be **considered a loan and** should be **forbidden.** Since coins cannot effect *ḥalifin*, the money changer does not immediately acquire the employer's money when the employer takes the money from him. The arrangement between the money changer and the employer is a loan, and when the employer later gives the money changer the extra tressis, he will be paying interest, which is forbidden.

אִשְׁתִּיק [6] Ulla **was silent,** because he had no answer to this objection.

RASHI

ואפרנסם — אעשה צרכיהם, כלומר: אסלקם מעלי. כל צורך סיפוק קרי פרנסה, *קונדרי״ר בלעז. **אם יש לו בביתו** — אותן מעות שהוא אומר. **מותר** — קא סלקא דעתך דכיון דיש לו הוו להו חליפין דהחליף אלו באלו אותן שבביתו באלו, ומחמת דוחקו אוזיל גביה לתת לו טריסית יותר, ואין כאן משום רבית, שהרי אין כאן שכר המתנה, שהרי אין ממתין לו כלום, שהרי הוא פורעו מיד, דמשמשך את מעות השולחני נקנה לו הדינר שבביתו בכל מקום שהוא. **ואם לאו אסור** — דכיון דאין לו הדינר בביתו — אין כאן חליפין, אלא כשאר מכר בעלמא שהוא מתחייב לו הדינר לאותו זמן, וטריסית מוסיף לו בשכר מעותיו שהמתין. **ואי אמרת אין מטבע נקנה בחליפין** — ואין מטבע נעשה חליפין, אפילו יש לו נמי אין קונין לו במקום שהם שם, ואין זו אלא הלואה, ואף על גב דדרך מקח וממכר הוא — קיימא לן לקמן: כללא דרביתא, כל אגר נטר ליה — אסור. אלא לאו שמע מינה מטבע נעשה חליפין, ונקנה בחליפין, דהא הכא תרוייהו מטבע נינהו, של שולחני נעשה חליפין, ושל בעל הבית נקנה בחליפין.

disciples of Rabbi Yoḥanan, and was responsible for conveying to Babylonia the Torah rulings laid down in Eretz Israel. He would likewise transmit the Halakhic teachings of the Babylonian scholars to Eretz Israel.

It would seem that Ulla made frequent journeys, and would travel from place to place teaching Torah. (For this reason Yalta, the wife of Rav Naḥman, described him as a "peddler" [*Berakhot* 51b].) In the eyes of the Babylonian scholars, Ulla was particularly important, and the scholars of the second generation of Amoraim there treated him with great respect. Thus Rav Ḥisda referred to him as "Our teacher who comes from Eretz Israel," and Rav Yehudah sent his son to learn Halakhic practice from Ulla's conduct.

In the Jerusalem Talmud, in which he is generally referred to as Rabbi Ulla the son of Yishmael (or "Ulla, the traveler down to Babylonia"), Torah rulings are recorded in his name. Many scholars of the next generation were his pupils.

Of his private life we know nothing. It is possible that the Amora Rabbah the son of Ulla was his son.

We know that he died in Babylonia on one of his journeys, and was brought back to Eretz Israel to be buried.

רַבִּי אַבָּא Rabbi Abba. An Amora of the third generation, Rabbi Abba was born in Babylonia. He was a disciple of Rav Huna and Rav Yehudah. He immigrated to Eretz Israel like his colleague Rabbi Zera, and probably settled in Tiberias.

LANGUAGE (RASHI)

קונדרי״ר* (read: קונידו״ר). From the Old French *conredier*, "to supply the needs of...."

NOTES

יָפֶה דִּינָר וּטְרֵיסִית A dinar and a tressis's worth of money. *Rashi* notes that this was not an instance of interest being paid on a loan. It would seem that the money changer, who served as a kind of banker, was receiving the tressis as a fee for the work involved in changing the money, and for his expertise in the quality of coins. It was common for money changers to receive commissions for their services.

HALAKHAH

וַאֲנִי אַעֲלֶה לְךָ יָפֶה דִּינָר "And I will repay you a dinar's worth." "If workers demand their wages, and the employer has no ready money to pay them, he may say to a money changer: 'Give me a dinar to pay the workers, and I will repay you more than a dinar of uncoined metal I have at home.' This is permitted only if the employer has small unminted coins at home worth at least an entire dinar, as such a transaction is considered a sale rather than an interest-bearing loan. According to *Rema* (citing *Tosafot* and *Rosh*,) even if the employer does not have a whole dinar's worth of unminted coins at home, such a transaction is permitted." (*Shulḥan Arukh, Yoreh De'ah* 173:6.)

TRANSLATION AND COMMENTARY

אֲמַר לֵיהּ [1]But Rabbi Abba, attempting to resolve the difficulty he himself had posed, **said to** Ulla: **Perhaps** the Baraita is referring specifically **to** a case where both the money given by the money changer and the money repaid by the employer are **small coins which** have **no impression on them,** rather than regular minted coins. [2]Hence, **both** the dinar and the dinar and the tressis **are considered merchandise** rather than money, [3]**and because of this they can be acquired through *ḥalifin*.** This being the case, the Baraita cannot serve as a proof that standard coins can also effect *ḥalifin*.

אֲמַר לֵיהּ [4]Ulla **said to** Rabbi Abba: **Yes,** this is the correct interpretation of the Baraita. [5]**This** interpretation **is also implicit** in the wording of the Baraita itself. **The Baraita states** that the employer undertakes to return "a dinar and a tressis's worth," [6]**but does not** state that he undertakes to return "**a good dinar and a tressis.**" Now, since the Baraita speaks of "a dinar's worth," we may assume that it refers not to ordinary coins but to unminted coins worth a dinar, which are considered merchandise and not money. [7]The Gemara concludes: Indeed, **conclude from** the wording of the Baraita that Rabbi Abba's interpretation is correct, and that this Baraita cannot be cited to resolve the issue of whether or not coins can effect *ḥalifin*.

רַב אַשִׁי אֲמַר [8]**Rav Ashi** suggested another interpretation of the Baraita, and **said: In fact,** the Baraita may even be dealing with a case where the money changer loaned money to the employer, and the money returned by the employer **is payment** for the money he received from the money changer, rather than a case where the transaction is an exchange of money by means of *ḥalifin*. In other words, the employer's money at home did not immediately become the property of the money changer as soon as the latter handed over the small coins to enable the employer to pay his workers. Nevertheless, if at the time he received the money from the money changer, the employer had money at home, he is permitted to repay more than he received. As

[1]אֲמַר לֵיהּ: דִּלְמָא אִידִי וְאִידִי בִּפְרוּטְטוֹת שָׁנוּ, דְּלֵיכָּא עֲלַיְיהוּ טִבְעָא, [2]וְאִידִי וְאִידִי פֵּירָא הָווּ, [3]וּמִשּׁוּם הָכִי נִקְנוּ בַּחֲלִיפִין. [4]אֲמַר לֵיהּ: אִין. [5]דַּיְקָא נַמִי, דְּקָתָנֵי, "יָפֶה דִּינָר וּטְרֵיסִית", [6]וְלָא קָתָנֵי, "דִּינָר יָפֶה וּטְרֵיסִית". [7]שְׁמַע מִינָּהּ. [8]רַב אַשִׁי אֲמַר: לְעוֹלָם בְּדָמִים

LITERAL TRANSLATION

[1]He said to him: Perhaps they taught this and that in [reference to] small coins which have no impression on them, [2]and this and that are [both considered] merchandise, [3]and because of that they can be acquired through *ḥalifin*.

[4]He said to him: Yes. [5]It is also precise, for it teaches, "A dinar and a tressis's worth," [6]but it does not teach, "A good dinar and a tressis." [7]Conclude from this.

[8]Rav Ashi said: In fact [it is] through payment and with

RASHI

אמר ליה – רבי אבא לעולא. **דלמא** – קאי אתרוייהו דהאי והאי בין דשולחני בין דבעל הבית. **בפרוטטות** – מעות של נחושת, שהם עדיין בלא צורה, כעין אסימון של כסף. **אמר ליה** – עולא: אין, שפיר תרצת לה. **ודיקא נמי,** מדקאמר "יפה דינר וטריסית" – דמשמע: אעלה לך מפרוטטות שבבית שוה דינר וטריסית. **ולא קתני דינר יפה** – דליםתמע דינר של כסף טוב וטבוע. **רב אשי אמר לעולם בפרוטטות** – היא, כדקאמרת. מדקתני "יפה דינר". ומיהו, טעמא לאו משום דנקנה בחליפין, שאפילו התנה עמו בתורת דמים – אין כאן רבית דאגר נטר ליה, שאפילו הלוהו אם יש לו בביתו – מותר לתת לו עודף, דהוה ליה "הלויני עד שיבא בני".

TERMINOLOGY

דַּיְקָא נַמִי, דְּקָתָנֵי **It is also precise, for it teaches....** An expression introducing a proof in support of the view previously stated, based on a precise examination of the wording of a Mishnah or a Baraita.

NOTES

בִּפְרוּטָטוֹת **In reference to small coins.** For Rabbi Abba's explanation of the Baraita to be valid, it is necessary for both the money changer and the employer to have been using small unminted coins rather than real money, for if one of the parties were using real money in a *ḥalifin* exchange, we would still be able to prove either that money can be used to effect *ḥalifin* — if the money changer used money — or that it can be acquired using *ḥalifin* — if the employer used money (*Rashi*). The Gemara's linguistic proof, however, refers only to the employer's use of unminted coins, for the expression יָפֶה דִּינָר rather than דִּינָר יָפֶה appears only there, and not in connection with the money changer's payment. Nevertheless, the Gemara felt that the linguistic argument supported Rabbi Abba's explanation, because if the employer was using small unminted coins, the money changer was probably also using them (*Ritva*).

According to Rav Ashi's explanation, however, there is no obvious need to use small unminted coins, and it would appear that the transaction could just as well have been performed with real money. Why, then, did Rav Ashi use the explanation that the coins were unminted?

According to *Rashi*, Rav Ashi retained the small unminted coins in his explanation merely in order to satisfy the Gemara's linguistic argument. Presumably, Rav Ashi too would explain that the unminted coins were used by both the employer and the money changer (see *Tosafot*). This leads to difficulties with the wording of Rav Ashi's explanation, for it literally reads: "In fact, it deals with payment and very small unminted coins." According to this explanation, Rav Ashi agrees with Rabbi Abba that both parties are using unminted coins. *Rashi* rewords Rav Ashi's statement thus: "In fact, it deals with an exchange of small unminted coins, but it could refer to a payment of money as well as to *ḥalifin*."

SAGES

רַב יְהוּדָה **Rav Yehudah.** A Babylonian Amora of the second generation. See *Bava Metzia,* Part II, p. 47.

TERMINOLOGY

הָכִי קָאָמַר **He says thus** — i.e., his statement should be interpreted as explained below. This term is used to introduce a new explanation or a textual emendation of a difficult passage in a Mishnah or a Baraita — usually proposed in order to resolve a problem raised by the Gemara regarding the passage.

TRANSLATION AND COMMENTARY

suggested above, the Baraita is referring to a case of **small**, unminted **coins,** which are considered merchandise. [1]**Since** the employer **has the money** at home, **it is considered as if he** had said to the money changer: [2]**"Lend me** money **until my son comes,"** or **"until I find the key** and can get to the money in my possession." Such a transaction is not considered a loan, and therefore raises no problem of interest.

תָּא שְׁמַע [3]The Gemara now cites another source in an attempt to determine whether or not coins can effect *ḥalifin*: **Come and hear** what we learned in the following Mishnah (*Kiddushin* 1:6, 28a), which discusses *ḥalifin*: "**Anything that can be used as payment for something else** can be used to effect *ḥalifin*. [4]**Once one** party **acquires** the article he wants, **the other** party acquires the merchandise he is to receive **in exchange**, and therefore **becomes liable** for that merchandise." Should the merchandise suffer damage before delivery, the party who is to receive it must suffer the loss, for he is already its legal owner.

כָּל הַנַּעֲשֶׂה דָּמִים בְּאַחֵר [5]The Gemara now seeks to understand this Mishnah: **What** is meant by the phrase **"anything that can be used as payment for something else,"** i.e., what sort of objects can be used as payment for others? [6]The Gemara answers: Presumably **coins,** for payment is usually made with money! Accordingly, the meaning of the Mishnah is as follows: When coins are given as payment for merchandise, they cannot effect a sale. But if a coin is not given as payment, but rather to effect *ḥalifin*, once one party acquires it, the other acquires the merchandise he is to receive in exchange, and immediately becomes liable for that merchandise should it be damaged. [7]Thus we may **infer from here that coins can effect *ḥalifin*!**

אֲמַר רַב יְהוּדָה [8]The Gemara rejects this proof: **Rav Yehudah said: What the Mishnah means is as follows:** [46B] [9]**"Anything that is appraised when given as payment for something else** can be used to effect *ḥalifin*. In other words, *ḥalifin* can be performed with any movable property whose value requires assessment before it

וּבִפְרוֹטְטוֹת. [1]כֵּיוָן דְּאִית לֵיהּ, נַעֲשֶׂה כְּאוֹמֵר, [2]"הַלְוֵינִי עַד שֶׁיָּבֹא בְּנִי", אוֹ "עַד שֶׁאֶמְצָא מַפְתֵּחַ".

[3]תָּא שְׁמַע: "כָּל הַנַּעֲשֶׂה דָּמִים בְּאַחֵר, [4]כֵּיוָן שֶׁזָּכָה זֶה, נִתְחַיֵּיב זֶה בַּחֲלִיפִין".

[5]"כָּל הַנַּעֲשֶׂה דָּמִים בְּאַחֵר" מַאי נִיהוּ? [6]מַטְבֵּעַ. [7]וּשְׁמַע מִינָּהּ מַטְבֵּעַ נַעֲשֶׂה חֲלִיפִין!

[8]אֲמַר רַב יְהוּדָה: הָכִי קָאָמַר: [46B] [9]"כָּל הַנִּישׁוֹם דָּמִים

LITERAL TRANSLATION

small coins. [1]Since he has [the money], it is as if he says, [2]"Lend me until my son comes," or "until I find the key."

[3]Come [and] hear: "Anything that can be used as payment for something else, [4]once this one acquires, the other is liable for its exchange."

[5]What is "anything that can be used as payment for something else"? [6]Coin. [7]And conclude from this [that] coin can be used for *ḥalifin*!

[8]Rav Yehudah said: He says thus: [46B] [9]"Anything that is appraised [when given as] payment

RASHI

כל הנעשה דמים באחר — משנה היא בקדושין (כח,א), וקא סלקא דעתך דהכי קאמר: כל הרגיל להיות ניתן דמים באחר, דהיינו מטבע. **כיון שזכה זה נתחייב זה בחליפין** — אם נתנה בעלים בתורת חליפין, בחליפי שור ופרה, כיון שמשך בעל הפרה את המטבע — נתחייב בעל המטבע בכל אונסין שיולדו בחליפין מעתה, אם מת השור — מת לו, אף על פי שלא משך כו׳, אלמא: קנה בחליפין של מטבע. **כל הנישום דמים באחר** — כל שרגילים לשום אותו כשנותנין אותן דמים באחר, דהיינו כל המטלטלים; אם בא אדם לתתם דמים בחפץ אחר דרכן לשומן בכמה יתנו לו.

NOTES

Other Rishonim reject this explanation. *Rosh* explains that, according to Rav Ashi, only the employer uses the small unminted coins, whereas the money changer uses ordinary money. This interpretation fits the language of Rav Ashi's explanation a little better, as it can be explained as follows: "In fact, it refers to money given in exchange for small unminted coins."

הַלְוֵינִי עַד שֶׁיָּבֹא בְּנִי **Lend me until my son comes.** The source of this law is a Mishnah (below, 75a). The Mishnah discusses the prohibition against lending "a *se'ah* for a *se'ah*" (see detailed explanation above, 44b). It is forbidden to lend commodities by weight or volume rather than by value, because if the commodity should go up in price, the difference would be a form of interest.

This prohibition is of Rabbinic origin, and has a number of exceptions. One of them is a loan "until my son comes." If the borrower already possesses a commodity he can use to repay the loan, but cannot get to it for some reason — "until my son comes," or "until I find the key" — he is permitted to borrow on the basis of weight or volume, as the Rabbis were willing to view the transaction as an exchange of goods rather than as a loan.

כָּל הַנִּישׁוֹם דָּמִים בְּאַחֵר **Anything that is appraised when given as payment for something else.** Our commentary follows *Rashi*, who explains that this clause is merely another way of saying "all movable goods." *Rabbenu Ḥananel*, however, explains that the Mishnah chose this expression in order to teach us that when articles are exchanged it is essential that they be appraised first, so that the parties know the relative value of the items involved. If the articles are not appraised, the *ḥalifin* exchange is not valid.

בְּאַחֵר, [1]כֵּיוָן שֶׁזָּכָה זֶה, נִתְחַיֵּיב זֶה בַּחֲלִיפִין".

[2]הָכִי נַמִי מִסְתַּבְּרָא, [3]מִדְּקָתָנֵי סֵיפָא: "כֵּיצַד? [4]הֶחֱלִיף שׁוֹר בְּפָרָה, אוֹ חֲמוֹר בְּשׁוֹר". [5]שְׁמַע מִינָּהּ.

[6]וּלְמַאי דְּסָלֵיק אַדַּעְתֵּיהּ מֵעִיקָּרָא — מַטְבֵּעַ — [7]מַאי "כֵּיצַד"?

LITERAL TRANSLATION

for something else, [1]once this one acquires, the other is liable for its exchange."

[2]So, too, it stands to reason, [3]since the latter clause teaches: "How so? [4][If] he exchanged an ox for a cow, or an ass for an ox." [5]Conclude from this.

[6]And according to what originally entered his mind — coin — [7]is "how so"?

TRANSLATION AND COMMENTARY

can be exchanged for other merchandise. [1]**Once one party acquires** the object whose value must be appraised, **the other** party acquires the merchandise he is to receive **in exchange,** and therefore **becomes liable** for it." If that merchandise is accidentally damaged before it is delivered to him, he must accept the loss, and cannot demand compensation.

הָכִי נַמִי מִסְתַּבְּרָא [2]The Gemara notes that Rav Yehudah's interpretation of the Mishnah **also stands to reason,** [3]**for the next clause** of the Mishnah **states: "How so?** What is an example of a *ḥalifin* exchange involving the items described in the first clause?" [4]The Mishnah continues: **"If a person exchanged an ox for a cow or an ass for an ox,** once one party acquires one of the animals, the other party acquires the other." Thus it would appear that the first clause of the Mishnah should be understood as dealing with "anything that is appraised when given as payment," i.e., movable property such as animals, and not coins. [5]Accordingly, the Gemara concludes: **Conclude from here** that the *ḥalifin* transaction described in the Mishnah was effected with movable goods and not with coins, and the Mishnah is teaching us that all movable goods other than coins — even animals — can be used to effect *ḥalifin.* As the Gemara will explain below, there is an opinion that only utensils can be used to effect *ḥalifin.* The Mishnah is informing us that this is not so.

וּלְמַאי דְּסָלֵיק אַדַּעְתֵּיהּ מֵעִיקָּרָא [6]The Gemara now asks: **And according to what we originally imagined** — that the Mishnah refers to a *ḥalifin* transaction effected with a **coin** — [7]**what** does the expression **"how so"** mean? How could anyone possibly have interpreted the words used in the first clause of the Mishnah — "anything that can be used as payment for something else" — as referring to coins, when the Mishnah itself explains that it refers to animals ("how so... an ox for a cow...")?

RASHI

כיון שזכה זה כו' – אם נתנם בתורת חליפין, כיון שמשכן זה כו'. ואשמועינן דמטלטלי ופרי נעשין חליפין, ולא בעינן כלי. "דשלף איש נעלו" (רות ד) לאו דוקא, ד"לקיים כל דבר" דרשינן: לקיים בכל דבר, כדלקמן (מז,א). **הכי נמי מסתברא** – דלאו במטבע עסקינן, דקתני סיפא: כיצד, החליף שור בפרה כו'.

NOTES

מַטְבֵּעַ פֵּירוֹת וְכֵלִים Coins, produce and utensils. Our commentary follows *Rashi,* who explains that in the context of *ḥalifin,* the term "produce" is not to be understood in its usual sense. In this context the term "produce" means any kind of movable property that is not a utensil, including animals and coins. A "utensil," on the other hand, is to be understood in the context of *ḥalifin* in its usual sense — as a tool, an article of clothing, or any other inanimate object that is physically utilized but not consumed.

According to *Rashi,* the entire discussion of the Gemara as to whether or not coins may be used in *ḥalifin* transactions is relevant only according to the viewpoint of Rav Sheshet, who maintains that "produce" can be used to effect *ḥalifin.* But according to Rav Naḥman, neither coins nor any other "produce" can be used to effect *ḥalifin,* and the entire discussion is irrelevant. *Rashi's* opinion is supported by the fact that when the Gemara explains the Mishnah according to Rav Naḥman, it makes no mention of the question of the status of coins or of the two ways of understanding the first clause of the Mishnah, as it does when explaining the Mishnah according to Rav Sheshet.

Nevertheless, many Rishonim disagree with *Rashi's* interpretation. They find it inconceivable that the Gemara's entire discussion about the status of coins should be irrelevant according to Rav Naḥman, whose view is generally accepted as the Halakhah. Moreover, the question as to whether or not a coin can be used in *ḥalifin* was first raised (above, 45b) by Rav and Levi, of the first generation of Amoraim, and it would be very unusual for Rav Naḥman to reject their opinions.

Accordingly, these Rishonim explain that in the context of *ḥalifin,* the term "produce" has its usual meaning — "foodstuffs" — and the term "utensils" is to be interpreted more broadly as meaning any item of movable property that serves a purpose and is not intended to be consumed. Thus, a coin and a live animal are both "utensils," but the meat

HALAKHAH

קִנְיַן חֲלִיפִין Acquisition through *ḥalifin.* "All movable objects can acquire each other through *ḥalifin,* and it makes no difference whether or not the parties verify the exact value of the merchandise being exchanged. For example, if one person has an ox and another an ass, and they assess the value of the animals and agree to exchange them, once one of the parties draws one of the animals into his possession, the other party acquires the other animal wherever it is, and neither party can withdraw from the transaction." *Gra* remarks that this is the opinion of

SAGES

רַב שֵׁשֶׁת Rav Sheshet. A Babylonian Amora of the third and fourth generations. See *Bava Metzia*, Part I, p. 36.

TRANSLATION AND COMMENTARY

הָכִי קָאָמַר [1]The Gemara answers: Even if we had explained the first clause of the Mishnah as referring to coins, we could still have explained the next clause as teaching us that all movable property other than coins, even animals, can be used to effect *ḥalifin*. **What the Mishnah means is as follows:** "Anything that can be used as payment for something else, i.e., coins, can be used to effect *ḥalifin*. **And** not only coins, but **produce too can** be used to **effect *ḥalifin***. [2]**How so?** [3]**If** a person **exchanged an ox for a cow or an ass for an ox,** once one party acquires one of the animals, the other party acquires the other." In other words, we can interpret the Mishnah's mention of "anything that can be used as payment" as referring to coins. The next clause then gives us the additional information that produce too can effect *ḥalifin*: "How so? If a person exchanged an ox for a cow...."

הָנִיחָא לְרַב שֵׁשֶׁת [4]The Gemara objects: Both explanations of the Mishnah offered above — the explanation of Rav Yehudah which follows the opinion that coins cannot be used to effect *ḥalifin*, and the Gemara's original explanation which follows the opinion that coins can be so used — assume that the second clause of the Mishnah comes to teach us that all movable property — including animals — can be used to effect *ḥalifin*. Now **these** explanations of the Mishnah **pose no problem according to Rav Sheshet, who said** (below, 47a) [5]that not only utensils, but even **produce, can effect *ḥalifin***. According to Rav Sheshet, we can understand how an animal can effect *ḥalifin*, for all "produce," including animals, can effect *ḥalifin*. [6]**But according to Rav Naḥman, who said** (ibid.): Only **utensils** can effect *ḥalifin*, [7]**but produce** or coins **cannot effect *ḥalifin***, [8]**what** does the later clause of the Mishnah — **"How so"** — mean? According to Rav Naḥman, since animals are not "utensils," one cannot be bartered for another in a *ḥalifin* exchange, and thus the Mishnah's ruling is problematic!

[1]הָכִי קָאָמַר: ״וּפֵירֵי נַמִי עָבְדִי חֲלִיפִין. [2]כֵּיצַד? [3]הֶחֱלִיף שׁוֹר בְּפָרָה אוֹ חֲמוֹר בְּשׁוֹר״.
[4]הָנִיחָא לְרַב שֵׁשֶׁת, דַּאֲמַר: [5]פֵּירֵי עָבְדִי חֲלִיפִין. [6]אֶלָּא לְרַב נַחְמָן, דַּאֲמַר: כְּלִי — אִין; [7]אֲבָל פֵּירֵי לָא עָבְדִי חֲלִיפִין, [8]מַאי ״כֵּיצַד״?

LITERAL TRANSLATION

[1]He says thus: "And produce, too, effects *ḥalifin*. [2]How so? [3][If] he exchanged an ox for a cow, or an ass for an ox."

[4]This is well according to Rav Sheshet, who said: [5]Produce can effect *ḥalifin*. [6]But according to Rav Naḥman, who said: A utensil — yes; [7]but produce cannot effect *ḥalifin*, [8]what is "how so"?

RASHI

הכי קאמר ופירי נמי — כל מטלטלין, אף על פי שאינו כלי עבדי חליפין, כיצד כו׳. והכי מפרשינן לה: כל העושה דמים באחר, דהיינו מטבע, אם נתנו בתורת חליפין, כיון שזכה זה — נתחייב זה בחליפין. כיצד חליפין, ומהו חליפין? כגון המחליף שור בפרה. ואשמועינן אגב אורחיה בסיפא, דפירי עושים חליפים. החליף שור בפרה גרסינן, ולא גרסינן בשר שור. **הניחא לרב ששת כו׳** — בין למאי דסליק אדעתין מעיקרא בין למאי דשני רב יהודה, סיפא דמתניתין אשמעינן דפירי עבדי חליפין, ולא בעינן כלי, והא פלוגתא דרב נחמן ורב ששת היא לקמן בשמעתין (מז,א) הניחא לרב ששת כו׳.

NOTES

of a slaughtered animal is "produce." Hence, the question as to whether or not coins may be used to effect *ḥalifin* is relevant both according to Rav Naḥman and according to Rav Sheshet (*Tosafot* and others).

הָכִי קָאָמַר He says thus. Our commentary follows *Rashi*'s interpretation, according to which live animals are considered "produce." Understood in this way, the Gemara's first two explanations of the Mishnah — the initial suggestion that coins may be used to effect *ḥalifin*, and Rav Yehudah's counter-explanation that the Mishnah was not referring to coins but to the exchange of animals — are both consistent with Rav Sheshet's view that produce may be used to effect *ḥalifin*. The difference between these explanations concerns only the first clause of the Mishnah, but according to both views, the second clause — presenting the example of an exchange of animals — specifically teaches us that animals and other "produce" may be used for *ḥalifin*. Moreover, according to *Rashi*, Rav Naḥman is of the opinion that coins cannot be used in *ḥalifin*. Hence the Gemara's subsequent consideration of Rav Naḥman's opinion has nothing to do with the question of whether or not the first clause of the Mishnah teaches us that coins may be used in *ḥalifin*. It is obvious that Rav Naḥman must explain the first clause along the lines of Rav Yehudah, and would thus avoid the implication that coins may be so used. Rather, Rav Naḥman's viewpoint is brought in only parenthetically, to avoid the implication that the second clause of the Mishnah is a refutation of his view.

Contrary to *Rashi*'s view, *Tosafot* argues (see previous note) that live animals are considered utensils because they are used for farm work, and coins are also considered utensils because they can be used in many ways. Thus the question about the status of coins is relevant according to Rav Naḥman as well as according to Rav Sheshet.

According to Tosafot, the Gemara initially understood the second clause of the Mishnah as permitting the use of live animals to effect *ḥalifin*. The Gemara explained the

HALAKHAH

Rabbenu Tam. *Rema* cites some opinions according to which even produce can be acquired through *ḥalifin*, provided the parties have assessed its value, but other authorities disagree. (*Shulḥan Arukh, Ḥoshen Mishpat* 203:1.)

TRANSLATION AND COMMENTARY

הָכִי קָאָמַר [1]The Gemara answers that Rav Naḥman can explain that the Mishnah is not referring to *ḥalifin* at all, but to a type of exchange that resembles it. According to this explanation, **what the Mishnah means is as follows:** "Anything that must be appraised before it can be used as money, can be used as money and can effect the transaction." In this clause, the Mishnah is telling us the following rule: "Even though, in general, payment of money does not effect a sale of movable property, [2]**there is** an exceptional type of **payment** which effects the transfer of ownership of property and causes the recipient of the goods being bought to become responsible for them even before he takes physical possession of them, just **like a *ḥalifin*** exchange." [3]The Mishnah proceeds to explain: "**How so?** [4]If a person **exchanged the value of an ox for a cow, or the value of an ass for an ox.**" The final clause of the Mishnah is thus to be understood as follows: Since one party has already completed his acquisition, the other party assumes responsibility for the animal he is acquiring; if the animal should suffer an accident before coming into his possession, he cannot demand compensation. This is how the transaction described by the Mishnah would take place: A sells B an ox. B takes possession of the ox, but does not yet pay for it. The parties then agree that, in lieu of payment, A will buy a cow from B with the money owed to him by B. The Mishnah teaches us that A acquires the cow immediately he comes to an agreement with B, without any need for a further act of acquisition, because the cancellation of the debt — which is the equivalent of a payment of money — serves as the act of acquisition. Even though it is ordinarily impossible to effect a sale of movable property by payment of money alone, this case is exceptional, as the Gemara will explain.

מַאי טַעְמֵיהּ דְּרַב נַחְמָן [5]The Gemara now goes on to explain why monetary payment is an effective mode of acquisition in this exceptional case. The Gemara asks: **What is Rav Naḥman's reasoning?**

LITERAL TRANSLATION

[1]He says thus: [2]"There is money that is like *ḥalifin*. [3]How so? [4][If] he exchanged the value of an ox for a cow, or the value of an ass for an ox."

[5]What is Rav Naḥman's reason?

[1]הָכִי קָאָמַר: [2]"יֵשׁ דָּמִים שֶׁהֵן כַּחֲלִיפִין. [3]כֵּיצַד? [4]הֶחֱלִיף דְּמֵי שׁוֹר בְּפָרָה, אוֹ דְּמֵי חֲמוֹר בְּשׁוֹר".

[5]מַאי טַעְמֵיהּ דְּרַב נַחְמָן?

RASHI

הכי קאמר יש דמים שהן כחליפין — רישא וסיפא חדא היא, ואשמעינן דיש תורת דמים, שהמעות קונות בלא משיכה כחליפין של סודר. **ביצד החליף דמי שור בפרה** — מכר לו שור בכך וכך מעות, ומשך את השור, ונתחייב לו המעות, אמר לו הלוקח: פרה יש לי שאני נותן לך בדמי השור, וניאותו יחד, וקבל עליו — נתחייב בעל הפרה לתת לו את הפרה, ואין אחד מהם יכול לחזור, והכי קאמר: כל הנישום דמים באחר; כל המטלטלין שאדם שם לחבירו ונותן לו שומת דמיהן בשביל חפץ אחר שהיה לו ללוקח. כיון שזכה זה — לוקח ראשון במטלטלין הראשונים שמשכן, ואפילו בתורת דמים, על מנת להקנות לו חפץ שלו בדמים, נתחייב זה — לוקח שני — בכל אונסי החליפין, לפי שקנו לו מעותיו כל אונסי החליפין. **ביצד החליף דמי שור בפרה** — שם לו השור בדמים על מנת שיתן לו זה פרה באותן מעות — קנה. **מאי טעמא דרב נחמן** — דאמר דמים כי האי גוונא קנו, ואנן תנן: מעות אינן קונות.

TERMINOLOGY

מַאי טַעְמֵיהּ דְּרַבִּי פְּלוֹנִי What is Rabbi X's reason? The Gemara often uses this expression when a Mishnah contains a difference of opinion between a majority of the Sages and a single dissenting Sage.

NOTES

first clause as ruling that coins may also be so used; then Rav Yehudah argued that the Mishnah reads better according to the opinion that coins may not be used to effect *ḥalifin*, with the first clause introducing the second clause. Both interpretations are quite acceptable according to Rav Naḥman, because the second clause refers to live animals, which are "utensils."

It is only when the Gemara looks for a way to resolve the linguistic difficulty ("how so") noted by Rav Yehudah that Rav Naḥman encounters a problem. The Gemara asks: According to the view that the first clause teaches that a coin can effect *ḥalifin*, how does the first clause relate to the second clause that speaks about animals? The Gemara answers that the second clause is not speaking about live animals, but rather about "produce" such as the meat of slaughtered animals. The Mishnah is thus to be understood as teaching that not only coins, but also "produce" may be used in *ḥalifin*.

It is at this point that the difference of opinion between Rav Naḥman and Rav Sheshet enters the discussion. The Gemara points out that this last explanation can be accepted only according to Rav Sheshet. But how would Rav Naḥman explain the connection between the two clauses of the Mishnah, according to the view that coins *can* be used to effect *ḥalifin*? (According to the view that coins cannot be so used, he would of course explain it as did Rav Yehudah.) The Gemara answers that, according to Rav Naḥman, the second clause is speaking about the value of the animals, rather than about their meat. Thus the Mishnah is to be understood as teaching that coins can not only effect *ḥalifin*, but can even be used as a mode of acquisition in a special case involving an exchange of animals (*Tosafot*).

יֵשׁ דָּמִים שֶׁהֵן כַּחֲלִיפִין There is money that is like *ḥalifin*. Our commentary follows *Rashi* and most Rishonim, and is based on a Geonic tradition (*Ramban*). According to this interpretation, the act of acquisition that finalizes the sale

HALAKHAH

יֵשׁ דָּמִים שֶׁהֵן כַּחֲלִיפִין There is money that is like *ḥalifin*. "If A sells movable property to B, and B draws the merchandise into his possession but has not yet paid for it, A can use the money B owes him to buy other goods from B.

BACKGROUND

נִשְׂרְפוּ חִטֶּיךָ בַּעֲלִיָּיה Your wheat was burnt in the upper story. The difference of opinion between Rabbi Yoḥanan and Resh Lakish is fully clarified below (47b), where we find that this general rule was established in order to ensure, as far as possible, that the buyer not lose the article on which he has spent his money. This regulation is therefore of a utilitarian nature, designed to reinforce trust between buyers and sellers.

TRANSLATION AND COMMENTARY

סָבַר לָהּ כְּרַבִּי יוֹחָנָן [1]The Gemara answers: Rav Naḥman **agrees with Rabbi Yoḥanan, who said: By Torah law, money acquires.** There is a difference of opinion (below, 47b) between Rabbi Yoḥanan and Resh Lakish. Our Mishnah ruled that in an exchange of money and merchandise, the merchandise acquires the money but the money does not acquire the merchandise. In other words, *meshikhah* — the buyer's drawing of the merchandise into his possession — is the act of acquisition that effects the sale and obligates the buyer to pay the agreed sum, whereas payment of money is not an act of acquisition at all. Resh Lakish is of the opinion that the Mishnah's ruling is a Torah law derived from a verse in Leviticus (25:14). Rabbi Yoḥanan, by contrast, is of the opinion that the Mishnah's ruling is a Rabbinic decree, whereas by Torah law payment of money is an act of acquisition, and the merchandise immediately becomes the property of the buyer; but merely picking up the purchased object is not an act of acquisition until the money has been paid. [2]**Why** then **did the Rabbis say that** monetary payment cannot effect a sale, and it is only *meshikhah* that **acquires** movable goods? [3]Rabbi Yoḥanan explains: **It was a preventive measure** taken by the Rabbis, **lest the seller say to** the buyer: **"Your wheat was burnt in the upper story** of my house after you paid me." By Torah law, once a person pays for his merchandise, he becomes the legal owner of the property — even before it enters his physical possession. If the property is damaged before he takes possession — for example, if a fire breaks out in the seller's home where the merchandise is being stored — the buyer's money is not refunded and he has to suffer the loss. The Rabbis, however, preferred that the party in physical possession of the merchandise be liable if the merchandise is damaged. Therefore they decreed that it is only *meshikhah* that effects the sale of movable goods. Even if the buyer has paid for his merchandise, the sale does not take effect until the merchandise comes into the buyer's physical possession. If the property is damaged before it is in

LITERAL TRANSLATION

[1]He agrees with Rabbi Yoḥanan, who said: By Torah law, money acquires. [2]And why did they say [that] *meshikhah* acquires? [3][It was] a preventive measure lest he [the seller] say to him: "Your wheat was burnt in the upper story."

[1]סָבַר לָהּ כְּרַבִּי יוֹחָנָן, דְּאָמַר: דְּבַר תּוֹרָה, מָעוֹת קוֹנוֹת. [2]וּמִפְּנֵי מָה אָמְרוּ מְשִׁיכָה קוֹנָה? [3]גְּזֵירָה, שֶׁמָּא יֹאמַר לוֹ: "נִשְׂרְפוּ חִטֶּיךָ בַּעֲלִיָּיה".

RASHI

סבר לה כרבי יוחנן — דאמר לקמן (מז,ב): דבר תורה מעות קונות, כדאשכחן גבי קונה מן ההקדש, שאמרה תורה "ונתן הכסף וקם לו". **ומפני מה אמרו משיכה קונה** — ולא מעות. **גזרה שמא** — יניחם לוקח בבית מוכר זמן מרובה, ותפול דליקה בשכונת המוכר, ולא יחוש לטרוח ולהציל, לפיכך העמידום ברשותו לחזור בו אם ירצה, דכיון שאם יתייקרו — ברשותו יתייקרו, ויחזור בו מן המכר ויהא השכר שלו — כי דידיה חשיב להו, וטרח ומציל. וכיון דתקנתא דרבנן בעלמא הוא, במכר דשכיח — עבוד רבנן תקנתא, במכר דלא שכיח, כגון האי שיהיו שמין דמי מטלטלין במטלטלין — לא עבוד רבנן תקנתא במשיכה.

NOTES

in this case is not even a payment of money. It is the cancellation of a debt arising from a previous sale.

The Rishonim ask: The Gemara (*Kiddushin* 6b) rules that in order to effect a betrothal, a man must place money, or an object that has monetary value, in the woman's possession; it is not sufficient for him to cancel a debt she owes him, as debt cancellation is not the equivalent of payment. How, then, is it possible to finalize a purchase by canceling a debt?

Tosafot explains that while it is not possible to effect a betrothal by canceling a debt, it is possible to do so with the gratification the bride has from having her debt canceled, as this is considered a service that has monetary value. Thus it is possible that in our case the animal is being purchased not with the cancellation of a debt, but with the gratification provided by the cancellation of the debt.

Ritva (see *Kiddushin* 28b) suggests that, in our case, the money to repay the original debt had already been set aside by the buyer and placed in escrow. Thus the money owed was no longer a debt but a deposit.

Meiri suggests an entirely different way of interpreting this passage, in which there is no debt cancellation. A sells an ox to B in exchange for a sum of money, but before B takes the ox into his possession, he suggests that A accept an ass instead of the money B has agreed to pay. The parties agree on the arrangement, and the Mishnah rules that as soon as B takes possession of the ox, A acquires the ass, just as in *ḥalifin*, even though the ass was really given in lieu of payment and not as *ḥalifin* for the ox. Moreover, the transaction is effective even according to Rav Naḥman — who does not permit *ḥalifin* with produce — because it is not actually a form of *ḥalifin*. There is some evidence that *Rashi* too would support this interpretation.

HALAKHAH

דְּבַר תּוֹרָה, מָעוֹת קוֹנוֹת By Torah law, money acquires. "By Torah law, movable property can be acquired with money. But the Rabbis enacted that movable property can be acquired only if the buyer draws it into his possession or lifts it up. This enactment was made because of the possibility that

Such a sale is effective even though A has not drawn the item into his possession. It is only by Rabbinic decree that money cannot be used to acquire movables, and this decree does not apply here, since people rarely buy things in this manner." (*Shulḥan Arukh, Ḥoshen Mishpat* 199:2.)

LITERAL TRANSLATION

[1] And in a thing that is frequent the Rabbis made a preventive measure; [2] in a thing that is not frequent, the Rabbis did not make a preventive measure.

[3] And according to Resh Lakish, who says: [4] *Meshikhah* is explicit from the Torah, [5] this is well if he agrees with Rav Sheshet; [6] he can explain this like Rav Sheshet.

[1] וּמִלְּתָא דִּשְׁכִיחָא גָּזְרוּ בֵּיהּ רַבָּנַן; [2] מִלְּתָא דְּלָא שְׁכִיחָא לָא גָּזְרוּ בֵּיהּ רַבָּנַן.

[3] וּלְרֵישׁ לָקִישׁ, דְּאָמַר: [4] מְשִׁיכָה מְפוֹרֶשֶׁת מִן הַתּוֹרָה, [5] הָנִיחָא אִי סָבַר לָהּ כְּרַב שֵׁשֶׁת; [6] מְתָרֵץ לָהּ כְּרַב שֵׁשֶׁת.

RASHI

ולריש לקיש דאמר — לקמן בפרקין (מז,ב). משיכה מפורשת מן התורה — וכיון דמדאורייתא מעות לא קנו — לא שנא מכר דשכיח ולא שנא מכר דלא שכיח מעות לא קנו. הניחא אי סבר לה כרב ששת דאמר פירי עבדי חליפין — מתרץ לה למתניתין כרב ששת, וכדשני רב יהודה: כל הנישום דמים באחר, כגון מטלטלין ופירי שאדם רגיל לשום כשנותנן דמים באחר, היכא דעשאם חליפין — כיון שזכה זה כו'.

TRANSLATION AND COMMENTARY

the buyer's possession, the seller must refund the money. Now, even according to Rabbi Yoḥanan, payment of money is a valid act of acquisition, but is rendered invalid by Rabbinic decree. Hence Rav Naḥman's explanation of the Mishnah in *Kiddushin* — according to which it is possible to buy an animal by canceling a debt without any further formal act of acquisition — should still not be tenable, even according to Rabbi Yoḥanan. However, the fact that by Torah law it is possible to buy an animal in this way does make a difference. The Rabbis did not always invalidate a sale performed with monetary payment. [1] For, as a general rule, **the Rabbis introduced a preventive measure** only **with regard to cases that occur frequently,** [2] but **with regard to cases that occur** only **infrequently, the Rabbis did not introduce a preventive measure.** Rather they allowed the Torah law to stand in these unusual cases. Now, people often buy merchandise with cash. Therefore the Rabbis issued a decree declaring that cash payment is an invalid mode of acquisition, and insisting on the use of *meshikhah*. However, people rarely buy merchandise with money owed to them from a previous sale. Therefore the Rabbis let the Torah law stand in this case, and it remains possible to effect such a sale on the basis of money alone without any further act of acquisition. Thus, provided we accept the opinion of Rabbi Yoḥanan, it is possible to explain the Mishnah in *Kiddushin* even according to Rabbi Naḥman, who is of the opinion that *ḥalifin* cannot be effected with animals or produce.

וּלְרֵישׁ לָקִישׁ [3] The Gemara now attempts to explain the Mishnah even according to the opinion of Resh Lakish, who disagrees with Rabbi Yoḥanan: How, asks the Gemara, can the Mishnah be explained **according to Resh Lakish, who says** [4] that ***meshikhah* is explicitly mentioned in the Torah** (see below, 47b)? If *meshikhah* is required by Torah law, no distinction can be made between cases that occur frequently and those that occur infrequently, for in all cases *meshikhah* is required. According to Resh Lakish, the rule that mere payment of money cannot effect a sale was established by Torah law, and has no exceptions. Thus it is impossible to buy an animal by canceling a debt without performing a formal act of acquisition. [5] Now the Mishnah in *Kiddushin* **poses no problem** for Resh Lakish **if he agrees with Rav Sheshet,** who maintains that produce can effect *ḥalifin*. For if Resh Lakish is of the opinion that even property other than utensils can effect *ḥalifin*, [6] **he can explain** the Mishnah — **like Rav Sheshet** did — as referring to *ḥalifin*. Accordingly, he can explain the last clause of the Mishnah as teaching us that *ḥalifin* can be performed with animals, even though

NOTES

מִלְתָא דְּלָא שְׁכִיחָא לָא גָּזְרוּ בֵּיהּ רַבָּנַן **In a thing that is not frequent, the Rabbis did not make a preventive measure.** As a general rule, Torah laws apply unconditionally. Even when they are not applicable in practice — for example, the laws of sacrifices which cannot be fulfilled in the absence of the Temple — they maintain their binding status. It is impossible to abrogate, repeal or modify a law of the Torah, except within certain very rigid limits set by the Torah itself (such as a case involving danger to human life).

Rabbinic decrees, by contrast, are the creation of human beings, and were enacted with a clearly defined purpose in mind. That purpose can be comprehended and challenged by human reason. Rabbinic decrees cannot be abrogated lightly. The authors of Rabbinic decrees enjoy immense prestige and authority, and only scholarship of similar weight can possibly challenge them. In fact, it is accepted that decrees enacted by the Talmudic Sages cannot in practice be abrogated until the Messiah comes. However, the fact that Rabbinic decrees are linked to specific purposes does, on occasion, make a difference in Halakhic rulings.

In particular, many Rabbinic decrees were enacted "for the good of the world" (מִפְּנֵי תִיקּוּן הָעוֹלָם). The Rabbis saw a

HALAKHAH

people might temporarily leave in the seller's possession merchandise for which they had paid. Thus, if payment were to effect a sale and the merchandise were at risk of loss, the seller might not make an effort to save it, since under Torah law it already belonged to the buyer," following Rabbi Yoḥanan, whose ruling is generally accepted. (Ibid., 198:1, 5.)

LANGUAGE

אַנְקָא Anka. Neither the source of this word nor its exact meaning is clear. Some authorities hold that it is connected with the Middle Persian word *anak*, meaning "dirty" or "blurred."

TRANSLATION AND COMMENTARY

they are not utensils. He can explain the first clause in one of the two ways suggested earlier by the Gemara — as referring either to coins or to the animals described in the next clause, as Rav Yehudah explained. [1]**But if** Resh Lakish **agrees with Rav Naḥman, who says** [2]that **produce cannot effect *ḥalifin***, he cannot explain the Mishnah in either of the ways suggested earlier by the Gemara. He cannot explain the second clause as referring to an exchange of animals effected by means of *ḥalifin*. [3]**And** since he maintains that by Torah law **money does not acquire** movable goods, he cannot explain the Mishnah as did Rav Naḥman — as referring to the acquisition of an animal with money owed from a previous sale. [4]So **how can** Resh Lakish **explain** the Mishnah's ruling?

עַל כָּרְחָךְ [5]The Gemara answers: **Of necessity,** you **must** say that Resh Lakish would **explain** the Mishnah **according to** the view of **Rav Sheshet.** It is impossible to maintain that *meshikhah* is a Torah law without also maintaining that *ḥalifin* can be performed with produce, and conversely it is impossible to maintain that *ḥalifin* can only be performed with a utensil without also maintaining that, by Torah law, payment of money is an act of acquisition.

תְּנַן [6]Having concluded its discussion of the Mishnah in *Kiddushin*, the Gemara now raises another objection from our Mishnah to the view that coins cannot effect *ḥalifin* or be acquired through *ḥalifin*: **We learned** in our Mishnah (above, 44a): **"All movable goods acquire each other."** [7]**And Resh Lakish** gave an authoritative interpretation of this clause, **saying:** The word "all" appears in the Mishnah to emphasize that "all" movable goods may be acquired in this way, and therefore **even a wallet full of coins** may be acquired by exchanging it **for** another **wallet full of coins.** Now, it is impossible to acquire a bag of coins in this way if the coins are being used as a means of payment, because mere payment of money is not recognized as a formal mode of acquisition. Thus, if the Mishnah is referring to an exchange of bags of coins, it must be referring to a *ḥalifin* exchange. If so, this is explicit proof from our Mishnah that coins can both effect *ḥalifin* and be acquired through *ḥalifin*.

תַּרְגְּמָא רַב אַחָא [8]The Gemara answers: **Rav Aḥa explained** Resh Lakish's statement **as referring to dinarim of Anka and Anigra** — coins which are no longer in use as money, and hence are treated like ordinary movable goods which can effect *ḥalifin* and can be acquired through *ḥalifin*. Parenthetically, the Gemara informs us

[1]אֶלָּא אִי סָבַר לָהּ כְּרַב נַחְמָן, [2]דְּאָמַר פֵּירֵי לָא עָבְדִי חֲלִיפִין [3]וּמַטְבֵּעַ לָא קָנֵי, [4]הֵיכִי מְתָרֵץ לַהּ? [5]עַל כָּרְחָךְ כְּרַב שֵׁשֶׁת מְתָרֵץ לַהּ.

[6]תְּנַן: "כָּל הַמִּטַּלְטְלִין קוֹנִין זֶה אֶת זֶה". [7]וְאָמַר רֵישׁ לָקִישׁ: וַאֲפִילּוּ כִּיס מָלֵא מָעוֹת בְּכִיס מָלֵא מָעוֹת.

[8]תַּרְגְּמָא רַב אַחָא בְּדִינָר אַנְקָא

LITERAL TRANSLATION

[1]But if he agrees with Rav Naḥman, who says [2][that] produce cannot effect *ḥalifin* [3]and money does not acquire, [4]how can he explain it?

[5]Of necessity (lit., "against your will") he must explain it like Rav Sheshet.

[6]We have learned: "All movable goods acquire each other." [7]And Resh Lakish said: And even a wallet full of coins for a wallet full of coins.

[8]Rav Aḥa explained [this as referring to] a dinar of Anka

RASHI

אלא אי סבר לה כרב נחמן דאמר – כלי בעינן. **ומטבע** – בתורת דמים נמי לריש לקיש לא קני, דניסני כרב נחמן דאמר יש דמים שהם כחליפין. דהא לריש לקיש מדאורייתא יליף דמעות אינן קונות, ואפילו במכר דלא שכיח נמי. **היכי מתרץ להאי** – "החליף שור בפרה" דמתניתין? לא בחליפין ולא בדמים. **ואפילו כיס מלא מעות** – ועל כרחך בחליפין קאמר. דאי בתורת דמים – מעות לא קנו. שמע מינה: מטבע נעשה חליפין, ונקנה חליפין. **תרגמא רב אחא** – בששתיהן מעות פסולות, דהוה ליה כשאר מטלטלין; מחליף כיס מלא דינרי אניקון בכיס מלא של דינרים אניגרא.

NOTES

particular problem arising in the course of normal social life, and sought to alleviate it by enacting a decree or ordinance. Such decrees may occasionally be optional, and if the parties involved prefer to act on the basis of Torah law, they may do so. In some cases, the decree has the status of a strong suggestion. But in most cases Rabbinic decrees are obligatory.

Even in a case where a decree is obligatory, such as the decree instituting *meshikhah* as an act of acquisition in place of the payment of money, the Rabbis generally applied their decrees only to common situations. In that way, they alleviated the social problem that had initially led to the decree, without abrogating the original Torah law entirely. Thus *meshikhah* takes the place of monetary payment for most transactions, but in a few unusual situations the original Torah law stands.

HALAKHAH

דִּינָר אַנְקָא וְאַנִיגְרָא A dinar of Anka and Anigra. "Coins that are no longer usable because they have been invalidated by the central government or by a province are treated like ordinary movables, and may therefore be acquired through *ḥalifin*." (*Shulḥan Arukh, Ḥoshen Mishpat* 203:8.)

TRANSLATION AND COMMENTARY

why the Anka and Anigra dinarim are not usable as money: [1]One of them refers to coins **invalidated by the state** — where the king has decreed that they may no longer be used — **and the other** refers to coins **invalidated by** the local population of **a province** — where the people refuse to use such coins, even though the money remains the official currency. But coins which are in actual use cannot effect *ḥalifin*, nor can they be acquired through *ḥalifin*.

וּצְרִיכָא [2]The Gemara now explains why **it was necessary** for Rav Aḥa to mention that **both** types of coins are treated like ordinary movable goods rather than money. [3]**For if** Rav Aḥa **had** only **taught us** that **coins** which have been **disqualified by the state** are no longer considered money, [4]**I might have thought that this is because** officially **they do not circulate at all,** for the king has decreed that they may not be used and have ceased to be legal tender. [5]**But** in the case of **coins invalidated by** the local population of a **province, since they** still **circulate in other provinces** where the inhabitants accept them, [6]**I might say: They are still** considered **coins** even in the province where they are not accepted, and therefore are governed by the rule that **coins cannot be acquired through *ḥalifin*.** [7]Conversely, **if** Rav Aḥa **had** only **taught us** that **coins invalidated by** the local population of **a province** are no longer considered money, [8]**I might have said that this is because** in the province in question **they do not circulate** at all, **neither in private nor in public,** since people refuse to use them. [9]**But** in the case of **coins invalidated by the state, which** despite their official cancellation still **circulate in private,** since the local population sees nothing wrong with them and expects the central government to change its policies, [10]I might **say: They are still** considered **coins, and** therefore are governed by the rule that **coins cannot be acquired through *ḥalifin*.** [11]**Therefore it was necessary** for Rav Aḥa to state explicitly that both types of coins are treated as ordinary movable goods, and not as money.

אָמַר רַבָּה אָמַר רַב הוּנָא [12]**Rabbah said in the name of Rav Huna: If** a buyer held up a bag of coins, pointed to an article on sale and **said** to a seller: [13]**"Sell me** this article in exchange **for these coins,"** and the seller did not ask how much money the bag contained, the buyer **acquires** the merchandise as soon as he pays the

וְאַנִיגְרָא, [1]אֶחָד שֶׁפְּסָלַתּוּ מַלְכוּת וְאֶחָד שֶׁפְּסָלַתּוּ מְדִינָה. [2]וּצְרִיכָא. [3]דְּאִי אַשְׁמוּעִינַן פְּסָלַתּוּ מַלְכוּת, [4]מִשּׁוּם דְּלָא סָגֵי כְּלָל; [5]אֲבָל פְּסָלַתּוּ מְדִינָה, דְּסָגֵי לֵיהּ בִּמְדִינָה אַחֲרִיתֵי, [6]אֵימָא: אַכַּתִּי מַטְבֵּעַ הוּא, וְאֵין מַטְבֵּעַ נִקְנֶה בַּחֲלִיפִין. [7]וְאִי אַשְׁמוּעִינַן פְּסָלַתּוּ מְדִינָה, [8]מִשּׁוּם דְּלָא סָגֵי לֵיהּ, לָא בְּצִנְעָא וְלָא בְּפַרְהֶסְיָא; [9]אֲבָל פְּסָלַתּוּ מַלְכוּת, דְּסָגֵי לֵיהּ בְּצִנְעָא, [10]אֵימָא: אַכַּתִּי מַטְבֵּעַ הוּא, וְאֵין מַטְבֵּעַ נִקְנֶה בַּחֲלִיפִין. [11]צְרִיכָא.

[12]אָמַר רַבָּה אָמַר רַב הוּנָא: [13]״מְכוֹר לִי בְּאֵלּוּ״, קָנָה,

LITERAL TRANSLATION

and Anigra, [1]one which the state invalidated, and one which a province invalidated.

[2]And [both were] necessary. [3]For if he had taught us [about coin] invalidated by the state, [4][I might have said that this is] because it does not circulate at all; [5]but [regarding coin] invalidated by a province, since it does circulate in another province, [6]I might say: It is still coin, and coin cannot be acquired through *ḥalifin*. [7]And if he had taught us [about coin] invalidated by a province, [8][I might have said that this is] because it does not circulate, neither in private nor in public; [9]but [regarding coin] invalidated by the state, since it circulates in private, [10]I might say: It is still coin, and coin cannot be acquired through *ḥalifin*. [11][Therefore both are] necessary.

[12]Rabbah said in the name of Rav Huna: [13][If he said:] "Sell [it] to me for these [coins]," he acquires,

RASHI

אחד מהם פסלתו מלכות ואחד מהם פסלתו מדינה — המלך גזר שלא יוציאו ובני מדינה לוקחין אותו בהצנע. ואחד מהם פסלתו מדינה — בני מדינה שנאוהו, אבל המלך לא צוה, ומוציאין אותם בשאר מדינות המלך. **דלא סגי כלל** — לשון הילוך הוא. **מכור לי באלו** — אחז בידו מעות, ואמר לחבירו: מכור לי חפץ שלך באלו שבידי, ולא הקפיד לשאול כמה הם, וקיבלם מיד הלוקח. **קנה** — לוקח החפץ במעות הללו, ואין אחד מהם יכול לחזור.

BACKGROUND

פְּסָלַתּוּ מַלְכוּת וּמְדִינָה Disqualification by the state or by the province. The government occasionally invalidated certain coins, usually for political reasons (i.e., because they did not want the coins of another country or another ruler to be used). However, the people frequently treated such coins as legal tender, often preferring them to the official currency, even though the government prohibited their use. On the other hand, the public occasionally refused to use coins issued by the government and recognized by the authorities, e.g., where the precious metal from which these coins were minted was adulterated with less expensive metals (usually in an attempt to devalue the currency).

LANGUAGE

פַּרְהֶסְיָא This word is derived from the Greek παρρησία *parresia*, the original meaning of which was "freedom of speech"; it was also used to describe a free political regime. As used by the Sages, the word means "in public," something visible to everyone.

SAGES

רַב הוּנָא Rav Huna. A Babylonian Amora of the second generation. See *Bava Metzia*, Part I, p. 52.

רַבָּה Rabbah. A Babylonian Amora of the third generation. See *Bava Metzia*, Part I, p. 25.

NOTES

שֶׁפְּסָלַתּוּ מַלְכוּת...שֶׁפְּסָלַתּוּ מְדִינָה Which the state invalidated... which a province invalidated. To understand this passage, it is important to bear in mind that the value of a coin in Talmudic times was closely linked to its

HALAKHAH

״מְכוֹר לִי בְּאֵלּוּ״, קָנָה "Sell it to me for these coins," he acquires. "If someone had some money in his hand but did not know the precise amount, and offered to buy an item and said to the seller: 'Sell me such-and-such an object for this money,' and the seller took the money without checking to see how much he was being paid, the sale is

BACKGROUND

אוֹנָאָה Fraud, overreaching. The laws of fraud are examined at length below (49b onwards). In the present case, the fraud (or mistake) took place in that the buyer overpaid. As explained below (56a onwards), fraud does not apply in every instance, and there are even cases where a person may say explicitly that he accepts the fraud, i.e., that he is prepared to pay more than the price agreed.

TRANSLATION AND COMMENTARY

seller, and there is no need for any further act of acquisition. [47A] [1]**But** if the money the buyer held in his hand was substantially less than the true value of the merchandise, **the seller** can press **a claim of fraud** (*ona'ah* — אוֹנָאָה) **against** the buyer. The buyer cannot argue that the seller agreed to accept the coins regardless of their value. Depending on how much he underpaid, the buyer may be required to reimburse the seller the amount he defrauded him, or the sale may be annulled. (The laws of *ona'ah* are discussed in detail later in this chapter, starting from 49b.)

קָנָה [2]The Gemara now considers the first part of Rabbah's statement in the name of Rav Huna. Rav Huna said that where the buyer and the seller agree that the buyer should pay with designated coins of unspecified value, the buyer **acquires** the merchandise. On this point the Gemara adds: The acquisition takes effect **even though** the buyer **has not** yet **drawn** the article into his possession by performing *meshikhah*. The sale has been effected by the delivery of the money to the seller. The Gemara explains: Even though the buyer gave the seller money for his merchandise, the transaction was not really a sale. It was a transaction closely resembling *ḥalifin*. For the characteristic of a *ḥalifin* exchange is the fact that the parties are *exchanging* property, and are not concerned about the exact value of the articles being exchanged. [3]Therefore, **since the seller was not particular** about how much money he was being offered, [4]**the buyer** immediately **acquires** the merchandise as soon as the seller picks up the coins he is receiving in exchange, **because** the transaction **is** considered to be like *ḥalifin*, although it is not in fact actual *ḥalifin*. (At this stage, the Gemara assumes that Rav Huna is of the opinion that coins can be used to effect *ḥalifin*. Later on the Gemara will adjust its explanation to make it consistent with the opinion that coins cannot be used to effect *ḥalifin*.)

וְיֵשׁ לוֹ עָלָיו אוֹנָאָה [5]The Gemara now turns to the second point made by Rabbah in the name of Rav Huna — that the seller may sue if the money transferred was substantially less than the value of the merchandise. The Gemara notes: The transaction is considered to be a sort of *ḥalifin* because the seller did not insist on knowing how much money he was being offered. Nevertheless, if the money transferred was substantially less than the value of the merchandise, Rabbah rules in the name of Rav Huna that **the seller** can press **a claim of fraud against** the buyer. [6]This is **because** the buyer **said to** the seller: **"Sell** the article to **me** in exchange **for these coins,"** explicitly using the word "sell." Since the transaction was explicitly termed a sale, the buyer must pay the full cost of the merchandise. Thus, according to Rabbah's version of Rav Huna's statement, if a seller accepts coins of unspecified value as payment for merchandise, the transaction is regarded as a kind

[47A] [1]וְיֵשׁ לוֹ עָלָיו אוֹנָאָה.
[2]"קָנָה" — אַף עַל גַּב דְּלָא מָשַׁךְ, [3]דְּכֵיוָן דְּלָא קָפֵיד, קָנָה, [4]דְּכִי חֲלִיפִין דָּמֵי.
[5]"וְיֵשׁ לוֹ עָלָיו אוֹנָאָה" — [6]דְּ"מְכוֹר לִי בְּאֵלּוּ" קָאָמַר לֵיהּ.

LITERAL TRANSLATION

[47A] [1]and he [the seller] has [a claim of] fraud against him.

[2]"He acquires" — although he did not draw [it], [3]for since he [the seller] was not particular, he [the buyer] acquires, [4]because it is like *ḥalifin*.

[5]"And he [the seller] has [a claim of] fraud against him" — [6]because he said to him: *"Sell* [it] to me for these [coins]."

RASHI

ויש לו לחבירו עליו דין אונאה — אם אין במעות כדי דמי החפץ, שפחתו שתות. **כחליפין דמי** — ולקמיה פריך: והא אין מטבע נעשה חליפין! **דמכור לי קאמר** — לשון ממכר ולא לשון חליפין.

NOTES

metallic content and did not entirely depend on the government's credit, as does modern currency.

Our translation and commentary follow *Rashi*, who explains that "the state" mentioned here refers to a king, such as the Roman emperor, who rules over many provinces. A coin invalidated by such a king would be invalid throughout the empire, but might well be honored in private, since its metallic content is unaffected by the decree. A coin invalidated by the inhabitants of a province is a coin that is not accepted locally for some reason — possibly because its metallic content is insufficient. Such a coin would not in practice be used anywhere in the province, neither in public nor in private. It would, however, be perfectly legal tender, and would presumably be accepted elsewhere in the empire.

HALAKHAH

valid, and neither party may retract. Since such transactions are infrequently performed, and Rabbinic decrees were instituted only for commonly encountered situations, the Rabbinic decree that *meshikhah* and not money effects acquisition does not apply here." (*Shulḥan Arukh, Ḥoshen Mishpat* 199:1.)

וְיֵשׁ לוֹ עָלָיו אוֹנָאָה And he has a claim of fraud against him. "If someone bought something, and the seller took the money without checking to see how much he was being paid, whoever underpaid or overcharged is subject to a claim of fraud and must reimburse the other party for the amount acquired by fraud. *Rema* (citing *Rosh*), however,

TRANSLATION AND COMMENTARY

of *ḥalifin* in that the transfer of ownership of the merchandise was effected by the seller accepting the coins; it is regarded as a regular sale for the purposes of the laws of fraud, because the buyer explicitly used the word "sell" in his proposal to the seller.

[1] But **Rav Abba** had a different version of the second part of Rav Huna's statement. He **said in the name of Rav Huna:** If the buyer held up a bag of coins and **said** to the seller: "**Sell me** this article in exchange **for these coins** I am offering you," and the seller agreed without asking how much money was being offered, [2] the buyer **acquires** the merchandise immediately without performing *meshikhah*, as it is considered to be a sort of *ḥalifin* exchange, as explained above. Up to this point, Rav Abba agrees with Rabbah's version. However, according to Rav Abba's version, the transaction is treated exactly like a case of *ḥalifin*, [3] **and even if the money transferred was substantially less than the value of the merchandise, the seller has no claim of fraud against** the buyer, since the laws of fraud do not apply to *ḥalifin*.

פְּשִׁיטָא [4] The Gemara now uses Rav Huna's statement as the point of departure for an inquiry into a basic issue involved in *ḥalifin*: Is *ḥalifin* effective in cases where the parties to the exchange are particular about the relative value of the items being exchanged? On this point the Gemara remarks: **It is obvious** what the law is **in a case** where the buyer gives the seller money or some object as **payment** and the seller **is not particular** about the value of what he is receiving. [5] **Surely we** have just **said that,** according to both versions, Rav Huna ruled that the buyer **acquires** the merchandise without performing *meshikhah*! **Because** the parties showed no concern about the value of the property being exchanged, the transaction **is considered like *ḥalifin*,** even though they called it a sale. [6] **But what about** the opposite situation? What is the law in a case where the buyer gives the seller an object, and stipulates that it should be used as *ḥalifin*, but the seller **is particular about**

LITERAL TRANSLATION

[1] Rav Abba said in the name of Rav Huna: [If he said:] "Sell [it] to me for these [coins]," [2] he acquires, [3] and he [the seller] has no [claim of] fraud against him. [4] It is obvious [that in a case of] payment where he is not particular about it, [5] surely we have said that he acquires because it is like *ḥalifin*. [6] [But] what [about] *ḥalifin* where he is particular about it?

רַב אַבָּא אָמַר רַב הוּנָא: ״מְכוֹר לִי בְּאֵלּוּ״, [2] קָנָה, [3] וְאֵין לוֹ עָלָיו אוֹנָאָה. [4] פְּשִׁיטָא דָמִים וְאֵין מַקְפִּיד עֲלֵיהֶן, [5] הָא קָאָמְרִינַן דְּקָנֵי, דִּכְחֲלִיפִין דָּמוּ. [6] חֲלִיפִין וּמַקְפִּיד עֲלֵיהֶן מַאי?

RASHI

פשיטא לן דמים ואין מקפיד עליהן — נתן לו מעות או חפץ בשביל חפץ אחר בתורת דמים ולא הקפיד עליהן לראות אם ישנן כדי שוויין. חליפין ומקפיד עליהן — נתן לו חפץ בחפץ בתורת חליפין, לקנות כדין קנין שקונין בסודר, וזה מקפיד לראות שיהא הסודר שוה כל כך. מהו — מי קנו תרוייהו במשיכה דהך מינייהו, או דלמא: הואיל והקפיד עליהם הרי הן כדמים, והוי להו מעות ואין קונה עד שימשוך גם השני.

NOTES

וְאֵין לוֹ עָלָיו אוֹנָאָה **And he has no claim of fraud against him.** Our commentary follows several Rishonim, who argue that the laws of fraud do not apply to any *ḥalifin* exchange, since with *ḥalifin* the parties are not concerned about the precise monetary value of the articles they are exchanging (Rif, Ri Migash, apparently also Rashi). This interpretation fits Rav Abba's version of Rav Huna's statement very well, since Rav Abba said that the seller in our Gemara may not press a claim of fraud even if the bag of coins turns out to be worth much less than the merchandise. But Rabbah's version, in which it is stated that the laws of fraud *do* apply to our case, needs explanation, so these Rishonim explain that Rabbah was making an exception to the general rule because the parties specifically used the word "sell" rather than "exchange."

Other Rishonim insist that in general the laws of fraud do apply to *ḥalifin* (Ritva, Ramban). They point out that, later in this passage, the Gemara declares that *ḥalifin* was not instituted solely for the benefit of fools, and that most people are concerned about the value of the articles they are

exchanging. Hence there would appear to be no reason why a party defrauded in a *ḥalifin* transaction should not be able to sue for redress.

According to this explanation, the reason Rav Abba ruled that the seller in the case discussed by Rav Huna could not press a claim of fraud was not because the transaction was a case of *ḥalifin*, but it was because the seller expressly accepted the stipulation that the sale would be for "these coins," and did not insist on counting them. Hence Rav Abba considered the seller to have waived his rights to sue for fraud. Rabbah, however, was of the opinion that the use of the word "sell" balances the effect of the use of the words "these coins," and the rule that the laws of fraud apply to *ḥalifin* remains in force.

חֲלִיפִין וּמַקְפִּיד עֲלֵיהֶן *Halifin* **where he is particular about it.** The Gemara's question is: Where a seller is particular about the value of the object he is to receive in exchange for the merchandise he is selling, is the transaction an act of *ḥalifin* or an ordinary sale? From the language of the question, it is not clear whether the Gemara

HALAKHAH

rules that the party guilty of fraud need not reimburse the party he defrauded, since it is not clear which version of

Rav Huna's statement (Rabbah's or Rav Abba's) is accepted." (Ibid., 227:19.)

TRANSLATION AND COMMENTARY

receiving something equal in value to that which he is selling? Do we follow the parties' language and consider the transaction to be one of *ḥalifin*, in which case the buyer acquires his merchandise as soon as the seller performs *meshikhah* on the object given in exchange? Or do we consider the transaction to be a sale, since the seller is particular about the value of the object he is to receive, and do we therefore view the object on which the seller performed *meshikhah* as money, in which case it cannot effect a sale, and the buyer does not acquire his merchandise until he himself performs *meshikhah* on the object he wants to buy?

[1]**אָמַר רַב אַדָּא בַּר אַהֲבָה** **Rav Adda bar Ahavah said** in reply: **Come and hear** the following Baraita, from which we can deduce the answer to this question: [2]**"Someone was standing** in the market **holding his cow, and another person came along and said to him, 'Why is your cow here?'** [3]The cow's owner replied, **'I need** to sell it in order to buy **an ass.'** [4]To which the other person responded, **'I have an ass that I can give you** for your cow. **How much is your cow?'** [5]The owner of the cow replied, **'So much,** and how **much is your ass?'** [6]The owner of the ass answered, **'So much.'** And the parties agreed to exchange the ass for the cow." Now, if the owner of the ass then took possession of the cow, and the owner of the cow took possession of the ass, the transaction is clearly final, and if anything subsequently happens to one of the animals, its new owner must sustain the loss. A problem arises, however, if the second animal dies after the first person takes possession of the first animal but before the second person takes possession of the second animal. [7]The Baraita continues: **"If the owner of the ass drew the cow** into his possession, [8]**but the owner of the cow did not manage to draw the ass** into his possession **before the ass died** — in such a case the sale is annulled, [9]and **the owner of the ass did not acquire the cow** even though he had already drawn it into his possession, as the transaction is not complete until *both* animals have been handed over to their respective new owners."

[1]אָמַר רַב אַדָּא בַּר אַהֲבָה: תָּא שְׁמַע: [2]״הֲרֵי שֶׁהָיָה תּוֹפֵשׂ פָּרָתוֹ וְעוֹמֵד, וּבָא חֲבֵירוֹ וְאָמַר לוֹ: ׳פָּרָתְךָ לָמָּה?׳ — [3]׳לַחֲמוֹר אֲנִי צָרִיךְ׳. [4]׳יֵשׁ לִי חֲמוֹר שֶׁאֲנִי נוֹתֵן לָךְ. פָּרָתְךָ בְּכַמָּה?׳ [5]׳בְּכָךְ וְכָךְ. חֲמוֹרְךָ בְּכַמָּה?׳ [6]׳בְּכָךְ וְכָךְ׳. [7]מָשַׁךְ בַּעַל הַחֲמוֹר אֶת הַפָּרָה, [8]וְלֹא הִסְפִּיק בַּעַל הַפָּרָה לִמְשׁוֹךְ אֶת הַחֲמוֹר עַד שֶׁמֵּת הַחֲמוֹר, [9]לֹא קָנָה בַּעַל הַחֲמוֹר אֶת הַפָּרָה״.

LITERAL TRANSLATION

[1]Rav Adda bar Ahavah said: Come [and] hear: [2]"If he was holding his cow and standing, and his fellow came and said to him: 'Why is your cow [here]?' [3]'I need an ass.' [4]'I have an ass that I can give you. How much is your cow?' [5]'So much and so much. How much is your ass?' [6]'So much and so much.' [7][If] the owner of the ass drew the cow, [8]but the owner of the cow did not manage to draw the ass before the ass died, [9]the owner of the ass did not acquire the cow."

RASHI

פרתך למה — הבאת בשוק.

SAGES

רַב אַדָּא בַּר אַהֲבָה Rav Adda bar Ahavah. A famous Babylonian Amora of the first and second generations. He was born (or circumcised) on the day Rabbi Yehudah HaNasi died. He was a disciple of Rav, and transmitted several teachings in his name. Among his colleagues were Rav Huna, Rav Hisda, Rav Naḥman and others. Many teachings are transmitted in his name in the Talmud. He was renowned for his piety, righteousness and modesty, and lived to an advanced age.

NOTES

is referring to a seller who insists on receiving an object equal in value to the merchandise, or to a seller who insists on ascertaining the value of the object before agreeing to the exchange, but does not necessarily expect the object to be equal in value to the merchandise.

Our commentary follows *Ramban* and others, who explain that the Gemara's question is restricted to a case where the seller insisted that the object be equal in value to the merchandise. Only in such a case does the Gemara examine the possibility that the exchange be considered a sale. In response, Rava points out that most sensible people do not exchange their property unless they receive something of equivalent value, and the parties' insistence on value does not detract from the transaction being regarded as an act of *ḥalifin*. But if the seller merely insisted on ascertaining the value of the object, and did not insist on its being equal to that of the merchandise he is selling, there can be no doubt that he is performing an act of *ḥalifin*.

Other Rishonim, however, disagree. They maintain that the Gemara's question concerns the special form of symbolic *ḥalifin* called *kinyan sudar* (קִנְיַן סוּדָר — "kerchief acquisition"), in which the buyer gives the seller his kerchief in exchange for merchandise (*Rashi, Nimmukei Yosef*). Now a *kinyan sudar* is purely symbolic; normally the seller does not even keep the kerchief he was given "in exchange" for the merchandise, and certainly does not care how much it is worth. Hence, if the seller did insist on ascertaining how much the kerchief was worth, even if he did not insist that it be equal in value to the merchandise, the Gemara questions whether he can still be considered to be engaging in an act of *ḥalifin*. Nevertheless, Rava declares that even in a case of kerchief acquisition, only fools would engage in *ḥalifin* without knowing that the kerchief they are to receive in exchange is worth something, and the Halakhah is that a seller who insists on ascertaining the value of the kerchief is still engaging in *ḥalifin*.

TRANSLATION AND COMMENTARY

שְׁמַע מִינָּהּ [1]Now, at first glance, the Baraita appears to be referring to a case of *ḥalifin*, in which one animal is bartered for another. But if this is so, the act of *meshikhah* performed on the cow should have finalized the exchange, and the loss of the ass should have been borne by its new owner. However, the Baraita is evidently treating the cow as monetary payment for the ass, and not as *ḥalifin*, presumably because each of the parties was concerned that he receive the full value of his animal. Therefore the transaction is not complete until the ass has been handed over, and since the ass died before being handed over, the transaction is null and void, and the cow must be returned. Accordingly, the Gemara concludes: **Infer from here that in a case of *ḥalifin* where** the parties are **particular about** receiving something equal in value to the merchandise they are offering, [2]the transaction is considered a sale and not *ḥalifin*, and neither party **acquires** the merchandise until he draws it into his possession.

אָמַר רָבָא [3]The Gemara dismisses this conclusion: **Rava said:** The reason the Baraita declares the exchange of the cow and the ass null and void cannot be because the parties to *ḥalifin* are unconcerned about the value of the articles they are to receive. For when Scripture says that *ḥalifin* is a valid mode of acquisition, **is it dealing** only **with *ḥalifin* performed by fools, who are not particular** about the worth of the merchandise they are exchanging? Even though *ḥalifin* is an exchange of actual articles, and not of their value, it is still obvious that each party will first assure himself that the article he is to receive is worth what it is supposed to be worth. [4]**Rather,** argues Rava, **in all** normal **cases of *ḥalifin*,** the parties **are certainly particular** about the value of the property they are to receive. Nevertheless, once one party to the exchange has taken possession of what he is to receive, the other party too **has acquired** through *ḥalifin* the object *he* is to receive. The fact that the parties inquired as to the value of the respective articles does not turn the *ḥalifin* into a sale. Thus the question of the Gemara — whether *ḥalifin* in which the parties are particular is still considered *ḥalifin* — must be answered in the affirmative. Why then did the Baraita rule that the exchange of the ass for the cow was not yet final at the time the ass died? [5]Rava explains: **With what are we dealing here** in this Baraita? [6]With a case **where** the owner of the ass **said to** the owner of the cow, "I am giving you **an ass** in exchange **for a cow and a lamb," and** the owner of the ass **drew the cow** into his possession, [7]**but had not yet drawn the lamb,** at which point the ass died. The Baraita rules that the transaction is invalid, as the owner of the cow had not yet acquired the ass when it died, [8]because the act of acquisition performed on the cow and the lamb **was not** a **proper**, complete *meshikhah*. *Ḥalifin* does not take effect unless one of the parties performs *meshikhah* on *all* the merchandise he is to receive. Thus the Baraita has no bearing on the Gemara's original question, and Rava's conclusion — that the parties to *ḥalifin* are particular as to the value of the merchandise being exchanged — stands.

[1]שְׁמַע מִינָּהּ: חֲלִיפִין וּמַקְפִּיד עֲלֵיהֶן, [2]לֹא קָנָה.

[3]אֲמַר רָבָא: אַטּוּ חֲלִיפִין בְּשׁוּפְטָנֵי עָסְקִינַן, דְּלָא קָפְדֵי? [4]אֶלָּא, כָּל חֲלִיפִין מִיקְפַּד קָפְדֵי, וְקָנָה. [5]וְהָכָא בְּמַאי עָסְקִינַן? [6]דְּאָמַר לֵיהּ: "חֲמוֹר בְּפָרָה וְטָלֶה", וּמָשַׁךְ אֶת הַפָּרָה, [7]וַעֲדַיִין לֹא מָשַׁךְ אֶת הַטָּלֶה, [8]דְּלָא הֲוָה לֵיהּ מְשִׁיכָה מְעַלְּיָא.

LITERAL TRANSLATION

[1]Infer from this [that in a case of] *ḥalifin* and he is particular about it, [2]he does not acquire.

[3]Rava said: Are we dealing with *ḥalifin* [performed] by fools, who are not particular? [4]Rather, [in] all [cases of] *ḥalifin* [people] are surely particular, and he acquires. [5]But with what are we dealing here? [6]Where he said to him: "An ass for a cow and a lamb," and he drew the cow, [7]but he did not yet draw the lamb, [8]which was not a proper *meshikhah*.

RASHI

אמר רבא אטו חליפין – דקרא. **בשופטני עסקינן** – דלא קפדי לדעת שיהו שוות קצת דמים, שייטב בעיניו לתת לו את שלו כנגדו, ואפילו הכי קאמר קרא דקנה?

LANGUAGE

בְּשׁוּפְטָנֵי **By fools.** There are differences of opinion regarding the source of the word שׁוּפְטָנֵי. Some authorities maintain that it comes from the Persian *seftan*, meaning frightened or confused. Other authorities believe it derives from the Aramaic טַפְשָׁנָא, with the key letters in reverse order. In the language of the Sages, it means an unintelligent person who acts foolishly.

TERMINOLOGY

הָכָא בְּמַאי עָסְקִינַן **With what are we dealing here?** i.e., the case we are referring to here is.... This expression is used by the Gemara to introduce an אוֹקִימְתָּא — an explanation whose purpose is usually to answer a previously raised objection, and to limit the application of the Mishnah or the Baraita under discussion to one particular set of circumstances.

NOTES

בְּפָרָה וְטָלֶה **For a cow and a lamb.** Our commentary follows *Ritva* and *Meiri,* who explain that when more than one article is used to effect *ḥalifin*, the seller must take possession of all the articles he is being given, as there is no such thing as partial *ḥalifin*.

Rashba, however, argues that this applies only where the parties are exchanging one indivisible item for two — as in our case, where they are exchanging an ass for a cow and a lamb. But if they were to exchange a cow and a lamb for a quantity of wheat, for example, and the owner of the wheat

HALAKHAH

חֲמוֹר בְּפָרָה וְטָלֶה **An ass for a cow and a lamb.** "If a person agrees to sell his ass in exchange for someone else's cow and lamb, and draws the cow into his possession but not the lamb, the sale is not yet binding, since the necessary act of *meshikhah* has not yet been completed." (Ibid., 203:2.)

TERMINOLOGY

אָמַר מָר It was said above (lit., "the master said"). A term used to cite a passage from a Mishnah or a Baraita previously mentioned, which will now be elucidated at greater length by the Talmud (usually as a continuation of the previous discussion).

[1]אָמַר מָר: "׳מְכוֹר לִי בְּאֵלּוּ׳, [2]קָנָה, [3]וְיֵשׁ לוֹ עָלָיו אוֹנָאָה". [4]לֵימָא סָבַר רַב הוּנָא: מַטְבֵּעַ נַעֲשֶׂה חֲלִיפִין?

[5]לָא! רַב הוּנָא סָבַר לָהּ כְּרַבִּי יוֹחָנָן, דְּאָמַר: [6]דְּבַר תּוֹרָה, מָעוֹת קוֹנוֹת. [7]וּמִפְּנֵי מַה אָמְרוּ מְשִׁיכָה קוֹנָה? [8]גְּזֵירָה, שֶׁמָּא יֹאמַר לוֹ: "נִשְׂרְפוּ חִטֶּיךָ בַּעֲלִיָּיה". [9]מִלְּתָא דִּשְׁכִיחָא גָּזְרוּ בָּהּ רַבָּנַן; [10]וּמִלְּתָא דְּלָא שְׁכִיחָא לָא גָּזְרוּ בָּהּ רַבָּנַן.

LITERAL TRANSLATION

[1]The master said: "[If he said:] 'Sell [it] to me for these [coins],' [2]he acquires, [3]and he has [a claim of] fraud against him." [4]Shall we say that Rav Huna maintains: Coin can be used for *ḥalifin*?

[5]No! Rav Huna agrees with Rabbi Yoḥanan, who said: [6]By Torah law, money acquires. [7]And why did they say that *meshikhah* acquires? [8][It was] a preventive measure, lest he [the seller] say to him: "Your wheat was burnt in the upper story." [9][And] in a thing that is common the Rabbis made a preventive measure; [10]but in a thing that is not common the Rabbis did not make a preventive measure.

TRANSLATION AND COMMENTARY

אָמַר מָר [1]Having considered the case where the parties to a *ḥalifin* exchange are particular about the value of the merchandise being exchanged, the Gemara now returns to Rav Huna's statement that if a buyer gives a seller a bag of coins and the seller expresses no interest in determining how much money is in the bag, the transaction is considered an act of *ḥalifin*. **The master said** above: **"If** a buyer **said** to a seller, **'Sell** this article **to me for these coins,'** and the seller agreed without asking how much money was being offered, [2]the buyer **acquires** the article as soon as he hands over the money, because the transaction is considered an act of *ḥalifin*. [3]**But the seller** can press a **claim of fraud against** the buyer if he was underpaid, because the parties did refer to the transaction as a sale." The Gemara now asks: Rav Huna's argument is that since the seller was not concerned about the amount of money being offered for the article, the transaction must have been an act of *ḥalifin*. But the transaction in fact was performed with a bag of coins. [4]**Shall we say** on the basis of this ruling **that Rav Huna is of the opinion** that **coins can be used for *ḥalifin*?**

לָא רַב הוּנָא סָבַר לָהּ [5]The Gemara answers: **No!** It is possible that Rav Huna is not referring to *ḥalifin* at all, but to a form of monetary payment that resembles *ḥalifin*. **Rav Huna agrees with Rabbi Yoḥanan, who said:** The Mishnah's ruling that movable property acquires money but money does not acquire movable property is a Rabbinic decree, [6]but **by Torah law** payment of **money** is an act of **acquisition,** and the merchandise immediately becomes the property of the buyer, just as in a case of *ḥalifin*. (A similar explanation was offered for an opinion expressed by Rav Naḥman — above, 46b. See our commentary there for a detailed explanation.) [7]**Why** then **did the Rabbis say that** monetary payment cannot effect a sale, and **it is** only *meshikhah* that **acquires** movable goods? [8]Rabbi Yoḥanan explains: **It was a preventive measure** taken by the Rabbis, **lest the seller say to** the buyer: **"Your wheat was burnt in the upper story** of my house after you paid me." But not in all cases did the Rabbis reverse the Torah procedure and invalidate a sale finalized by monetary payment. [9]Only **in a case that occurs frequently** — for example, where the buyer and the seller agree on the price of the article being sold — **did the Rabbis enact a preventive measure** that money cannot acquire movable property. [10]**In a case that occurs** only **infrequently** — for example, where the seller accepts payment without knowing how much money he is receiving — **the Rabbis did not enact a preventive measure,** and the original Torah law remains in force. Thus, when Rav Huna ruled that the transaction was finalized as soon as the buyer handed over the money — as in a case of *ḥalifin* — what he may have meant was that the Torah law applies to this unusual case, and the payment of money is sufficient in this case to finalize the transaction as though it were a case of *ḥalifin*. Hence Rav Huna's ruling does not prove that he is of the opinion that coins can be used for *ḥalifin*.

RASHI

לימא קסבר רב הונא כו׳ — דהא יהב טעמא למלתיה משום דכחליפין דמו. **סבר לה כרבי יוחנן** — כלומר אין מטבע נעשה חליפין. והני לאו חליפין נינהו אלא דמים, דהא "מכור לי" קאמר, ודמים כי האי גוונא קנו בלא משיכה כחליפין דקנין סודר, משום דזביני דלא שכיח נינהו, וכרבי יוחנן כו׳.

NOTES

were to draw the cow into his possession, but before he could take the lamb the wheat was destroyed by fire, the owner of the animals would nevertheless have already acquired part of the wheat and would have to take a proportional share of the loss.

TRANSLATION AND COMMENTARY

אֲמַר לֵיהּ [1]**Mar Huna the son of Rav Naḥman said to Rav Ashi:** Your tradition with regard to Rav Huna's opinion as to whether coins can be used for *ḥalifin* differs from ours. [2]**You report** Rav Huna's view as stated above in the case where merchandise is bought with an unspecified number of coins. From this you attempt to infer his opinion about using coins to effect *ḥalifin*, and you are unable to arrive at any conclusion. [3]But **we report** Rav Huna's explicit opinion about using coins to effect *ḥalifin* **as follows: "And similarly Rav Huna said: [4]Coins cannot be used for *ḥalifin*."** The expression "and similarly" refers to the list of Amoraim mentioned above (46a) who ruled this way. In the version of that passage transmitted by Mar Huna the son of Rav Naḥman, Rav Huna's name also appeared in the list.

[1]אֲמַר לֵיהּ מָר הוּנָא בְּרֵיהּ דְּרַב נַחְמָן לְרַב אַשִׁי: [2]אַתּוּן הָכִי מַתְנִיתוּ לָהּ. [3]אֲנַן הָכִי מַתְנִינַן לָהּ: "וְכֵן אָמַר רַב הוּנָא: [4]אֵין מַטְבֵּעַ נַעֲשֶׂה חֲלִיפִין".

[5]בַּמֶּה קוֹנִין?

[6]רַב אָמַר: בְּכֵלָיו שֶׁל קוֹנֶה,

LITERAL TRANSLATION

[1]Mar Huna the son of Rav Naḥman said to Rav Ashi: [2]You teach it thus. [3]We teach it as follows: "And similarly Rav Huna said: [4]Coins cannot be used for *ḥalifin*."

[5]With what does one acquire?

[6]Rav said: With the buyer's utensils,

RASHI

אתון הכי מתניתו לה — לדרב הונא, דמספקא לכו אי סבר ליה מטבע נעשה חליפין ואם לאו, ודחיתו דחוי בעלמא. **אנן** — בהדיא מתנינן רב הונא בהדי הנך רבנן דלעיל (מו,א), וכן אמר רב הונא כו', ולא מספקא לן הכא מידי, דולאי טעמיה משום דסבירא ליה כרבי יוחנן הוא. **במה קונין** — קנין חליפין דכתיב בקרא "שלף איש נעלו", מי שלף ונתן?

SAGES

מָר הוּנָא בְּרֵיהּ דְּרַב נַחְמָן Mar Huna the son of Rav Naḥman. A Babylonian Amora of the fourth generation, Mar Huna was the son of Rav Naḥman bar Ya'akov. In the present context, however, in which Mar Huna is reported as being a contemporary of Rav Ashi (sixth generation), it is more likely that the reference is to Rav Huna the son of Rav Nehemyah. This Sage is quoted several times in the Talmud in discussion with Rav Ashi, and seems to have been the same age as or a little older than Rav Ashi.

בַּמֶּה קוֹנִין [5]Having concluded its discussion as to whether coins can be used for *ḥalifin*, the Gemara now proceeds to discuss some other laws of *ḥalifin*. The most common case of *ḥalifin* is called *kinyan sudar* (קִנְיַן סוּדָר) — "the transfer of ownership by means of a kerchief." In this transaction, A wishes to buy B's cow, but it is not convenient for him to take immediate physical possession. In order to finalize the sale, a symbolic form of *ḥalifin* is performed in which the cow is "exchanged" for a kerchief or a similar article of clothing. The Gemara asks: **With** whose kerchief **does one acquire** merchandise through *ḥalifin*? Is *ḥalifin* a true "exchange" — as the name would seem to indicate — in which A gives B his kerchief and acquires B's cow in return? Or does B give A his own kerchief, and give him the cow together with it?

רַב אָמַר [6]This question was the subject of a difference of opinion between Amoraim. **Rav said:** *Ḥalifin* is performed by exchanging the merchandise for **the buyer's utensils.** As implied by its name, *ḥalifin* is effected by the buyer giving an article such as a kerchief to the seller in exchange for the merchandise he is buying. Once the seller draws the kerchief into his possession, thereby acquiring it, the sale is effected and the buyer acquires his merchandise in exchange. According to this viewpoint, the mechanism of *ḥalifin* works in the

NOTES

בַּמֶּה קוֹנִין With what does one acquire? Throughout this passage, the Gemara is referring to *kinyan sudar* ("kerchief acquisition") or symbolic *ḥalifin*, in which inexpensive merchandise is exchanged for a kerchief or another inexpensive article of clothing. However, most Rishonim agree that there is no substantial difference between the laws governing *kinyan sudar* and those governing other forms of *ḥalifin*.

Rabbenu Tam, however, disagrees. He interprets the verse from Ruth (4:7), cited later in the passage, as defining three different types of transaction: *Selling* merchandise for money or for other merchandise of equal value; *exchanging* merchandise for other merchandise of comparable value; and performing a *kinyan sudar* to *formalize* a transaction. The latter two transactions are forms of *ḥalifin*.

According to *Rabbenu Tam*, *ḥalifin* is considered an act of "exchanging" when the two parties exchange animals or pieces of land and the like. Although the exchanged properties may not be precisely equal in value, there is still a rough equivalency between them. But when the two properties are not at all comparable in value, and the *ḥalifin* is performed purely in order to finalize the transaction, the *ḥalifin* is considered to be "formalizing." The restrictions placed by the Gemara on *ḥalifin* generally apply only to the latter case.

Thus, according to *Rabbenu Tam*, if the two parties genuinely wish to *exchange* property, they may do so almost without restriction, and the moment one party takes possession of the property he is acquiring, the second party acquires the other property, even if the properties involved consist of land or produce. It is only when the *ḥalifin* is purely symbolic, as in *kinyan sudar*, that the formal act of acquisition must be performed with a utensil. Likewise, the dispute between Rav and Levi applies only to *kinyan sudar*, and according to Levi the kerchief must be given by the seller to the buyer. But in a genuine exchange of property of comparable value, even Levi would agree that "the buyer" gives "the seller" his property in exchange for the merchandise he is acquiring.

HALAKHAH

קִנְיָן בְּכֵלָיו שֶׁל קוֹנֶה An act of acquisition performed with the buyer's utensils. "*Ḥalifin* is performed by the buyer giving the seller a utensil. Produce, however, cannot be used to perform *ḥalifin*, following Rav Naḥman, whose views on

SAGES

רַב הוּנָא מִדִּסְקַרְתָּא Rav Huna of Diskarta. A fourth-generation Babylonian Amora.

TRANSLATION AND COMMENTARY

following way: [1]**It pleases the buyer that the seller should acquire** his kerchief, [2]**so that** in accepting the kerchief the seller **will** mentally **resolve to transfer the merchandise to** the buyer in exchange. Thus, as soon as the seller receives the symbolic consideration he agreed to accept, the transaction ceases to be a mere promise and becomes legally binding.

וְלֵוִי אָמַר [3]**But Levi said:** *Ḥalifin* is performed **with the seller's utensils.** *Ḥalifin* is effected by having the seller give his own kerchief to the buyer. Once the buyer draws it into his possession, he simultaneously acquires the merchandise that he wants to buy. According to this view, the mechanism of *ḥalifin* is less clear, as the seller is not receiving any consideration at all, and there is no obvious reason why he should feel obligated to fulfill his promise. [4]The Gemara **will have occasion to explain** the mechanism of *ḥalifin* according to Levi's view **later** in the passage.

אֲמַר לֵיהּ [5]At this point the Gemara assumes that, according to Levi, symbolic *ḥalifin* is effective in much the same way as the act of acquisition known as *kinyan agav* (קִנְיַן אַגַּב), in which movable property is acquired by means of and together with immovable property. Just as movable property be acquired together with real estate, so too may both real estate and movable property may be acquired by means of and together with the symbolic transfer of a kerchief from the seller to the buyer. But if this assumption is correct, certain Halakhic difficulties seem to result. **Rav Huna of Diskarta said to Rava:** [6]**According to Levi, who said** that *ḥalifin* is performed **with the seller's utensils,** the act of *ḥalifin* is not an exchange of property at all! The seller gives the buyer his kerchief, at which point the buyer acquires the merchandise as well, without giving the seller anything in return. But if this is how *ḥalifin* works, according to Levi, [7]**surely** a case can occur where **the buyer acquires land by way of** movable property, namely **a cloak** or a kerchief! In other words, in *ḥalifin* the act of acquisition is performed on the movable property, and its effect is extended to the real estate as well. For, according to Levi, where *ḥalifin* is used in order to transfer ownership of land, the buyer acquires an article of movable property (the kerchief) belonging to the seller by picking it up, and thereby also acquires the seller's land. Now, picking up an object is a valid act of acquisition for movable property, but not for land. Thus what Levi appears to be proposing is that *ḥalifin* is a kind of *kinyan agav*, whereby a mode of acquisition that is effective for one type of property is used to acquire another type of property together with it. As mentioned above, it is possible to sell a piece of land and include together with it an article of

[1]דְּנִיחָא לֵיהּ לְקוֹנֶה דְּלֶהֱוֵי מַקְנֶה קוֹנֶה, [2]כִּי הֵיכִי דְּלִגְמַר וְלַקְנֵי לֵיהּ.

[3]וְלֵוִי אָמַר: בְּכֵלָיו שֶׁל מַקְנֶה, [4]כִּדְבָעֵינַן לְמֵימַר לְקַמָּן.

[5]אֲמַר לֵיהּ רַב הוּנָא מִדִּסְקַרְתָּא לְרָבָא: [6]וּלְלֵוִי, דְּאָמַר: בְּכֵלָיו שֶׁל מַקְנֶה, [7]הָא קָא קָנֵי אַרְעָא אַגַּב גְּלִימָא!

LITERAL TRANSLATION

[1]for it pleases the buyer that the seller should acquire, [2]so that he will resolve and transfer [the merchandise] to him.

[3]But Levi said: With the seller's utensils, [4]as we shall have [occasion] to say below.

[5]Rav Huna of Diskarta said to Rava: [6]But according to Levi, who said: With the seller's utensils, [7]surely he [the buyer] is acquiring land by way of a cloak!

RASHI

דליהוי מקנה קונה — את הכלי. **קא קני ארעא אגב גלימא** — הנותן קרקע לחבירו בקנין סודר, והמקבל מתנה מושך הסודר מיד הנותן, ונקנה לו הקרקע עם הסודר במשיכת הסודר שנקנה במשיכה.

NOTES

דְּלֶהֱוֵי מַקְנֶה קוֹנֶה That the seller should acquire. An act of acquisition is a formal procedure finalizing a transaction, thus transforming it from a promise into a legally enforceable contract. Most acts of acquisition symbolize the resolve of the parties to honor their commitment. In many cases, the act of acquisition is the seller's receipt of some symbolic consideration. By accepting the consideration, the seller demonstrates his resolve to transfer his merchandise to the buyer, and the transaction is final. Accordingly, Rav explains that when a kerchief is used to effect *ḥalifin*, the buyer's kerchief should be used, so that it can serve as symbolic payment and finalize the transaction.

Levi, on the other hand, maintains that the *seller's* kerchief is used. According to this view, it would appear that in *ḥalifin* the seller receives no symbolic consideration at all. Hence Rav Huna of Diskarta suggests a different interpretation of symbolic *ḥalifin*, called *kinyan agav* (קִנְיַן אַגַּב). According to this interpretation, when the seller gives the buyer his kerchief, the property is symbolically delivered to the buyer together with the kerchief. However, the Gemara is forced to reject this explanation because it is incompatible with a Mishnah which teaches that land cannot be acquired

HALAKHAH

questions of civil law are accepted where they differ with those of Rav Sheshet. The buyer then declares that he is giving the utensil to the seller in exchange for the merchandise. (*Rema*, however, rules that it is not customary to make a declaration.) The seller then draws the utensil into his possession, thereby consummating the sale," following Rav. (*Shulḥan Arukh, Ḥoshen Mishpat* 195:1,2.)

movable property. In such a case, both the land and the movable property are acquired as soon as the buyer performs an act of acquisition that is valid for the purchase of land, even if this act of acquisition is not normally valid for the purchase of movable property. But, Rav Huna of Diskarta points out, this concept cannot apply here. [1]For **if** it were **so, we would have** a case of **mortgagable property** — real estate — [2]that **is acquired** by being included in a sale together **with non-mortgageable property** — movables! Thus, according to this explanation, an act of acquisition performed on non-mortgageable movable property also acquires the mortgageable real estate included in the sale. [3]But **in the Mishnah** (*Kiddushin* 1:5, 26a), **we have learned** exactly **the opposite:** [4]**"Non-mortgageable property is acquired** when included in a sale **with mortgageable property"!** Thus it is possible to acquire movables along with land by acquiring the land, but not land along with movables by acquiring the movables, as seems to be Levi's opinion!

אֲמַר לֵיהּ [5]Rava **said to** Rav Huna of Diskarta in reply: **If Levi were here, he would strike you** with **lashes of fire** for having asked such an ill-founded question. He would answer you with a stinging reply, because the assumption underlying your question is completely incorrect. [6]**Do you** really **think** that, according to Levi's understanding of the function of *ḥalifin*, it is the *meshikhah* performed on the seller's **cloak** that **transfers ownership** of the merchandise to the buyer, with the merchandise being acquired along with the cloak? In fact, says Rava, even according to Levi, *ḥalifin* is based on an exchange between buyer and seller. For even if *ḥalifin* is performed with the seller's kerchief, an exchange is still taking place, and the buyer is still giving something to the seller as consideration for transferring ownership of the merchandise to him. For when the buyer accepts the seller's kerchief from him, the seller has a sense of gratification, which is regarded by the Halakhah as having a certain monetary value.

[1]אִם כֵּן, הָווּ לֵיהּ נְכָסִים שֶׁיֵּשׁ לָהֶן אַחֲרָיוּת, [2]וְנִקְנִין עִם נְכָסִים שֶׁאֵין לָהֶן אַחֲרָיוּת. [3]וַאֲנַן אִיפְּכָא תְּנַן: [4]״נְכָסִים שֶׁאֵין לָהֶן אַחֲרָיוּת נִקְנִין עִם נְכָסִים שֶׁיֵּשׁ לָהֶן אַחֲרָיוּת״!

[5]אֲמַר לֵיהּ: אִי הֲוָה לֵוִי הָכָא, הֲוָה מַפֵּיק לְאַפָּךְ פּוּלְסֵי דְנוּרָא. [6]מִי סָבְרַתְּ גְּלִימָא מַקְנֶה לֵיהּ?

LITERAL TRANSLATION

[1]If so, this is mortgageable property (lit., "property with responsibility"), [2]and it is acquired with non-mortgageable property. [3]But we have learned the opposite: [4]"Non-mortgageable property is acquired with mortgageable property"!

[5]He said to him: If Levi were here, he would strike you with (lit., "bring out against you") lashes of fire. [6]Do you think [it is] the cloak [that] transfers ownership for him?

RASHI

אם כן הוו להו קרקעות נקנין עם מטלטלין — במשיכה, בדבר שהוא קנין למטלטלין ואינו קנין לקרקע. **נכסים שאין להן אחריות נקנין עם נכסים שיש להן אחריות** — בדבר שהוא קנין לקרקע ואינו קנין למטלטלין, כדקתני: בכסף ובשטר ובחזקה. **מפיק לאפך פולסא דנורא** — ניצוצות של אור, *אשטנצל״ש, שהן עגולות כפולסא. דאמרינן לקמן אסימון פולסא, ולשון שמתא קאמר ליה, שחשדתו בזו. **מי סברת** — דאמר ליה אגב שעל ידי משיכת הכלי שנקנה לו במשיכה יקנה לו הקרקע עם הכלי, אין אלו אלא כחליפין. כאילו זה מוסר לו חפץ אחר תחת קרקע, ומהו מסירתו — הנאת קבלתו ממנו מתנת הכלי, שחשבו לקבל ממנו מתנה — נוח לו כאילו נותן לו זה הקונה מתנה רבה, וגמר נותן ומקנה לו הקרקע.

CONCEPTS

נְכָסִים שֶׁיֵּשׁ לָהֶן אַחֲרָיוּת Mortgageable property. This refers to real estate, immovable property or land, which can be mortgaged to guarantee a loan, and from which debts may ultimately be paid. Written contracts normally establish a lien on all of a person's *landed* property (though the Geonim subsequently decreed that debts may be collected from *movable* property as well). Special modes of acquisition must be used to purchase land, although one who purchases land can acquire movable property together with it. One who buys land can acquire separate lots located in different areas, or even in different countries, simultaneously.

הֲוָה מַפֵּיק לְאַפָּךְ פּוּלְסֵי דְנוּרָא He would strike you with lashes of fire. These "lashes of fire" are an expression borrowed from the Aggadah, which speaks of spiritual punishments meted out by angels or the like. The expression means "the full severity of judgment," or "great severity." *Rashi* in this instance applied a more exact definition to the term — excommunication or a ban. In the present case, Rava tells Rav Huna of Diskarta that the challenge he raised to one of the greatest Sages was not well founded, and that Levi would have been justified in responding to him harshly.

LANGUAGE

פּוּלְסֵי This word is apparently derived from the Latin *pulsus,* meaning "a blow."

LANGUAGE (RASHI)

אשטנצל״ש* From the Old French *estenceles,* "sparks."

NOTES

"by means of" or "along with" (אַגַּב) movable property. Hence, the Gemara returns to the idea of symbolic consideration, and concludes that the consideration received by the seller in *ḥalifin* is his gratification that the buyer is willing to accept his kerchief. Thus, according to Levi, the seller commits himself to complete the transaction in exchange for the gratification he receives.

Rabbenu Yehonatan points out that, according to both Rav and Levi, *kinyan sudar* is only a form of symbolic payment; it is not the equivalent of purchasing with money or with objects of value. The seller expects to be paid in full for the merchandise, and the value of the kerchief is not to be deducted from the expected payment. Rather, exchange of the kerchief is regarded as an additional consideration. This additional symbolic payment — above and beyond the purchase price of the merchandise — is given in exchange for a commitment to complete the transaction (see also *Ri Migash*).

פּוּלְסֵי דְנוּרָא Lashes of fire. As explained in our commentary, Rava means that Levi would have made a stinging rejoinder to Rav Huna of Diskarta's objection. According to *Rashi,* the "lashes of fire" refer to a form of excommunication. Rava felt that the way Rav Huna of Diskarta posed his question was an insult to Levi's honor, deserving of severe punishment.

Other Rishonim insist that a question, however bad, is not

HALAKHAH

נְכָסִים שֶׁאֵין לָהֶן אַחֲרָיוּת נִקְנִין עִם נְכָסִים שֶׁיֵּשׁ לָהֶן אַחֲרָיוּת Movable property can be acquired together with immovable property. "If a person transfers land to someone else, whether by selling it, giving it or leasing it — and the transfer includes movable property — the movable property is acquired by the buyer through the acquisition of the land." (Ibid., 202:1.)

TRANSLATION AND COMMENTARY

[1] And it is **in exchange for the gratification** felt by **the seller — that** the buyer is willing to **accept** the seller's **cloak from him** — that the seller **resolves to transfer the merchandise to** the buyer. Thus, Rav and Levi basically agree about the mechanism of *ḥalifin*: The buyer wants the seller to receive a consideration so that the seller will resolve to transfer the merchandise in exchange. As soon as the seller receives the consideration agreed upon, the transaction ceases to be a mere promise and becomes final. The only difference between Rav and Levi is that, according to Rav, the consideration is the kerchief itself, whereas according to Levi it is the gratification the seller receives from having his kerchief accepted by the buyer.

כְּתַנָּאֵי [2] Having explained the reasoning of Rav and Levi, the Gemara notes that their dispute **is like** an earlier **dispute between Tannaim,** cited at the end of the following Baraita. [3] The Baraita considers a verse in the Book of Ruth (4:7): "**'And this was the custom in former time in Israel concerning redeeming and concerning changing to confirm all matters:** [4] **a man pulled off his shoe and gave it to his neighbor.'"** According to this verse, "redeeming" and "changing" can be effected by handing over a shoe. [5] The Baraita now defines these terms: "The expression '**redeeming**' (גְּאוּלָּה) used in the verse **means selling,** i.e., it describes a situation where merchandise is sold for money." [6] The Baraita proves this definition by quoting a verse from the Torah: "For this is what **the Torah, too, states** (Leviticus 27:28): Consecrated property 'shall not be sold and **shall not be redeemed,'"** and the parallelism between "selling" and "redeeming" in this verse implies that the terms are synonymous. Thus the verse in Ruth teaches us that when merchandise is sold for money, the sale can be finalized by performing an act of symbolic *ḥalifin* through the transfer of a shoe. [7] The Baraita now defines another term used in the verse in Ruth: "The expression '**changing**' (תְּמוּרָה) used in the verse **means** *ḥalifin*, i.e., it describes a situation where merchandise is exchanged for other merchandise." [8] The Baraita proves this definition, too, by quoting a verse from the Torah: "For this is what **the Torah states** (Leviticus 27:10): **'He shall not barter** an animal

[1] בְּהַהִיא הֲנָאָה דְּקָא מְקַבֵּל מִינֵּיהּ, גָּמַר וְאַקְנֵי לֵיהּ.
[2] כְּתַנָּאֵי: [3] ״׳וְזֹאת לְפָנִים בְּיִשְׂרָאֵל עַל הַגְּאוּלָּה וְעַל הַתְּמוּרָה לְקַיֵּם כָּל דָּבָר: [4] שָׁלַף אִישׁ נַעֲלוֹ וְנָתַן לְרֵעֵהוּ׳.
[5] ׳גְּאוּלָּה׳ — זוֹ מְכִירָה, [6] וְכֵן הוּא אוֹמֵר: ׳לֹא יִגָּאֵל׳.
[7] ׳תְּמוּרָה׳ — זוֹ חֲלִיפִין, [8] וְכֵן הוּא אוֹמֵר: ׳לֹא יַחֲלִיפֶנּוּ וְלֹא

LITERAL TRANSLATION

[1] In [exchange for] that gratification [felt by the seller] that he [the buyer] accepts [the cloak] from him, he resolves and transfers [the merchandise] to him.

[2] [This is] like [a dispute between] Tannaim. [3] "'And this was [the custom] in former time in Israel concerning redeeming and concerning changing to confirm all matters: [4] a man pulled off his shoe and gave it to his neighbor.' [5] 'Redeeming' — this is selling, [6] and so too [the Torah] says: 'It shall not be redeemed.' [7] 'Changing' — this is *ḥalifin*, [8] and so too [the Torah] says: 'He shall not barter it nor

RASHI

גאולה זו מכירה — שמכר לו מכירה גמורה בדמים, ולא קיבל מעות, ובאין לקיים דברי מכירתן על ידי קנין. **זו חליפין** — שמחליף כלי זה בחפץ שכנגדו.

TERMINOLOGY

כְּתַנָּאֵי Like the Tannaim. When an Amoraic controversy is shown to parallel a Tannaitic dispute, the Talmud states: "This Amoraic controversy is like the dispute of the Tannaim." When the Gemara uses this expression without qualification (i.e., without preceding it with the interrogative word לֵימָא — "shall we say"), the identification of the Amoraic controversy with a previous Tannaitic controversy is usually accepted.

NOTES

worthy of punishment, let alone excommunication. They explain that Levi would have used sharp language, likened to lashes of fire, if he had had to answer Rav Huna's question, as the question was not worthy of a student of Rav Huna's intelligence (*Rosh, Ritva*).

בְּהַהִיא הֲנָאָה In exchange for that gratification. To understand this passage, it is important to note that the Halakhah considers an action that gives a person pleasure to be the equivalent of payment, if the person would have been willing to pay a perutah for the pleasure he enjoyed. This issue is discussed in detail in tractate *Kiddushin* (7a, 63a).

The Rishonim ask: Gratification is the equivalent of payment only if the gratified person would be willing to pay a perutah for it. Gratification worth less than a perutah has no Halakhic significance. On what basis, then, does Levi claim that the gratification felt by the seller when the buyer accepts his kerchief is worth at least a perutah, and is sufficient to effect the transaction? (*Ritva, Ramban* and *Ran* in *Kiddushin*.) This question is strengthened by the fact that the kerchief is usually returned to its owner immediately after symbolic *ḥalifin* has been performed with it (*Ramban*).

Some Rishonim explain that even the slightest gratification has significance. *Ḥalifin* can be performed even with a utensil that is not worth a perutah. Hence, according to Levi, even the minuscule gratification felt by the seller when the buyer grasps his kerchief for an instant is sufficient to effect the transaction (*Ramban, Ran*).

Ritva states that, in *ḥalifin*, the handing over of a shoe or a kerchief is not intended as payment for anything, not even symbolic payment; it is simply a ritual that Scripture prescribes to finalize a transaction. Thus there is no need for the utensil or the gratification to have any measurable value. Rav and Levi are not explaining the mechanics of *ḥalifin*; they are, rather, trying to explain the symbolic meaning of an act mandated by Scripture. According to Levi, when a seller transfers merchandise to a buyer by handing

TRANSLATION AND COMMENTARY

consecrated as a sacrifice, **nor change it.'"** Here too the parallelism between "barter" and "change" in this verse implies that the terms are synonymous. Thus the verse in Ruth teaches us that merchandise can be acquired by exchanging it for a shoe in a *ḥalifin* transaction. [1]The Baraita now considers the next part of the verse from Ruth: **"'To confirm all matters: a man pulled off his shoe and gave it to his neighbor.'"** [2]The Baraita asks: "In the story described in the Book of Ruth, **who gave the shoe to whom?** The first Tanna said: It was **Boaz,** the buyer, who **gave** his shoe **to** the seller, described in Ruth as **'the redeemer.'"** Clearly this Tanna agrees with Rav's opinion that *ḥalifin* must be performed with the buyer's utensil. [3]"But **Rabbi Yehudah says: The redeemer gave** his shoe **to Boaz,"** implying that *ḥalifin* is performed with the seller's property, as Levi maintained. Thus we see that the Tannaim already differed as to whose property was to be used to effect *ḥalifin*.

תָּנָא [4]The Gemara now considers another aspect of the laws of *ḥalifin* (already mentioned above, 46b). **A Tanna taught** in a Baraita: "In a *ḥalifin* transaction **one acquires** merchandise **by means of a utensil, even if** that utensil **is not worth a perutah** — the coin of lowest denomination in Talmudic times. For *ḥalifin* is an exchange of the items themselves, not of their value, and the fact that one of the items is worthless is immaterial.

אָמַר רַב נַחְמָן [5]The Gemara now cites an Amoraic dispute regarding this Baraita: **Rav Naḥman said:** This Baraita **taught** that **only a utensil** — a tool or an article of clothing — can be used to perform *ḥalifin*, and the act of *ḥalifin* is effective even if the utensil is worth very little; [6]**but produce** — anything that is not a utensil — **cannot** be used to effect *ḥalifin* no matter how much it is worth. [7]**Rav Sheshet said: Even produce** can be used to perform *ḥalifin*, and the Baraita's use of the term "utensil" does not exclude other articles.

מַאי טַעְמָא דְּרַב נַחְמָן [8]The Gemara asks: **What is Rav Naḥman's reason?** Why should only a utensil be used to effect *ḥalifin*?

אָמַר קְרָא [9]The Gemara answers: **The verse** from which we learn the laws of *ḥalifin* (Ruth 4:7) **states** that Boaz and the redeemer used **a shoe** to effect the act of *ḥalifin* between them. [10]From this we may infer that **a shoe** can be used to effect *ḥalifin*, and by extension the same rule applies to other objects similar to shoes, i.e., all utensils. But **other things cannot** be used to effect *ḥalifin*.

LITERAL TRANSLATION

change it.' [1]'To confirm all matters: a man pulled off his shoe and gave it to his neighbor.' [2]Who gave to whom? Boaz gave to the redeemer. [3]Rabbi Yehudah says: The redeemer gave to Boaz."

[4][A Tanna] taught: "One acquires with a utensil, even if it is not worth a perutah."

[5]Rav Naḥman said: They only taught 'with a utensil,' [6]but not with produce. [7]Rav Sheshet said: Even with produce.

[8]What is Rav Naḥman's reason?

[9]The verse said: "His shoe." [10]A shoe — yes; something else — no.

יָמִיר אוֹתוֹ׳. [1]׳לְקַיֵּם כָּל דָּבָר שָׁלַף אִישׁ נַעֲלוֹ וְנָתַן לְרֵעֵהוּ׳. [2]מִי נָתַן לְמִי? בּוֹעַז נָתַן לַגּוֹאֵל. [3]רַבִּי יְהוּדָה אוֹמֵר: גּוֹאֵל נָתַן לְבוֹעַז״.

[4]תָּנָא: ״קוֹנִין בִּכְלִי, אַף עַל פִּי שֶׁאֵין בּוֹ שָׁוֶה פְּרוּטָה״.

[5]אָמַר רַב נַחְמָן: לֹא שָׁנוּ אֶלָּא ׳בִּכְלִי׳, [6]אֲבָל בְּפֵירֵי לֹא. [7]רַב שֵׁשֶׁת אָמַר: אֲפִילּוּ בְּפֵירוֹת.

[8]מַאי טַעְמָא דְּרַב נַחְמָן? [9]אָמַר קְרָא: ״נַעֲלוֹ״. [10]נַעַל — אִין; מִידֵּי אַחֲרִינָא — לָא.

RASHI

לא שנו – דקונין קנין אלא בכלי. **אבל בפירי** – כל דבר שאינו כלי. **לא** – ואפילו שוה הרבה.

SAGES

רַבִּי יְהוּדָה Rabbi Yehudah (bar Il'ai). A Tanna of the fifth generation. See *Bava Metzia*, Part II, p. 4.

TERMINOLOGY

תָּנָא (occasionally **תָּאנָא**) Lit., **he taught.** A term used to introduce Baraitot and Tosefot. Usually the Baraitot introduced by this expression are very short (one or two sentences), and they clarify, supplement or limit statements in the Mishnah.

NOTES

him a shoe, the symbolism is unconnected with the value of the shoe, but relates to the pleasure felt by the seller, even though neither the shoe nor the pleasure is worth a perutah.

קוֹנִין בִּכְלִי One acquires with a utensil. In Talmudic literature, the term "utensil" refers to any manufactured, movable, inanimate object of immediate practical use. Included in this category are clothes, toys, tools, containers and furniture. Not included are food and fuel which are intended to be consumed; raw materials which must be processed before they can be used; coins whose usefulness consists of their symbolic rather than their physical properties; animals; buildings; growing plants, etc. Thus a shoe is a utensil, but produce is not.

אַף עַל פִּי שֶׁאֵין בּוֹ שָׁוֶה פְּרוּטָה Even if it is not worth a perutah. *Tosafot* asks: Under Torah law, the perutah is the smallest possible measure of value. An object not worth one perutah is worthless for all Halakhic purposes. Such an object cannot be used, for example, to betroth a woman. If someone steals such an object, he is not subject to the regular laws of theft. Damages worth less than a perutah have no legal standing. How then can the handing over of a worthless utensil be considered "giving"?

Tosafot answers that financial obligations and payment must be at least one perutah in value. But when the "giving" is ceremonial in nature, and not in any sense a monetary obligation, the object given need not be worth a perutah. Thus, when a farmer gives a priest terumah, he may give him less than one perutah's worth. But if the same farmer

TRANSLATION AND COMMENTARY

מַאי טַעְמֵיהּ דְּרַב שֵׁשֶׁת [1]The Gemara asks: **What is Rav Sheshet's reason?** Why does he not interpret the Baraita and the verse as did Rav Naḥman?

אָמַר קְרָא [2]The Gemara answers: **The verse** (ibid.) also **states: "To confirm all matters."** The Gemara interprets this expression as if it read: "To confirm *with* all things," implying that *ḥalifin* can be effected with produce, and not just with utensils. Thus Rav Sheshet argues that the word "shoe" used in the verse was not intended to forbid the use of produce as a means of effecting *ḥalifin*.

לְרַב נַחְמָן [3]The Gemara objects: But **according to Rav Naḥman, too, surely** the verse **uses the expression: "To confirm all matters"!** How does Rav Naḥman interpret Rav Sheshet's textual proof?

הַהוּא לְקַיֵּם כָּל דָּבָר [4]The Gemara answers: Rav Naḥman can explain the verse as follows: The expression "to confirm all matters" does not refer to the object used to effect *ḥalifin*; that object must be a shoe or something similar. Rather, the expression **means: To confirm all things** that are acquired through *ḥalifin*. Thus the verse is informing us that *all* commodities — produce, utensils and land — **can be acquired** through *ḥalifin* **by means of a shoe** or a similar utensil. There is no restriction on the type of merchandise that can be acquired in this way, even though the act of acquisition itself can only be effected with a utensil.

וְרַב שֵׁשֶׁת נַמִי [5]The Gemara objects: **But according to Rav Sheshet too, surely** the verse **uses the expression "his shoe,"** which is clearly intended to place a restriction on the kind of article that can be used to effect *ḥalifin*! How would Rav Sheshet interpret Rav Naḥman's textual proof? If even produce can be used, what kind of object *cannot* be used to effect *ḥalifin*?

אָמַר לָךְ רַב שֵׁשֶׁת [6]The Gemara answers: **Rav Sheshet** can **say to you** that we may infer from the mention of "shoe" in this verse [7]that, **just as a shoe** — which **is a distinct** and whole **object** — can be used to effect *ḥalifin*, [8]**so too all distinct**, unbroken **objects can be used** to effect *ḥalifin*, but incomplete objects cannot be used. [9]Thus, the mention of "shoe" comes **to exclude** incomplete objects such as **half a pomegranate or half a nut.** [10]Even according to Rav Sheshet, these **cannot** be used to effect *ḥalifin*.

This concludes the Gemara's detailed analysis of the laws of *ḥalifin*. To summarize the subject, the Gemara now examines the standard formula used in documents written to record acts of *ḥalifin*. In such formulae, each word carries special significance. Thus, an examination of the standard formula used for *ḥalifin* can illustrate how the issues considered by the Gemara above were resolved in practice.

[1]מַאי טַעְמֵיהּ דְּרַב שֵׁשֶׁת? [2]אָמַר קְרָא: ״לְקַיֵּם כָּל דָּבָר״. [3]לְרַב נַחְמָן נַמִי, הָכְתִיב: ״לְקַיֵּם כָּל דָּבָר״! [4]הַהוּא לְקַיֵּם כָּל דָּבָר דְּנִיקְנִין בְּמִנְעָל. [5]וְרַב שֵׁשֶׁת נַמִי, הָכְתִיב: ״נַעֲלוֹ״! [6]אָמַר לָךְ רַב שֵׁשֶׁת: [7]מַה ״נַעֲלוֹ״ דָּבָר הַמְסוּיָּים, [8]אַף כָּל דָּבָר הַמְסוּיָּים, [9]לְאַפּוּקֵי חֲצִי רִמּוֹן וַחֲצִי אֱגוֹז, [10]דְּלָא.

LITERAL TRANSLATION

[1]What is Rav Sheshet's reason?

[2]The verse said: "To confirm all matters."

[3]According to Rav Naḥman, too, surely it is written: "To confirm all matters"!

[4]That [means]: To confirm all matters that are acquired with a shoe.

[5]And [according to] Rav Sheshet, too, surely it is written: "His shoe"!

[6]Rav Sheshet can say to you: [7]Just as "his shoe" is a distinct thing, [8]so too anything that is distinct [can be used], [9]to exclude half a pomegranate and half a nut, [10]which cannot [be used].

RASHI

לקיים כל דבר – לקיים בכל דבר. **ההוא לקיים כל דבר** – גאולה ותמורה במנעל. **המסויים** – שלם.

BACKGROUND

דָּבָר הַמְסוּיָּים A distinct thing. The term מְסוּיָּם — "distinct" — comes from the verb לְסַיֵּם, meaning "to finish," so that something which is מְסוּיָּם has a boundary or a limit. Most objects are bounded, which is what makes them distinct or discrete. However, an unweighed, unmeasured part of a piece of fruit is not distinct, for there is no way of defining it as a separate entity. An object's indistinctness does not affect its monetary value; but its undefined status denies it significance in its own right. Something undefined cannot be acquired: Just as a person cannot sell an unspecified "part of a field" or "part of a thing," acquisition also cannot be effective with regard to such an undefined article.

NOTES

were to eat the terumah by mistake, he would not be required to replace it unless it was worth at least one perutah.

חֲצִי רִמּוֹן Half a pomegranate. According to Rav Sheshet, the word "shoe" in the Book of Ruth teaches us that a piece of fruit such as half a pomegranate may not be used to effect *ḥalifin*. Even though Rav Sheshet is of the opinion that it is not necessary to use a utensil, and that a fruit may be used instead, the fruit must at least resemble a utensil in being a complete and distinct object.

It is not clear from the Gemara whether this rule applies only to fruit, according to Rav Sheshet, or whether Rav Naḥman would accept that a similar rule applies to utensils as well. Can *ḥalifin* be effected by handing over a piece broken off from a utensil, or must the utensil be whole and distinct, like a shoe?

The Gemara (above, 7a) rules that when performing *ḥalifin* with a kerchief, it is sufficient for the two parties to grasp the kerchief at the same time. This practice is based on the idea that the piece of cloth in the seller's hand is regarded as having been severed from the rest of the cloth and given to him. Thus, it would appear that it is not necessary to hand over a whole and distinct utensil.

On the other hand, some Rishonim understand Rav Sheshet's ruling that an object used in *ḥalifin* must be whole and distinct as applying even according to the Halakhah, which follows Rav Naḥman. To explain the Gemara's ruling above

TRANSLATION AND COMMENTARY

אָמַר רַב שֵׁשֶׁת בְּרֵיהּ דְּרַב אִידִי [1]**Rav Sheshet the son of Rav Idi asked:** [2]**Whose** opinions are we following **nowadays** when **we write** in documents mentioning *ḥalifin* that the transaction was finalized **"with a utensil with which it is fit to acquire"?**

בְּמָנָא [3]He answered: Each term used in this clause indicates a restriction on the kind of object that may be used to effect *ḥalifin*. The purpose of the expression **"with a utensil"** is **to exclude the viewpoint of Rav Sheshet, who said** that **one may** perform the act of *ḥalifin* and **acquire** property **by means of produce.** For the Halakhah is in accordance with the viewpoint of Rav Naḥman, who ruled that only utensils can be used to effect *ḥalifin*. [4]The purpose of the expression **"it is fit"** is **to exclude the viewpoint of Shmuel, who said** that **one may acquire** [47B] **with *maroka*** — discarded date pits. Date pits are technically a kind of utensil, since tanners use them in the preparation of parchment. Thus Shmuel is of the opinion that they can be used to effect *ḥalifin*. But the Halakhah is that *maroka* may not be used, since it is essentially worthless refuse. [5]The purpose of the expression **"to acquire"** is **to exclude the viewpoint of Levi, who said** that *ḥalifin* is performed **with the seller's utensils.** [6]**Hence** the customary formula **informs us** that the utensil is used by the buyer **"to acquire"** the merchandise, **and not** by the seller **"to transfer ownership"** of it to the buyer. In other words, the buyer gives his kerchief to the seller, as Rav maintained, and not vice versa, as maintained by Levi. [7]The expression **"with which"** is to be understood as meaning "not with something else," but there is a difference of opinion between Amoraim as to the identity of the thing being excluded. **Rav Pappa said:** The purpose of the expression is **to exclude coins,** since it implies that only the items specified (i.e., utensils) can be used to

[1]אֲמַר רַב שֵׁשֶׁת בְּרֵיהּ דְּרַב אִידִי: [2]כְּמַאן כָּתְבִינַן הָאִידָּנָא: ״בְּמָנָא דִּכְשַׁר לְמִקְנְיָא בֵּיהּ״? [3]״בְּמָנָא״ — לְאַפּוּקֵי מִדְּרַב שֵׁשֶׁת, דַּאֲמַר: קוֹנִין בְּפֵירוֹת. [4]״דִּכְשַׁר״ — לְאַפּוּקֵי מִדִּשְׁמוּאֵל, דְּאָמַר: קוֹנִין [47B] בְּמָרוֹקָא. [5]״לְמִקְנְיָא — לְאַפּוּקֵי מִדְּלֵוִי, דַּאֲמַר: בְּכֵלָיו שֶׁל מַקְנֶה. [6]קָא מַשְׁמַע לָן: ״לְמִקְנְיָא״, וְלָא לְקַנּוּיֵי. [7]״בֵּיהּ״ — רַב פַּפָּא אֲמַר: לְמַעוּטֵי מַטְבֵּעַ.

LITERAL TRANSLATION

[1]Rav Sheshet the son of Rav Idi said: [2]According to whom do we write nowadays: "With a utensil with which it is fit to acquire"?

[3]"With a utensil" — to exclude [the viewpoint] of Rav Sheshet, who said: One may acquire with produce. [4]"It is fit" — to exclude [the viewpoint] of Shmuel, who said: One may acquire [47B] with *maroka*. [5]"To acquire" — to exclude [the viewpoint] of Levi, who said: With the seller's utensils. [6][Hence] it tells us: "To acquire," and not to transfer ownership. [7]"With which" — Rav Pappa said: To exclude coin.

RASHI

מרוקא – כלי העשוי מגללי בקר. **למקניא** – משמע לקנות בו, ולא משמע להקנות בו. אלמא: כליו של קונה קאמר. **ביה** – משמע מיעוט, בו ולא בדבר אחר.

NOTES

(7a), *Tosafot* suggests that the piece of cloth in the seller's hand is considered to be whole and distinct. *Rashi* points out that a small piece of cloth is a utensil in its own right, since, if it were torn off, it could still be used as a small handkerchief. According to these explanations, it would appear that the Gemara's ruling applies only to kerchiefs and the like, but a piece of a utensil that is completely useless by itself, such as a part of a shoe, could not be used to effect *ḥalifin*.

Ritva, however, insists that Rav Sheshet's ruling that the object used in *ḥalifin* must be whole and distinct applies only to fruit, and not to utensils such as kerchiefs. A piece of fruit is not in any sense the same as a whole fruit; hence it may not be used, according to Rav Sheshet. A piece of a utensil, on the other hand, is still a utensil in its own right, since it can be used together with the other part. Thus Rav Sheshet's ruling has no relevance according to the Halakhah, which follows Rav Naḥman.

כְּמַאן כָּתְבִינַן According to whom do we write...? The document to which Rav Sheshet the son of Rav Idi refers is not the deed used to effect a transaction (קִנְיַן שְׁטָר) when buying real estate. Rather, it is merely a written record of that transaction, serving as proof that the property mentioned in the document was legally transferred from one party to the other, and now belongs to its new owner.

To effect *ḥalifin* it is not necessary to write anything, nor, according to most Rishonim, is it necessary to perform *ḥalifin* in the presence of witnesses (*Rambam*, *Tosafot* and others). The parties must only agree to the terms and hand over one of the articles being exchanged. Nevertheless, the custom of writing a document to serve as evidence of a transaction was so widespread that the Sages ruled that whenever a party stipulates that he wants to effect a transaction by exchanging a kerchief, we must assume that he also wants the transaction to be recorded in a document of this type (*Bava Batra* 40a).

מָרוֹקָא *Maroka.* The Rishonim agree that *maroka* must be a sort of utensil. Our commentary follows *Tosafot,* who explains that *maroka* means discarded date pits. Such pits were used in the treatment of parchment, but were nevertheless considered worthless refuse.

Rashi explains that *maroka* means an ordinary utensil made of cow dung. It is not obvious why such a utensil should be unacceptable for the purposes of *ḥalifin*. *Rabbenu Yehonatan* explains that a utensil made of dung cannot be used with hot water. Hence, even though it looks like a utensil, it cannot really be used as one.

Ra'avad suggests that *maroka* may mean a utensil the

SAGES

רַב שֵׁשֶׁת בְּרֵיהּ דְּרַב אִידִי Rav Sheshet the son of Rav Idi. This Babylonian Amora of the fourth generation was also known as Rav Shisha. He and his brother, Rav Yehoshua, were the sons of Rav Idi bar Avin, a disciple of Rav Hisda. Rav Sheshet the son of Rav Idi discussed the Halakhah with other Sages of his generation, in particular with Rav Pappa.

שְׁמוּאֵל Shmuel. A Babylonian Amora of the first generation. See *Bava Metzia*, Part II, p. 48.

BACKGROUND

כְּמַאן כָּתְבִינַן הָאִידָּנָא According to whom do we write nowadays...? The proof here derives from the wording used by court scribes in writing official documents. Conventional wording of this kind generally reflected the conclusion of many scholars who dealt with such matters professionally, and derived from accepted rulings based on the agreement of many Sages during the period when the wording was in use.

LANGUAGE

מָרוֹקָא *Maroka.* Commentators have proposed various explanations of this term. *Rashi*'s interpretation may be based on the word מַרְקָה found in the Mishnah, meaning a kind of mud mixed with hair, or mud mixed with egg white. The interpretation offered by *Rabbenu Ḥananel* derives the term from the word for scouring (from the root מרק), so that מָרוֹקָא would thus be material used in scouring.

TRANSLATION AND COMMENTARY

effect *ḥalifin*, but not coins. [1]**Rav Zevid — and some say Rav Ashi** — disagreed, and **said:** [2]The purpose of the expression "with which" is **to exclude things from which benefit is forbidden.** Only ordinary utensils may be used to effect *ḥalifin*, but not utensils from which it is Halakhically forbidden to derive any benefit (e.g., idols).

אִיכָּא דְּאָמְרִי [3]**There are some who give** a slightly different version of the Amoraim's interpretation of the expressions used in these formal documents: [4]Regarding the expression **"with which," Rav Pappa said:** This comes **to exclude coins.** This statement by Rav Pappa is identical to that stated in his name in the first version. Moreover, in this version, no one differs with Rav Pappa about the explanation given for the use of this term. [5]It was regarding the expression **"it is fit"** that **Rav Zevid — and some say Rav Ashi — said:** [6]This expression comes **to exclude things from which benefit is forbidden.** In the previous version, the expression "it is fit" was used to exclude *maroka*, [7]**but** in this version, **it was not** considered **necessary to** mention any special phrase to **exclude *maroka*,** since it is obvious that *maroka* is absolutely worthless and cannot be used to effect *ḥalifin*.

אֲסִימוֹן קוֹנֶה אֶת הַמַּטְבֵּעַ [8]The Gemara now considers the next clause of the Mishnah: "An *asimon* **acquires** a minted **coin,**" because an *asimon* is considered merchandise relative to any minted coin, even though it is considered a coin relative to ordinary merchandise.

מַאי אֲסִימוֹן [9]The Gemara asks: **What does** the word ***"asimon"*** **mean?** What kind of coin is merchandise even relative to "bad coins," but is still a coin relative to merchandise?

אֲמַר רַב [10]**Rav said** in reply: The word "*asimon*" refers to **coins that are given as** admission **tokens at the bathhouse.** According to Rav, when the Mishnah said that an *asimon* is considered merchandise relative to all other coins, but a coin relative to regular merchandise, it was referring to these tokens.

מֵיתִיבֵי [11]**An objection was raised** to this interpretation of the term *asimon* from the following Baraita: "One **may not redeem second-tithe produce with an *asimon*,** [12]**nor with coins that are given as tokens at the bathhouse,"** because the Torah insists that only proper, minted coins can be used for this purpose (see above, 44b, for

[1]וְרַב זְבִיד — וְאִיתֵּימָא רַב אַשִׁי — אֲמַר: [2]לְמַעוּטֵי אִיסּוּרֵי הֲנָאָה.

[3]אִיכָּא דְּאָמְרִי: [4]״בֵּיהּ״ — אֲמַר רַב פַּפָּא: לְמַעוּטֵי מַטְבֵּעַ. [5]״דִּכְשַׁר״ אֲמַר רַב זְבִיד — וְאִיתֵּימָא רַב אַשִׁי: [6]לְמַעוּטֵי אִיסּוּרֵי הֲנָאָה. [7]אֲבָל מוֹרִיקָא לָא אִצְטְרִיךְ.

[8]״אֲסִימוֹן קוֹנֶה אֶת הַמַּטְבֵּעַ, וכו׳״.

[9]מַאי אֲסִימוֹן?

[10]אֲמַר רַב: מָעוֹת הַנִּיתָּנוֹת בְּסִימָן לְבֵית הַמֶּרְחָץ.

[11]מֵיתִיבֵי: ״אֵין מְחַלְּלִין מַעֲשֵׂר שֵׁנִי עַל אֲסִימוֹן, [12]וְלֹא עַל מָעוֹת הַנִּיתָּנוֹת בְּסִימָן לְבֵית הַמֶּרְחָץ״.

LITERAL TRANSLATION

[1]And Rav Zevid — and some say Rav Ashi — said: [2]To exclude things from which benefit is forbidden.

[3]There are [some] who say: [4]"With which" — Rav Pappa said: To exclude coin. [5]"It is fit" — Rav Zevid — and some say Rav Ashi — said: [6]To exclude things from which benefit is forbidden. [7]But *maroka* it was not necessary [to exclude].

[8]"An *asimon* acquires a coin, etc."

[9]What is an *asimon*?

[10]Rav said: Coins that are given as a token at the bathhouse.

[11]They objected: "One may not redeem second tithe with an *asimon*, [12]nor with coins that are given as a token at the bathhouse."

RASHI

לא אצטריך — למימר דלא קני. **הניתנות בסימן** — הבלן מקבל סימנין מיד הנכנין לרחוץ בבית המרחץ, לדעת כמה הם, ולפיהם יחם המים ויכין אלונטיאות. ונותנין לו מעות פחותות ורעות בסימן.

SAGES

רַב זְבִיד **Rav Zevid.** A fifth generation Babylonian Amora. See *Bava Metzia*, Part II, p. 36.

CONCEPTS

אִיסּוּרֵי הֲנָאָה **Things from which benefit is forbidden.** Things from which one is forbidden to derive any kind of benefit or profit — not only that conferred by eating them, but by any other use, including selling them, even to a non-Jew. Some אִיסּוּרֵי הֲנָאָה are prohibited by Torah law, others only by Rabbinic decree. Some must be disposed of by burning, others by burial. Among the things covered by this prohibition are idols and pagan sacrifices; the male first-born of an ass before it has been redeemed and after its neck has been broken (פֶּטֶר חֲמוֹר); an animal sentenced to stoning (שׁוֹר הַנִּסְקָל); and a heifer whose neck has been broken (עֶגְלָה עֲרוּפָה). Today the prohibition applies specifically to wine used for idolatrous purposes (יֵין נֶסֶךְ), meat of kosher domesticated animals (not undomesticated animals or birds) which has been cooked in milk (בָּשָׂר בְּחָלָב), and leaven (חָמֵץ) on Pesaḥ.

LANGUAGE

אֲסִימוֹן *Asimon.* Rabbi Yoḥanan interprets the first syllable of this word (a-) like the Greek prefix meaning "non-," also used in English, so that an *asimon* is thus a coin (סִימָן) without a sign. In Rav's opinion, however, the root of the word is indeed סִימָן, and is related to the Greek σῆμα, *sema*, found in English words such as "semantics." It can mean a token used in payment.

BACKGROUND

אֲסִימוֹן *Asimon.*

A Roman bathhouse token, made of metal, from the Talmudic period.

NOTES

sole purpose of which is to collect urine or dung. Since the purpose for which it is designed is indelicate, *maroka* does not have the status of a utensil for the purpose of *ḥalifin*.

אֲבָל מוֹרִיקָא לָא אִצְטְרִיךְ **But *maroka* it was not necessary to exclude.** The Aḥaronim ask: Why was it not necessary to exclude *maroka*? After all, Shmuel is of the opinion that *maroka* can be used to effect *ḥalifin*. Why is it so obvious that he was mistaken (*Leḥem Abirim*)?

It is interesting to note that *Meiri* explains the Gemara in a slightly different way. According to his interpretation, the Gemara should be explained as follows: The word "fit" is mentioned to exclude items from which benefit is forbidden; it is not necessary to say that it also excludes *maroka*, which is even less "fit" than items from which it is forbidden to benefit.

HALAKHAH

אִיסּוּרֵי הֲנָאָה **Things from which it is forbidden to benefit.** "*Ḥalifin* may not be performed with objects from which it is forbidden to derive benefit." (*Shulḥan Arukh, Ḥoshen Mishpat* 19 5:2.)

LITERAL TRANSLATION

[1] [This proves] by implication that an *asimon* is not [the same as] coins that are given as a token at the bathhouse.

[2] And if you say it is explaining, [3] but surely [the Tanna] did not teach thus [but as follows]: "One may redeem second tithe with an *asimon*. [4] [These are] the words of Rabbi Dosa. [5] But the Sages say: One may not redeem. [6] But they agree that one may not redeem with coins that are given as a token at the bathhouse."

[7] Rather, Rabbi Yoḥanan said: What is an *asimon*? [8] Unminted metal. [9] And Rabbi Yoḥanan follows his argument, [10] for Rabbi Yoḥanan said: Rabbi Dosa and Rabbi Yishmael said the same thing. [11] Rabbi Dosa — that which we [just] said. [12] What is Rabbi Yishmael's [statement]?

[1] מִכְּלָל דַּאֲסִימוֹן לָאו מָעוֹת הַנִּיתָּנוֹת בְּסִימָן לְבֵית הַמֶּרְחָץ.
[2] וְכִי תֵּימָא פֵּרוּשֵׁי קָמְפָרֵשׁ,
[3] וְהָא לָא תָּנָא הָכִי: "מְחַלְּלִין מַעֲשֵׂר שֵׁנִי עַל אֲסִימוֹן. [4] דִּבְרֵי רַבִּי דּוֹסָא. [5] וַחֲכָמִים אוֹמְרִים: אֵין מְחַלְּלִין. [6] וְשָׁוִין שֶׁאֵין מְחַלְּלִין עַל מָעוֹת הַנִּיתָּנוֹת בְּסִימָן לְבֵית הַמֶּרְחָץ".
[7] אֶלָּא אָמַר רַבִּי יוֹחָנָן: מַאי אֲסִימוֹן? [8] פּוּלְסָא.
[9] וְאָזְדָא רַבִּי יוֹחָנָן לְטַעְמֵיהּ,
[10] דְּאָמַר רַבִּי יוֹחָנָן: רַבִּי דּוֹסָא וְרַבִּי יִשְׁמָעֵאל אָמְרוּ דָּבָר אֶחָד.
[11] רַבִּי דּוֹסָא — הָא דַּאֲמָרַן.
[12] רַבִּי יִשְׁמָעֵאל מַאי הִיא?

RASHI

פולסא — מחוסר צורה, וקורין לו *פלדו"ן. **אזדא רבי יוחנן לטעמיה** — מדאוקי לרבי ישמעאל, דפליג על כל דבר שאין עליה צורה להתיר חילול עליו, דאמר כרבי דוסא, אשמועינן רבי יוחנן דאסימון דרבי דוסא דבר שאין עליו צורה הוא.

TRANSLATION AND COMMENTARY

further information about the redemption of second-tithe produce). [1] But, argues the Gemara, surely the wording of this Baraita **proves by implication that an** ***asimon*** **is not the same as a coin that is given as a token at the bathhouse!**

וְכִי תֵּימָא פֵּרוּשֵׁי קָמְפָרֵשׁ [2] The Gemara first considers an obvious solution to this objection: It is true that **if you say** that the second clause of the Baraita **is** no more than **an explanation** of the first — i.e., the Baraita is defining terms, and "coins given as tokens at the bathhouse" is merely a definition of the term *"asimon"* and does not denote a different item — you can explain the Baraita in this way, with a minor but acceptable emendation to remove the word "nor." [3] **But** examination of other sources proves that this interpretation is incorrect, for **surely the following Baraita did not teach that way, but as follows: "One may redeem second-tithe produce with an** ***asimon***. [4] **These are the words of Rabbi Dosa.** Rabbi Dosa disagrees with the Baraita quoted previously, and rules that an *asimon* is sufficiently like a proper, minted coin that it be used to redeem second-tithe produce. [5] **But the Sages** agree with the previous Baraita, and **say:** One **may not redeem** second-tithe produce with an *asimon*. [6] **But** both Rabbi Dosa and the Sages **agree that one may not redeem** second-tithe produce **with coins that are given as tokens at the bathhouse."** Thus it is clear that an *asimon* is not a bathhouse token as Rav suggested, for according to Rabbi Dosa, second-tithe produce can be redeemed with an *asimon*, but not with a token!

אֶלָּא אָמַר רַבִּי יוֹחָנָן [7] **Rather,** concludes the Gemara, a different definition of *asimon* must be sought: **Rabbi Yoḥanan said: What is an** ***asimon***? [8] A disk of **unminted metal** — i.e., a piece of metal shaped like a coin and having the same metallic content as a coin, but which has not yet been stamped by the government. In Talmudic times, the value of a coin was closely linked to its metallic content, and an *asimon* might well be accepted as a substitute for a minted coin. According to Rabbi Yoḥanan, such a coin is considered merchandise when exchanged for minted coins, although it is considered money when exchanged for ordinary merchandise.

וְאָזְדָא רַבִּי יוֹחָנָן לְטַעְמֵיהּ [9] The Gemara notes that **Rabbi Yoḥanan's** definition of *"asimon"* **is in accordance with his** usual line of **argument** as expressed in a related matter discussed elsewhere. [10] **For Rabbi Yoḥanan said: Rabbi Dosa and Rabbi Yishmael** made two different statements regarding the Halakhic status of unminted money, but their statements really **mean the same thing.** [11] **Rabbi Dosa** made the statement **that we** have **just cited,** namely that an *asimon* is considered sufficiently like a coin that it can be used to redeem second-tithe produce. [12] And **where is Rabbi Yishmael's** parallel **statement** recorded?

HALAKHAH

חִילּוּל מַעֲשֵׂר שֵׁנִי Redeeming second tithe. "Second tithe can only be redeemed with coins bearing an impression (or inscription), but not with unminted metal and the like." (*Rambam, Sefer Zeraim, Hilkhot Ma'aser Sheni* 4:9.) *Ḥatam Sofer* writes that paper money may be used to redeem second tithe, but his view is not accepted by any other authority.

LANGUAGE

פּוּלְסָא Unminted metal. Some authorities believe that this word is derived from the Greek φόλλις, *follis,* which is related to the Latin *"follis,"* meaning a small coin used in the Roman Empire during Talmudic times.

BACKGROUND

פּוּלְסָא Unminted metal.

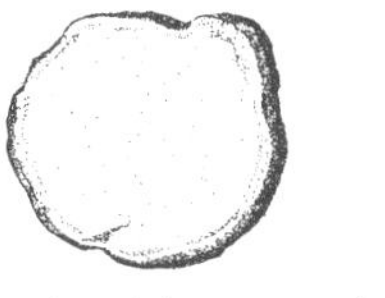

Uncoined metal, or a coin whose impression was worn away, so that it could no longer be used as money.

SAGES

רַבִּי דּוֹסָא Rabbi Dosa (ben Horkinas). Rabbi Dosa ben Horkinas seems to have been a contemporary of Rabban Yoḥanan ben Zakkai and is said to have known the leading scholars of the generation of Yavneh (Rabbi Eliezer and Rabbi Yehoshua) when they were still in their infancy. It is probable that in the period during which the Sanhedrin convened in Yavneh, Rabbi Dosa was no longer active and did not take part in its sessions. But his opinions were still influential at that time. We know that he lived to a most advanced age and was very wealthy. Rabbi Dosa was one of the senior Sages of Bet Hillel, although he had a younger brother, Yonatan, who was one of the heads of Bet Shammai. It seems that references in the Mishnah to Rabbi Dosa without a patronymic are to Rabbi Dosa ben Horkinas.

רַבִּי יִשְׁמָעֵאל Rabbi Yishmael (ben Elisha). A Tanna of the fourth generation. See *Bava Metzia*, Part II, p. 313.

TERMINOLOGY

אָמְרוּ דָּבָר אֶחָד They said one [i.e., the same] thing. An expression used to note that two scholars (usually Tannaim) held similar opinions about the subject under discussion.

LANGUAGE (RASHI)

פלדו"ן* From the Old French *fladon,* which means "a round piece of uncoined metal."

TRANSLATION AND COMMENTARY

[1]It is included in **the following Baraita** explaining the verse (Deuteronomy 14:25) that is the source for the law permitting the redemption of second-tithe produce with money. "The verse says: **'And you shall bind up the money in your hand.'** This verse describes the money permitted to be used for this purpose as being 'bound up in the hand.' [2]This teaches that **any** coin **that can be bound up in the hand is included** in the term 'money' for the purpose of redeeming second-tithe produce. [3]**These are the words of Rabbi Yishmael.** [4]But **Rabbi Akiva** disagrees with Rabbi Yishmael. He interprets the verse in a nonliteral manner, and translates the Hebrew word וְצַרְתָּ — 'and you shall bind up' — from the root צרר, as though it meant 'and you shall stamp,' from the root צור. Hence Rabbi Akiva **says:** This verse teaches us that **any** coin **bearing an impression on it is included** in the term 'money' for the purpose of redeeming second-tithe produce." Thus, according to Rabbi Akiva, only minted coins which bear impressions may be used for tithe-redemption.

In this Baraita, Rabbi Yishmael rules that any coin that can be bound up in the hand can be used to redeem second-tithe produce, even if the coin was not minted with an official stamp. Now, Rabbi Yoḥanan identifies the view of Rabbi Yishmael with that of Rabbi Dosa, who permitted the use of an *asimon* to redeem second-tithe produce. Thus it is clear that, according to Rabbi Yoḥanan, an *asimon* and an unminted coin are one and the same.

כֵּיצַד [5]The Gemara now considers the next clause of the Mishnah: **"How so? If the buyer has drawn** the seller's **merchandise** into his possession, **but has not** yet **given** the seller the purchase **money, neither he** nor the seller **can retract,"** because *meshikhah* — drawing merchandise into one's possession — is an act of acquisition that finalizes a sale and obligates the buyer to pay the agreed sum. But if the buyer has not yet drawn the merchandise into his possession, either party may retract, even if the money has already been paid, because payment of money is not an act of acquisition, and does not finalize a sale.

אָמַר רַבִּי יוֹחָנָן [6]The Gemara now investigates why it is that *meshikhah* is an effective act of acquisition whereas payment of money is not. This question was the subject of a difference of opinion between Rabbi Yoḥanan and Resh Lakish. **Rabbi Yoḥanan said:** The Mishnah's ruling is a Rabbinic decree, whereas **by Torah law,** payment of **money** is an effective act of acquisition that **acquires** movable property, and the purchased merchandise immediately becomes the property of the buyer; merely picking up a purchased object is not an act of acquisition until the money has been paid. [7]**Why,** then, according to Rabbi Yoḥanan, **did** the

[1]דְּתַנְיָא: "'וְצַרְתָּ הַכֶּסֶף בְּיָדְךָ' — [2]לְרַבּוֹת כָּל דָּבָר הַנִּצְרָר בַּיָּד. [3]דִּבְרֵי רַבִּי יִשְׁמָעֵאל. [4]רַבִּי עֲקִיבָא אוֹמֵר: לְרַבּוֹת כָּל דָּבָר שֶׁיֵּשׁ עָלָיו צוּרָה".

[5]"כֵּיצַד? מָשַׁךְ הֵימֶנּוּ פֵּירוֹת וְלֹא נָתַן לוֹ מָעוֹת, אֵינוֹ יָכוֹל לַחֲזוֹר בּוֹ וכו'".

[6]אָמַר רַבִּי יוֹחָנָן: דְּבַר תּוֹרָה, מָעוֹת קוֹנוֹת. [7]וּמִפְּנֵי מָה אָמְרוּ

LITERAL TRANSLATION

[1]As it has been taught: "'And you shall bind up the money in your hand' — [2]to include everything that can be bound up in the hand. [3][These are] the words of Rabbi Yishmael. [4]Rabbi Akiva says: To include everything that has an impression on it."

[5]"How so? [If] he [the buyer] drew produce from him [the seller] but did not give him money, he cannot retract, etc."

[6]Rabbi Yoḥanan said: By Torah law, money acquires. [7]And why did they say

SAGES

רַבִּי עֲקִיבָא **Rabbi Akiva.** A Tanna of the fourth generation. See *Bava Metzia*, Part II, p. 314.

BACKGROUND

וְצַרְתָּ הַכֶּסֶף **And you shall bind up the money.** The word כֶּסֶף can mean either the metal silver or money of any kind. Here Rabbi Yishmael takes the term to mean the metal — something of intrinsic value. Rabbi Akiva's words, however, must be taken not only as an interpretation of the expression וְצַרְתָּ — "and you shall bind up" — thus giving the silver a form (צוּרָה), but also as meaning that the very necessity of binding up the money implies that the verse does not refer to a piece of metal but rather to silver coins — pieces of silver with a fixed value.

מָעוֹת קוֹנוֹת **Money acquires.** *Ḥatam Sofer* has an original suggestion. He argues that symbolic acts of acquisition need to be performed only when it is necessary to formally finalize a transaction that the parties have yet to complete. But if the parties have completed their transaction — i.e., the buyer has paid the seller the entire purchase price and has taken delivery of the merchandise — there is no need for any further ceremonial act of acquisition. According to this view, when the Torah declares that payment of money, and not *meshikhah*, is the necessary act of acquisition, this means that a sale can be finalized through payment of money even if the entire price is not yet paid, and the object has not yet been delivered. But a sale that is complete in all its details is obviously valid. Thus it is possible to make a gift that is valid by Torah law by simply giving the recipient the object and having him take it home — not because the recipient has performed *meshikhah*, but because all the details of the transaction are complete and there is no need for a formal act of acquisition.

NOTES

דְּבַר תּוֹרָה, מָעוֹת קוֹנוֹת **By Torah law, money acquires.** Our commentary follows most Rishonim, who explain that, according to Rabbi Yoḥanan, by Torah law money alone acquires and *meshikhah* is of no effect. According to this view, the Rabbis instituted *meshikhah* in place of the payment of money, which they invalidated. This explanation finds support in the parallel passage in tractate *Bekhorot* (13b) which reads: "By Torah law it is money that acquires and not *meshikhah*" (see *Ramban*, *Rashba* and others).

The Rishonim ask: Not every transfer of ownership involves sale; it is also possible to give property away. How then, according to the Torah law as understood by Rabbi Yoḥanan — in which *meshikhah* was not a valid act of acquisition — could a person transfer ownership of movable property as a gift rather than as a sale?

As a result of this objection, *Tosafot* (*Avodah Zarah* 71a) suggests that even Rabbi Yoḥanan would agree that *meshikhah* is valid by Torah law for the transfer of gifts and the like. *Ramban*, however, insists that, according to Rabbi Yoḥanan, *meshikhah* is of absolutely no effect by Torah law. He suggests that a person wishing to make a gift before the Rabbinic enactment would have had to use some other act of acquisition, such as transferring the ownership of movable property together with land.

מָעוֹת קוֹנוֹת **Money acquires.** The Rishonim ask: The Gemara insists on finding a Scriptural source for Resh Lakish's statement that *meshikhah* is a valid act of acquisition by Torah law. But what is Rabbi Yoḥanan's source for saying that payment of money is a valid act of acquisition for movable property by Torah law? Why does the Gemara assume that the payment of money is a valid

TRANSLATION AND COMMENTARY

Rabbis **say that** it is ***meshikhah*** that **acquires** movable goods, and not monetary payment? What reason did the Rabbis have to reverse the Torah procedure? [1]Rabbi Yoḥanan explains: **It was a preventive measure** taken by the Rabbis, **lest the seller say to** the buyer: **"Your wheat was burnt in the upper story** of my house after you paid me." By Torah law, a sale is finalized upon payment of money. Thus, if a buyer pays a seller for a quantity of wheat, for example, the wheat immediately becomes the property of the buyer, and any subsequent damage it may suffer is the buyer's responsibility. Hence, if a fire breaks out in the seller's attic, where the wheat is stored, the buyer has to suffer the loss, and cannot demand a refund. By contrast, under the law of the Mishnah, it is the act of *meshikhah* that finalizes the sale. Hence, if the wheat is destroyed by fire after the buyer has paid for it but before he has had a chance to collect it from the seller, the seller has to refund him the money. The Rabbis preferred that the person in physical possession of merchandise be responsible for it, for reasons the Gemara will presently explain. Therefore the Rabbis reversed the Torah procedure and introduced the law of *meshikhah*.

מְשִׁיכָה קוֹנָה? [1]גְּזֵירָה, שֶׁמָּא יֹאמַר לוֹ: ״נִשְׂרְפוּ חִטֶּיךָ בַּעֲלִיָּיה״.

LITERAL TRANSLATION

[that] *meshikhah* acquires? [1][It was] a preventive measure, lest he [the seller] say to him: "Your wheat was burnt in the upper story."

NOTES

act of acquisition, unless formally invalidated by a verse (according to Resh Lakish) or by Rabbinic decree (according to Rabbi Yoḥanan)?

Many Rishonim explain that the Gemara's assumption is based on an *a fortiori* argument from the purchase of a Hebrew slave. An Israelite in extreme poverty could sell himself for a period of six years as a slave, and the transaction was effected by the payment of money. Now, if it is possible to purchase a person as a Hebrew slave by paying him money, it should also be possible to purchase in the same way any kind of property a person may own (*Rif, Ramban*, others).

Rashi suggests another *a fortiori* argument, based on movable property dedicated to the Temple. Such property could be redeemed from the Temple treasury by payment of money. Now, if movable property can be acquired from the Temple by mere payment of money, it should certainly be possible to acquire it from an ordinary owner in the same way.

Some Rishonim suggest that there is no need of a special source for the Gemara's assumption that payment of money is a valid act of acquisition for movable property unless proven otherwise. They note that payment of money is a valid act of acquisition for many other purposes, notably for buying real estate, as well as for buying slaves and redeeming property dedicated to the Temple. Therefore, although the Torah did not explicitly state that paying money is a valid mode of acquisition of movable property, it appeared obvious to the Gemara that we should assume it to be valid unless the Torah or the Sages formally invalidated it (*Rosh*).

וּמִפְּנֵי מָה אָמְרוּ מְשִׁיכָה קוֹנָה And why did they say that *meshikhah* acquires? The Rishonim ask: Why did the Sages invalidate money payment altogether? Why did they not require both acts — payment of money *and meshikhah* — to finalize a sale?

Rosh answers that the Sages did not want to complicate business transactions by requiring a double act of acquisition. Since payment of money was deemed unsuitable, it was entirely replaced by *meshikhah*.

Tosafot answers that if the Sages were to require two acts of acquisition, a problem would arise if the buyer performed *meshikhah* before paying for the merchandise. In such a case, the merchandise would still be the property of the seller, even though it would already be in the physical possession of the buyer. Hence, if a fire were to break out in the buyer's attic, the seller would suffer unfairly. Therefore the Rabbis declared *meshikhah* alone to be the legal way of finalizing a sale of movable property.

גְּזֵירָה, שֶׁמָּא יֹאמַר לוֹ נִשְׂרְפוּ חִטֶּיךָ בַּעֲלִיָּיה It was a preventive measure, lest the seller say to the buyer: "Your wheat was burnt in the upper story." The Rishonim ask: Why did the Rabbis apply this decree only to monetary payments? Why is *kinyan sudar* — kerchief acquisition — effective even before the buyer picks up his merchandise? Why were the Rabbis not concerned that the seller might say to the buyer: "After you handed me your kerchief, your merchandise was destroyed in a fire in my attic"?

Ramban explains that a *kinyan sudar* is ordinarily used in a case where the buyer still owes the seller money. Hence, the seller will take exceptional care not to let the merchandise be damaged, lest the buyer refuse to pay his debt and force the seller to sue him in court.

Alternatively, *Ramban* explains that *kinyan sudar* is merely a special kind of *ḥalifin*. In theory, *ḥalifin* is supposed to be an exchange of two objects of similar value, and in such a case, as soon as one of the objects is exchanged, the transaction is considered complete, even before the other object is handed over. Thus at the stage when *ḥalifin* takes effect, both items are in the possession of one of the parties, and if a fire breaks out in that party's attic and destroys both items, the other party will lose, regardless of whether or not the sale is complete. Because in such a situation it is impossible to avoid the risk of loss, there is no reason to depart from the procedure established by Torah law.

HALAKHAH

מָעוֹת וּמְשִׁיכָה Money and *meshikhah*. "By Torah law, monetary payment effects a sale. But the Rabbis decreed that a sale is valid only if the buyer draws the merchandise into his possession or lifts it up," following Rabbi Yoḥanan, whose opinion is generally accepted when he differs with Resh Lakish. (*Shulḥan Arukh, Ḥoshen Mishpat* 198:1.)

TERMINOLOGY

סוֹף סוֹף At all events (lit., "the end," "finally"). In the course of a Talmudic discussion, after an objection has been made to a statement and a response has been offered to that objection, the Gemara may then restate its original objection by pointing out the weak point of the answer: "However much I wish to accept your answer, nevertheless my previous objection still stands."

TRANSLATION AND COMMENTARY

סוֹף סוֹף [1]The Gemara objects to Rabbi Yoḥanan's explanation: The Rabbis would not have reversed the Torah procedure and introduced *meshikhah* as an act of acquisition merely in order to save the buyer from loss under these particular circumstances. For even if we had followed Torah procedure, the buyer's interests would still be protected, because **ultimately the** person **who caused the fire** is liable for the damage, and **must pay** the buyer for his wheat.

אֶלָּא [2]**Rather,** Rabbi Yoḥanan's explanation should be amended slightly as follows: Why did the Rabbis reverse the Torah procedure and introduce *meshikhah* as an act of acquisition? **It was a preventive measure lest a fire break out by accident,** in circumstances where nobody is liable for the damage. In such a case, under the original Torah law, the buyer would have to accept the loss, whereas following the Rabbinic decree, the seller is responsible and must refund the money. The Gemara goes on to explain why the Rabbis considered it important that the seller should bear the risk of accidental loss and not the buyer: When the fire breaks out, the wheat is in the seller's physical possession, in his attic, as the buyer has not yet had an opportunity to collect it. The seller was not responsible for the fire; it broke out by accident. But as soon as the fire breaks out, it is the duty of the seller, as guardian of the wheat, to retrieve it from his attic and save it from the fire. Moreover, it is important that the seller move quickly, or the wheat will be lost. [3]Now, **if you place** the wheat **in** the seller's **ownership** and hold him liable for any damage it may suffer, however caused, [4]**he will take pains** and go to the **trouble** needed to **save it** before it is too late. [5]**But if not, he will not.** Therefore the Rabbis preferred that the merchandise remain the responsibility of the person who has it in his physical possession. Accordingly, they decreed that sales of movable property should take effect only after the buyer has performed *meshikhah* and physically drawn the merchandise into his possession.

רֵישׁ לָקִישׁ אָמַר [6]But **Resh Lakish** disagreed with Rabbi Yoḥanan and **said:** *meshikhah* **is** mentioned **explicitly in the Torah.** According to Resh Lakish, the Mishnah's ruling that *meshikhah* but not monetary payment is an effective act of acquisition was not a preventive measure instituted by the Rabbis to protect the interests of the buyer. It was the Torah itself that enacted that *meshikhah* and not monetary payment should finalize a sale.

[1]סוֹף סוֹף מַאן דִּשְׁדָא דְּלֵיקָה בָּעֵי שַׁלּוּמֵי!

[2]אֶלָּא, גְּזֵירָה, שֶׁמָּא תִּפּוֹל דְּלֵיקָה בְּאוֹנֶס. [3]אִי מוֹקְמַתְּ לְהוּ בִּרְשׁוּתֵיהּ, [4]מָסַר נַפְשֵׁיהּ, טָרַח וּמַצִּיל. [5]וְאִי לָא, לָא מָסַר נַפְשֵׁיהּ, טָרַח וּמַצִּיל.

[6]רֵישׁ לָקִישׁ אָמַר: מְשִׁיכָה מְפוֹרֶשֶׁת מִן הַתּוֹרָה.

LITERAL TRANSLATION

[1][But] ultimately the one who caused the fire must pay!

[2]Rather, [it was] a preventive measure, lest a fire break out by accident. [3]If you place it in his ownership, [4]he will take pains (lit., "deliver his soul"), trouble himself and save [it]. [5]But if not, he will not take pains, trouble himself and save [it].

[6]Resh Lakish said: *Meshikhah* is explicit from the Torah.

NOTES

מַאן דִּשְׁדָא דְּלֵיקָה בָּעֵי שַׁלּוּמֵי The one who caused the fire must pay. Our translation and commentary follow the text of the standard Vilna edition. According to this reading, the Gemara originally understood that the Rabbis invalidated the sale if a fire caused by some third party destroyed the merchandise which had been paid for but not yet delivered. The Rabbis did so in order to spare the buyer the difficulty of suing the third party for damages. The Gemara then objected that it was unreasonable to take such radical action merely to spare the buyer some inconvenience, since in any case the third party would have to pay. If the buyer did not sue him, the seller would have to do so. Therefore the Gemara explained that the Rabbis were concerned lest a fire break out by accident (*Magen Gibborim*).

The Rishonim, however, appear to follow the reading found in *Rif*, in which the words "the one who caused the fire" do not appear. According to this version, the Gemara never suggested that there was a third party involved, but assumed all along that the fire had broken out by itself. Initially, however, the Gemara assumed that the seller might have been negligent in some way. Therefore it objected that even if the Rabbis had not instituted *meshikhah*, the seller would still have had to refund the money, because he had the wheat in his custody and was thus a bailee, and a bailee must pay compensation for damage due to negligence. Accordingly, the Gemara suggested that the fire might have broken out by accident, in which case the bailee would not be responsible, and it was for this reason that the Rabbis instituted *meshikhah* (*Ritva*).

מְשִׁיכָה מְפוֹרֶשֶׁת מִן הַתּוֹרָה *Meshikhah* is explicit from the Torah. The primary dispute between Rabbi Yoḥanan and Resh Lakish is theoretical, because in practice, according to both opinions, *meshikhah* and not monetary payment is the valid act of acquisition for movable property. However, the Rishonim note that this dispute does have several practical ramifications.

Thus, in an unusual case where the Rabbis did not apply their decrees, the original Torah law remains in force, and according to Rabbi Yoḥanan payment of money is a valid

TRANSLATION AND COMMENTARY

[1]The Gemara asks: **What is Resh Lakish's reasoning?** Where in the Torah did he find any mention of acquisition by means of *meshikhah*? [2]The Gemara replies: **The verse states** (Leviticus 25:14): **"And if you sell anything to your neighbor or buy anything from the hand of your neighbor,** do not defraud one another." The expression, "buying from the hand of your neighbor" indicates that the verse is speaking about the sale of movable objects — objects that can be held in one's hand. [3]Moreover, according to Resh Lakish, this choice of words also suggests that these **objects are acquired** when an act of *meshikhah* is performed, and the merchandise is transferred **from** the **hand** of the seller **to** the **hand** of the buyer. Thus it was the Torah itself that established the rule that *meshikhah*, and not monetary payment, finalizes the sale of movable property.

וְרַבִּי יוֹחָנָן אָמַר [4]**But Rabbi Yohanan said:** The expression "buying **from the hand of** your neighbor" does indeed indicate that the verse is speaking about movable property that can be held in one's hand. But it does not teach us anything about how movable property is to be acquired; rather, these words were mentioned to teach us that this verse, which deals with the laws of fraud, applies specifically to movable property. [5]The expression "buying from the hand of your neighbor" had to be mentioned in the verse in order **to exclude land, which is not subject to a claim of fraud,** from the purview of the verse. Thus, according to Rabbi Yoḥanan, the verse cited by Resh Lakish does not refer to *meshikhah* at all, and the law of the Mishnah is a Rabbinic institution. The verse is simply teaching us that claims of fraud can be brought only with respect to movable objects that can be passed from hand to hand, but not with respect to land. Accordingly, if a seller overcharged or a buyer underpaid in a sale of land, the defrauded party cannot normally sue for redress. (The details of the law exempting real estate from claims of fraud can be found below, 56a–57a.)

וְרֵישׁ לָקִישׁ [6]The Gemara asks: **And** how can **Resh Lakish** derive from this verse that movables are acquired by *meshikhah*? Surely Resh Lakish also agrees that the inclusion of the phrase "from the hand" was needed to teach us that claims of fraud cannot be brought with respect to land?

אִם כֵּן [7]The Gemara answers: **If so** — if the purpose of the verse was limited to teaching us that claims of fraud cannot be brought with respect to land — **the verse should have stated:** [8]**"And if you sell** anything **from** the hand of **your neighbor,** do **not defraud,"** leaving out the words "or buy anything." [9]**Why** did the Torah **need** to include the words **"or buy anything** from the hand of your neighbor"? [10]We can therefore **conclude from here that** the words are **needed** to teach us that movable property is acquired by performing the act of ***meshikhah***. Since the verse speaks not merely of "selling from one's hand" but rather of "selling and buying from one's hand," we may conclude from here that the Torah wished to teach us two things about movable property: (1) that claims of fraud can be brought only with respect to movable property, and (2) that movable property is acquired through *meshikhah*.

וְרַבִּי יוֹחָנָן [11]The Gemara asks: **And what does Rabbi Yoḥanan do with** the expression **"or buy anything"?** How does he interpret these seemingly superfluous words?

[1]מַאי טַעְמָא דְּרֵישׁ לָקִישׁ? [2]אָמַר קְרָא: "וְכִי תִמְכְּרוּ מִמְכָּר לַעֲמִיתֶךָ אוֹ קָנֹה מִיַּד עֲמִיתֶךָ" — [3]דָּבָר הַנִּקְנֶה מִיָּד לְיָד.
[4]וְרַבִּי יוֹחָנָן אָמַר: "מִיַּד" — [5]לְמַעוּטֵי קַרְקַע, דְּלֵית בָּהּ אוֹנָאָה.
[6]וְרֵישׁ לָקִישׁ?
[7]אִם כֵּן, לִכְתּוֹב קְרָא: [8]"וְכִי תִמְכְּרוּ מִמְכָּר מִיַּד עֲמִיתֶךָ אַל תּוֹנוּ". [9]"אוֹ קָנֹה" לָמָּה לִי? [10]שְׁמַע מִינָּהּ לִמְשִׁיכָה.
[11]וְרַבִּי יוֹחָנָן "אוֹ קָנֹה" מַאי עָבֵיד לֵיהּ?

LITERAL TRANSLATION

[1]What is Resh Lakish's reason? [2]The verse said: "And if you sell anything to your neighbor or buy anything from the hand of your neighbor" — [3]an object that is acquired from hand to hand.

[4]But Rabbi Yoḥanan said: "From the hand of" — [5]to exclude land, which is not subject to [a claim of] fraud.

[6]And Resh Lakish?

[7]If so, let the verse write: [8]"And if you sell anything from your neighbor's hand, do not defraud." [9]Why do I need: "Or buy anything"? [10]Conclude from this [that it is needed for] *meshikhah*.

[11]And what does Rabbi Yoḥanan do with "or buy anything"?

RASHI

למעוטי קרקע מאונאה — דאישתעי ביה קרא אתי, דכיון דאינה נקחת מיד ליד אין בו אונאה. **נכתוב כי תמכרו ממכר מיד עמיתך אל תונו** — מאי "או קנה"? להכי כתביה — למסמך קנין ל"מיד", לומר שאין נקנה עד שיצא מיד זה ליד זה.

BACKGROUND

דָּבָר הַנִּקְנֶה מִיָּד לְיָד An object that is acquired from hand to hand. The difference of opinion between Rabbi Yoḥanan and Resh Lakish concerns the issue of whether the expressions קָנֹה מִיַּד — "buying from the hand" — and מִמְכָּר מִיַּד — "selling from the hand" — should be taken literally, or whether "hand" has an extended meaning, as it does in the laws of acquisition of possession or ownership. In Rabbi Yoḥanan's view, the literal meaning of the phrase מִיַּד — "from the hand of" — has only negative force, meaning that this refers only to something which could literally be placed in someone's hand. However, in Resh Lakish's view, the term must be taken as meaning an actual hand, so that the transfer of ownership is a transfer from hand to hand, which is acquisition by *meshikhah*.

NOTES

means of acquisition (see above, 46b and 47a). Moreover, in cases connected with ritual law, it is sometimes necessary to determine the status of property by Torah law, disregarding subsequent Rabbinic decrees (*Rashi, Ritva*).

TRANSLATION AND COMMENTARY

מִיבָּעֵי לֵיהּ לִכְדְתַנְיָא [1]The Gemara answers: This expression **was necessary** according to Rabbi Yoḥanan to teach us another detail in the laws of fraud. For these words serve as the basis **of what has been taught in the following Baraita: "'And if you sell anything...do not defraud.'** [2]From these words alone, **I would only know** that the laws of fraud apply **where the buyer was defrauded,** i.e., where the seller overcharged, as it is the duty of the seller to inform the buyer of the true value of the merchandise he is selling so that the buyer can make an informed decision. [3]But **from where do we know** that these laws apply even **where the seller was defrauded** — i.e., where the buyer underpaid? How do we know that the buyer, too, must inform the seller if he is charging too little for his merchandise, and must not take advantage of the seller's mistake by arguing that the seller should have known how much his merchandise was really worth?" [4]The Baraita answers: **"The Torah states: 'Or buy anything... do not defraud,'** implying that the laws of fraud also apply if it is the buyer who is defrauding the seller." Thus the entire verse is needed to teach us the laws of fraud, and the mention of buying "from the hand" is needed to teach us that claims of fraud — both with respect to buying and with respect to selling — apply specifically to movable property. Thus there is no room for Resh Lakish's inference.

וְרֵישׁ לָקִישׁ [5]The Gemara asks: **And** how could **Resh Lakish** infer from this verse that movable property is acquired through *meshikhah*? Surely Resh Lakish also agrees that the inclusion of the phrase "or buy anything" was needed to teach us that the laws of fraud apply even where the buyer defrauded the seller?

תַּרְתֵּי גָּמַר מִינֵּיהּ [6]The Gemara answers: Resh Lakish **learns two things from** the additional words "or buy anything." (1) The words themselves inform us that the buyer is forbidden to defraud the seller. (2) The fact that the phrase "from the hand" — which teaches us that the verse is referring only to movable property — was inserted immediately after the words "or buy," rather than earlier in the verse, informs us that movable property is "bought from the hand," through *meshikhah*.

תְּנַן [7]The Gemara now raises an objection to Resh Lakish's view: **We have learned in the Mishnah** (above, 44a): **"Rabbi Shimon** disagrees with the first opinion cited in the Mishnah, according to which both parties may withdraw from the transaction even after payment has been made as long as *meshikhah* has not yet been performed, and **says:** [8]**Whoever has the money in his hand** — i.e., the seller who has received payment — **has the upper hand** and may retract. But the buyer may not retract once he has paid, even if he has not yet performed *meshikhah*." If the buyer has neither paid for the merchandise nor performed *meshikhah*, it is obvious that both parties can retract, because the transaction has not yet taken place. Thus Rabbi Shimon is clearly referring specifically to a case where the buyer has already paid the money but has not yet performed *meshikhah*. [9]According to Rabbi Shimon, if the buyer has paid for the merchandise but has not yet performed *meshikhah*, it is only **the seller who may retract,** because he has the money in his hand, [10]but **the buyer may not retract,** since the payment of money has the effect of finalizing the sale from the point of view of the

[1]מִיבָּעֵי לֵיהּ לִכְדְתַנְיָא: "'וְכִי תִמְכְּרוּ מִמְכָּר אַל תּוֹנוּ'. [2]אֵין לִי אֶלָּא שֶׁנִּתְאַנָּה לוֹקֵחַ; [3]נִתְאַנָּה מוֹכֵר מִנַּיִן? [4]תַּלְמוּד לוֹמַר: 'אוֹ קָנֹה... אַל תּוֹנוּ'".

[5]וְרֵישׁ לָקִישׁ?

[6]תַּרְתֵּי גָּמַר מִינֵּיהּ.

[7]תְּנַן: "רַבִּי שִׁמְעוֹן אוֹמֵר: [8]כָּל שֶׁהַכֶּסֶף בְּיָדוֹ יָדוֹ עַל הָעֶלְיוֹנָה". [9]מוֹכֵר הוּא דְּמָצֵי הָדַר בֵּיהּ; [10]לוֹקֵחַ לָא מָצֵי הָדַר בֵּיהּ.

LITERAL TRANSLATION

[1]He needs it for that which has been taught: "'And if you sell anything...do not defraud.' [2]I have only where the buyer was defrauded; [3]from where [do I have] where the seller was defrauded? [4]The Torah says: 'Or buy anything...do not defraud.'"

[5]And Resh Lakish?

[6]He learns two things from it.

[7]We have learned: "Rabbi Shimon says: [8]Whoever has the money in his hand has the upper hand. [9]It is the seller who may retract; [10]the buyer may not retract.

RASHI

תרתי גמר מיניה — אונאת מוכר מ"או קנה", "אל תונו", ומשיכה מדסמכן "מיד" ללשון קנין, ולא סמכיה ל"ממכר". **כל שהכסף בידו** — פליג אדרבנן דאמרי נתן לו מעות יכול לחזור בו זה וזה, ופליג רבי שמעון ואמר: לא יחזור אלא מוכר.

HALAKHAH

אוֹנָאַת מוֹכֵר **Defrauding the seller.** "It is forbidden both for the buyer to underpay and for the seller to overcharge, as the Torah states: 'Do not defraud,' and one who does so violates a Torah prohibition." (*Shulḥan Arukh, Ḥoshen Mishpat* 227:1.)

[1]אִי אָמְרַתְּ בִּשְׁלָמָא מָעוֹת קוֹנוֹת, [2]מִשּׁוּם הָכִי מוֹכֵר מָצֵי הָדַר בֵּיהּ, [3]לוֹקֵחַ לֹא מָצֵי הָדַר בֵּיהּ. [4]אֶלָּא אִי אָמְרַתְּ מָעוֹת אֵינָן קוֹנוֹת, [5]לוֹקֵחַ נָמֵי לִיהֲדַר בֵּיהּ!

[6]אָמַר לָךְ רֵישׁ לָקִישׁ: אַלִּיבָּא דְּרַבִּי שִׁמְעוֹן לָא קָאָמִינָא; [7]כִּי קָאָמִינָא אַלִּיבָּא דְּרַבָּנַן.

[8]בִּשְׁלָמָא לְרֵישׁ לָקִישׁ, הַיְינוּ דְּאִיכָּא בֵּין רַבִּי שִׁמְעוֹן לְרַבָּנַן. [9]אֶלָּא לְרַבִּי יוֹחָנָן, מַאי אִיכָּא בֵּין רַבִּי שִׁמְעוֹן לְרַבָּנַן?

LITERAL TRANSLATION

[1]Granted if you say [that] money acquires, [2]because of this the seller may retract [3][and] the buyer may not retract. [4]But if you say [that] money does not acquire, [5]let the buyer also retract!

[6]Resh Lakish can say to you: I do not say [this] according to Rabbi Shimon; [7]I say [it] according to the Sages.

[8]Granted according to Resh Lakish, this is [the issue] between Rabbi Shimon and the Sages. [9]But according to Rabbi Yoḥanan, what [issue] is there between Rabbi Shimon and the Sages?

TRANSLATION AND COMMENTARY

buyer. [1]Now, **if you say that money acquires** by Torah law, [2]**it is** quite clear why Rabbi Shimon maintains that **it is** only **the seller who may retract** [3]**and** that **the buyer may not retract.** If by Torah law a sale can be effected through monetary payment, then by right neither party should be able to retract. It is true that the Rabbis invalidated monetary payment as an act of acquisition, in order to insure the buyer against loss by fire before delivery. But there is no reason to grant the buyer additional privileges. The seller, who must accept the responsibilities of ownership, is entitled to its privileges as well. Since he remains liable for accidental damage, he can also withdraw from the sale. But the buyer, who will not suffer a loss if the merchandise is damaged, should continue to be governed by Torah law, and there is no reason to permit him to retract. [4]**But if you say that money does not acquire** movable property even by Torah law, [5]**let the buyer also** have the right to **retract,** since the payment of the money by the buyer was totally without legal validity! How, then, can Resh Lakish explain Rabbi Shimon's opinion?

אָמַר לָךְ רֵישׁ לָקִישׁ [6]The Gemara answers: **Resh Lakish** can **say to you** in reply: **I did not state** my view **according to Rabbi Shimon;** [7]**I stated** my view only **according to the Sages.** According to Resh Lakish, it is the Sages who maintain that *meshikhah* acquires movable property by Torah law. They therefore rule that both parties may retract as long as *meshikhah* has not been performed. But even Resh Lakish would agree that, according to Rabbi Shimon, *meshikhah* is a Rabbinic decree, and by Torah law it is money that acquires. This is why Rabbi Shimon rules that only the seller may retract.

בִּשְׁלָמָא לְרֵישׁ לָקִישׁ [8]The Gemara now raises an objection to Rabbi Yoḥanan's view: **According to Resh Lakish, it is** quite **clear what the issue in dispute is between Rabbi Shimon and the Sages.** According to Resh Lakish, the dispute between Rabbi Shimon and the Sages in the Mishnah is precisely the same as that between Rabbi Yoḥanan and Resh Lakish. [9]**But according to Rabbi Yoḥanan, what is the issue in dispute between Rabbi Shimon and the Sages?** Rabbi Yoḥanan must maintain that the Sages agree with Rabbi Shimon that *meshikhah* is a Rabbinic decree. Why, then, are the Sages of the opinion that both the seller and the buyer may retract? Why do they not accept Rabbi Shimon's argument in this matter?

RASHI

אי אמרת בשלמא דבר תורה מעות קונות – ומשיכה תקנתא דרבנן היא, אתא רבי שמעון למימר דיינו אם אמרינן חזרה במוכר, דמכי מוקמת להו ברשותיה לחזור בו אם הוקרו, מסר נפשיה לאצוליניהו, מימר אמר: עדיין שכרי תלוי בהם, שאם יתייקרו אחזור בי, ולוקח לא מצי הדר ביה, דמעות קונות. אלא אי אמרת מן התורה מעות אינן קונות, לוקח נמי יחזור! **אליבא דרבי שמעון ודאי לא קאמינא** – דרבי שמעון סבירא ליה משיכה תקנתא דרבנן היא. **כי קאמינא אליבא דרבנן** – דאמרי לוקח נמי חוזר, משום דמעות אינן קונות כלל. **בשלמא לריש לקיש** – דאמר לרבנן משיכה דאורייתא היא. **היינו דאיכא בין רבי שמעון לרבנן** – כלומר בהא פליגי, והאי טעם יהבו למלתייהו, דרבנן סברי משיכה דאורייתא, והלכך לא שנא מוכר ולא שנא לוקח מצי הדרי. ורבי שמעון סבר משיכה תקנתא דרבנן היא, משום דנטרח בהו, הלכך למוכר הוא דעבוד רבנן תקנתא דליהדר, ולא לוקח. **אלא לרבי יוחנן** – דאמר לרבנן נמי משיכה תקנתא דרבנן היא. **מאי איכא בין רבי שמעון לרבנן** – כלומר במאי קמיפלגי, ומה טעם נותנים לדבריהם?

NOTES

אִי אָמְרַתְּ בִּשְׁלָמָא מָעוֹת קוֹנוֹת Granted if you say that money acquires. Our commentary follows *Rabbenu Ḥananel*, who explains that the prerogative of retracting was granted to the seller in consideration of his liability for accidental damage, and there is no reason to grant a similar prerogative to the buyer.

Rashi, however, explains that the purpose of the decree was to encourage the seller to save the wheat if a fire broke out. The decree did not expressly shift liability for loss to the seller, but created a situation which encouraged the seller to look after the wheat as long as it was still in his possession. During this period the seller could take advantage of any increase in the market price of the wheat and sell it to someone else at the higher price. By giving the seller this advantage, the Rabbis encouraged him to look after the wheat.

[1]אִיכָּא בֵּינַיְיהוּ דְּרַב חִסְדָּא. [2]דְּאָמַר רַב חִסְדָּא: כְּדֶרֶךְ שֶׁתִּקְּנוּ מְשִׁיכָה בַּמּוֹכְרִין, [3]כָּךְ תִּקְּנוּ מְשִׁיכָה בַּלָּקוֹחוֹת. [4]רַבִּי שִׁמְעוֹן לֵית לֵיהּ דְּרַב חִסְדָּא; [5]רַבָּנַן אִית לְהוּ דְּרַב חִסְדָּא.
[6]תְּנַן: "אֲבָל אָמְרוּ: [7]מִי שֶׁפָּרַע מִדּוֹר הַמַּבּוּל הוּא עָתִיד לִיפָּרַע מִמִּי שֶׁאֵינוֹ עוֹמֵד בְּדִיבּוּרוֹ". [8]אִי אָמְרַתְּ בִּשְׁלָמָא מָעוֹת קוֹנוֹת, [9]מִשּׁוּם הָכִי קָאֵי בַּ"אֲבָל", [10]אֶלָּא אִי אָמְרַתְּ מָעוֹת אֵינָן קוֹנוֹת, [11]אַמַּאי קָאֵי בַּ"אֲבָל"?

LITERAL TRANSLATION

[1]There is [a disagreement] between them [regarding] that which Rav Ḥisda [said]. [2]For Rav Ḥisda said: In the [same] way as they enacted *meshikhah* for sellers, [3]so too they enacted *meshikhah* for buyers. [4]Rabbi Shimon does not accept [the ruling] of Rav Ḥisda; [5]the Sages do accept [the ruling] of Rav Ḥisda.

[6]We have learned: "But they said: [7]He who punished the generation of the flood will punish him who does not stand by his word." [8]Granted if you say [that] money acquires, [9]because of this he is subject to "But...." [10]But if you say [that] money does not acquire, [11]why is he subject to "But..."?

TRANSLATION AND COMMENTARY

אִיכָּא בֵּינַיְיהוּ דְּרַב חִסְדָּא [1]The Gemara explains: Even according to Rabbi Yoḥanan, **there is an issue in dispute between** Rabbi Shimon and the Sages. They differ **regarding** the following ruling issued by **Rav Ḥisda.** [2]**For Rav Ḥisda said: In the same way as** the Rabbis **enacted** ***meshikhah*** **for sellers,** [3]**so too did they enact** ***meshikhah*** **for buyers,** because the Rabbis declared *meshikhah*, and not monetary payment, to be the valid act of acquisition for movable property. Even though, as Rabbi Shimon argued, there is no logical reason for the Rabbis to allow the buyer to retract, because the rationale behind the enactment pertains to the seller alone, nevertheless according to Rav Ḥisda the enactment was absolute and is not dependent on the rationale behind it. Thus, until the buyer performs *meshikhah*, both parties may retract. The Gemara now explains the dispute between Rabbi Shimon and the Sages according to Rabbi Yoḥanan: Both Rabbi Shimon and the Sages agree that *meshikhah* is a Rabbinic enactment, [4]but **Rabbi Shimon did not accept the ruling of Rav Ḥisda,** [5]whereas **the Sages did.** Therefore Rabbi Shimon is of the opinion that the buyer may not retract, whereas the Sages are of the opinion that both parties may retract until the sale is finalized by *meshikhah*.

תְּנַן [6]The Gemara now raises an objection to Resh Lakish's view, from our Mishnah. **We** have **learned** in the Mishnah: **"But** the Sages **said:** [7]God **who** punished **the generation of the flood will punish anyone who does not stand by his word."** Even though both parties have the prerogative of retracting before *meshikhah* is performed, the Rabbis declared that the party who retracts is subject to a curse. (From now on, the Gemara will refer to this curse — "But the Sages said: God who punished..." — in an abbreviated form as "But....")
[8]The Gemara explains its objection: **If you say that money acquires** movable property by Torah law, [9]then **it is clear why** a party who retracts **is subject to the "But..."** curse mentioned in the Mishnah. For monetary payment, though invalid by Rabbinic decree, is nevertheless binding by Torah law. Therefore, by Torah law the retractor is guilty of taking advantage of the Rabbis' enactment to commit what would otherwise be a crime, and this carries a severe moral stigma. [10]**But if you say that** even by Torah law **money does not acquire** movable property, [11]**why is** a party who retracts after paying money **subject to the "But..."** curse? Until a transaction is completed, it is certainly permissible for a party to it to change his mind. Why should the Rabbis curse him for doing so? There is surely nothing objectionable about withdrawing from a transaction that is not yet binding!

RASHI

כדרך שתקנו משיכה למוכרין – לחזור בו המוכר כל זמן שלא משך הלוקח.
כך תקנו חכמים משיכה ללוקח – לחזור בו בשביל אותה תקנה עצמה ד"נשרפו חטיך", דכל שכן כי מוקמת לחזרה נמי ברשות לוקח מסר נפשיה המוכר וטרח ומציל, שאם יראה הלוקח דליקה באה יאמר: חוזרני בי. ולקמן (מט,ב) אמרה רב חסדא גבי ההוא דיהב זוזי אמרא, שמע דבעו למינסביה דבי פרזוק רופילא והדר ביה.

NOTES

אִיכָּא בֵּינַיְיהוּ דְּרַב חִסְדָּא There is a disagreement between them regarding that which Rav Ḥisda said. The expression אִיכָּא בֵּינַיְיהוּ — "there is a difference between them" — usually indicates that the Gemara is seeking to determine the practical ramifications of a theoretical dispute. Here, however, the phrase clearly cannot be explained in this way, as the dispute between Rabbi Shimon and the Sages has obvious practical ramifications. According to Rabbi Shimon, the buyer may not retract, whereas according to the Sages, he may. In fact, the Gemara is really trying to determine the theoretical basis of a practical dispute! Thus the phrase should be explained as though it read מַאי קָמִיפַּלְגִי — "about what do they disagree?" (*Rashi* and others.)

כְּדֶרֶךְ שֶׁתִּקְּנוּ מְשִׁיכָה בַּמּוֹכְרִין, כָּךְ תִּקְּנוּ מְשִׁיכָה בַּלָּקוֹחוֹת In the same way as they enacted ***meshikhah*** **for sellers, so too they enacted** ***meshikhah*** **for buyers.** Our commentary follows *Ramban,* who explains that there is no compelling

SAGES

רַב חִסְדָּא Rav Ḥisda. Considered among the greatest Babylonian Amoraim of the second generation, Rav Ḥisda, a priest, was one of Rav's younger students. After Rav's death he remained a colleague and student of Rav's student, Rav Huna. Throughout his life Rav Ḥisda showed great affection for Rav's words, and tried to add to his knowledge of Rav's teachings. Though he was poor as a youth, he became wealthy and lived most of his life in comfort. He was affable towards his fellowmen, and devoted to his students, to his sons, and to his daughters, guiding them along the right path in both spiritual and worldly matters.
Rav Ḥisda is regarded as one of the most sharp-witted and profound thinkers of his generation, while his friend and colleague, Rav Sheshet, was known for his wide knowledge.
Rav Ḥisda served as a judge in Sura for many years, together with Rav Huna, and both of them continued the tradition of Rav's school. After Rav Huna's death, Rav Ḥisda took his place as head of the Sura Yeshivah. Much is told of his deeds of charity.
He lived to the age of ninety-two. Many of the Sages of the following generation were his students, and he had many sons who became Sages: Rav Ḥanan bar Rav Ḥisda, Mar Yenuka and Mar Keshisha, Rav Mari, Rav Pinḥas and Rav Taḥlifa. However, Rav Ḥisda used to say that he preferred his daughters to his sons because they married the greatest Sages of the generation, Mar Ukva bar Ḥama and his brother, Rami bar Ḥama. The daughter referred to as "the daughter of Rav Ḥisda," who married Rami bar Ḥama, later married Rava.

TRANSLATION AND COMMENTARY

מִשּׁוּם דְּבָרִים [1]The Gemara answers: The Rabbis cursed the party who retracts **because of his words.** Since the buyer promised to buy and the seller to sell, they are expected to fulfill their promises. Hence, if one of the parties does not keep his word, he is subject to the "But..." curse, even though the sale was not yet finalized and the party who retracted is not guilty of any crime, either by Torah law or by Rabbinic law.

וּבִדְבָרִים [2]The Gemara now objects: **But is** a person **subject to the "But..."** curse **because of** mere **words?** Violation of a promise, though morally reprehensible, should not be subject to any sanction whatsoever, as long as the transaction has not been completed! [3]**Surely it has been taught** in the following Baraita: [48A] **"Rabbi Shimon says:** [4]**Even though** the Rabbis **said that a garment acquires a gold dinar,** because the act of *meshikhah* finalizes the sale of movable goods and creates an obligation to pay, [5]but **a gold dinar does not acquire a garment,** because monetary payment without *meshikhah* does not finalize a sale, nevertheless the matter is not quite so simple. [6]**It is true that this is the law,** and as long as *meshikhah* has not been performed, either party can retract and the courts will not enforce the sale. [7]**But** the Rabbis cursed the person who withdrew from a transaction at this point, **saying: God, who punished the men of the generation of the flood,** [8]**and the men of the generation of the dispersion, and the people of Sodom and Gomorrah, and the Egyptians at the Red Sea,** [9]**will punish** anyone who **does not stand**

[1]מִשּׁוּם דְּבָרִים.

[2]וּבִדְבָרִים מִי קָאֵי בְּ"אֲבָל"? [3]וְהָתַנְיָא: [48A] "רַבִּי שִׁמְעוֹן אוֹמֵר: [4]אַף עַל פִּי שֶׁאָמְרוּ טַלִּית קוֹנָה דִּינַר זָהָב, [5]וְאֵין דִּינַר זָהָב קוֹנֶה טַלִּית, [6]מִכָּל מָקוֹם כָּךְ הֲלָכָה, [7]אֲבָל אָמְרוּ: מִי שֶׁפָּרַע מֵאַנְשֵׁי דוֹר הַמַּבּוּל, [8]וּמֵאַנְשֵׁי דוֹר הַפַּלָּגָה, וּמֵאַנְשֵׁי סְדוֹם וַעֲמוֹרָה, וּמִמִּצְרַיִם בַּיָּם, [9]הוּא עָתִיד לִיפָּרַע מִמִּי שֶׁאֵינוֹ עוֹמֵד

LITERAL TRANSLATION

[1]Because of [his] words.

[2]But is one subject to "But..." because of words? [3]But surely it has been taught: [48A] "Rabbi Shimon says: [4]Even though they said [that] a garment acquires a gold dinar, [5]but a gold dinar does not acquire a garment, [6]at all events that is the law, [7]but they said: He who punished the men of the generation of the flood, [8]and the men of the generation of the dispersion, and the men of Sodom and Gomorrah, and the Egyptians at the Sea, [9]He will punish him who does not stand by

RASHI

ואין דינר זהב קונה טלית — דלגבי פירות הוי דהכא טבעא. מכל מקום — כלומר, אף לפי פורענות העתידה לבוא על החוזר. כן הלכה — שאין בית דין יכולין לעכב בידו.

BACKGROUND

מִכָּל מָקוֹם כָּךְ הֲלָכָה **At all events, that is the law.** The expression "that is the law" means that this is how a court rules: Once the act of *meshikhah* has been performed, the court uses every means of coercion available to it and forces the parties to complete the transaction, but when the act of *meshikhah* has not yet taken place, the court is unable to compel the reluctant party to complete the transaction, though it is empowered to use other means of persuasion short of actual coercion.

NOTES

reason to allow the buyer to withdraw from the transaction if the price of the merchandise drops, since the prerogative of withdrawal was granted in compensation for assuming the risk of loss in the event that the wheat was destroyed, and it is only the seller who assumes this risk. Nevertheless, since the Rabbis ruled that monetary payment should not be considered an act of acquisition at all, they applied their decree equally to both the seller and the buyer.

Rashi, however, argues that it is perhaps even more important to allow the buyer to retract than it is to allow the seller. Since the purpose of the decree was to encourage the seller to do his duty and save the wheat from a fire, the seller will be even more anxious to do so if he knows that the buyer too can cancel the sale at any time (see also previous note).

מִכָּל מָקוֹם כָּךְ הֲלָכָה **At all events, that is the law.** This phrase literally means: "In every instance the Halakhah is so." Our translation and commentary is based on *Rashi*, who explains the phrase in context as follows: "Even though I am about to say that reneging on a promise is subject to a severe curse, nevertheless (מִכָּל מָקוֹם) I concede that, according to the strict Halakhah, the contract is unenforceable."

The Gemara (below, 74b) uses the literal translation of the phrase to suggest that according to Rabbi Shimon there are other circumstances, not explicitly stated, where the curse is applied. Accordingly, the Gemara suggests that Rabbi Shimon's ruling — that only the seller may retract — applies only to retraction without grounds; however, if prices fluctuate greatly, Rabbi Shimon would agree that the buyer can also retract, although he too is subject to the curse of the Mishnah for doing so.

מֵאַנְשֵׁי דוֹר הַמַּבּוּל וּמֵאַנְשֵׁי דוֹר הַפַּלָּגָה **The men of the generation of the flood, and the men of the generation of the dispersion.** The Baraita lists a number of instances mentioned in the Torah in which God intervened directly to punish evildoers. The story of Noaḥ and the flood is found in Genesis, chapters 6-8. The story of the building of the Tower of Babel and the dispersion that followed is found in Genesis, chapter 11. The story of the destruction of the evil cities of Sodom and Gomorrah is found in Genesis, chapters 18-19. The story of the destruction of Pharaoh and

HALAKHAH

הַחוֹזֵר מִקִּנְיַן מָעוֹת **One who reneges on a sale effected with monetary payment.** "If someone has paid for something but has not yet drawn the merchandise into his possession, the sale is not valid. However, if one of the parties retracts, he is subject to the curse of 'He who punished....'" (*Shulḥan Arukh, Ḥoshen Mishpat* 204:1.)

TRANSLATION AND COMMENTARY

by this word." Up to this point, the Baraita has done nothing more than state the law of our Mishnah (above, 44a) in slightly different words. [1]Now, however, the Baraita considers a slightly different case: **"And someone who does business with** mere **words,** and promises to buy or sell something but has not yet given or received any money or performed any formal act of acquisition, **does not acquire** or transfer ownership of the merchandise he has promised to buy or sell, because a formal act of acquisition must be performed to finalize any transaction. [2]**But** nevertheless, **if he goes back on his word** and reneges on his promise, **the spirit of the Sages is displeased with him** — i.e., his behavior meets with the disapproval of the Sages, because it is unethical to break a promise." Thus we see from this Baraita that violation of a promise, though morally reprehensible, is not subject to any sanction, as long as the sale is not complete.

LITERAL TRANSLATION

his word. [1]And someone who does business with words does not acquire, [2]but someone who goes back on [his word], the spirit of the Sages is not pleased with him."

בְּדִיבּוּרוֹ. [1]וְהַנּוֹשֵׂא וְנוֹתֵן בִּדְבָרִים לֹא קָנָה, [2]וְהַחוֹזֵר בּוֹ, אֵין רוּחַ חֲכָמִים נוֹחָה הֵימֶנּוּ."

RASHI

אין רוח חכמים נוחה הימנו — אין נחת רוח לחכמי ישראל במעשיו של זה, אין דעתם נוחה עליהם. הימנו = על ידו.

BACKGROUND

דְּבָרִים Words. The central issue with regard to obligations (whether oral or written) in which a person promises to do something, although these obligations are not legally binding, is discussed in various places in the Talmud.

It is necessary to distinguish between an obligation to contribute to charity, which is a form of consecration of property, and one person's promise to someone else that he will complete a certain business transaction with him or give him a present. In the first instance, simply making the promise creates an absolute obligation (from the viewpoint of the Halakhah as well). In the second instance, however, the Halakhah distinguishes between intentionally telling a lie and taking back a promise which was initially meant sincerely.

Telling a lie is only punishable if the liar was aware at the time he told the lie or made the promise that he was telling an untruth. It is not a punishable transgression if a person sincerely meant what he said and intended to keep his promise, or if he believed that what he was saying was true at the time he said it. Nevertheless, failure to keep one's word is immoral, and a violation of trust between people. Therefore the Sages are pleased with people of good faith who keep their word and who feel obligated to act as they said they would. Moreover, a virtue highly praised by the Sages is that of fulfilling one's tacit commercial obligations, even if they were not stated explicitly.

Although failure to keep a promise or an obligation is a moral and social fault, the Sages only rarely issue Halakhic rulings in civil suits that are not firmly based in law. When issues touch upon inner moral qualities or on matters of ritual law — which are essentially issues of man's relations with his Creator — the Sages *do* pronounce strict rulings even when they are based on moral considerations which may not be central to the Torah law. However, in civil suits — in which every case has two sides, and a strict ruling

NOTES

the Egyptian army at the Red Sea is found in Exodus, chapter 14.

The Rishonim ask: It is clear that in all these cases, the people concerned were guilty of serious crimes against their fellowmen, but why are these four cases appropriate to the case discussed here in the Mishnah and the Gemara? *Rosh* and *Meiri* explain two of these cases. Pharaoh was singled out because he regularly broke his promises (throughout the events narrated in chapters 8, 9 and 10 of Exodus). *Rosh* points out that the generation of the flood were known for their deceit (Genesis 6:13). *Meiri* adds that the Jerusalem Talmud explains that the generation of the flood used to take advantage of legal loopholes to steal in such a way that they could not be penalized in court. Thus, these instances were singled out to deter a buyer or a seller who is contemplating doing the same.

As to the other two examples, it is interesting to note that the people of Sodom are said by the Sages to have had no pity on their fellowmen, and to have insisted on taking even the smallest amount to which they had a legal claim (*Avot* 5:13). Concerning the generation of the dispersion, a Midrash (Pirkei DeRabbi Eliezer) says that God destroyed the Tower of Babel because He saw that its builders cared more about a fallen brick than about a fallen person. Thus the people of Sodom and the builders of the Tower may have been singled out in order to deter a buyer or a seller who is concerned only with his legal prerogatives and not with his fellowmen, and is thus prepared to cause another person distress in order to make a profit.

וְהַחוֹזֵר בּוֹ, אֵין רוּחַ חֲכָמִים נוֹחָה הֵימֶנּוּ But someone who goes back on his word, the spirit of the Sages is not pleased with him. The following is a summary of the rules applicable to a person who reneges on a promise, according to *Tosafot* and most Rishonim: (1) If the merchandise is destroyed before *meshikhah* has been performed, even if money has already been paid, the transaction is voided according to all opinions, and there is nothing unethical in demanding one's money back.

(2) If the price of the merchandise fluctuated greatly after the money was paid, and *meshikhah* has not yet been performed, either party has the right to withdraw, according to all opinions. However, anyone who does so is subject to the curse of the Sages, "God, who punished...." Nevertheless, under unusually severe circumstances, a person may choose to suffer the curse to save himself from financial loss (see below, 49a).

(3) If the price of the merchandise is not fluctuating greatly, and the money has already been paid but *meshikhah* has not yet been performed, the seller still has the right to withdraw if he wishes to do so for personal reasons, subject to the "But..." curse. The buyer has the same right according to the Sages, but according to Rabbi Shimon the buyer cannot renege unless the price fluctuates greatly.

(4) If the money has not yet been paid, and *meshikhah* has not yet been performed, but the parties have agreed to the terms of the sale, it is considered unethical to withdraw from the transaction, yet a person who chooses to do so is not subject to any sanction. If the contract concerns a large sum of money, and the parties have no confidence in it until it is formalized, there is an Amoraic dispute as to whether there is any ethical objection to retracting before money is paid (see below, 49a).

(5) Once *meshikhah* has been performed, regardless of whether or not the money has already been paid, the sale is final and may not be revoked unilaterally. The buyer must pay the seller the agreed sum, and neither party can make any changes in the terms of the sale. If either party refuses to fulfill his part in the transaction, he may be sued.

HALAKHAH

הַנּוֹשֵׂא וְנוֹתֵן בִּדְבָרִים Verbal agreements. "A sale cannot be consummated by verbal agreement, even if the agreement was made in the presence of witnesses. As long as the sale was not finalized using one of the standard modes of acquisition, either party may retract." (*Shulḥan Arukh, Ḥoshen Mishpat* 199:1.)

הַחוֹזֵר בּוֹ אֵין רוּחַ חֲכָמִים נוֹחָה הֵימֶנּוּ One who reneges on an agreement arouses the displeasure of the Sages. "A person who enters a verbal agreement must keep his word. If he fails to do so, he arouses the displeasure of the Sages." (Ibid., 204:7.)

¹וְאָמַר רָבָא: אָנוּ אֵין לָנוּ אֶלָּא ״אֵין רוּחַ חֲכָמִים נוֹחָה הֵימֶנּוּ״. ²דְּבָרִים וְאִיכָּא בַּהֲדַיְיהוּ מָעוֹת קָאֵי בַּ״אֲבָל״; ³דְּבָרִים וְלֵיכָּא בַּהֲדַיְיהוּ מָעוֹת לָא קָאֵי בַּ״אֲבָל״.

⁴אֲמַר רָבָא: קְרָא וּמַתְנִיתָא מְסַיֵּיעַ לֵיהּ לְרֵישׁ לָקִישׁ.

⁵קְרָא, דִּכְתִיב: ״וְכִחֵשׁ בַּעֲמִיתוֹ בְּפִקָּדוֹן, ⁶אוֹ בִתְשׂוּמֶת יָד אוֹ בְגָזֵל, ⁷אוֹ עָשַׁק אֶת עֲמִיתוֹ״.

LITERAL TRANSLATION

[1] And Rava said: We have only [that] "the spirit of the Sages is not pleased with him."

[2] Words that have money together with them are subject to "But..."; [3] words that do not have money together with them are not subject to "But...."

[4] Rava said: A [Scriptural] verse and a Baraita support Resh Lakish.

[5] A verse, for it is written: "And lie to his neighbor regarding a deposit, [6] or regarding a loan (lit., "in the putting out of a hand"), or regarding robbery, [7] or he oppressed his neighbor."

TRANSLATION AND COMMENTARY

וְאָמַר רָבָא [1] Now, to prevent us from imagining that the Baraita's two expressions of censure — "the spirit of the Sages is displeased with him," and "But they said: He who punished..." — mean the same thing, and that a person who withdraws from a merely verbal agreement is also subject to the "But..." curse, **Rava said:** The Baraita is to be understood literally as making no condemnation of the person who breaks his verbal undertaking. It **only** states **that "the spirit of the Sages is displeased with him."** But the Sages did not subject him to any curse. Thus we see that violation of a promise, though morally reprehensible, is not subject to the "But..." curse. Why, then, should the Rabbis regard the payment of money followed by withdrawal from the transaction as a situation requiring the more severe response of the curse? Does this not prove that Rabbi Yoḥanan is correct, and that monetary payment does finalize a sale by Torah law?

דְּבָרִים וְאִיכָּא בַּהֲדַיְיהוּ מָעוֹת [2] The Gemara answers: Resh Lakish would explain this Baraita as follows: **Words together with money are subject to the "But..."** curse; [3] **words without money are not subject to the "But..."** curse. If a person merely reneges on a promise, he incurs the disapproval of the Sages, but is not subject to any sanctions. If a person reneges on a promise that has already led to the payment of money, however, he is subject to the "But..." curse — not because payment of money is an act of acquisition, but because violating a promise that has already begun to be fulfilled is much more unethical than violating an ordinary promise. Thus the Baraita cannot serve as proof of the correctness of Rabbi Yoḥanan's opinion.

אֲמַר רָבָא [4] **Rava said: Support for Resh Lakish's** viewpoint — that by Torah law *meshikhah* and not monetary payment finalizes a sale — can be found in two sources: one, a Scriptural **verse, and** the other, **a Baraita.**

קְרָא [5] Rava now explains his statement: The following is **the verse** that supports Resh Lakish's viewpoint. **For it is written** (Leviticus 5:21): "If a person sins... **and lies to his neighbor regarding a deposit,** [6] **or regarding a loan, or regarding robbery,** [7] **or if he oppresses his neighbor."** This verse deals with the special guilt-offering brought by someone who owes another person money, denies his debt, and then swears falsely to support his denial. Such a person is obliged to repay the money he owes, to add an additional fifth, and to bring a guilt-offering. Whoever embezzles money by taking a false oath falls under the purview of this verse.

This verse and the one following it describe five situations in which a person denies a claim against himself, and takes a false oath in order to embezzle money. "A deposit" (פִּקָּדוֹן) refers to a bailee who denies having received a deposit from a depositor. "A loan" — described by the verse as "putting out a hand" (תְּשׂוּמֶת יָד)

RASHI

אנו אין לנו — קללה אחרת, אלא אינו הגון בעיני חכמים. **קאי באבל** — משום דברים שבאו על כך לכלל מעשה. אבל מעות לא קנו מדאורייתא, ונפקא מינה לענין איסורא, כגון אם קידש בו את האשה, לרבי יוחנן הוו קדושין, דמדאורייתא קנייה, ודידיה הוא. לריש לקיש לא הוו קדושין. **מסייע לריש לקיש** — דמדאורייתא נמי לא קנו מעות להדיוט.

NOTES

וְאָמַר רָבָא אָנוּ אֵין לָנוּ And Rava said: We have only.... Our commentary follows *Tosafot*, who explains that Rava was delivering an authoritative interpretation of the Baraita. According to *Tosafot*, Rava was simply explaining that the two expressions of censure — "the spirit of the Sages is displeased" and "But they said: He who punished..." — are not synonymous.

Rashba suggests that Rava was explaining that a person who reneges on an agreement where no money has yet been paid is not subject to any curse.

Rosh suggests that Rava was not referring to the Baraita at all. In fact, Rava was not even aware of the Baraita, and his statement shows that he came to the same conclusion independently. According to this interpretation, the Gemara quotes Rava together with the Baraita as additional support for the idea that violating a promise, while morally reprehensible, is not subject to any sanction.

אֲמַר רָבָא קְרָא וּמַתְנִיתָא מְסַיֵּיעַ לֵיהּ לְרֵישׁ לָקִישׁ Rava said: A Scriptural verse and a Baraita support Resh Lakish. It would appear from this passage that Rava is ruling in favor of Resh Lakish. Rava was one of the later Amoraim who summarized the earlier traditions, and his opinions carried great authority. This led certain Rishonim, including *Rashi*, to conclude that the Halakhah here is in accordance with

against one side is a lenient ruling for the other — the Sages do not employ external coercion. Nonetheless, as explained here, when the transaction has reached the stage where one side has already given money to the other, the Sages exert moral pressure on the recalcitrant party through the curse, "But He who punished...." When the transaction has remained at the verbal stage, however — when it can be claimed that the parties are still negotiating — the Sages merely express their firm opinion that not keeping one's word is dishonest.

All the foregoing remarks relate to the Torah law as explained here in the Gemara. From the Halakhic point of view, however, there is another consideration. When agreement has been reached — either explicitly, in the form of a regulation passed by a community or a group, or tacitly, that certain ceremonial signs of obligation are binding (such as expressing agreement through a handshake) — the side that does not wish to keep the agreement may not argue that he insists on applying the modes of acquisition stipulated by the Torah, and the court will compel him to fulfill his obligation.

BACKGROUND

אֵין רוּחַ חֲכָמִים נוֹחָה הֵימֶנּוּ The spirit of the Sages is not pleased with him. This expression refers to various acts that do not constitute a violation of the Halakhah but are morally flawed or have some other deficiency. A person who behaves in a manner of which the Sages disapprove cannot be forced by the court to change his ways, either by physical coercion or by the application of open social pressure (such as the curse, "But He who punished..."). Nevertheless, the Sages make it clear that they are displeased, and anyone who knows of the Sages' opinion should refrain from such action.

BACKGROUND

תְּשׂוּמֶת יָד וְעוֹשֶׁק A loan and oppression. The term תְּשׂוּמֶת יָד — the misappropriation of a loan — is interpreted here as being different from the illegal taking of a pledge (which is explicitly mentioned in the verse) that someone leaves or promises to leave with his fellow as security for a loan. The term עוֹשֶׁק — oppression — is also interpreted here not as a general expression, but as a term with a narrow meaning based on its use in other verses such as Deuteronomy 24:14: "You shall not oppress a hired laborer who is poor and needy" (see also Malachi 3:5), meaning failure to pay a worker's salary.

[1] "תְּשׂוּמֶת יָד" — אָמַר רַב חִסְדָּא: [2] כְּגוֹן שֶׁיִּחֵד לוֹ כְּלִי לַהֲלְוָאָתוֹ.

[3] "עָשַׁק" — אָמַר רַב חִסְדָּא: [4] כְּגוֹן שֶׁיִּחֵד לוֹ כְּלִי לְעָשְׁקוֹ.

LITERAL TRANSLATION

[1] "A loan" — Rav Ḥisda said: [2] For example, if he designated for him a utensil for his loan.

[3] "Oppressed" — Rav Ḥisda said: [4] For example, if he designated for him a utensil for his oppression.

RASHI

תשומת יד — הלואה. ואמר רב חסדא כגון שיחד לו הלוה כלי עליה, דהוי דומיא דפקדון. דאילו כפר בהלואה גרידתא לא מיחייב קרבן שבועה, הואיל וניתנה להוצאה. עשק — שכר שכיר. שיחד לו כלי לעשקו — ואי לא, לא מיחייב אכפירת שכר שכיר קרבן שבועה, דלא מייחד ליה באפי נפשיה כפקדון וגזל ואבידה.

TRANSLATION AND COMMENTARY

— refers to a borrower who denies a loan granted to him by a lender. "Robbery" (גָּזֵל) refers to a robber or thief who steals someone else's property and then denies having done so. "Oppression" (עֹשֶׁק) refers to an employer who oppresses an employee by denying him his wages. And the next verse mentions the case of someone who finds a lost object and then denies having it in his possession.

In three of the five cases — "the deposit," "the robbery," and "the lost object" — the person who denies the claim has actually embezzled a specific piece of property. The Gemara has a tradition that the penalties prescribed in this passage — the surcharge of a fifth and the guilt-offering — apply only in cases similar to these. But if the person who denies the claim merely owes money and denies his debt, without embezzling a specific piece of property, he is not required to pay the surcharge or to bring the sacrifice. Now, "the loan" and "the oppression" (unpaid wages) do not appear to meet this criterion. They seem to be ordinary financial obligations which the denier is trying to evade, and there does not appear to be a specific piece of embezzled property involved. In order to classify these two terms under the same category as the other three, Rav Ḥisda offered an authoritative interpretation of them according to which they too refer to identifiable items of embezzled property rather than to ordinary debts.

תְּשׂוּמֶת יָד [1] **"The loan"** mentioned in the verse, **says Rav Ḥisda,** [2] refers, **for example,** to a case **where** the borrower **designated a** particular **utensil** to be used as collateral **for** the repayment of **his loan,** and then denied under oath that he owed any money. Only in such a case has the borrower actually embezzled the creditor's property. But if the borrower had merely denied a debt, without embezzling an object designated as collateral for it, he would not be required to pay the surcharge or bring the sacrifice.

עָשַׁק [3] Likewise with regard to the term **"oppression,"** which according to Halakhic tradition refers to withheld wages, **Rav Ḥisda said:** The guilt-offering must be brought only, [4] **for example,** in a case **where** the employer **designated a utensil** to pay **for his oppression** — i.e., the worker's wages — and then denied owing the worker any money.

NOTES

Resh Lakish, even though in general the Halakhah follows Rabbi Yoḥanan in his disputes with Resh Lakish.

Most Rishonim, however, insist that the Halakhah follows Rabbi Yoḥanan, even though Rava ruled in favor of Resh Lakish (*Rif, Rambam*, and others). *Rosh* points out that at the end of this passage the Gemara quotes Rav Naḥman as ruling in favor of Rabbi Yoḥanan, and the Halakhah always follows Rav Naḥman in monetary questions.

Rabbenu Tam suggests that even Rava may not actually be ruling in favor of Resh Lakish. He points out that Rava's arguments are suggestive but not conclusive, so that he may not have been ruling in Resh Lakish's favor, but merely pointing out that a particular verse and Mishnah read more smoothly according to Resh Lakish's view.

שְׁבוּעָה עַל הַלְוָאָה A false oath denying a loan. Our commentary follows *Rashi* and other Rishonim (*Tosafot, Rosh*), who explain Rav Ḥisda's argument in the following way: A person who falsely denies a debt under oath is not required to pay the additional fifth or bring the special guilt-offering unless the oath concerns a specific item of property.

Rashi's explanation is based on a distinction made by the Torah between a person who swears falsely about facts and obligations (שְׁבוּעַת בִּיטּוּי), and one who swears falsely in order to misappropriate another person's property (שְׁבוּעַת הַפִּקָּדוֹן). The penalty in the latter case is generally more severe. According to the Halakhah, repayment of a debt is considered a general obligation unrelated to specific funds. Once a loan has been made, the money ceases to be the property of the creditor, as it is assumed that the debtor will spend the proceeds of the loan. Therefore, since there is no specific fund to which the debtor's false oath refers, his oath is regarded as a denial of the fact of a debt, or of the duty to repay it, but not as an attempt to misappropriate specific property.

Many Rishonim, however, disagree with *Rashi*'s explanation, as it appears from several other sources (see *Tosafot*) that a person who swears falsely to deny any sort of financial obligation is required to pay the surcharge and bring the guilt-offering, even if he was only evading his duty to pay and was not actually misappropriating his creditor's property.

אָמַר רַב חִסְדָּא: כְּגוֹן שֶׁיִּחֵד לוֹ כְּלִי Rav Ḥisda said: For example, if he designated for him a utensil. Our commentary follows *Rashi* (see previous note), who explains that if the debtor had not designated a utensil as collateral, he would not be required to bring the guilt-offering. Most Rishonim, however, agree that any debtor who swears falsely in order to evade a financial obligation is required to bring this sacrifice, even if he did not designate a specific

[1]וְכִי אֲהַדְרֵיהּ קְרָא, [2]כְּתִיב: "וְהָיָה כִּי יֶחֱטָא וְאָשֵׁם, [3]וְהֵשִׁיב אֶת הַגְּזֵלָה אֲשֶׁר גָּזָל, [4]אוֹ אֶת הָעֹשֶׁק אֲשֶׁר עָשָׁק, [5]אוֹ אֶת הַפִּקָּדוֹן אֲשֶׁר הָפְקַד אִתּוֹ". [6]וְאִילּוּ "תְשׂוּמֶת יָד" לָא אֲהַדְרֵיהּ.

[7]מַאי טַעְמָא? [8]לָאו מִשּׁוּם דִּמְחַסְּרָא מְשִׁיכָה?

LITERAL TRANSLATION

[1]But when the [Scriptural] verse repeats it, [2]it is written: "And it shall be, because he has sinned and is guilty, [3]and he shall return the robbed object that he robbed, [4]or the oppression that he oppressed, [5]or the deposit that was deposited with him." [6]Whereas it does not repeat "a loan."

[7]What is the reason? [8]Is it not because it lacks *meshikhah*?

RASHI

וכי אהדריה קרא – להישבון לאחר שהודה "כי יחטא ואשם". **לאו משום דמחוסר משיכה** – אותו כלי, ולא קנאו מלוה.

TRANSLATION AND COMMENTARY

וְכִי אֲהַדְרֵיהּ קְרָא [1]Rava now demonstrates how this verse, as authoritatively explained by Rav Ḥisda, supports Resh Lakish: Later on in the same passage, when the Torah orders an embezzler to return the embezzled property, the Torah repeats the same list of situations in which a person denies a claim against him and takes a false oath. **But when the Scriptural verse repeats** the list, the case of "the loan" is omitted. [2]For **it is written** (Leviticus 5:23): **"And it shall be, because he has sinned and is guilty, [3]and he shall return the robbed object that he robbed, [4]or the oppression that he oppressed, [5]or the deposit that was deposited with him,** or the lost object that he found." [6]**But** by contrast, the verse **did not repeat** the case of **"a loan,"** even though that case was mentioned in the earlier verse.

מַאי טַעְמָא [7]**What is the reason** for the distinction between the case of "the loan" and the other four cases? [8]**Is it not because** the object designated as collateral still **lacks *meshikhah*?** Even if the borrower designated an object as collateral, there is still a difference between "a loan," on the one hand, and "a deposit," "robbery," or "a lost object" on the other ("oppression" will be considered by the Gemara below). The embezzled deposit or stolen or lost object belongs to the victim, whereas the collateral for the loan was merely designated, and the borrower can still change his mind unilaterally and give the lender something else, as long as the lender has not yet taken possession of it. According to Rabbi Yoḥanan, there is no room for such a distinction; since money is an effective mode of acquisition by Torah law, the existence of the loan should be sufficient to give the lender proprietary rights in the designated object — without need for any other act of acquisition. But, according to Resh Lakish, Torah law makes a distinction between a designated object and an object already drawn into the lender's possession by the act of *meshikhah*. Now, from the fact that the Torah did not repeat "the loan," Rava infers that the Torah is implying that there are indeed two kinds of loan — one

NOTES

piece of property as collateral. According to these Rishonim, Rav Ḥisda is not saying, as *Rashi* suggests, that the debtor must have designated a utensil in order to be subject to the penalty for a false oath concerning property. Rather he is saying that the verse is stating the general rule regarding one who swears falsely to deny a loan, and illustrates this by means of a case where the debtor designated a specific item as collateral.

Ritva explains that the additional information conveyed by Rav Ḥisda's ruling is not merely an application of the general rule, but teaches us the law in a case where the argument concerned the collateral rather than the debt itself. According to this explanation, Rav Ḥisda maintains that the Torah is teaching us that even if the debtor did not swear falsely about the debt itself, but merely denied his obligation to give the creditor the designated utensil upon which the creditor had performed *meshikhah*, he is still liable, because the utensil has already become the property of the creditor.

Many Rishonim (*Ramban, Rashba, Ran*) follow another interpretation proposed by *Rabbenu Ḥananel, who* notes that in Leviticus 5:23 the Torah says: "And he shall *return* the robbed object that he robbed, or the oppression that he oppressed, or the deposit that was deposited with him, or the lost object that he found." But how is it possible to "return" a loan or unpaid wages, since the funds to be paid to the creditor or employee never belonged to the intended recipient in the first place? In order to explain this anomaly, *Rabbenu Ḥananel* maintains that Rav Ḥisda insisted that the Torah was referring to the special case where the dishonest debtor designated a utensil as collateral. If he had not designated a utensil, he would still be required to pay the surcharge and bring the sacrifice, but the language of the verse suggests that the dishonest debtor has a specific piece of property which already belongs to his creditor and which he must "return."

According to this view, Rava deduces from the fact that the Torah did not mention "the loan" in the verse dealing with restitution that sometimes the debtor is not required to return the utensil itself, but merely to repay the debt. This suggests that a utensil designated as collateral does not become the creditor's property automatically, until *meshikhah* is performed, from which it follows that *meshikhah* is required by Torah law. The Gemara then objects that Rabbi Shimon inferred from the word "anything" that the debtor is in fact required to return the utensil itself, even in a case of a loan. But the Gemara answers that the fact that the Torah did not explicitly order him to return "the loan," but rather included it in the general term "anything," is sufficient to indicate that there is indeed a case in which the dishonest debtor is not required to return the utensil itself.

TRANSLATION AND COMMENTARY

of which, if denied, is subject to the guilt-offering, while the other is not. Presumably the Torah is teaching us that designation of an object as collateral is not sufficient by itself. The lender must also perform a formal act of *meshikhah*. Verse 21, which mentions "the loan," must be referring to a case where the creditor performed *meshikhah* on the designated collateral, whereas verse 23, which does not mention "the loan," must be referring to a case where he did not. Hence, Rava argues, these verses support Resh Lakish's view that, by Torah law, *meshikhah* is a valid act of acquisition.

אֲמַר לֵיהּ רַב פַּפָּא לְרָבָא [1]The Gemara now raises an objection to Rava's proof: **Rav Pappa said to Rava:** Perhaps we can **say** that even though the Torah does not explicitly mention the case of "the loan" when it repeats the list of cases (verse 23), [2]**it can** nevertheless **be inferred from** the mention of **"oppression," which the verse** ***does*** **repeat!** The same problem that troubled Rava regarding "the loan" also applies to "the oppression" (the withholding of wages). In each case, Rav Ḥisda explained that the person denying the claim must have designated an object as collateral, and in both cases it is questionable whether such designation alone, without a formal act of *meshikhah*, is sufficient. Yet the Torah *did* repeat the case of "oppression." Thus we see that all kinds of "oppression" fall under the purview of this verse, whether or not *meshikhah* was performed. Apparently, designation of an object as collateral is sufficient even without *meshikhah*. Hence, even though the Torah does not explicitly state that designating an object as collateral for "a loan" is also sufficient, this can be inferred from the analogous case of "oppression." Thus it would appear that *meshikhah* is *not* necessary to acquire movables by Torah law, as Rabbi Yoḥanan argued, and the viewpoint of Resh Lakish is refuted!

הָכָא בְּמַאי עָסְקִינַן [3]The Gemara answers: There is no reason to assume that "the oppression" and "the loan" are referring to the same case; "the oppression" may be referring to a case where the worker did perform *meshikhah*. For **with what** case **are we dealing here,** when the Torah repeats the case of the "oppression" (the employer who denies owing money to his worker)? [4]**For instance, where** the worker first performed *meshikhah* and **took** the utensil **from** the employer as payment, **and** later **returned and deposited it with him.** By contrast, the case of "the loan" was not repeated, so as to imply that if the lender did not perform *meshikhah*, a sacrifice need not be brought.

הַיְינוּ פִּקָּדוֹן [5]Once again the Gemara raises an objection: According to this explanation, the case of "oppression" **is the same as** the case of **"deposit"!** If "the oppression" refers to a case where the worker took possession of the article and then left it temporarily in the employer's custody, then "oppression" is simply a special case of "deposit." In both cases, the embezzler is liable because he refuses to return property entrusted to him by its owner!

תְּרֵי גַּוְונֵי פִּקָּדוֹן [6]The Gemara answers: The Torah chose to mention **two** different **types of deposit** — one where the deposit had always belonged to the depositor ("deposit"), and one where it had initially belonged to the bailee ("oppression"). Both cases fall under the purview of the verse. By not repeating the case of "the loan," the Torah informs us that if the embezzled property never actually belonged to the victim, the law stated in the verse does not apply. Thus Rava's proof in support of Resh Lakish — that *meshikhah* is needed to acquire movables by Torah law — still stands.

אִי הָכִי [7]The Gemara again objects: According to Rava's original explanation, verse 21 refers to cases in which *meshikhah* has already been performed, and verse 23 refers to cases in which it has not. Therefore, verse 21 includes all five cases, whereas verse 23 leaves out the case of "the loan" and includes only the cases of "deposit," "robbery" and "lost object," in which *meshikhah* is not necessary. But **if** verse 23 is also referring to a case — "oppression" — in which *meshikhah* has been performed, then **let** that verse **repeat** the

[1]אֲמַר לֵיהּ רַב פַּפָּא לְרָבָא: [2]אֵימָא: מֵעוֹשֶׁק הוּא דַּהֲדַר קְרָא! [3]הָכָא בְּמַאי עָסְקִינַן? [4]כְּגוֹן שֶׁנְּטָלוֹ מִמֶּנּוּ וְחָזַר וְהִפְקִידוֹ אֶצְלוֹ. [5]הַיְינוּ פִּקָּדוֹן! [6]תְּרֵי גַּוְונֵי פִּקָּדוֹן. [7]אִי הָכִי, "תְּשׂוּמֶת יָד" נַמִי לִיהַדְרֵיהּ,

LITERAL TRANSLATION

[1]Rav Pappa said to Rava: [2]Say: This is [inferred] from oppression, which the verse *does* repeat!

[3]With what are we dealing here? [4]For example, where he took it from him and returned and deposited it with him.

[5]This is the same as a deposit!

[6]Two types of deposits.

[7]If so, let it repeat "a loan" as well,

RASHI

מעושק דאהדריה קרא — מכיון דאהדריה קרא לעושק, דמחסר נמי משיכה — לא אצטריך לאהדורי לתשומת יד, דמעושק נילף ליה. **הכא במאי עסקינן** — עושק דאהדריה קרא משתעי בשנטלו שכיר לכלי ממנו, וחזר והפקידו אצלו. **אי הכי** — דמאי לאהדר קרא מוקמת בדלא מחוסר משיכה, נהי נמי דמשיכה בעינן, ליהדריה קרא נמי לתשומת יד, ונוקמה בהכי!

TRANSLATION AND COMMENTARY

case of **"a loan" as well,** just as it did with the case of "oppression." [1]**And we can** then **explain** that when the verse mentions "the loan," it is referring, **for example,** to a case **where** the lender first **took** the pledge **from** the borrower **and** later **returned and deposited it with him.** Why mention "oppression," and refer to a case where *meshikhah* has been performed, and not mention "loan," and hint at a case where *meshikhah* was *not* performed?

אִי אֲהַדְרֵיהּ קְרָא [2]The Gemara answers: If **the verse had repeated** the case of "loan," **it would be neither refutation of nor support** for Resh Lakish. For while Resh Lakish can interpret both the case of "oppression" and that of "loan" as referring to cases in which *meshikhah* has been performed, and can thus argue that *meshikhah* is necessary before an article may be considered as having been embezzled, Rabbi Yoḥanan can explain both as cases in which there has been no act of *meshikhah*, and can argue that designation alone is sufficient. [3]**Now,** however, **since the verse does not repeat** the case of "loan," but only the case of "oppression," **it supports** the viewpoint of Resh Lakish. For we can only account for the omission of "loan" if we say that the Torah is using the case of "oppression" to illustrate the law when *meshikhah* has been performed, and the case of "loan" to illustrate the law when it has not. In the case of oppression — or a loan, for that matter — where *meshikhah* has been performed, a guilt-offering must be brought if the defendant denies his obligations under oath; whereas in the case of a loan — or oppression, for that matter — where *meshikhah* has not been performed, a guilt-offering is not required if the defendant denies his obligations under oath. Thus we see that there is a distinction between a situation where *meshikhah* has been performed and a situation where it has not, and it follows that *meshikhah* is valid by Torah law, as Resh Lakish maintains.

וּתְשׂוּמֶת יָד [4]The Gemara objects: **But did the verse not repeat** the case of **"a loan"?** Even though the case of "a loan" does not appear explicitly in verse 23, it can be inferred from the words appearing at the beginning of verse 24, as the Gemara now explains: [5]**But surely** this very point **has been taught in** the following Baraita: **"Rabbi Shimon said:** Verse 21 lists all the cases that come under the purview of this law, and verse 23 lists all the cases in which the embezzler is required to make restitution. [6]**From where do we know that** all the cases mentioned **above,** in verse 21, **apply below,** in verse 23, even if such cases were not mentioned explicitly in verse 23? How do we know that the embezzler is always required to make restitution? [7]Rabbi Shimon answers: We learn it **from what is written** at the beginning of verse 24: **'Or concerning *anything* about which he swore falsely.'"** Since this verse states that the embezzler must make restitution for *anything* about which he swore falsely, we can infer that all the cases mentioned in verse 21 are included — some directly, but all by implication — in verse 23 as well.

וְאָמַר רַב נַחְמָן [8]Now, concerning this Baraita, **Rav Naḥman said in the name of Rabbah bar Avuha in the name of Rav:** To which case was Rabbi Shimon referring? Which case appears to be included in verse 21 and omitted in verse 23? [9]The answer is that this statement by Rabbi Shimon **comes to include** the case of **a loan, with regard to restitution.** In other words, a loan which was falsely denied must be repaid to the lender, even though the case of "the loan" was not mentioned specifically in verse 23, which deals with restitution. By the use of the word "anything" in verse 24 the Torah does in fact repeat the case of "the loan" as well. But we have already noted above that if the verse *does* repeat the case of "the loan," it provides neither

[1]וְלוֹקְמֵיהּ כְּגוֹן שֶׁנְּטָלוֹ הֵימֶנּוּ וְחָזַר וְהִפְקִידוֹ אֶצְלוֹ! [2]אִי אֲהַדְרֵיהּ קְרָא, לָא תְּיוּבְתָּא וְלָא סַיְיעְתָּא. [3]הָשְׁתָּא, דְּלָא אֲהַדְרֵיהּ קְרָא, מְסַיֵּיעַ לֵיהּ. [4]וּ״תְשׂוּמֶת יָד״ לָא אֲהַדְרֵיהּ קְרָא? [5]וְהָתַנְיָא: ״אָמַר רַבִּי שִׁמְעוֹן: [6]מִנַּיִן לִיתֵּן אֶת הָאָמוּר לְמַעְלָה לְמַטָּה? [7]דִּכְתִיב: ׳אוֹ מִכֹּל אֲשֶׁר יִשָּׁבַע עָלָיו לַשֶּׁקֶר׳״. [8]וְאָמַר רַב נַחְמָן אָמַר רַבָּה בַּר אֲבוּהּ אָמַר רַב: [9]לְרַבּוֹת תְּשׂוּמֶת יָד לְהִישָּׁבוֹן.

LITERAL TRANSLATION

[1]and let it be explained, for example, where he took it from him and returned and deposited it with him! [2]If the verse had repeated it, it would be neither a refutation nor a support. [3]Now, since the verse does not repeat it, it supports him.

[4]But did the verse not repeat "a loan"? [5]But surely it has been taught: "Rabbi Shimon said: [6]From where [do we know] to apply (lit., "give") what was said above below? [7]For it is written: 'Or concerning anything about which he swore falsely.'"

[8]And Rav Naḥman said in the name of Rabbah bar Avuha in the name of Rav: [9][This comes] to include a loan with regard to restitution.

RASHI

אי אהדריה קרא לא הוה גמרינן לא תיובתא ולא סייעתא — דרבי יוחנן לוקמה בדלא משך, וריש לקיש לוקמיה במשך. **השתא דלא אהדריה מסייע ליה** — דמדלאהדריה לעוסק ופקדון וגזל ואבידה, ולא אהדריה לתשומת יד — איכא למילף תשומת יד במחוסר משיכה, ועסק כשמשך.

SAGES

רַבָּה בַּר אֲבוּהּ Rabbah bar Avuha. A Babylonian Amora of the second generation, pupil of Rav, and transmitted many teachings in his name. Rabbah bar Avuha was a member of the Exilarch's family, and Rav Naḥman was his pupil and son-in-law.

LANGUAGE

בַּלָּן A bathhouse attendant. This word is derived from the Greek βαλανεύς, *balaneus*, meaning "bathhouse attendant."

TRANSLATION AND COMMENTARY

refutation of nor support for the position of Resh Lakish. Thus Rava's argument is apparently unfounded.

בְּהֶדְיָא [1]The Gemara replies: **Nevertheless,** despite the inclusion of the general term "anything" in verse 24, **verse** 23 **did not repeat** the case of "the loan" **explicitly.** It may therefore be inferred that, by not explicitly repeating the case of "the loan," the Torah is implying that there are circumstances under which a debtor who denies his debt under oath need not bring a sacrifice, and the inclusion of "the loan" in the repetition, by the use of the word "anything," refers only to those instances when the debtor must indeed bring a sacrifice. In this way Rava has demonstrated that verse 23 supports Resh Lakish's view that, even according to Torah law, movable goods are acquired through *meshikhah*.

מַתְנִיתָא מְנָלַן [2]Rava stated above that there is also a Baraita which supports Resh Lakish's viewpoint that by Torah law *meshikhah* is a valid mode of acquisition for movable property. The Gemara now investigates this part of Rava's statement: **Where is there** such **a Baraita?** [3]The Gemara answers: Support for Resh Lakish is to be found in the following Baraita (it is in fact a Mishnah, *Me'ilah* 20a), in which **it has been taught: "If** the Temple treasurer unwittingly **gives** money consecrated to the Temple **to a bathhouse attendant** as payment for a bath — even if the treasurer has not yet used the bath — **he has committed *me'ilah*.** The law of *me'ilah* — trespass, unlawful use of property consecrated to the Temple — is as follows: Whenever a person inadvertently derives personal benefit from Temple property, he must repay the value of the property to the Temple treasury, add a fifth, and bring a guilt-offering (see Leviticus 5:14-16). The key conditions are that the trespasser must derive benefit from the trespass, and that the trespass must be inadvertent. When more than one person is involved in *me'ilah,* it is important to determine who was the first to derive benefit from the property inadvertently, as only the first trespasser is subject to the penalties of this law. When the treasurer inadvertently spends the money for his own private purposes, he is guilty of *me'ilah*. On the other hand, if he merely places the money in someone else's hand — without transferring ownership of the money or effecting any other transaction — he is not guilty of *me'ilah*. Thus, when the Mishnah tells us that a Temple treasurer who pays a bath attendant with Temple funds is guilty of *me'ilah,* we learn that paying the bath attendant is itself a legal transaction, at least by Torah law. Thus, this Mishnah would at first glance appear to support the viewpoint of Rabbi Yoḥanan.

LITERAL TRANSLATION

[1]Nevertheless, the verse did not repeat it explicitly. [2]From where [do we have] a Baraita? [3]As it has been taught: "[If] he gave it to a bathhouse attendant, he has committed *me'ilah*."

[1]בְּהֶדְיָא מִיהָא לָא אֲהַדְרֵיהּ קְרָא. [2]מַתְנִיתָא מְנָלַן? [3]דְּתַנְיָא: "נְתָנָהּ לַבַּלָּן, מָעַל".

RASHI

בהדיא מיהא לא אהדריה קרא — שיהא חייב להשיבו ולהביא קרבן, וכי הדר רבייה קרא — דומיא דפקדון רבייה, שנטלו הימנו וחזר והפקידו אצלו. **נתנה** — לפרוטה של הקדש בשוגג. **לבלן** — בשכר שירחצנו בבית המרחץ. **מעל** — ואף על פי שעדיין לא רחץ.

NOTES

מְעִילָה *Me'ilah*, trespass. *Ra'avad* and other Rishonim maintain that having Temple property in one's possession without authorization is itself *me'ilah*. This presents a problem in relation to our passage because, according to this view, the trespasser in our passage committed a crime the moment he took the money, before spending it on a bathhouse or a barber. Hence, these Rishonim (followed in our commentary) explain that the various Mishnaic sources and Baraitot cited by our Gemara refer only to a case in which it was the Temple treasurer himself who inadvertently paid for his personal needs with Temple funds. For the treasurer is entitled to carry consecrated money on his person, and commits *me'ilah* only when he spends it on his personal needs.

According to this view, whenever the Mishnah or the Baraita rules that no transaction took place, and the man who paid the money — the treasurer — is not guilty of *me'ilah*, it only means that the treasurer is not guilty, but the person who received the money has committed *me'ilah*, since he has taken possession of consecrated money. Thus, if the treasurer paid the bathhouse attendant with Temple funds, the treasurer has committed *me'ilah*, because the act of paying the attendant is itself an unauthorized use of the money. On the other hand, if the treasurer paid the Jewish barber, it is the barber who commits *me'ilah*, because the treasurer was allowed to have consecrated money in his possession, and did not effect a transaction by paying the barber, whereas the barber is not authorized to have the money in his possession and commits *me'ilah* as soon as he receives it.

According to *Rambam* (*Sefer Avodah, Hilkhot Me'ilah* 6:7-9), a person is not guilty of *me'ilah* simply by having Temple property in his physical possession. Rather, he must have asserted ownership over the consecrated property by damaging it or deriving benefit from it, or transferring ownership of it to another person. According to this explanation, the various Mishnaic sources and Baraitot cited by the Gemara need not be referring to the treasurer; they could be referring to anyone who inadvertently pocketed money consecrated to the Temple.

TRANSLATION AND COMMENTARY

וְאָמַר רַב [1]Rav gave an authoritative interpretation **of this** Mishnah, and **said:** The reason the Temple treasurer is guilty of *me'ilah* is not because paying money is in general an act of acquisition by Torah law. [2]Rather, this Mishnah **refers specifically to** money paid to **a bathhouse attendant.** Ordinarily, the payment of money is not an act of acquisition, and *meshikhah* is required. [3]But **since** in the case of a bathhouse there is nothing upon which *meshikhah* could be performed, ***meshikhah* is not lacking,** i.e., not necessary — and the bathhouse attendant's services are acquired as soon as he receives the money. Therefore the transaction takes effect and *me'ilah* is committed as soon as the money is paid — even before the Temple treasurer takes his bath. [4]**But regarding any** other kind of hired worker, **where** there *is* something upon which *meshikhah* can be performed, ***meshikhah* is lacking** — i.e., necessary. [5]Therefore, the person paying the money **has not** committed ***me'ilah* until he performs *meshikhah*,** at which time the transaction takes effect. But if money acquires by Torah law, then *me'ilah* should take place as soon as the worker is paid the money, even in a case where there is something upon which to perform *meshikhah*, for the Rabbinic decree invalidating such a transaction should not free a person from liability for *me'ilah*. Therefore, since according to Rav's authoritative interpretation the Temple treasurer is not liable until he performs *meshikhah* — except in a case of a bathhouse attendant and the like — *meshikhah* must be a Scriptural enactment, as claimed by Resh Lakish. Thus this Mishnah supports Resh Lakish.

וְהָתַנְיָא [6]The Gemara raises an objection: **But surely** the opposite **has been taught** in the following Baraita: **"If** the Temple treasurer unwittingly **gave** money consecrated to the Temple **to a barber** so that he should cut his hair, **he has committed *me'ilah*."** [7]**But surely, with regard to a barber,** the customer **needs to perform *meshikhah* on the scissors!** Now, since the Baraita states that *me'ilah* is committed as soon as the barber receives the consecrated money — even if *meshikhah* has not been performed — we can infer that, according to Torah law, the barber's services are acquired by means of the money, and *meshikhah* is only required by Rabbinic decree, as claimed by Rabbi Yoḥanan.

[1]וְאָמַר רַב: [2]דַּוְקָא בַּלָּן הוּא, [3]דְּלָא מְחַסְּרָא מְשִׁיכָה. [4]אֲבָל מִידֵּי אַחֲרִיתָא, דִּמְחַסְּרָא מְשִׁיכָה, [5]לֹא מָעַל עַד דְּמָשֵׁיךְ. [6]וְהָתַנְיָא: ״נְתָנָהּ לַסַּפָּר, מָעַל״. [7]וְסַפָּר, הָא בָּעֵי לְמִמְשַׁךְ תִּסְפּוֹרֶת!

LITERAL TRANSLATION

[1]And Rav said: [2]Specifically a bathhouse attendant, [3]since *meshikhah* is not lacking. [4]But [regarding] something else, where *meshikhah* is lacking, [5]he does not commit *me'ilah* until he has performed *meshikhah*.

[6]But surely it has been taught: "[If] he gave it to a barber, he has committed *me'ilah*." [7]But surely [with regard to] a barber, he has to perform *meshikhah* on the scissors!

RASHI

ואמר רב – גרסינן. **דוקא בלן** – קתני דמעל הנותן, משום דשכירות גמורה היא בנתינת הפרוטה, ואין יכול לחזור בו, שאין כאן למשוך. אבל אם נתנה על דבר שיש בה מה למשוך, לא מעל עד דמשיך. **הא בעי למשוך** – האי שוכר התספורת, דבכל מידי דאית ביה מה למשוך לא קני עד דמשיך.

BACKGROUND

לְמִמְשַׁךְ תִּסְפּוֹרֶת To perform *meshikhah* on the scissors. Since the barber does his work on a specific object — his customer's hair — the transaction between the barber and his customer does not take effect from the moment the customer enters the barber's shop (if the barber indeed has a shop, for it seems that many barbers used to go to their customers' houses to cut their hair). Rather, the transaction takes effect with a particular act of *meshikhah* which represents the agreement of both parties. In other contexts, the Sages said that a haircut begins from the moment the barber places a sheet on his customer to keep clipped hair off his clothing.

NOTES

שְׂכִירוּת בַּלָּן וְסַפָּר Hiring a bathhouse attendant or a barber. Our commentary follows *Rashi,* who explains that the trespasser hired the bathhouse attendant to wait on him, and the barber to cut his hair. According to this interpretation, the Gemara apparently had a tradition that the laws applying to the purchase of movable property also apply to the hiring of workmen, and it is necessary to perform *meshikhah* on their tools in order to formalize the contract. Moreover, according to this view, even Resh Lakish would agree that money acquires whenever there is no practical way of performing *meshikhah*, since the Gemara says that money acquires the labor of a bathhouse attendant.

Ritva explains that the trespasser is renting the bathhouse and the barber's implements, but not the bathhouse attendant and the barber. According to this explanation, the reason *meshikhah* is not necessary in the case of the bathhouse is because the bathhouse is real estate, and real estate can be acquired, or rented, for money, but in the case of the barber, the trespasser is not guilty of *me'ilah* until he performs *meshikhah* on the barber's implements, since these are movable property.

HALAKHAH

נְתָנָהּ לַבַּלָּן... נְתָנָהּ לַסַּפָּר Paying consecrated money to a bathhouse attendant or to a barber. "If a person gives consecrated money to a bathhouse attendant, he is guilty of *me'ilah* even if he has not yet used the baths, since he can gain admission to the baths immediately if he so desires. Similarly, someone who gives consecrated money to a worker when hiring him is guilty of *me'ilah,* even if the worker has not yet begun working. However, someone who uses consecrated money to buy something is not guilty of *me'ilah* until he draws the merchandise into his possession, unless he bought it from a non-Jew, in which case he is guilty of *me'ilah* immediately. (*Rambam, Sefer Avodah, Hilkhot Me'ilah* 6:9, but see *Kesef Mishneh* ad loc.)

TRANSLATION AND COMMENTARY

הָכָא בְּמַאי עָסְקִינַן [1]The Gemara replies: **With what are we dealing here** in this Baraita? [2]**With a non-Jewish barber, who is not subject to the laws of *meshikhah*.** Even according to Resh Lakish, a transaction involving a non-Jew is effected by monetary payment, and not by *meshikhah*. For, according to Resh Lakish, *meshikhah* is derived from the verse (Leviticus 25:14): "Or buy anything from your neighbor's hand," and any verse in the Torah which refers to "your neighbor" applies specifically to Jews and not to non-Jews. Therefore the Baraita rules that *me'ilah* is committed as soon as the barber receives the money.

תַּנְיָא נַמִּי הָכִי [3]The Gemara now provides additional support for this explanation from another Baraita: **This** principle **has also been taught** in the following Baraita: [4]**"If** the Temple treasurer unwittingly **gave** money consecrated to the Temple **to a barber or to a sailor or to any** other **artisan,** [5]**he has not** committed *me'ilah* **until he performs *meshikhah*."** Now, the previous Baraita ruled that the treasurer is guilty of *me'ilah* as soon as he pays the barber money, whereas this Baraita rules that he must first have performed *meshikhah*. [6]Do these Baraitot **contradict each other?** Surely not!

אֶלָּא לָאו שְׁמַע מִינָּהּ [7]**Rather,** says the Gemara, the two Baraitot must be explained as referring to different cases. Thus **may we not conclude from here** that **the Baraita** which states that he commits *me'ilah* immediately **refers to a non-Jewish barber,** [8]while the Baraita which states that he does not commit *me'ilah* until he performs *meshikhah* **refers to a Jewish barber?** And does this not mean that where *meshikhah* is appropriate, it is valid by Torah law, as Resh Lakish argued?

שְׁמַע מִינָּהּ [9]The Gemara answers: We may indeed **conclude from here** that the distinction suggested above between Jewish and non-Jewish barbers is correct, and the Baraitot support Resh Lakish.

וְכֵן אָמַר רַב נַחְמָן [10]Having explained Rava's argument in favor of the viewpoint of Resh Lakish in detail, the Gemara now considers the viewpoint of Rabbi Yoḥanan. **And similarly Rav Naḥman said: By Torah law, money acquires.** Thus Rav Naḥman supports the view of Rabbi Yoḥanan. (See also above, 46b, where the Gemara proved that Rav Naḥman must be of this opinion.)

[1]הָכָא בְּמַאי עָסְקִינַן? [2]בְּסַפָּר נָכְרִי, דְּלָאו בַּר מְשִׁיכָה הוּא. [3]תַּנְיָא נַמִּי הָכִי: [4]"נְתָנָהּ לְסַפָּר אוֹ לְסַפָּן אוֹ לְכָל בַּעֲלֵי אוּמָּנוּת, [5]לֹא מָעַל עַד דְּמָשַׁךְ. [6]קַשְׁיָין אַהֲדָדֵי!

[7]אֶלָּא לָאו שְׁמַע מִינָּהּ: כָּאן בְּסַפָּר נָכְרִי; [8]כָּאן בְּסַפָּר יִשְׂרָאֵל?

[9]שְׁמַע מִינָּהּ.

[10]וְכֵן אָמַר רַב נַחְמָן: דְּבַר תּוֹרָה, מָעוֹת קוֹנוֹת.

LITERAL TRANSLATION

[1]With what are we dealing here? [2]With a non-Jewish barber, who is not subject to [the laws of] *meshikhah*.

[3]It has also been taught thus: [4]"[If] he gave it to a barber or to a sailor or to any artisans, [5]he has not committed *me'ilah* until he has performed *meshikhah*. [6]They contradict each other!

[7]Rather, [may we] not conclude from this: Here [the Baraita refers] to a non-Jewish barber; [8]here [it refers] to a Jewish barber?

[9]Conclude from this.

[10]And similarly Rav Naḥman said: By Torah law, money acquires.

RASHI

נכרי – לא שייך ביה דין משיכה, ד"מיד עמיתך" כתיב (ויקרא כה). **קשיין אהדדי** – ספר אספר. **וכן אמר רב נחמן** – כרבי יוחנן.

NOTES

סַפָּר נָכְרִי **A non-Jewish barber.** The Gemara accepts the argument that a distinction must be made between a non-Jewish and a Jewish barber, as it is otherwise impossible to explain the fact that one Baraita rules that a customer commits *me'ilah* by paying the barber money, while the other Baraita rules that he does not commit *me'ilah* until he performs *meshikhah*. The Rishonim ask: Since the argument indeed appears to be a conclusive proof of Resh Lakish's position, how does Rabbi Yoḥanan account for these Baraitot?

It is possible to explain Rabbi Yoḥanan's position, based on a passage in tractate *Bekhorot* (13b). The Gemara derives from the word "neighbor" appearing in the verse "or buy from your neighbor's hand" (Leviticus 25:14) that, by Torah law, a non-Jew does not acquire in the same way as a Jew. The Gemara explains: According to Resh Lakish, a Jew acquires through *meshikhah* and a non-Jew acquires by paying money, whereas according to Rabbi Yoḥanan, the reverse is true: a Jew acquires by paying money and a non-Jew acquires through *meshikhah*.

On this basis, Rabbi Yoḥanan can explain the contradiction between the Baraitot in our Gemara by simply reversing Resh Lakish's explanation: The Baraita that says that *me'ilah* is committed as soon as the barber is paid can be explained as referring to a Jewish barber, whereas the Baraita that says that the customer must first draw the scissors into his possession can be explained as referring to a non-Jewish barber (*Tosafot*).

[1]וּבְדָקָהּ לֵוִי בְּמַתְנִיתֵיהּ וְאַשְׁכַּח: [2]״נְתָנָהּ לְסִיטוֹן, מָעַל״.
[48B] [3]אֶלָּא קַשְׁיָא לְרֵישׁ לָקִישׁ!
[4]אָמַר לָךְ רֵישׁ לָקִישׁ: הָא מַנִּי? [5]רַבִּי שִׁמְעוֹן הִיא.
[6]אֲבָל אָמְרוּ: ״מִי שֶׁפָּרַע וכו׳״.
[7]אִיתְּמַר: אַבַּיֵי אֲמַר: אוֹדוּעֵי מוֹדְעִינַן לֵיהּ. [8]רָבָא אֲמַר: מֵילָט לָיְיטִינַן לֵיהּ.

LITERAL TRANSLATION

[1]And Levi searched for it in his Baraita [collection] and found: [2]"[If] he gave it to a wholesaler, he has committed *me'ilah*."

[48B] [3]But [this is] a difficulty for Resh Lakish!

[4]Resh Lakish can say to you: [According to] whom is this? [5]It is [according to] Rabbi Shimon.

[6]"But they said: He who punished, etc."

[7]It was stated: Abaye said: We inform him. [8]Rava said: We curse him.

TRANSLATION AND COMMENTARY

וּבְדָקָהּ לֵוִי בְּמַתְנִיתֵיהּ [1]The Gemara observes: **And Levi** too **searched for** a ruling on this question **in his Baraita** collection, **and found** the following: [2]**"If** a person **gives** money consecrated to the Temple **to a wholesaler, he has committed *me'ilah*."** It was customary for retailers to pay wholesalers a down payment and then take a large supply of produce on credit. The Baraita tells us that if a retailer inadvertently gave a wholesaler consecrated money, he committed *me'ilah* immediately, even though the money was paid before he could draw the produce into his possession. Thus we see that, according to Torah law, movable goods *can* be acquired with money, and *meshikhah* is not necessary to consummate a sale.

אֶלָּא קַשְׁיָא לְרֵישׁ לָקִישׁ [48B] [3]The Gemara objects: **But this** Baraita poses **a difficulty for** the viewpoint of **Resh Lakish!**

אָמַר לָךְ רֵישׁ לָקִישׁ [4]The Gemara answers: **Resh Lakish can say to you** in reply: **According to whose** viewpoint **is this** Baraita stated? [5]**It is** stated **according to** the viewpoint of **Rabbi Shimon,** who is of the opinion that, by Torah law, movable property is acquired by monetary payment and not by *meshikhah*. But the Sages, who disagree with Rabbi Shimon, maintain that even by Torah law movable property can be acquired only through *meshikhah,* as Resh Lakish ruled. For the Gemara has already explained (above, 47b) that, according to Resh Lakish, his difference of opinion with Rabbi Yoḥanan is identical with the difference of opinion between Rabbi Shimon and the Sages in our Mishnah. Thus no objection can be raised against Resh Lakish from Levi's Baraita.

אֲבָל אָמְרוּ מִי שֶׁפָּרַע וכו׳ [6]The Gemara now considers the next clause of the Mishnah. We learned in the Mishnah that in a purchase of movable property, payment of money is not an act of acquisition, and both parties can still retract, **"but** this is considered so unethical that the Rabbis **said: God, who punished** the generation of the flood and the generation of the dispersion, will punish anyone who does not stand by his word and takes the opportunity to renege on a transaction after money has been paid." We see that, although monetary payment does not effect a fully binding sale, it does create a situation in which the parties cannot renege without submitting to the "He who punished" curse. In the following passage, for reasons of brevity, the Gemara will sometimes refer to money "acquiring" movable property, even though the law is that money does not acquire movable property. When this expression appears, it should be understood as meaning that in a transaction where the payment of money has already taken place, one may not arbitrarily cancel without suffering the penalty of the Mishnah's curse.

אִיתְּמַר [7]**It was stated** that Amoraim disagreed about the meaning of this clause in the Mishnah. **Abaye said** that the Mishnah means: The court **informs** the person who is thinking of withdrawing from a transaction that, if he does so, God will punish him, just as He punished the generation of the flood, etc. According to this interpretation, "He who punished..." is a warning rather than a curse. [8]But **Rava said:** The court **curses** the person who reneges. According to this interpretation, "He who punished..." is to be understood as a curse.

RASHI

ובדקה לוי במתניתיה — הגיהה והוסיפה בתוספתא שסידר ושנה בה. **נתנה לסיטון מעל** — סיטון = חנוני גדול, ומוכר פירות הרבה לחנונים עניים, ונותנים לו המעות על יד על יד כשהם מוכרים, ובתחלת הקנייה נותנין ערבון דמים מועטין על הכל. **מעל** — אף על גב דלא משך כל הפירות, שהרי הרבה פוסק עמו בבת אחת. **אלא קשיא** — הך מתניתין דלוי לריש לקיש. **רבי שמעון היא** — דאמר במתניתין לוקח לא מצי הדר ביה, דקסבר מעות קונות. **מודעינן ליה** — דע שאתה תחזור — סופך להפרע ממך.

LANGUAGE

סיטון Wholesaler. This word is derived from the Greek σιτώνης, *sitones*, meaning "an official buyer of corn for the public."

TERMINOLOGY

הָא מַנִּי Whose is this? I.e., in accordance with whose viewpoint is this Mishnah or Baraita?

NOTES

וּבְדָקָהּ לֵוִי בְּמַתְנִיתֵיהּ And Levi searched for it in his Baraita collection. *Rashi* explains that Levi, one of the editors of the Tosefta, decided after careful investigation of conflicting texts that the version of the Baraita which accorded with Rabbi Yoḥanan's view was the correct one, and should be included in the Tosefta (see also *Ramban, Rashash*).

אוֹדוּעֵי מוֹדְעִינַן לֵיהּ We inform him. According to Abaye, we may not curse a person who reneges on a transaction, because of the Scriptural prohibition against cursing a

TRANSLATION AND COMMENTARY

אַבַּיֵי אָמַר [1]The Gemara now explains the basis of this dispute: **Abaye said: We inform** the person who is about to renege that he will be punished, but we do not curse him, [2]**for it is written** (Exodus 22:27): **"And a prince among your people you shall not curse,"** and from here the Rabbis inferred that it is forbidden to curse any Jew.

רָבָא אָמַר [3]**Rava said: We curse** the person who is about to renege, as the prohibition against cursing other Jews does not apply here. [4]**For** in this verse a qualification **is written** — the words **"among your people"** — from which we learn: You are only forbidden to curse Jews **who act in the manner of "your people,"** i.e., Jews who keep the laws of the Torah. But it is permissible to curse Jews who violate the laws of the Torah. Rava is of the opinion that this applies even to people who do not technically violate the law but merely behave improperly, such as those who renege on their promises.

אָמַר רָבָא [5]Rava now produces support for his view: **Rava said: From where do I know** that the "He who

[1]אַבַּיֵי אָמַר: אוֹדוּעֵי מוֹדְעִינַן לֵיהּ, [2]דִּכְתִיב: "וְנָשִׂיא בְעַמְּךָ לֹא תָאֹר".

[3]רָבָא אָמַר: מֵילַט לָיְיטִינַן לֵיהּ, [4]דִּכְתִיב: "בְּעַמְּךָ" — בְּעוֹשֶׂה מַעֲשֵׂה עַמְּךָ.

[5]אָמַר רָבָא: מְנָא אָמֵינָא לָהּ?

LITERAL TRANSLATION

[1]Abaye said: We inform him, [2]for it is written: "And a prince among your people you shall not curse." [3]Rava said: We curse him, [4]for it is written: "Among your people" — where he does the deeds of your people.

[5]Rava said: From where do I say this?

RASHI

בעושה מעשה עמך – "בעמך" דרשינן הכי. והאי לאו עושה מעשה עמך הוא, דכתיב (צפניה ג) "שארית ישראל לא יעשו עולה ולא ידברו כזב".

NOTES

fellow Jew. Rava counters that it is permitted to curse a Jew who does not behave "in the manner of your people." It should be noted that Abaye does not dispute the law cited by Rava. But according to Abaye, the behavior of a person who reneges on a transaction is not sufficiently bad to justify a curse. Abaye assumes that the person who reneges on the agreement is not being deliberately deceitful, and that he initially meant to keep his promise. He only changed his mind when prices changed unexpectedly. Although his reaction is certainly unethical, it does not belong in the category of behavior that is "not in the manner of your people" (*Ritva*). In contrast, Rava is of the opinion that dishonest business practice, even where there is no technical violation of the law, is so anti-social that it is "not in the manner of your people" (*Rashi*).

Tosafot adds that even Rava does not claim that to renege is equivalent to behaving "not in the manner of your people." A truly wicked person may be cursed at any time with impunity, as he is not protected by the Scriptural injunction against cursing a fellow Jew. A person who reneges, however, may not ordinarily be cursed; it is only with regard to the specific unethical act itself that a curse is justified.

וְנָשִׂיא בְעַמְּךָ לֹא תָאֹר And a prince among your people you shall not curse. The Talmud (*Sanhedrin* 66a) notes that there are three Scriptural injunctions against cursing another person: (1) "A prince among your people you shall not curse" (Exodus 22:27), which refers to cursing a ruler. (2) "You shall not curse God" (ibid.), which includes a prohibition against cursing a judge. (3) "You shall not curse a deaf man" (Leviticus 19:14), which includes a prohibition against cursing a person who is not present. Judges, rulers and deaf people have nothing in common, other than their humanity, and there appears to be no reason why it should be forbidden to curse them while it is permitted to curse other people. Therefore the Gemara infers that the prohibition against cursing applies to all Jews.

Rambam explains that the reason the Torah referred specifically to a deaf person is to teach us that it is forbidden to curse even a person who does not know he is being cursed, and will not take offense. *Ramban* (Leviticus 19:14) adds that the Torah may have singled out the ruler, the judge and the deaf man because people are more tempted to curse them than to curse ordinary people.

לֹא תָאֹר You shall not curse. Strictly speaking, the Torah's prohibition against cursing one's fellow Jew is not violated unless God's name is used in the curse (*Shevuot* 35a). However, it is considered improper to curse even without referring to God (*Rambam*). Moreover, according to most opinions, the Torah prohibition includes curses using an indirect reference to God (e.g., the Merciful One), and it is possible that the curse described in the Mishnah in the name of "He who punished" falls under the category of a curse using an indirect reference to God's name (*Meiri*).

בְּעוֹשֶׂה מַעֲשֵׂה עַמְּךָ Where he does the deeds of your people. The Scriptural verse dealing with rulers contains a qualification on the prohibition against cursing: The person cursed must be "among your people." From here we learn that the prohibition applies only to Jews. However, the Torah did not say "your neighbor," as it usually does when a law

HALAKHAH

קִלְלַת מִי שֶׁפָּרַע The curse of "He who punished...." "How is someone subjected to the 'He who punished' curse? If a person reneges on a transaction, the court pronounces the following curse on him: 'He who punished the men of the generation of the flood, and the men of the generation of the dispersion, and the men of Sodom and Gomorrah, and the Egyptians at the Red Sea, will ultimately punish anyone who does not keep his word.' *Rema* writes that, according to some authorities, the conclusion of the curse is phrased in the second person — 'He will punish you if you do not keep your word,' and some maintain that this curse is pronounced publicly." (*Shulḥan Arukh, Ḥoshen Mishpat* 204:4.)

BACKGROUND

וְנָשִׂיא בְעַמְּךָ לֹא תָאֹר And a prince among your people you shall not curse. Although the Torah does not explicitly prohibit cursing another Jew, it does contain two explicit prohibitions related to this: (1) It is forbidden to curse a deaf person (Leviticus 19:14). (2) It is forbidden to curse a prince among one's people (Exodus 22:27). Since the first of these verses speaks of Jews of low status while the second speaks of those of high status, the Rabbis infer that it is forbidden to curse any Jew, whatever his status. Although the prohibition against cursing, which is punishable by lashes, applies specifically to a curse using the name of God, anyone who curses a fellow Jew in any fashion is committing a transgression.

מֵילַט לָיְיטִינַן לֵיהּ We curse him. Rava is of the opinion that it is not sufficient to warn a person that if he does not keep his word he will be punished by God. It is necessary that the formula of "He who punished..." be recited in court as a curse, so that God will punish the offender for acting dishonestly. Regarding the objection that it is forbidden to curse another Jew, Rava stated that the qualification applied only to Jews who behaved properly, but a Jew who does not behave as befits a Jew may be cursed, and this is not at all forbidden. (See Nehemiah 13:25, where Nehemiah cursed the Jews who violated the laws of the Torah.)

[1] דְּרַבִּי חִיָּיא בַּר יוֹסֵף יָהֲבוּ לֵיהּ זוּזֵי אַמִּלְחָא. [2] לְסוֹף, אִיַּיקַר מִלְחָא. [3] אֲתָא לְקַמֵּיהּ דְּרַבִּי יוֹחָנָן. [4] אֲמַר לֵיהּ: ״זִיל, הַב לְהוּ, [5] וְאִי לָא, קַבֵּיל עָלֶיךָ ׳מִי שֶׁפָּרַע׳״.

[6] וְאִי אָמְרַתְּ אוֹדוּעֵי מוֹדְעִינַן לֵיהּ, [7] רַבִּי חִיָּיא בַּר יוֹסֵף בַּר אוֹדוּעֵי הוּא?

[8] וְאֶלָּא מַאי? מֵילָט לָיְיטִינַן לֵיהּ? [9] רַבִּי חִיָּיא בַּר יוֹסֵף אָתֵי לְקַבּוּלֵי עֲלֵיהּ לְטוּתָא דְּרַבָּנַן?

[10] אֶלָּא, רַבִּי חִיָּיא בַּר יוֹסֵף עֵרָבוֹן הוּא דְּיָהֲבִי לֵיהּ.

LITERAL TRANSLATION

[1] For Rabbi Ḥiyya bar Yosef was [once] given money for salt. [2] Later, salt went up in price. [3] He came before Rabbi Yoḥanan. [4] He said to him: "Go, give [it] to them, [5] and if not, accept upon yourself 'He who punished.'"

[6] But if you say [that] we inform him, [7] was Rabbi Ḥiyya bar Yosef in need of (lit., "subject to") being informed?

[8] But what then? Do we curse him? [9] Would Rabbi Ḥiyya bar Yosef come to accept a curse of the Sages upon himself?

[10] Rather, it was a down payment that they gave Rabbi Ḥiyya bar Yosef.

TRANSLATION AND COMMENTARY

punished" formula is a curse? [1] From the following story: **Rabbi Ḥiyya bar Yosef was once given money** as payment **for** a supply of **salt.** [2] **Later, salt went up in price,** and Rabbi Ḥiyya bar Yosef, being the seller, was tempted to retract. [3] **He came before Rabbi Yoḥanan** to ask him what to do. [4] Rabbi Yoḥanan **said to him: "Go and give** the buyers the salt they paid for, as you have no moral right to retract after receiving payment. [5] Moreover, **if** you do **not** do so, you must **accept** the **'He who punished'** curse **on yourself."**

וְאִי אָמְרַתְּ [6] Rava now explains how this story proves that the formula "He who punished..." is a curse: **If you say** that the court merely **informs** the person who is about to retract that his impending action is unethical and will lead to Divine displeasure, [7] **was Rabbi Ḥiyya bar Yosef in need of being informed** of this? A Talmudic Sage must surely have known this statement of the Mishnah without needing to be told about it by Rabbi Yoḥanan. Hence, it would seem that "He who punished" cannot be a warning, as Abaye explained, but a curse, as Rava explained. Rabbi Yoḥanan must have been cautioning Rabbi Ḥiyya bar Yosef not to carry out his intention of reneging on the transaction, lest he bring upon himself the "He who punished" curse.

וְאֶלָּא מַאי [8] **But** the Gemara rejects this proof: If you find it unlikely that Rabbi Yoḥanan was informing Rabbi Ḥiyya bar Yosef of the law of the Mishnah, **what then** would you rather say? **That** Rabbi Yoḥanan threatened to **curse him?** [9] This explanation is as implausible as the other, for **would Rabbi Ḥiyya bar Yosef submit himself to a curse of the Sages?** Surely a Talmudic Sage would not do something that justified a curse merely in order to save money!

אֶלָּא [10] **Rather,** the Gemara concludes, in this case Rabbi Yoḥanan needed to inform Rabbi Ḥiyya bar Yosef of the law, as his was not the standard case considered by the Mishnah and familiar to all Talmudic scholars, in which one party chooses to withdraw from a transaction after money has been paid. This particular case was unusual enough for Rabbi Ḥiyya bar Yosef to feel he needed to inquire of a greater authority. For, in this case, the buyer had not yet paid for the salt in full. Instead, he **gave Rabbi Ḥiyya bar Yosef** a **down payment,** with the understanding that he would pay the remainder later. But before the buyer could perform *meshikhah* on the salt, the price rose, and Rabbi Ḥiyya bar Yosef regretted that he had agreed to the transaction.

RASHI

אייקר מלחא — ורצה לחזור. **בר אודועי הוא** — בתמיה. וכי היה צריך להודיעו שהוא נפרע מן השקרנים? והלא תלמיד חכם היה! **ערבון** — מקצת המעות נתן לו על פיסוק מרובה.

SAGES

רַבִּי חִיָּיא בַּר יוֹסֵף **Rabbi Ḥiyya bar Yosef.** A second generation Babylonian Amora who later immigrated to Eretz Israel, Rabbi Ḥyya bar Yosef was one of Rav's outstanding students and transmitted many of his teachings. After Rav's death, Rabbi Ḥiyya studied with Shmuel and later immigrated to Eretz Israel, where he became a student-colleague of Rabbi Yoḥanan (with whom he had many Halakhic discussions). He may also have served as a Rabbinical judge in Tiberias.

From the Gemara here, and from other sources as well, it appears that Rabbi Ḥiyya bar Yosef earned his living as a merchant.

NOTES

refers to Jews alone. Rather, it says "among your people." From here we learn that it is permitted to curse Jews who are not behaving "in the manner of your people."

In several places the Gemara extends the permission to curse sinners. Thus the command to honor and revere one's parents does not apply to parents who "are not behaving in the manner of your people." The prohibition against striking another person also does not apply to sinners who "do not behave in the manner of your people." In our Gemara, Rava extends this idea further. According to Rava, even a person who is scrupulous in his adherence to the law may be cursed if he takes advantage of a legal technicality to behave in a manner the Rabbis considered unethical.

אָתֵי לְקַבּוּלֵי עֲלֵיהּ לְטוּתָא **Would he come to accept a curse upon himself...?** Why did Rava think it more likely that Rabbi Ḥiyya bar Yosef would behave in a manner that would bring a curse upon himself, than that he would be unaware of a statement of the Mishnah?

Rosh explains that Rava thought Rabbi Ḥiyya might have been willing to risk behaving unethically because he knew the buyers personally and was confident that they would forgive him for not going beyond the letter of the law. However, the Gemara insisted that even if Rabbi Ḥiyya bar Yosef was confident that he would not actually be cursed, he would still not have behaved in so unethical a manner as to deserve a curse.

LANGUAGE (RASHI)

אייר״ש* From the Old French *eres,* "advance," i.e., an initial payment towards part of a debt.

פרמנינ״ן** (פרמנינ״ץ) From the Old French *fermance,* "surety, security."

TRANSLATION AND COMMENTARY

הוּא סָבַר [1]The question then arose as to whether Rabbi Hiyya bar Yosef was permitted to withdraw from the transaction. There was no dispute that Rabbi Ḥiyya bar Yosef was required, under pain of the Mishnah's curse, to supply the buyers with a quantity of salt corresponding to the amount of money he had received. But there was room to query whether he was required to supply *all* the salt for which he had contracted, or whether he was entitled to change his mind about that portion that corresponded to the as-yet-unpaid money. Rabbi Ḥiyya bar Yosef **maintained**: A down payment **acquires** an amount of **merchandise corresponding to its** own value, and no more. Therefore Rabbi Ḥiyya bar Yosef was not afraid of being subject to the "He who punished" curse for reneging on a transaction. He was willing to provide the buyers with an amount of salt corresponding to the amount of the down payment, and only wanted to renege on the amount in excess of the down payment.

וַאֲמַר לֵיהּ רַבִּי יוֹחָנָן [2]**But Rabbi Yoḥanan said to** Rabbi Ḥiyya bar Yosef: Your understanding of the law is mistaken. In fact, a down payment **acquires all of the merchandise.** Once the buyer has paid the seller any money at all, the parties may not withdraw from the transaction without submitting to the "He who punished" curse. They may not even renege on that part of the merchandise that exceeds the value of the down payment. Thus this story cannot be used to resolve the dispute between Abaye and Rava regarding the proper interpretation of the Mishnah.

אִתְּמַר [3]The Gemara continues its discussion of the effectiveness of a partial payment in a sale of movable property or real estate: **It was stated** that the Amoraim differed about this issue: [4]**Rav said: A pledge acquires** an amount of **merchandise corresponding to its** own value, and no more. Hence, if one of the parties wishes to renege on the rest of the transaction (as Rabbi Ḥiyya bar Yosef did in the previous story), he may do so without having to submit to the "He who punished" curse. [5]**But Rabbi Yoḥanan said:** A pledge **acquires all of the merchandise,** as Rabbi Yoḥanan ruled above in the story of Rabbi Ḥiyya bar Yosef.

מֵיתִיבֵי [6]**An objection was raised** against Rav's view from a Baraita. The Baraita deals with the concept called *asmakhta* (אַסְמַכְתָּא — lit., "reliance"). If two people make an agreement and A shows signs of a lack of confidence in B's sincerity, B may then make an extravagant promise to reassure A. For example, he may say: "If I do not fulfill my part of the agreement, you can take my house away." The language used is the language of a conditional contract. B is, as it were, contracting to give A his house if he does not fulfill a certain agreement. But the intent of *asmakhta* is entirely different from that of a conditional contract. B does not for a moment contemplate actually giving A his house. He merely wants to impress upon A that he has every intention of fulfilling his part of the agreement. There is a Tannaitic dispute as to whether or not *asmakhta* is legally binding in the event that B does not fulfill his part of the agreement. In other words, do we follow the language of the *asmakhta* and treat it like any other conditional contract, or do we follow the intent of the *asmakhta* and treat it as mere words of reassurance, having no legal significance? The Halakhah is that *asmakhta* is not legally binding. Thus, even if B fails to fulfill his part of the agreement, A has no claim on his house. It is therefore important, when writing a contract, to consider clauses specifying penalties for non-fulfillment very carefully, as these clauses may sometimes be valid, and may sometimes be nothing more than an empty *asmakhta*.

The Baraita says: "A person was buying landed property, and the parties were not yet ready to perform an act of acquisition to finalize the transaction, but they wished nevertheless to commit themselves to it. [7]The buyer **gave the** seller a sum of money as **a pledge** — a guarantee, not a down payment — **and** then made

[1]הוּא סָבַר: כְּנֶגְדּוֹ הוּא קוֹנֶה. [2]וַאֲמַר לֵיהּ רַבִּי יוֹחָנָן: כְּנֶגֶד כּוּלּוֹ הוּא קוֹנֶה.
[3]אִתְּמַר: עֵרָבוֹן, [4]רַב אוֹמֵר: כְּנֶגְדּוֹ הוּא קוֹנֶה. [5]וְרַבִּי יוֹחָנָן אָמַר: כְּנֶגֶד כּוּלּוֹ הוּא קוֹנֶה.
[6]מֵיתִיבֵי: [7]"הַנּוֹתֵן עֵרָבוֹן

LITERAL TRANSLATION

[1]He maintained: It acquires [merchandise] corresponding to itself.

[2]But Rabbi Yoḥanan said to him: It acquires [merchandise] corresponding to all of it.

[3]It was stated: [Regarding] a deposit, [4]Rav says: It acquires [merchandise] corresponding to itself. [5]But Rabbi Yoḥanan said: It acquires [merchandise] corresponding to all of it.

[6]They raised an objection: [7]"Someone who gives a pledge

RASHI

הוא סבר כנגדו הוא קונה — אי מכירת קרקע הוא שנקנית בכסף קונה קנין גמור, ואי מכירת מטלטלין הוא קונה כנגדו להתחייב ב"מי שפרע". **ורבי יוחנן אמר כו'** — בקרקע לקנין גמור, ובמטלטלין לקבל "מי שפרע". **הנותן ערבון** — לא דמי להיא דלעיל, דזה אינו פריעת מקצת מעות שקורין *אייר"ש, אלא ערבון ומשכון לקנוס את החוזר בו **פרמנינ"ן בלעז.

TRANSLATION AND COMMENTARY

a declaration (an *asmakhta*) to reassure the seller, [1]**saying to him: 'If I go back on my word, my pledge is forfeited to you** without my receiving anything in return.' [2]**The** seller then likewise made a declaration (an *asmakhta*) to reassure the buyer, **saying to him: 'If I go back on my word, I will return to you double** the amount of **your pledge.'** [3]The law in this case is as follows: **The conditions** that were stipulated **are** in effect, and must be **fulfilled.** The buyer is allowed to retract, but if he does so, he forfeits the pledge. Likewise, if the seller retracts, he must return to the buyer twice the amount of the pledge. [4]**These are the words of Rabbi Yose."**

רַבִּי יוֹסֵי לְטַעְמֵיהּ [5]The Gemara interrupts its presentation of the Baraita and explains the basis of Rabbi Yose's opinion: In this ruling, **Rabbi Yose follows his own opinion** cited elsewhere in the Talmud (*Bava Batra* 168a), **for he says** that ***asmakhta* acquires.** Rabbi Yose is of the opinion that we treat an *asmakhta* like any other conditional transaction, and the specified penalties are valid and enforceable.

רַבִּי יְהוּדָה אוֹמֵר [6]The Gemara resumes its quotation from the Baraita, which it had interrupted to explain Rabbi Yose's view: **"Rabbi Yehudah said:** If one of the parties retracts, the pledge is neither forfeited nor doubled, for Rabbi Yehudah maintains that *asmakhta* does not acquire, and the extravagant promises the parties made to each other have no binding force. The mutual promises of the parties are to be ignored, and this case is to be treated like an ordinary case in which a buyer gives a seller a pledge without attaching any *asmakhta* conditions to it. The law in such a case is as follows: To the extent that the pledge acquires, it is impossible to retract at all, and to the extent that it does not acquire, both parties may retract without penalty. But to what extent does the pledge acquire? [7]**It is sufficient that** the buyer **acquires** a part of the **property** equal **to the value of his pledge,** but not all of it." Thus, with respect to property corresponding to the value of the pledge, neither party can retract at all, for the sale on this part of the property was effected with the pledge. But with respect to property in excess of the value of the pledge, both parties may still retract without penalty, as the pledge does not acquire the rest of the property, and the *asmakhta* is legally unenforceable." At first glance, it would appear that Rabbi Yehudah agrees with Rav that a pledge acquires property corresponding to its

לַחֲבֵירוֹ, [1]וְאָמַר לוֹ, 'אִם אֲנִי חוֹזֵר בִּי, עֵרְבוֹנִי מָחוּל לְךָ', [2]וְהַלָּה אָמַר לוֹ, 'אִם אֲנִי אֶחֱזוֹר בִּי, אֶכְפּוֹל לְךָ עֵרְבוֹנְךָ', [3]נִתְקַיְּימוּ הַתְּנָאִים. [4]דִּבְרֵי רַבִּי יוֹסֵי".

[5]רַבִּי יוֹסֵי לְטַעְמֵיהּ, דְּאָמַר: אַסְמַכְתָּא קַנְיָא.

[6]"רַבִּי יְהוּדָה אוֹמֵר: [7]דַּיּוֹ שֶׁיִּקְנֶה כְּנֶגֶד עֵרְבוֹנוֹ.

LITERAL TRANSLATION

to his fellow [1]and said to him, 'If I go back on my [word], my pledge is forfeited to you,' [2]and the other [party] said to him, 'If I go back on my [word], I will double your pledge for you,' [3]the conditions are fulfilled. [4][These are] the words of Rabbi Yose."

[5]Rabbi Yose [follows] his [own] opinion, for he said: *asmakhta* acquires.

[6]"Rabbi Yehudah says: [7]It is sufficient that he acquires [property] corresponding to [the value of] his pledge.

RASHI

רבי יוסי לטעמיה דאמר – בבבא בתרא בפרק "גט פשוט" (קסח,א). **אסמכתא קניא** – הבטחת גוזמא, שאדם מבטיח את חבירו לסמוך עליו, שאם לא יקיים תנאו יתן כך וכך. **דיו שיקנה כו'** – לא זה ימחול ולא זה יכפול, אלא לא זה ולא זה יכולין לחזור מלקיים מן המכירה כנגד הערבון, וחוזרים על השאר.

SAGES

רַבִּי יוֹסֵי Rabbi Yose (ben Ḥalafta). A Tanna of the generation before the completion of the Mishnah. See *Bava Metzia*, Part I, pp. 21-22.

NOTES

אַסְמַכְתָּא *Asmakhta* (lit., "reliance"). The word *asmakhta* has several meanings in Talmudic literature, and its precise definition depends on the context. In our Gemara, *asmakhta* refers to an exaggerated promise to pay damages, given as reassurance that an agreement will be honored. The language of an *asmakhta* is the language of a conditional contract, but the intent is entirely different. The person giving the *asmakhta* does not really believe he will ever be called upon to fulfill it. He merely wishes to impress upon the other party that he has every intention of fulfilling the agreement.

The dispute between Rabbi Yehudah and Rabbi Yose with respect to *asmakhta* revolves around the fundamental question of whether it is the language of the *asmakhta* or the intent of the parties that should be followed. The question of how to rule in the Tannaitic dispute between Rabbi Yose and Rabbi Yehudah is itself subject to an Amoraic dispute (below, 66a). However, the Rishonim agree that the Halakhah is that *asmakhta* is not legally binding.

Sometimes the parties to a contract may wish to include a stipulation of damages in the event of non-fulfillment. Often these stipulations are a mere *asmakhta,* and have no validity, but there are similar arrangements whose validity has been upheld.

כְּנֶגֶד עֵרְבוֹנוֹ Corresponding to the value of his pledge. Our commentary follows *Rashi,* as explained by *Ran* and *Nimmukei Yosef.* According to this explanation, the pledge discussed in the Baraita by Rabbi Yose, Rabbi Yehudah and Rabban Shimon ben Gamliel is not the same as the pledge discussed by Rabbi Yoḥanan and Rav. The latter was given as a *down payment,* whereas the pledge discussed in the Baraita was given as a *guarantee* in lieu of payment.

In a sale of real estate, if the parties agree on a price and the buyer pays a small sum of money as a down payment, intending to pay the remainder over a period of time,

TRANSLATION AND COMMENTARY

own value and no more. [1]However, the Baraita continues, **"Rabban Shimon ben Gamliel said: Regarding which case was the statement** of Rabbi Yehudah **made?** When does the pledge acquire property corresponding to its own value and no more? [2]Only **when** the buyer **said to** the seller: **'Let my pledge** serve as an act of **acquisition** on the entire property, with no connection to the actual payment.' If the buyer states that he wants the pledge to serve as a *substitute* for an act of acquisition, and uses the pledge as a guarantee that he will fulfill his part of the agreement, the buyer only acquires merchandise worth the value of the pledge, because the pledge was not intended to serve as a down payment. [3]**But** if the buyer gave the seller a pledge as a down payment, without stating that he wanted to use it as a substitute for an act of acquisition for all the property — for

[1]אָמַר רַבָּן שִׁמְעוֹן בֶּן גַּמְלִיאֵל: בַּמֶּה דְּבָרִים אֲמוּרִים? [2]בִּזְמַן שֶׁאָמַר לוֹ, ׳עֵרָבוֹנִי יִקּוֹן׳. [3]אֲבָל מָכַר לוֹ בַּיִת אוֹ שָׂדֶה בְּאֶלֶף זוּז,

LITERAL TRANSLATION

[1]Rabban Shimon ben Gamliel said: In what [case] are these words said? [2]When he said to him, 'Let my pledge acquire.' [3]But if he sold him a house or a field for a thousand zuz,

RASHI

במה דברים אמורים — שאינו קונה אלא כנגד ערבונו. **בזמן שאמר לו ערבוני יקון** — יקנה. שלא נתנה לו בתורת תחילת פירעון והשאר עליו מלוה, אלא בתורת שערבון זה יקנה את הכל, והא לאו מלתא היא. **אבל מוכר לו כו׳** — **ונותן לו מהן** מתש מאות זוז לשם פירעון, או סתם — **קנה כו׳**. והיא דאיפלגו בה רב ורבי יוחנן — כי האי גונא הוא, שזה הערבון תחילת הדמים הפירעון של פיסוק כי יהב ליה סתם.

BACKGROUND

עֵרָבוֹן וּמַשְׁכּוֹן A pledge and a pawn. Although a pledge and a pawn are quite similar, there is a difference between them. A pawn (מַשְׁכּוֹן) is something given to a lender by a borrower, either as security — so that the lender can take the pawn if the borrower does not return the loan — or as a means of applying pressure on the borrower, who wants the pawn back and will therefore make an effort to repay his debt speedily. In contrast, a pledge is not connected to a loan, but guarantees some undertaking (such as a commercial transaction or an agreement to perform a certain task). One party gives a pledge as a guarantee that he will carry out the agreement. We see that there is a dispute among the Tannaim as to the legal right of the recipient to keep the pledge.

CONCEPTS

אַסְמַכְתָּא ***Asmakhta.*** An obligation which a person undertakes but does not expect to be called upon to fulfill. An example of this is a seller's acceptance of exaggerated fines for failure to deliver merchandise by a certain time. The Sages disagreed as to whether or not such a commitment is binding.

NOTES

the sale is complete, and neither party may subsequently retract. This is because the payment of money is an act of acquisition for the purpose of purchasing real estate, and even a small payment is sufficient to make the sale irreversible.

According to Rabbi Yoḥanan, the law is the same in relation to sale of movable property. Once a sum of money, however small, has been given as a down payment, the parties cannot renege on the sale without submitting to the "He who punished" curse. But according to Rav, the law is different for movable property, and the curse is applied only with reference to that part of the merchandise that corresponds to the value of the down payment.

In the case described by the Baraita, on the other hand, the parties had not yet agreed on a price for the real estate being sold, but wished to commit themselves in principle to the transaction, with the details to be worked out later. Therefore the buyer gave the seller a sum of money as a *guarantee* of payment, and agreed that if he subsequently withdrew, the pledge would be forfeit, and if the seller withdrew, he would have to return double the value of the pledge. The formula used in such a case is as follows: "Handing over my pledge to you will serve as a substitute for an act of acquisition on all the property, regardless of the actual payment, which has yet to be worked out" (עֵרָבוֹנִי יִקּוֹן).

This arrangement would appear to be an ideal way of committing oneself to an agreement before the details are worked out. The problem is that it is an *asmakhta.* When they made this promise, the parties had no intention of reneging on the deal and actually paying the specified damages. Therefore, Rabbi Yose, who is of the opinion that *asmakhta* is legally binding, maintains that this is a good way to finalize an agreement, and if either party reneges, he must fulfill his promise concerning the pledge. Rabbi Yehudah, by contrast, is of the opinion that *asmakhta* is not legally binding. We therefore ignore the promises made by the parties, and treat the pledge like an ordinary payment of money.

But even though, according to Rabbi Yehudah, we ignore the parties' promises, the law is not the same as in a case where no promises were made. Since the parties did stipulate that the pledge would serve only as a guarantee of payment, and since they may not have agreed on a purchase price, the pledge cannot be considered a down payment, even according to Rabbi Yehudah. Therefore it acquires only an amount corresponding to its own value. But if the parties had stipulated that the pledge would serve as a down payment, or even if they had said nothing at all, the pledge would have acquired the entire property.

There are many other interpretations of *Rashi*'s explanation. Many Rishonim, however, explain this passage entirely differently (see following note).

עֵרָבוֹנִי יִקּוֹן Let my pledge acquire. Our commentary follows *Rashi* (see previous note). *Tosafot* and many other Rishonim explain this Baraita quite differently.

HALAKHAH

קִנְיָן בְּעֵרָבוֹן Buying with a pledge. "If someone agreed to the price of a land purchase and gave a pledge to secure the purchase, both parties may retract. *Rema* adds that if the buyer told the seller to acquire the pledge itself to the extent of the agreed price, then the pledge acquires the land." (*Shulḥan Arukh, Ḥoshen Mishpat* 190:9.)

עֵרָבוֹן וְאַסְמַכְתָּא A pledge and *asmakhta.* "If a buyer gives a seller a pledge, specifying that the seller may keep the pledge if he, the buyer, retracts, and at the same time he secures the agreement of the seller to return double the pledge if the seller should retract, the seller may keep the pledge if the buyer retracts, because the pledge is already in his possession. But if the seller retracts, he need not return double the value of the pledge, for this is regarded as an *asmakhta*, which is not enforceable (*Rambam*). *Rema* (in the name of *Rashi*, *Ra'avad* and *Rosh*) maintains that if the buyer retracts, the seller does not acquire the pledge which he has in his possession, since such a transaction is also considered an *asmakhta*." (*Shulḥan Arukh, Ḥoshen Mishpat* 207:11.)

¹וּפָרַע לוֹ מֵהֶם חֲמֵשׁ מֵאוֹת זוּז, קָנָה, ²וּמַחֲזִיר לוֹ אֶת הַשְּׁאָר אֲפִילּוּ לְאַחַר כַּמָּה שָׁנִים״.
³מַאי לָאו הוּא הַדִּין לְמִטַּלְטְלִין — ⁴בִּדְסְתָמָא קָנֵי לְהוּ לְכוּלְּהוּ?
⁵לָא, מִטַּלְטְלִין, בִּדְסְתָמָא, לָא קָנֵי.
⁶וּמַאי שְׁנָא?
⁷קַרְקַע, דִּבְכַסְפָּא קָנֵי לֵיהּ מַמָּשׁ, ⁸קָנֵי לֵיהּ לְכוּלָּהּ. ⁹מִטַּלְטְלֵי,

LITERAL TRANSLATION

[1] and he paid him five hundred zuz of them, he acquires, [2] and he pays him back the remainder even after several years."

[3] Is it not that the same law [applies] to movable property — [4] that where it is unspecified it acquires everything?

[5] No, movable property, where it is unspecified, it does not acquire.

[6] But what is the difference?

[7] Land, which one actually acquires with money, [8] it acquires all of it. [9] Movable property,

TRANSLATION AND COMMENTARY

example, if the seller **sold** the buyer **a house or a field for a thousand zuz,** [1] **and** the buyer **paid** the seller **five hundred of** the thousand **zuz** as a down payment — then the buyer immediately **acquires** the entire property. [2] He may then **pay back the remainder**, the other five hundred zuz, **even after several years,** as the balance is treated as an ordinary debt independent of the sale."

מַאי לָאו [3] We see, according to the authoritative ruling of Rabban Shimon ben Gamliel, that when a buyer gives a seller a sum of money as a down payment on the purchase of real estate, he immediately acquires the entire property, and the parties have no right to withdraw from the transaction. It would appear, therefore, that this Baraita contradicts Rav's ruling that a pledge given as a down payment only acquires the amount of merchandise that corresponds to the value of the pledge. It is true that the Baraita is referring to real estate, whereas the difference of opinion between Rav and Rabbi Yoḥanan concerns movable property. But nevertheless the Gemara suggests: **Why not assume that the same law applies to movable property** as well? [4] There, too, a pledge given as a down payment on the merchandise **should acquire everything,** at least with respect to the "He who punished" curse, provided, as Rabban Shimon ben Gamliel explained, that the buyer **did not specify** that the pledge was intended to serve as a guarantee and not as a down payment.

לָא [5] The Gemara answers: **No,** a pledge **does not acquire movable property** in full, even **where** the buyer **did not specify** that the pledge was intended to serve as a guarantee. For there is a difference between the use of a down payment to acquire land and its use to acquire movable property.

וּמַאי שְׁנָא [6] **But what is the difference** between real estate and movable property? In both cases the down payment should be effective!

קַרְקַע דִּבְכַסְפָּא קָנֵי לֵיהּ מַמָּשׁ [7] The Gemara answers: **Land is actually acquired with money,** since monetary payment is a valid act of acquistion for the purchase of real estate. [8] Therefore money **acquires everything** included in the sale, even when there was only a symbolic down payment. [9] But monetary payment is not a

RASHI

מאי לאו — כי היכי דאמר רבן שמעון בן גמליאל בקרקע, הקנוי בכסף לגמרי, דמכי יהיב ליה מקלת מעות סתם — קנה לגמרי, והוא הדין למטלטלי הקנויס בכסף לענין "מי שפרע" בסתמא קני ליה ערבון לכוליה לחייבו ב"מי שפרע". **לא קני ליה כוליה** — לקבל "מי שפרע" אם נתן לו כנגד ערבונו. **ומאי שנא** — מטלטלין לענין "מי שפרע" מקרקע לענין קנין גמור? ומשנינן: קרקע דיפה כח הכסף בקניינה לקנות לגמרי קנין גמור מלחזור — יפה נמי כח מקלת פריעתו לקנות הכל. אבל מטלטלין, שהורע הכסף בהן, דאי פרע הכל לא קני אלא לקבל "מי שפרע" — בסתמא נמי לא קני פרעון מקלת לכולו, לקבל "מי שפרע" על השאר, אלא כנגד הערבון.

NOTES

According to *Tosafot,* the *asmakhta* agreement between the parties was as follows: The buyer agreed that if he reneged, the pledge would be *acquired* by the seller without anything being given in exchange, and the seller agreed that if *he* reneged, the pledge would *acquire* a part of the real estate corresponding to double the value of the pledge. Both parties thus used the words עֲרָבוֹנִי יִקּוֹן — "let my pledge acquire."

According to Rabbi Yose, an *asmakhta* is a valid agreement, and the parties must fulfill their promises if they renege on the purchase. According to Rabbi Yehudah, *asmakhta* is not valid; therefore we reduce the extravagant damages stipulated in the contract, and award only those damages that are justified. Thus, if the buyer reneges, the seller cannot retain the pledge without giving the buyer a part of the field corresponding to the value of the pledge, and if the seller reneges, the buyer can insist on receiving that part, but no more. Thus, in effect, the pledge acquires a part corresponding to its own value.

Rabban Shimon ben Gamliel then points out that this applies only if the parties made an agreement in which the pledge was supposed to acquire a part of the field. In such a case, Rabbi Yose follows the language of the agreement and awards the injured party the enlarged part stipulated in the contract, whereas Rabbi Yehudah adjusts the size of the part so that the damages are justified. But if the parties had made no stipulation at all, the pledge would be treated like a down payment and would acquire the entire field.

TRANSLATION AND COMMENTARY

valid act of acquistion for the purchase of **movable property; it only "acquires" for purposes of receiving** the **"He who punished"** curse. [1]Therefore, since the acquisition of movables with money has only limited validity, partial payment **does not acquire everything** for purposes of receiving the curse. Whatever effects it has are restricted to a portion of the merchandise corresponding in value to the amount of the down payment. There is, therefore, no contradiction between the Baraita, which deals with landed property, and Rav's ruling, which deals with movables.

לֵימָא כְּתַנָּאֵי [2]The Gemara now considers another Baraita, dealing with the laws of the Sabbatical Year. The Torah declared that, at the close of the Sabbatical Year, all outstanding debts are canceled (Deuteronomy 15:1-3). Debts that have already begun to be collected, however, are not canceled. This includes a case where the creditor pressed the debtor for his money, and the debtor gave him a utensil to place in pawn, pending payment of the debt. Once the debtor gives the creditor a pawn, the debt is no longer affected by the Sabbatical Year. The Gemara asks: **Shall we say** that the dispute between Rav and Rabbi Yoḥanan regarding acquisition with a pledge **parallels an** earlier, **Tannaitic dispute** recorded in the following Baraita: [3]"If **someone lends money to another person against** a pawn, **and the** end of the Sabbatical **Year,** when debts are canceled, **arrives,** the debt is not canceled, because a debt secured by a pawn is not affected by the Sabbatical Year. Moreover, [4]**even if the pawn is only worth half** the loan, [5]the obligation to repay **the loan is** still **not canceled.** [6]**These are the words of Rabban Shimon ben Gamliel.** [7]But **Rabbi Yehudah HaNasi says: If the pawn corresponded to the loan** — i.e., if it was worth as much as the entire loan — then indeed the loan **is not canceled.** [8]**But if** the pawn is **not** worth as much as the loan, then the loan **is canceled,** because according to Rabbi Yehudah HaNasi the law that the Sabbatical Year does not cancel a loan secured by a pawn applies only to a pawn worth as much as the loan."

דְּלָא קָנֵי אֶלָּא לְקַבּוּלֵי "מִי שֶׁפָּרַע", [1]לָא קָנֵי לֵיהּ כּוּלֵּיהּ.
[2]לֵימָא כְּתַנָּאֵי: [3]"הַמַּלְוֶה אֶת חֲבֵירוֹ עַל הַמַּשְׁכּוֹן, וְנִכְנְסָה הַשְּׁמִיטָּה, [4]אַף עַל פִּי שֶׁאֵינוֹ שָׁוֶה אֶלָּא פְּלָג, [5]אֵינוֹ מְשַׁמֵּט.
[6]דִּבְרֵי רַבָּן שִׁמְעוֹן בֶּן גַּמְלִיאֵל.
[7]רַבִּי יְהוּדָה הַנָּשִׂיא אוֹמֵר: אִם הָיָה מַשְׁכּוֹן כְּנֶגֶד הַלְוָאָתוֹ, אֵינוֹ מְשַׁמֵּט, [8]וְאִם לָאו, מְשַׁמֵּט".

LITERAL TRANSLATION

which one only acquires for [purposes of] receiving "He who punished," [1]it does not acquire all of it.

[2]Shall we say [it is] like [a dispute of] Tannaim: [3]"Someone who lends [money] to his fellow against a pawn, and the Sabbatical Year arrived, [4]even if it is only worth half, [5]it does not cancel. [6][These are] the words of Rabban Shimon ben Gamliel. [7]Rabbi Yehudah HaNasi says: If the pawn corresponded to his loan, it does not cancel, [8]but if not, it does cancel."

RASHI

המלוה על המשכון אין שביעית משמטת — דלא קרינא ביה "לא יגוש" שהרי אינו תובעו כלום. **אלא פלג** — חצי החוב. **אינו משמט** — לקמן מפרש לה.

TERMINOLOGY

לֵימָא כְּתַנָּאֵי **Shall we say that this dispute is the same as the following dispute between Tannaim?** Sometimes, in an attempt to understand an Amoraic controversy, the Gemara may suggest that each of the Amoraic viewpoints parallels a corresponding Tannaitic viewpoint. This suggestion is usually rejected by the Gemara, which proceeds to show that the Amoraim are in fact discussing a previously unconsidered aspect of law. The expression לֵימָא — "shall we say" — generally introduces a proposition which is rejected at the end of the discussion. In any event, presenting a difference of opinion between Amoraim as an exact parallel to an earlier difference of opinion among Tannaim entails a difficulty, for even if the Amoraim are divided in their opinion as to which of the Tannaim they support, they each ought to have stated initially, "I agree with Rabbi X (or Y)," and they should not have presented their difference of opinion as though it were a new one.

BACKGROUND

הַשְּׁמִיטָּה **The Sabbatical Year.** The Torah specifically says (Deuteronomy 15:1-3) that when the last day of the Sabbatical Year arrives, all debts are canceled. The Sages explained that this law applies only to those debts that are unsecured, but when the creditor has a lien on the debtor's property, his right to collect the loan is not canceled. There are also other ways of ensuring the payment of loans after the Sabbatical Year. Hillel the Elder simplified these procedures by instituting the prosbul, whereby a lender authorizes the court to collect all his debts.

NOTES

לֵימָא כְּתַנָּאֵי **Shall we say it is like a dispute of Tannaim?** The Rishonim ask: The Gemara has just explained that the dispute between Rav and Rabbi Yoḥanan revolves around the question of whether the law regarding the "He who punished" curse for movable property is analogous to the laws of acquisition for real estate. Rabbi Yoḥanan maintains that it is analogous, while Rav maintains that it is not. But everyone agrees that in a sale of real estate, a down payment acquires the entire property. However, the dispute between Rabban Shimon ben Gamliel and Rabbi Yehudah HaNasi concerns a different subject — a pawn taken against a loan. How can the Gemara compare this dispute with the Amoraic dispute about the "He who punished" curse?

Shittah Mekubbetzet explains that, according to *Rosh,* the dispute between Rabban Shimon ben Gamliel and Rabbi Yehudah HaNasi also concerns a pawn given at the time of a loan, which may not be retained by the creditor as payment on his loan. Such a pawn is merely a token of good faith, a reinforcement of the debtor's promise to repay; it is not itself a form of repayment. Therefore, it is analogous to the payment of money in a purchase of movables, which creates a strong moral obligation — supported by the "He who punished" curse — but is not in itself an act of acquisition.

הַמַּלְוֶה אֶת חֲבֵירוֹ עַל הַמַּשְׁכּוֹן **Someone who lends money to his fellow against a pawn.** Talmudic literature considers two kinds of pawn: מַשְׁכּוֹן בִּשְׁעַת הַלְוָאָה — a pawn given to the creditor as collateral at the time of the loan, and מַשְׁכּוֹן שֶׁלֹּא בִּשְׁעַת הַלְוָאָה — a pawn given to the creditor when he comes to demand repayment of the loan, if the debtor is unable to pay. The first kind of pawn is considered a private arrangement between the parties, and has little Halakhic significance. The creditor has no right to retain such a pawn or to sell it. There are no restrictions on which types of objects may be used as pawns, and there are no restrictions on how the pawn is to be collected.

HALAKHAH

הַשְּׁמִיטָּה בְּהַלְוָאָה בְּמַשְׁכּוֹן **Cancellation by the Sabbatical Year of loans given against pledges.** "If someone lends money against a pledge, the Sabbatical Year does not cancel the loan, and the debtor is still required to repay the creditor

[1]מַאי ״אֵינוֹ מְשַׁמֵּט״ דְּקָאָמַר רַבָּן שִׁמְעוֹן בֶּן גַּמְלִיאֵל? [2]אִילֵימָא: כְּנֶגְדוֹ, [3]מִכְּלָל דְּרַבִּי יְהוּדָה הַנָּשִׂיא סָבַר: [4]לְהַךְ פַּלְגָּא נַמִי מְשַׁמֵּט! [49A] [5]אֶלָּא מַשְׁכּוֹן דְּנָקֵיט לָמָּה לֵיהּ?

LITERAL TRANSLATION

[1]What is "it does not cancel" that Rabban Shimon ben Gamliel said?

[2]If we say: Corresponding to its own [value], [3][this proves] by implication that Rabbi Yehudah HaNasi maintains: [4]That half, too, it cancels!

[49A] [5]Then why does he need the pawn he is holding?

TRANSLATION AND COMMENTARY

מַאי אֵינוֹ מְשַׁמֵּט [1]The Gemara now clarifies the dispute between Rabban Shimon ben Gamliel and Rabbi Yehudah HaNasi: **What is** the meaning of the expression **"it is not canceled" that Rabban Shimon ben Gamliel used?** Which part of the loan is not canceled when the pawn is worth only half as much as the loan?

אִילֵימָא [2]**If we say** that Rabban Shimon ben Gamliel only meant that the half of the loan which **corresponds to** the pawn's **own value** is not cancelled — because it is covered by the pawn, and a debt covered by a pawn is not canceled by the Sabbatical Year, but the rest of the loan, which is not covered by the pawn, is indeed canceled even according to Rabban Shimon ben Gamliel — then about which half do Rabban Shimon ben Gamliel and Rabbi Yehudah HaNasi disagree? They do not disagree about the half of the loan that is not covered by the pawn. Both agree that that half is canceled. [3]Therefore, **this proves by implication** that they disagree about the half of the loan that *is* covered by the pawn. In other words, **Rabbi Yehudah HaNasi maintains** [4]that even **that half** of the loan which corresponds to the pawn's value **is also canceled!** Thus everyone agrees that the half not covered by the pawn is canceled by the Sabbatical Year, but Rabban Shimon ben Gamliel maintains that the half covered by the pawn is unaffected by the Sabbatical Year, whereas Rabbi Yehudah HaNasi maintains that a pawn worth less than a loan has no legal significance, and the entire loan remains subject to cancellation by the Sabbatical Year.

אֶלָּא מַשְׁכּוֹן דְּנָקֵיט לָמָּה לֵיהּ [49A] [5]The Gemara rejects this interpretation as unacceptable. The reason a creditor usually takes a pawn is to make certain that a loan is repaid. In the event that the debt remains unpaid after a certain period of time, the creditor is entitled to retain the pawn or sell it. But any debt secured by such a pawn has in a sense already been collected, and is not subject to cancellation by the Sabbatical Year. Thus, if Rabbi Yehudah HaNasi insists that no part of the loan is secured by the pawn, he is in effect saying that the pawn has no legal significance at all, and that the creditor may not retain it or sell it. But if the pawn has no legal significance, **then why does** the creditor **need the pawn he is holding** in the first place?

RASHI

אילימא — ד״אינו משמט״ כנגד חצי החוב שהוא תופס משכון עליו אינו משמט, אבל משמט הוא השאר. **מכלל דרבי יהודה הנשיא** — אתא למימר דכיון דאינו משכונו כנגד הלוואתו משמט כל החוב? בתמיה. **אלא משכון דתפס** — למאי תפס אם לא להיות משכון תחת שוויו? וההיא מיהא לא קרינא ביה ״לא יגוש״.

NOTES

Most of the discussion on this subject in the Talmud revolves around the type of pawn given to the creditor after the debt falls due. This pawn is considered a form of collection, and if the debtor does not pay his debt promptly, the creditor may sell the pawn or take it for himself. Since this pawn is imposed on the debtor, rather than offered voluntarily, it must be collected by a court, with proper respect for the dignity of the debtor, and only certain types of property may be used (see, for example, Deuteronomy 24:6,10-14).

Our commentary follows *Rashi,* who explains that a debt is exempt from cancellation by the Sabbatical Year only if it is secured by a pawn given after the time of the loan; when a creditor takes such a pawn, the debt has already, in a sense, been collected.

Rosh, by contrast, quotes the Sifrei (*Re'eh* 131), which says that a debt secured by a pawn given at the time of the loan is also exempt from cancellation by the Sabbatical Year. According to this view, the reason why the debt is not canceled is because of a specific Scriptural decree exempting from the Sabbatical laws any debt in which two parties have claims against one another. For if the creditor is holding a pawn belonging to the debtor, even if the pawn was given at the time of the loan, the debtor has a counterclaim against the creditor; hence, both the claim and the counterclaim are exempt from cancellation.

HALAKHAH

after the Sabbatical Year is over. If the pledge was worth less than the loan, the Sabbatical Year does not cancel that part of the loan that corresponds to the value of the pledge, but the rest of the loan is canceled. Some authorities maintain that the loan is not canceled at all, even though the pledge does not cover the full value of the loan." (*Shulḥan Arukh, Ḥoshen Mishpat* 67:12.)

[1]אֶלָּא לָאו שְׁמַע מִינַּהּ: [2]מַאי "אֵינוֹ מְשַׁמֵּט" דְּקָאָמַר רַבָּן שִׁמְעוֹן בֶּן גַּמְלִיאֵל? [3]אֵינוֹ מְשַׁמֵּט בְּכוּלּוֹ.
[4]וּמַאי "מְשַׁמֵּט" דְּקָאָמַר רַבִּי יְהוּדָה הַנָּשִׂיא? [5]לְהַךְ פַּלְגָּא דְּלָא נָקֵיט עֲלֵיהּ מַשְׁכּוֹן.
[6]וּבְהָא קָמִיפַּלְגִי: [7]דְּרַבָּן שִׁמְעוֹן בֶּן גַּמְלִיאֵל סָבַר: כְּנֶגֶד כּוּלּוֹ הוּא קוֹנֶה. [8]וְרַבִּי יְהוּדָה הַנָּשִׂיא סָבַר: כְּנֶגְדּוֹ הוּא קוֹנֶה.
[9]לָא! מַאי "אֵינוֹ מְשַׁמֵּט" דְּקָאָמַר רַבָּן שִׁמְעוֹן בֶּן גַּמְלִיאֵל? [10]לְהַךְ פַּלְגָּא דְּנָקֵיט עֲלֵיהּ מַשְׁכּוֹן.
[11]מִכְּלָל דְּרַבִּי יְהוּדָה הַנָּשִׂיא סָבַר: [12]לְהַךְ פַּלְגָּא דְּנָקֵיט עֲלֵיהּ מַשְׁכּוֹן נַמִי מְשַׁמֵּט. [13]אֶלָּא מַשְׁכּוֹן דְּנָקֵיט לָמָּה לֵיהּ?

LITERAL TRANSLATION

[1]Rather, is it not [correct] to conclude from this: [2]What is "it does not cancel" that Rabban Shimon ben Gamliel said? [3]It does not cancel at all.
[4]And what is "it does cancel" that Rabbi Yehudah HaNasi said? [5]That half against which he does not hold a pawn.
[6]And they disagree about this: [7]Rabban Shimon ben Gamliel maintains: [A down payment] acquires [merchandise] corresponding to all of it. [8]But Rabbi Yehudah HaNasi maintains: It acquires [merchandise] correponding to itself.
[9]No! What is "it does not cancel" that Rabban Shimon ben Gamliel said? [10]That half against which he holds a pawn.
[11][This proves] by implication that Rabbi Yehudah HaNasi maintains: [12]That half against which he holds a pawn, too, it cancels. [13]Then why does he need the pawn he is holding?

RASHI

אינו משמט בכולו – כלומר, אינו משמט כלל. **מכלל דרבי יהודה כו'** – קושיא הוא.

TRANSLATION AND COMMENTARY

אֶלָּא לָאו שְׁמַע מִינַּהּ [1]**Rather,** the Gemara argues, **is it not correct to conclude from here** that the difference of opinion between Rabban Shimon ben Gamliel and Rabbi Yehudah HaNasi should be explained as follows? [2]**What is** the meaning of the expression "the loan **is not canceled**" used **by Rabban Shimon ben Gamliel?** [3]He must have meant that the loan **is not canceled at all,** not even the part unsecured by a pawn. For, according to Rabban Shimon ben Gamliel, a loan partly secured by a pawn is entirely exempt from being canceled by the Sabbatical Year.

וּמַאי מְשַׁמֵּט [4]**And what is** the meaning of the expression "the loan **is canceled" used by Rabbi Yehudah HaNasi?** [5]He must have been referring only to **that half** of the loan **against which** the creditor **is not holding a pawn.** But even he would agree that the half secured by the pawn is not canceled by the Sabbatical Year. Thus both Sages agree that the part of the loan that is secured by the pawn is not canceled by the Sabbatical Year, but Rabban Shimon ben Gamliel is of the opinion that the entire loan is secured by the pawn, whereas Rabbi Yehudah HaNasi is of the opinion that the pawn secures only that part of the loan which corresponds to its own value.

וּבְהָא קָמִיפַּלְגִי [6]The Gemara now explains how the dispute between Rabban Shimon ben Gamliel and Rabbi Yehudah HaNasi corresponds to the later dispute between Rav and Rabbi Yoḥanan concerning a pledge: If the reasoning used above is correct, Rabban Shimon ben Gamliel and Rabbi Yehudah HaNasi **disagree about the following principle:** [7]**Rabban Shimon ben Gamliel maintains** that **a down payment** given as partial payment for the purchase of movable goods **acquires all of the merchandise.** Therefore a pawn that is worth only half the loan secures the entire loan, so that no part of it is canceled by the Sabbatical Year. [8]**But Rabbi Yehudah HaNasi** maintains that a pledge only **acquires an amount** of merchandise **corresponding to** the pledge's **own value.** Therefore the pawn only secures that part of the loan corresponding to its own value, and the rest of the loan is canceled by the Sabbatical Year. Thus it would appear that the difference of opinion between Rav and Rabbi Yoḥanan is identical to the earlier Tannaitic dispute, with Rabbi Yoḥanan holding the same opinion as Rabban Shimon ben Gamliel, and Rav holding the same opinion as Rabbi Yehudah HaNasi.

לָא [9]The Gemara now rejects this conclusion, and reconsiders the interpretation it suggested earlier: **No,** says the Gemara, it is not necessary to explain the Baraita in this way. **When Rabban Shimon ben Gamliel uses** the expression **"it is not canceled"** he is referring only **to** [10]**that half** of the loan **against which** the creditor **is holding the pawn,** but Rabban Shimon ben Gamliel would agree with Rabbi Yehudah HaNasi that the rest of the loan is indeed canceled. According to this explanation, Rabban Shimon ben Gamliel is of the opinion that a pawn worth only half as much as the loan secures that half, whereas Rabbi Yehudah HaNasi is of the opinion that a pawn worth less than a loan has no legal significance.

מִכְּלָל דְּרַבִּי יְהוּדָה הַנָּשִׂיא סָבַר [11]Once again the Gemara objects: But as we pointed out before, if **this** explanation is true, it **proves by implication that Rabbi Yehudah HaNasi maintains** [12]**that half** of the loan **against which** the creditor **holds a pawn is also canceled,** since a pawn worth less than a loan has no legal significance. [13]But in that case, **why does** the creditor **need the pawn he is holding** in the first place?

[1] לְזִכְרוֹן דְּבָרִים בְּעָלְמָא. [2] רַב כָּהֲנָא יָהֲבֵי לֵיהּ זוּזֵי אַכִּיתָּנָא. [3] לַסּוֹף, אִיַּיקַּר כִּיתָּנָא. [4] אֲתָא לְקַמֵּיהּ דְּרַב. [5] אֲמַר לֵיהּ: בְּמַאי דְּנָקִיטַתְּ זוּזֵי, הַב לְהוּ, [6] וְאִידָךְ — דְּבָרִים נִינְהוּ, [7] וּדְבָרִים אֵין בָּהֶן מִשּׁוּם מְחוּסְּרֵי אֲמָנָה. [8] דְּאִיתְּמַר: דְּבָרִים, רַב אָמַר: [9] אֵין בָּהֶן מִשּׁוּם מְחוּסְּרֵי אֲמָנָה. [10] וְרַבִּי יוֹחָנָן אָמַר: יֵשׁ בָּהֶם מִשּׁוּם מְחוּסְּרֵי אֲמָנָה. [11] מֵיתִיבֵי: ״רַבִּי יוֹסֵי בְּרַבִּי יְהוּדָה אוֹמֵר: [12] מַה תַּלְמוּד

LITERAL TRANSLATION

[1] As a mere reminder of words.

[2] Rav Kahana was given money for flax. [3] Later, flax went up in price. [4] He came before Rav. [5] He said to him: For that [part against] which you are holding money, give them, [6] but the rest — they are words, [7] and words do not involve a lack of [good] faith.

[8] For it was stated: Words, said Rav, [9] do not involve a lack of [good] faith. [10] But Rabbi Yoḥanan said: They do involve a lack of [good] faith.

[11] They raised an objection: "Rabbi Yose the son of Rabbi Yehudah says: [12] What does the

RASHI

במאי דנקיטת זוזי הב להו — ואי לא, מקבלת ״מי שפרע״. **ואידך** — המותר. **דברים נינהו** — בלא מעות. רב לטעמיה דאמר כנגדו הוא קונה.

TRANSLATION AND COMMENTARY

לְזִכְרוֹן דְּבָרִים בְּעָלְמָא [1] The Gemara answers: According to Rabbi Yehudah HaNasi, such a pawn serves **merely as a reminder** of the **terms of the transaction.** A pawn worth less than a loan is not an instrument of collection, but merely a token of the borrower's recognition of his debt, and of his sincere intent to repay. Thus it is possible to explain the Baraita in such a way that it has no bearing on the dispute between Rav and Rabbi Yoḥanan.

רַב כָּהֲנָא [2] It was related that **Rav Kahana was** once **given money as** a down payment **for flax** that he was selling. [3] **Later, flax went up in price,** and Rav Kahana, as the seller, wanted to retract. But being a Talmudic Sage, he did not wish to do anything that would be even slightly unethical. [4] **He came before Rav** to ask him what to do. Now, in the previous passage of the Gemara it was stated that Rav is of the opinion that, with respect to the "He who punished" curse, a down payment acquires only that part of the merchandise which corresponds to its own value. [5] Accordingly, Rav **said to him:** Clearly you must **give** the buyers **part of the flax** they ordered — namely, a quantity corresponding to **the money that you are holding** — for if not, you will be subject to the "He who punished" curse. [6] **But the rest** of the flax — that exceeding the value of the down payment — you need not give them, for a down payment acquires only that quantity of merchandise that corresponds to its own value. Your agreement to sell the buyers the rest of the flax, for which they have not yet paid, **is** no more than **a verbal agreement,** unsupported by a formal act of acquisition or by payment of money, [7] **and one is not considered lacking in good faith for going back on a verbal agreement.** Until an act of acquisition, or at least monetary payment, is performed, you are under no legal or even moral obligation to fulfill your part of the agreement. When you made your agreement you were no doubt sincere, but circumstances changed and prices went up, and you are not even morally bound to adhere to your original agreement to give the buyers the flax they ordered at the originally agreed price.

דְּאִיתְּמַר [8] Thus we see that Rav is of the opinion that a verbal agreement does not have even moral significance. The Gemara now reports that this question was the subject of disagreement between these same Amoraim, Rav and Rabbi Yoḥanan: **For it was stated: Rav said: For going back on an** unsupported **verbal agreement,** [9] **one is not considered to be lacking in good faith.** [10] **But Rabbi Yoḥanan said: One is considered to be lacking in good faith** if one violates such an agreement.

מֵיתִיבֵי [11] **An objection was raised** against Rav's view from the following Baraita (Sifra, *Kedoshim* 86): **"Rabbi Yose the son of Rabbi Yehudah says:** The Torah (Leviticus 19:36) said: 'Just balances, just weights, a just ephah and a just hin shall you have,' the ephah being a dry measure (of approx. one bushel) and the hin a liquid measure (approx. six quarts). The Torah thus commands us to be honest in our business dealings. [12] But **what does**

HALAKHAH

מְחוּסְּרֵי אֲמָנָה בִּדְבָרִים **Violation of verbal agreements.** "Someone who makes a verbal agreement without making a monetary payment or delivering a pledge should keep his word. If he reneges on his promise, he is considered lacking in good faith, and such conduct met with the disapproval of the Sages," following Rabbi Yoḥanan's view. *Rema* writes that if a person reneges on a promise because prices have changed, no breach of faith is involved (*Razah, Rosh,* and *Tur*). Others, however disagree (*Ramban* and *Rashba*). *Arukh HaShulḥan* agrees that no breach of faith is involved if a person reneges after prices change, but it is nevertheless not considered pious conduct to violate one's promise in such cases. (*Shulḥan Arukh, Ḥoshen Mishpat* 204:7,11.)

SAGES

רַב כָּהֲנָא **Rav Kahana.** Many Sages bore the name of "Rav Kahana," but the one mentioned here is the Babylonian Amora of the second generation who was a disciple and colleague of Rav.

Rav Kahana was still a young man when he came to study with Rav, but he had already attained such a high level that "he needed Rav's learning but not his opinion" (הֲוָה צָרִיךְ לִגְמָרָא דְּרַב וְלָא לִסְבָרָה). Nevertheless, he was a devoted and respectful disciple. On one occasion he was so zealous for the honor of his teacher that he struck and caused the death of a known informer who had threatened to inform on Rav. For this reason he had to flee to Eretz Israel. There he joined the company of the greatest Sages — Rabbi Yoḥanan and Resh Lakish — who called him "the lion who came up from Babylonia." However, it seems that many people in Eretz Israel did not honor him, and he returned to Babylonia.

רַבִּי יוֹסֵי בְּרַבִּי יְהוּדָה **Rabbi Yose the son of Rabbi Yehudah.** A Tanna of the last generation, Rabbi Yose was the son of the Tanna Rabbi Yehudah (ben Il'ai). He was apparently a close disciple of his father, though he occasionally disagreed with him about the Halakhah, and he was a colleague of Rabbi Yehudah HaNasi. He also discussed the Halakhah with other Sages of his generation. In his activity as a Halakhic authority he was apparently closely associated with Rabbi Yehudah HaNasi, and his teachings are mentioned a number of times in the Mishnah, and very often in the Tosefta and elsewhere. He was also very prolific in the area of Aggadah, and some well-known sayings are transmitted in his name. He seems to have died before Rabbi Yehudah HaNasi, for he referred to him in his will.

BACKGROUND

מְחוּסְּרֵי אֲמָנָה **Lacking in good faith.** Although violation of trust is not a criminal offense, in that a court cannot force the offending party to

לוֹמַר: ׳הִין צֶדֶק׳? [1]וַהֲלֹא הִין בִּכְלָל אֵיפָה הָיָה? [2]אֶלָּא, לוֹמַר לְךָ שֶׁיְּהֵא ׳הֵן׳ שֶׁלְּךָ צֶדֶק, [3]וְ׳לָאו׳ שֶׁלְּךָ צֶדֶק״.

[4]אָמַר אַבַּיֵי: הַהוּא שֶׁלֹּא יְדַבֵּר אֶחָד בַּפֶּה וְאֶחָד בַּלֵּב.

LITERAL TRANSLATION

verse teach by saying: 'A just hin'? [1]Was not a hin included in an ephah? [2]Rather, to say to you that your 'yes' should be just, [3]and your 'no' should be just."

[4]Abaye said: That [means] that he should not say one [thing] with his mouth and one [thing] in his heart.

RASHI

הין בכלל איפה — שההין שנים עשר לוגין, והאיפה שלשה סאין שהן שבעים ושנים לוגין. **אלא שיהא הן שלך כו'** — כלומר, כשאתה מדבר הן או לאו, קיים דבריך והצדק אותם. **שלא ידבר אחד בפה כו'** — בשעה שהוא אומר הדבור לא יהא בדעתו לשנות. אבל אם נשתנה השער לאחר זמן והוא חוזר בו לפי שינוי השער, אין כאן חסרון אמנה.

TRANSLATION AND COMMENTARY

the verse **teach** us **by saying, 'a just hin'** as well as 'a just ephah'? Why mention both of them? [1]**Was not** the law concerning **a hin included in** that of **an ephah,** so that if the ephah must be just, so too must the hin? If the Torah mentioned both measures even though only one was necessary to teach us to be honest in business, the Torah must be hinting at some other law as well. [2]Accordingly, says Rabbi Yose the son of Rabbi Yehudah, we should **rather** interpret the word *'hin'* as though it were *'hen'* — 'yes' — and say that the verse means **to tell us: Your 'yes' should be just,** [3]**and your 'no' should be just,** because a righteous person should never break his word." We see from this statement that Rabbi Yose the son of Rabbi Yehudah is of the opinion that a person who makes a verbal agreement has a moral duty to keep his word, even if the agreement was not in any way legally binding. Thus it would appear that this Baraita contradicts the view of Rav!

אָמַר אַבַּיֵי [4]**Abaye said** in reply: Rabbi Yose the son of Rabbi Yehudah **means that** an ethical person **should not say one thing with his mouth and** think **another thing in his heart.** It is wrong to speak insincerely and make promises which one does not intend to keep. But if a verbal agreement has been made in good faith, and circumstances change later, it is not forbidden to withdraw from such an agreement. Thus Rav's ruling is not contradicted by this Baraita.

NOTES

וַהֲלֹא הִין בִּכְלָל אֵיפָה הָיָה **Was not a hin included in an ephah?** The hin is a liquid measure and the ephah is a dry measure. Why, then, was Rabbi Yose the son of Rabbi Yehudah of the opinion that it was superfluous to mention both of them, especially since the verse mentions other measures of different kinds, such as weights and scales (*Maharsha*)?

Ritva explains that the ephah has a capacity six times that of the hin. Hence, Rabbi Yose reasoned that if the Torah prohibited even the slightest deviation in a large measure, it is obvious that a deviation in a small measure is also prohibited, since a slight deviation is much more significant in a small measure than in a large one.

אָמַר אַבַּיֵי **Abaye said.** Abaye's statement has obvious ethical appeal, but does it also have operative Halakhic force? According to our commentary, Abaye's interpretation was introduced in order to remove the difficulty presented by the Baraita to the view of Rav, who maintains that going back on one's word does not make a person "lacking in good faith." But according to Rabbi Yoḥanan, the Baraita presents no difficulty. Hence Abaye's statement is superfluous. Since the Halakhah is in accordance with Rabbi Yoḥanan — one who goes back on his word *is* regarded as "lacking in good faith" — Abaye's statement on behalf of sincerity is sound moral advice, but no more.

Most Rishonim, however, follow *Rif*, who quotes Abaye's statement as Halakhah. This would imply that the Baraita of the "just hin" presents a position that is also difficult to reconcile with the view of Rabbi Yoḥanan, and that Abaye was quoted in order to defend Rabbi Yoḥanan as well as Rav.

The Rishonim differ as to what difficulty the Baraita poses to Rabbi Yoḥanan. According to *Ra'avad* and *Rosh*, the difficulty arises from the Baraita's implication that a dishonest person violates a command of the Torah. By contrast, Rabbi Yoḥanan failed to appeal to Scripture to prove his point, limiting himself to the observation that a dishonest person evokes the displeasure of the Sages.

Ramban and *Rosh* perceive another difficulty in the Baraita for Rabbi Yoḥanan. The Gemara concludes that Rabbi Yoḥanan forbade reneging on a promise only in the case of a promise to give a small gift. In the case of a large gift, however, he would agree with Rav that there is nothing unethical about changing one's mind. This distinction is of course inconsistent with the Baraita, which on the face of it deplores commercial dishonesty in all cases.

No matter how we understand the difficulty posed by the Baraita to Rabbi Yoḥanan, Abaye's understanding of the Baraita as referring to sincerity and not commercial honesty removes a significant obstacle to the recognition of Rabbi Yoḥanan's view as normative Halakhah. This explains why *Rif* cited the views of both these Amoraim as Halakhah.

אֶחָד בַּפֶּה וְאֶחָד בַּלֵּב **Saying one thing and thinking another.** Insincerity — "saying one thing with the mouth

HALAKHAH

הֵן צֶדֶק וְלָאו צֶדֶק **A just "yes" and a just "no."** "All people — and Torah scholars in particular — should do business in good faith, and scrupulously keep their word." (*Rambam, Sefer HaMad'a, Hilkhot De'ot* 5:13.)

אֶחָד בַּפֶּה וְאֶחָד בַּלֵּב **Saying one thing and thinking another.** "It is forbidden to deceive others by saying one thing if one really means another." (Ibid., 2:6.)

keep his word, or punish him for breaking it, nevertheless it is a serious religious and moral infraction. Throughout the Bible we find praise for trustworthiness and for trustworthy people. See, for example, Isaiah's praise of Jerusalem as "the city of righteousness, the faithful city" (1:26). He also speaks of "the righteous nation, which keeps faith" (26:2). Conversely, the violation of trust is condemned by the Torah (Deuteronomy 32:20), by the Prophets (Jeremiah 7:28) and in many other places. The Sages also praised trustworthy people, and severely condemned those who are not trustworthy. However, because people bargain with each other in commerce and may legitimately change their minds, it is necessary to define the point at which a person is considered to have broken his promise.

אֵיפָה וְהִין **Ephah and hin.** In the Bible it is written "just balances, just weights, a just ephah, and a just hin shall you have" (Leviticus 19:36). This verse refers to measuring devices used in commerce — scales and stone weights, dry and liquid measures. The ephah unit of dry measure was quite large, containing three *se'ahs*. A hin is a smaller unit, equal to one-sixth of an ephah. The hin was mainly used during the Biblical period, and even before Mishnaic times had become archaic. The log, which was one-twelfth of a hin, was generally used instead.

הִין בִּכְלָל אֵיפָה **A hin was included in an ephah.** Since the ephah was a unit of dry measure, it could not be absolutely precise, for various materials compress to different degrees, and it is also possible to overfill the measure. In fact, the Sages distinguish between heaped measures and level measures in a number of cases. By contrast, liquid measures can be much more precise. Since the Bible reinforced its mention of the ephah (a unit of dry measure) by also mentioning the hin (a unit of liquid measure), this indicates that the measurements must be exact.

LITERAL TRANSLATION

[1]They raised an objection: "Rabbi Shimon says: [2]Even though they said [that] a garment acquires a gold dinar, [3]but a gold dinar does not acquire a garment, [4]at all events that is the law, [5]but they said: He who punished the men of the generation of the flood and the men of the generation of the dispersion, [6]He will punish him who does not stand by his word."

[7]It is [a dispute between] the Tannaim, [8]for we have learned: "It once happened that Rabbi Yoḥanan ben Matya said to his son, 'Go out and hire workers for us.' [9]He went and promised them food. [10]But when he came to his father, he said to him: [11]'My son, even if you make [a meal] for them like Solomon's feast in his time,

[1]מֵיתִיבֵי: ״רַבִּי שִׁמְעוֹן אוֹמֵר: [2]אַף עַל פִּי שֶׁאָמְרוּ טַלִּית קוֹנָה דִּינָר זָהָב, [3]וְאֵין דִּינָר זָהָב קוֹנֶה טַלִּית, [4]מִכָּל מָקוֹם כָּךְ הֲלָכָה, [5]אֲבָל אָמְרוּ: מִי שֶׁפָּרַע מֵאַנְשֵׁי דוֹר הַמַּבּוּל וּמֵאַנְשֵׁי דוֹר הַפַּלָּגָה, [6]הוּא עָתִיד לִיפָּרַע מִמִּי שֶׁאֵינוֹ עוֹמֵד בְּדִיבּוּרוֹ״.

[7]תַּנָּאֵי הִיא, [8]דִּתְנַן: ״מַעֲשֶׂה בְּרַבִּי יוֹחָנָן בֶּן מַתְיָא שֶׁאָמַר לִבְנוֹ, ׳צֵא וּשְׂכוֹר לָנוּ פּוֹעֲלִים׳. [9]הָלַךְ וּפָסַק לָהֶם מְזוֹנוֹת. [10]וּכְשֶׁבָּא אֵצֶל אָבִיו, אָמַר לוֹ: [4]׳בְּנִי, אֲפִילוּ אַתָּה עוֹשֶׂה לָהֶם כִּסְעוּדַּת שְׁלֹמֹה בְּשַׁעְתּוֹ,

RASHI

אבל אמרו חכמים כו׳ — סיפא קתני החוזר בו אין רוח חכמים נוחה הימנו, אלמא יש בהן משום מחוסרי אמנה. **תנאי היא** — דאשכחן רבי יוחנן בן מתיא דפליג. **מעשה ברבי יוחנן כו׳** — משנה היא ב״השוכר את הפועלים״ שצוה את בנו לחזור בתנאו עד שלא יתחילו המלאכה, ולפסוק להם מזונות קלים.

TRANSLATION AND COMMENTARY

מֵיתִיבֵי [1]Another **objection was raised** against Rav from a different Baraita (also quoted above, 48a). Only the beginning of the Baraita is quoted here, but the objection is really based on the part that is not quoted: **"Rabbi Shimon says:** [2]**Even though** the Rabbis **said that a garment acquires a gold dinar,** because the act of *meshikhah* finalizes the sale of movable goods and creates an obligation to pay, [3]**but a gold dinar does not acquire a garment,** because monetary payment without *meshikhah* does not finalize a sale, [4]**nevertheless** the matter is not quite so simple. **It is true that this is the law,** and as long as *meshikhah* has not been performed, both parties can retract and the courts will not enforce the sale. [5]**But the Rabbis** cursed the person who withdraws from a transaction at this point, **saying: 'God, who punished the men of the generation of the flood and the men of the generation of the dispersion,** [6]**will punish anyone who does not stand by his word.'"** The Baraita goes on to consider another case: "And someone who does business with mere words, and promises to buy or sell something, but has not yet given or received any money or performed any formal act of acquisition, does not acquire or transfer ownership of the merchandise he has promised to buy or sell, because a formal act of acquisition must be performed to finalize any transaction. Nevertheless, if he goes back on his word and reneges on his promise, his behavior arouses the disapproval of the Sages." Thus it would appear that any violation of a verbal agreement arouses the displeasure of the Sages, even if it is not supported by the "He who punished" curse. Clearly, then, this Baraita is not consistent with Rav's view.

תַּנָּאֵי הִיא [7]The Gemara replies that the question of whether a person must keep his word under all circumstances **is the** subject of **a dispute between Tannaim.** Thus, even though it is true that Rabbi Shimon, in the Baraita quoted above, supports Rabbi Yoḥanan, there is another Tanna, Rabbi Yoḥanan ben Matya, who supports Rav and is of the opinion that it is permitted to withdraw from a verbal agreement. [8]The Gemara explains: **For we have learned** in the following Mishnah (below, 83a): **"It once happened that Rabbi Yoḥanan ben Matya said to his son, 'Go out and hire workers for us.'** [9]The son **went and** hired workers, and negotiated a tentative wage agreement with them, subject to his father's approval. As one of the conditions of employment, he **promised** to give the workers **food,** but did not specify what kind of food or how much. [10]**But when** the son **came** back **to his father,** the father **said to him:** [11]**'My son,** I cannot accept these terms. For **even if you make an** extremely lavish **meal for** the workers, **like the feasts given by King Solomon in his time,**

TERMINOLOGY

תַּנָּאֵי הִיא It is a Tannaitic controversy, i.e., the matter under discussion by Amoraim is in fact the subject of a Tannaitic controversy.

SAGES

רַבִּי יוֹחָנָן בֶּן מַתְיָא Rabbi Yoḥanan ben Matya. A Tanna about whom nothing is known beyond the incident described here and below (83a). Rabbi Yoḥanan ben Matya probably belonged to the third generation of Tannaim.

BACKGROUND

וּפָסַק לָהֶם מְזוֹנוֹת And he promised them food. Working conditions for day laborers were not fixed, but depended on the specific agreement between the employer and his workers. Sometimes workers brought their own food from home, and sometimes the employer would supply a single meal.

כִּסְעוּדַּת שְׁלֹמֹה בְּשַׁעְתּוֹ Like Solomon's feast in his time. The provisions for the meals of a single day eaten at King Solomon's palace are described in detail by the Bible: "Thirty kor of fine flour and sixty kor of meal, ten fat oxen, and twenty grazing oxen and a hundred sheep beside harts, and roebucks, and fallow-deer, and fatted fowl" (I Kings 5:2-3). The expression "in his time" is explained by the Sages as a reference to the legend that Solomon abdicated for a time, and the provisions mentioned here were those consumed at the palace at the height of his power and glory.

NOTES

and thinking another in the heart" in Talmudic terminology — is a general moral defect that can appear in a variety of contexts. Our commentary follows *Rashi*, who understood Abaye to be interpreting the Baraita as referring to the case of a person who knows full well at the time he makes a promise that he will not keep it.

Rambam rules that "a person must not train himself to flatter, and must not say one thing and think another, and must not engage in trickery." Insincerity of this kind is forbidden even outside the area of business. *Rabbi Zvi Ḥayyot* suggests that *Rambam* did not learn this law from our Gemara, but rather derived it from an incident concerning Joseph and his brothers, who according to the verse (Genesis 37:4) "could not speak to Joseph peacefully." The Sages (*Bereshit Rabbah* 84:8) see this verse as praising Joseph's brothers for not engaging in insincere flattery.

TRANSLATION AND COMMENTARY

[1]you will not have fulfilled your obligation towards them, [2]for they are the children of Abraham, Isaac and Jacob, and it befits them to receive the most lavish meal in the world. [3]Rather, before they begin work, go out and say to them, [4]"I am employing you on condition that you will only have a claim on me to receive bread and beans, the customary fare for laborers." But you must do it quickly, because after they begin to work it will be impossible to make any further changes in the terms of employment, since the act of beginning work finalizes a labor contract.'"

וְאִי סָלְקָא דַּעְתָּךְ [5]It is clear that Rabbi Yoḥanan was not legally bound by the terms his son agreed to with the workers. But his son should still have been morally bound by his agreement. And if it should enter your mind that a person who goes back on his word is considered to be lacking in good faith, as the previous Baraita asserted, [6]how could Rabbi Yoḥanan ben Matya have said to his son, "Go and speak to the workers again and go back on your word"? Accordingly, we may infer that Rabbi Yoḥanan ben Matya was of the opinion that there is nothing wrong with withdrawing from a verbal agreement that has not yet been legally finalized. Thus Rav's ruling is supported by this Tannaitic opinion.

שָׁאנֵי הָתָם [7]But the Gemara refutes this argument: In fact, all the Tannaim agree that it is wrong to go back on a verbal agreement. But the case of Rabbi Yoḥanan ben Matya was different, for the workers themselves did not rely on the son's promise, and it is permitted to withdraw if the would-be beneficiary of a promise knows that it is not to be taken seriously.

מַאי טַעְמָא [8]The Gemara explains: What is the reason that the workers did not take the son's promise seriously? [9]It is because they knew that he relied on his father. In other words, the promise was obviously made subject to his father's approval, so no agreement contracted by the son was binding until it received the father's approval.

אִי הָכִי [10]The Gemara objects: If so, if the son's promise was wholly dependent on his father's approval, he should also have been able to retract even if the workers had already begun work. If the entire contract was conditional, then it would not have been binding even after the workers had begun work. Why, then, did Rabbi Yoḥanan ben Matya insist that his son alter the conditions of employment before the workers began?

הִתְחִילוּ בִּמְלָאכָה [11]The Gemara answers: Once the contract was finalized — when the workers began working — the promise ceased to be conditional. For once the workers began to work, they certainly relied on the terms they had negotiated with the son. [12]For they said: He must certainly have told his father about the employment conditions he discussed with us, and the father must have agreed to them. Thus the conditional element in the son's promise extended only until the workers began to work, and Rabbi Yoḥanan ben Matya's son had to notify the workers of the change before they began to work.

וּמִי אָמַר רַבִּי יוֹחָנָן הָכִי [13]The Gemara now asks: But did Rabbi Yoḥanan really say that someone who

[1]לֹא יָצָאתָ יְדֵי חוֹבָתְךָ עִמָּהֶם, [2]שֶׁהֵן בְּנֵי אַבְרָהָם יִצְחָק וְיַעֲקֹב. [3]אֶלָּא, עַד שֶׁלֹּא יַתְחִילוּ בִּמְלָאכָה, צֵא וֶאֱמוֹר לָהֶם: [4]עַל מְנָת שֶׁאֵין לָכֶם עָלַי אֶלָּא פַּת וְקִטְנִית בִּלְבַד״. [5]וְאִי סָלְקָא דַּעְתָּךְ דְּבָרִים יֵשׁ בָּהֶן מִשּׁוּם מְחוּסְּרֵי אֲמָנָה, [6]הֵיכִי אֲמַר לֵיהּ, ״זִיל, הֲדַר בָּךְ״? [7]שָׁאנֵי הָתָם, דְּפוֹעֲלִים גּוּפַיְיהוּ לָא סָמְכָא דַּעְתַּיְיהוּ. [8]מַאי טַעְמָא? [9]מֵידַע יָדְעֵי דְּעַל אֲבוּהּ סָמַךְ. [10]אִי הָכִי, אֲפִילּוּ הִתְחִילוּ בִּמְלָאכָה נַמִי! [11]הִתְחִילוּ בִּמְלָאכָה, וַדַּאי סָמְכֵי דַּעְתַּיְיהוּ, [12]אָמְרוּ: מֵימַר אֲמַר קַמֵּיהּ דַּאֲבוּהּ, וְנִיחָא לֵיהּ. [13]וּמִי אָמַר רַבִּי יוֹחָנָן הָכִי?

LITERAL TRANSLATION

[1]you have not fulfilled your obligation towards them, [2]for they are the children of Abraham, Isaac and Jacob. [3]Rather, before they begin work, go out and say to them: [4]On condition that you have no [claim] on me except for bread and beans alone.'"

[5]And if it should enter your mind that words involve a lack of [good] faith, [6]how could he say to him, "Go, retract"?

[7]It is different there, for the workers themselves did not rely [on the promise].

[8]What is the reason? [9]They know that he relied on his father.

[10]If so, even if they began work also!

[11][If] they began work, they certainly do rely, [12][for] they say: He surely said [this] before his father, and he agreed.

[13]But did Rabbi Yoḥanan say this?

RASHI

לא סמכא דעתייהו — על דברי הבן. **מימר אמר קמיה** — ככל הודיעו מה פסק לנו, ונתרלה. **מי אמר רבי יוחנן הכי** — דיש בדברים משום חסרון אמנה.

BACKGROUND

בְּנֵי אַבְרָהָם יִצְחָק וְיַעֲקֹב The children of Abraham, Isaac and Jacob. The Sages said that "all Israel are the sons of kings," meaning that, because of the Patriarchs, every Jew is considered a nobleman, worthy of every honor and pleasure in the world. In the same vein, the Torah says, "and you shall be a treasure to me above all peoples," and the Prophets say similar things. Therefore Rabbi Yoḥanan ben Matya believed that if one promises "a meal" to Jewish workers, there is no limit to what one must give them, as befits their honor. However, according to the Halakhah, there is no need to go back and tell them what food will be provided, since in such matters one follows the local custom, providing the kind of meal to which the workers are accustomed.

פַּת וְקִטְנִית Bread and beans. A meal of this kind was the normal daily fare for simple people, who used to eat a more ample meal in the evening, when those who could afford it also ate meat. קִטְנִית refers to any edible seed, especially cooked legumes such as beans or lentils.

1 וְהָאָמַר רַבָּה בַּר בַּר חָנָה אָמַר רַבִּי יוֹחָנָן: 2 הָאוֹמֵר לַחֲבֵירוֹ, ״מַתָּנָה אֲנִי נוֹתֵן לְךָ״, יָכוֹל לַחֲזוֹר בּוֹ.
3 ״יָכוֹל״?! 4 פְּשִׁיטָא!
5 אֶלָּא, מוּתָּר לַחֲזוֹר בּוֹ.
6 אָמַר רַב פַּפָּא: 7 וּמוֹדֶה רַבִּי יוֹחָנָן בְּמַתָּנָה מוּעֶטֶת, 8 דְּסָמְכָא דַּעְתַּיְיהוּ.

LITERAL TRANSLATION

1 But surely Rabbah bar Bar Ḥanah said in the name of Rabbi Yoḥanan: 2 Someone who says to his fellow, "I am giving you a present," can retract.
3 "Can"?! 4 This is obvious!
5 Rather, he is permitted to retract.
6 Rav Pappa said: 7 But Rabbi Yoḥanan agrees about a small gift, 8 since they rely.

TRANSLATION AND COMMENTARY

withdraws from a verbal agreement is regarded as dishonest? 1 **But surely, Rabbah bar Bar Ḥanah said in the name of Rabbi Yoḥanan: 2 If someone says to another person, "I am giving you a present," he can retract.**

יָכוֹל 3 The Gemara asks what Rabbi Yoḥanan meant when he said that the donor can retract: ***Can*** retract?! 4 Surely **it is obvious** that he is *able* to retract if he so desires, and he cannot be compelled to give the present. For the recipient has not yet performed an act of acquisition, and the gift is still the exclusive property of the donor!

אֶלָּא מוּתָּר לַחֲזוֹר בּוֹ 5 **Rather,** explains the Gemara, Rabbi Yoḥanan meant that the donor **is *permitted* to retract.** Thus we see that, according to Rabbi Yoḥanan, a person is permitted to go back on a promise to give someone else a present, and there is nothing unethical about breaking such a promise.

אָמַר רַב פַּפָּא 6 **Rav Pappa said** in reply that there is no contradiction between Rabbi Yoḥanan's statement that one may not go back on a verbal agreement and his ruling allowing the donor to retract, for they refer to different cases. When a person promises to make a large donation, he is permitted to go back on his promise if circumstances change. The recipient realizes that the donor may not be able to fulfill his commitment, and since he does not take the promise totally seriously it is not ethically binding and the donor may go back on it. 7 **But Rabbi Yoḥanan agrees** that a person may not go back on a promise if it concerns a sale, or even **a small gift.** 8 **Since** the recipient **relies** on the promise and expects to receive the gift or the merchandise, the promise must be fulfilled.

RASHI

יכול לחזור בו – וקשיא לן: יכול? פשיטא! דהא לא משך ואין כח בבית דין לכופו. **אלא** – ודאי על כרחך מותר לחזור בו קאמר, ואשמעינן דאפילו חסרון אמנה ליכא. **מודה רבי יוחנן במתנה מועטת** – שאין מותר לחזור, משום דסמכא דעתיה דמקבל אדיבוריה, וכי אמר מותר לחזור בו, במתנה מרובה קאמר, דלא סמכא דעתיה דמקבל דלקיימיה לדיבוריה.

BACKGROUND

בְּמַתָּנָה מוּעֶטֶת About a small gift. There is no absolute Halakhic definition of "a small gift," since this depends on the time and place, as well as on the economic status of the donor and the recipient. For what one person considers a small gift may well be a large one for someone else. This is shown by the following discussion about a kor of grain, which was a large amount. When given to a Levite it was regarded as a small gift, because it had to be given in any event. The giving of a kor to one Levite rather than to another was, in these circumstances, merely a small gift.

NOTES

וּמוֹדֶה רַבִּי יוֹחָנָן בְּמַתָּנָה מוּעֶטֶת But Rabbi Yoḥanan agrees about a small gift. Rav Pappa's report of Rabbi Yoḥanan's "agreement" appears out of place. Rabbi Yoḥanan, after all, champions the view that a person must honor his word in all circumstances. Why, then, is he said to "agree" that a person who promises to give a small gift may not go back on his promise? In order to account for the use of the word מוֹדֶה — "agrees," "concedes" — several Aḥaronim interpolate a stage in the exposition of Rabbi Yoḥanan's opinion that does not appear in our text. The line of development is as follows: Rabbi Yoḥanan says that a person who does not honor his word is untrustworthy. The Gemara then asks: But did not Rabbah bar Bar Ḥanah report that Rabbi Yoḥanan himself said that a person may revoke a promise to give a gift? The Gemara's answer to this seeming contradiction, which does not appear in our texts, was as follows: Rabbi Yoḥanan distinguishes between promises made in the course of business dealings (which must always be honored), and promises to give gifts (which may be freely revoked). At this point Rav Pappa interjects his understanding that Rabbi Yoḥanan, despite his general view that promises to make gifts may be revoked, concedes that a promise to make a small gift may not be revoked.

מַתָּנָה מוּעֶטֶת A small gift. Our commentary follows *Tosafot* and other Rishonim (*Ra'avad, Ramban, Rashba*), who agree that the dispute between Rabbi Yoḥanan and Rav focuses on the case of an agreement to sell where prices changed before any money was paid. Rabbi Yoḥanan is of the opinion that it is unethical to renege because of price fluctuations, whereas Rav is of the opinion that in such circumstances there is nothing wrong with reneging before money is paid. This interpretation is supported by the fact that the Gemara illustrates the dispute between Rav and Rabbi Yoḥanan with the story of Rav Kahana, who wished to renege on a sale because of a price rise. According to this explanation, it is arguable that Rav permits reneging on a sale only if prices rise; he may well agree that it is unethical to renege on a sale for no sound commercial reason. Similarly, in the case of a promise to give a gift, Rav may agree that one may not revoke a promise to give a small gift, and Rabbi Yoḥanan

HALAKHAH

חֲזָרָה מִמַּתָּנָה Reneging on a gift. "If a person promises someone a small gift, he is forbidden to renege on his promise, since this is behavior lacking in good faith. But if he promises to give a large gift, he is permitted to renege, since the recipient is not really certain that he will receive the gift until he actually acquires it." (*Shulḥan Arukh, Ḥoshen Mishpat* 204:8.) "It is forbidden to renege on a promise to give a gift to a poor person, since a promise of this kind is considered tantamount to vowing money to charity." (Ibid., 243:2, and see *Sma*.)

TRANSLATION AND COMMENTARY

הָכִי נַמִּי מִסְתַּבְּרָא [1]The Gemara now provides additional support for the distinction between large and small gifts: **This** distinction is not merely a means of resolving the seeming contradiction between the two statements of Rabbi Yoḥanan quoted above. **It also stands to reason,** as it has independent support in the following statement of Rabbi Yoḥanan. [2]**For Rabbi Abbahu said in the name of Rabbi Yoḥanan:** [3]**If an Israelite said to a Levite, "You have a kor of tithe in my possession,"** i.e., I promise to give you a kor (a dry measure, approximately ten bushels) of first tithe from my produce, [4]**the Levite is permitted to** treat this kor of produce as though it were already his own, even though he has not yet received it. Thus, he may use it by **making it "terumah of tithe" on produce** that he has **elsewhere.** Before a Levite is permitted to eat the first-tithe produce that he receives from an Israelite, he must set aside a tenth of it and give it to a priest. The produce that he gives the priest is called "terumah of tithe" (תְּרוּמַת מַעֲשֵׂר). Before the Levite sets aside the terumah of tithe, the first-tithe produce he has received is considered untithed as far as he is concerned, and he may not eat it. Rabbi Yoḥanan is of the opinion that the Levite may designate first-tithe produce that has merely been promised to him as "terumah of tithe" for first-tithe produce he has already received and stored somewhere else.

אִי אָמְרַתְּ בִּשְׁלָמָא [5]Now, this ruling **presents no problem if you say that** a person who promises to give a small gift **may not go back on his word.** Since the donor is required to give the Levite the first-tithe produce he promised him, the Levite is entitled to assume that the donor will fulfill his obligation, [6]and **this is why** the Levite **is permitted** to use produce that he has not received for "terumah of tithe." First-tithe produce is treated as a small gift, regardless of how much produce is involved, because its value to the original owner is minimal. Before the Israelite gives the tithe to the Levite, he may not make use of it for himself. His sole interest in the produce is his right to choose which Levite will receive it. Therefore, since Rabbi Yoḥanan agrees that in the case of a small gift the donor may not retract, the Levite is permitted to designate first tithe that has merely been promised to him as "terumah of tithe" for other first-tithe produce that he has already received and stored. [7]**But if you say** that the donor **may go back on his word** even if he promised a small gift, [8]**why is** the Levite **permitted** to use for "terumah of tithe" produce that he has not yet actually received? [9]Perhaps the donor will retract, and **it may happen that** the Levite **will** unintentionally **eat untithed produce!** For if the donor fails to keep his word and give this first-tithe produce to the Levite, the Levite's own action in rendering it "terumah of tithe" will be without effect. How can the Levite rely on the donor's word if the donor is under no moral obligation to keep it?

[1]הָכִי נַמִּי מִסְתַּבְּרָא. [2]דְּאָמַר רַבִּי אַבָּהוּ אָמַר רַבִּי יוֹחָנָן: [3]יִשְׂרָאֵל שֶׁאָמַר לְבֶן לֵוִי: "כּוֹר מַעֲשֵׂר יֵשׁ לְךָ בְּיָדִי", [4]בֶּן לֵוִי רַשַּׁאי לַעֲשׂוֹתוֹ תְּרוּמַת מַעֲשֵׂר עַל מָקוֹם אַחֵר.

[5]אִי אָמְרַתְּ בִּשְׁלָמָא לָא מָצֵי לְמִיהֲדַר בֵּיהּ, [6]מִשּׁוּם הָכִי רַשַּׁאי, [7]אֶלָּא אִי אָמְרַתְּ מָצֵי לְמִיהֲדַר בֵּיהּ, [8]אַמַּאי רַשַּׁאי? [9]אִישְׁתַּכַּח דְּקָא אָכֵיל טְבָלִים!

LITERAL TRANSLATION

[1]This also stands to reason. [2]For Rabbi Abbahu said in the name of Rabbi Yoḥanan: [3][If] an Israelite said to a Levite: "You have a kor of tithe in my possession," [4]the Levite is permitted to make it terumah of tithe on [produce] elsewhere.

[5]Granted if you say [that] he may not retract, [6]because of this he is permitted. [7]But if you say he may retract, [8]why is he permitted? [9]It may happen that he will eat untithed produce!

RASHI

לבן לוי – כל לוי קרוי בן לוי. כור מעשר יש לך בידי – שעישרתי פירותי, ואתננו לך. תרומת מעשר – שהלוי מפריש מעשר לכהן מעשר מן המעשר. משום הכי רשאי – שיש לו לסמוך על מה שכתוב (צפניה ג) "שארית ישראל לא יעשו עולה ולא ידברו כזב" ולא יתננו ללוי אחר. והא מתנה מועטת היא, שאין לישראל במעשר זה אלא טובת הנאה, שהיה בידו מתחילה לתת לכל בן לוי שירצה.

SAGES

רַבִּי אַבָּהוּ **Rabbi Abbahu.** A Palestinian Amora of the third generation. See *Bava Metzia*, Part I, p. 100.

BACKGROUND

תְּרוּמַת מַעֲשֵׂר עַל מָקוֹם אַחֵר **Terumah of tithe on produce elsewhere.** Once the owner of produce has given terumah to the priest, first tithe to the Levites and the appropriate gifts to the poor, his produce may be eaten. However, the Torah requires the Levite who receives first tithe to set aside one-tenth of it — "terumah of tithe" (תְּרוּמַת מַעֲשֵׂר) — and to give it to the priest. Until he has set aside this "terumah of tithe" from the first tithe he has received, that produce is untithed (טֶבֶל) and may not be eaten. Although the proper way of setting aside this "terumah of tithe" is to take it from the tithe itself, nevertheless the Levite may take it from any other first-tithe produce in his possession.

NOTES

may agree that one may revoke a promise to give a large gift. Thus, the dispute between Rav and Rabbi Yoḥanan revolves around the right to revoke a verbal commercial promise in a case where keeping the promise will result in financial loss.

Ba'al HaMa'or defines the argument differently. According to him, breaking a promise as a result of a change in price is the equivalent of breaking a promise to make a large gift. Thus, in the case of Rav Kahana, Rabbi Yoḥanan would agree with Rav's ruling, and that story has no bearing on the dispute between them. Rather, the dispute concerns two cases: (1) a small gift, and (2) a sale in which the prices have not changed. According to Rav, it is permitted to change one's mind about a small gift, and it is permitted to renege on a sale even if the prices have not changed, whereas according to Rabbi Yoḥanan it is forbidden to break a promise unless the gift is large or the prices have fluctuated.

יִשְׂרָאֵל שֶׁאָמַר לְבֶן לֵוִי **If an Israelite said to a Levite.** *Rosh* asks: Even if the Levite is entitled to rely on the Israelite's

[1]הָכָא בְּמַאי עָסְקִינַן? [2]כְּגוֹן שֶׁנְּטָלוֹ מִמֶּנּוּ, וְחָזַר וְהִפְקִידוֹ אֶצְלוֹ.

[3]אִי הָכִי, אֵימָא סֵיפָא: [4]נְתָנוֹ לְבֶן לֵוִי אַחֵר, אֵין לוֹ עָלָיו אֶלָּא תַּרְעוֹמֶת.

[5]וְאִי סָלְקָא דַּעְתָּךְ, [6]כְּגוֹן שֶׁנְּטָלוֹ מִמֶּנּוּ וְחָזַר וְהִפְקִידוֹ אֶצְלוֹ, [7]אַמַּאי אֵין לוֹ עָלָיו אֶלָּא תַּרְעוֹמֶת? [8]כֵּיוָן דְּמְשָׁכֵיהּ, מָמוֹנָא אִית לֵיהּ גַּבֵּיהּ!

[9]אֶלָּא לָאו שְׁמַע מִינָּהּ בִּדְלָא נְטָלוֹ?

[10]שְׁמַע מִינָּהּ.

LITERAL TRANSLATION

[1]With what are we dealing here? [2]For example, where he took it from him, and returned and deposited it with him.

[3]If so, say the last clause: [4][If] he gave it to another Levite, he has nothing but resentment against him.

[5]But if it should enter your mind [that it refers], [6]for example, [to] where he took it from him and returned and deposited it with him, [7]why does he have nothing but resentment against him? [8]Once he drew it, he has [a claim of] money against him!

[9]Is it not [correct] to conclude from this [that it is a case] where he did not take it?

[10]Conclude from it.

RASHI

אין לו עליו – אין לו לבן לוי ראשון על ישראל זה. **אלא תרעומת** – שהבטיחו בתוחלת נכזבה. **אלא שמע מינה בדלא נטלו** – ויש בדברים משום חסרון אמנה.

TRANSLATION AND COMMENTARY

הָכָא בְּמַאי עָסְקִינַן [1]The Gemara attempts to rebut this proof: **With what are we dealing here?** [2]With a case, **for example, where** the Levite **took** possession of the tithe **from** the donor **and returned and deposited it with him.** Once the Levite has actually acquired the first tithe by drawing it into his possession, he is certainly permitted to designate it as "terumah of tithe" for other first-tithe produce. But until he has acquired it, Rabbi Yoḥanan would not allow him to make use of it in this way because Rabbi Yoḥanan permits a donor to retract, even if the gift was small.

אִי הָכִי [3]The Gemara objects to this interpretation: **If so,** if the circumstances are as just described, **consider the last clause** of Rabbi Yoḥanan's statement about the Levite: [4]**If** the donor broke his promise and **gave** the first tithe **to another Levite,** rather than to the Levite to whom he had originally promised it, the first Levite can do **nothing** more **than** feel **resentment towards him.** In other words, the Levite to whom the first-tithe produce was initially promised certainly has grounds for resentment towards the Israelite for breaking his promise, but he cannot retrieve the first tithe promised him by recourse to law.

וְאִי סָלְקָא דַּעְתָּךְ [5]**But if it should enter your mind** to think **that** Rabbi Yoḥanan **was referring to a case,** [6]**for example, where** the Levite **took** the tithe **from** the donor **and returned and deposited it with him,** [7]**why** can he do **nothing** more **than** feel **resentment towards** the donor, if the latter then gives the first tithe to another Levite? Why does the first Levite — to whom the tithe had initially been promised — have no legal recourse? [8]**Once he has drawn** the tithe into his possession, **he** has acquired it, and **has a monetary claim against** the donor. Thus, if the donor fails to return the tithe, he is guilty of theft, and not merely of failing to keep his promise!

אֶלָּא לָאו שְׁמַע מִינָּהּ [9]Since we cannot explain Rabbi Yoḥanan's statement as referring to a case where the Levite redeposited the first tithe with the donor, **is it not correct to conclude from here that** our original interpretation of Rabbi Yoḥanan's view was correct, and that Rabbi Yoḥanan was referring **to a case where** the Levite **had not** yet **taken** the promised first-tithe produce into his possession, but proceeded to designate it as "terumah of tithe" solely on the basis of the Israelite's promise that he would give it to him? Since Rabbi Yoḥanan permitted the Levite to designate the promised tithe as "terumah of tithe" for other produce, may we not infer that Rabbi Yoḥanan is of the opinion that a person may not go back on a promise to give a small gift?

שְׁמַע מִינָּהּ [10]The Gemara concludes: We may, indeed, **draw this conclusion from here.**

NOTES

promise to give him the tithe, the produce is not his until he actually receives it. How, then, can he use it as "terumah of tithe" for his own produce? *Rosh* resolves the problem by referring to a passage in tractate *Gittin* (30a), where the Gemara establishes that if an Israelite always gives his tithes to a particular Levite, the tithes are considered to be that Levite's property even before they are given to him. *Rosh* suggests that in our Gemara we may be dealing with a similar situation.

Alternatively, *Rosh* suggests that the Israelite's promise to give the produce to the Levite included an implicit authorization for this Levite to separate the "terumah of tithe."

BACKGROUND

הַהוּא גַּבְרָא A certain man. This expression is often used by the Gemara to introduce an incident in which an individual claimant appeared before a scholar or before a Rabbinical Court to receive a decision on a point of law.

SAGES

רַב פַּפִּי Rav Pappi. A Babylonian Amora of the fifth generation, Rav Pappi was a disciple of Rava. He was a colleague of Rav Pappa, Rav Huna the son of Rav Yehoshua, Rav Bibi bar Abaye, and Rav Kahana. His most famous disciples were Rav Ashi and Mar Zutra.

רָבִינָא Ravina. A Babylonian Amora of the fifth and sixth generations. See *Bava Metzia*, Part II, p. 71.

רַב טָבוֹת Rav Tavot. A Babylonian Amora of the fifth generation, Rav Tavot is mentioned only a few times in the Talmud. He was a disciple of Rava, and discussed the Halakhah with him. Rav Tavot was famous for his devotion to telling the truth, and in tractate *Sanhedrin* (97a) a remarkable story is told about him to show how difficult it is to attain absolute truth.

רַב שְׁמוּאֵל בַּר זוּטְרָא Rav Shmuel bar Zutra. A Babylonian Amora of the fifth generation, Rav Shmuel bar Zutra transmitted teachings in the name of Rava.

[1]הַהוּא גַּבְרָא דְּיָהֵיב זוּזֵי אַשּׁוּמְשְׁמֵי. [2]לְסוֹף, אִיַּיקַּר שׁוּמְשְׁמֵי. [3]הֲדַרוּ בְּהוּ וַאֲמַרוּ לֵיהּ: [4]״לֵית לָן שׁוּמְשְׁמֵי; שְׁקוֹל זוּזָךְ״. [5]לָא שָׁקֵיל זוּזֵיהּ. [6]אִיגְנוּב. [7]אָתוּ לְקַמֵּיהּ דְּרָבָא. [8]אֲמַר לֵיהּ: ״כֵּיוָן דְּאָמְרִי לָךְ, ׳שְׁקוֹל זוּזָךְ׳, וְלָא שַׁקְלִית, [9]לָא מִבָּעֲיָא שׁוֹמֵר שָׂכָר דְּלָא הָוֵי, [10]אֶלָּא אֲפִילּוּ שׁוֹמֵר חִנָּם נַמִי לָא הָוֵי״. [11]אֲמַרוּ לֵיהּ רַבָּנַן לְרָבָא: [12]וְהָא בָּעֵי לְקַבּוּלֵי עֲלֵיהּ ״מִי שֶׁפָּרַע״! [13]אֲמַר לְהוּ: הָכִי נַמִי. [14]אֲמַר רַב פַּפִּי: אֲמַר לִי רָבִינָא: [15]לְדִידִי אֲמַר לִי הַהוּא מֵרַבָּנַן וְרַב טָבוֹת שְׁמֵיהּ, וְאָמְרִי לָהּ, רַב שְׁמוּאֵל בַּר זוּטְרָא שְׁמֵיהּ,

LITERAL TRANSLATION

[1]A certain man gave money for sesame seeds. [2]Later, sesame seeds went up in price. [3][The sellers] retracted and said to him: [4]"We have no sesame seeds; take your money." [5]He did not take his money. [6]It was stolen. [7]They came before Rava. [8]He said to him: "Since they said to you, 'Take your money,' and you did not take it, [9]there is no need [to state] that he is not a paid bailee, [10]but he is not even an unpaid bailee."

[11]The Rabbis said to Rava: [12]But surely he must accept "He who punished" upon himself!

[13]He said to them: Indeed so.

[14]Rav Pappi said: Ravina said to me: One of the Rabbis said to me, and Rav Tavot was his name, [15]and some say, Rav Shmuel bar Zutra was his name,

RASHI

אפילו שומר חנם נמי לא הוי — ואפילו פשעו בשמירתן פטורין. והא בעי לקבולי כו׳ — ודלמא לא הוי מקבל, ואישתכח דזוזי דידיה הוה. הכי נמי — או משלם השומשמין, או יקבל ״מי שפרע״.

TRANSLATION AND COMMENTARY

הַהוּא גַּבְרָא [1]The Gemara relates the following incident: **A certain man gave money** as payment **for sesame seeds.** [2]**Later,** before he had a chance to collect his purchase, **sesame seeds went up in price.** [3]**The seller went back on his word and said to** the buyer, [4]**"I have no sesame seeds** for sale, so **take** back **your money."** [5]But the buyer **did not take** back **his money** immediately. [6]In the meantime, the money **was stolen** from the seller's house.

אָתוּ לְקַמֵּיהּ דְּרָבָא [7]The two parties **came before Rava** to receive a ruling about the stolen money. The buyer claimed that the seller was responsible for the money, because a seller who receives money has the status of a paid bailee, and a paid bailee is liable for damage caused by theft. [8]But Rava **said to** the buyer: **"Since** the seller **said to you, 'Take** back **your money,' and you did not take it** back, [9]**there is no question that** the seller **is no** longer considered **a paid bailee,** as you wished to claim. The seller is in no way liable for the theft of the deposit, and is not required to reimburse you for the money he received. [10]As a matter of fact, the seller **is not even** considered **an unpaid bailee,** who is at least liable for a loss caused by his own negligence. Hence, the seller would not be liable even if the money was lost due to negligence on his part, because the seller was under no obligation whatsoever to safeguard your money."

אֲמַרוּ לֵיהּ רַבָּנַן לְרָבָא [11]Hearing this ruling, **the Rabbis said to Rava:** [12]**But surely** the seller reneged on the deal, and **he must submit himself to** the **"He who punished"** curse! If he decides to submit to the curse, he will indeed be free from liability for the stolen money, for he did tell the buyer to take back his money. But if he decides not to submit to the curse, he must deliver the merchandise *and* bear the loss of the stolen money, for then it will be his money that has been stolen.

אֲמַר לְהוּ [13]Rava **said to them: Indeed so.** The seller must either submit to the curse or deliver the sesame seeds for which he received payment.

אֲמַר רַב פַּפִּי [14]The Gemara now relates another incident: **Rav Pappi said: Ravina said to me:** There was **a certain Rabbi whose name was Rav Tavot,** [15]**and some say** his name was **Rav Shmuel bar Zutra.**

NOTES

לְדִידִי אֲמַר לִי הַהוּא מֵרַבָּנַן One of the Rabbis said to me. The Gemara presents two versions of this story. The two versions bear a certain superficial similarity, but the issues with which they deal are totally different. It appears from the Gemara that the second version is authoritative, and that the events described in the first version never happened.

The Rishonim disagree as to whether the ruling attributed to Rava in the first version would be applied if the hypothetical case described were actually to arise. Suppose the seller reneged on the sale and told the buyer to reclaim his deposit, which was subsequently stolen from the seller's possession. Is the seller liable for the stolen deposit money like a paid bailee? Is he liable for negligence, like an unpaid bailee? Or is he free of liability as a bailee, as Rava was supposed to have ruled?

Ran quotes *Tosafot* as saying that Rava's ruling is valid, even though the incident itself never took place. *Ra'avad* also supports this view.

In *Eruvin* (81b), *Tosafot* raises a related question: Consider a case similar in all details to the case of Rava, except that the seller did *not* say, "take back your money." In such a case, Rava clearly would not exempt the seller from all liability. But on what basis would his liability be determined?

TRANSLATION AND COMMENTARY

[1]**who would not break his word** even **if they gave him all the treasures of the world. He said to me:** [2]**"That incident** involving sesame seeds **happened to me.** The person who wished to buy sesame seeds, and whose money was stolen, made his claim against me, and it was in my favor that Rava issued his ruling. But the story did not happen in the way it was reported. [3]This is what actually happened: **It was Sabbath eve** (Friday afternoon) **towards sunset,** [4]**and I was sitting** at home when **a certain man came and stood at the gate.** [5]**He said to me, 'Do you have sesame seeds to sell?'** [49B] [6]**I said to him, 'No.** I have no sesame seeds.' [7]**He said to me: 'Let this money** that I have with me **be deposited with you** over the Sabbath, **for it is getting dark,** and I am not likely to reach home before the Sabbath. I cannot keep the money with me, because it is forbidden to handle or carry money on the Sabbath, and I have nowhere to leave it in this town.' [8]In response, **I said to him:** 'My **house** stands **before you.** You may leave your money in my house until after the Sabbath.' [9]So the owner of the money **put** his money **in my house.** Unfortunately, on that particular Sabbath, a thief broke into my house **and** the man's money **was stolen.** The man considered me responsible for his money. I denied responsibility. [10]So **he came before Rava** seeking compensation for the loss. [11]But Rava **said to him: In any case** where someone asks another person to accept a deposit, and the other person responds by saying, 'My **house** stands **before you,'** [12]**there is no question that** the owner of the house **is not** considered **a paid bailee,** who is liable in a case of theft. [13]**And moreover, he is not even** considered **an unpaid bailee,** who is at least liable for loss caused by his own negligence. Hence you have no grounds to demand compensation from the Rabbi who kept your money over the Sabbath. He never assumed responsibility for your money. Hence, he is not liable for the theft."

[1]דְּאִי הָווּ יָהֲבֵי לֵיהּ כָּל חֲלָלָא דְּעָלְמָא לָא הָוֵי קָא מְשַׁנֵּי בְּדִבּוּרֵיהּ: [2]״בְּדִידִי הֲוָה עוּבְדָא. [3]הַהוּא יוֹמָא אַפַּנְיָא דְּמַעֲלֵי שַׁבְּתָא הֲוָה, [4]וַהֲוָה יָתֵיבְנָא, וַאֲתָא הַהוּא גַּבְרָא וְקָאֵי אַבָּבָא. [5]אֲמַר לִי: ׳אִית לָךְ שׁוּמְשְׁמֵי לְזַבּוֹנֵי?׳ [49B] [6]אֲמַרִי לֵיהּ: ׳לָא׳. [7]אֲמַר לִי: ׳לֶיהֱווּ הָנָךְ זוּזֵי בְּפִקָּדוֹן גַּבָּךְ, דְּהָא חֲשְׁכָה לִי׳. [8]אֲמַרִי לֵיהּ: ׳הָא בֵּיתָא קַמָּךְ׳. [9]אוֹתְבִינְהוּ בְּבֵיתָא, וְאִיגְּנוּב. [10]אֲתָא לְקַמֵּיהּ דְּרָבָא. [11]אֲמַר לֵיהּ: כָּל ׳הָא בֵּיתָא קַמָּךְ׳, [12]לָא מִיבַּעְיָא שׁוֹמֵר שָׂכָר דְּלָא הָוֵי, [13]אֶלָּא אֲפִילּוּ שׁוֹמֵר חִנָּם נַמִי לָא הָוֵי״.

LITERAL TRANSLATION

[1]who would not break his word if they gave him all the treasures (lit., "space") of the world: [2]"That incident happened to me. [3]That day was Sabbath eve toward sunset, [4]and I was sitting, and a certain man came and stood at the gate. [5]He said to me: 'Do you have sesame seeds to sell?' [49B] [6]I said to him: 'No.' [7]He said to me: 'Let this money be a deposit with you, for it has become dark for me.' [8]I said to him: 'Here is the house before you.' [9]He put it in the house, and it was stolen. [10]He came before Rava. [11]He said to him: [In] any [case of] 'Here is the house before you,' [12]there is no need [to state] that he is not a paid bailee, [13]but he is not even an unpaid bailee."

RASHI

בדידי הוה עובדא — אותו מעשה דשומשמין על ידי היה. ולא כן היה, שאילו קיבלתים לתת השומשמין לא הייתי חוזר בי בכל חללו של עולם, ולא על כן באנו לדין, אלא כך היה.

CONCEPTS

שׁוֹמֵר שָׂכָר A paid bailee. One of the four categories of bailee (see also Exodus 22:9-12). A person who accepts an article for safekeeping for a fee. In addition to the responsibilities imposed on an unpaid bailee (שׁוֹמֵר חִינָּם), a paid bailee must reimburse the owner of the article if it is lost or stolen. But he is free of liability if the article is taken by robbers or damaged by forces beyond his control.

שׁוֹמֵר חִנָּם An unpaid bailee. One of the four categories of bailee (see also Exodus 22:6-8). A person who accepts an article for safekeeping without remuneration, and without permission to use it for his own benefit. An unpaid bailee is not required to recompense the owner of the article if it is lost or stolen from him, or taken away by forces beyond his control. He is only liable if he is criminally negligent, or if he takes the article for himself.

NOTES

Would Rava consider the seller a paid bailee or an unpaid bailee? *Tosafot* leaves the question unresolved.

Unlike *Tosafot*, most Rishonim accept a tradition, reported by *Rav Hai Gaon*, that Rava's "ruling" is to be rejected together with the story. According to this tradition, a seller who receives money is not a bailee of any kind, since he is not required to return the same coins he received as a deposit. Rather, he is considered to be a lender, who is entitled to spend the money he borrows. Now, the law is that a borrower is always liable for his debt, even if the money is lost in circumstances beyond his control. Moreover, a borrower remains liable for his debt until he actually pays it, and cannot escape liability by saying to the lender: "Take back your money."

שׁוֹמֵר שָׂכָר דְּלָא הָוֵי He is not a paid bailee. The Rishonim ask: Rava ruled that the person from whom the money was stolen (the seller in the first story, and Rav Tavot in the second) was exempted from liability as a paid bailee because he said, "Take back your money" (or "here is the house before you" in the second version). It appears,

HALAKHAH

הָא בֵּיתָא קַמָּךְ Here is the house before you. "If someone declared that he would take care of something — even if he only said: 'Place the object before me' — he is considered an unpaid bailee. But if he simply said: 'Leave it in front of you,' or 'leave it' (or 'here is the house before you' — *Rema*) without specifying anything else, he is not even considered an unpaid bailee, and need not take an oath if the object was damaged," following the Gemara's ruling. (*Shulhan Arukh, Hoshen Mishpat* 291:2.)

¹אֲמַרִי לֵיהּ: ²״וְהָא אֲמַרוּ לֵיהּ רַבָּנַן לְרָבָא: ³אִיבָּעֵי לֵיהּ לְקַבּוּלֵי עֲלֵיהּ ׳מִי שֶׁפָּרַע׳״! ⁴וַאֲמַר לִי: ״לֹא הָיוּ דְּבָרִים מֵעוֹלָם״.

⁵״רַבִּי שִׁמְעוֹן אוֹמֵר: כָּל שֶׁהַכֶּסֶף בְּיָדוֹ יָדוֹ עַל הָעֶלְיוֹנָה וכו׳״. ⁶תַּנְיָא: ״אָמַר רַבִּי שִׁמְעוֹן: ⁷אֵימָתַי? ⁸בִּזְמַן שֶׁהַכֶּסֶף וְהַפֵּירוֹת בְּיַד מוֹכֵר. ⁹אֲבָל כֶּסֶף בְּיַד מוֹכֵר וּפֵירוֹת בְּיַד לוֹקֵחַ, ¹⁰אֵינוֹ יָכוֹל לַחֲזוֹר בּוֹ, ¹¹מִפְּנֵי שֶׁכַּסְפּוֹ בְּיָדוֹ״.

¹²בְּיָדוֹ? ¹³בְּיַד מוֹכֵר הוּא!

LITERAL TRANSLATION

¹I said to him: ²"But surely the Rabbis said to Rava: ³He must accept 'He who punished' upon himself!" ⁴But he said to me: "This never happened (lit., 'there were never such things')."

⁵"Rabbi Shimon says: Whoever has the money in his hand has the upper hand, etc."

⁶It was taught: "Rabbi Shimon said: ⁷When? ⁸At a time when the money and the produce are in the seller's hand. ⁹But [if] the money is in the seller's hand and the produce is in the buyer's hand, ¹⁰he cannot retract, ¹¹because his money is in his hand."

¹²In his hand? ¹³It is in the seller's hand!

TRANSLATION AND COMMENTARY

אֲמַרִי לֵיהּ ¹Ravina, relating this story, continued: I **said to** Rav Tavot (or Rav Shmuel bar Zutra): "The two versions of the story certainly bear a superficial similarity, and I can see how the story you describe may have been distorted into the first version. ²**But surely,** in the first version, **the Rabbis said to Rava:** ³The person who retracted **must submit himself to** the curse of **'He who punished'!** So the case must have involved a sale where one of the parties retracted. What is your version of that part of the story?"

וַאֲמַר לִי ⁴**But,** Ravina continued, **he said to me** in reply: **"This never happened.** The Rabbis never said such a thing to Rava, because there was no transaction and no retraction."

רַבִּי שִׁמְעוֹן אוֹמֵר ⁵The Gemara now proceeds to analyze the last clause of our Mishnah: **"Rabbi Shimon says: Whoever has the money in his hand has the upper hand.** As the Gemara explained above (47b), what Rabbi Shimon means is that the seller can withdraw from the sale even after receiving his money — until *meshikhah* has been performed — but the buyer cannot. For Rabbi Shimon agrees with Rabbi Yoḥanan that by Torah law, monetary payment acquires, and that *meshikhah* is a Rabbinic enactment to protect the buyer in the event that the merchandise is damaged. Therefore the Rabbis empowered the seller to retract, since he bears the risk in the event of damage, but they did not so empower the buyer (see above, 47b, for details).

תַּנְיָא ⁶With reference to this clause in the Mishnah, the Gemara notes: The following **was taught in a Baraita: "Rabbi Shimon said:** ⁷**When** can the seller retract? ⁸**When** both **the money and the produce are in the seller's possession** — in other words, after the purchase money has been paid but before the buyer has performed *meshikhah* on the produce. In such a case, Rabbi Shimon is of the opinion that the seller can retract, but not the buyer. ⁹**But if the money is in the seller's possession** — i.e., payment has been made — **and the produce is in the buyer's possession** — i.e., *meshikhah* has been performed — the seller **cannot** ¹⁰then **retract,** ¹¹**because the money is in** the buyer's **possession."**

בְּיָדוֹ ¹²The Gemara objects to the language of the Baraita: Is the money **in** the *buyer's* **possession?** ¹³Surely this clause of the Baraita began by positing that the money **is in the *seller's* possession** ("But if the money is in the seller's possession...")!

RASHI

אמרי ליה והא אמרו ליה רבנן לרבא — רבינא אמר להא מילתא. אמרתי לו לההוא מרבנן: היכי אמרת דלאו חזרת מקח וממכר הוא? והא אמרו ליה רבנן לרבא איבעי ליה לקבל ״מי שפרע״. **אימתי** — יש חזרה בדבר. **בזמן שהכסף ופירות ביד המוכר** — דיכול מוכר לחזור בו, דאוקמינהו רבנן ברשותיה לחזרה, כי היכי דליטרח ולציל. **מפני שבכספו בידו** — משמע שהלוקח קיבל כבר כספו.

NOTES

therefore, that had he not made that remark, he would indeed be considered a paid bailee. Why is this so? After all, what benefit did the seller (or Rav Tavot) receive for looking after the money?

Tosafot (*Eruvin* 81a) explains that the seller's benefit derives from the fact that he is entitled to spend the deposit money as soon as he receives it. Moreover, the seller derives benefit from the very fact of the sale, and this may be sufficient for him to be considered a paid bailee of the purchased merchandise as well as the money.

The second version of Rava's ruling is more difficult. Why would anyone have thought that Rav Tavot should be considered a paid bailee for allowing the man to leave his money in his house over the Sabbath?

Talmid Rabbenu Peretz explains that Rav Tavot took money from the man as rent for the room in which the money was stored. Nevertheless, the money was only to pay for the use of the space, and Rav Tavot took no responsibility for theft.

TRANSLATION AND COMMENTARY

אֶלָּא [1]**Rather,** answers the Gemara, the Baraita must be amended to read as follows: "If the money is in the seller's possession and the produce is in the buyer's possession, then the seller cannot retract **because** the buyer's **money's worth** — i.e., the produce, which was given in exchange for the money — is already **in the buyer's possession.**" In other words, since meshikhah has been performed, the transaction is now final and irreversible.

פְּשִׁיטָא [2]**The Gemara objects: But surely this is obvious!** If the buyer has already acquired the produce by drawing it into his possession, it is obvious that the seller cannot retract!

אָמַר רָבָא [3]**Rava said** in reply: **With what are we dealing here** in the Baraita? Not with a case where the produce was already acquired through meshikhah, but rather with a case, [4]**for example, where** the produce was paid for but not yet acquired, and the seller placed it in his attic until the buyer would come to collect it. Ordinarily, in such a case the seller has the power to retract. But in this case it happened that **the attic** where the produce was stored **had been rented by the seller from the buyer.** This is what Rabbi Shimon meant when he said that the produce was "in the buyer's possession," since the produce was in the attic of the house where the buyer was living. Now, even though the attic belonged to the buyer, it was technically considered the property of the seller, since he had rented it. Thus, placing the merchandise in the attic had no effect on the transaction itself. The significance of the fact that the merchandise was placed in an attic rented from the buyer lies in the fact that both parties had an obvious interest in protecting such an attic from fire. For Rabbi Shimon maintains that movable goods are acquired through monetary payment, by Torah law, and meshikhah was enacted to protect the buyer in the event of a fire breaking out in the seller's attic. Thus the Baraita is teaching us that, where both parties have an interest in the attic where the merchandise is stored, the Rabbis did not apply their enactment.

טַעְמָא מַאי תַּקִּינוּ רַבָּנַן מְשִׁיכָה [5]**Rava continues: What is the reason that the Sages enacted** meshikhah instead of monetary payment as a mode of acquisition? [6]**It was a preventive measure** taken by the Sages, **lest the seller say to** the buyer: [7]**"Your wheat was burnt in the upper story** of my house after you paid me." The Sages feared that if payment were to effect a sale, the seller would make no attempt to save the purchased merchandise from damage, since the merchandise had already been acquired by the buyer and was no longer the responsibility of the seller. Therefore they enacted that meshikhah must be performed, and decreed that the merchandise is the property of the party who has it in his physical possession.

LITERAL TRANSLATION

[1]Rather: Because his money's worth is in his hand.
[2]This is obvious!
[3]Rava said: With what are we dealing here? [4]For example, where the buyer's upper story was rented by the seller.
[5]What is the reason [that] the Sages enacted meshikhah? [6][It was] a preventive measure, lest he [the seller] say to him:
[7]"Your wheat was burnt in the upper story."

אֶלָּא: מִפְּנֵי שֶׁדְּמֵי כַסְפּוֹ בְּיָדוֹ. [2]פְּשִׁיטָא! [3]אָמַר רָבָא: הָכָא בְּמַאי עָסְקִינַן? [4]כְּגוֹן שֶׁהָיְתָה עֲלִיָּיה שֶׁל לוֹקֵחַ מוּשְׂכֶּרֶת בְּיַד מוֹכֵר. [5]טַעְמָא מַאי תַּקִּינוּ רַבָּנַן מְשִׁיכָה? [6]גְּזֵירָה, שֶׁמָּא יֹאמַר לוֹ: [7]"נִשְׂרְפוּ חִטֶּיךָ בַּעֲלִיָּיה".

RASHI

פשיטא — הרי משיכה יש, ואפילו רבנן מודו. מושכרת ביד מוכר — והיו הפירות מונחין ביד הלוקח. ולא שתקנה לו חצירו בנתינת המעות, דכיון דקבל השכר ניקנה המקום למוכר כל ימי השכירות, וחצירו של מוכר הוא. אלא רבי שמעון אית ליה "מעות קונות דבר תורה" כדאמרינן (בבא מציעא מו,ב), ומשיכה תקנתא דרבנן היא. והכא לא איצטריך תקנתא, דטעמא מאי תקון רבנן כו'. אי נמי שמא תפול כו' — לא גרס ליה, אלא לישנא אחרינא הוא, והיא היא.

NOTES

שֶׁהָיְתָה עֲלִיָּיה שֶׁל לוֹקֵחַ מוּשְׂכֶּרֶת בְּיַד מוֹכֵר **Where the buyer's upper story was rented by the seller.** One of the methods of acquiring movable property is to place it in a field or a house belonging to the buyer. This is called "courtyard-acquisition" (קִנְיַן חָצֵר). At first glance, it would appear that our Gemara is referring to this procedure when it says that the buyer acquires the merchandise immediately

if it was placed in an attic that he had leased to the seller.

However, Rashi and most Rishonim agree that the attic plays no role in the transaction in our Gemara. For even though the attic belongs to the buyer, once he leases it to the seller it is regarded as the seller's property, and merchandise placed there cannot be acquired by the buyer through courtyard-acquisition. Rather, the buyer in our

HALAKHAH

בֵּיתוֹ שֶׁל לוֹקֵחַ מוּשְׂכֶּרֶת בְּיַד מוֹכֵר **Where the house of the buyer is rented to the seller.** "If the buyer's house was rented to the seller, the buyer acquires merchandise located there by paying for it, without the need to perform

meshikhah. In such a case we rely upon Torah law that monetary payment acquires." (Shulhan Arukh, Hoshen Mishpat 198:5.)

LITERAL TRANSLATION

[1]Here they are on the buyer's premises. [2]If a fire breaks out by accident, [3]he himself will take the trouble and bring it.

[4]A certain person gave money [as payment] for an ass. [5]Later he heard that [the men of] the house of Parzak the general wanted to take it. [6]He said to him: "Give me the money. I do not want the ass." [7]He came before Rav Ḥisda. [8]He said to him: "In the same way as they enacted *meshikhah* for sellers, [9]so too they enacted *meshikhah* for buyers."

[1]הָכָא בִּרְשׁוּתֵיהּ דְּלוֹקֵחַ נִינְהוּ. [2]אִי נָפְלָה דְּלֵיקָה בְּאוֹנֶס, [3]אִיהוּ טָרַח וּמַיְיתֵי לַהּ.

[4]הַהוּא גַּבְרָא דְּיָהֵיב זוּזֵי אַחֲמָרָא. [5]לְסוֹף שְׁמַע דְּקָא בָּעֵי לְמִנְסְבֵיהּ דְּבֵי פַּרְזָק רוּפִילָא. [6]אֲמַר לֵיהּ: "הַב לִי זוּזֵי. לָא בְּעֵינָא חֲמָרָא". [7]אֲתָא לְקַמֵּיהּ דְּרַב חִסְדָּא. [8]אֲמַר לֵיהּ: "כְּדֶרֶךְ שֶׁתִּיקְּנוּ מְשִׁיכָה בְּמוֹכְרִין, [9]כָּךְ תִּיקְּנוּ מְשִׁיכָה בַּלָּקוֹחוֹת".

RASHI

פרזק — שם השר. **רופילא** = משנה למלך. **כדרך שתקנו משיכה** — לחזור בו המוכר כל זמן שלא משך הלוקח. **כך תקנו משיכה** — לחזור בהן הלקוחות.

TRANSLATION AND COMMENTARY

[1]But **here** there is no reason for the Rabbis to apply their decree. For the attic where the merchandise is stored **is in the buyer's possession** for the purposes of protection from fire. Even though the attic is now technically the seller's — since he rented it from the buyer — the buyer still has an obvious interest in protecting it from fire. [2]Therefore, **if a fire breaks out by accident,** [3]the buyer **himself will take the trouble and save** the merchandise from danger. Therefore Rabbi Shimon is of the opinion that the Rabbis did not apply their decree to this case, and if the merchandise is stored in an attic rented by the seller from the buyer, the merchandise is acquired by monetary payment, without any need for *meshikhah*.

הַהוּא גַּבְרָא [4]The Gemara relates further: **A certain person gave money as payment for an ass.** [5]**Later,** before the ass was delivered to him, **he heard that the men of the house of Parzak the general wanted to seize it.** [6]The buyer **said to** the seller: **"Give me** back **my money. I do not want the ass,** since it will presumably be seized."

אֲתָא לְקַמֵּיהּ דְּרַב חִסְדָּא [7]The seller **came before Rav Ḥisda,** seeking a ruling as to whether the buyer was entitled to retract, [8]and Rav Ḥisda **said to him: In the same way as** the Rabbis **enacted *meshikhah*** for the benefit of **sellers** — allowing them to retract as long as *meshikhah* had not been performed — [9]**so too they enacted *meshikhah* for** the benefit of **buyers.** Therefore, since the buyer has not yet performed *meshikhah* on the ass, he is permitted to retract.

BACKGROUND

בָּעֵי לְמִנְסְבֵיהּ Wanted to take it. The authorities in various countries used to seize beasts of burden belonging to private individuals in order to use the animals for public works or military service. Occasionally they would force the owners of these animals to work with them. When soldiers or other authorities passed through places, they would often confiscate the first beasts of burden they came across. However, for works being carried out in a permanent installation, regular lists were drawn up. Therefore when the purchaser of an ass found out that it was on a list for seizure, he would naturally wish to withdraw from the purchase.

פַּרְזָק רוּפִילָא Parzak the general. *Rashi* and other commentators explain that Parzak was the name of a certain minister. Others derive it from the Middle Persian word *vazurg*, meaning "great," "someone in high office." However, on linguistic grounds, this seems to be an unlikely parallel.

LANGUAGE

רוּפִילָא The general. This word is apparently derived from the Latin *rufulus*, which denotes a military officer of relatively high rank. Certain types of high-ranking officers in other armies were also called *rufuli*.

NOTES

Gemara is acquiring the merchandise through monetary payment. For even though the Rabbis invalidated the giving of money as an act of acquisition, it is still valid when the merchandise is placed in the rented attic. Since the situation is such that there is no need to insure the buyer against fire, the Rabbis did not apply their decree, and the original Torah law applies, according to which money acquires.

Rambam, however, disagrees with the other Rishonim on this matter. According to *Rambam*, when a field is rented out, both the owner and the renter can use it to acquire movable property placed in it, through courtyard-acquisition. Accordingly, *Rambam* also explains our Gemara in this way. He rules that if merchandise is placed in a room owned by the buyer and rented to the seller, or owned by the seller and rented to the buyer, the sale is legally finalized as soon as money is paid. *Maggid Mishneh* explains that *Rambam* understands our Gemara to be referring to courtyard-acquisition. Thus, if the attic where the seller stored the merchandise was rented from the buyer, the merchandise is acquired immediately by virtue of the fact that it is in the rented room.

כָּךְ תִּיקְּנוּ מְשִׁיכָה בַּלָּקוֹחוֹת So, too, they enacted *meshikhah* for buyers. According to Rav Ḥisda's ruling, the buyer is entitled to demand his money back, since he will in any case not receive the ass.

The Rishonim ask: Is the buyer subject to the "He who punished" curse for reneging on his promise to buy the ass? Or is he permitted to annul the transaction without penalty, since the seller cannot carry out his part of the agreement?

Rid quotes *Rabbenu Shlomo ben HaYatom,* who says that even in a case such as this, the buyer cannot renege without submitting to the "He who punished" curse. *Rid* himself disagrees. He compares this case with one in which the merchandise was destroyed by fire before the buyer could collect it. In that situation most Rishonim agree that the buyer is permitted to demand his money back without penalty. Similarly, even if the merchandise was not actually destroyed but it became impossible to carry out the transaction, the buyer is permitted to renege without penalty.

Meiri agrees with the ruling of *Rid.* He adds, however, that this applies only if it is clear that the transaction cannot go forward, or if the merchandise has been destroyed or has become worthless. If, however, it is uncertain whether or not the merchandise is still worth purchasing, the situation

HALAKHAH

מְשִׁיכָה בַּלָּקוֹחוֹת *Meshikhah* for buyers. "If someone paid for merchandise and it was accidentally damaged before he was able to draw it into his possession, the buyer may retract, even though the seller was not responsible for the damage. Moreover, the buyer is not subject to the curse of 'He who punished' in such a case." (*Shulḥan Arukh, Ḥoshen Mishpat* 204:2.)

TRANSLATION AND COMMENTARY

MISHNAH The Torah states (Leviticus 25:14): "And if you sell anything to your neighbor or buy anything from the hand of your neighbor, do not defraud one another." From here the Sages derived that it is not permitted to sell an article for more than its market value, or to buy an article for less than its market value. There are three degrees of *ona'ah* (fraud), depending on the discrepancy between the market value of the article and the price actually paid: (1) a discrepancy that need not be returned; (2) a discrepancy that must be returned but does not necessarily invalidate the sale; and (3) a discrepancy that invalidates the sale. The following Mishnah discusses the second degree of *ona'ah* — where the discrepancy must be returned. From it we learn that any overcharging or underpaying involving *less* than this discrepancy does not need to be remedied, and that any overcharging or underpaying *more* than this invalidates the sale.

הָאוֹנָאָה אַרְבָּעָה כֶּסֶף [1]The Mishnah begins: **Fraud** is said to occur in a sales transaction when the buyer's overpayment or underpayment with respect to the market value of the merchandise **is four silver ma'ot out of** the **twenty-four silver ma'ot in a sela** — i.e., **one-sixth of the purchase price.** In such a case the seller must refund the overpayment to the buyer, and if he was underpaid he can demand the extra payment from the buyer. If the fraud was less than one-sixth, the transaction stands. If the fraud was more than one-sixth, the entire sale is invalidated.

עַד מָתַי מוּתָּר לְהַחֲזִיר [2]**Until when is** the person who was defrauded **permitted to** demand compensation or to **retract?** [3]**Until he can show the merchandise to a merchant or to his relative,** who is more knowledgeable than he about how much the merchandise is really worth. After this time, however, he may neither demand compensation nor retract, for it may be assumed that he has already determined how much the merchandise is worth, and since he has not demanded compensation, he must have waived his rights.

משנה [1]הָאוֹנָאָה אַרְבָּעָה כֶּסֶף מֵעֶשְׂרִים וְאַרְבָּעָה כֶּסֶף לְסֶלַע — שְׁתוּת לַמִּקָּח. [2]עַד מָתַי מוּתָּר לְהַחֲזִיר? [3]עַד כְּדֵי שֶׁיַּרְאֶה לַתַּגָּר אוֹ לִקְרוֹבוֹ.

LITERAL TRANSLATION

MISHNAH [1]Fraud is four silver [ma'ot] out of twenty-four silver [ma'ot] to a sela — one-sixth of the purchase.

[2]Until when is it permitted to revoke? [3]Until he can show [the merchandise] to a merchant or to his relative.

RASHI

משנה האונאה ארבעה כסף – מעות כסף, שהם שש בדינר. מעשרים וארבעה כסף לסלע – אם היה המקח בדמי הסלע, שהוא עשרים וארבע מעות, דהשתא הויא אונאה שתות למקח – חייב להשיב לו כל אונאתו, ארבעה כסף. עד מתי מותר להחזיר – מי שנתאנה. והא דנקט לשון "מותר", לאשמועינן דליכא אפילו "מי שפרע" להחזיר המקח, או שיתן לו אונאתו. עד כדי שיראה המקח לתגר או לאחד מקרוביו – ואם שהה יותר, מחל על אונאתו.

BACKGROUND

עַד כְּדֵי שֶׁיַּרְאֶה לַתַּגָּר **Until he can show the merchandise to a merchant.** Someone who buys an item for the first time does not generally know its fair price. Hence he cannot know whether he has been overcharged. For this reason the Sages said that people are permitted to check with an expert after they have made their purchase; the expert can be a merchant who specializes in the article purchased or merely someone who is knowledgeable about goods and prices in general.

NOTES

is comparable to a case of price fluctuation, and the buyer may not renege without submitting to the curse. On the other hand, if the merchandise was destroyed, or if it was obviously rendered worthless, as in our Gemara, it is not even considered unethical for the buyer to cancel the transaction, and even the most scrupulous person may do so without qualms.

הָאוֹנָאָה אַרְבָּעָה כֶּסֶף מֵעֶשְׂרִים וְאַרְבָּעָה כֶּסֶף לְסֶלַע **Fraud is four silver ma'ot out of twenty-four silver ma'ot to a sela**. The Mishnah could theoretically have given other examples involving smaller sums of money (e.g., four perutot out of twenty-four perutot), in which the overcharge also comes out to one-sixth of the sale price. However, *Torat Ḥayyim* explains that the Mishnah chose to speak of sela'im because this is the coin most commonly mentioned in the Torah, since the shekel mentioned in the Torah is the same as the Mishnaic sela.

שְׁתוּת לַמִּקָּח **One-sixth of the purchase.** The Mishnah rules that a discrepancy of one-sixth between the market worth of an article and the price paid constitutes *ona'ah* and must be refunded, but if the discrepancy amounts to less than one-sixth, the overcharge is waived and need not be returned. This ruling applies only if the seller provided the merchandise concerning which the two parties had initially agreed and the discrepancy resulted from the seller's charging either more or less than the general market price. If, however, the fair market price was charged, but an error was made when measuring, weighing or counting the merchandise. or when counting out the money, the resulting mistake must be rectified no matter how small (see below, 56b). Similarly, if the seller promised to provide high-quality merchandise and later supplied merchandise of poor quality, the buyer may cancel the transaction even if the difference in value amounts to less than one-sixth (see *Bava Batra* 83b).

עַד כְּדֵי שֶׁיַּרְאֶה לַתַּגָּר אוֹ לִקְרוֹבוֹ **Until he can show the merchandise to a merchant or to his relative.** The time limit mentioned in the Mishnah appears to be subjective. In

HALAKHAH

עַד מָתַי מוּתָּר לְהַחֲזִיר? **Until when is it permitted to revoke?** "If the buyer was defrauded, he may demand a refund (if the overcharge was one-sixth of the value of the merchandise) or cancel the sale entirely (if the overcharge was more than one-sixth) during the length of time allowed him to show the merchandise to a merchant or a relative." (Ibid., 227:7.)

TRANSLATION AND COMMENTARY

הוֹרָה רַבִּי טַרְפוֹן בְּלוֹד [1]**Rabbi Tarfon** disagreed with the view of the Sages, and **ruled in Lod:** [2]**Fraud** is said to occur in a sales transaction if the discrepancy between the market value of the merchandise and the price paid for it **is eight silver ma'ot out of** the **twenty-four silver ma'ot in a sela,** i.e., **one-third of the purchase price.** If the fraud was less than one-third, the injured party need not be compensated. If the fraud was more than one-third, the entire sale is invalidated. [3]**The merchants of Lod were happy** to hear this ruling, for it enabled them to charge up to one-third more than the fair price of the article without fear that the sale would be invalidated. [4]But Rabbi Tarfon **said to them:** The person who was defrauded **is permitted to** demand compensation or to **retract** during **the entire day,** and not just until he can show the merchandise to a merchant or a relative. [5]The merchants **said to him: Let Rabbi Tarfon leave us** alone **in our place,** for despite your "lenient" method of calculating fraud, we cannot accommodate ourselves to the extended period you give the buyer to demand a refund or void the sale. [6]**And they reverted to the ruling of the Sages** — that an overcharge of one-sixth must be returned, and a greater overcharge invalidates the sale.

GEMARA אִתְּמַר [7]**It was stated** that the Amoraim disagreed about the interpretation of the Mishnah's expression: "One-sixth of the purchase." [8]**Rav said: We learned** in the Mishnah that fraud occurs where the discrepancy is **"one-sixth of the** true value of the **purchase."** When the Mishnah stated that the discrepancy between the real value of the merchandise and the price actually paid must be returned, it was only in a case where the buyer overpaid or underpaid one-sixth of the market value of that merchandise. [9]**But Shmuel said: We also learned** in the Mishnah that fraud occurs where the discrepancy is **"one-sixth of the money** actually paid." Not only must the money be returned when the discrepancy amounts to one-sixth of the *real value* of the merchandise, but in a case where the amount of money *actually paid* is one-sixth more or less than the real value of the merchandise, the discrepancy must also be returned.

[1]הוֹרָה רַבִּי טַרְפוֹן בְּלוֹד: [2]הָאוֹנָאָה שְׁמוֹנָה כֶּסֶף מֵעֶשְׂרִים וְאַרְבַּע כֶּסֶף לַסֶּלַע, שְׁלִישׁ לַמִּקָּח. [3]וְשָׂמְחוּ תַּגָּרֵי לוּד. [4]אָמַר לָהֶם: כָּל הַיּוֹם מוּתָּר לַחֲזוֹר. [5]אָמְרוּ לוֹ: יַנִּיחַ לָנוּ רַבִּי טַרְפוֹן בִּמְקוֹמֵינוּ. [6]וְחָזְרוּ לְדִבְרֵי חֲכָמִים.

גמרא [7]אִתְּמַר: [8]רַב אָמַר: ״שְׁתוּת מִקָּח״ שָׁנִינוּ. [9]וּשְׁמוּאֵל אָמַר: ״שְׁתוּת מָעוֹת״ נַמִי שָׁנִינוּ.

LITERAL TRANSLATION

[1]Rabbi Tarfon ruled in Lod: [2]Fraud is eight silver [ma'ot] out of twenty-four silver [ma'ot] to a sela — one-third of the purchase. [3]And the merchants of Lod rejoiced. [4]He said to them: It is permitted to retract the whole day. [5]They said to him: Let Rabbi Tarfon leave us in our place. [6]And they reverted to the words of the Sages.

GEMARA [7]It was stated: [8]Rav said: We learned: "One-sixth of the purchase." [9]And Shmuel said: We also learned: "One-sixth of the money."

RASHI

ושמחו תגרי לוד — שהיו בקיאין בסחורה, ומוכרין ביוקר.

גמרא שתות מקח שנינו — דוקא קתני מתניתין ״שתות למקח״, שאם האונאה שתות לשויו של מקח הויא אונאה, אבל אם פחות או יותר היא, אף על פי שישנה שתות אצל מעות שנתן זה, אין זה קרוי שתות להיות בו דין אונאה. וזהו דין אונאה שתות, להיות המקח קיים, ואין אחד יכול לחזור, אלא מחזיר אונאה. אבל אם פחות משתות — מחילה היא, ואין מחזיר לו כלום. ואם יותר על שתות — שניהם חוזרין, אפילו רצה להחזיר לו האונאה — הרשות ביד שניהם לחזור, הכי מוקמינן לה לקמן (נ,ב). **ושמואל אמר שתות מעות נמי שנינו** — מתניתין דקתני שתות למקח — לאו אשויו של מקח דוקא קאי, אלא כל התנאי קרוי מקח, בין מעות שניתנו בו בין דמי החפץ. וכל צד שאתה מוצא שם שתות אונאה, בין לצד מעות ובין לצד שויו של חפץ, יש שם אונאה, ואין כאן לא מחילה ולא ביטול מקח. והשתא מפרש פלוגתייהו.

BACKGROUND

תַּגָּרֵי לוּד **The merchants of Lod.** Lod (Lydda) is an ancient city (according to the Talmud, it dates back to the time of Joshua). Because of its central position in the lowlands near the Mediterranean, Lod was an important center of Jewish life, as well as a major commercial and administrative center, for many generations. During the Talmudic period, many types of industry flourished in Lod — weaving, the manufacture of pottery, etc. The merchants of Lod were known to be extremely astute.

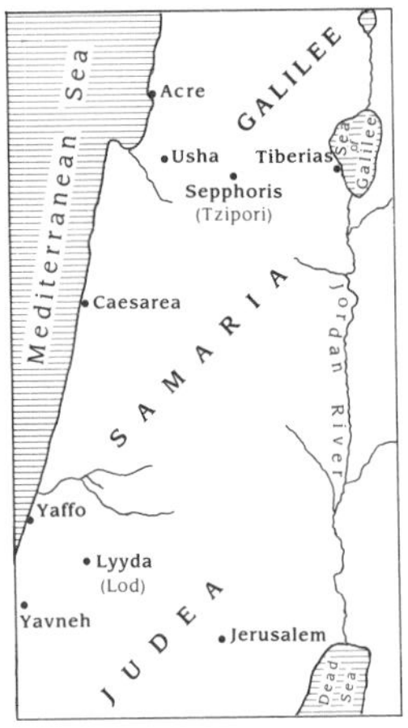

יַנִּיחַ לָנוּ רַבִּי טַרְפוֹן **Let Rabbi Tarfon leave us.** Whenever there is no fixed Halakhic ruling on a certain subject and there are various opinions with regard to it, a person may adopt the ruling of that Sage whose approach he wishes to follow. However, once the Halakhah has been determined, either by an institution with the proper authority, such as the Sanhedrin, or by general agreement, or by a permanent local custom, one must follow that Halakhah. Since in Rabbi Tarfon's time there were still differences of opinion regarding the degree of price difference that constitutes fraud, the merchants of Lod were permitted to accept his approach as opposed to that of the Sages. However, it is a general rule that when one follows the approach of a certain Sage, one must do so in full, and one is not permitted to pick and choose among the features of various systems. Hence, the merchants of Lod learned that Rabbi Tarfon's approach also included a feature that was

NOTES

other words, in order to establish whether or not the buyer can still demand a refund for the overcharge, it must be determined whether or not in that particular case the buyer had the opportunity to show the merchandise to a merchant or a relative. *Tosafot,* however, points out that the Rabbis generally avoided allowing the Halakhah to be dependent upon subjective criteria. Rather, objective guidelines were created that could be applied universally. According to *Tosafot,* the time limit mentioned in the Mishnah is the time normally required to show the merchandise to a merchant or a relative.

Rosh disagrees and rules that the deadline for demanding a refund may differ from case to case. If the buyer was prevented from showing the merchandise to a merchant or a relative because of circumstances beyond his control, he is still entitled to a refund even after the time normally required to show the merchandise to an expert has elapsed, for in such a case there is no presumption that the buyer waived the overcharge.

HALAKHAH

שְׁתוּת מִקָּח וּמָעוֹת **"One-sixth of the merchandise and the money.** *"Ona'ah* must be refunded whether it was one-sixth of the value of the merchandise or one-sixth of the value of the money paid. Thus, whether a person sold something

LITERAL TRANSLATION

[1] [If something] worth six [is sold] for five, [or if something] worth six [is sold] for seven, [2] everyone agrees that we follow the purchase, and it is fraud. [3] Where they disagree is [if something] worth five [is sold] for six, or [if something] worth seven [is sold] for six. [4] According to Shmuel, who said [that] we follow the money, both are fraud. [5] According to Rav, who said [that] we follow the purchase, [6] [something] worth five [sold] for six is cancellation of the purchase; [7] [something] worth seven [sold] for six is a waiver. [8] But Shmuel said: When we say [that there is] a waiver or a cancellation of the purchase, [9] [it is] where there is not one-sixth on both sides, [10] but where there is one-sixth on one side, it is fraud.

[1] שָׁוֵי שִׁיתָּא בְּחַמְשָׁא, שָׁוֵי שִׁיתָּא בְּשִׁבְעָה, [2] כּוּלֵּי עָלְמָא לָא פְּלִיגֵי דְּבָתַר מִקָּח אָזְלִינַן, וְאוֹנָאָה הָוְיָא. [3] כִּי פְּלִיגֵי שָׁוֵי חַמְשָׁא בְּשִׁיתָּא, וְשָׁוֵי שִׁבְעָה בְּשִׁיתָּא. [4] לִשְׁמוּאֵל, דְּאָמַר בָּתַר מָעוֹת אָזְלִינַן, אִידִי וְאִידִי אוֹנָאָה הָוֵי. [5] לְרַב, דְּאָמַר בָּתַר מִקָּח אָזְלִינַן, [6] שָׁוֵי חַמְשָׁא בְּשִׁיתָּא בִּיטּוּל מִקָּח הָוְיָא, [7] שָׁוֵי שִׁבְעָה בְּשִׁיתָּא מְחִילָה הָוְיָא. [8] וּשְׁמוּאֵל אָמַר: כִּי אָמְרִינַן מְחִילָה וּבִיטּוּל מִקָּח, [9] הֵיכָא דְּלֵיכָּא שְׁתוּת מִשְּׁנֵי צְדָדִים, [10] אֲבָל הֵיכָא דְּאִיכָּא שְׁתוּת מִצַּד אֶחָד, אוֹנָאָה הָוְיָא.

RASHI

שוי שיתא בחמשא — ונתאנה מוכר, או שוי שיתא בשבעה ונתאנה לוקח. **כולי עלמא** — בין לרב בין לשמואל אונאה הוא, דהא שתות היא לגד מקח. ושמואל שתות מעות נמי קאמר, וכל שכן שתות מקח. **כי פליגי שוי חמשא בשיתא** — ונתאנה לוקח בזוז שהוא חומש למקח, ויותר משתות הוא זה. אבל אצל מעות שנתן, שתות הוא. אי נמי, שוי שבעה בשיתא, ונתאנה מוכר בזוז, לגבי מקח — אין כאן שתות אלא שביעית, ופחות משתות היא, ולגבי מעות הוי שתות. **אידי ואידי** — בין שוי שבעה בשיתא, בין שוי חמשא בשיתא. **משני צדדין** — באחד משני לצדדין.

TRANSLATION AND COMMENTARY

שָׁוֵי שִׁיתָּא בְּחַמְשָׁא [1] The Gemara now explains this difference of opinion between Rav and Shmuel in greater detail: **If something worth six** ma'ot **is sold for five, or if something worth six** ma'ot **is sold for seven,** [2] **all** authorities — both Rav and Shmuel — **agree that we follow the** real value of the **purchase,** that **fraud has taken place,** and that the discrepancy must be returned. If the buyer underpaid by one-sixth of the merchandise's real value (paying five ma'ot for something worth six) or if he overpaid by one-sixth of its true value (paying seven ma'ot for something worth six), both Rav and Shmuel agree that the discrepancy must be returned to the defrauded party. [3] **Where they disagree is if** something **worth five** ma'ot **is sold for six, or if something worth seven** ma'ot **is sold for six.**

לִשְׁמוּאֵל [4] **According to Shmuel, who said that we** also **follow the money** actually paid, both of these cases **are** considered cases of **fraud,** and the discrepancy between the real value of the merchandise and the amount actually paid must be returned. If the amount actually paid was one-sixth more than the real value of the merchandise (where six ma'ot were paid for something worth five), or if the amount actually paid is one-sixth less than the real value of the merchandise (where six ma'ot were paid for something worth seven), the discrepancies must be returned. [5] But **according to Rav, who said that we** only **follow the** real value of the **merchandise,** [6] if something **worth five** ma'ot is **sold for six,** the sale **is canceled,** since the seller defrauded the buyer by more than one-sixth of the real value of the merchandise (by one-fifth), and an overcharge greater than one-sixth is grounds for canceling the sale. [7] Similarly, if **something worth seven** ma'ot is **sold for six,** this **constitutes a waiver.** Since the seller was defrauded by less than one-sixth of the real value of the sale (by one-seventh), he waives the discrepancy, and hence the buyer need not refund the extra money. [8] **But Shmuel said: When we say** that the person defrauded **waives** the discrepancy **or that the sale is canceled,** [9] **it is where there is not** a discrepancy of **one-sixth on either side** (either one-sixth of the real value of the purchase or one-sixth of the money actually paid, as explained above). [10] **But where there is** a discrepancy of **one-sixth on** at least **one side** (according to either of the above methods of calculation), **it is** considered **fraud,** and the discrepancy must be refunded.

inconvenient for them, they decided to revert to the system of the Sages in its entirety.

TERMINOLOGY

כּוּלֵּי עָלְמָא לָא פְּלִיגֵי... כִּי פְּלִיגֵי... Everyone agrees [lit., does not disagree] about X; where they disagree is about Y. Sometimes the Gemara attempts to delimit an issue in dispute by first stating the points agreed upon by both sides: "Everyone agrees [i.e., both parties agree] that the law in case X is such-and-such; the disputants differ about case Y...."

CONCEPTS

בִּיטּוּל מִקָּח The nullification of a transaction. If unfair advantage (אוֹנָאָה) was taken of one of the parties to a commercial transaction, and the other party made a profit greater than one-sixth (שתות) of the market value of the goods, the transaction may be nullified, and the wronged party (according to some authorities: either party) may demand the return of the goods or the amount paid.

BACKGROUND

מְחִילָה Waiver. This means a waiver by a person of certain of his rights, or of damages due him for some wrong committed against him. The waiver may be conscious and explicit, as when someone announces that he has waived a claim. However, a waiver may occasionally be tacit — when it is assumed that, in the given circumstances, people generally waive certain rights. The waiver in question here is restricted to a proportion of the entire price paid, regarding which one may assume that an ordinary person would normally waive his claim.

NOTES

מְחִילָה Waiving an overcharge. The Rabbis assumed that small overcharges are automatically waived. Since it is difficult to appraise merchandise with absolute precision (because of constant fluctations in prices), and since even

HALAKHAH

worth six ma'ot for five, or worth seven for six, or worth five for six, or worth six for seven, all such cases constitute *ona'ah,* and the person defrauded is entitled to compensation." (Ibid., 227:2.)

מְחִילָה וּבִיטּוּל מִקָּח Waiver of fraud and cancellation of sale. "A fraudulent sale involving less than one-sixth need not be refunded, as the injured party is considered to waive his right to compensation. However, if the fraudulent transaction involved more than one-sixth, the person who was defrauded may cancel the sale." (*Shulḥan Arukh, Ḥoshen Mishpat* 227:3,4.)

TERMINOLOGY

אֵימָא סֵיפָא Say the last clause, i.e., read the last clause in the source under discussion, and then you will realize that your interpretation of the first clause is incorrect.

TRANSLATION AND COMMENTARY

תְּנַן [1]The Gemara now attempts to adduce support for Shmuel's viewpoint from what **we have learned** in our Mishnah: **"Fraud** occurs when there **is** a discrepancy of **four silver ma'ot out of the twenty-four silver ma'ot in a sela** —, i.e., **one-sixth of the purchase."** [2]**Is not** the case described here one **where a person sold something worth twenty ma'ot for twenty-four,** and thus the overcharge amounts to one-sixth of the money actually paid, which is one-fifth of the real value of the merchandise? [3]Surely we may **conclude from here that** the Mishnah **is also referring to** a discrepancy of **one-sixth of the money** actually paid, as Shmuel stated!

לָא [4]But the Gemara rejects this proof: **No,** the Mishnah is referring to a case **where a person sold something worth twenty-four** ma'ot **for twenty,** i.e., where the underpayment amounts to one-sixth of the real value of the merchandise. Thus Shmuel interprets the Mishnah as referring to a case of *overcharging*. The Gemara denies this, and interprets the Mishnah as referring to a case of *underpaying*.

מִי נִתְאַנָּה [5]The Gemara is unconvinced that Shmuel's interpretation can be so easily set aside, and objects: **Who was defrauded** according to the Gemara's own explanation? **The seller.** [6]But if this is so, **consider the next clause** of the Mishnah and you will see that this explanation is untenable: **"Until when is** the person defrauded **permitted to retract?** [7]**Until he can show the merchandise to a merchant or to his relative."** [8]Concerning this time limit, **Rav Naḥman noted:** The Mishnah **is only referring to** a case where **the buyer** wants to retract, **but the seller may always retract.** Thus it is clear that the Mishnah is referring to a case where the buyer, not the seller, was defrauded, as we just explained!

אֶלָּא [9]The Gemara concludes that the Mishnah is indeed referring to a case where the buyer was defrauded, but nevertheless the Mishnah need not support Shmuel: **Rather,** says the Gemara, the Mishnah is referring to a case **where a person sold something worth twenty-four** ma'ot **for twenty-eight,** i.e., where the buyer's overpayment amounts to one-sixth of the real value of the merchandise.

תְּנַן [10]The Gemara now attempts to support Shmuel's viewpoint from the next clause of the Mishnah, where **we learned: "Rabbi Tarfon ruled in Lod: Fraud** occurs when there **is** a discrepancy of **eight silver ma'ot out of**

[1]תְּנַן: ״הָאוֹנָאָה אַרְבָּעָה כֶּסֶף מֵעֶשְׂרִים וְאַרְבָּעָה כֶּסֶף לַסֶּלַע — שְׁתוּת לַמִּקָּח״. [2]מַאי לָאו דִּזְבֵין שָׁוֵי עֶשְׂרִים בְּעֶשְׂרִין וְאַרְבָּעָה, [3]וּשְׁמַע מִינָּהּ ״שְׁתוּת מָעוֹת״ נַמִי שָׁנִינוּ!

[4]לָא, דִּזְבֵין שָׁוֵי עֶשְׂרִים וְאַרְבָּעָה בְּעֶשְׂרִים.

[5]מִי נִתְאַנָּה? מוֹכֵר. [6]אֵימָא סֵיפָא: ״עַד מָתַי מוּתָּר לְהַחֲזִיר? [7]בִּכְדֵי שֶׁיַּרְאֶה לַתַּגָּר אוֹ לִקְרוֹבוֹ״. [8]וְאָמַר רַב נַחְמָן: לֹא שָׁנוּ אֶלָּא לוֹקֵחַ, אֲבָל מוֹכֵר לְעוֹלָם חוֹזֵר.

[9]אֶלָּא דִּזְבֵין שָׁוֵי עֶשְׂרִים וְאַרְבָּעָה בְּעֶשְׂרִין וּתְמַנְיָא.

[10]תְּנַן: ״הוֹרָה רַבִּי טַרְפוֹן בְּלוֹד: הָאוֹנָאָה שְׁמוֹנָה כֶּסֶף מֵעֶשְׂרִים וְאַרְבָּעָה כֶּסֶף לְסֶלַע

LITERAL TRANSLATION

[1]We have learned: "Fraud is four silver [ma'ot] out of twenty-four silver [ma'ot] to a sela — one-sixth of the purchase." [2]Is it not where he sold [something] worth twenty for twenty-four, [3]and conclude from this that we also learned: "One-sixth of the money"!

[4]No, where he sold [something] worth twenty-four for twenty.

[5]Who was defrauded? The seller. [6]Say the latter clause: "Until when is it permitted to revoke? [7]Until he can show [the merchandise] to a merchant or to his relative." [8]And Rav Nahman said: They only taught [this regarding] the buyer, but the seller may always retract.

[9]Rather, where he sold [something] worth twenty-four for twenty-eight.

[10]We have learned: "Rabbi Tarfon ruled in Lod: Fraud is eight silver [ma'ot] out of twenty-four silver [ma'ot] to a sela

RASHI

מאי לאו דזבין שוי עשרים בעשרים וארבע — ונתאנה לוקח, דהוה ליה חומש לגבי מקח, דארבעה הוי חומש של עשרים, וקרי ליה אונאה, ולא קרי ליה ביטול מקח. **לא דזבין שוי עשרים וארבע בעשרים** — דהוה ליה שתות למקח. **ופרכינן** — ומי נתאנה מוכר? בתמיה. **לא שנו** — דבכדי שיראה ותו לא, אלא לוקח. **אבל אם נתאנה מוכר לעולם מוכר חוזר** — ולקמן מפרש טעמא. **אלא דזבין כו'** — דהוה ליה שתות למקח, ונתאנה לוקח.

NOTES

similar objects are not always identical in value, buyers do not generally mind paying slightly more than what the merchandise is really worth.

שְׁתוּת מָעוֹת נַמִי שָׁנִינוּ We also learned: "One-sixth of the money." According to *Tosafot*, both Rav and Shmuel agree that the actual value of the merchandise is the most appropriate basis for determining whether or not a given transaction involves *ona'ah*. This is so because *ona'ah* by definition involves an error concerning the value of the merchandise, with the buyer either overpaying or

TRANSLATION AND COMMENTARY

the **twenty-four silver ma'ot in a sela, or one-third of the purchase.**" [1]Is not the case described here one **where** a **person sold something worth sixteen ma'ot for twenty-four,** and the overcharge amounts to one-third of the money actually paid? [2]Thus surely we may **conclude from here that** the Mishnah **is also referring to** a discrepancy of **one-third of the money** actually paid, as Shmuel stated!

לָא [3]But the Gemara rejects this proof: **No,** the Mishnah is referring to a case **where a person sold something worth twenty-four** ma'ot **for sixteen** ma'ot, i.e., where the underpayment amounts to one-third of the real value of the merchandise, the seller being the injured party.

מִי נִתְאַנָּה [4]But the Gemara again objects in the same manner as before: **Who was defrauded** according to this explanation? **The seller.** [5]But if this is so, **consider the next clause** of the Mishnah and you will see that this explanation is untenable: [6]"Rabbi Tarfon **said to** the merchants of Lod: The person who was defrauded **is permitted to retract** during **the entire day.**" [7]Concerning this ruling, **Rav Naḥman noted:** The Mishnah **is only referring to** a case where **the buyer** wants to retract, **but the seller may always retract.** Thus it is clear that the Mishnah is referring to a case where the buyer, not the seller, was defrauded, and it can legitimately be cited in support of Shmuel's viewpoint!

אֶלָּא [8]The Gemara concludes that the Mishnah is indeed referring to a case where the buyer was defrauded, but nevertheless the Mishnah need not support Shmuel. **Rather,** says the Gemara, the Mishnah is referring to a case **where a person sold something worth twenty-four** ma'ot **for thirty-two,** i.e., where the overcharge amounts to one-third of the real value of the merchandise.

תַּנְיָא כְּוָותֵיהּ דִּשְׁמוּאֵל [9]The Gemara now observes that a Baraita **has been taught in accordance with Shmuel's** viewpoint: **"The person who was wronged has the upper hand.** [10]**How so? If a person sold something worth five** ma'ot **for six, who was defrauded? The buyer.** [11]**Therefore the buyer has the upper hand. If he wishes, he can say: 'Give me** back all **my money,'** for the sale is entirely voided, [12]**or** he may say: **'Give me what you defrauded me of,'** i.e., the overcharge of one ma'ah. [13]**If he sold him something** [50A] **worth six** ma'ot **for five,**

— שְׁלִישׁ לַמִּקָּח״. [1]מַאי לָאו דִּזְבִין שָׁוֵי שִׁיתְּסָרֵי בְּעֶשְׂרִים וְאַרְבָּעָה, [2]וּשְׁמַע מִינָּהּ ״שְׁלִישׁ מָעוֹת״ נַמִּי שָׁנִינוּ!

[3]לָא, דִּזְבִין שָׁוֵי עֶשְׂרִים וְאַרְבָּעָה בְּשִׁיתְּסַר.

[4]מִי נִתְאַנָּה? מוֹכֵר. [5]אֵימָא סֵיפָא: [6]״אָמַר לָהֶם: כָּל הַיּוֹם מוּתָּר לַחֲזוֹר״. [7]וְאָמַר רַב נַחְמָן: לֹא שָׁנוּ אֶלָּא לוֹקֵחַ, אֲבָל מוֹכֵר לְעוֹלָם חוֹזֵר.

[8]אֶלָּא דִּזְבִין שָׁוֵי עֶשְׂרִים וְאַרְבָּעָה בִּתְלָתִין וּתְרֵין.

[9]תַּנְיָא כְּוָותֵיהּ דִּשְׁמוּאֵל: ״מִי שֶׁהוּטַּל עָלָיו יָדוֹ עַל הָעֶלְיוֹנָה. [10]כֵּיצַד? מָכַר לוֹ שָׁוֶה חֲמִשָּׁה בְּשִׁשָּׁה, מִי נִתְאַנָּה? לוֹקֵחַ. [11]יַד לוֹקֵחַ עַל הָעֶלְיוֹנָה. רָצָה, אוֹמֵר: ׳תֵּן לִי מָעוֹתַי, [12]אוֹ תֵּן לִי מַה שֶּׁאוֹנִיתַנִי׳. [13]מָכַר לוֹ [50A] שָׁוֶה שֵׁשׁ בְּחָמֵשׁ, מִי

LITERAL TRANSLATION

— one-third of the purchase." [1]Is it not where he sold [something] worth sixteen for twenty-four, [2]and conclude from this that we also learned: "One-third of the money"!

[3]No, where he sold [something] worth twenty-four for sixteen.

[4]Who was defrauded? The seller. [5]Say the last clause: [6]"He said to them: It is permitted to retract the whole day." [7]And Rav Naḥman said: They only taught [this regarding] the buyer, but the seller may always retract.

[8]Rather, where he sold [something] worth twenty-four for thirty-two.

[9]It was taught in accordance with Shmuel: "The one who was wronged has the upper hand. [10]How so? [If] he sold him [something] worth five for six, who was defrauded? The buyer. [11]The buyer has the upper hand. [If] he wishes, he may say: 'Give me my money, [12]or give me that of which you defrauded me.' [13][If] he sold him [something] [50A] worth six for five, who

RASHI

תניא כוותיה דשמואל — דכין שתות מקח בין שתות מעות. **מי שהוטל עליו** — מי שהאונאה עליו, מי שנתאנה. **שוה שש בחמש** — שתות מקח, שוה חמש בשש — שתות מעות.

TERMINOLOGY

תַּנְיָא כְּוָותֵיהּ דְּרַבִּי פְּלוֹנִי It was taught in accordance with Rabbi X, i.e., the Baraita that follows supports the view of Rabbi X, an Amora whose view has previously been stated and is the subject of disagreement.

BACKGROUND

מִי שֶׁהוּטַּל עָלָיו The one who was wronged. The verb להטיל means "to place" or "to throw" something. Here it appears to have a special, idiomatic meaning: someone upon whom a certain burden has been placed. That is to say, someone who has been cheated and upon whom an unwanted burden has been imposed.

NOTES

underpaying for his purchase, and not an error with regard to the value of the money used as payment. For this reason, Rav maintains that the true value of the merchandise is the sole basis for calculating *ona'ah.* Shmuel disagrees and maintains that *ona'ah* can also be calculated on the basis of the amount of money actually paid for the purchase.

TRANSLATION AND COMMENTARY

who was defrauded? The seller. [1]Therefore **the seller has the** upper hand. [2]**If he wishes, he can say to** the buyer: **'Give me** back **my merchandise,'** thereby canceling the sale, [3]**or** he can say: **'Give me what you defrauded me of,'** in which case the buyer must pay the seller another ma'ah." Thus we see from this Baraita that it makes no difference whether the buyer underpaid by one-sixth of the value of the goods or overpaid by one-sixth of the total price paid; both are considered cases of fraud in which the discrepancy between the real value of the merchandise and the amount actually paid must be returned, as is maintained by Shmuel.

אִיבַּעְיָא לְהוּ [4]In our Mishnah the Sages ruled that if the buyer is overcharged by one-sixth, the amount overpaid must be refunded. They added that the buyer may demand his refund only during the limited period of time it takes him to show the merchandise to a merchant or to his relative to determine its true value. After that period of time has elapsed, it may be assumed that the buyer has waived his right to a refund. The following **question was raised** concerning a situation where the overpayment was less than one-sixth: **According to the Sages, is** the right to a refund in the case of an overpayment of **less than one-sixth waived immediately,** so that the act of *meshikhah* performed by the buyer finalizes the sale, and even if the buyer immediately demands the return of the overpayment he is not entitled to a refund, [5]**or** is the law here, too, that the buyer does not waive his right to a refund of the overpayment **until he has had time to show** the merchandise **to a merchant or to his relative**?

וְאִם תִּמְצֵי לוֹמַר [6]Before attempting to resolve this question, the Gemara presents a possible objection and refutes it: **Now, if you should argue** that, where the overcharge is less than one-sixth, the waiver must be immediate — for if an overcharge of less than one-sixth is not waived **until** the buyer **can show** the merchandise **to a merchant or to his relative,** [7]**what difference is there between** an overpayment of **one-sixth and** one of **less than one-sixth**, for in both cases the right to a refund is only waived after the buyer can show the merchandise to a merchant or to a relative — this argument can be refuted.

נִתְאַנָּה? מוֹכֵר. [1]יַד מוֹכֵר עַל הָעֶלְיוֹנָה. [2]רָצָה, אוֹמֵר לוֹ: 'תֵּן לִי מִקָּחִי', [3]אוֹ 'תֵּן לִי מַה שֶּׁאוֹנִיתַנִי'".

[4]אִיבַּעְיָא לְהוּ: פָּחוֹת מִשְּׁתוּת לְרַבָּנַן, לְאַלְתַּר הָוְיָא מְחִילָה, [5]אוֹ בִּכְדֵי שֶׁיַּרְאֶה לַתַּגָּר אוֹ לִקְרוֹבוֹ?

[6]וְאִם תִּמְצֵי לוֹמַר: בִּכְדֵי שֶׁיַּרְאֶה לַתַּגָּר אוֹ לִקְרוֹבוֹ, [7]מַאי אִיכָּא בֵּין שְׁתוּת לְפָחוֹת מִשְּׁתוּת?

LITERAL TRANSLATION

was defrauded? The seller. [1]The seller has the upper hand. [2][If] he wishes, he may say to him: 'Give me my merchandise,' [3]or 'Give me that of which you defrauded me.'"

[4]A question arose (lit., "it was asked of them"): Is less than one-sixth according to the Sages an immediate waiver, [5]or until he can show [it] to a merchant or to his relative?

[6]And if you say [there is no waiver] until he can show [it] to a merchant or to his relative, [7]what [difference] is there between one-sixth and less than one-sixth?

RASHI

לאלתר הויא מחילה — אפילו יחזור לאלתר. **ואם תמצא לומר בכדי שיראה לתגר או לקרובו מאי איכא כו'** — ואם באת לומר דודאי פשיטא דלאלתר הויא מחילה, דאי בכדי שיראה — מאי איכא בין שתות כו'.

LANGUAGE

לְאַלְתַּר Immediately. This word used in Mishnaic Hebrew is actually an Aramaic term, עַל אֲתַר, meaning, "on the place." It came to refer to time rather than place and to mean "immediately," as in the English idiom "on the spot."

BACKGROUND

לְאַלְתַּר הָוְיָא מְחִילָה Is it an immediate waiver? The difference of opinion here concerns how the waiver is to be understood. Is the waiver a voluntary act, by which the person defrauded waives his rights, and therefore as long as he does not know he has been defrauded or made a mistake, he cannot waive his rights? Or perhaps the waiver takes effect immediately and automatically, because we assume that in such circumstances people normally waive their rights, and therefore it is not at all dependent on the knowledge or wishes of the person defrauded?

NOTES

יַד מוֹכֵר עַל הָעֶלְיוֹנָה The seller has the upper hand. The Rishonim (*Rosh*, *Talmid Rabbenu Peretz* and *Meiri*) explain that this entire discussion in the Gemara is in accordance with the opinion of Rabbi Yehudah HaNasi (below, 50b-51a), who is of the opinion that the party defrauded has the option either of requesting a refund or of having the sale revoked. According to Rabbi Natan, however, an overcharge of exactly one-sixth must be refunded, but the sale cannot be revoked.

פָּחוֹת מִשְּׁתוּת Less than one-sixth. If the discrepancy between the real value of the merchandise and the price actually paid is less than one-sixth of the value of the merchandise, the difference need not be refunded. The Gemara states that this ruling is based on the concept of waiver (*mehilah*), i.e., the surrender of the right to claim a refund by the party against whom the fraud was committed. The Rishonim disagree as to how the concept of waiver applies to fraud. Some Rishonim explain that when the fraud amounts to less than one-sixth, we assume that the defrauded party actually waived his claim, since in fact most people would not insist on a refund in such a situation. Others maintain that since most people are willing to waive a small difference in price, prices may legitimately fluctuate by up to one-sixth. Accordingly, a waiver is not actually required, for fraud was not committed.

These two basic approaches are reflected in a number of disputes among the Rishonim concerning fraud amounting to less than one-sixth:

(1) The Rishonim disagree as to whether the prohibition "Do not wrong one another" (Leviticus 25:14) applies when the fraud amounts to less than one-sixth. If prices may legitimately fluctuate by up to one-sixth, it stands to reason that the prohibition is not violated if the overcharge is less than one-sixth (*Sefer HaHinnukh*, *Rosh*). But if the reason why such an overcharge need not be refunded is only because we assume that it is waived, there is room to argue that the Biblical prohibition applies (*Ramban*, *Rosh*).

(2) What is the ruling where the defrauded party is legally

TRANSLATION AND COMMENTARY

אִיכָּא [1]The Gemara now explains how the objection presented above can be refuted: **There is** still **a difference** between an overcharge of one-sixth and one of less than one-sixth. [2]**For** we can say that **in the case of one-sixth,** the person defrauded **has the upper hand,** as was maintained by the Baraita cited earlier. [3]**If he wishes, he can retract** and cancel the sale completely, [4]**and if he wishes, he can keep** the merchandise **and the** seller must **return the overcharge.** [5]**Whereas if** the overcharge **was less than one-sixth,** [6]the buyer **must keep** the merchandise, his only remedy being that **the** seller **must return the overpayment.**

מַאי [7]The Gemara now returns to its original question: **What is the answer** to the question raised? At what point is an overcharge of less than one-sixth waived, according to the Sages?

תָּא שְׁמַע [8]The Gemara now attempts to solve this problem by analyzing a passage from our Mishnah. **Come and hear:** "Rabbi Tarfon ruled in Lod: Fraud is ... one-third of the purchase. If the fraud was more than one-third, the entire sale is invalidated. The merchants of Lod were happy to hear this ruling. He said to them: The person defrauded is permitted to retract during the entire day ... and **they reverted to the ruling of the Sages."** [9]The Amoraim who wished to resolve their question from our Mishnah **at first assumed that** an overpayment of **less than one-third, according to Rabbi Tarfon, is** treated **like** an overpayment of **less than one-sixth according to the Sages,** i.e., it is waived. They accounted for the initial satisfaction of the merchants of Lod with the ruling of Rabbi Tarfon, and their subsequent displeasure, as follows: [10]There is **no problem**

[1]אִיכָּא, [2]דְאִלּוּ שְׁתוּת, יָדוֹ עַל הָעֶלְיוֹנָה. [3]רָצָה, חוֹזֵר, [4]רָצָה, קוֹנֶה וּמַחֲזִיר אוֹנָאָה. [5]וְאִילּוּ פָּחוֹת מִשְּׁתוּת, [6]קָנָה וּמַחֲזִיר אוֹנָאָה.

[7]מַאי?

[8]תָּא שְׁמַע: "חָזְרוּ לְדִבְרֵי חֲכָמִים". [9]סַבְרוּהָ: פָּחוֹת מִשְּׁלִישׁ לְרַבִּי טַרְפוֹן כְּפָחוֹת מִשְּׁתוּת לְרַבָּנַן דָּמֵי. [10]אִי אָמְרַתְּ

LITERAL TRANSLATION

[1]There is [a difference], [2]for [in the case of] one-sixth, he has the upper hand. [3][If] he wishes, he may retract, [4][and if] he wishes, he acquires and [the other party] returns the fraud. [5]Whereas [if it was] less than one-sixth, [6]he acquires, and [the other party] returns the fraud.

[7]What [is the answer]?

[8]Come [and] hear: "They reverted to the words of the Sages." [9]They [first] assumed: Less than one-third according to Rabbi Tarfon is like less than one-sixth according to the Sages. [10]Granted if you say

RASHI

איכא דאילו שתות — קתני מתניתין מי שהוטל עליו ידו על העליונה, רצה חוזר בו. **ואילו פחות משתות** — אם חזר בתוך כדי שיראה לתגר או לקרובו — קנה, ומחזיר לו אונאה. **חזרו לדברי חכמים** — גבי תגרי לוד במתניתין. **סברוה** — רבנן דבי מדרשא, דבעו למיפשט מינה בעיין. **פחות משליש לרבי טרפון** — לאו אונאה היא, אלא כפחות משתות לרבנן.

TERMINOLOGY

סַבְרוּהָ They thought, they assumed [that].... This term introduces an assumption proposed at the beginning of a discussion, but later found to be erroneous.

NOTES

incapable of waiving his claim? *Rambam* and *Ra'avad* disagree as to whether a minor can demand a refund for an overcharge amounting to less than one-sixth. *Ra'avad* argues that, since the waiver of a minor has no legal effect, a minor can sue for a refund even if the overcharge amounts to less than one-sixth. *Rambam* disagrees and apparently maintains that discrepancies amounting to less than one-sixth need not be returned because prices may legitimately fluctuate by up to one-sixth. Since an actual waiver is not required, the law concerning a minor is the same as that for an adult.

(3) What is the law if the claimant can convincingly argue that he did not waive his claim? If we require an actual waiver, then when we are convinced that in fact there was no such waiver, the defrauded party retains his right to demand a refund. However, if an overcharge of less than one-sixth is considered a legitimate fluctuation in price, the claimant's argument that he never waived the overcharge is irrelevant (*Maḥaneh Efraim*). The possibility considered by the Gemara — that in cases of fraud amounting to less than one-sixth, the overcharge is not waived until the buyer has had an opportunity to show the merchandise to a merchant or to a relative — can only be understood if it is assumed that an actual waiver is necessary. For if prices may legitimately fluctuate by up to one-sixth, no waiver is required and therefore a time limit is meaningless.

דְאִלּוּ שְׁתוּת, יָדוֹ עַל הָעֶלְיוֹנָה For in the case of one-sixth he has the upper hand. The Gemara's statement here — that in the case of "one-sixth" the defrauded party may opt to void the transaction — requires clarification. In the introduction to our commentary on the Mishnah, we stated that in the case of overcharging by "one-sixth" the sale may not be voided, the only remedy being a refund of the overcharge. In fact, this point is the subject of a disagreement between the Tannaim, Rabbi Natan and Rabbi Yehudah HaNasi (below, 50b-51a). Our introduction to the Mishnah follows the viewpoint of Rabbi Natan, which is accepted as the normative Halakhah. According to Rabbi Natan, if the fraud amounts to one-sixth, the sale is binding. Therefore, he must maintain that when the fraud is less than one-sixth, the waiver is immediate, for if not, there would be no difference between an overcharge of one-sixth and one of less than one-sixth. The possibility raised by the Gemara — that even if the overcharge is less than one-sixth there is no waiver until the defrauded party can show the merchandise to an expert — assumes the position of Rabbi Yehudah HaNasi, according to whom the defrauded party may opt to void the sale when the overcharge amounts to one-sixth (*Rosh*, *Talmid Rabbenu Peretz*).

סַבְרוּהָ They assumed. At first glance, the Gemara's assumption that Rabbi Tarfon treats an overcharge of less

TRANSLATION AND COMMENTARY

understanding the merchants' reaction **if you say that** the time limits mentioned in the Mishnah apply even to an overpayment of less than one-sixth. Thus, **according to the Sages,** an overpayment of **less than one-sixth is not waived until** the buyer has had an opportunity to **show** the merchandise **to a merchant or to his relative,** [1]**whereas according to Rabbi Tarfon** the merchant has to wait **the entire day** before the waiver of the overpayment takes effect. [2]**This is why** the merchants **reverted** to the ruling of the Sages. The merchants were pleased with the first part of Rabbi Tarfon's ruling, which permitted an excess payment of as much as one-third of the real value of their merchandise without the sale being automatically canceled — unlike the ruling of the Sages, according to whom any overpayment greater than one-sixth cancels the sale. However, when they learned that Rabbi Tarfon gave customers all day to demand a refund, they were disappointed, because they were now at a disadvantage regarding an overpayment of one-sixth or less, which according to the Sages is waived once the buyer has had time to show the merchandise to a merchant or to his relative, whereas according to Rabbi Tarfon the whole day must pass before the waiver takes effect. The merchants calculated that this disadvantage outweighed the potential advantage granted by Rabbi Tarfon with regard to an overpayment greater than one-sixth. [3]**But if you say that** the time limits mentioned in the Mishnah apply only to overpayments of one-sixth (according to the Sages) or one-third (according to Rabbi Tarfon) but an overpayment of **less than one-sixth according to the Sages is waived immediately,** [50B] [4]**and similarly according to Rabbi Tarfon** an overcharge of less than one-third **is waived immediately, why did** the merchants of Lod **revert** to the Sages' ruling? [5]After all, **Rabbi Tarfon's ruling was more to** the merchants' **advantage,** [6]**for** an overpayment which **the Sages considered fraud** — requiring a refund of the overpayment (in the case of overpayment by one-sixth) or canceling the sale (in the case of overpayment by more than one-sixth) — **is waived** completely **according to Rabbi Tarfon** (as long as the overpayment is less than one-third). The merchants' preference for the ruling of the Sages and their decision to forgo the opportunities for profit offered by the ruling of Rabbi Tarfon can only be accounted for if the merchants considered Rabbi Tarfon's extended time limit for retraction as a particularly harsh measure that canceled out whatever advantages they might gain from his relatively lenient attitude towards overcharging. This would indeed be the case if we were to assume that the waiver does not occur immediately in the case of overpayment by less than one-sixth (according to the Sages) or by less than one-third (according to Rabbi Tarfon). The merchants were simply not prepared to take the risk of their customers being given an entire

בִּשְׁלָמָא פָּחוֹת מִשְּׁתוּת לְרַבָּנַן בִּכְדֵי שֶׁיַּרְאֶה לַתַּגָּר אוֹ לִקְרוֹבוֹ, [1]וּלְרַבִּי טַרְפוֹן כָּל הַיּוֹם, [2]מִשּׁוּם הָכִי חָזְרוּ. [3]אֶלָּא אִי אָמְרַתְּ פָּחוֹת מִשְּׁתוּת לְרַבָּנַן לְאַלְתַּר הָוְיָא מְחִילָה, [50B] [4]וּלְרַבִּי טַרְפוֹן נַמִי לְאַלְתַּר הָוְיָא מְחִילָה, אַמַּאי חָזְרוּ? [5]בִּדְרַבִּי טַרְפוֹן נִיחָא לְהוּ טְפֵי, [6]דְּמַאי דְּרַבָּנַן קָא מְשַׁוֵּי לְהוּ אוֹנָאָה, לְרַבִּי טַרְפוֹן הָוְיָא מְחִילָה!

LITERAL TRANSLATION

[that for] less than one-sixth according to the Sages [there is no waiver] until he can show it to a merchant or to his relative, [1]but according to Rabbi Tarfon [he has] the whole day, [2]this is why they reverted. [3]But if you say [that] less than one-sixth according to the Sages is an immediate waiver, [50B] [4]and according to Rabbi Tarfon too it is an immediate waiver, why did they revert? [5]Rabbi Tarfon's [ruling] was more to their advantage, [6]for what the Sages considered (lit., "made") fraud is a waiver according to Rabbi Tarfon!

RASHI

אי אמרת בשלמא — מחילה דרבנן בכדי שיראה הוא, כי אמר להו רבי טרפון במחילה דידיה "כל היום" — דהיינו מפרוטה ועד שליש. **משום הכי חזרו** — מעיקרא שמחו, דשתות ויתר על שתות עד שליש, לרבנן הויא חזרה בתוך כדי שיראה, ואם רצה לחזור מן המקח — חוזר וחשיב ליה איהו מחילה וקנה ומחזיר אונאה, וכי אמר להו "כל היום" — מפסיד להו טובא, דפחות משתות או שתות דלרבנן בכדי שיראה, משוי ליה איהו כל היום, וצריכין להחזיר אונאה, ואי משום דלרבנן הויא שתות ויתר על שתות חזרה, ולדידיה קנה ומחזיר אונאה — נוח להם שתהא חזרה בתוך כדי שיראה, ואם לא בא בכדי שיראה — הויא מחילה, מקנה ומחזיר אונאה והיה לו שהות כל היום. **ולרבי טרפון נמי לאלתר הוי מחילה** — פחות משליש. **אמאי חזרו** — הא כל היום דרבי טרפון בשליש הוא דקאמר להו, ויזהרו מאונאת שליש ויהא הכל מחילה לאלתר.

NOTES

than one-third in the same way as the Sages treat an overcharge of less than one-sixth may seem strange, since the Gemara generally assumes that the differences of opinion mentioned in the Mishnah are minimal (and thus we would expect Rabbi Tarfon to treat an overcharge of less than one-third in the same way as the Sages treat an overcharge of exactly one-sixth). However, since the wording of Rabbi Tarfon's statement in the Mishnah exactly parallels that of the Sages, it seems reasonable to assume that Rabbi Tarfon treated an overcharge of less than one-third in the same way as the Sages treated an overcharge of less than one-sixth (*Shittah Mekubbetzet*).

TRANSLATION AND COMMENTARY

day to reconsider the wisdom of their purchase, even where the overcharge was less than one-third. If this was how the merchants understood Rabbi Tarfon's opinion, we may conclude by analogy that an overpayment of less than one-sixth is not waived immediately, and the waiver only takes effect, according to the Sages, after the buyer has waited long enough to show the merchandise to a merchant or to a relative.

מִי סָבְרַתְּ [1]But the Gemara now questions the assumption underlying the above argument: **Do you think that** an overpayment of **less than one-third according to Rabbi Tarfon is** treated **like** an overpayment of **less than one-sixth according to the Sages**? Is the Gemara's analogy between the two legitimate? [2]**No,** says the Gemara. The opinions of the Sages and Rabbi Tarfon are not parallel. [3]An overpayment ranging **from one-sixth to** one-**third according to Rabbi Tarfon is treated like** an overpayment of **exactly one-sixth according to the Sages.** According to Rabbi Tarfon, overpayment falling within that range entitles the buyer to a refund — and is not waived, as we had earlier assumed. Thus, with regard to overpayment by one-sixth, the Sages maintain that a refund may be demanded only until the buyer has had time to show the merchandise to a merchant or to a relative, whereas Rabbi Tarfon maintains that the refund may be demanded anytime that day. Even though Rabbi Tarfon's ruling may be advantageous to the merchants with regard to an overcharge greater than one-sixth, this is outweighed by the disadvantage with regard to an overcharge of one-sixth. This is why the merchants of Lod accepted the Sages' ruling. No inference can be drawn from their preference as to whether, in the case of overpayment by less than one-sixth, the waiver is immediate or occurs only after the buyer has shown the merchandise to a merchant or to a relative.

אִי הָכִי [4]However, this interpretation is difficult to reconcile with the story as reported in the Mishnah: **If so, why were the merchants happy** with Rabbi Tarfon's **first** ruling? For according to this explanation, even before Rabbi Tarfon issued his second ruling with regard to the length of time during which the buyer could retract, the merchants should have preferred the viewpoint of the Sages. Both the Sages and Rabbi Tarfon agreed that overpayment by less than one-sixth is waived immediately, and that an overpayment of one-sixth must be refunded provided the buyer did not yet have time to show the merchandise to a merchant or a relative. They only disagreed with regard to an overcharge greater than one-sixth. The Sages maintained that the sale was canceled, while Rabbi Tarfon maintained that the overcharge had to be refunded. The merchants of Lod should have preferred the Sages' ruling, which would allow them to cancel the sale, rather than obligate them to refund the overcharge.

LITERAL TRANSLATION

[1]Do you think [that] less than one-third according to Rabbi Tarfon is like less than one-sixth according to the Sages? [2]No. [3]From one-sixth to one-third according to Rabbi Tarfon is like one-sixth itself according to the Sages.

[4]If so, why did they [the merchants] rejoice at first?

[1]מִי סָבְרַתְּ פָּחוֹת מִשְּׁלִישׁ לְרַבִּי טַרְפוֹן כְּפָחוֹת מִשְּׁתוּת לְרַבָּנַן דָּמֵי? [2]לָא. [3]מִשְּׁתוּת וְעַד שְׁלִישׁ לְרַבִּי טַרְפוֹן כִּשְׁתוּת עַצְמָהּ לְרַבָּנַן דָּמֵי.

[4]אִי הָכִי, בְּמַאי שָׂמְחוּ מֵעִיקָּרָא?

RASHI

משתות ועד שליש לרבי טרפון — הויא אונאה כשתות עצמה לרבנן, ואינו חולק על חכמים אלא דבטול מקח דידהו משוי להו אונאה וידו על העליונה, ואליבא דרבנן שניהם חוזרין. **אי הכי** — דרבי טרפון אבטול מקח לחודיה פליג. **במאי שמחו** — מעיקרא.

TERMINOLOGY

מִי סָבְרַתְּ Do you think that...? An expression used by the Gemara to introduce the refutation of an argument based on a mistaken interpretation of an authoritative text: "Do you really think that such-and-such is the correct interpretation of the text you are quoting, when in fact it is not, because...?"

NOTES

מִי סָבְרַתְּ פָּחוֹת מִשְּׁלִישׁ Do you think that less than one-third...? The Gemara here rejects its previous assumption that an overcharge of less than one-third according to Rabbi Tarfon is treated like an overcharge of less than one-sixth according to the Sages, because we generally assume that disagreements between the Rabbis were relatively limited in scope. Thus it is more reasonable to assume that Rabbi Tarfon treated an overcharge of less than one-third (but more than one-sixth) in the same way as the Sages treated an overcharge of exactly one-sixth, than to assume that these authorities disagreed completely about an overcharge of less than one-third — Rabbi Tarfon maintaining that it is waived, the Sages maintaining that the sale is canceled (*Shittah Mekubbetzet*).

מִשְּׁתוּת וְעַד שְׁלִישׁ לְרַבִּי טַרְפוֹן כִּשְׁתוּת עַצְמָהּ לְרַבָּנַן דָּמֵי From one-sixth to one-third according to Rabbi Tarfon is like one-sixth itself according to the Sages. According to this interpretation of the dispute, Rabbi Tarfon's statement that "fraud...is one-third" does not mean that less than one-third is not considered fraud and is automatically waived, but that an overcharge of up to one-third is not grounds for canceling the sale. I.e., "one-third" is the maximum overcharge that does not void a sale, rather than the minimal refundable overcharge (*Talmid Rabbenu Peretz*).

TRANSLATION AND COMMENTARY

תִּפְשׁוֹט דְּבִטּוּל מִקָּח לְרַבָּנַן [1]In order to account for the merchants' initial satisfaction, the Gemara now suggests that we can deduce a new rule from the Mishnah: Let us **conclude** that in the case of an overcharge exceeding one-sixth — **where according to the Sages the sale is null and void** — the injured party **can always retract** without any limitation of time (an issue which arises later in the Gemara). [2]**For when Rabbi Tarfon told** the merchants **that** an overpayment ranging from one-sixth to one-third **is fraud** which is waived if the buyer does not demand a refund within the time it takes him to show the merchandise to a merchant or to his relative, the merchants **were happy,** since this was more to their advantage than the viewpoint of the Sages, who maintained that such an overpayment was grounds for canceling the sale no matter how much time had passed. [3]**But when** Rabbi Tarfon **told** the merchants that the customer had **all day** to demand his refund, **they reverted** to the Sages' ruling. For if the overpayment was one-sixth, the buyer could demand his refund all day, according to Rabbi Tarfon, whereas according to the Sages he had only as long as it takes to show the merchandise to a merchant or to a relative. And even though Rabbi Tarfon's ruling was more advantageous to the merchants with regard to an overpayment greater than one-sixth, such an overpayment was unusual, and therefore that advantage was outweighed by the disadvantage with regard to an overpayment of one-sixth. [4]**But if it should enter your mind that** in the case of an overcharge greater than one-sixth, **cancellation of the sale is possible according to the Sages only until** the customer **can show** the merchandise **to a merchant or to his relative,** [5]**why were** the merchants **happy** with Rabbi Tarfon's first ruling? The only difference between the Sages and Rabbi Tarfon would then be with regard to an overcharge greater than one-sixth — in which case the Sages maintain that the sale is canceled and each party may retract, whereas Rabbi Tarfon maintains that the overpayment must be refunded. The merchants of Lod should therefore have preferred the Sages' ruling to that of Rabbi Tarfon, because the Sages gave them the opportunity to withdraw entirely from a fraudulent sale rather than pay their customers a refund.

[1]תִּפְשׁוֹט דְּבִטּוּל מִקָּח לְרַבָּנַן לְעוֹלָם חוֹזֵר. [2]דְּכֵיוָן דְּאָמַר לְהוּ רַבִּי טַרְפוֹן הָוְיָא אוֹנָאָה, שָׂמְחוּ, [3]כִּי אָמַר לְהוּ: ״כָּל הַיּוֹם״, חָזְרוּ. [4]דְּאִי סָלְקָא דַּעְתָּךְ דְּבִטּוּל מִקָּח לְרַבָּנַן בִּכְדֵי שֶׁיַּרְאֶה לַתַּגָּר אוֹ לִקְרוֹבוֹ, [5]בְּמַאי שָׂמְחוּ?

LITERAL TRANSLATION

[1]Conclude that according to the Sages [where there is] cancellation of a sale one can always retract. [2]For when Rabbi Tarfon said to them [that] it is fraud, they rejoiced, [3][but] when he said to them: "The whole day," they reverted. [4]For if it should enter your mind that cancellation of a sale [is only possible] according to the Sages until he can show [it] to a merchant or to his relative, [5]why did they rejoice?

RASHI

תפשוט – דמדשמחו. **ביטול מקח לרבנן** – דמיבעיא לן לקמן, אי לעולם חוזר או בכדי שיראה, תפשוט דמדשמחו דלרבנן לעולם חוזר, וכי אמר להו רבי טרפון אונאה, והם היו סבורין דבכדי שיראה סבירא ליה באונאה, שמחו. **כי אמר להו כל היום חזרו** – אלא דבין לעולם חוזר ובין שהות כל היום הנאה פורתא היא לדידהו, דשהות הרבה יש לימלך כל היום, ועוד: אונאה יתר על שתות לא שכיחא, וקמפסיד להו בשתות עצמה, לרבנן – בכדי שיראה ולדידיה – כל היום. **דאי סלקא דעתך בטול מקח לרבנן** – כאונאה בכדי שיראה, ואין בין אונאה לבטול מקח אלא דבאונאה ידו על העליונה, ובבטול מקח שניהם חוזרין, כי משוי רבי טרפון לבטול מקח אונאה, אין זו טובה להם.

NOTES

בְּטוּל מִקָּח **Cancellation of a sale.** The discussion here must be considered in the light of guidelines formulated in the Mishnah (*Bava Batra* 5:6) for the cancellation of a sale on the grounds that the transaction was made in error (מִקַּח טָעוּת). If inferior merchandise is sold as being of superior quality, the buyer may retract. If superior merchandise is sold as being of inferior quality, the seller may retract. Even though the basic terms of the agreement between the two parties were fulfilled, the party who was mistaken about the quality of the merchandise is given the right to retract. If the mistake is not limited to a question of quality, but rather concerns the very nature of the merchandise sold, both parties may retract. Since the merchandise that was delivered is so different from the merchandise upon which the two parties agreed, the transaction is considered as a purchase made in error, and is thus void.

The question arises with regard to *ona'ah* of more than one-sixth — in which case the sale is canceled — as to whether the defect in the transaction should be compared to a mistake in quality, and thus only the defrauded party should be entitled to retract, or whether it should be likened to a mistake regarding the very nature of the merchandise, in which case either party may retract, since the transaction is void. Some Rishonim claim that an overcharge exceeding one-sixth constitutes a significant deviation from the original terms, for the parties only agreed on a price appropriate for the merchandise. The sale is therefore not binding (*Tosafot*). Others maintain that, since the merchandise promised was delivered and the price charged was paid, the basic terms of the agreement were fulfilled. Thus it is only the defrauded party who is given the right to retract (*Rif*).

The Gemara's question concerning the time limit seems to depend on these two approaches. If the transaction is void, there should be no time limit after which the defrauded party may no longer demand that the sale be canceled. If

[1]שָׂמְחוּ בִּשְׁתוּת עַצְמָהּ. [2]דִּלְרַבִּי טַרְפוֹן מְחִילָה, [3]וּלְרַבָּנַן אוֹנָאָה.
[4]אִיבַּעֲיָא לְהוּ: [5]בִּטּוּל מִקָּח לְרַבָּנַן לְעוֹלָם חוֹזֵר, [6]אוֹ דִּלְמָא בִּכְדֵי שֶׁיַּרְאֶה לַתַּגָּר אוֹ לִקְרוֹבוֹ? [7]וְאִם תִּמְצָא לוֹמַר: בִּכְדֵי שֶׁיַּרְאֶה לַתַּגָּר אוֹ לִקְרוֹבוֹ, [8]מָה אִיכָּא בֵּין שְׁתוּת לְיָתֵר עַל שְׁתוּת?
[9]אִיכָּא, [10]דְּאִילּוּ שְׁתוּת, מִי שֶׁנִּתְאַנָּה חוֹזֵר, [11]וְאִילּוּ יָתֵר עַל שְׁתוּת, שְׁנֵיהֶם חוֹזְרִים.

LITERAL TRANSLATION

[1]They rejoiced about one-sixth itself. [2]For according to Rabbi Tarfon it is a waiver, [3]but according to the Sages it is fraud.

[4]A question arose: [5][Where there is] cancellation of a sale according to the Sages can one always retract, [6]or perhaps [only] until he can show [it] to a merchant or to his relative?

[7]And if you say: [Only] until he can show [it] to a merchant or to his relative, [8]what [difference] is there between one-sixth and more than one-sixth?

[9]There is [a difference], [10]for [in the case of] one-sixth, the one who has been defrauded may retract, [11]whereas [in the case of] more than one-sixth, both may retract.

TRANSLATION AND COMMENTARY

שָׂמְחוּ בִּשְׁתוּת עַצְמָהּ [1]However, the Gemara refutes this conclusion: We may explain that the merchants **were happy about** Rabbi Tarfon's ruling as applied to overpayment of **exactly one-sixth.** [2]Such an overpayment, **according to Rabbi Tarfon,** is treated not like an overpayment of more than one-sixth, as we originally thought, but rather **it is waived** immediately, [3]whereas **according to the Sages it is** considered **fraud**, which is waived only after the buyer has had time to show the merchandise to a merchant or to a relative. Accordingly, the merchants of Lod were happy with Rabbi Tarfon's first ruling. However, when they heard Rabbi Tarfon's second ruling — allowing the buyer all day to demand a refund on an overcharge greater than one-sixth — they reverted to the ruling of the Sages, according to whom the buyer can retract only until he has had time to show the merchandise to a merchant or a relative.

אִיבַּעֲיָא לְהוּ [4]In our Mishnah the Sages ruled that, if a buyer is overcharged by one-sixth, he may demand a refund of the overcharge only for so long as it takes him to show the merchandise to a merchant or to his relative. After that time it is assumed that the buyer has waived his rights. If, however, the overcharge is more than one-sixth, the sale can be canceled by either party. The Gemara now discusses whether the right to cancel the sale is subject to any time limit. This is an issue not touched on explicitly by our Mishnah, which deals with fraud of one-sixth. The Gemara wonders, however, whether the time limits laid down in the Mishnah also apply in the case of fraud in excess of one-sixth. The following **question was raised** concerning such an overcharge: [5]If the overcharge is more than one-sixth — **where the sale is canceled according to the Sages — can** the injured party **always retract,** [6]**or** can the sale be canceled only in the period it would **take him to show** the merchandise **to a merchant or to his relative?**

וְאִם תִּמְצָא לוֹמַר [19]Before attempting to resolve this question, the Gemara presents a potential objection and refutes it: **Now, if you should argue** that cancellation of the sale must always be possible — for if the buyer can cancel the sale only **during the time it takes him** to **show** the merchandise **to a merchant or to his relative,** [8]**what difference is there between** overcharging by **one-sixth and** overcharging by **more than one-sixth?** In both cases the buyer may cancel the sale during the period granted him to show the merchandise to a merchant or a relative — what practical difference would there then be between the two levels of overpayment, which are Halakhically recognized as two different categories?

אִיכָּא [9]The Gemara answers: **There would** still **be a difference** between an overcharge of one-sixth and an overcharge of more than one-sixth. [10]**For** we could say that, **in the case of one-sixth,** only **the person who has been defrauded may retract,** [11]**but** if the overcharge was **more than one-sixth, both** parties **may retract.** Thus, we

RASHI

שמחו בשתות עצמה כו׳ – דהא דאמרן משתות ועד שליש לרבי טרפון כשתות לרבנן, משתות ומעלה אמרו, ולא שתות עצמה. **אם תמצא לומר כו׳** – כלומר, אם באת לומר פשיטא דלעולם חוזר, דאי בכדי שיראה מאי איכא כו׳. **איכא דאילו שתות כו׳** – כי נמי אמרינן תרוייהו בכדי שיראה, עדיין יש חילוק זה ביניהם.

NOTES

the transaction is binding, but the defrauded party is given the right to retract, it is reasonable that this right be limited in time. Rava's conclusion that there is in fact a time limit for the cancellation of the sale is understandable according to *Rif*, who maintains that though the transaction is not void, the defrauded party has the right to retract. Since he had time to ascertain whether the transaction involved *ona'ah* but still did not retract, he forfeits that right. Rava's conclusion can also be explained according to *Tosafot*, who maintains that the transaction is void because it lacks the necessary agreement of the two parties. If the defrauded party becomes aware of the *ona'ah* and does not lodge a complaint within the specified time, he thereby finalizes the transaction (*Rashbam* and *Ramban*).

שְׁנֵיהֶם חוֹזְרִים **Both may retract.** As was explained in the previous note, the Rishonim disagree about a case in which

¹מַאי?
²תָּא שְׁמַע: ״חָזְרוּ לְדִבְרֵי חֲכָמִים״. ³אִי אָמְרַתְּ בִּשְׁלָמָא בִּטּוּל מִקָּח לְרַבָּנַן בִּכְדֵי שֶׁיַּרְאֶה לַתַּגָּר אוֹ לִקְרוֹבוֹ, ⁴וּלְרַבִּי טַרְפוֹן כָּל הַיּוֹם, ⁵מִשּׁוּם הָכִי חָזְרוּ.
⁶אֶלָּא אִי אָמְרַתְּ בִּטּוּל מִקָּח

LITERAL TRANSLATION

¹What [is the answer]?

²Come [and] hear: "They reverted to the words of the Sages." ³Granted if you say [that] cancellation of the sale according to the Sages is [possible only] until he can show [it] to a merchant or to his relative, ⁴but according to Rabbi Tarfon [he has] the whole day, ⁵this is why they reverted.

⁶But if you say [that where there is] cancellation of a sale

TRANSLATION AND COMMENTARY

are unable to draw conclusions as to the period during which a fraudulent sale may be canceled.

מַאי ¹So the Gemara must return to its original question: **What is the answer?** Until when, according to the Sages, can the sale be canceled if the overpayment exceeded one-sixth?

תָּא שְׁמַע ²The Gemara now attempts to solve this problem by analyzing a passage from our Mishnah: **Come and hear:** "Rabbi Tarfon ruled in Lod: Fraud is ... one-third of the purchase. If the fraud was more than one-third, the entire sale is invalidated. The merchants of Lod were happy to hear this ruling. He said to them: The person defrauded is permitted to retract during the entire day ... and **they reverted to the words of the Sages.**" ³The Gemara's argument is as follows: There is **no problem** understanding the merchants' reaction **if you say that** the Sages apply the time limits mentioned in the Mishnah even to an overcharge greater than one-sixth, and that therefore cancellation **of the sale according to the Sages is possible only until** the buyer has had time **to show** the merchandise **to a merchant or to his relative,** ⁴**whereas according to Rabbi Tarfon he has the entire day** to retract. ⁵**This is why** the merchants **reverted** to the ruling of the Sages. The merchants were initially pleased with Rabbi Tarfon's ruling, because they reasoned that if they overcharged by exactly one-sixth, the overcharge would be waived immediately according to Rabbi Tarfon (who ruled that a price discrepancy of one-sixth did not constitute fraud), whereas the Sages would say that the buyer could demand a refund. But then they learned that Rabbi Tarfon's ruling was not as favorable to them as they had supposed, for Rabbi Tarfon also ruled that in cases of overpayment by more than one-sixth but less than one-third the defrauded party had the entire day to demand a refund. Having grasped the full implication of Rabbi Tarfon's ruling, the merchants reverted to the Sages' ruling, that in no case could the buyer demand a refund until he had time to show the merchandise to a merchant or to a relative. The merchants realized that Rabbi Tarfon's ruling did not give them a clear-cut advantage over their customers. The advantage to the merchants of Rabbi Tarfon's ruling was obvious where the overcharge was exactly one-sixth. In that case, Rabbi Tarfon left the customer without remedy. But in cases of overpayment by more than one-sixth, the advantage of Rabbi Tarfon's ruling for the merchants was questionable. True, in such a case Rabbi Tarfon only entitled the customer to a refund, whereas the Sages permitted him to cancel the sale. But the merchants viewed this as a benefit of dubious value if the buyer had all day to seek his refund. The merchants preferred to face the risk of cancellation for a limited period rather than the risk of refund for an entire day. The upshot of this argument is that the Mishnah appears to imply that, according to the Sages, a fraudulent sale can only be canceled until the defrauded party has had time to show his purchase to a merchant or to a relative.

אֶלָּא אִי אָמְרַתְּ ⁶**But if you say** that the time limit mentioned in the Mishnah applies only to an overpayment

RASHI

משום הכי חזרו — מעיקרא כי שוי להו רבי טרפון יתר על שתות אונאה, דלרבנן בטול מקח ולא הרחיב זמן החזרה, שמחו בשתות עצמה דמחילה לאלתר, כדאמרן, וכי הדר אמר להו כל היום, חזרו, דהחמיר להם ביתר על שתות ופגם להם יותר ממה שהשביחם בשתות עצמה, כדפרישית. **אלא אי אמרת לעולם חוזר** — נהי נמי דשתות עצמה משוי להו אונאה כרבנן, דהאי דאמר לעיל ״שמחו בשתות עצמה״ שינויא דחיקא הוה משום שמחה דמעיקרא, דקשיא לן במאי שמחו, והשתא אמרת לי דשמחה מעיקרא משום בטול מקח היא דהואי, דלרבנן לעולם ולרבי טרפון היו סבורין בכדי שיראה כדין אונאה דרבנן, כי הדר אמר להו כל היום, אכתי שמחה איכא, דלרבנן לעולם

NOTES

the *ona'ah* exceeds one-sixth. According to *Tosafot*, the transaction is void, and therefore each side may retract. According to *Rif*, the transaction is valid, but the defrauded party has the right to retract. At first glance, the Gemara's statement — "In the case of one-sixth, the one who has been defrauded may retract, whereas in the case of more than one-sixth, both may retract" — would seem to support *Tosafot*. According to *Rif*, this passage can be explained as follows: If the *ona'ah* is one-sixth, only the defrauded party may retract and demand a refund for the overcharge or underpayment. If the *ona'ah* is more than one-sixth, the defrauded party may retract and cancel the transaction. If, instead of retracting, he demands that the overcharge be refunded, the other party can claim that the terms of the transaction differ significantly from the terms upon which the two originally agreed. If the defrauded party insists on the refund, the other party may retract and cancel the sale altogether (see *Rivam* quoted in *Tosafot*).

TRANSLATION AND COMMENTARY

of one-sixth (or one-third, according to Rabbi Tarfon), but in the case of an overpayment by more than one-sixth, **where** the result of the overpayment **is the cancellation of the sale, and according to the Sages it is always possible to retract** no matter how much time has passed, [1]**why did** the merchants of Lod **revert** to the Sages' ruling? [2]**Rabbi Tarfon's ruling was more to their advantage,** [3]**since he considered** an overpayment of more than one-sixth **fraud**, for which the buyer can demand a refund that **entire day, but not longer!** By contrast, in that same case, the Sages would not only impose the harsher remedy of cancellation, but would leave that remedy available indefinitely. Why then should the merchants have reverted to the ruling of the Sages?

בִּטּוּל מִקָּח לָא שְׁכִיחַ [4]The Gemara cannot find fault with this reasoning, but rejects it nonetheless as being out of touch with the way business was actually conducted at the Lod marketplace. In the specific case of overcharging by more than one-sixth, Rabbi Tarfon's ruling is more to the merchants' advantage than the ruling of the Sages, who maintain that the remedy of cancellation, where applicable, is available indefinitely. In such a case the Sages would grant the customer the permanent right to cancel the sale, whereas Rabbi Tarfon would permit him a refund only, and only on the day of the purchase. Nevertheless, looking at the general impact of Rabbi Tarfon's ruling, the merchants of Lod preferred the Sages' ruling over that of Rabbi Tarfon. Although Rabbi Tarfon's ruling is advantageous to the merchants when the buyer is overcharged by more than one-sixth, such an overcharge — which, according to the Sages, leads to the **cancellation of the sale — is not common.** The merchants would therefore derive little benefit from Rabbi Tarfon's ruling, because the case where it was most advantageous to them — overcharging by more than one-sixth — did not frequently occur. By contrast, the merchants stood to derive benefit from the Sages' ruling in a case where the buyer was overcharged by exactly one-sixth. In such a case, Rabbi Tarfon would maintain that the buyer can demand a refund the entire day, whereas according to the Sages, the buyer may only demand a refund until he has had time to show the merchandise to a merchant or a relative. In assessing the relative merits of Rabbi Tarfon's position and that of the Sages, the merchants focused on the case of overcharge by exactly one-sixth, and found that in such circumstances the Sages' ruling was more to their advantage than that of Rabbi Tarfon. The Gemara fails to bring conclusive proof from our Mishnah regarding the initial question, whether cancellation of the sale is always possible or whether it is limited to the period mentioned in the Mishnah.

אֲמַר רָבָא [5]The Gemara concludes the previous discussion by presenting an actual decision regarding the laws governing overcharging: **Rava said: The law is** that if the overcharge was **less than one-sixth, the sale is valid,** and the overcharge is waived immediately. [6]If the overcharge was **more than one-sixth, the sale is**

LITERAL TRANSLATION

according to the Sages one can always retract, [1]why did they revert? [2]Rabbi Tarfon's [ruling] was more to their advantage, [3]since he considered it fraud the whole day but not more!

[4]Cancellation of a sale is not common.

[5]Rava said: The Halakhah is: Less than one-sixth, the sale is valid (lit., "acquired"). [6]More than one-sixth is cancellation of the sale. One-sixth,

לְרַבָּנַן לְעוֹלָם חוֹזֵר, [1]אַמַּאי חָזְרוּ? [2]בְּדְרַבִּי טַרְפוֹן נִיחָא לְהוּ טְפֵי, [3]דְּקָא מְשַׁוֵּי לְהוּ אוֹנָאָה כָּל הַיּוֹם וְתוּ לֹא!

[4]בִּטּוּל מִקָּח לָא שְׁכִיחַ.

[5]אֲמַר רָבָא: הִלְכְתָא: פָּחוֹת מִשְּׁתוּת, נִקְנָה מִקָּח. [6]יוֹתֵר עַל שְׁתוּת, בִּיטּוּל מִקָּח. שְׁתוּת,

RASHI

ולרבי טרפון כל היום ותו לא, ואי משום שתות עצמה, דלרבנן בכדי שיראה ולדידיה כל היום, הרבה הוא שבח שמשביח רבי טרפון ביתר על השתות, מפגם שפוגם בשתות עצמה, שהרי יכולין ליזהר בשתות עצמה, יפחתו לו מעט ותהא מחילה, נמצאו משתכרין בשל רבי טרפון כל אונאה שיתר על שתות. **בטול מקח לא שכיח** — ואין שבח זה חשוב להם במידי דלא שכיח, וכי מיקרי והוי נמי — הרי נתן לו שהות כל היום לחזור, ורוב הנמלכים נמלכים בו ביום, הלכך פגם דשתות עצמה עדיף להו. **הלכתא פחות משתות נקנה מקח** — לאלתר. **יתר על שתות בטל מקח** — ושניהם חוזרין.

HALAKHAH

אוֹנָאָה וּבִטּוּל מִקָּח Fraud and the cancellation of a sale. "An overcharge or an underpayment of one-sixth must be refunded, whereas an overcharge or an underpayment of more than one-sixth constitutes grounds for cancellation of the sale. But the overcharge need not be refunded (or the sale canceled) if the buyer waited longer than it takes to show the merchandise to a merchant or a relative before demanding the refund (or cancellation of the sale). These laws (which follow Rava's ruling) apply only if the buyer was defrauded. However, if the seller was defrauded, he may demand a refund (or have the sale canceled) no matter how much time has passed. Nevertheless, if the buyer underpaid for merchandise whose price ordinarily does not vary, the sale is finalized, and hence the seller cannot demand a refund once the seller waited long enough to ask how much merchandise of this type costs. Similarly, if it can be proved that the seller had seen similar merchandise and knew how much it cost (and thus realized that he had been defrauded)

BACKGROUND

בִּטּוּל מִקָּח לָא שְׁכִיחַ Cancellation of a sale is not common. A transaction is invalidated when there was a large deviation from the normal price. Since most people do not purposely cheat each other, such a large margin of error is unusual. Generally, people have a fair notion regarding the prices of things, and fall into error only when the difference is small.

TERMINOLOGY

הִלְכְתָא The Halakhah is.... An expression used to introduce the Talmud's decision about a Halakhic issue left unresolved in the previous discussion.

קָנָה וּמַחֲזִיר אוֹנָאָה, [1]וְזֶה וְזֶה בִּכְדֵי שֶׁיַּרְאֶה לְתַגָּר אוֹ לִקְרוֹבוֹ.
[2]תַּנְיָא כְּוָותֵיהּ דְּרָבָא: [3]״אוֹנָאָה פָּחוֹת מִשְּׁתוּת, נִקְנָה מִקָּח. [4]יָתֵר עַל שְׁתוּת, בָּטֵל מִקָּח. [5]שְׁתוּת, קָנָה וּמַחֲזִיר אוֹנָאָה. [6]דִּבְרֵי רַבִּי נָתָן. [7]רַבִּי יְהוּדָה הַנָּשִׂיא אוֹמֵר: יַד מוֹכֵר עַל הָעֶלְיוֹנָה. [8]רוֹצֶה, אוֹמֵר לוֹ: ׳תֵּן לִי מִקָּחִי׳, [9]אוֹ, ׳תֵּן לִי מַה שֶּׁאִנִּיתַנִי׳. [10]וְזֶה וְזֶה בִּכְדֵי שֶׁיַּרְאֶה לְתַגָּר אוֹ לִקְרוֹבוֹ״.

LITERAL TRANSLATION

he acquires and he returns the overcharge, [1]and [in] both [cases] until he can show [it] to a merchant or to his relative.

[2]It was taught in accordance with Rava: [3]"[In a case of] fraud less than one-sixth, the sale is valid. [4]More than one-sixth is cancellation of the sale. [5]One-sixth, he acquires and returns the overcharge. [6][These are] the words of Rabbi Natan. [7]Rabbi Yehudah HaNasi says: The seller has the upper hand. [8][If] he wishes, he may say to him: 'Give me my merchandise,' [9]or 'Give me that of which you defrauded me.' [10]And [in] both [cases] (lit., 'this and this'), until he can show [it] to a merchant or to his relative."

TRANSLATION AND COMMENTARY

canceled at the option of either party. If the overcharge was exactly **one-sixth,** the buyer **acquires** the merchandise, but the seller must **refund the overcharge.** [1]**And** in **both** cases — where the overcharge was exactly one-sixth and where it was greater than one-sixth — a refund can only be demanded (or the sale canceled) **until** the buyer has had time **to show** the merchandise **to a merchant or to a relative.** After this time, however, the overcharge is assumed to have been waived.

תַּנְיָא כְּוָותֵיהּ דְּרָבָא [2]The Gemara now adduces support for Rava's ruling, citing a Baraita that **was taught in accordance with Rava's** view: [3]"If the **fraud was less than one-sixth, the sale is valid** and the overcharge is waived immediately. [4]If the overcharge was **more than one-sixth, the sale is canceled** at the option of either party. [5]If the overcharge was exactly **one-sixth,** the buyer **acquires** the merchandise, and the seller must **refund the overcharge.** [6]**These are the words of Rabbi Natan.** [7]**Rabbi Yehudah HaNasi says:** If the fraud was exactly one-sixth, and it was the seller who was defrauded, **the seller has the upper hand.** [8]**If he wishes, he may say to the buyer, 'Give me my merchandise,'** in which case the sale is revoked entirely, [9]**or** he may say, **'Give me what you defrauded me** of,' in which case the buyer must pay the amount of the underpayment. (The same would, of course, apply if it was the buyer who was defrauded.) [10]**And in both cases** — where the overcharge was equal to one-sixth and where it was greater than one-sixth — a refund can only be demanded (or the sale canceled) **until** the buyer has had time **to show** the merchandise **to a merchant or to a relative.** After this time, however, the overcharge is assumed to have been waived." Thus we see that Rava's ruling is supported by the viewpoint of Rabbi Natan in the Baraita just quoted.

RASHI

שתות קנה — ואין אחד מהן יכול לחזור. **ומחזיר אונאה** — ולית ליה לרבא ידו על העליונה דמתניתין דסבירא ליה כרבי נתן דברייתא, דקיימא לן רבי נתן דיינא הוא ונחית לעומקא דדינא, בפרק "הכית והעלייה" (בבא מציעא קיז,ב, ובבבא קמא נג,א). **זה וזה** — אונאה ובטול מקח. **יד מוכר על העליונה** — אם נתאנה מוכר, והוא הדין אם נתאנה לוקח, יד לוקח על העליונה, והכי מוקמינן לה לקמן (נא), מאי דשייר במתניתין תני בברייתא. **זה וזה** — אונאה ובטול מקח.

NOTES

שְׁתוּת קָנָה וּמַחֲזִיר אוֹנָאָה **One-sixth, he acquires and returns the overcharge**. Rava rules that, if the overcharge is exactly one-sixth, the buyer acquires the merchandise and the overcharge is refunded. The Gemara brings support for Rava's ruling from a Baraita which records a dispute between Rabbi Natan and Rabbi Yehudah HaNasi concerning an overcharge of one-sixth. Rabbi Natan maintains that the defrauded party can demand a refund of the overcharge, but the transaction itself is binding. According to Rabbi Yehudah HaNasi, the defrauded party may choose whether to void the sale or accept a refund of the overcharge.

The question arises as to which of the two opinions — that of Rabbi Natan or that of Rabbi Yehudah HaNasi — is brought in support of Rava. Most Rishonim maintain that Rava rules in accordance with Rabbi Natan that the claimant can demand reimbursement but cannot nullify the sale, for there is no mention in Rava's ruling that the defrauded party can choose between two options.

Rabbenu Tam objects that it is difficult to maintain that Rava rules like Rabbi Natan, for the Halakhah should be in accordance with Rabbi Yehudah HaNasi, whose view is recorded anonymously in the next Mishnah (below, 51a) and is generally accepted when he disagrees with a colleague. Moreover, Rava himself interprets the next Mishnah according to Rabbi Yehudah HaNasi, and presumably rules accordingly. Therefore *Rabbenu Tam* explains that, when Rava states that in a case of one-sixth the

HALAKHAH

but did not demand a refund or cancellation of the sale, he is not entitled to a refund or cancellation, since we assume that he waived his rights," following Rav Naḥman's ruling. (*Shulḥan Arukh, Ḥoshen Mishpat* 227:7-8.)

SAGES

רַבִּי נָתָן **Rabbi Natan.** This is Rabbi Natan the Babylonian, who immigrated to Eretz Israel and was one of the greatest Tannaim of the generation before the completion of the Mishnah. Rabbi Natan was the son of the Exilarch in Babylonia, a member of a family descended from King David. Because of his greatness as a Torah scholar and his noble lineage, he was named deputy to the president of the Sanhedrin. He was famous for his profound knowledge of civil law. Similarly, he was known for his piety, and it is told that Elijah the Prophet used to appear to him.

Rabbi Natan, together with Rabbi Meir, tried to alter the procedure for choosing the president of the Sanhedrin. This effort failed, and as a kind of punishment it was decreed that Rabbi Natan should not be mentioned by name in the Mishnah, but that his teachings be introduced with the phrase, "Some say." However, this decision was not always observed in practice.

Rabbi Natan edited a number of collections of Mishnaic teachings, and the tractate *Avot DeRabbi Natan* is named after him. Many Sages of the following generation were his students, the most prominent of whom was Rabbi Yehudah HaNasi.

[1]״עַד מָתַי מוּתָּר לְהַחֲזִיר כו׳״. [2]אָמַר רַב נַחְמָן: לֹא שָׁנוּ אֶלָּא לוֹקֵחַ, [3]אֲבָל מוֹכֵר לְעוֹלָם חוֹזֵר. [4]נֵימָא מְסַיֵּיעַ לֵיהּ ״חָזְרוּ לְדִבְרֵי חֲכָמִים״? [5]אִי אָמְרַתְּ בִּשְׁלָמָא מוֹכֵר לְעוֹלָם חוֹזֵר, [51A] מִשּׁוּם הָכִי חָזְרוּ. [6]אֶלָּא אִי אָמְרַתְּ מוֹכֵר נַמִי כְּלוֹקֵחַ דָּמֵי, [7]מַאי נָפְקָא לְהוּ מִינָּהּ? [8]כִּי הֵיכִי דְּעָבְדִי לֵיהּ רַבָּנַן תַּקַּנְתָּא לַלּוֹקֵחַ, [9]הָכִי נַמִי עָבְדִי לֵיהּ רַבָּנַן תַּקַּנְתָּא לַמּוֹכֵר! [10]תַּגָּרֵי לוּד לָא שְׁכִיחַ דְּטָעוּ.

LITERAL TRANSLATION

[1]"Until when is it permitted to revoke, etc.?" [2]Rav Naḥman said: They only taught [this concerning] the buyer, [3]but the seller may always retract. [4]Shall we say "they reverted to the words of the Sages" supports him? [5]Granted if you say [that] the seller may always retract, [51A] this is why they reverted. [6]But if you say [that] the seller is also like the buyer, [7]what difference does it make to them? [8]Just as the Rabbis made an enactment for the buyer, [9]so too the Rabbis made an enactment for the seller!

[10]It was not often that the merchants of Lod made mistakes.

RASHI

לא שנו — בכדי שיראה. אלא לוקח — שמקחו בידו, ויכול להראותו. מוכר — שאין בידו מה להראות ולימלך אינו מכיר באונאתו עד שיראה טלית אחרת כדמותה נמכרת בדמים יקרים, הלכך לעולם חוזר, אם לא נתייקרו טליתות בינתים. משום הכי חזרו — שהם היו מוכרין, ואינן נהנין בהרחבת זמן החזרה דרבי טרפון, שהרי אפילו לרבנן לעולם חוזרים. אמאי חזרו — לדידהו נמי מהני הרחבת זמן החזרה, דאי טעו אינהו, נהדרו בהו.

TRANSLATION AND COMMENTARY

עַד מָתַי מוּתָּר לְהַחֲזִיר כו׳ [1]The Gemara now analyzes the next clause of the Mishnah, which stated: **"Until when is** the person who was defrauded **permitted to** demand compensation or to **retract?** Until enough time has passed to allow him to show the merchandise to a merchant or a relative." [2]Concerning this limitation, **Rav Naḥman noted**: The authors of this Mishnah **spoke only of the buyer.** Only the buyer's right to demand a refund or revoke a sale is restricted to this limited period. [3]**But the seller may always retract,** no matter how much time has already passed.

נֵימָא מְסַיֵּיעַ לֵיהּ [4]The Gemara asks: **Shall we say** that the Mishnah's statement, that the merchants of Lod **"reverted to the words of the Sages," supports** Rav Naḥman's distinction between the buyer and the seller? [5]The Gemara explains: There is **no problem if you say that the seller can always retract,** [51A] and **this is why** the merchants **reverted** to the Sages' ruling. If we assume, as does Rav Naḥman, that there is no symmetry between the periods of time granted to the buyer and to the seller to retract, then we can well understand why the merchants preferred the Sages' ruling, which limited the buyer's right to retract but left the merchants with an indefinite period in which to retract. [6]**But if you say that the seller is** considered **like the buyer,** and both parties have only a limited time in which to retract, [7]**what difference did it make to** the merchants when Rabbi Tarfon extended the period during which the parties could retract? [8]**Just as the Rabbis** — here, Rabbi Tarfon — **made an enactment for** the benefit of **the buyer,** enabling him to retract all day if he discovered that he had overpaid, [9]**so too the Rabbis** — again, Rabbi Tarfon — **made an enactment for** the benefit of **the seller,** enabling him to retract all day if he discovered that he had been underpaid. If there is symmetry between the periods of time granted to the buyer and to the seller to retract, why did the merchants revert to the ruling of the Sages? After all, the merchants were as much the beneficiaries of Rabbi Tarfon's enactment as were their customers!

תַּגָּרֵי לוּד [10]The Gemara answers: No inference can be drawn from our Mishnah with regard to Rav Naḥman's distinction between buyers and sellers. It is quite possible that, in principle, the periods of time laid down in the Mishnah apply equally to both buyers and sellers. Nevertheless, the merchants of Lod preferred the restricted period of time for withdrawal laid down by the Sages, because **it was not often that the merchants of Lod made mistakes.** They were astute businessmen, and Rabbi Tarfon's ruling allowing both parties to a transaction all day to retract was of greater practical benefit to their customers than it was to them. Our Mishnah, therefore, need not be understood as supporting Rav Naḥman's distinction between the buyer and the seller.

BACKGROUND

תַּגָּרֵי לוּד לָא שְׁכִיחַ דְּטָעוּ It was not often that the merchants of Lod made mistakes. The commentators ask: According to the Gemara's previous assumption — that the merchants of Lod often *did* make mistakes — why were these merchants initially pleased with Rabbi Tarfon's ruling (assuming that the same laws apply to both the seller and the buyer)? For according to Rabbi Tarfon, an overcharge of up to one-third is not considered fraud, and thus the merchants stood to lose by following his ruling! *Tosafot Ḥitzoniyyot* in *Shittah Mekubbetzet* answers that the merchants were initially pleased with Rabbi Tarfon's ruling because they wanted the sale to be valid. In this way they would receive at least the payment due them, and possibly earn a higher profit on the merchandise. However, according to the Sages, such a sale would be canceled completely, and the merchants would not earn any profit at all (see also *Rosh* and *Ritva*).

NOTES

merchandise is acquired and the overcharge is refunded, he is referring to a case where the defrauded party chooses not to void the sale; but if he so chooses, the transaction is cancelled, in accordance with the view of Rabbi Yehudah HaNasi. Rava did not feel it necessary to explain this in detail, because the options available to the defrauded party are fully clarified in the Mishnah. Rava's primary concern here was to establish that when the *ona'ah* exceeds one-sixth, the sale can only be canceled as long as the buyer has not yet had time to show the merchandise to a merchant or a relative. The Baraita is thus cited to support this aspect of Rava's statement, since the Mishnah is unclear on this point.

מוֹכֵר לְעוֹלָם חוֹזֵר **The seller may always retract.** The Gemara does not literally mean that the seller may retract no matter how much time has passed. Rather, he may only retract until he is able to find out how much the merchandise he sold was worth. However, the Gemara says that the seller may "always" retract, because there is no fixed time limit after which the seller may no longer retract.

BACKGROUND

אוּשְׁפִּיזִיכְנֵיהּ **His host.** When Sages came to visit the major yeshivot — during the special study sessions (יַרְחֵי כַּלָּה) or at other times — they generally used to stay with a host, who would occasionally refuse to accept money for his hospitality because he viewed it as a privilege to have a great person stay in his home. Even when they were paying guests, the Sages were treated with respect and would help their hosts by offering them sound advice.

SAGES

רָמִי בַּר חָמָא **Rami bar Ḥama.** A Babylonian Amora of the fourth generation. See *Bava Metzia*, Part I, p. 83.

LANGUAGE

וַרְשְׁכֵי **Strips of silk.** This word is derived from the Persian *barsak*, meaning "belt" or "girdle."

LANGUAGE (RASHI)

בינדיל״ש* From the Old French *bendels*, meaning "belts" or "straps."

TRANSLATION AND COMMENTARY

אוּשְׁפִּיזִיכְנֵיהּ דְּרָמִי בַּר חָמָא [1]Continuing the previous discussion, the Gemara relates that **the keeper of the inn where Rami bar Ḥama was staying sold an ass and made a mistake** by selling it for less than it was worth. [2]Rami bar Ḥama **noticed that** the innkeeper **was sad,** so **he said to him, "Why are you depressed?"** [3]The innkeeper **replied, "I sold an ass and I made a mistake** about the price." [4]Rami bar Ḥama **told him to go and retract.** [5]**"But I waited longer than the time it takes to show it to a merchant or to my relative,"** the **innkeeper said.** [6]Rami bar Ḥama then **sent** the innkeeper **to Rav Naḥman,** [7]**who said to him:** "When the Sages limited the time during which one may retract, **they spoke only of the buyer, but the seller may always retract,** no matter how much time has passed. Thus you are still entitled to retract."

מַאי טַעְמָא [8]The Gemara asks: **What is the reason** for the distinction between the limited time during which a buyer can retract and the unlimited time given to a seller? [9]The Gemara answers: Since **the buyer has the merchandise in his possession, he shows it** wherever he goes, so people **tell him whether or not he made a mistake** about the price. [10]But **the seller, who does not have the merchandise in** his possession — because he has sold it — has no way of determining how much it was really worth, [11] and **must wait until he comes across** other **goods like the goods** he sold **and learns whether or not he made a mistake** about the price.

הַהוּא גַּבְרָא [12]The Gemara now relates another incident illustrating the laws governing overcharging: **A certain person had strips of silk to sell.** [13]**He was asking six** zuzim, even though **they were** really only **worth five;** [14]however, **if people would have given him five-and-a-half, he would have** been willing to **accept** their offer.

[1]אוּשְׁפִּיזִיכְנֵיהּ דְּרָמִי בַּר חָמָא זַבִּין חֲמָרָא וְטָעָה. [2]אַשְׁכְּחֵיהּ דַּהֲוָה עֲצִיב. אֲמַר לֵיהּ: "אַמַּאי עֲצִיבַתְּ?" [3]אֲמַר לֵיהּ: "זַבֵּינִי חֲמָרָא וּטְעַאי". [4]אֲמַר לֵיהּ: "זִיל הֲדַר בָּךְ". [5]אֲמַר לֵיהּ: "הָא שְׁהַאי לִי יוֹתֵר מִכְּדֵי שֶׁאַרְאֶה לַתַּגָּר אוֹ לִקְרוֹבִי". [6]שַׁדְרֵיהּ לְקַמֵּיהּ דְּרַב נַחְמָן. [7]אֲמַר לֵיהּ: לֹא שָׁנוּ אֶלָּא לוֹקֵחַ, אֲבָל מוֹכֵר לְעוֹלָם חוֹזֵר.

[8]מַאי טַעְמָא? [9]לוֹקֵחַ מִקָּחוֹ בְּיָדוֹ. כָּל הֵיכָא דְּאָזֵיל, מַחֲוֵי לֵיהּ, וְאָמְרִי לֵיהּ אִי טָעָה אִי לָא טָעָה. [10]מוֹכֵר, דְּלָא נָקֵט מִקָּחֵיהּ בִּידֵיהּ, [11]עַד דְּמִיתְרְמֵי לֵיהּ זְבִינְתָא כִּזְבִינְתֵיהּ, וְיָדַע אִי טָעָה וְאִי לָא טָעָה.

[12]הַהוּא גַּבְרָא דַּהֲוָה נָקֵט וַרְשְׁכֵי לְזַבּוּנֵי. [13]קָרֵי "שִׁיתָּא", וְשַׁוְיָא חַמְשָׁא, [14]וְאִי הֲווּ יָהֲבִי לֵיהּ חַמְשָׁא וּפַלְגָּא, הֲוָה שָׁקֵיל.

LITERAL TRANSLATION

[1]Rami bar Ḥama's host sold an ass and made a mistake. [2]He found him [and saw] that he was sad. He said to him: "Why are you sad?" [3]He said to him: "I sold an ass and I made a mistake." [4]He said to him: "Go [and] retract." [5]He said to him: "But I waited longer than [the time it takes] to show [it] to a merchant or to my relative." [6]He sent him before Rav Naḥman. [7]He said to him: They only taught [this concerning] a buyer, but a seller may always retract.

[8]What is the reason? [9]The buyer [has] his merchandise in his hand. Wherever he goes, he shows it, and they tell him whether he made a mistake or did not make a mistake. [10]The seller, who does not have his merchandise in his hand, [11][must wait] until he comes across goods like his goods, and knows whether he made a mistake or did not make a mistake.

[12]A certain person had strips of silk to sell. [13]He called out, "Six," but they were worth five, [14]and if [people] would have given him five-and-a-half, he would have accepted.

RASHI

ורשכי — קשורי משי, שקורין *בינדיל״ש. **קרי שיתא** — שואל בדמיהם ששה זוזים.

NOTES

עַד דְּמִיתְרְמֵי לֵיהּ זְבִינְתָא כִּזְבִינְתֵיהּ **Until he comes across goods like his goods.** According to Rav Naḥman, the time limit mentioned in the Mishnah applies only to the buyer, but the seller can always retract. Nevertheless, many Rishonim maintain that the seller's right to demand additional payment or cancel a sale is also limited. Based on the Gemara's argument that until the seller comes across similar merchandise he is unable to ascertain whether or not the sale involved *ona'ah*, *Rif* claims that if in fact witnesses testify that the seller came across such merchandise, he may no longer retract. *Rambam*, too, maintains that if similar merchandise can readily be found in the marketplace, the seller can only retract for as long as it would take him to determine the market price. According to both, the seller must retract as soon as he realizes he was underpaid, or else he forfeits that right.

Rashba points out that, if this is correct, Rav Naḥman's statement — "The seller may always retract" — is imprecise. He therefore argues that the seller may always retract, even

TRANSLATION AND COMMENTARY

[1]**Someone came and said** to himself: **"If I give him five-and-a-half** — the price for which he is willing to settle — [2]the overcharge **will be waived** automatically, since it amounts to less than one-sixth, and I will not be able to get a refund. Therefore, I will now lay the foundation which will make it possible to recover the overcharge. [3]**I will give him** the **six** he is asking for **and sue him** later for a refund of the overcharge." [4]After the buyer had bought the silk for six zuzim, **he came before Rava,** confident of receiving a ruling requiring the seller to refund the overcharge. [5]But Rava surprised the buyer and **said to him:** When the Rabbis made their rulings on the laws of fraud, **they were only speaking of a person who buys from a merchant.** [6]**But if someone buys from a** private **householder,** the buyer **has no claim of fraud against him,** because the buyer knows that people do not ordinarily part with their personal belongings unless they can sell them at a premium. And since the seller here was a private householder, not a merchant, he is not required to refund the overcharge. Thus Rava frustrated the buyer's plan by ruling that the Halakhah does not treat all sellers equally. Merchants, who set prices solely on an economic basis, are held to the strict laws of fraud. Householders, who have a sentimental attachment to their own possessions, are not considered fraudulent if they succeed in selling them at a premium.

[1]אֲתָא הַהוּא גַּבְרָא וַאֲמַר: ״אִי יָהֵיבְנָא לֵיהּ חַמְשָׁא וּפַלְגָּא, [2]הָוְיָא מְחִילָה. [3]אֶתֵּן לֵיהּ שִׁיתָּא וְאֶתְבְּעֵיהּ לְדִינָא״. [4]אֲתָא לְקַמֵּיהּ דְּרָבָא. [5]אֲמַר לֵיהּ: לֹא שָׁנוּ אֶלָּא בְּלוֹקֵחַ מִן הַתַּגָּר, [6]אֲבָל בְּלוֹקֵחַ מִבַּעַל הַבַּיִת, אֵין לוֹ עָלָיו אוֹנָאָה.

LITERAL TRANSLATION

[1]Someone came and said: "If I give him five-and-a-half, [2]it will be a waiver. [3]I will give him six and sue him at law." [4]He came before Rava. [5]He said to him: They only taught [this] concerning someone who buys from a merchant, [6]but concerning someone who buys from a householder, he has no [claim of] fraud against him.

RASHI

מבעל הבית – תכשיטין וכלי תשמיש שלו חביבין עליו ואינו מוכרן אלא ביוקר, והוה ליה כמפרש ״יודע אני שיש בו אונאה״ דאמרינן לקמן אין לו עליו אונאה, כך מצאתי בשאילתות דרב אחאי (פרשת בהר סימן קיג).

NOTES

if he became aware of the *ona'ah* and failed to retract immediately. Since no objective time limit can be set for the seller to retract, the Rabbis allowed him unlimited time to retract.

וְאֶתְבְּעֵיהּ לְדִינָא **And I will sue him at law.** It may be inferred from this passage that, even if at the time of the purchase the buyer knows he is being overcharged, he may complete the transaction and later demand a refund; and the seller may not claim that the buyer must have waived the overcharge (*Rabbenu Ḥananel*). This seems to contradict the Mishnah's principle regarding reimbursement for *ona'ah*, that the buyer may only retract until the merchandise can be shown to a merchant or a relative — in other words, only as long as it takes the buyer to ascertain that he has been overcharged. If within that time the buyer does not exercise his right to retract, the right is forfeited, for we assume that he waived the overcharge.

Baḥ suggests that the Gemara is referring to a case where witnesses testify that at the time of the purchase they heard the buyer say that he intended to sue. In such a case the buyer's completion of the transaction does not prove that he has waived the overcharge.

אֵין אוֹנָאָה בבַּעַל הַבַּיִת **There is no fraud for a householder.** Many Rishonim follow the explanation offered by *Rav Ahai Gaon* that, since the buyer knows that a private person generally overcharges, the buyer implicitly agrees to a condition allowing *ona'ah*. Thus our case is similar to a sale made on condition that the buyer will not claim *ona'ah*, i.e., where the seller stated explicitly that he was overcharging. In such a case the sale is valid and the buyer is not entitled to bring a claim of *ona'ah* against the seller (see below, 51b). Following this explanation, *Rashba* maintains that the buyer cannot cancel the sale if he was overcharged by more than one-sixth, for the implicit condition allowing *ona'ah* applies to all claims of *ona'ah*. *Rosh* disagrees and argues that the buyer expects a private person to overcharge, but only by one-sixth. Therefore he retains the right to cancel the sale if the overcharge exceeds that amount. *Rosh* also notes that, if the private person sold his property through a middleman, the buyer can register a claim of *ona'ah* since he was unaware that the seller was a private person, and therefore did not implicitly agree to the overcharge.

Rambam appears to have understood the ruling concerning a private person differently. According to *Rambam*, a person values his personal property above the general market price. Therefore, while he may be overcharging by market standards, he is charging a legitimate price according to the property's special worth to

HALAKHAH

בְּלוֹקֵחַ מִבַּעַל הַבַּיִת **Someone who buys from a householder.** "If a private householder sells his personal belongings, the buyer cannot demand indemnification for fraud, since he realizes that people ordinarily sell their possessions for much more than their market value. Some authorities maintain that the buyer may demand that the sale be canceled if the seller overcharged by more than one-sixth, although others disagree." (*Shulḥan Arukh, Ḥoshen Mishpat* 227:23-24.)

TRANSLATION AND COMMENTARY

הַהוּא גַּבְרָא [1]The Gemara now relates another story highlighting the distinction between merchants and householders: **A certain person had jewels to sell.** [2]**He was asking sixty** zuzim, even though **they were** only **worth fifty;** however, **if people would have given him fifty-five, he would have** been willing to **accept** their offer. [3]**Someone came and said** to himself: **"If I give him fifty-five** — the price for which he is willing to settle — the overcharge **will be waived** automatically, since it amounts to less than a sixth, and I will not be able to get a refund. [4]Therefore, **I will give him the sixty** he is asking for **and sue him** later for a refund of the overcharge." [5]After the buyer had bought the jewels for sixty zuzim, **he came before Rav Ḥisda,** who **said to him:** When the Rabbis gave their rulings on the laws of fraud, **they were only speaking of a person who buys from a merchant.** [6]**But if someone buys from a** private **householder,** the buyer **has no claim of fraud against him.** In this case, therefore, the overcharge need not be refunded.

אֲמַר לֵיהּ רַב דִּימִי [7]**Rav Dimi said to** Rav Ḥisda: Your ruling is **correct.** [8]**And similarly Rabbi Elazar said:** This ruling is **correct.**

וְהָא אֲנַן תְּנַן [9]The Gemara now objects to this distinction between a merchant and a private householder: **But surely we have learned** in the next Mishnah: **"Just as there is fraud for** a layman, **so too there is fraud for a merchant"** — the laws of fraud apply whether the person who overcharged was a merchant or a layman. [10]The Gemara clarifies further: **What** is meant by the word "layman" mentioned in the Mishnah? **Is it not** the same as the **"householder"** mentioned by Rav Ḥisda? Thus it appears from the following Mishnah that the rulings by Rava and Rav Ḥisda — that the laws of overcharging apply only to merchants and not to private individuals — contradict the ruling of a Mishnah!

אֲמַר רַב חִסְדָּא [11]The Gemara answers: **Rav Ḥisda said:** The next Mishnah's ruling that the laws of fraud apply even to laymen refers to people selling items such as **rough** linen **clothes,** which are frequently sold even by non-merchants and have no special sentimental value. Buyers of such clothing do not assume that the seller is charging more than they are worth, and they will not waive an excessive overcharge. [12]**But Rava's** and Rav Ḥisda's statements apply where the seller overcharged for **articles used** or worn **by the seller** himself

[1]הַהוּא גַּבְרָא דַּהֲוָה נָקֵיט כֵּיפֵי לְזַבּוּנֵי. [2]קָרֵי, "שִׁתִּין", וְשָׁוֵי חַמְשִׁין, וְאִי הָווּ יָהֲבִי לֵיהּ חַמְשִׁין וְחַמְשָׁא, הֲוָה שָׁקֵיל. [3]אֲתָא הַהוּא גַּבְרָא וְאָמַר: "אִי יָהֵיבְנָא לֵיהּ חַמְשִׁין וְחַמְשָׁא, הָוְיָא מְחִילָה. [4]אֶתֵּן לֵיהּ שִׁיתִּין וְאֶתְבְּעֵיהּ לְדִינָא". [5]אֲתָא לְקַמֵּיהּ דְּרַב חִסְדָּא. אֲמַר לֵיהּ: לֹא שָׁנוּ אֶלָּא בְּלוֹקֵחַ מִן הַתַּגָּר, [6]אֲבָל בְּלוֹקֵחַ מִן בַּעַל הַבַּיִת, אֵין לוֹ עָלָיו אוֹנָאָה.

[7]אֲמַר לֵיהּ רַב דִּימִי: "יִשַׁר!" [8]וְכֵן אָמַר רַבִּי אֶלְעָזָר: "יִשַׁר!" [9]וְהָא אֲנַן תְּנַן: "כְּשֵׁם שֶׁאוֹנָאָה לְהֶדְיוֹט, כָּךְ אוֹנָאָה לַתַּגָּר"! [10]מַאן "הֶדְיוֹט"? לָאו בַּעַל הַבַּיִת? [11]אֲמַר רַב חִסְדָּא: בְּצַדְרָיָיתָא. [12]אֲבָל מָאנֵי תַּשְׁמִישְׁתֵּיהּ,

LITERAL TRANSLATION

[1]A certain person had jewels to sell. [2]He called out, "Sixty," but they were worth fifty, and if [people] would have given him fifty-five, he would have accepted. [3]Someone came and said: "If I give him fifty-five, it will be a waiver. [4]I will give him sixty and sue him at law." [5]He came before Rav Ḥisda. He said to him: They only taught [this] concerning someone who buys from a merchant, [6]but concerning someone who buys from a householder, he has no [claim of] fraud against him.

[7]Rav Dimi said to him: "Correct!" [8]And similarly Rabbi Elazar said: "Correct!"

[9]But surely we have learned: "Just as there is fraud for a layman, so too there is fraud for a merchant"! [10]Who is "a layman"? Is it not a householder?

[11]Rav Ḥisda said: [That applies] to rough clothes. [12]But things for his own use,

RASHI

כיפי = נזמים. הוי מחילה – לאלתר, דהוה ליה פחות משתות. ואתבעיה בדינא – כגדי שיחזיר לי תגר. בצדרייתא = בגדי קנבוס העומדים לימכר.

LANGUAGE

כֵּיפֵי Jewels. *Rashi* interprets this word as rings, and other commentators think it means precious stones, for the main meaning of כֵּיפֵי is "stones," and this is the common usage of the word in several languages.

צַדְרָיָיתָא Rough clothes. This word may have been derived from the Persian *cadar*, meaning "kerchief" or "veil."

SAGES

רַב דִּימִי Rav Dimi. An Amora of the third and fourth generations, Rav Dimi lived both in Babylonia and in Eretz Israel. He seems to have been a Babylonian who moved to Eretz Israel in his youth. He returned to Babylonia several times, bringing with him the teachings of Eretz Israel. Rav Dimi was responsible for the transmission of these teachings, and in the Jerusalem Talmud he is called Rav Avdimi (or Avduma) Nehuta. He was one of the Sages who were given the title רַבָּנַן נְחוּתֵי — "the emigrant Rabbis" — because they carried the teachings of Eretz Israel to Babylonia, mainly the teachings of Rabbi Yoḥanan, Resh Lakish, and Rabbi Elazar. Others who shared in this task were Rabbah bar Bar Hanah and Ulla, and later Ravin, Rav Shmuel bar Yehudah, and others. The Talmud reports dozens of laws that Rav Dimi brought from one Torah center to the other, and he debates with the greatest Sages of his generation about them. At the end of his life he is believed to have returned to Babylonia, where he died.

רַבִּי אֶלְעָזָר Rabbi Elazar (ben Pedat). An Amora of the second generation. See *Bava Metzia*, Part I, p. 103.

TERMINOLOGY

וְהָא אֲנַן תְּנַן But surely we have learned.... The Talmud uses this expression to introduce a question from a Mishnah in another context against a Halakhah stated in the current discussion: "But surely we have learned differently elsewhere in a Mishnah...."

NOTES

him, and thus there is no *ona'ah*. According to this explanation, even if the overcharge exceeded one-sixth, the price charged may still be considered legitimate by subjective standards. It also follows that if a private person was underpaid, he should be entitled to sue.

A third explanation for the exemption of a private person is simply that personal property is excluded from the laws of *ona'ah*. The Biblical verse (Leviticus 25:14) refers to מִמְכָּר, which can be understood as meaning merchandise which is marketed, and not personal property. According to this explanation, there should be no difference whether the private person overcharged or was underpaid, for in either case the laws of *ona'ah* do not apply to personal property (*Ha'amek She'elah*).

דִּיַקִּירֵי עֲלֵיהּ, [1]לָא מְזַבֵּין לְהוּ אִי לָאו בְּדָמֵי יְתֵירֵי.

משנה [2]אֶחָד הַלּוֹקֵחַ וְאֶחָד הַמּוֹכֵר יֵשׁ לָהֶן אוֹנָאָה. [3]כְּשֵׁם שֶׁאוֹנָאָה לְהֶדְיוֹט, כָּךְ אוֹנָאָה לַתַּגָּר. [4]רַבִּי יְהוּדָה אוֹמֵר: אֵין אוֹנָאָה לַתַּגָּר. [5]מִי שֶׁהוּטַּל עָלָיו יָדוֹ עַל הָעֶלְיוֹנָה. [6]רָצָה, אוֹמֵר לוֹ: "תֵּן לִי מָעוֹתַי", [7]אוֹ "תֵּן לִי מַה שֶּׁאִנֵּיתַנִי".

גמרא [8]מְנָהָנֵי מִילֵּי? [9]דְּתָנוּ רַבָּנַן: "'וְכִי תִמְכְּרוּ מִמְכָּר לַעֲמִיתֶךָ אַל תּוֹנוּ'. [10]אֵין לִי אֶלָּא שֶׁנִּתְאַנָּה לוֹקֵחַ. [11]נִתְאַנָּה מוֹכֵר מִנַּיִן? [12]תַּלְמוּד לוֹמַר: 'אוֹ קָנֹה... אַל תּוֹנוּ'".

[13]וְאִיצְטְרִיךְ לְמִכְתַּב "לוֹקֵחַ", וְאִיצְטְרִיךְ לְמִכְתַּב "מוֹכֵר".

LITERAL TRANSLATION

which are dear to him, [1]he will not sell except at higher prices.

MISHNAH [2]Both the buyer and the seller have [claims of] fraud.

[3]Just as there is fraud for a layman, so too there is fraud for a merchant. [4]Rabbi Yehudah says: There is no fraud for a merchant.

[5]The one who was wronged has the upper hand. [6][If] he wishes, he may say to him: "Give me my money," [7]or "Give me that of which you defrauded me."

GEMARA [8]From where are these things [derived]?

[9]As our Rabbis taught: "'And if you sell anything to your neighbor, do not oppress.' [10]I only [know] where the buyer was defrauded. [11]From where [do I know this] if the seller was defrauded? [12]The Torah says: 'Or if you buy... do not oppress.'"

[13]And it was necessary to write "buyer," and it was necessary to write "seller."

TRANSLATION AND COMMENTARY

or by his family. [1]These articles **are dear to him,** and hence the buyer expects the seller to **sell** them **for a higher price** than they are actually worth. Thus the buyer waives the application of the standard laws of fraud to such a sale.

MISHNAH אֶחָד הַלּוֹקֵחַ וְאֶחָד הַמּוֹכֵר [2]**Both the buyer and the seller** are entitled to **bring claims of fraud** against each other if one of them overpaid or undercharged.

כְּשֵׁם שֶׁאוֹנָאָה לְהֶדְיוֹט [3]**Just as the laws of fraud apply to a lay person, so too do the laws of fraud apply to a merchant.** Even a merchant, who is an expert in the valuation of merchandise, can claim that he was deceived by a buyer as to the value of what he was selling. [4]**Rabbi Yehudah says: There is no** claim of **fraud for a merchant.** In other words, a merchant cannot claim that he was defrauded, since he presumably knew the true value of the merchandise he was selling, and it is reasonable to assume that he voluntarily sold the merchandise at a discount.

מִי שֶׁהוּטַּל עָלָיו [5]**The person who was defrauded has the upper hand** when he seeks compensation. [6]**If he wishes, he can say to** the person who defrauded him: **"Give me** back all **my money,"** canceling the sale entirely, [7]**or** he can say: **"Give me** back what **you defrauded me of,"** i.e., the amount of the overcharge.

GEMARA מְנָהָנֵי מִילֵּי [8]The Gemara asks: **From where** in the Torah **does the** Mishnah **derive its ruling** that both the buyer and the seller are subject to claims of fraud?

דְּתָנוּ רַבָּנַן [9]The Gemara answers: **Our Rabbis taught** in the following Baraita: "The verse (Leviticus 25:14) says: **'And if you sell anything to your neighbor, do not oppress,'** i.e., do not commit fraud. [10]**I might think that this** verse refers **only to a case where the buyer was defrauded,** for it forbids the seller to commit fraud. [11]**From where do we learn** that fraud is prohibited **where the seller was defrauded?** [12]**The Torah states** in the same verse: **'Or if you buy... do not oppress,'"** implying that the buyer, too, is forbidden to defraud the seller.

וְאִיצְטְרִיךְ לְמִכְתַּב לוֹקֵחַ [13]We see from this verse that the Torah expressly forbids both the buyer and the seller from engaging in fraudulent dealing. But why was it necessary to state this law in relation to both the buyer and the seller? Could not the Torah have forbidden fraud by one party to a sale and allowed us to infer that the prohibition applies to the other party as well? The Gemara now explains why the Torah had to state explicitly that the laws of fraud apply to both the buyer and the seller: **It was necessary to mention** that the

TERMINOLOGY

מְנָהָנֵי מִילֵּי From where are these things derived? I.e., what verse in the Torah is the source of the statement just made? This question by the Gemara is usually followed either by a specific Biblical text or, as in this case, by a Midrashic interpretation of Biblical verses from which the Halakhic ruling is derived.

RASHI

משנה **רבי יהודה אומר אין אונאה לתגר** — לקמיה מפרש לה. **מי שהוטל עליו** — מי שנתאנה. **תן לי מעותי** — אם נתאנה לוקח.

HALAKHAH

לוֹקֵחַ וּמוֹכֵר בְּאוֹנָאָה Fraud involving buyers and sellers. "It is forbidden to defraud others when buying or selling. Both the seller who overcharges and the buyer who underpays violate the Torah's prohibition against fraud." (*Shulḥan Arukh, Ḥoshen Mishpat* 227:1.)

אוֹנָאָה לַתַּגָּר Fraud involving merchants. "The laws of fraud apply to merchants as well as to ordinary people; we do not assume that merchants invariably know how much the merchandise they are selling is worth and that they cannot therefore be defrauded." (Ibid. 227:14.)

BACKGROUND

זְבַנְתְּ, קְנֵית.... זַבֵּין, אוֹבִיד If you bought, you acquired.... If he sold, he lost. These words were spoken in the context of an economic system which was very distant from developed capitalism — a system in which products still had a true value, and money was largely a convenient medium of exchange, but was not viewed as actual property. Therefore the buyer received something with intrinsic value, whereas the seller received only money, which could only be used to obtain something else and had no use of its own. Very few people during the Talmudic period engaged in commerce on such a large scale that money could be considered as actual property, as capital.

[1]דְּאִי כָּתַב רַחֲמָנָא "מוֹכֵר", מִשּׁוּם דְּקִים לֵיהּ בִּזְבִינְתֵּיהּ, [2]אֲבָל לוֹקֵחַ, דְּלָא קִים לֵיהּ בִּזְבִינְתֵּיהּ, אֵימָא לָא אַזְהֲרֵיהּ רַחֲמָנָא בְּ"לֹא תוֹנוּ". [3]וְאִי כָּתַב רַחֲמָנָא "לוֹקֵחַ", מִשּׁוּם דְּקָא קָנֵי, [4]דְּאָמְרִי אִינָשֵׁי: "זְבַנְתְּ, קְנֵית". [5]אֲבָל מוֹכֵר, דְּאַבּוּדֵי קָא מוֹבִיד — [6]דְּאָמְרִי אִינָשֵׁי: "זַבֵּין, אוֹבִיד" — [7]אֵימָא לָא אַזְהֲרֵיהּ רַחֲמָנָא בְּ"לֹא תוֹנוּ". [8]צְרִיכָא.

[9]"רַבִּי יְהוּדָה אוֹמֵר: אֵין אוֹנָאָה לַתַּגָּר". [10]מִשּׁוּם שֶׁהוּא תַּגָּר אֵין לוֹ אוֹנָאָה?

LITERAL TRANSLATION

[1]For if the Torah had written "seller," [I might have thought it was] because he is familiar with his goods, [2]but [as for] a buyer, who is not familiar with his goods, I might say [that] the Torah did not warn him with "do not oppress." [3]And if the Torah had written "buyer," [it might have been] because he acquires, [4]as people say: "[If] you bought, you acquired." [5]But [as for] a seller, who loses — [6]as people say: "[If] he sold, he lost" — [7]I might say [that] the Torah did not warn him with "do not oppress." [8][Therefore] it was necessary [to mention both].

[9]"Rabbi Yehudah says: There is no fraud for a merchant." [10]Because he is a merchant he has no [claim of] fraud?

TRANSLATION AND COMMENTARY

prohibition against fraud applies both to **the buyer and** to **the seller.** [1]**For if the Torah had** only **mentioned** that **the seller** is forbidden to defraud the buyer, **I might have thought** that the prohibition applied **because** the seller **is familiar with** the value of **his merchandise,** and when he overcharges, he does so with intent to defraud the buyer. [2]**But** with regard to **the buyer, who is not familiar with** the value of **the merchandise, I might have said** that **the Torah did not warn him with** the words **"do not oppress"** that fraud on his part is forbidden. Since the buyer is unlikely to commit fraud intentionally, we might mistakenly suppose that the Torah did not subject him to the prohibition against fraud. In order to prevent us from making this error of reasoning, the Torah saw fit to prohibit the buyer expressly from underpaying for his purchases. [3]Conversely, **if the Torah had** only **mentioned** that **the buyer** is forbidden to defraud the seller, **I might have thought** that the buyer was commanded not to commit fraud **because he acquires** the merchandise and benefits from the transaction, [4]**as the popular proverb says: "If you have bought** durable merchandise, **you have gained,"** because your money is now invested in something of permanent value. [5]**But** with regard to **the seller, who loses** when he sells something, [6]**as the popular proverb says: "If he sells** merchandise, **he has lost** both the merchandise and the money acquired through the sale," because that money will soon be spent, [7]**I might have said** that **the Torah did not** warn **him with** the words **"do not oppress"** that fraud on his part is forbidden. [8]Accordingly **it was necessary** for the Torah **to state** explicitly that **both** the buyer and the seller are forbidden to commit fraud.

רַבִּי יְהוּדָה אוֹמֵר [9]The Gemara proceeds to analyze the next clause of our Mishnah, which states: **"Rabbi Yehudah says: There is no** claim of **fraud for a merchant."** The meaning of this clause is unclear. At this point the Gemara understands it to mean that, according to Rabbi Yehudah, a merchant is not permitted to demand extra payment from a customer who underpaid. [10]Regarding this the Gemara asks: **Because he is a merchant, does he have no claim of fraud?** Why should a merchant be dealt with more harshly than anyone else?

RASHI

גמרא דאי כתב רחמנא מוכר — שהוא מוזהר ב"לא תונו". דקים ליה בזבינתיה — כמה נתן בה, ובמזיד הוא עושה. זבנת קנית — אם לקחת חפץ המתקיים — שכר הוא אצלך, שלא הוצאת המעות ביציאה, והרי הוא מתקיים לך. זבין אוביד — מכרת חפץ שלך — הרי אתה נפסד, שיכלו המעות ביציאה.

NOTES

זַבֵּין, אוֹבִיד If he sold, he lost. *Rashi* explains that one who sells his property is considered to have lost, because after liquidating his property he is likely to spend the money he received and be left with nothing. Therefore, if the Torah had not explicitly stated that the laws of *ona'ah* apply also to the seller, one might have thought that they apply only to the buyer. Now, to which type of seller does the Gemara here refer? It cannot be referring to a private person selling his personal property, for it was established above that such a person is not subject to claims of *ona'ah*. And it is equally difficult to understand the Gemara as referring to a merchant, for a merchant selling merchandise for profit cannot be considered as having lost.

Ra'avad understands that the Gemara is referring to a private person, and that the verse teaches that even though a private person is not subject to claims of *ona'ah*, he nevertheless violates a Biblical prohibition when he overcharges.

Rosh suggests that the verse refers to a private person who sells merchandise through a middleman. Since he sells his personal property, he is considered to have lost, but since he sold through a middleman, he is nevertheless subject to claims of *ona'ah* (see previous note).

Rashba argues that, since a private person who sells is considered as having lost, one might have claimed that all sellers are excluded from the laws of *ona'ah*. It was therefore necessary for the Torah to state that the laws of *ona'ah* apply to a professional merchant.

[1]אָמַר רַב נַחְמָן אָמַר רַב: בְּתַגָּר סַפְסָר שָׁנוּ. [2]מַאי טַעְמָא? [3]מֵידַע יָדַע זְבִינְתֵיהּ כַּמָּה שַׁוְיָא, [4]וְאַחוּלֵי אַחֵיל גַּבֵּיהּ. [5]וְהַאי דְּזַבְּנָא הָכִי מִשּׁוּם דְּאִתְרַמְיָא לֵיהּ זְבִינְתָא אַחֲרִיתִי, [6]וְהָשְׁתָּא מִיהָא קָא הָדַר בֵּיהּ.

[7]רַב אַשִׁי אֲמַר: מַאי "אֵין לַתַּגָּר אוֹנָאָה"? [8]אֵינוֹ בְּתוֹרַת אוֹנָאָה, שֶׁאֲפִילּוּ פָּחוֹת מִכְּדֵי אוֹנָאָה חוֹזֵר.

[10]תַּנְיָא כְּוָותֵיהּ דְּרַב נַחְמָן: "רַבִּי יְהוּדָה אוֹמֵר: [10]תַּגָּר אֵין לוֹ אוֹנָאָה, מִפְּנֵי שֶׁהוּא בָּקִי".

[11]"מִי שֶׁהוּטַּל עָלָיו יָדוֹ עַל הָעֶלְיוֹנָה" וכו׳. [12]מַנִּי מַתְנִיתִין?

LITERAL TRANSLATION

[1]Rav Naḥman said in the name of Rav: They taught [this] concerning a merchant [who is] a middleman. [2]What is the reason? [3]He certainly knows how much his goods are worth, [4]and he surely made a waiver to him. [5]And the [reason] that he sold it thus was that he chanced upon other goods, [6]but now, nevertheless, he is retracting.

[7]Rav Ashi said: What does "there is no fraud for a merchant" [mean]? [8]He is not subject to the law of fraud, for he may retract even for less than [the minimum] fraud.

[9]It was taught in accordance with Rav Naḥman: [10]"Rabbi Yehudah says: [11]A merchant has no fraud, because he is an expert."

[11]"The one who was wronged has the upper hand." [12][According to] whom is our Mishnah?

RASHI

ספסר — קונה ומוכר מיד תמיד. **מידע ידע זבינתיה כמה שויא** — שהרי לא שהה בין קנייתה למכירתה. **שאפילו פחות מכדי אונאה חוזר** — אם נתאנה, דחייו תלויין בכך, ותקנו לו שיחזור. **תניא כוותיה דרב נחמן** — דאפילו בכדי אונאה אינו חוזר בו ואין מחזירין לו אונאה, מדתלי טעמא מפני שהוא בקי, כגון ספסר.

TRANSLATION AND COMMENTARY

אָמַר רַב נַחְמָן [1]The Gemara explains: **Rav Naḥman said in the name of Rav:** A retail merchant is indeed protected by the laws of fraud. But this statement in our Mishnah **is referring to a merchant who is a middleman.** The merchant referred to by Rabbi Yehudah is a broker, who regularly buys merchandise from one party and sells it to another. [2]**What is the reason** why a broker may not claim fraud if he was underpaid? [3]It is because, being constantly in the market, **he certainly knows how much his goods are worth;** [4]**and** if he was underpaid, it was not because he was taken advantage of, but because he made an informal decision to accept the low price offered and **waived the difference to** the buyer. Now why should the broker agree to accept a price he knows is too low? [5]**The reason that he sold** the merchandise at a discount in the first place **was that,** at the time of the sale, **he chanced upon other goods** and was willing to take a loss on the first item in order to raise the money necessary to buy the second, [6]**and** it is only **now** that **he** regrets his decision to sell at a low price and **wishes to retract.** Rabbi Yehudah, as understood by Rav Naḥman, teaches that in such circumstances a middleman may not look to the law for assistance.

רַב אַשִׁי אֲמַר [7]Rav Naḥman understood Rabbi Yehudah's statement in the Mishnah as placing certain types of merchant at a severe disadvantage under the laws of fraud. The Gemara now cites Rav Ashi's opinion that Rabbi Yehudah actually intends to place merchants in a favored position: **Rav Ashi said: What does "there is no fraud for a merchant" mean?** [8]It means that a merchant **is not subject to the laws of fraud, as he may retract even** when the fraud committed against him was **less than** the degree of **fraud** usually required for a claim to be accepted — one-sixth. Since a merchant earns his livelihood from the profit on what he sells, the Rabbis enacted a decree in order to protect the merchant's profit margin. Accordingly, the merchant may demand reimbursement even if he was underpaid by the slightest amount. In other words, Rabbi Yehudah's statement that "a merchant has no fraud" should not be understood as meaning that a merchant has *no claim* for fraud, as we earlier thought, but that the merchant *always* has a claim for fraud, even when underpayment was less than one-sixth.

תַּנְיָא כְּוָותֵיהּ דְּרַב נַחְמָן [9]The Gemara notes that a Baraita **was taught in accordance with Rav Naḥman's** interpretation of the Mishnah: [10]**"Rabbi Yehudah says: A merchant has no** claim of **fraud, because he is an expert."** Since he knew at the time of the sale how much the merchandise was worth, he cannot later claim that he was paid less than he should have been. This Baraita is in accordance with Rav Naḥman's interpretation of Rabbi Yehudah's statement as dealing harshly with merchants, and is incompatible with Rav Ashi's interpretation.

מִי שֶׁהוּטַּל עָלָיו [11]The Gemara now discusses the next clause of the Mishnah, which stated: **"The one who was subjected to the fraud has the upper hand."** [12]The Gemara asks: **Whose point of view does our Mishnah**

BACKGROUND

תַּגָּר סַפְסָר **A merchant who is a middleman.** Many of the "merchants" mentioned in this and other passages were not actually professional merchants, but marketed products that they themselves had manufactured, such as agricultural produce, clothing or tools. Although a merchant of this kind carried out some trade, he nevertheless did not draw up a professional reckoning of expenses and income. By contrast, a middleman was a true merchant, constantly engaged in buying and selling. He could estimate the market price of an article, and also had a clear picture of the costs and profits involved in every transaction.

אֵינוֹ בְּתוֹרַת אוֹנָאָה **He is not subject to the laws of fraud.** That is to say, the laws and regulations concerning fraud do not apply to him. The laws of fraud lay down clear limits regarding degree and time, and in certain cases we say that these laws do not apply, meaning that these limits are not relevant to the case.

TERMINOLOGY

אֵינִי יוֹדֵעַ מִי שְׁנָאָהּ I do not know who taught it. This expression is occasionally used as a polite way of saying that a Baraita or a Mishnah is so imprecisely formulated that it cannot be relied upon. The expression does not refer to the problem of attributing the teaching to a specific Sage, but rather indicates that the ruling is not consistent with any known framework of rulings. Occasionally it may also mean that there is no possibility of inserting a third opinion between two conflicting ones. Sometimes a Sage will say the same thing in a much clearer and sharper way: "This is not a Mishnah."

TRANSLATION AND COMMENTARY

represent? [1]The Gemara now explains that this clause is consistent with **neither Rabbi Natan nor Rabbi Yehudah HaNasi,** whose views were cited above (50b). [2]**If** you try to explain the Mishnah according to **Rabbi Natan,** there is a difficulty, for **our Mishnah states "if he wishes,"** and this indicates that if the overcharge was exactly one-sixth, the party who was defrauded may at his option choose whether to demand a refund or cancel the sale altogether. [3]**By contrast, the Baraita** (above, 50b) which cites Rabbi Natan's view **does not state "if he wishes."** Rabbi Natan as quoted in the Baraita maintains that if the overcharge was exactly one-sixth, the sale is valid, and the only remedy available is that the overcharge be refunded. Thus the Mishnah cannot represent the viewpoint of Rabbi Natan. But it also appears inconsistent with the viewpoint of Rabbi Yehudah HaNasi. [4]For **if** you explain the Mishnah according to **Rabbi Yehudah HaNasi,** this too is problematic, for **the** Mishnah's statement that "the defrauded party has the upper hand" clearly **refers to** a case where **the buyer** was wronged, as is shown by the Mishnah's own statement that the party who was defrauded demands: "Give me my money." The demand for a refund of money only makes sense if it comes from the mouth of the buyer. [5]**By contrast, the Baraita** which cites Rabbi Yehudah HaNasi's statement that "the defrauded party has the upper hand" clearly **speaks of** a case where **the seller** was defrauded, as is shown by the Baraita's words: "The seller has the upper hand." This implies that according to Rabbi Yehudah HaNasi a defrauded buyer does not have the upper hand. This is, of course, incompatible with our Mishnah. We thus remain with the question: Whose point of view does our Mishnah represent?

(סִימָן: ז״ב ר״ש) [6]Before proceeding with the remainder of the discussion, the Gemara provides a mnemonic for the names of the Sages who are about to be quoted with regard to this problem: **Z** (for Rabbi Elazar), **B** (for Rabbah), **R** (for Rava), and **Sh** (for Rav Ashi).

אָמַר רַבִּי אֶלְעָזָר [7]**Rabbi Elazar said: I do not know** which Tanna **taught this Mishnah about** the laws of **fraud,** as it does not seem to accord with the views of any known Tanna.

רַבָּה אֲמַר [8]But **Rabbah said: In fact,** the Mishnah rules in accordance with **Rabbi Natan.** Our earlier objection to the hypothesis that our Mishnah reflects the viewpoint of Rabbi Natan can be removed if we amend the **Baraita to read** (in conformity with the Mishnah): **"If he wishes,** the sale is valid, and the overcharge is refunded." Thus our Mishnah and Rabbi Natan as cited in the amended Baraita apply the same rule in the case of fraud amounting to exactly one-sixth — the defrauded party may, at his option, demand either compensation or cancellation of the sale.

[1]לָא רַבִּי נָתָן וְלָא רַבִּי יְהוּדָה הַנָּשִׂיא. [2]אִי רַבִּי נָתָן, מַתְנִיתִין קָתָנֵי ״רָצָה״, [3]וּבָרַיְיתָא לָא קָתָנֵי ״רָצָה״. [4]אִי רַבִּי יְהוּדָה הַנָּשִׂיא, מַתְנִיתִין קָתָנֵי ״לוֹקֵחַ״, [5]בָּרַיְיתָא קָתָנֵי ״מוֹכֵר״.
[6](סִימָן: ז״ב ר״ש).
[7]אָמַר רַבִּי אֶלְעָזָר: אוֹנָאָה זוֹ, אֵינִי יוֹדֵעַ מִי שְׁנָאָהּ.
[8]רַבָּה אֲמַר: לְעוֹלָם רַבִּי נָתָן הִיא, וּתְנֵי נַמִּי בְּבָרַיְיתָא: ״רָצָה״.

LITERAL TRANSLATION

[1]Neither Rabbi Natan nor Rabbi Yehudah HaNasi. [2]If Rabbi Natan, our Mishnah teaches "[if] he wishes," [3]but the Baraita does not teach "[if] he wishes." [4]If Rabbi Yehudah HaNasi, our Mishnah teaches [about] "a buyer," [5][but] the Baraita teaches [about] "a seller."

[6](Mnemonic: Z. B. R. Sh.)

[7]Rabbi Elazar said: This [Mishnah about] fraud, I do not know who taught it.

[8]Rabbah said: In fact, it is Rabbi Natan, and teach in the Baraita too: "[If] he wishes."

RASHI

קתני רצה – דידו על העליונה. **ברייתא** – כדרבי נתן. **לא קתני רצה** – אלא על כרחו קנה, ומחזיר לו אונאה. **מתניתין קתני לוקח** – היכא דנתאנה לוקח – קתני דידו על העליונה, כדקתני "תן לי מעותי". **ברייתא** – כרבי יהודה הנשיא. **קתני מוכר** – דהיכא דנתאנה מוכר, הוא דידו על העליונה; אבל אם נתאנה לוקח, לא. **אונאה זו** – משנתינו זו. **ותני נמי בברייתא** – כרבי נתן רצה ובלוקח ומוכר הוא דפליגי.

NOTES

אֵינִי יוֹדֵעַ מִי שְׁנָאָהּ I do not know who taught it. *Ritva* explains that this Mishnah apparently reflects the view of a third Tanna, who disagrees with both Rabbi Natan and Rabbi Yehudah HaNasi. The fact that the identity of this third Tanna remains unknown does not necessarily challenge the validity of his view. *Rashi*, however, suggests (*Yevamot* 27b) that the expression "I do not know who taught this Mishnah" means that the text of the Mishnah (or the Baraita) in question is corrupt, and must therefore be rejected.

וּתְנֵי נַמִּי בְּבָרַיְיתָא: ״רָצָה״ And teach in the Baraita too: "If he wishes." According to Rabbah, Rabbi Natan agrees with Rabbi Yehudah HaNasi that if the *ona'ah* amounts to one-sixth, the defrauded party is given the choice of whether to demand a refund or cancel the sale. The two Tannaim disagree as to which party is granted the option of canceling the sale. Rabbi Yehudah HaNasi clearly limits his ruling to a case where the seller was underpaid. The Rishonim disagree about the position of Rabbi Natan. According to *Ritva*, Rabbi

TRANSLATION AND COMMENTARY

רָבָא אָמַר [1]**Rava said: In fact,** our Mishnah may be explained according to **Rabbi Yehudah HaNasi.** Our earlier objection, that our Mishnah explicitly favors a defrauded buyer while the Baraita explicitly favors a defrauded seller, is not valid. The Mishnah and the Baraita should be read as complementing rather than contradicting each other. [2]**What the Mishnah omitted the Baraita specified.** It is true that the Mishnah speaks of a case where the buyer was defrauded, and the Baraita of a case where the seller was defrauded, but the two sources are complementary. They do not contradict each other.

אָמַר רַב אַשִׁי [3]**Rav Ashi said:** There is evidence from the wording of the Mishnah that this interpretation by Rava is correct. [4]**For** the Mishnah first **states** that the laws of fraud apply to **"both the buyer and the seller,"** [5]**yet it** goes on to **explain** only **the laws of the buyer.** [6]Accordingly, we may **conclude from here that** the Mishnah simply **omitted the laws of the seller** in the last clause, but in fact, as the first clause of the Mishnah says, the same laws apply if the seller is defrauded. [7]The Gemara concludes: Indeed, **conclude from here** that Rava's interpretation is correct, and no significance is to be attached to the fact that the case of the seller is left out in the Mishnah's exposition.

אִיתְּמַר [8]**It was stated** that the Amoraim differed regarding a case where **someone says to another person,** "I am selling you merchandise **on condition that you waive any claim of fraud against me."** [9]**Rav said:** The sale is valid, but the condition is unenforceable and the buyer **retains his right** to lodge **a claim of fraud against him.** [10]**But Shmuel said:** The buyer **does not retain the right to** lodge **a claim of fraud against** the seller, since he accepted the seller's condition invalidating potential claims of fraud.

לֵימָא רַב דְּאָמַר כְּרַבִּי מֵאִיר [11]Attempting to explain this dispute by referring to a seemingly parallel Tannaitic dispute, the Gemara asks: **Shall we say that Rav ruled like Rabbi Meir, and Shmuel ruled like Rabbi Yehudah,** whose views are cited in the following Baraita? [12]**For it was taught: "If someone says to a woman,**

[1]רָבָא אָמַר: לְעוֹלָם רַבִּי יְהוּדָה הַנָּשִׂיא הִיא, [2]וּמַאי דְּשַׁיַּיר בְּמַתְנִיתִין קָא מְפָרֵשׁ בְּבָרַיְיתָא.

[3]אָמַר רַב אַשִׁי: [4]דַּיְקָא נַמִי, דְּקָתָנֵי: ״אֶחָד הַלּוֹקֵחַ וְאֶחָד הַמּוֹכֵר״, [5]וּמְפָרֵשׁ לֵיהּ לַלּוֹקֵחַ. [6]שְׁמַע מִינָּהּ שִׁיּוּרֵיהּ שַׁיְּירֵיהּ לַמּוֹכֵר. [7]שְׁמַע מִינָּהּ.

[8]אִיתְּמַר: הָאוֹמֵר לַחֲבֵירוֹ: ״עַל מְנָת שֶׁאֵין לְךָ עָלַי אוֹנָאָה״, [9]רַב אָמַר: יֵשׁ לוֹ עָלָיו אוֹנָאָה. [10]וּשְׁמוּאֵל אָמַר: אֵין לוֹ עָלָיו אוֹנָאָה.

[11]לֵימָא רַב דְּאָמַר כְּרַבִּי מֵאִיר, וּשְׁמוּאֵל דְּאָמַר כְּרַבִּי יְהוּדָה? [12]דְּתַנְיָא: ״הָאוֹמֵר לְאִשָּׁה:

LITERAL TRANSLATION

[1]Rava said: In fact, it is Rabbi Yehudah HaNasi, [2]and what he left out in our Mishnah he explained in the Baraita.

[3]Rav Ashi said: [4]It is also precise, for it teaches: "Both the buyer and the seller," [5]and it explains [the laws of] the buyer. [6]Conclude from this [that] it left out [the laws of] the seller. [7]Conclude from this.

[8]It was stated: Someone who says to his fellow: "On condition that you do not have [a claim of] fraud against me," [9]Rav said: He has [a claim of] fraud against him. [10]But Shmuel said: He does not have [a claim of] fraud against him.

[11]Shall we say [that] Rav said like Rabbi Meir, and Shmuel said like Rabbi Yehudah? [13]For it was taught: "Someone who says to a woman:

TERMINOLOGY

וּמַאי דְּשַׁיַּיר בְּמַתְנִיתִין.... And what he left out in the Mishnah.... This explanation fits in well with the general way in which the Mishnah and the Baraitot are worded. The Mishnah is written in extremely condensed form, and often does not mention all the possibilities and aspects inherent in a certain matter. The Baraitot expand on the subject, and even though they were not specifically written as supplements to the Mishnah (unlike the various Toseftot, which are intended to be explanations and elaborations of the Mishnaic text), their expanded formulation often clarifies matters not presented in sufficient detail by the Mishnah.

RASHI

דיקא נמי — דמתניתין במוכר נמי סבירא ליה הכי, ומפרש ללוקח ולא פירש למוכר. **לימא רב דאמר כרבי מאיר** — דאמר מתנה על מה שכתוב בתורה תנאו בטל, אפילו בדבר שבממון.

NOTES

Natan maintains that the defrauded party is always granted the option of canceling the sale, whether he was the buyer or the seller. *Ritzbash* disagrees, and maintains that according to Rabbi Natan, only the buyer may cancel the sale. If the seller was underpaid by one-sixth, his only option is to demand reimbursement.

HALAKHAH

עַל מְנָת שֶׁאֵין לְךָ עָלַי אוֹנָאָה On condition that you do not have a claim of fraud against me. "In a transaction where one party said to another: 'On condition that you do not have a claim of fraud against me,' the defrauded party can still pursue a claim of fraud, and can certainly do so if there was a stipulation that this transaction should not involve the laws of fraud (*Sma* adds that such a stipulation nullifies a commandment of the Torah — which, of course, cannot be done). However, if the seller explicitly informed the buyer that what he was selling for two hundred zuz was only worth one hundred, and the buyer agreed to waive the overcharge, the buyer cannot lodge a claim of fraud against the seller," following Rava and the Baraita. (*Shulḥan Arukh, Ḥoshen Mishpat* 227:21.)

TRANSLATION AND COMMENTARY

[1] **'Behold, you are betrothed to me on condition that you do not have a claim against me for food, clothing or conjugal relations,'** [2] **she is betrothed, but his condition is void,** since it runs counter to the Torah law which requires a husband to provide his wife with food and clothing and to have sexual relations with her. [3] **These are the words of Rabbi Meir.** [4] But **Rabbi Yehudah** disagrees and **says: Concerning monetary matters,** such as the husband's obligation to provide his wife with food and clothing, **a condition** that runs counter to Torah law but that has nevertheless been accepted **is binding."** Concerning other matters, however, Rabbi Yehudah agrees that a condition that runs counter to Torah law is not valid. Now if we compare the viewpoints of these Tannaim with the views of Rav and Shmuel expressed above, we reach the following conclusion: Rav, who says that a person may not include as a condition of sale that he be exempt from the laws of fraud, shares the same viewpoint as Rabbi Meir, who maintains that conditions running counter to Torah law are generally void, even in monetary matters. And Shmuel, who says that one may include such an exemption as a condition of sale, shares the same viewpoint as Rabbi Yehudah, who maintains that in monetary matters a condition that runs counter to Torah law is binding.

אָמַר לָךְ רַב [5] But the Gemara rejects this interpretation: **Rav can say to you: I expressed my opinion even according to Rabbi Yehudah.** Rabbi Yehudah would agree with me that, although they involve financial matters, the laws of fraud cannot be abrogated by agreement of the parties. Our case can easily be distinguished from the case of the conditional betrothal. [6] **Rabbi Yehudah only stated his opinion** in the case dealt with **there,**

[1] 'הֲרֵי אַתְּ מְקוּדֶּשֶׁת לִי עַל מְנָת שֶׁאֵין לָךְ עָלַי שְׁאֵר כְּסוּת וְעוֹנָה', [2] הֲרֵי זוֹ מְקוּדֶּשֶׁת, וּתְנָאוֹ בָּטֵל. [3] דִּבְרֵי רַבִּי מֵאִיר. [4] רַבִּי יְהוּדָה אוֹמֵר: בְּדָבָר שֶׁבְּמָמוֹן תְּנָאוֹ קַיָּים".

[5] אָמַר לָךְ רַב: אֲנָא דַּאֲמַרִי אֲפִילּוּ לְרַבִּי יְהוּדָה. [6] עַד כָּאן לֹא קָאָמַר רַבִּי יְהוּדָה הָתָם,

LITERAL TRANSLATION

[1] 'Behold, you are betrothed to me on condition that you have no [claims] on me for food, clothing or conjugal relations,' [2] she is betrothed, but his condition is void. [3] [These are] the words of Rabbi Meir. [4] Rabbi Yehudah says: In monetary matters, his condition stands."

[5] Rav can say to you: I [said] what I said even according to Rabbi Yehudah. [6] Rabbi Yehudah only stated [his opinion] there,

RASHI

רבי יהודה אומר בדבר שבממון — כגון שאר וכסות — ניתן למחילה, והרי מחלה; אבל עונה, שהיא צער הגוף, לא ניתן למחילה.

NOTES

הֲרֵי זוֹ מְקוּדֶּשֶׁת, וּתְנָאוֹ בָּטֵל **She is betrothed, but his condition is void.** The Rishonim raise the following question: According to Rabbi Yehudah, who maintains that a condition that runs counter to Torah law is void, why should the marriage not be void as well? The husband imposed certain conditions on his agreement to the marriage, and those conditions were not fulfilled. Thus the basic element of all transactions — mutual agreement — is lacking!

Rabbenu Tam suggests that a condition which runs counter to Torah law is treated like one that cannot possibly be fulfilled. Such a condition is assumed not to have been intended seriously. Thus the condition imposed by the man is disregarded, and we view his agreement to marry the woman as unconditional.

Ri argues that even if the condition was meant seriously, the marriage is still binding even though the condition remains unfulfilled. Once a person agrees to a certain transaction, it is by no means self-evident that he can qualify that agreement with a verbal condition. Had the Torah not stated otherwise, a condition attached to a transaction would always have been void, and the transaction itself would have been valid even though the condition was not fulfilled. We derive the law that a condition can qualify an agreement from the condition imposed by Moses concerning the land to be allocated to the tribes of Reuven and Gad (Numbers 32:29-30). However, the ability to qualify a transaction is limited to conditions similar to the condition imposed in the case of the tribes of Reuven and Gad. All other conditions (e.g., a condition that runs counter to the Torah) are void. Nevertheless, the transactions to which they remain attached are valid. Therefore, when a condition that runs counter to Torah law is imposed on a marriage, the condition is void but the marriage is binding.

דָּבָר שֶׁבְּמָמוֹן תְּנָאוֹ קַיָּים **In monetary matters his condition stands.** *Rashi* explains that the wife's rights to food and clothing are considered "monetary matters" (which may therefore be canceled by a condition), but her right to conjugal relations is not. However, the Jerusalem Talmud,

HALAKHAH

עַל מְנָת שֶׁאֵין לָךְ עָלַי שְׁאֵר כְּסוּת וְעוֹנָה **On condition that you have no claims on me for food, clothing or conjugal relations.** "If a man says to a woman: 'I am betrothing you on condition that I be exempt from providing you with food, clothing and conjugal relations,' his condition is valid insofar as monetary matters (i.e., food and clothing) are concerned. However, he is not exempt from marital relations, since a condition made in violation of Torah law is null and void with regard to matters of a non-monetary nature," following Rabbi Yehudah. (*Shulḥan Arukh* 38:5.)

¹אֶלָּא דְּיָדְעָה וְקָא מָחֲלָה. [51B] ²אֲבָל הָכָא, מִי יָדַע דְּמָחֵיל? ³וּשְׁמוּאֵל אָמַר: אֲנָא דַּאֲמַרִי אֲפִילּוּ לְרַבִּי מֵאִיר. ⁴עַד כָּאן לָא קָאָמַר רַבִּי מֵאִיר הָתָם, ⁵אֶלָּא דְּוַדַּאי קָא עָקַר. ⁶אֲבָל הָכָא, מִי יֵימַר דְּקָא עָקַר מִידֵּי?

LITERAL TRANSLATION

¹where she knew and waived [her rights]. [51B] ²But here, does he know, so that he waives [the overcharge]?

³And Shmuel can say: I [said] what I said even according to Rabbi Meir. ⁴Rabbi Meir only stated [his opinion] there, ⁵where he definitely abrogates [the law]. ⁶But here, who can say that he abrogated anything?

TRANSLATION AND COMMENTARY

¹**where** a man betrothed a woman on condition that she not receive food, clothing or conjugal rights from him, because **she knew** that she was waiving what was due her, **and** she made an informal decision to **waive her rights.** In the case of fraud, however, the injured party does not consent to being defrauded. Rather, he is waiving his right to a remedy if it is later discovered that the transaction into which he entered was fraudulent. This waiver is not enforceable because it was not offered by someone who had accurate knowledge of its consequences. Thus, says Rav, Rabbi Yehudah would agree that application of the laws of fraud is not subject to conditions stipulated by the parties to a sale, and I would agree with Rav Yehudah that a woman is betrothed even if she waives her rights to food, clothing and conjugal relations. [51B] ²**But here,** where the seller has stipulated that the sale is conditional on the buyer's waiver of whatever claims of fraud may arise, **does** the buyer really **know** at the time he enters into the transaction that he is being defrauded and **that he is waiving the overcharge?** Surely the buyer does not know that he is being defrauded. Thus we cannot say that his acquiescence in the waiver was the result of an agreement.

וּשְׁמוּאֵל אָמַר ³**And Shmuel** can **say: I expressed** my opinion that the waiver is effective, **even according to Rabbi Meir.** Rabbi Meir's seemingly differing opinion in the case of the conditional betrothal can readily be explained. ⁴**Rabbi Meir only stated his opinion** that a condition that runs counter to Torah law is invalid even in monetary matters in the case dealt with **there,** where a man betrothed a woman on condition that he be exempted from his marital obligations. ⁵The reason why Rabbi Meir ruled there that the condition is void is because in that case the man **definitely abrogates the law** of the Torah by betrothing her under such conditions. ⁶**But here,** where a person sells on condition that the buyer waive potential claims of fraud, **who says that he is abrogating any** principle of Torah law? The parties are not agreeing that they are permitted to defraud each other. They are merely saying that they are prepared to waive their rights in the event of an overcharge or underpayment. Perhaps the seller will not overcharge. Thus his condition does not necessarily contravene Torah law.

RASHI

מי ידע — דאיכא אונאה. הוא סבור דאין בו אונאה. דודאי עקר — בשעת התנאי עוקר דברי תורה, שהטילה עליו שאר כסות ועונה, וזה עוקר החובה מעליו. ואפילו הוא נותן לאחר זמן — מתנה בעלמא הוא. אבל הכא מי יימר דעקר — שמא לא יהא בו אונאה.

NOTES

followed by many Rishonim, maintains that even a woman's right to conjugal relations is considered a "monetary matter," which can be canceled by a condition, according to Rabbi Yehudah. (According to this view, marrying a woman on condition that the marriage can be annulled without a divorce would constitute a non-monetary condition that runs counter to Torah law.)

מִי יָדַע דְּמָחֵיל Does he know, so that he waives? *Ramban* explains that the same reasoning applies even to conditions that do not run counter to Torah law. If someone agrees to waive something because he is not certain that he will incur a loss, the waiver is not binding. For example, if a person stipulates that he will not inherit his wife's estate if she dies before him, his stipulation is not binding, since the husband does not know whether his wife will die first.

Other commentators disagree, however, arguing that a waiver issued where it is not clear whether one is necessary is voided only if the stipulation runs counter to Torah law (*Ritva*). These authorities are of the opinion that conditions regarding monetary matters are valid even if they run counter to Torah law, because a person may willingly forgo money due him. However, if it was not clear whether a waiver was necessary in the first place, the person presumably did not want to waive the money due him, but to make his transaction contingent upon the stipulation; and since his condition runs counter to Torah law, it is not valid (see *Birkat Shmuel*).

מִי יֵימַר דְּקָא עָקַר מִידֵּי Who says that he is abrogating anything? Shmuel's reasoning requires explanation. Since Rabbi Meir is of the opinion that even conditions relating to monetary matters cannot run counter to Torah law, what has been gained by the fact that we are initially unaware that this will occur? The end result remains the same — because of the condition, Torah law has been breached. *Rabbi Ḥayyim of Brisk* explained that, according to Shmuel, a condition relating to monetary matters does have the power to abrogate Torah law. However, if a person intentionally attempts to abrogate the law, his condition is void. Therefore, where it is unclear whether Torah law will be breached, the intention to abrogate the law is considered ambiguous and the condition is not void. (*Birkat Shmuel.*)

[1]אָמַר רַב עָנָן: לְדִידִי מְפָרְשָׁא לִי מִינֵּיהּ דְּמָר שְׁמוּאֵל: [2]הָאוֹמֵר לַחֲבֵירוֹ, ״עַל מְנָת שֶׁאֵין לְךָ עָלַי אוֹנָאָה״, [3]אֵין לוֹ עָלָיו אוֹנָאָה. [4]״עַל מְנָת שֶׁאֵין בּוֹ אוֹנָאָה״, [5]הֲרֵי יֵשׁ בּוֹ אוֹנָאָה.

[6]מֵיתִיבֵי: ״הַנּוֹשֵׂא וְהַנּוֹתֵן בֶּאֱמָנָה [7]וְהָאוֹמֵר לַחֲבֵירוֹ, ׳עַל מְנָת שֶׁאֵין לְךָ עָלַי אוֹנָאָה׳, [8]אֵין לוֹ עָלָיו אוֹנָאָה״. [9]לְרַב, דְּאָמַר: אֲנָא דַּאֲמַרִי אֲפִילּוּ לְרַבִּי יְהוּדָה, [10]הָא מַנִּי?

LITERAL TRANSLATION

[1]Rav Anan said: [The matter] was explained to me by Mar Shmuel: [2]Someone who says to his fellow, "On condition that you do not have [a claim of] fraud against me," [3][his fellow] does not have [a claim of] fraud against him. [4]"On condition that there is no fraud in it," [5]there is fraud in it.

[6]They raised an objection: "Someone who trades on trust [7]or who says to his fellow, 'On condition that you do not have [a claim of] fraud against me,' [8][his fellow] does not have [a claim of] fraud against him." [9]According to Rav, who said: I [said] what I said even according to Rabbi Yehudah, [10]whose [view] is this?

TRANSLATION AND COMMENTARY

אָמַר רַב עָנָן [1]The Gemara now clarifies our understanding of Shmuel's opinion that a waiver of one's rights under the laws of fraud is effective: **Rav Anan said: The matter was explained to me by Mar Shmuel** himself: [2]**If one person says to another,** "I am selling you something **on condition that you do not have** any **claims of fraud against me,"** [3]the condition is valid and the buyer **does not have** the right to lodge **a claim of fraud against him.** [4]But if the seller stipulates that he is selling something **"on condition that** the sale **does not entail fraud,"** [5]**then,** if the seller overcharges, the sale **does entail fraud,** thus violating the condition of the sale, and the buyer is entitled to demand a refund or cancellation of the sale, as the case may be.

מֵיתִיבֵי [6]**An objection was raised** to Rav's view from the following Tosefta (*Bava Metzia* 3:22): **"If a person trades on trust,** i.e., if the buyer agrees to pay the seller a certain amount above what the seller himself paid for his merchandise, relying on the seller's word as to how much he paid, the buyer cannot later lodge a claim of fraud against him if it turns out that the seller had initially overpaid for the merchandise, thereby causing the price to the buyer to be one-sixth or more above the market value of the merchandise. [7]Similarly, **if one person says to another,** 'I am selling you merchandise **on condition that you do not have a claim of fraud against me,'** [8]the condition is valid and the buyer **does not have** the right to lodge **a claim of fraud against him."** [9]Now **according to Rav, who said: "I expressed my view even according to Rabbi Yehudah,"** [10]**whose view is** represented by **this** Tosefta? This Tosefta explicitly maintains that the laws of fraud can be waived if a condition to that effect is agreed to by the parties to the sale. Yet Rav interpreted the previous Baraita in such a way as to conclude that all the Tannaim, including Rabbi Yehudah, maintained that the laws of fraud cannot be waived by the imposition of a condition.

RASHI

אין לו עליו אונאה — כדפרישית, דמי יימר דעקר? **שאין בו אונאה** — אם אמר לו בלשון זה — אין זה לשון מחילת אונאה אלא לשון תביעת אונאה, ד״על מנת שאין בו אונאה״ אמר — והרי יש בו. ומקח טעות נמי הוי, ואם רצה לחזור, חוזר לגמרי. **הנושא ונותן באמנה** — ״מכור במה שתוכל, ותן לי המעות לזמן פלוני, והנני סומך עליך״. ונותן לו שכר טרחו כדלקמן. **אין לו עליו אונאה** — לומר ״יותר היה שוה״ ואם מכר זה בדמים רבים, אין זה יכול לומר ״לא אתן אלא דמיו״.

NOTES

אָמַר רַב עָנָן **Rav Anan said.** The commentary here follows *Rashi*'s interpretation. According to *Rashi*, Rav Anan's ruling is as follows: A sale was made under a certain condition. Since that condition was not fulfilled, the sale is canceled. Rav Anan's purpose was to distinguish between two similar conditions which could otherwise have been confused. Most Rishonim, however, interpret Rav Anan's statement differently. "On condition that the sale does not entail fraud" means "on condition that the laws of fraud are suspended regarding this sale." Such a condition is not binding, even according to Shmuel, for it is not within the power of men to agree to the abrogation of Torah law. The stipulation that "you do not have any claims of fraud against me," on the other hand, is binding according to Shmuel, for in this case the condition focuses on the individual's claim and not on the objective law.

HALAKHAH

הַנּוֹשֵׂא וְהַנּוֹתֵן בֶּאֱמָנָה **Someone who trades on trust.** "If a person trades on trust, e.g., if a seller tells a buyer: 'I purchased this merchandise for a certain amount of money, and my profit is so-much,' the buyer cannot claim that he was defrauded." *Shakh* adds that the seller also cannot claim that he was defrauded if he discovers that the merchandise was worth more. (*Shulḥan Arukh, Ḥoshen Mishpat* 227:27.)

SAGES

רַב עָנָן **Rav Anan.** A Babylonian Amora of the second generation, Rav Anan was a disciple of Shmuel, many of whose teachings he transmitted. He also transmitted teachings in the name of Rav. After Shmuel's death, Rav Anan became one of the judges of the city of Neharde'a. Rav Anan was a younger contemporary of Rav Huna and an older contemporary of Rav Naḥman. Rav Anan's teachings, both in the name of Shmuel and in his own name, are found in several places in the Talmud, and several Sages of the following generation cite teachings in his name.

מִינֵּיהּ דְּמָר שְׁמוּאֵל **By Mar Shmuel.** Although Shmuel was one of the greatest Sages of his generation, he never received official ordination, as is explained later in this tractate (85b). In mentioning his name, his disciples wished to honor him with a title. Hence they frequently call him Mar ("Master") Shmuel. The title "Mar" (not only as a form of direct address) designated in particular the Exilarch and members of his family. In the Jerusalem Talmud Shmuel is often also called Rav Shmuel.

BACKGROUND

בַּאֲמָנָה **On trust.** Generally, merchants buy merchandise as cheaply as possible and sell it at its market price. It is possible to earn large profits in this way, but losses are incurred if one cannot procure merchandise cheaply, or if for some reason one does not manage to sell the merchandise. Because of this, some dealers worked on the system of "trust," making an agreement based on a cost-plus system, and adding a set percentage of profit to the price they paid for the merchandise. Agreements of this kind are known as "trust" agreements, because the person who pays the money must trust that the merchant indeed paid the sum that he says he has.

TRANSLATION AND COMMENTARY

אָמַר אַבָּיֵי [1]On the basis of this Tosefta, **Abaye said: It is clear that Rav ruled like Rabbi Meir, [2]and Shmuel like Rabbi Yehudah.** We must discard our earlier interpretation that Rabbi Yehudah's opinion is consistent with Rav's view, and we must acknowledge that the issue as to whether claims of fraud can be conditionally waived or not is indeed the subject of a Tannaitic dispute. Rav can then explain that this Tosefta reflects the view of Rabbi Yehudah (which he does not accept).

רָבָא אֲמַר [3]An alternative explanation was suggested by **Rava,** who **said: There is** really **no difficulty.** When Rav said that all Tannaim would agree that a condition exempting a person from claims of fraud is void, [4]he was **referring to a case without specification,** where the seller merely stipulated that the buyer could not lodge claims of fraud against him. As stated above, this condition is void because the buyer does not know, at the time he agrees to the condition, by how much the seller is overcharging him. Therefore we cannot convincingly argue that he is waiving his rights. [5]But the Tosefta is referring to a case **where** the seller **specified** explicitly that he was overcharging the buyer. In such a case the buyer knows that he is overpaying and knowingly waives the overcharge.

[1]אֲמַר אַבָּיֵי: מְחַוַּורְתָּא רַב אֲמַר כְּרַבִּי מֵאִיר, [2]וּשְׁמוּאֵל דַּאֲמַר כְּרַבִּי יְהוּדָה.
[3]רָבָא אֲמַר: לָא קַשְׁיָא. [4]כָּאן בִּסְתָם; [5]כָּאן בִּמְפָרֵשׁ.
[6]דְּתַנְיָא: ״בַּמֶּה דְּבָרִים אֲמוּרִים? [7]בִּסְתָם. [8]אֲבָל בִּמְפָרֵשׁ — [9]מוֹכֵר שֶׁאָמַר לַלּוֹקֵחַ, ׳חֵפֶץ זֶה שֶׁאֲנִי מוֹכֵר לְךָ בְּמָאתַיִם, יוֹדֵעַ אֲנִי בּוֹ שֶׁאֵינוֹ שָׁוֶה אֶלָּא מָנֶה, [10]עַל מְנָת שֶׁאֵין לְךָ עָלַי אוֹנָאָה׳ — [11]אֵין לוֹ עָלָיו אוֹנָאָה. [12]וְכֵן, לוֹקֵחַ שֶׁאָמַר לַמּוֹכֵר, ׳חֵפֶץ זֶה שֶׁאֲנִי לוֹקֵחַ מִמְּךָ בְּמָנֶה, יוֹדֵעַ אֲנִי בּוֹ שֶׁשָּׁוֶה מָאתַיִם, [13]עַל מְנָת שֶׁאֵין לְךָ עָלַי אוֹנָאָה׳ — [14]אֵין לוֹ עָלָיו אוֹנָאָה״.

LITERAL TRANSLATION

[1]Abaye said: It is clear [that] Rav said as Rabbi Meir, [2]and Shmuel said as Rabbi Yehudah.

[3]Rava said: There is no difficulty. [4]Here [it refers to a case] without specification; [5]here, [to] where he specified.

[6]For it has been taught: "In what [case] are these things said? [7]Where it is without specification. [8]But where he specified — [9]a seller who said to the buyer, 'This object that I am selling you for two hundred, I know of it that it is only worth a maneh, [10]on condition that you do not have [a claim of] fraud against me' — [11]he does not have [a claim of] fraud against him. [12]And likewise, a buyer who said to the seller, 'This object that I am buying from you for a maneh, I know of it that it is worth two hundred, [13]on condition that you do not have [a claim of] fraud against me' — [14]he does not have [a claim of] fraud against him."

TERMINOLOGY

לָא קַשְׁיָא **There is no difficulty.** An expression used by the Gemara to introduce a response to the objection that two authoritative sources are in conflict with each other. The Gemara responds: "There is no difficulty. The two sources refer to two different situations." The answer often continues: ...כָּאן...כָּאן — "In the one case the circumstances are X, whereas in the other case the circumstances are Y."

RASHI

מחוורתא כו׳ — ורב מוקי לה כרבי יהודה, דאפילו היכא דלא ידע ומחיל נמי אמר. **סתם** — על מנת שאין לך עלי אונאה, דלא ידע דניחול. **מפרש** — שפירש לו: יודע אני שיש אונאה ואני מוכרו לך על מנת שאין לך עלי אונאה. דהא אמר רבי יהודה דמתנה ותנאו קיים, דדמי לשאר וכסות. **במה דברים אמורים** — דיש אונאה לזה על זה. **בסתם** — מכר. **אבל במפרש** — כגון מוכר כו׳.

דְּתַנְיָא [6]The Gemara now cites a Baraita in support of this distinction: **For it has been taught** in a Baraita: **"When does this apply?** When are waivers of the remedies for fraud ineffective? [7]In a case **lacking specification,** where the seller and the buyer agreed in general terms that they waived claims of fraud against each other. [8]**But** in a case **where** one of the parties **indicated** that he was overcharging or underpaying the other, the party who waived his rights after having been so informed cannot lodge a claim of fraud. [9]For example, **if the seller said to the buyer:** 'I know that **this object that I am selling you for two hundred** zuz **is only worth a maneh** (one hundred zuz), [10]but I am selling it to you **on condition that you have no claims of fraud against me**' — [11]in such a case, the condition is valid and the buyer **has no claims of fraud against him,** since he knew that he was being overcharged. [12]**Similarly, if the buyer said to the seller:** 'I know that **this object that I am buying from you for a maneh is worth two hundred** zuz, [13]but I am buying it for a maneh **on condition that you have no claims of fraud against me** — [14]in such a case, the condition is valid, and the seller **has no claims of fraud against him."** Thus this Baraita explicitly supports Rava's distinction, with regard to the efficacy of waivers, between cases in which a person specified that he was overcharging or underpaying, and cases in which he did not.

NOTES

כָּאן בִּסְתָם כָּאן בִּמְפָרֵשׁ **Here it refers to a case without specification; here to where he specified.** The commentary here offers the accepted explanation linking specification with immunity from later claims. *Rid,* however, offers a novel explanation. He claims that the prohibition of fraud applies only where the victim was deceived. If the victim was told the true value, he can make no claim of fraud, even if he was subsequently cheated, since the

BACKGROUND

שְׂכַר כַּתָּף.... Payment for the porter.... These are the expenses incurred by those dealing with large quantities of merchandise and their transportation over long distances. The payments to the porters who loaded and unloaded the camels were called "porter wages," the costs of transportation were called "camel fees," and the sums for lodging and storage at way stations were called "inn fees."

LANGUAGE

פּוּנְדָּק Inn. This word is derived from the Greek πανδοκεῖον, *pandokeion*, which means "lodging house" or "inn."

LITERAL TRANSLATION

1 Our Rabbis taught: "Someone who trades on trust should not calculate the bad on trust and the good at value, 2 but either both on trust, 3 or both at value. 4 And he gives him payment for the porter, payment for the camel driver, [and] payment for the inn. 5 [But] he does not receive payment for himself, since he has already given him his payment in full."

1 תָּנוּ רַבָּנַן: "הַנּוֹשֵׂא וְהַנּוֹתֵן בַּאֲמָנָה הֲרֵי זֶה לֹא יְחַשֵּׁב אֶת הָרַע בַּאֲמָנָה וְאֶת הַיָּפֶה בְּשָׁוֶה, 2 אֶלָּא אוֹ זֶה וְזֶה בַּאֲמָנָה, 3 אוֹ זֶה וְזֶה בְּשָׁוֶה. 4 וְנוֹתֵן לוֹ שְׂכַר כַּתָּף, שְׂכַר גַּמָּל, שְׂכַר פּוּנְדָּק. 5 שְׂכַר עַצְמוֹ אֵינוֹ נוֹטֵל, שֶׁכְּבָר נָתַן לוֹ שְׂכָרוֹ מְשֻׁלָּם".

TRANSLATION AND COMMENTARY

תָּנוּ רַבָּנַן 1 The Gemara now returns to the topic of trading on trust mentioned above and cites a related Baraita: **Our Rabbis taught: "Someone who trades on trust should not calculate the bad on trust and the good at value."** The case discussed here occurs when a seller buys a batch of merchandise of uneven quality, paying a fixed price per unit. He then sorts the merchandise by quality and seeks to calculate the cost of each grade of goods. For example, suppose the seller bought a batch of merchandise at an overall price of one dinar per unit. The inferior portion was really worth only half a dinar, but the superior portion was worth one-and-a-half dinarim. The seller may not resell the merchandise "on trust" by claiming the inferior merchandise cost one dinar per unit and the superior merchandise cost one-and-a-half dinar per unit ("at value"). 2 The Baraita continues: **"Rather, he** must **either** sell **both** the inferior and the superior merchandise **on trust,** calculating his cost as a dinar per unit for both the inferior and the superior merchandise, 3 **or** sell **both at** their real **value."** The Baraita now instructs the seller "on trust" how to account for his overhead expenses, and permits him to include certain costs in the asking price of the merchandise he is selling: 4 **"And** the buyer **pays** the seller his expenses **for the cost of** hiring **a porter** and **a camel driver,** and **payment for storage.** 5 But the seller **does not receive payment for himself, since he has already been paid in full."** The seller is not entitled to wages because he is adequately compensated by his profits. The price that the buyer pays covers both the cost of the merchandise to the seller and his overhead, as well as providing for the seller's wages in full.

RASHI

הנושא ונותן באמנה כו׳ — כדפרישית. **הרי זה לא יחשוב לו את הרע באמנה ואת היפה בשוה** — להיות לו המתנת מעות היפה בשכר טרחו, כגון היה לו שני יינות, יפה שיש לו עליו קופלים ללקחו בבת אחת, והרע שאינו נמכר אלא בחנות, לא יאמר לו — הרי לך יפה בשויו, על מנת שתמכור לי הרע בחנות כמה שתוכל, ולכשימכר תן לי מעות שניהם. ופוטר עצמו בהמתנת מעות של דמי היפה מלתת שכר טרחו על הרע, והוי כרבית. **אלא או זה וזה באמנה** — ויתן לו כדרך הנותן באמנה, ששכר קצוב היה להם כדמפרש לקמן, ארבעה למאה. **או זה וזה בשוה** — והשכר יהא של מקבל. **ונותן לו שכר כתף שכר גמל** — אם נתן באמנה, כשיבואו לחשבון ינכה לו שכר כתף המוליכו מביתו לחנות, ואם הוצרך לגמלים — נותן לו שכר גמל.

NOTES

prohibition was not violated.

הַנּוֹשֵׂא וְהַנּוֹתֵן בַּאֲמָנָה Someone who trades on trust. The commentary is based on *Rabbenu Ḥananel*'s explanation, which is followed by most Rishonim. *Rashi,* however, describes the case differently. While according to *Rabbenu Ḥananel* the buyer trusts the seller, *Rashi* claims that it is the seller who trusts the buyer. The buyer in this case is a merchant who purchases produce in order to sell it at a higher price. When trading on trust, this merchant is allowed to take the merchandise without payment, and is trusted to pay the seller the money he receives upon completion of his sale. As an incentive, the merchant is given a commission. Since the price that was fixed relates to the eventual sale by the merchant and not the objective value of the merchandise, claims of fraud are inappropriate.

Rashi proceeds to explain the next statement, that one should not appraise the bad on trust and the good at value: The "good" is merchandise which due to its superior quality can be sold at the higher price without the services of the merchant. Since the seller can demand the full price immediately, by allowing the merchant to pay this price only when he has himself sold the merchandise, the seller has in fact provided the merchant with a loan. This is what is meant by "selling the good at value." One cannot simultaneously "sell the bad on trust," for then in exchange for the loan the merchant is expected to make a concerted effort to receive a high price for the bad produce. Receiving services in exchange for a loan falls under the prohibition of taking interest.

HALAKHAH

לֹא יְחַשֵּׁב אֶת הָרַע בַּאֲמָנָה Should not calculate the bad on trust. "A person who sells merchandise on trust (see above) should not appraise the inferior merchandise separately on trust and the better merchandise at value, but should appraise all the merchandise on trust, taking into account both how much he paid and all his expenses (the cost of a porter, storage, etc.), to which he may add the profit he had specified to the buyer." (*Shulḥan Arukh, Ḥoshen Mishpat* 227:28.)

TRANSLATION AND COMMENTARY

שְׂכָרוֹ מִשָּׁלֵם מֵהֵיכָא קָא יָהֵיב לֵיהּ [1]The Gemara objects: **From where did he receive his payment in full?** How can you say that the seller's profit margin represents his full wages? Wages are typically regarded as a fixed expense, much like the cost of porters, camels and storage, whose cost may be passed on directly to the buyer. In what sense can we say that the seller's profits are to be regarded as fixed wages?

אָמַר רַב פַּפָּא [2]**Rav Pappa said:** The Baraita refers to **clothing merchants, who** ordinarily **give** a fixed commission of **4 percent** to the people who actually sell the merchandise. The Baraita is referring to a case where the seller received a bonus of 4 percent on the merchandise, but sold it without including this bonus in the price. This fixed bonus or guaranteed commission is regarded by the Baraita as the seller's wages.

MISHNAH כַּמָּה תְּהֵא הַסֶּלַע חֲסֵירָה [3]In addition to the fraud discussed in the previous two Mishnayot, which involved overcharging or underpaying for merchandise, fraud may also be committed when coins that have been worn away through extended use, thereby losing a portion of their value, are given as payment for merchandise or exchanged for other coins at their nominal value. The Mishnah asks: **By how much** of its metal content **may a** worn **sela be defective, and yet not entail fraud** if the coin is used at its nominal value? [4]**Rabbi Meir says:** Up to **four isars** per sela or **one isar per dinar**, which is one twenty-fourth of the coin's value (1 sela = 4 dinarim = 24 ma'ot = 48 pundyons = 96 isars; hence 4 isars = 1/24 of a sela, 1 isar = 1/24 of a dinar). [5]**Rabbi Yehudah says:** Up to **four pundyons** per sela or **one pundyon per dinar**, which is one-twelfth of the

[1]שְׂכָרוֹ מִשָּׁלֵם מֵהֵיכָא קָא יָהֵיב לֵיהּ?
[2]אָמַר רַב פַּפָּא: בְּצַדְרוּיֵי, דְּיָהֲבִי אַרְבַּע לְמֵאָה.
משנה [3]כַּמָּה תְּהֵא הַסֶּלַע חֲסֵירָה וְלֹא יְהֵא בָּהּ אוֹנָאָה? [4]רַבִּי מֵאִיר אוֹמֵר: אַרְבַּע אִיסָּרוֹת, אִיסָּר לְדִינָר. [5]וְרַבִּי יְהוּדָה אוֹמֵר: אַרְבַּע פּוּנְדְּיוֹנוֹת,

LITERAL TRANSLATION

[1]From where did he give him his payment in full?
[2]Rav Pappa said: In [the case of] people who sell rough clothing, who give four per hundred.
MISHNAH [3]How much may a sela be defective and [yet] not entail [4]fraud? Rabbi Meir says: Four isars, one isar per dinar. [5]And Rabbi Yehudah says: Four pundyons,

RASHI

בצדרויי = מוכרי בגדי קנבוס, שסכר קצוב להם ליתן ארבעה למאה למי שטורח במכירתן. **משנה כמה תהא הסלע חסירה** — מטבע היוצא, ותמיד הוא שוחק וחסר כמה תחסר, ואם הוציאה לא תהא אונאה. **ארבע איסרין** — לסלע. **איסר לדינר** — והוא אחד מעשרים וארבעה בו, דשש מעה כסף — דינר, מעה — שני פונדיונים, פונדיון — שני איסרין. ובגמרא מפרש מאי שנא דגבי שאר סחורה אמרינן שתות, וכאן יש אומרים כך ויש אומרים כך. **ארבעה פונדיונים** — אחד משנים עשר.

BACKGROUND

בְּצַדְרוּיֵי **In the case of people who sell rough clothing.** This was the name for those who dealt in צַדְרָיָיתָא (see above, 51a) — cheap garments manufactured in semi-industrial fashion and sold in large quantities. Since this was a widespread business, there were fixed agreements regarding the fees paid to agents involved.

LANGUAGE

פּוּנְדְּיוֹן **Pundyon.** This word is derived from the Latin *dupondium*, and referred to a coin worth two isars.

REALIA

פּוּנְדְּיוֹן **Pundyon.**

A pundyon from Talmudic times.

NOTES

כַּמָּה תְּהֵא הַסֶּלַע חֲסֵירָה **How much may a sela be defective?** The previous two Mishnayot dealt with *ona'ah* relating to merchandise. This Mishnah deals with *ona'ah* relating to coins. One might expect that the laws of *ona'ah* relating to coins should parallel the laws concerning merchandise. Thus it would follow that when the Mishnah sets the amount of metal which a coin may lack without involving *ona'ah*, it is referring to the degree of *ona'ah* that would obligate a refund to the defrauded party. If less than that amount of metal were missing, a claim of *ona'ah* would not be accepted. If the coin showed greater wear than that, there would be valid grounds for nullifying the sale (see above, 50b).

However, some Rishonim distinguish between *ona'ah* relating to merchandise and *ona'ah* concerning worn coins. For example, *Rosh* distinguishes between merchandise and coins with regard to *ona'ah* that amounts to less than the amount that would require a refund. In the case of merchandise, even though the buyer cannot demand a refund when the overcharge amounts to less than one-sixth, the seller nevertheless violates the Biblical prohibition against *ona'ah*, for he in fact overcharged and cheated the buyer. The law in the case of worn coins is different, for coins that are slightly worn still retain their face value (even though there may be some people who are wary of accepting such coins). Therefore, if the coin was only slightly worn, nobody was cheated and a prohibition was not violated.

Ritva distinguishes between *ona'ah* relating to merchandise and *ona'ah* concerning coins in the opposite direction. He maintains that, with regard to merchandise, a refund cannot be demanded if the overcharge amounts to less than one-sixth, whereas in the case of a worn coin, a claim of *ona'ah* is legitimate even if the wear is minimal. This ruling reflects a basic difference between the two cases. Even where the seller overcharges, he nevertheless delivers the merchandise on which the two parties agreed. Therefore, if the overcharge was minimal, no claim can be made. In the case of a worn coin, however, the seller expected currency which circulates easily. Since the seller did not receive such currency, he has grounds for a claim of *ona'ah* even if the coin was only slightly worn.

וְלֹא יְהֵא בָּהּ אוֹנָאָה **And yet not entail fraud.** Even though an overcharge that amounts to less than one-sixth need not be refunded, if an error resulted from incorrect measuring, weighing or counting, the mistake must be corrected, no matter how small (see below, 56b). For example, if someone agreed to buy a silver article weighing one hundred grams, he can cancel the agreement if the article delivered weighed only ninety-nine grams, even though the discrepancy is much less than one-sixth.

Tosafot asks why this ruling should not apply to the case

TRANSLATION AND COMMENTARY

coin's value. [1]**And Rabbi Shimon says:** [52A] Up to **eight pundyons** per sela or **two pundyons per dinar**, which is one-sixth of the coin's value.

עַד מָתַי מוּתָּר לְהַחֲזִיר [2]A person who has bought merchandise and later realizes that he has been overcharged by one-sixth may demand a refund, provided he does so within the time it would take him to show the merchandise to a merchant or to a relative (see above, 49b). The Mishnah now asks: **Until when may** a person who has received a worn coin **return it** and demand that it be exchanged for a coin of full weight? [3]The Mishnah answers: **In cities**, where there are money changers, he has **until he can show** the coin **to a money changer**, who can judge whether or not the coin is still usable. [4]**In villages**, where there are no money changers, the holder of the coin has **until Sabbath eve** to return the coin, since Friday is the day that villagers ordinarily spend their money, and only then will he be able to find out whether or not the coin is acceptable. After these times, however, he may no longer demand that the coin be exchanged, for it is assumed that he has waived the difference. [5]The Mishnah adds: **If** the person who gave the worn coin **recognizes it, he should accept it from** the person who now holds it, **even after twelve months** have passed since the transaction between them. [6]If he refuses to accept it, the holder of the coin **has no** legal claim **against him, but** is entitled to feel **resentment** at his behavior, as the Gemara explains below.

וְנוֹתְנָהּ לְמַעֲשֵׂר שֵׁנִי [7]**A person may use** a worn coin **for** redeeming **second-tithe** produce, **and need not be concerned** that he is redeeming his second tithe with an unfit coin, [8]**for** such a coin is Halakhically acceptable, and **someone who refuses** to accept such a coin on the grounds that it weighs marginally less than the official amount **is merely a miserly person.**

פּוּנְדְיוֹן לְדִינָר. [1]וְרַבִּי שִׁמְעוֹן אוֹמֵר: [52A] שְׁמוֹנָה פּוּנְדְיוֹנוֹת, שְׁנֵי פּוּנְדְיוֹנוֹת לְדִינָר.
[2]עַד מָתַי מוּתָּר לְהַחֲזִיר? [3]בַּכְּרַכִּים, עַד כְּדֵי שֶׁיַּרְאֶה לַשּׁוּלְחָנִי. [4]בַּכְּפָרִים, עַד עַרְבֵי שַׁבָּתוֹת. [5]אִם הָיָה מַכִּירָהּ, אֲפִילּוּ לְאַחַר שְׁנֵים עָשָׂר חֹדֶשׁ, מְקַבְּלָהּ הֵימֶנּוּ, [6]וְאֵין לוֹ עָלָיו אֶלָּא תַּרְעוֹמֶת.
[7]וְנוֹתְנָהּ לְמַעֲשֵׂר שֵׁנִי וְאֵינוֹ חוֹשֵׁשׁ, [8]שֶׁאֵינוֹ אֶלָּא נֶפֶשׁ רָעָה.

LITERAL TRANSLATION

one pundyon per dinar. [1]And Rabbi Shimon says: [52A] Eight pundyons, two pundyons per dinar. [2]Until when is he permitted to return [it]? [3]In cities, until he can show [it] to a money changer. [4]In villages, until Sabbath eves. [5]If he recognized it, even after twelve months he should accept it from him, [6]and he has nothing against him but resentment.

[7]And he may give it for second tithe and he need not be concerned, [8]for he [who refuses] is nothing but a miserly person (lit., "a wicked soul").

RASHI

שמונה פונדיונות – שתות, כשאר אונאה. **בכרכים** – שיש שם שולחני, עד כדי שיראה לשולחני. **בכפרים** – שאין שם שולחני. **עד ערבי שבתות** – שבא להוציאה בערב שבת לסעודת שבת, אז ידע אם יוכל להוציאה, ויקבלוה ממנו. **ואם היה** – הנותן מכירה. **אפילו לאחר שנים עשר חודש כו'** – בגמרא פריך: הא אמרת עד ערבי שבתות! **ואין לו עליו אלא תרעומת** – מפרש בגמרא. **ונותנה** – בחילול מעשר שני ובגמרא מפרש אם בשויה, אם בסלע יפה, לפי שאינה מדה זו של פוסלי מטבע בשביל חסרון מעט אלא נפש רעה.

NOTES

of our Mishnah, so that a coin that is even minimally deficient with regard to its metallic content should be returnable, for in such a case there is a discrepancy caused by inaccurate weighing. *Tosafot* answers that a coin is not accepted as a specific amount of silver, but rather as a coin. As long as the deterioration does not reach the amounts mentioned in the Mishnah, the coin remains acceptable currency, and hence the ruling concerning incorrect measurement does not apply.

HALAKHAH

כַּמָּה תְּהֵא הַסֶּלַע חֲסֵירָה **How much may a sela lack?** "The prohibition against fraud applies not only to merchandise, but also to defective coins. Specifically, it is forbidden to use a coin if one-sixth of it has been worn away. (*Shulḥan Arukh*, who follows Rabbi Shimon's view, following *Rif* and *Rambam*, who adopt Rava's interpretation of the Mishnah against that of Abaye.) *Rema*, however, writes that, according to some authorities, the minimum quantity for fraud with coins is one-twelfth (following Rabbi Yehudah, whose opinions are ordinarily accepted against those of Rabbi Meir and Rabbi Shimon; this view assumes that we read 'Rabbah' in the Gemara instead of 'Rava.' According to this interpretation, Abaye's view is accepted, since he lived later than Rabbah, and the views of later authorities are followed when they conflict with those of earlier scholars, beginning with Abaye and Rava — *Rosh*)." (*Shulḥan Arukh, Ḥoshen Mishpat* 227:16.)

עַד מָתַי מוּתָּר לְהַחֲזִיר **Until when is he permitted to return it?** "A defective coin may be returned in cities until it can be shown to a money changer, or in villages (where there are generally no money changers) until Friday afternoon, when such coins are usually spent. After this time, one who

גמרא ¹וּרְמִינְהִי: ²״עַד כַּמָּה תְּהֵא הַסֶּלַע חֲסֵירָה וִיהֵא בָּהּ אוֹנָאָה״? ³אָמַר רַב פַּפָּא: לָא קַשְׁיָא. ⁴תַּנָּא דִּידָן קָא חָשֵׁיב מִמַּטָּה לְמַעְלָה. ⁵תַּנָּא בָּרָא קָא חָשֵׁיב מִלְמַעְלָה לְמַטָּה. ⁶מַאי שְׁנָא בְּסֶלַע דִּפְלִיגִי, ⁷וּמַאי שְׁנָא בְּטַלִּית דְּלָא פְּלִיגִי? ⁸אֲמַר רָבָא: מַאן תְּנָא טַלִּית? ⁹רַבִּי שִׁמְעוֹן הִיא.

LITERAL TRANSLATION

GEMARA [1]A contradiction was raised (lit., "cast them together"): [2]"How much must a sela lack to entail fraud?"

[3]Rav Pappa said: There is no difficulty. [4]Our Tanna calculates from below upwards. [5]The Tanna of the Tosefta (lit., "the external Tanna") calculates from above downwards.

[6]What is the difference in [the case of] a sela that they disagree, [7]and what is the difference in [the case of] a garment that they do not disagree?

[8]Rava said: Who taught a garment? [9]It was Rabbi Shimon.

TRANSLATION AND COMMENTARY

GEMARA וּרְמִינְהִי [1]**A contradiction was raised** by the Gemara between our Mishna and a Tosefta (*Bava Metzia* 3:17): Our Mishnah asks how much metal a sela may lack and still be used without entailing fraud. In other words, according to the formulation of our Mishnah, a coin may lack one twenty-fourth, one-twelfth, or one-sixth of its value (depending on the opinions of the various Sages) and may still be used as currency. [2]The Tosefta frames the question differently. **"How much must a sela lack** for its use **to entail fraud?"** it asks, and then proceeds to list the same amounts of wear mentioned in the Mishnah (one twenty-fourth, etc.)! This formulation implies that coins with these amounts of wear are unacceptable and their use constitutes fraud. How is this contradiction to be resolved?

אָמַר רַב פַּפָּא [3]**Rav Pappa** resolved the contradiction in the following way: **There is** really **no difficulty**. Both the Mishnah and the Tosefta agree that the amounts of wear mentioned are inclusive, and the use of coins worn to that extent does indeed constitute fraud. [4]**Our Tanna** — the author of the Mishnah — **calculates from below upwards,** and gives the maximum level of deterioration a coin may sustain and still be used without violating the laws of fraud. Any level of deterioration up to but not including the percentages mentioned in the Mishnah does not constitute fraud. [5]But **the Tanna of the Tosefta calculates from above downwards.** The Tosefta asks what the minimum level of deterioration is that will result in the violation of the laws of fraud. The amounts listed in response are inclusive. Thus, properly understood, the Mishnah and the Tosefta do not contradict each other. They both arrive at the same result, but from different directions.

מַאי שְׁנָא [6]The Gemara now asks **why** there is **a difference** between a sela and a garment. Why, **in the case of a sela,** do the Tannaim of our Mishnah **disagree** as to how much a coin must be worn before its use constitutes fraud, [7]whereas **in the case of a garment** or other merchandise **there is no disagreement,** for all the Tannaim (with the exception of Rabbi Tarfon) seem to agree that an overcharge of one-sixth constitutes fraud (see Mishnah above, 49b)?

אָמַר רָבָא [8]The Gemara reports two answers to its question: **Rava said: Who** is the author of the previous Mishnah about overcharging for **a garment** and other merchandise? [9]**It is Rabbi Shimon,** who is of the opinion in our Mishnah that use of a coin whose value has been debased by one-sixth constitutes fraud. However, those Tannaim who disagree with Rabbi Shimon in our Mishnah would also disagree with the anonymous ruling of the previous Mishnah concerning an overcharge. The previous Mishnah does not, according to Rava, give a full account of the various Tannaitic opinions on this subject. Thus there is no necessary difference between the application of the laws of fraud to merchandise in general and to coins in particular.

RASHI

גמרא ורמינהי כמה תהא סלע חסירה ויהא בה אונאה — אלמא: בהני שיעורי הויא אונאה. ומתניתין קתני ולא יהא, אלמא בהני שיעורי לאו אונאה היא עד דאיכא טפי! **אמר רב פפא** — לעולם אימא לך בהני שיעורי הויא אונאה, ו״לא יהא״ דמתניתין — לאו אשיעורא קאי, אלא אפחות מכשיעור קאי. **מלמטה למעלה קחשיב** — והכי קאמר: סלע הפוחתת והולכת, עד כמה יכול להוציאה — עד שתפחת שיעור כך וכך, ומכיון שהגיעה לשיעור הזה — יהא בה אונאה. **ותנא ברא** — דנקט ״ויש בה״. **מלמעלה למטה חשיב** — סלע שפחתה, כמה פחתה להיות בה אונאה? מפרש כל פחיתה גדולה שבה, כגון שבע איסרות או שש או חמש — הויא אונאה עד ארבע והיא בכלל. אבל לתנא דידן אין ארבעה בכלל ״לא יהא״, ועל כרחך לא מיתוקמא אלא בהכי. **ומאי שנא בטלית** — סתם סחורה, דתנן בהו לעיל (מט,ב) שתות למקח. **רבי שמעון היא** — דגבי סלע אית ליה שתות.

TERMINOLOGY

תַּנָּא דִּידָן Our Tanna, i.e., the Tanna whose view is cited in the Mishnah under discussion, as opposed to the Tanna whose view is cited in another Mishnah, or as opposed to תַּנָּא בָּרָא — "the external Tanna, the author of the Baraita under discussion."

תַּנָּא בָּרָא The external Tanna, i.e., the Tanna who is the author of the Baraita under discussion, as opposed to תַּנָּא דִּידָן — "our Tanna, the Tanna of our Mishnah."

HALAKHAH

paid with defective coins is not required to take them back, although it is praiseworthy to do so if he still recognizes them (provided that they still circulate, if only with difficulty)." (Ibid., 227:17.)

TRANSLATION AND COMMENTARY

אַבַּיֵי אָמַר [1] Abaye resolved the difficulty differently. He said that a distinction can be drawn between the laws governing garments and those governing coins. In the case of a garment, a person is willing to waive an overcharge of up to one-sixth, [2] and follows the popular advice: "Overpay for your back but pay value for your stomach." People consider that it is worthwhile to overpay for clothing in order to maintain a respectable appearance. But it is not worthwhile to overpay for food, which is in any event consumed. Thus, people are willing to waive a fairly substantial overcharge — up to one-sixth — when buying clothing. [3] By contrast, people are particular about receiving debased coins and will not waive their right to compensation if paid with a worn sela, since such a coin does not readily circulate. Therefore, concerning garments and similar merchandise, all the Tannaim agree that an overcharge of up to one-sixth is waived. Concerning worn coins, however, they disagree about the degree of wear that renders a coin unacceptable.

גּוּפָא [4] The Gemara now proceeds to quote at great length the Tosefta that was cited above in part: Returning to our subject, the Tosefta stated: "How much of its metal content must a sela lack so that using the coin at its nominal value entails fraud? [5] Rabbi Meir says: Four isars per sela, or one isar per dinar, which is one twenty-fourth of the coin's value. [6] Rabbi Yehudah says: Four pundyons per sela, or one pundyon per dinar, which is one-twelfth of the coin's value. [7] Rabbi Shimon says: Eight pundyons per sela, or two pundyons per dinar,

[1] אַבַּיֵי אָמַר: טַלִּית עַד שְׁתוּת מָחֵיל אִינִישׁ, [2] דְּאָמְרִי אֱינָשֵׁי: "עֲשִׁיק לְגַבָּךְ וְשַׁוֵּי לְכְרֵסָךְ". [3] סֶלַע, כֵּיוָן דְּלָא סָגֵי לֵיהּ, לָא מָחֵיל.

[4] גּוּפָא: "עַד כַּמָּה תְּהֵא הַסֶּלַע חֲסֵירָה וִיהֵא בָּהּ אוֹנָאָה? [5] רַבִּי מֵאִיר אוֹמֵר: אַרְבָּעָה אִיסָרוֹת, אִיסָר לְדִינָר. [6] רַבִּי יְהוּדָה אוֹמֵר: אַרְבָּעָה פּוּנְדְּיוֹנוֹת, פּוּנְדְּיוֹן לְדִינָר. [7] רַבִּי שִׁמְעוֹן אוֹמֵר: שְׁמוֹנָה פּוּנְדְּיוֹנוֹת, שְׁנֵי פּוּנְדְּיוֹן

LITERAL TRANSLATION

[1] Abaye said: [In the case of] a garment, a person waives up to one-sixth, [2] as people say: "Overpay for your back but pay value for your stomach." [3] [But with regard to] a sela, since it does not circulate, he does not waive.

[4] Returning to the statement quoted above (lit., "the thing itself"): "How much must a sela lack to entail fraud? [5] Rabbi Meir says: Four isars, one isar per dinar. [6] Rabbi Yehudah says: Four pundyons, one pundyon per dinar. [7] Rabbi Shimon says: Eight pundyons, two pundyons

RASHI

עשיק לגביך – הצריך לכסות גופך וגביך, קנה ביוקר. ושוי לכריסך – למאכלך לא תקנה אלא בשווין. עשיק – לשון יוקר הוא, ותבירו ב״איזהו נשך״ (בבא מציעא עד,א): באתרא דלאמימר עשיק עפרא. כיון דלא סגי ליה – שאינו יוצא בהוצאה.

TERMINOLOGY

דְּאָמְרִי אֱינָשֵׁי **As people say.** This expression is used in the Talmud to introduce popular proverbs. Even though such proverbs cannot serve as official proof-texts, much can still be learned from popular wisdom. Hence, adages of this sort are frequently cited to provide additional support for an idea already suggested, or to prove that a given viewpoint is widely accepted.

גּוּפָא **Returning to the statement quoted above** (lit., "the body, the thing itself"). An expression used to introduce a quotation from a source cited in passing in the previous discussion, which will now be analyzed at length. Generally, גּוּפָא introduces a new theme.

BACKGROUND

"עֲשִׁיק לְגַבָּךְ וְשַׁוֵּי לְכְרֵסָךְ" **"Overpay for your back, but pay value for your stomach."** This proverb resembles a Rabbinic saying (*Hullin* 84b): "A person should eat and drink with less than what he has and dress with what he has" (cf. *Rambam, Sefer HaMada, Hilkhot De'ot* 5:10). The reason why the Sages distinguished between food and clothing is that one can survive without eating expensive food; by contrast, since people are judged by their clothes, wearing inexpensive clothing creates a bad impression, and those who dress poorly are likely to be rejected by society.

NOTES

טַלִּית וְסֶלַע **A garment and a sela.** The commentators were puzzled by Abaye's explanation of the difference between garments and coins (i.e., that people are willing to overpay for clothing, but not for coins). For according to such reasoning, even fraud that amounts to less than one-sixth should warrant a refund (or a voiding of the sale) if the merchandise was fruit (since people are not willing to overpay for produce), or if the seller was defrauded.

Ramban and others explain that the essence of Abaye's distinction is that people are unwilling to accept coins that do not circulate. Hence, even a minor deviation of one twenty-fourth renders them unfit for use, since people will not accept them. By contrast, people are willing to suffer a minor loss (i.e., up to one-sixth) on overpriced merchandise (see also *Ritva* and *Ran*).

עֲשִׁיק לְגַבָּךְ וְשַׁוֵּי לְכְרֵסָךְ **Overpay for your back but pay value for your stomach.** This popular saying is cited in support of Abaye's position, which distinguishes between *ona'ah* involving merchandise and that involving worn coins. The Rishonim point out that while the saying may explain why a person is willing to waive a substantial overcharge with regard to clothing, it does not account for the law regarding food — for which, according to the saying, a person ought not to overpay. Moreover, the saying only accounts for the difference between merchandise and coins when it is the buyer who is overcharged. It does not explain why the seller would be willing to waive a discrepancy when he is underpaid by less than one-sixth.

Tosafot explains that the laws of *ona'ah* were based on a common case, i.e., where the buyer was overcharged for the purchase of clothing. Those laws were then applied to all transactions, even those involving the purchase of foodstuffs, and even to those in which the seller was underpaid. Alternatively, *Tosafot* suggests that, according to Abaye, *ona'ah* involving merchandise is different from *ona'ah* involving worn coins, in that merchandise has inherent value, so one is willing to waive a substantial overcharge, whereas a coin's value is based on its currency, so a person is not willing to accept a coin which does not readily circulate. The popular saying that people are willing to overpay for garments is unrelated to this distinction. It was mentioned by Abaye only to disprove the position of Rava, according to which the Tannaim who disagree with Rabbi Shimon with regard to coins would also disagree with the earlier Mishnah concerning an overcharge of less than one-sixth. Abaye argues that if people are willing to waive a substantial overcharge when buying clothing, it is unlikely that Rabbi Meir would allow a claim of *ona'ah* where the discrepancy in price was only one twenty-fourth (see *Ramban*).

TRANSLATION AND COMMENTARY

which is one-sixth of the coin's value. [1]But if the coin is still worth **more than this,** i.e., has deteriorated less than the degree that constitutes fraud (one twenty-fourth, one-twelfth or one-sixth, depending on the opinion), its holder is entitled to **sell it at its** face **value** as a coin of full weight." On the other hand, there are times when a debased coin must be withdrawn from circulation. Such a situation can arise when, because of excessive deterioration, a worn coin of a larger denomination may become confused with a full-weight coin of a smaller denomination. In such cases, the worn coin may not even be sold for the value of the metal it contains. [2]The Baraita now inquires: **"What is the maximum decrease** in the metal content of a coin **that would still permit a person to keep it** and use it? [3]**In the case of a sela,** the metal content of the coin may be reduced **as far as a shekel** (half a sela); **in the case of a dinar, as far as a quarter."** (The Gemara explains below what is meant by "a quarter".) But if these coins are further debased, they may no longer be used, because they may be confused with a full-weight shekel (in the case of a debased sela) or a quarter (in the case of a debased dinar). [4]The Baraita continues: "If the coin was worn **an isar less than this** (the Gemara explains below what this means), **it is forbidden to use it.** [5]**One may not sell** it **to a merchant, to a robber or to a murderer, because they** are likely to **deceive others with it** by attempting to pass it off as being worth more than it is. [6]**Rather, he should pierce it and hang it around his son's or his daughter's neck** as an ornament."

LITERAL TRANSLATION

per dinar. [1]More than that, he sells it at its value. [2]By how much may it decrease and he will be permitted to keep it? [3]In [the case of] a sela, as far as a shekel; in [the case of] a dinar, as far as a quarter. [4]An isar less than this, it is forbidden to spend it. [5]He may not sell it either to a merchant or to a robber or to a murderer, because they deceive others with it. [6]Rather, he should pierce it and hang it round the neck of his son or round the neck of his daughter."

לַדִּינָר. [1]יָתֵר עַל כֵּן, מוֹכְרָהּ בְּשָׁוְיָהּ. [2]עַד כַּמָּה תִּיפָּחֵת וִיהֵא רַשַּׁאי לְקַיְּימָהּ? [3]בְּסֶלַע, עַד שֶׁקֶל; בְּדִינָר, עַד רוֹבַע. [4]פָּחוֹת מִכֵּן אִיסָּר, אָסוּר לְהוֹצִיאָהּ. [5]הֲרֵי זֶה לֹא יִמְכְּרֶנָּה לֹא לַתַּגָּר וְלֹא לְחָרָם וְלֹא לֶהָרָג, מִפְּנֵי שֶׁמְּרַמִּין בָּהּ אֶת אֲחֵרִים. [6]אֶלָּא, יִקְבֶנָּה וְיִתְלֶנָּה בְּצַוָּאר בְּנוֹ אוֹ בְּצַוָּאר בִּתּוֹ".

RASHI

יתר על כן מוכרה בשוויה — לקמיה מפרש לה: יתירה על כן — שלא פחתה כדי אונאה. **מוכרה בשוויה** — כסלע יפה. **בסלע עד שקל** — סלע הטבוע ופוחת והולך עד שקל — מותר לקיימו, שאין עשוי לרמות בו בני אדם למוכרו בסלע יפה, לפי שפחת שלו ניכר. אבל משפחת משקל, לא יקיימנו, לפי שבא לרמות ולמוכרו בתורת שקל, שאין פחת שלו ניכר לגבי שקל, מתוך שהוא רחב שבתחילה היה סלע אינו נראה חסר. משקל שקל הוא מטבע של חצי סלע, ודינר מטבע קטן, שנים מהם יש בשקל. **בדינר עד רובע** — ואם היה דינר נפחת עד שעמד על רובע — מותר לקיימו. קא סלקא דעתך רובע דינר קאמר, ולקמיה פריך: מאי שנא סלע — דלא מצי לשהויי אלא עד חציו, ודינר עד רובע. משחסר ועמד על פחות מרובע — לא יקיימנו, דאתי לאפוקיה ברובע. **פחות מכאן איסור אסור** — לקמיה מפרש. **לא ימכרנה** — זו שאמרו אסור לקיימה, לא התירו לו שימכרנה בדמיה, לא לתגר. **ולא לחרם** — אדם אנס. **ולא להרג** — רוצח. **שמרמין בה את אחרים** — ומיראה יקבלוה מידם ביפה.

BACKGROUND

חָרָם A violent person, a robber. This word is derived from the root חרם, which means "forfeit" or "destroy." Thus, "a violent person" is one who oppresses others and forces them to do as he wishes. *Rav Naḥshon Gaon* explains that a *ḥaram* was a type of tax collector, an official appointed by the king and authorized to expropriate property. Since tax collectors during this period were not subject to formal supervision, they often took advantage of people, forcing them to pay more than they had to and keeping the extra money for themselves.

הָרָג A murderer. People are usually afraid of a murderer, so they do not argue when a murderer offers to pay them with defective coins. Alternatively, this expression may denote another type of tax collector.

וְיִתְלֶנָּה בְּצַוָּאר בְּנוֹ וכו׳ And hang it around the neck of his son.... In the Middle East, women's jewelry, and young women's jewelry in particular, was manufactured from coins, which were used to make bracelets, earrings and necklaces. This practice continued until modern times. Older women usually preferred wearing coins of value, which served both as jewelry and as a sort of savings box. Younger people, however, did not care whether the coins were worth anything or not, and hence were willing to use defective coins as jewelry.

NOTES

פָּחוֹת מִכֵּן אָסוּר Less than this, it is forbidden. Our commentary follows *Rashi*, who explains that, according to Abaye, the Tosefta teaches that one may not use a worn sela at its face value if the wear on the coin is an isar more than the quantities mentioned in the Mishnah. Other Rishonim object that, according to this explanation, the Tosefta permits fraud, for it permits the use of a coin at its nominal value even though it is worn to the degree of *ona'ah* and up to an isar beyond it.

Tosafot suggests that, according to *Rashi,* one may use a coin worn to the point of *ona'ah* only if at the time he spends the coin, he has in mind to return the *ona'ah*. However, many Rishonim disagree and maintain that, even in such a case, the use of a coin worn to the point of *ona'ah* would be forbidden even according to Abaye.

Ramban explains that the Tosefta does not refer to the prohibition of spending a worn coin at its face value, but rather to the prohibition against keeping such a coin in one's possession. This explanation assumes that both Abaye and Rava agree with Rav Huna (below) that a coin must be cut in two even if it has not yet been worn down to half its weight. According to Abaye, the coin must be cut only if it is worn an isar beyond the point of *ona'ah*, while Rava requires the coin to be cut as soon as it reaches the point of *ona'ah*.

שֶׁמְּרַמִּין בָּהּ אֶת אֲחֵרִים Because they deceive others with it. It is obvious why one may not sell defective coins to a robber or a murderer. They will use these coins to pay

HALAKHAH

עַד כַּמָּה תִּיפָּחֵת וִיהֵא רַשַּׁאי לְקַיְּימָהּ By how much may it decrease and he will be permitted to keep it? "If a coin has become worn away to the point where using it constitutes fraud, it is forbidden to keep it, since one might easily deceive others with it. Likewise, one may not give such a coin to a robber or a merchant, since he is likely

TERMINOLOGY

מִלְּתָא אַגַּב אוֹרְחֵיהּ קָא מַשְׁמַע לָן **He teaches us something incidentally.** Sometimes the Gemara raises an objection to a certain form of expression used in a Mishnah or a Baraita, claiming that the text could have used a different, clearer, expression. The reply to such an objection may begin as follows: "The Tanna chose to use that particular expression in the Mishnah or the Baraita in order to teach us something else incidentally, namely that...."

[1]אָמַר מָר: [2]״בְּסֶלַע, עַד שֶׁקֶל; בְּדִינָר, עַד רוֹבַע״. [3]מַאי שְׁנָא בְּסֶלַע עַד שֶׁקֶל, [4]וּמַאי שְׁנָא בְּדִינָר עַד רוֹבַע?

[5]אָמַר אַבַּיֵי: מַאי ״רוֹבַע״ דְּקָתָנֵי נַמִי רוֹבַע שֶׁקֶל.

[6]אֲמַר רָבָא: דַּיְקָא נַמִי, דְּקָא תָּנֵי ״רוֹבַע״ וְלָא קָתָנֵי ״רְבִיעַ״. [7]שְׁמַע מִינָּהּ.

[8]לָמָּה לֵיהּ לְמִתְלְיֵיהּ לְדִינָר בְּשֶׁקֶל?

[9]מִלְּתָא אַגַּב אוֹרְחֵיהּ קָא מַשְׁמַע לָן: דְּאִיכָּא דִינָר דְּאָתֵי מִשֶּׁקֶל.

LITERAL TRANSLATION

[1]The master said: [2]"In [the case of] a sela, as far as a shekel; in [the case of] a dinar, as far as a quarter." [3]What is the difference in [the case of] a sela [that it is] as far as a shekel, [4]and what is the difference in [the case of] a dinar [that it is] as far as a quarter?

[5]Abaye said: What is the "quarter" that it teaches? Also a quarter of a shekel.

[6]Rava said: There is evidence, too (lit., "it is also precise"), for it teaches "a quarter" and does not teach "a fourth." [7]Conclude from this.

[8][But] why did he connect a dinar to a shekel?

[9]He teaches us something incidentally: That there is a dinar that comes from a shekel.

RASHI

רובע שקל — מטבע קטן של חצי דינר, והוא הקרוי בגמרא סלע מדינה. למה ליה למתלייה לדינר בשקל — לימא בדינר עד חצי זוז. דאתי משקל — אם פיחת השקל עד חציו ונעשה דינר.

TRANSLATION AND COMMENTARY

אָמַר מָר [1]The Gemara now proceeds to analyze this Tosefta: **It was said above** in the Tosefta (lit., "the master said" — a formula often used by the Talmud to introduce a quotation from a passage cited previously): "What is the maximum decrease in the metal content of a coin that would still permit a person to keep it and use it? [2]**In the case of a sela,** the content may be reduced **as far as a shekel** (half a sela); **in the case of a dinar, as far as a quarter."** As noted above, it is unclear what the term "quarter" describes. At this point, the Gemara assumes that a quarter refers to a quarter of a dinar. [3]This leads to an obvious question. The Gemara asks: How do we explain this **difference, that in the case of a sela,** the coin may wear down only **as far as a shekel** — one-half of a sela — before it must be withdrawn from circulation, [4]**whereas in the case of a dinar,** the coin may wear down **as far as a quarter** of its value before it must be withdrawn from circulation?

אָמַר אַבַּיֵי [5]**Abaye said** in reply: **What is the "quarter"** that the Tosefta **mentions**? It is not a quarter of a dinar, as we first assumed, but **a quarter of a shekel**, which is equivalent to half a dinar. Thus, the maximum permissible amount of wear in both the case of a sela and that of a dinar is one-half.

אֲמַר רָבָא [7]**Rava said: There is evidence, too,** from the Tosefta itself that this interpretation is correct, **because** the Tosefta **uses the expression "a quarter" and not "a fourth."** "A quarter" (*rova* — רוֹבַע) designates a particular type of coin worth one-quarter of a shekel (= half a dinar), while "one-fourth" (*revi'a* — רְבִיעַ) denotes one-fourth of the particular type of currency mentioned in the context (here, a dinar). [7]Accordingly, the Gemara says: **Conclude from this** that the correct interpretation of the expression "a quarter" is as Abaye suggested, and the maximum permissible wear in the case of a sela *and* of a dinar is one-half.

לָמָּה לֵיהּ לְמִתְלְיֵיהּ לְדִינָר בְּשֶׁקֶל [8]The Gemara now questions Abaye's interpretation: **Why**, according to Abaye, **did** the Tosefta **relate the dinar to the shekel?** Why did the Tosefta describe the maximum permissible debasement of a dinar in terms of shekalim, rather than in terms of dinarim? The Tosefta should have read: "In the case of a dinar, as far as half a dinar"!

מִלְּתָא אַגַּב אוֹרְחֵיהּ קָא מַשְׁמַע לָן [9]The Gemara answers: The Tosefta expressed the maximum amount of wear permitted for dinarim in terms of shekalim in order **to teach us an incidental matter,** namely, **that there is a dinar that is derived from a** worn **shekel.** If a shekel loses half its metal content and is now worth a

NOTES

others, who will have no choice but to accept them. Why, though, should merchants be suspected of deceiving others? *Ein Yitzhak* explains that, since merchants often give their customers change, they can easily slip defective coins into the change without being noticed.

דְּקָא תָּנֵי ״רוֹבַע״ **For it teaches "a quarter."** The commentators object, noting that elsewhere (see *Keritot* 8a) the expression "a quarter" denotes a type of coin worth

HALAKHAH

to deceive others with it. Such a coin must be melted down, or pierced in the middle and used as a trinket. However, if the coin has been worn away to the point where it is only worth half its designated value, it may be kept, since it is impossible to deceive others with it. *Rema* adds that coins which circulate by weight may be kept, no matter how much has been worn away." (*Shulḥan Arukh, Ḥoshen Mishpat* 227:18.)

¹מְסַיֵּיע לֵיהּ לְרַבִּי אַמִי, דְּאָמַר רַבִּי אַמִי: דִּינָר הַבָּא מִשֶּׁקֶל, מוּתָּר לְקַיְּימוֹ; ²דִּינָר הַבָּא מִסֶּלַע, אָסוּר לְקַיְּימוֹ.

⁴״פָּחוּת מִכֵּן אִיסָּר, אָסוּר לְהוֹצִיאָהּ״.

⁵מַאי קָאָמַר?

⁶אָמַר אַבַּיֵי: הָכִי קָאָמַר: פָּחֲתָה סֶלַע יוֹתֵר מִכְּדֵי אוֹנָאָה אִיסָּר, אָסוּר.

⁷אָמַר לֵיהּ רָבָא: אִי הָכִי, אֲפִילּוּ מַשֶּׁהוּ נַמִי!

⁸אֶלָּא אֲמַר רָבָא: פָּחֲתָה סֶלַע אִיסָּר לַדִּינָר, אָסוּר, ⁹וּסְתָמָא כְּרַבִּי מֵאִיר.

¹⁰תְּנַן הָתָם: ¹¹״סֶלַע שֶׁנִּפְסְלָה,

LITERAL TRANSLATION

[1] This supports Rabbi Ammi, for Rabbi Ammi said: [2] A dinar that comes from a shekel, it is permitted to keep it; [3] a dinar that comes from a sela, it is not permitted to keep it.

[4] "An isar less than this, it is forbidden to spend it." [5] What is he saying?

[6] Abaye said: This is what he is saying: If a sela decreased [by] an isar more than the rate of fraud, it is forbidden.

[7] Rava said to him: If so, even a minute amount (lit., "anything") as well!

[8] Rather, Rava said: If a sela decreased [by] an isar per dinar, it is forbidden, [9] and the anonymous view is as Rabbi Meir [maintains].

[10] We learned there: [11] "A sela that became unfit,

TRANSLATION AND COMMENTARY

dinar, the coin may be used as a dinar. This point is not related directly to the subject matter of the Tosefta, but was considered of sufficient interest to be included incidentally.

מְסַיֵּיע לֵיהּ לְרַבִּי אַמִי [1] The Gemara notes that the Tosefta's indication that a deficient shekel may be used as a dinar **corroborates** the viewpoint of **Rabbi Ammi, for Rabbi Ammi said:** [2] **It is permitted to keep a dinar that is derived from a** worn **shekel** and spend it as if it were an ordinary dinar, for people will not make a mistake about its value and think it is a shekel. [3] But **it is not permitted to keep a dinar that is derived from a** worn **sela,** because a sela has a larger diameter than a dinar (since it is four times as large), and therefore the deficient sela may pass as a shekel rather than as a dinar.

פָּחוּת מִכֵּן אִיסָּר [4] The Gemara now proceeds to explain another difficult statement found in the above Tosefta. The Tosefta stated: "If the coin was worn **an isar less than this, it is forbidden to use it."** [5] **What does this mean?**

אָמַר אַבַּיֵי [6] **Abaye said: This is what** the Tosefta is **saying: If a sela deteriorated** through wear by **an isar in excess of the amount** which would constitute **fraud, it is forbidden** to use the coin at its nominal value. According to this interpretation of the Tosefta, the levels of deterioration mentioned by the Tannaim in the Mishnah and the Tosefta include a margin of error of an isar.

אָמַר לֵיהּ רָבָא [7] **Rava** objected and **said to** Abaye: There is no indication that the Mishnah intended to provide a margin of error of an isar. **If so** — if a coin deteriorates beyond the amounts mentioned in the Mishnah by **even a minute amount** (even less than an isar) this should **also** render the coin unusable at its nominal value!

אֶלָּא אֲמַר רָבָא [8] **Rather, Rava said:** The above expression of the Tosefta should be explained as follows: **If** the wear on **a sela** was such that it **decreased by an isar per dinar, it is forbidden** to pass it off as a sela of full weight. [9] **And** the Tosefta's **anonymous ruling follows** the opinion of **Rabbi Meir,** who ruled in our Mishnah that using a coin that has become deficient by one isar per dinar (a ratio of one to twenty-four) constitutes fraud.

תְּנַן הָתָם [10] The Gemara now cites a related Mishnah and explains it: **We learned elsewhere** (*Kelim* 12:7): "A coin that is still current is not susceptible to ritual impurity because it is not considered a utensil, and only utensils can become ritually impure. [11] **If a sela** became sufficiently debased that it **was disqualified** as

RASHI

מותר לקיימו — ולהוציאו בדינר. **דינר הבא מסלע אסור לקיימו** — אפילו להוציאו בדינר, דמתוך שהוא בא ממטבע עבה ורחבה — טועין בו לאמדו בשקל, ואתי לקבולי בתורת שקל. **מאי קאמר** — הא ליכא למימר פחות מיכן, דאם עמד סלע על פחות משקל או אם עמד דינר על פחות מרובע איסר אסור לקיימו, דמאי איריא איסר? אפילו משהו נמי, דהא אמר בסלע עד שקל, ותו לא. **יתר מכדי אונאתה** — לרבי מאיר כדאית ליה, לרבי יהודה כדאית ליה. **אסור להוציאה** — ביפה.

SAGES

רַבִּי אַמִי Rabbi Ammi. A Palestinian Amora of the third generation. See *Bava Metzia*, Part II, p. 298.

TERMINOLOGY

מַאי קָאָמַר What is he saying? I.e., what is the meaning of this Tannaitic statement? This expression is used by the Gemara when a complete sentence or statement in a Mishnah or a Baraita appears unclear. The Gemara usually introduces the answer to such a question with the words הָכִי קָאָמַר — "This is what he means...."

NOTES

one-fourth of a dinar, rather than one-fourth of a shekel (as the Gemara assumes here). *Tosafot* answers that if the Tosefta were referring to such a "quarter" (i.e., one worth one-fourth of a dinar), it would have used the less ambiguous expression *ravi'a* (i.e., one-fourth of the dinar mentioned previously in the Tosefta), rather than the potentially obscure *rova*.

BACKGROUND

וְהִתְקִינָהּ שֶׁיְּהֵא שׁוֹקֵל בָּהּ And he fixed it so that he could weigh things with it. Even though defective coins may not be used as money, they still contain precious metal which their owners obviously do not want to waste. Hence, such coins were occasionally cut up and made into small weights. Now, while broken metal utensils (e.g., broken coins) are not ordinarily susceptible to ritual impurity, once they are designated for a new use — for example, for weighing things — they can contract ritual impurity.

REALIA

מַטְבֵּעַ חָתוּךְ בְּצִדּוֹ A coin cut on its edge.

TERMINOLOGY

מַאי לָאו Is it not...? This expression is used to suggest an interpretation of material found in the preceding passage: "Why not say that the following interpretation is correct?" The reply to this usually begins with the word לָא and continues: "This is not the way to interpret the passage under discussion. Rather, the following is the correct interpretation...."

TRANSLATION AND COMMENTARY

currency, **and a person prepared it for use as a weight,** [1]**it becomes susceptible to ritual impurity,** like any other metal utensil. [2]**By how much may** the metal content of a coin **decrease while a person is still permitted to keep it** and continue using it? [3]**In the case of a sela,** the coin may depreciate until it is worth only **two dinarim** (= one shekel) — half its original value. [4]However, if the wear was so great that the coin is now worth even **less than** a shekel, **he must cut it up** in such a way that it no longer has the appearance of a coin, because it might otherwise be confused with a shekel."

יָתֵר עַל כֵּן מַאי [5]The Gemara asks: **What** is the law if the coin has not deteriorated by half its value, and so is still worth **more than this,** i.e., more than two dinars (one shekel)?

אָמַר רַב הוּנָא [6]**Rav Huna said:** If the coin has deteriorated so much that it is now worth **less than this,** the owner **must cut it up** and no longer use it as a coin. [7]Likewise, if it is still worth **more than this, he must cut it up.** In other words, if the coin was sufficiently impaired that its use could constitute fraud, it must be cut up. It may not be used as a coin, even if only at its diminished value. [8]But **Rabbi Ammi said:** If the impaired coin is now worth **less than this,** the owner **must cut it up,** because it might be confused with a shekel. [9]But if it is still worth **more than this, he may keep it** and use it as a coin at its true value, since people will realize that it is defective, and not mistake it for a sela.

מֵיתִיבֵי [10]**An objection was raised** [52B] to Rav Huna's view from the Tosefta cited above: "If the coin has depreciated **more than this,** i.e., if the value of the coin has dropped beyond the amount that constitutes fraud, its holder **sells it at its** actual **value,** after taking into account its deterioration." [11]The Gemara now explains how this Tosefta contradicts Rav Huna's position: **Does this** statement of the Tosefta **not mean that,** even though a sela has **depreciated more than the minimum degree of** wear which constitutes **fraud,** it may still be used at its actual value as long as it is still worth more than half its original worth, i.e., more than two dinarim? On what basis, then, does Rav Huna maintain that an impaired sela — even one worth more than two dinarim — must be cut up and no longer used? This position appears to be in clear contradiction to the Tosefta.

וְהִתְקִינָהּ שֶׁיְּהֵא שׁוֹקֵל בָּהּ מִשְׁקָלוֹת, [1]טְמֵאָה. [2]עַד כַּמָּה תִּיפָּחֵת וִיהֵא רַשַּׁאי לְקַיְּימָהּ? [3]לְסֶלַע, שְׁנֵי דִינָרִים. [4]פָּחוֹת מִכֵּן, יָקוֹץ".

[5]יָתֵר עַל כֵּן מַאי?

[6]אָמַר רַב הוּנָא: פָּחוֹת מִכֵּן, יָקוֹץ; [7]יָתֵר עַל כֵּן, יָקוֹץ. [8]רַבִּי אַמִּי אָמַר: פָּחוֹת מִכֵּן, יָקוֹץ; [9]יָתֵר עַל כֵּן, יְקַיֵּים.

[10]מֵיתִיבֵי: [52B] "יָתֵר עַל כֵּן, מוֹכְרָהּ בְּשָׁוְיָהּ". [11]מַאי לָאו שֶׁפָּחֲתָה יוֹתֵר מִכְּדֵי אוֹנָאָתָהּ?

LITERAL TRANSLATION

and he fixed it so that he could weigh things with it, [1]is susceptible to ritual impurity (lit., 'impure'). [2]By how much may it decrease and while he is [still] permitted to keep it? [3]In [the case of] a sela, two dinarim. [4]Less than this, he must cut [it up]."

[5]What [if it's] more than this?

[6]Rav Huna said: Less than this, he must cut [it up]; [7]more than this, he must cut [it up]. [8]Rabbi Ammi said: Less than this, he must cut [it up]; [9]more than this, he may keep it.

[10]They raised an objection: [52B] "More than that, he sells it at its value." [11]Is it not that it decreased more than the [minimum] amount of fraud?

RASHI

טמאה – מקבלת טומאה מעתה, שהרי עשאה כלי. **יקוץ** – יחתכנה לשנים, דאתי לאפוקה בשקל. **יתר על כן יקיים** – דלגבי סלע מנכרא פחיתתה, ולא מחליפה בסלע. **יתר על כן מוכרה בשויה** – לעיל קתני לה גבי סלע שפיחתה – מוכרה בשויה, לפי דמיה ולא ביפה, אלמא מותר לקיימה.

NOTES

שֶׁיְּהֵא שׁוֹקֵל בָּהּ מִשְׁקָלוֹת And he fixed it so that he could weigh things with it. *Rosh* explains that one need not "fix" the coin by physically altering it; it is enough to designate it verbally for use as a weight, since anything can be rendered a "utensil" (which is susceptible to ritual impurity) by verbal declaration (cf. *Kelim* 25:9).

פָּחוֹת מִכֵּן, יָקוֹץ Less than this, he must cut it up. According to *Rashi*, a coin must be destroyed as soon as it is worn down by more than half of its original metal content. According to *Rashba*, however, a coin may be kept even if it is worn down by more than half, as long as the wear has not exceeded the half by the amount that entails *ona'ah*. *Rashba* argues that a sela worn down to the value of a shekel should be treated no differently than an ordinary shekel, which does not have to be destroyed unless it is worn down by the amount that constitutes *ona'ah*.

יָתֵר עַל כֵּן More than that. The Gemara's objection ("is it not that it decreased") was based on the assumption that

HALAKHAH

סֶלַע שֶׁנִּפְסְלָה, וְהִתְקִינָהּ לְמִשְׁקָל A sela that became unfit, and he fixed it so that he could weigh things with it. "A coin that does not circulate and has been designated for use as a weight is susceptible to ritual impurity, like any other metal utensil." (*Rambam, Sefer Tohorah, Hilkhot Kelim* 9:10.)

TRANSLATION AND COMMENTARY

לָא [1]The Gemara refutes this objection: **No.** The Tosefta presents no difficulty for Rav Huna since it does not deal with the case discussed by him. Rav Huna's ruling applies to a coin worn to such a degree that its use would be fraudulent. [2]The Tosefta, however, deals with a coin which, though somewhat worn, is still worth **more,** i.e., **it** has **not yet depreciated** to **the degree** that its use would constitute **fraud.** [3]The Tosefta teaches that, in such a case, and only in such a case, **one may sell** the coin **at its** face **value.**

מֵיתִיבֵי [4]Another **objection was raised** against Rav Huna from the continuation of the same Tosefta (above, 52a): **"What is the maximum decrease** in the metal content of a coin **that would still permit** a person **to keep it** and use it? [5]**In the case of a sela,** the metal content of the coin may be reduced **as far as** the value of **a shekel** (half a sela)." [6]The Gemara explains how this contradicts Rav Huna's position: **Does this** statement of the Tosefta **not mean** that, in a case **where** the sela **depreciated gradually,** it may be kept and used at its actual value until it depreciates to the value of a shekel — half its original value? Typically, a coin depreciates slowly. Thus the Tosefta implies that, as long as the value of the coin has not decreased by half, it may be kept and used as a coin. Again, this appears to be a direct contradiction of the viewpoint of Rav Huna, who is of the opinion that, once the coin has depreciated to the point where its use would constitute fraud, it must be withdrawn from circulation.

לָא [7]The Gemara answers: **No.** The Tosefta here refers to a case **where** the sela **fell into a fire and was worn away** all **at once.** In such a case even Rav Huna would admit that the coin may be kept and used at its actual value as long as it has not lost half its value, because the coin was disfigured in so drastic a way that no one would confuse it with a sela of full value. On the other hand, if the coin wears away gradually, Rav Huna maintains that one is forbidden to use it once the deterioration has reached the level where the use of the coin would result in fraud. Since the deterioration is gradual, the danger exists that the debased sela may be confused with a sela of full value.

אָמַר מָר [8]The Gemara proceeds to analyze the next clause of the Tosefta cited previously: It was said above in the Tosefta concerning a coin that is so worn that it may no longer be used as currency: **"He should pierce** the coin **and hang it around his son's neck or his daughter's neck** as an ornament." [9]**A contradiction was raised** between this Tosefta and the following Baraita: **"One may not use** the defective coin **as a weight, or throw it away among his scrap metal,** [10]**or pierce it and hang it around his son's neck or his daughter's neck,** as it may again come to be used as a coin, and may be confused with a coin of full weight.

[1]לָא. [2]״יְתֵירָה״ דְּאַכַּתִּי לֹא פָּחֲתָה בִּכְדֵי אוֹנָאָתָהּ, [3]מוֹכְרָהּ בְּשָׁוְיָהּ.

[4]מֵיתִיבֵי: ״עַד כַּמָּה תִּיפָּחֵת וִיהֵא רַשַּׁאי לְקַיְּימָהּ? [5]בְּסֶלַע, עַד שֶׁקֶל״. [6]מַאי לָאו דְּפָחֵית פּוּרְתָּא פּוּרְתָּא?

[7]לָא. דְּנָפֵיל לְנוּרָא וְאִפְחוּת בַּחֲדָא זִימְנָא.

[8]אָמַר מָר: ״יִקְבֶנָּה וְיִתְלֶנָּה בְּצַוָּאר בְּנוֹ אוֹ בְּצַוַּאר בִּתּוֹ״. [9]וּרְמִינְהוּ: ״לֹא יַעֲשֶׂנָּה מִשְׁקָל בֵּין מִשְׁקְלוֹתָיו, וְלֹא יִזְרְקֶנָּה בֵּין גְּרוּטוֹתָיו, [10]וְלֹא יִקְבֶנָּה וְיִתְלֶנָּה בְּצַוַּאר בְּנוֹ וּבְצַוַּאר בִּתּוֹ.

LITERAL TRANSLATION

[1]No. [2]"More" [means] that [if] it has not yet decreased the [minimum] amount of fraud, [3]he sells it at its value.

[4]They raised an objection: "By how much may it decrease while he is [still] permitted to keep it? [5]In [the case of] a sela, as far as a shekel." [6]Is it not that it decreased bit by bit?

[7]No. Where it fell into a fire and decreased at one time.

[8]The Master said: "He should pierce it and hang it round the neck of his son or round the neck of his daughter." [9]A contradiction was raised: "He may not make it a weight among his weights, and he may not throw it among his scrap metal, [10]and he may not pierce it and hang it round the neck of his son or the neck of his daughter.

RASHI

יתר על כן — על כדי אונאה, דלא פחתה כדי אונאה, לכל חד וחד כדאית ליה. **מוכרה בשויה** — ביפה. **מאי לאו דפחתא פורתא פורתא** — וקאמר: מותר לקיימה עד שקל. אלמא: לא מיחלפא בסלע, ותיובתא דרב הונא. **גרוטותיו** — שברי כלי כסף.

LANGUAGE

גְּרוּטוֹתָיו His scrap metal. This word is apparently derived from the Greek γρύτη, *grutee*, which means "trash."

REALIA

מַטְבֵּעַ נָקוּב A perforated coin.

NOTES

דְּאַכַּתִּי לֹא פָּחֲתָה בִּכְדֵי אוֹנָאָתָהּ מוֹכְרָהּ בְּשָׁוְיָהּ That if it has not yet decreased the minimum amount of fraud, he sells it at its value. *Rashi* maintains that when a coin is only slightly worn, i.e., where the wear has not yet reached the point of *ona'ah*, the coin may be used at its full face value. *Ritva*, however, argues that even if the wear is

"more than that" refers to the decrease in the coin's value, i.e., the coin decreased by "more than" the minimum amount constituting fraud. Hence, the Gemara answered that "more than that" refers to what the coin weighs, i.e., the coin weighs "more than" what would be considered fraud (*Ritva*).

[1] אֶלָּא, אוֹ יִשְׁחוֹק אוֹ יִתּוֹךְ אוֹ יָקוֹץ אוֹ יוֹלִיךְ לְיַם הַמֶּלַח״.
[2] אֲמַר רַבִּי אֶלְעָזָר — וְאָמְרִי לָהּ רַב הוּנָא אֲמַר רַבִּי אֶלְעָזָר: [3] לָא קַשְׁיָא. כָּאן בְּאֶמְצַע; [4] כָּאן מִן הַצַּד.
[5] ״עַד מָתַי מוּתָּר לְהַחֲזִיר? [6] בִּכְרַכִּים, עַד שֶׁיַּרְאֶה לַשּׁוּלְחָנִי. בִּכְפָרִים, עַד עַרְבֵי שַׁבָּתוֹת״.
[7] מַאי שְׁנָא בְּסֶלַע דְּמַפְלִיג, [8] וּמַאי שְׁנָא בְּטַלִּית דְּלָא מַפְלִיג? [9] אֲמַר אַבַּיֵי: כִּי תְּנַן נַמִי מַתְנִיתִין בְּטַלִּית, בִּכְרַכִּין תְּנַן.

LITERAL TRANSLATION

[1] Rather, he must either grind [it] down or melt [it] or cut [it] up or throw [it] into the Dead Sea."

[2] Rabbi Elazar said — and some say [it was] Rav Huna in the name of Rabbi Elazar: [3] There is no difficulty. Here [it is] in the middle; [4] here [it is] on the edge.

[5] "Until when is he permitted to return [it]? [6] In cities, until he can show [it] to a money changer. In villages, until Sabbath eve." [7] What is the difference that in [the case of] a sela, it distinguishes, [8] and what is the difference that in [the case of] a garment it does not distinguish?

[9] Abaye said: When we also taught our Mishnah about a garment, we taught [it] with regard to cities.

RASHI

הכי גרסינן: **או יקוץ או יתוך** — לשון התכה. ולא גרסינן יחתוך. **באמצע** — יקבנה, דמשנקבה לא סגיא. **מן הצד לא יקבנה** — לפי שהרמאי שימלאנה יקוץ אותה סביב עד שיוציא את הנקב, ומרמה בה את האחרים, ויוציאנה בשקל. **דמפליג** — בין כפרים לכרכים. **ומאי שנא טלית דלא מפליג** — דקתני בכדי שיראה לתגר או לקרובו, לא שנא כרך לא שנא כפר.

TRANSLATION AND COMMENTARY

[1] **Rather, he should grind it down, or melt it, or cut it up, or throw it into the Dead Sea**, so that it is never again used as a coin." This Baraita stands in clear contradiction to the Tosefta we have been discussing, which suggests that defective coins be made into ornaments.

אֲמַר רַבִּי אֶלְעָזָר [2] **Rabbi Elazar said — and some say it was Rav Huna in the name of Rabbi Elazar:** [3] **There is** really **no difficulty. Here,** in the Tosefta which permits piercing the defective coin and making it into jewelry, it is referring to a case where it is pierced **in the middle** in such a way that it will never again be used as a coin. [4] But **there** in the Baraita, which forbids making the coin into an ornament, it refers to a case where the coin is pierced **near its edge.** Someone could conceivably cut off the edge of the coin, thereby removing the perforation, and use it to deceive others, who would not realize that the coin is defective and has been removed from circulation.

עַד מָתַי מוּתָּר לְהַחֲזִיר [5] The Gemara now proceeds to discuss the next clause in the Mishnah, which stated: **"Until when may** a person who has received a worn coin **return** it and demand that it be exchanged for a coin of full weight? [6] **In cities,** where there are money changers, he has **until he can show** the coin **to a money changer. In villages,** where there are no money changers, he has **until Sabbath eve."** [7] The Gemara asks: **Why** does the Mishnah make **a distinction** between cities and villages **in the case of a sela,** with regard to how long one may return a defective sela, [8] whereas **in the case of a garment** or other merchandise, **no** such **distinction is made.** For we learned above (49b) that someone who was overcharged for merchandise may return it for only as long as it takes to show it to a merchant or to a relative, and this time period presumably applies both in cities and villages.

אֲמַר אַבַּיֵי [9] **Abaye said** in reply: The distinction between cities and villages is as valid in the case of fraud involving merchandise as it is in fraud involving coins, and indeed **the** earlier **Mishnah** — concerning fraud in the sale of **a garment** or other merchandise — **applies** only **in cities.** In a village, however, the defrauded buyer can return the merchandise or demand a refund until Sabbath eve. The earlier Mishnah simply did not see fit to discuss all the circumstances in which differing time periods might apply.

NOTES

minimal, the coin cannot be used as if it were a coin of full weight. Therefore, in this context, "at its value" means according to the current value of the silver it contains.

כָּאן בְּאֶמְצַע; כָּאן מִן הַצַּד Here it is in the middle; here it is on the edge. *Rashi*, followed by our commentary, explains that "the middle" and "the edge" refer to the place in which the coin is pierced. *Rif* and *Rambam*, however, explain that "the middle" and "the edge" refer to the parts of the coin that were worn. According to this view, it is forbidden to keep a coin that is worn away on its edge, even if one pierces it in the middle.

HALAKHAH

כָּאן בְּאֶמְצַע Here it is in the middle. "If a sela has been worn away to the point where it may no longer be used as a coin, and the owner wants to convert it to jewelry, he must not pierce it near its edge, since the edge itself may wear away and the hole will disappear. Rather, he must make a hole in the middle of the coin." (*Shulḥan Arukh, Ḥoshen Mishpat* 227:18.)

REALIA

מַטְבֵּעַ נָקוּב מִן הַצַּד A coin perforated on its edge.

BACKGROUND

אוֹ יוֹלִיךְ לְיַם הַמֶּלַח Or throw it into the Dead Sea. Elsewhere in the Talmud we find that certain objects (e.g., idols, which a person is forbidden to retain in his possession) must be destroyed by "throwing them into the Dead Sea." Practically speaking, throwing such items into the Dead Sea serves a double purpose. First, the high concentration of salts and bromides in the Dead Sea helps destroy the unwanted object. Moreover, since there are no fish in the Dead Sea, there is no reason to assume that fishermen will accidentally pick up what was discarded.

כְּרַכִּים וּכְפָרִים Cities and villages. The "cities" (כְּרַכִּים) referred to here were large cities (usually surrounded by a wall). Such cities were centers of commerce and administration, and each city usually had one or more money changers to take care of its financial needs. There were also smaller urban settlements (not necessarily surrounded by a wall), the inhabitants of which generally earned their livelihood from industry and commerce. However, business in these towns was usually carried out in small shops, while large, wholesale businesses flourished in the larger cities.

By contrast, "villages" (כְּפָרִים) were small, agricultural settlements which often did not engage in any sort of commerce and at best had a small shop to provide residents with basic necessities. The villagers therefore bought most of their goods from traveling salesmen, or purchased what they needed when they went to the city to sell their own merchandise.

TERMINOLOGY

כִּי תְּנַן נַמִי מַתְנִיתִין When

TRANSLATION AND COMMENTARY

רָבָא אָמַר [1]Rava said that a distinction must be drawn between worn coins and garments: **In the case of a garment, everyone knows** how much it is worth. Therefore, anyone who has overpaid for a garment can discover his error within the time it takes to show the garment to a merchant or to a relative. [2]But **in the case of a sela, since not everyone knows** how much it is worth, **except for a money changer,** a distinction must be drawn between cities and villages. [3]**In cities, where there are money changers,** the defective coin may be returned only **until** the recipient **can show it to a money changer** who can inform him whether or not the coin is still current. [4]But **in villages, where there** are **no money changers,** the coin may be returned **until** the **Sabbath eve,** (i.e., Friday), [5]the time **when people** in the village **go to the market.** Only then will the recipient of the coin find out whether or not it is acceptable.

וְאִם הָיָה מַכִּירָהּ [6]The Gemara now proceeds to analyze the next clause in the Mishnah: **"And if** the person who gave the defective coin still **recognizes it,** he should take it back **even after twelve months** have passed." [7]The Gemara asks: **Where** does this ruling apply? [8]**If** we assume that the Mishnah here is referring **to cities, surely** the previous clause **said** that the recipient has only **until he can show it to a money changer,** but after that time the defective coin need not be replaced. [9]And **if** we assume that the Mishnah here is referring **to villages, surely** that very same clause of the Mishnah **said** that the recipient may demand that the coin be replaced only **until the Sabbath eve!**

אָמַר רַב חִסְדָּא [10]**Rav Ḥisda said** in reply: **In this instance** the Mishnah **was teaching** us **pious behavior.** Even though a person is not obligated to take back a defective coin after the time allotted for showing it to a money changer has passed or the Sabbath eve has passed, as the case may be, a pious person should take it back even after twelve months have passed since he gave it as payment.

[1]רָבָא אָמַר: טַלִּית, כָּל אִינִישׁ קִים לֵיהּ בְּגַוָּהּ. [2]סֶלַע, כֵּיוָן דְּלָאו כָּל אִינִישׁ קִים לֵיהּ בְּגַוָּהּ אֶלָּא שׁוּלְחָנִי, [3]הִלְכָּךְ, בִּכְרַכִּים, דְּאִיכָּא שׁוּלְחָנִי, "עַד שֶׁיַּרְאֶה לַשּׁוּלְחָנִי". [4]בִּכְפָרִים, דְּלֵיכָּא שׁוּלְחָנִי, "עַד עַרְבֵי שַׁבָּתוֹת", [5]דְּסָלְקִין לְשׁוּקָא.

[6]"וְאִם הָיָה מַכִּירָהּ, אֲפִילּוּ לְאַחַר שְׁנֵים עָשָׂר חֹדֶשׁ" כו׳. [7]הֵיכָא? [8]אִי בִּכְרַכִּין, הָא אָמְרַתְּ: "עַד שֶׁיַּרְאֶה לַשּׁוּלְחָנִי". [9]אִי בִּכְפָרִים, הָא אָמְרַתְּ: "עַד עַרְבֵי שַׁבָּתוֹת".

[10]אָמַר רַב חִסְדָּא: מִידַּת חֲסִידוּת שָׁנוּ כָּאן.

LITERAL TRANSLATION

[1]Rava said: [In the case of] a garment, everyone is knowledgeable about it. [2][In the case of] a sela, since not everyone is knowledgeable about it except a money changer, [3]therefore, in cities, where there is a money changer, "until he can show it to a money changer." [4]In villages, where there is no money changer, "until Sabbath eves," [5]when they go to the market.

[6]"And if he recognized it, even after twelve months," etc. [7]Where? [8]If in cities, surely you said: "Until he can show [it] to a money changer." [9]If in villages, surely you said: "Until Sabbath eves."

[10]Rav Ḥisda said: They taught pious behavior here.

RASHI

דסלקין לשוקא – לקנות צורך סעודת שבת. **מדת חסידות** – והכי קאמר: אם חסיד הוא – מקבלה.

we also taught our Mishnah.... Sometimes the Talmud resolves an objection based on a Mishnah by arguing that the law in the Mishnah also applies to the case under discussion: "When we also taught our Mishnah," the Mishnah did in fact refer to this case, although it was not explicitly mentioned.

BACKGROUND

מִידַּת חֲסִידוּת Pious behavior. A person who acts more strictly than required by the letter of the law (both towards God and towards his fellow man) is called a pious person (חָסִיד), and his behavior is considered "pious behavior" (מִידַּת חֲסִידוּת).

NOTES

עַד עַרְבֵי שַׁבָּתוֹת דְּסָלְקִין לְשׁוּקָא Until Sabbath eve, when they go to the market. Villagers ordinarily spent their money on Fridays, when they bought food for the Sabbath, at which time they would be able to determine whether or not the coins in their possession were acceptable. *Sma* notes that even wealthy people, who presumably did not have to spend all their money on Fridays, were given only until Friday to check their money. These people, also presumably tried to get rid of their defective coins as soon as possible (i.e., by Friday), saving the better coins for use at a later date.

מִידַּת חֲסִידוּת Pious behavior. Rav Ḥisda distinguishes between the letter of the law — according to which a defective coin must be taken back only until it can be shown to a money changer — and pious conduct, according to which the coin should be taken back even after twelve months have passed. According to *Rambam*, this distinction applies only as long as the defective coin still circulates, even if it only circulates with difficulty. If the coin does not

HALAKHAH

וְאִם הָיָה מַכִּירָהּ And if he recognized it. "Even though the Rabbis limited the amount of time during which a person is permitted to return a defective coin, if the person who gave it still recognizes it, it is proper to exchange it (as an act of piety), even after the period of time laid down by the Rabbis. However, if he refuses, the recipient has no legal recourse, and only has grounds for resentment against him, since the person who gave him the coin is acting according to the law." (Ibid., 227:17.)

TRANSLATION AND COMMENTARY

אִי הָכִי [1]The Gemara objects: **If so,** if the Mishnah's statement that a person who recognizes a defective coin that he gave as payment should take it back even after twelve months have passed is read as describing pious conduct beyond the strict requirements of the law, then we can raise an objection by **citing the next clause** of the Mishnah: **"He has nothing against him except resentment."** What does this enigmatic statement mean? [2]**Who** has grounds for resentment here? Let us assume that the person entitled to harbor resentment is the pious person who, having acted beyond the requirements of the law, now finds himself in possession of a defective coin. [3]But **if** we assume that it is referring to **the pious person, let him not take** back the coin **from** the person to whom he gave it, **and let him harbor no resentment!** Surely we expect more from a pious person than to bear resentment against the very person to whom he has acted kindly! Thus it would appear that Rav Ḥisda's explanation cannot be correct.

וְאֶלָּא לְהָאֵיךְ דְּקִבְּלָהּ מִינֵּיהּ [4]The Gemara now rejects another possible explanation of this clause in the Mishnah: **On the other hand,** shall we assume that the person **referred to** in the Mishnah as being entitled to harbor resentment **is the one from whom** the person who gave the defective coin **took it back**, i.e., the one who received the worn coin in the first place? This explanation is also problematic. [5]**After** the person who originally gave the coin as payment **has accepted it back, can** the original recipient of the coin still **have reason for resentment?!**

הָכִי קָאָמַר [6]Rather, explains the Gemara, what the Mishnah **means** is **as follows:** A pious person should indeed replace a defective coin even after twelve months, and in such a case nobody has reason for resentment. But the Mishnah is referring to **another person** — who is not exceptionally pious — who, more than twelve months previously gave a defective coin as payment for merchandise. The recipient of the coin only now seeks to return it. **Even if** the "non-pious" person **does not accept** the defective coin back **from him,** the current holder of the coin has no legal recourse. [7]**All he has is reason for resentment against** the person who gave him the coin, since the latter is not required to take it back after enough time has passed for the recipient to show it to a money changer.

וְנוֹתְנָהּ לְמַעֲשֵׂר שֵׁנִי [8]The Gemara now proceeds to analyze the next clause of the Mishnah, which states: **"A person may use** a worn coin **for** redeeming **second-tithe** produce, **and need not be concerned** that he is redeeming his second tithe with an unfit coin, [9]**for** such a coin is Halakhically acceptable, and **someone who refuses** to accept such a coin on the grounds that it is marginally less than the official weight **is merely a miserly person."** (With regard to the institution of redeeming second-tithe produce, see above 44b-45a.)

[1]אִי הָכִי, אֵימָא סֵיפָא: "אֵין לוֹ עָלָיו אֶלָּא תַּרְעוֹמֶת". [2]לְמַאן? [3]אִי לְחָסִיד, לָא קַבּוּלֵי לִיקַבְּלָהּ מִינֵּיהּ, וְלָא תַּרְעוֹמֶת תֶּיהֱוֵי לֵיהּ! [4]וְאֶלָּא לְהָאֵיךְ דְּקִבְּלָהּ מִינֵּיהּ? [5]וּלְבָתַר דִּמְקַבְּלָהּ מִינֵּיהּ, תַּרְעוֹמֶת תֶּיהֱוֵי לֵיהּ?! [6]הָכִי קָאָמַר: הָא אַחֵר, אַף עַל פִּי שֶׁאֵין מְקַבְּלָהּ הֵימֶנּוּ, [7]"אֵין לוֹ עָלָיו אֶלָּא תַּרְעוֹמֶת". [8]"וְנוֹתְנָהּ לְמַעֲשֵׂר שֵׁנִי וְאֵינוֹ חוֹשֵׁשׁ, [9]שֶׁאֵינוֹ אֶלָּא נֶפֶשׁ רָעָה".

LITERAL TRANSLATION

[1]If so, say the latter clause: "He has nothing against him but resentment." [2]To whom [does this refer]? [3]If to the pious person, let him not accept it from him, and let him have no resentment!

[4]But [does it refer] to the one from whom he accepted it? [5]After he accepted it from him, can he have [reason for] resentment?!

[6]He says thus: But [in the case of] another person, even if he does not accept it from him, [7]"he has nothing against him but resentment."

[8]"And he may give it for second tithe and he need not be concerned, [9]for he [who refuses] is nothing but a miserly person (lit., 'an evil soul')."

RASHI

למאן — מי המתרעם. **אם לחסיד** — קאמר דיש לו תרעומת על המחזיר, מי כופהו לקבל שיתרעם? טוב לו שלא יקבלנה משיקבלנה ויוליא דיבה על חבירו. **ואחר שאינו חסיד** — ולא רצה לקבלה, אין לזה עליו אלא תרעומת, דאיהו הוא דאפסיד אנפשיה שלא החזירו בזמנו.

BACKGROUND

נֶפֶשׁ רָעָה A miserly person. This refers to a petty person, who is unwilling to forgo anything he thinks he deserves, even if he would not suffer any loss by doing so. For the purposes of the discussion here, a person who insists on being paid with coins in perfect condition (even though others would be willing to accept defective coins) is considered miserly. Such conduct is not forbidden, technically speaking, but is certainly reprehensible.

NOTES

circulate at all, then by the letter of the law it must be taken back, no matter how much time has already passed.

According to *Perishah,* if a coin is so defective that it does not circulate at all, not only is there no obligation to take it back after the time needed to show the coin to a money changer has passed, but even a pious person need not take it back. Pious conduct is only recommended if it will not entail a financial loss for the pious individual, i.e., as long as the coin still circulates. A question arises as to whether in the case of *ona'ah* relating to merchandise a pious individual ought to refund an overcharge if the legal period of claim has already passed. Following his own argument, *Perishah* rules that such "pious conduct" is not necessary, for such a refund would cause him financial loss.

נֶפֶשׁ רָעָה A miserly person. This expression — literally, "an evil soul" — is apparently derived from Ecclesiastes 6:1-2, where a miser's conduct is described as "evil under the heaven... an evil disease" (*Torat Ḥayyim*).

[1]אֲמַר רַב פַּפָּא: שְׁמַע מִינָּהּ הַאי מַאן דְּמוֹקֵים אַזּוּזֵי מִיקְּרֵי נֶפֶשׁ רָעָה. [2]וְהָנֵי מִילֵּי הוּא דְּסַגֵּי לְהוּ. [3]מְסַיֵּיעַ לֵיהּ לְחִזְקִיָּה, דְּאָמַר חִזְקִיָּה: בָּא לְפוֹרְטָהּ, פּוֹרְטָהּ בְּשָׁוְיָהּ. [4]בָּא לְחַלְּלָהּ, מְחַלְּלָהּ בְּיָפָה.

[5]מַאי קָאָמַר? הָכִי קָאָמַר:

LITERAL TRANSLATION

[1]Rav Pappa said: Conclude from this [that] he who is exacting about money is called a miserly person. [2]And this [only] applies if it circulates.

[3]This supports Ḥizkiyah, for Ḥizkiyah said: [If] he comes to exchange it, he exchanges it at its value. [4][If] he comes to redeem [with] it, he redeems [with] it as a good [coin].

[5]What is he saying? [7]He says thus:

TRANSLATION AND COMMENTARY

[1]**Rav Pappa said:** We can **conclude from this** statement **that a person who is exacting about money** and insists on being paid with coins that do not show any wear at all **is called a miserly person.** While the law protects the rights of the miserly, it does not encourage their behavior. [2]The Gemara notes that **this** statement — that a person who refuses to accept slightly worn coins is considered a miserly person — **only applies** to a person who refuses to accept worn coins that are good enough to **circulate** and are accepted by others. Refusal to accept worn coins that have been withdrawn from circulation, however, is by no means characteristic of a miserly person. It is reasonable conduct.

מְסַיֵּיעַ לֵיהּ לְחִזְקִיָּה [3]The Gemara notes further: **This** Mishnah, which rules that a worn coin may be used to redeem second tithe, **supports** the viewpoint of **Ḥizkiyah.** [4]**For Ḥizkiyah said: If a person wishes to exchange** a worn coin for smaller coins, **he** may only **exchange it** at **its** true, rather than its nominal, **value,** and he will thus receive small coins of less value than the face value of the coin. [4]However, **if he wishes to redeem** second-tithe produce with a worn coin, **he** may **redeem** such produce **with it as** if it were **a coin of full weight,** i.e., at its nominal value.

מַאי קָאָמַר [5]The Gemara asks: **What does this statement mean?** The Gemara answers: **It means the following:**

RASHI

דמוקי אזוזא — מעמיד עצמו מלקבלם, כשמוצא בהם פגם. **מסייע ליה** — מתניתין דקתני נותנה למעשר שני. **בא לפורטה** — בא להחליף סלע חסירה בפרוטות. **פורטה בשויה** — לפי חסרונה, ולא ירמה את חבירו לפורטה ביפה. **בא לחללה** — לחלל מעשר שני עליה. **מחלל עליה** — מעשר בדמי סלע יפה. **ביפה** — כאילו היא יפה. **מאי קאמר** — בא לפורטה פורטה בשויה — מתניתין אתא לאשמועינן, דכיון דפיחתה כדי אונאה אסור להוציאה ביפה. **הכי קאמר** — אף על פי שכשבא לפורטה בירושלים בפרוטות, ליקח סעודת מעשר, על כרחו יפרטנה בשויה ולא ביפה, אפילו הכי, סלע שמה, שאינה אלא נפש רעה. וכשחילל מעשר עליה מחלל ביפה. ואשמועינן חזקיה דמתניתין דקתני נותנה למעשר שני — כאילו היא יפה קאמר.

SAGES

חִזְקִיָּה **Ḥizkiyah.** The son of Rabbi Ḥiyya, Ḥizkiyah was a first-generation Amora. He and his twin brother Yehudah immigrated to Eretz Israel from Babylonia while they were still young. In Eretz Israel they studied with Rabbi Yehudah HaNasi, even though they were already considered important scholars in their own right. Rabbi Yehudah HaNasi held Rabbi Ḥiyya and his sons in high esteem, and maintained a warm relationship with them because of his high regard for their learning and piety.

Ḥizkiyah's brother, Yehudah, died young. Ḥizkiyah edited collections of Baraitot (as his father Rabbi Ḥiyya had done before him), and these are often cited by the Gemara as "the teachings of Ḥizkiyah's school" (תָּנָא דְּבֵי חִזְקִיָּה). Ḥizkiyah engaged in Halakhic discussions with other leading disciples of Rabbi Yehudah HaNasi. His own students included the noted Sage Rabbi Yoḥanan, as well as other Amoraim of that generation. Ḥizkiyah and his brother apparently earned their livelihood from commerce, and from their extensive real-estate holdings. Ḥizkiyah lived in Tiberias and was buried there, near his father's grave.

NOTES

הַאי מַאן דְּמוֹקֵים אַזּוּזֵי מִיקְּרֵי נֶפֶשׁ רָעָה **He who is exacting about money is a miserly person.** At first sight, it would appear that Rav Pappa does not add anything to what was stated explicitly in the Mishnah — "for he who refuses is nothing but a miserly person." The commentaries, however, explain that if not for Rav Pappa's statement, the Mishnah could have been interpreted differently. Specifically, we might have thought that, while coins that are slightly defective must be accepted, they must be accepted at their actual value (i.e., based on how much precious metal they contain), rather than at their official, designated value, which is greater. Thus Rav Pappa's statement teaches us that such coins must be accepted at their official, designated value, and one who fails to accept them as such is considered a miserly person (*Rashba, Ran*). Others, however, maintain that the Mishnah refers to coins that have become worn, whereas Rav Pappa speaks of coins that have other defects (*Torat Ḥayyim* according to *Rashi*).

מְסַיֵּיעַ לֵיהּ לְחִזְקִיָּה **This supports Ḥizkiyah.** The commentators disagree about what the Gemara means here (see *Rashi, Tosafot, Ramban, Ritva, Rashba,* and especially *Rosh*). According to *Rashi,* followed by our commentary, the Mishnah supports Ḥizkiyah. Specifically, the Mishnah teaches us that even a coin that has become so worn that the laws of fraud apply to it may be used to redeem second-tithe produce. Hence, we may infer that such a coin is still considered "money" Halakhically speaking, and may therefore be used to redeem second tithe, as Ḥizkiyah stated.

Ramban and others, however, interpret the Mishnah differently, and maintain that only coins that have been worn by *less* than one-sixth may be used to redeem second-tithe produce. By contrast, coins worn by more than one-sixth are not considered "money," Halakhically speaking, and one is even forbidden to retain such coins in one's possession. According to this view, the support for Ḥizkiyah was adduced from Rav Pappa's statement rather than from the Mishnah.

Specifically, we may infer from Rav Pappa's statement that a coin worn away by less than one-sixth must not only

HALAKHAH

וְהָנֵי מִילֵּי הוּא דְּסַגֵּי לְהוּ **And this only applies if it circulates.** "It is permitted to pay with a coin that is slightly worn, provided that it is still in circulation." (Ibid., 227:6.)

[1]אַף עַל פִּי כְּשֶׁבָּא לְפוֹרְטָהּ — פּוֹרְטָהּ בְּשָׁוְיָהּ, [2]כְּשֶׁהוּא מְחַלְּלָהּ — מְחַלְּלָהּ בְּיָפָה. [3]לְמֵימְרָא דְּסָבַר חִזְקִיָּה דִּמְזַלְזְלִינַן בְּמַעֲשֵׂר שֵׁנִי? [4]וְהָאָמַר חִזְקִיָּה: מַעֲשֵׂר שֵׁנִי שֶׁאֵין בּוֹ שָׁוֶה פְּרוּטָה, [5]אוֹמֵר: ״הוּא וְחוּמְשׁוֹ מְחוּלָּל עַל מָעוֹת הָרִאשׁוֹנוֹת״, [5]לְפִי שֶׁאִי אֶפְשָׁר לוֹ לְאָדָם לְצַמְצֵם מָעוֹתָיו.

LITERAL TRANSLATION

[1]Even though if he comes to exchange it, he exchanges it at its value, [2]if he redeems [with] it, he redeems [with] it as a good [coin].

[3][Do you mean] to say that Ḥizkiyah maintains that we minimize [the value of] second tithe? [4]But surely Ḥizkiyah said: [If a person has] second tithe that is not worth a perutah, [5]he says: "It and its fifth is redeemed with the first money," [6]because it is impossible for a man to calculate [value for] his money exactly.

TRANSLATION AND COMMENTARY

[1]**Even though a person who wishes to exchange** a worn coin for smaller coins may **exchange it** only **at its** true **value,** i.e., less than its face value, [2]nevertheless **if he wishes to redeem** second tithe **with it, he** is permitted to **redeem with it as** if it were **a coin of full weight.**

לְמֵימְרָא דְּסָבַר חִזְקִיָּה [3]The Gemara asks: **Do you mean to say that Ḥizkiyah** maintains **that it is permitted to minimize the value of second tithe** by permitting people to redeem it with coins worth less than the true value of the tithe? The result of Ḥizkiyah's permission to use worn coins at their nominal value is to undervalue the second-tithe produce being redeemed. For example, if a shekel's worth of produce is redeemed with a worn shekel coin that is worth only 90 percent of a good shekel, the produce is being undervalued by 10 percent. [4]**But,** says the Gemara, this result is inconsistent with another ruling given by Ḥizkiyah. **Surely Ḥizkiyah said** elsewhere: Redeeming **second-tithe** produce **worth less than a perutah** presents a special problem. Second-tithe produce valued at less than a perutah may not be redeemed by a coin, even with a perutah, because the coin cannot receive the sanctity of the tithe when the tithe is worth less than a perutah. Ḥizkiyah offers a solution to the problem of redeeming second-tithe produce worth less than a perutah by suggesting that it be redeemed by means of a coin (referred to here as "first money") that has already been used to redeem other second-tithe produce. Such a coin has already received second-tithe sanctity, and stands available to receive a little more. [5]Thus the owner of the second-tithe produce worth less than a perutah should take a coin that has already been used to redeem second-tithe produce, and **say:** "This tithe **and** the **fifth of it** that must be added to the cost of the redemption when a person redeems his own tithe **are** hereby **redeemed with** the **first money** that I used earlier to redeem other second-tithe produce." Ḥizkiyah's suggestion will only be effective if the "first money" being used has not already been used to redeem second-tithe produce exactly equal to its value. From Ḥizkiyah's suggestion it appears that he is confident that all "first money" can be used to redeem second-tithe produce worth less than a perutah. [6]This is indeed so, because people never use a coin to redeem produce up to the coin's exact value, **since it is impossible for a person to calculate exactly the value** he is receiving **for his money.** Since it is impossible to determine the exact value of the produce, people redeem their second tithe with a coin of

BACKGROUND

מְזַלְזְלִינַן בְּמַעֲשֵׂר שֵׁנִי We minimize the value of second tithe. Second tithe is sacred, and must therefore be eaten in Jerusalem. Nevertheless, since second tithe belongs to the person who separated it, the laws governing its redemption are not very strict, because the money used to redeem it will eventually be spent by the owner.

RASHI

דמזלזלינן — לפחות דמי פדיונו. **שאין בו שוה פרוטה** — ואין בו כח לתפוס פדיונו שיתן פרוטה ויחללנה, כדאמר לקמן: ממעשרו ולא כל מעשר כו׳. **אומר הוא וחומשו** — שאני צריך להוסיף עליו. **יהא מחולל על מעות הראשונות** — שחיללתי עליה מעשר שני ועודן בידי, יהא אף זה מחולל על אותו מעשר. **שאי אפשר לאדם לצמצם מעותיו** — לחלל בשוין בצמצום, שמתוך שהוא ירא מלפחות ונמצא אוכלו בלא חילוף — הוא מוסיף על דמיו. הילכך, פחות משוה פרוטה זה מחלל על אותו עודף, אלמא: לא פרקינן בצמצום, וכל שכן בפחות.

NOTES

be accepted, but must be accepted at its face value, i.e., as if it has not been worn away at all. Thus it follows that such a coin may also be used at its official, designated value to redeem second-tithe produce.

אַף עַל פִּי כְּשֶׁבָּא לְפוֹרְטָהּ Even though if he comes to exchange it. According to *Ramban*'s interpretation of the Gemara (see previous note), Ḥizkiyah's statement means the following: Even though money changers may not be willing to accept slightly defective coins at face value, since they want to make a profit, such coins may still be used to redeem second tithe at their official, designated value (see *Ritva*).

HALAKHAH

בְּאֵיזֶה מַטְבֵּעַ פּוֹדֶה מַעֲשֵׂר שֵׁנִי? Which coins may be used to redeem second tithe? "It is permitted to redeem second tithe with a coin that is worn out, as long as the coin circulates and the wear is no greater than the amount specified in our Mishnah (above, 51b-52a)," following the Mishnah. (*Rambam, Sefer Zeraim, Hilkhot Ma'aser Sheni* 4:19.)

הוּא וְחוּמְשׁוֹ מְחוּלָּל עַל מָעוֹת הָרִאשׁוֹנוֹת It and its fifth is redeemed with the first money. "One may redeem second tithe, a fifth of which is worth less than a perutah (see below, 53b), with money that has already been used to redeem

TRANSLATION AND COMMENTARY

slightly greater value than necessary, to ensure that they do not underestimate the value of the produce. A portion of that coin (the difference between the value of the coin and the true value of the produce) remains unused in the redemption, and may therefore be used to redeem second tithe worth less than a perutah. Thus we see that Ḥizkiyah is of the opinion that it is *not* permitted to undervalue tithes by redeeming them for less than their actual value, because he assumes that a person ordinarily redeems second-tithe produce with coins worth more than the second-tithe produce!

מַאי בְּיָפָה [1]The Gemara answers: **What** does Ḥizkiyah mean when he says that a worn coin, when used for redemption of second-tithe produce, should be valued **as a good coin?** [2]He means: **According to** the coin's **real value,** and no *less*. Ḥizkiyah never intended to suggest that the worn coin be used at its nominal value. To do so would indeed be considered dealing contemptuously with second-tithe produce. All Ḥizkiyah meant to say was that a worn coin may be used at its true value. The point of Ḥizkiyah's statement is that using the worn coin is not regarded as contemptuous treatment of second tithe. [3]However, using a worn coin at its face value is unacceptable **because we do not minimize the value** of second-tithe produce **twice,** both by permitting the use of a worn coin and then using it at its nominal value. Instead, the actual value of the worn coin is assessed, and it may be used to redeem the corresponding amount of second tithe.

גּוּפָא [4]The Gemara had earlier cited Ḥizkiyah's statement in the context of its discussion as to whether a worn coin can be used at its nominal or at its real value. The Gemara now **returns to** analyze Ḥizkiyah's **statement** in its own context in greater detail. [5]**Ḥizkiyah said: Regarding second-tithe** produce **that is worth less than a perutah,** [6]**one says:** "This tithe **and the fifth of it** that must be added to the cost of the redemption when a person redeems his own tithe **are** hereby **redeemed with** the **first money** that I used earlier to redeem other second-tithe produce," [7]**since it is impossible for a person** to **calculate his money exactly**. Accordingly, the value of the second tithe originally redeemed with the "first money" is likely to have been overestimated.

מֵיתִיבֵי [8]**An objection** to this ruling **was raised** from a Mishnah (*Bikkurim* 2:1), which lists some of the ways in which terumah and first fruits — both gifts of produce given to the priests — differ from second tithe. Many of the laws with regard to terumah — the portion of produce set aside and given to a priest — apply equally to *bikkurim*, the first fruits of the harvest. [9]The Mishnah states: "The following laws apply in common to **terumah and to *bikkurim***: Terumah and *bikkurim* may be eaten only by a priest who is in

LITERAL TRANSLATION

[1]What is "as a good [coin]"? [2]At its real value, [3]for we do not minimize its value twice.

[4]Returning to the statement quoted above (lit., "the thing itself"): [5]Ḥizkiyah said: [If a person has] second tithe that is not worth a perutah, [6]he says: "It and its fifth is redeemed with the first money," [7]because it is impossible for a man to calculate [value for] his money exactly.

[8]They raised an objection: [9]"For terumah and first fruits

[1]מַאי "בְּיָפָה"? [2]בְּתוֹרַת יָפָה, [3]דִּתְרֵי זִילֵי לָא מְזַלְזְלִינַן בֵּיהּ. [4]גּוּפָא: [5]אָמַר חִזְקִיָּה: מַעֲשֵׂר שֵׁנִי שֶׁאֵין בּוֹ שָׁוֶה פְּרוּטָה, [6]אוֹמֵר: "הוּא וְחוּמְשׁוֹ מְחוּלָּל עַל מָעוֹת הָרִאשׁוֹנוֹת", [7]לְפִי שֶׁאִי אֶפְשָׁר לוֹ לְאָדָם לְצַמְצֵם מָעוֹתָיו.

[8]מֵיתִיבֵי: [9]"הַתְּרוּמָה וְהַבִּיכּוּרִים

RASHI

בתורת יפה — בשויה, והכי קאמר: כסף שכשבא לפורטה בירושלים לא יקבלוה הימנו להדיא אלא בשויה, ויש מזלזלין בדמיה יותר מכדי פחתה — כך כשבא לחללה מחללה בשויה, דמים פחותים. **בתורת יפה** — משחלל עליה כפי דמים ודאין שלה, כך לא יחלל על זו אלא בדמים ודאין שלה. **דתרי זילי לא מזלזלינן ביה** — דאף על גב דתנן נותן למעשר שני — חד זילותא אשמועינן דמתחלל על סלע חסירה, ולא אמרינן הרי הוא כאסימון או כמעות הניתנות באסימון. אבל תרי זילי, לחלל עליה מעשר בדמי סלע יפה לא. **ביכורים** — הוקשו לתרומה, דקרינהו רחמנא תרומה, דאמר מר (מכות יז,א): "ותרומת ידך אלו ביכורים".

CONCEPTS

בִּיכּוּרִים First fruits. The first fruits of the new harvest were given to the priests. (See Deuteronomy 26:1.) In Temple times, a farmer would select the first-fruits (according to Rabbinic decree, at least one-sixtieth of the harvest) from the seven types of fruit with which Eretz Israel is specially favored (Deuteronomy 8:8). He would bring them to the Temple in a basket, place them before the altar, and recite prayers of thanks to God. Afterwards the fruit was given to the priests and eaten under the same conditions that govern terumah. The first fruits were brought to the Temple between the Festivals of Shavuot and Sukkot. If they were not brought within this period, an extension was granted until Ḥanukkah. An entire tractate of the Mishnah, *Bikkurim*, is devoted to the laws and practices governing this commandment.

HALAKHAH

other second tithe. Specifically, the owner of the produce must declare that he is redeeming its fifth with the money he used to redeem the other second tithe. Since it is impossible to determine exactly how much money is necessary to redeem any particular amount of second tithe, there is usually money left over when doing so, and this remainder may be used to redeem other second tithe." (Ibid., 5:5.)

הַתְּרוּמָה וְהַבִּיכּוּרִים חַיָּיבִין עֲלֵיהֶן מִיתָה For terumah and first fruits one is liable to death. "If a non-priest intentionally ate terumah (regardless of whether it was ritually pure) or first fruits (if they had entered the walls of ancient Jerusalem), he is liable to death by the hand of God." (*Rambam, Hilkhot Terumot* 6:6; ibid., *Bikkurim* 3:1.)

TRANSLATION AND COMMENTARY

a state of ritual purity. If a non-priest or a ritually impure priest willfully eats terumah or *bikkurim,* **he is liable to** the punishment of **death** by the hand of Heaven. If a non-priest ate terumah or *bikkurim* unintentionally, he must restore the value of the produce he ate, adding **one-fifth** of its value as a fine. [53A] [1]**And** both terumah and *bikkurim* **are forbidden to non-priests.** [2]**They are** considered **the** private **property of the priest to whom they** were given, so that he can sell them to other priests and use the money for any purpose, or use them to betroth a woman. [3]**And they are neutralized** — rendered permissible for consumption by non-priests — **in a mixture of one hundred and one.** That is, if terumah or first fruits are inadvertently mixed with food permitted to be eaten by non-priests, and cannot be distinguished from the other food, a non-priest is not allowed to eat the resulting mixture unless there are at least one hundred parts of permissible food for each part of the terumah or first fruits. [4]**And** terumah and *bikkurim* **require washing of the hands.** The priest must purify his hands by ritually washing them before eating terumah or *bikkurim.* [5] If the priest is ritually impure, he may not eat terumah or *bikkurim* even after immersing in a ritual bath, until after **sunset** on the day of his immersion. [6]**These laws apply**

חַיָּבִין עֲלֵיהֶן מִיתָה וְחוֹמֶשׁ, [53A] [1]וַאֲסוּרִים לְזָרִים, [2]וְהֵן נִכְסֵי כֹהֵן, [3]וְעוֹלִים בְּאֶחָד וּמֵאָה, [4]וּטְעוּנִין רְחִיצַת יָדַיִם, [5]וְהַעֲרֵב שֶׁמֶשׁ. [6]הֲרֵי אֵלּוּ

LITERAL TRANSLATION

one is liable to death and [to] one-fifth, [53A] [1]and they are forbidden to non-priests, [2]and they are the property of the priest, [3]and they are annulled (lit., 'they go up') in [a mixture of] one hundred and one, [4]and they require washing of the hands, [5]and the setting of the sun. [6]These [laws] apply

RASHI

חייבין עליהן מיתה — זר או כהן טמא האוכלו במזיד. **וחומש** — זר האוכלן בשוגג, דכתיב (ויקרא כב) "ואיש כי יאכל קדש בשגגה וגו׳". **ואסורים לזרים** — ב"לא יאכל", ואצטריך למתנייה, משום דבעי למתנייה "מה שאין כאן במעשר", דאפילו איסור ליכא. **והן נכסי כהן** — לקדש בהן את האשה, מה שאין כן במעשר, סתם משנה כרבי מאיר, דאמר: מעשר ממון גבוה הוא, והמקדש בו, לא קידש. **וטעונים רחיצת ידים** — לפירות, שהידים טמאות שניות גזרו בהן רבנן, ושני עושה שלישי בתרומה. מה שאין כן במעשר, שאין טעון רחילת ידים לפירות, דאמר מר: הנוטל ידיו לפירות — הרי זה מגסי הרוח, והכי מוקמינן לה בחגיגה בפרק שני (יח,ב). **והערב שמש** — לטומאה דאורייתא. מה שאין כן במעשר, דאמר מר: טבל ועלה — אוכל במעשר, ומקרא ילפינן לה ביבמות בפרק "הערל" (עד,ב). **ועולין באחד ומאה** — צריכין אחד ומאה לבטל, ואין בטלין ברוב, מה שאין כן במעשר, דבטיל ברוב

BACKGROUND

חַיָּבִין עֲלֵיהֶן מִיתָה וְחוֹמֶשׁ One is liable to death and to one-fifth. According to the Torah, ritually pure terumah may only be eaten by a priest. A non-priest who willfully eats terumah is subject to death at the hands of Heaven, but not by a human court. This punishment is similar to, though less severe than, "excision" (כָּרֵת). Since terumah is considered sacred property (even though it belongs to the priest to whom it was given, who may therefore derive personal benefit from it), a non-priest who inadvertently eats terumah must pay an extra fifth of its value to atone for his sin.

וְעוֹלִים בְּאֶחָד וּמֵאָה And they are annulled in a mixture of one hundred and one. The expression עוֹלִים — literally "they go up" — used here for nullification or neutralization — was apparently employed because the food "goes up" and leaves its original status as prohibited food. Indeed, this term is frequently used by the Gemara to describe the neutralization of forbidden food that was inadvertently mixed with permissible food.

According to Torah law, terumah or *bikkurim* mixed with ordinary food is neutralized (and the resulting mixture may therefore be eaten) as long as the mixture contains more ordinary food than the terumah or the *bikkurim.* By Rabbinic decree, however, terumah or *bikkurim* is neutralized only if it was mixed with at least one hundred parts of ordinary food (other prohibited foods, however, need only be mixed with sixty parts of ordinary food to be nullified).

וּטְעוּנִין רְחִיצַת יָדַיִם And they require washing of the hands. "Washing the hands" refers here to ritually washing the hands, i.e., pouring water from a cup over each hand (as is done before eating bread). Thus the Mishnah teaches that a person must wash his hands before eating any kind of terumah or first fruits (and not just bread).

The requirement to wash one's hands before eating bread, terumah and first fruits is of Rabbinic origin, although allusions to this practice are

NOTES

וַאֲסוּרִים לְזָרִים And they are forbidden to non-priests. Since the Mishnah has already established that a non-priest who willfully ate terumah and *bikkurim* is liable to death, why does the Mishnah add the seemingly self-evident information that terumah and *bikkurim* are forbidden to non-priests? *Rashi* explains that for terumah and *bikkurim* alone this addition is unnecessary. But the Mishnah continues by contrasting these laws to the laws of second tithe. Regarding second tithe, it is necessary to establish not only that there is no penalty of death if it is eaten by non-priests, but that it is entirely permitted.

Tosafot objects that a parallel redundancy is found in another Mishnah (*Hallah* 1:9), where the contrast to second tithe is not mentioned. Therefore, a reason for the addition must be found in connection with terumah and *bikkurim* themselves. The Jerusalem Talmud (*Bikkurim* 2:1) answers that the punishment of death applies only if the amount of an olive's bulk or more were eaten. The Mishnah goes on to state that it is even prohibited to eat less than this amount.

Similarly, *Meiri* answers that the purpose of the addition is to establish that it is prohibited for a non-priest to use terumah and *bikkurim* for purposes other than food, although the death penalty applies specifically to eating.

HALAKHAH

וְחַיָּבִין עֲלֵיהֶן חוֹמֶשׁ The fine of one-fifth for eating terumah and first fruits. "If a non-priest unintentionally ate terumah or first fruits, he must pay the priest the value of the produce plus one-fifth (when the Talmud speaks of an extra one-fifth, it refers to one-fifth of the total payment, i.e., a quarter of the actual loss)." (*Rambam, Sefer Zeraim, Hilkhot Terumot* 6:6.)

וַאֲסוּרִים לְזָרִים And they are forbidden to non-priests. "People who are not priests are forbidden to eat terumah and first fruits, even in Jerusalem." (Ibid., *Hilkhot Terumot* 6:5; ibid., *Hilkhot Bikkurim,* 3:1, 4:15.)

וְהֵן נִכְסֵי כֹהֵן And they are the property of the priest. "First fruits and terumah are the property of the priest to whom they were given, and he may use them to buy slaves, land, or non-kosher animals. Likewise, first fruits and terumah may be collected from priests in payment of their debts, and a woman may accept them in payment of her ketubah." (Ibid., *Hilkhot Bikkurim* 4:14.)

וְעוֹלִים בְּאֶחָד וּמֵאָה And they are annulled in a mixture of one hundred and one. "If a *se'ah* of terumah or first fruits fell into a hundred *se'ah* of ordinary produce, the terumah or first fruits is neutralized by the other produce, and the mixture may be eaten even by non-priests. However, one *se'ah* of the mixture must be given to a priest, since one *se'ah* of the contents of the mixture belongs to him." (Ibid., *Hilkhot Terumot* 13:1; *Hilkhot Bikkurim* 4:15.)

וּטְעוּנִין רְחִיצַת יָדַיִם And they require washing of the hands. "A person who wishes to eat any kind of terumah — bread or fruit — must wash his hands before doing so, even if he is ritually pure. This law was instituted by the Rabbis to safeguard ritual purity." (Ibid., *Hilkhot Terumot* 11:7.)

וְהַעֲרֵב שֶׁמֶשׁ And the setting of the sun. "A person who was ritually impure may not eat terumah until the sun has set (i.e., until three medium-sized stars have appeared), even

בִּתְרוּמָה וּבְכּוּרִים, מַה שֶּׁאֵין כֵּן בְּמַעֲשֵׂר״.

1 מַאי ״מַה שֶּׁאֵין כֵּן בְּמַעֲשֵׂר״?

2 לָאו מִכְּלָל דְּמַעֲשֵׂר בָּטֵיל בְּרוּבָּא?

3 וְאִם אִיתָא דְּחִזְקִיָּה, הֲוָה לֵיהּ

LITERAL TRANSLATION

to terumah and first fruits, which is not the case with tithe."

[1] What is "which is not the case with tithe"? [2] [Does this] not [prove] by implication that tithe is annulled in a majority?

[3] But if Ḥizkiyah's [ruling] is [correct], [4] it is

RASHI

ולא בעי אחד ומאה, ועל כרחך במעשר שאין לו תקנתא לא בפדייה ולא להעלותו לירושלים קאמר, דאי אית ליה תקנתא — אמור רבנן דבר שיש לו מתירין לא בטיל! והכא כגון שנטמא, דלית ליה תקנתא באכילה. ואין בו שוה פרוטה, דלאו בר פדייה הוא, אם איתא לדחזקיה כו'.

TRANSLATION AND COMMENTARY

to terumah and first fruits, but they do not **apply to** second **tithe."** Obviously there is no death penalty or fine if a non-priest eats second tithe, for second tithe is intended to be eaten in Jerusalem by its owner. And although second tithe may not be eaten in a state of ritual impurity, the penalty for so doing is lashes, and not death at the hands of Heaven. Second tithe is considered divine property, and therefore its owner may not use it to betroth a woman, for which one's personal property is required. The law requiring a hundred parts of permitted food in order to neutralize each part of forbidden food does not apply to second tithe, as the Gemara explains in detail below. A person need not wash his hands before eating second-tithe fruit, and a person who was ritually impure may partake of second tithe immediately after he has purified himself by immersion in a ritual bath.

מַאי מַה שֶּׁאֵין כֵּן בְּמַעֲשֵׂר [1] Having quoted this Mishnah in which the differences between terumah and *bikkurim,* on the one hand, and second tithe on the other, are listed, the Gemara now focuses on one of these differences, which it interprets as being in contradiction to the ruling of Ḥizkiyah regarding second-tithe produce worth less than a perutah: **What,** it asks, is meant by the expression **"but they do not apply to** second **tithe"** used by the Mishnah to teach that the laws of neutralization that apply to terumah and *bikkurim* are different from those that apply to second-tithe produce? [2] **Does this** expression **not prove by implication that,** whereas an inadvertent mixture of terumah and *bikkurim* with other food may not be eaten by a non-priest unless the ratio of the other food to the terumah or *bikkurim* is at least a hundred to one, second **tithe** is governed by more lenient rules of neutralization and **can be** neutralized **by a** simple **majority**? If some second-tithe produce was inadvertently mixed with ordinary produce, may not the resulting mixture be eaten outside Jerusalem if the ratio of ordinary produce to second-tithe produce is greater than one to one?

וְאִם אִיתָא דְּחִזְקִיָּה [3] The Gemara now argues that Ḥizkiyah's ruling cannot be reconciled with this understanding of the Mishnah. There is a Halakhic principle that the rules permitting the neutralization of forbidden foods do not apply to those forbidden foods that can be rendered permissible by some other means. Non-kosher meat, for example, is irrevocably forbidden, so that if some non-kosher meat were inadvertently mixed with kosher meat, the only way that the mixture could become permitted would be if the relevant conditions of neutralization were met. By contrast, the prohibition against eating second-tithe produce outside Jerusalem is conditional. If a person wishes to render his second-tithe produce permitted to be eaten even outside Jerusalem, all he has to do is redeem it for money. Thus the implication in the Mishnah that the rules of neutralization *do* apply to mixtures containing second-tithe produce is seemingly problematic. One possible way of resolving the difficulty is to say that second-tithe produce does not fall within the category of forbidden food that can be rendered permissible, since redemption is not effective in all cases — for example, where the value of the second-tithe produce is less than a perutah. But this answer is not available to Ḥizkiyah, for **if Ḥizkiyah's ruling is correct,** and it is possible to redeem second-tithe produce worth less than a perutah with money that was previously used to redeem other second-tithe produce, then

NOTES

בָּטֵיל בְּרוּבָּא **Annulled in a majority.** When forbidden food is inadvertently mixed with permitted food, under certain circumstances the forbidden food becomes neutralized and can be eaten. One example is where the mixture is fluid and a homogeneous combination is formed. If the forbidden food is identical to the permitted food, Torah law requires a simple majority to achieve neutralization. Rabbinic law however, demands that the permitted food be sixty times

HALAKHAH

if he has already immersed himself that day in a ritual bath." (Ibid., 7:2.)

מַה שֶּׁאֵין כֵּן בְּמַעֲשֵׂר **Which is not the case with tithe.** "Second tithe is considered as if it were God's property, and hence cannot be acquired as a gift, sold, or used to buy other things or to betroth a woman." (Ibid., *Hilkhot Ma'aser Sheni* 3:17.) "However, it may be eaten immediately after immersion before sunset — and by non-priests, too." (Ibid., 7:11.)

found in the Torah. For example, the Torah states (Exodus 30:19 and elsewhere) that the priests had to wash their hands before performing the Temple service. The laws that apply to washing the hands for the Temple service, for eating terumah, and for eating bread differ slightly from one another, despite certain fundamental similarities.

הָעֶרֶב שֶׁמֶשׁ **Sunset.** A person who is ritually impure has to immerse himself in a ritual bath in order to regain his ritual purity. However, even after immersing in a ritual bath he remains partially impure until nightfall. Such a person is called a *tevul yom* (טְבוּל יוֹם — literally, "one who immersed during the day"; cf. Leviticus 22:7). A *tevul yom* may not eat terumah or sacrifices, although he may eat second tithe (even though it is sacred) immediately after immersing himself, without waiting for nightfall.

The Mishnah here speaks of sunset (הָעֶרֶב שֶׁמֶשׁ) as the end of the day. In fact, however, the Gemara explains elsewhere that הָעֶרֶב שֶׁמֶשׁ does not mean sunset, but nightfall, i.e., after three middle-sized stars have appeared (this time is also known as צֵאת הַכּוֹכָבִים, "the appearance of three stars").

CONCEPTS

בִּיטּוּל אִיסּוּרִים **The nullification of prohibitions.** The neutralization of the prohibition on a forbidden item when it becomes mixed with other entities; for example, when forbidden food is mixed with permitted food. When a prohibited item is mixed together with other items and can no longer be singled out as an individual unit, the mixture may sometimes be permitted for use. The circumstances under which the mixture containing the prohibited item becomes permitted depend upon the nature of the prohibition and the nature of the mixture. Some prohibited items become permitted in a mixture: (1) where there is a simple majority of permitted substances; or (2) where the taste of the forbidden substance is no longer

דָּבָר שֶׁיֵּשׁ לוֹ מַתִּירִין, [1]וְכָל דָּבָר שֶׁיֵּשׁ לוֹ מַתִּירִין אֲפִילּוּ בְּאֶלֶף לָא בָּטֵיל!

[2]וּמִמַּאי דְּ״מַה שֶּׁאֵין כֵּן בְּמַעֲשֵׂר״ דְּבָטֵיל בְּרוּבָּא?

[3]דִּלְמָא לָא בָּטֵיל כְּלָל!

[4]לָא מָצֵית אָמְרַתְּ הָכִי, דִּלְגַבֵּי תְּרוּמָה חוּמְרֵי דִּתְרוּמָה קָתָנֵי, [5]קוּלֵּי דִּתְרוּמָה לָא קָתָנֵי.

LITERAL TRANSLATION

a thing that can become permitted, [1]and anything that can become permitted is not annulled, even in a thousand!

[2]But from what [do we know] that "which is not the case with tithe" [means] that it is annulled in a majority?

[3]Perhaps it is not annulled at all!

[4]You cannot say so, for regarding terumah it teaches the stringencies of terumah, [5][but] it does not teach the leniencies of terumah.

TRANSLATION AND COMMENTARY

second tithe **is** in all cases considered **something** that **can be rendered permissible**. [1]**And** the rule is that **anything that can become permitted** through means other than inadvertent neutralization **is not neutralized even** if it is mixed **with a thousand** times as much permissible food! Thus, if, as the Mishnah implies, second tithe can be neutralized if it is inadvertently mixed with a quantity of other produce greater than its own, we must conclude — against Ḥizkiyah — that second tithe worth less than a perutah cannot be redeemed.

וּמִמַּאי [2]The Gemara attempts to rebut this objection: **But from where do we know that** when the Mishnah states that the rule of one-hundred-to-one neutralization applies to terumah and *bikkurim*, **"but does not apply to tithe,"** the implication is that second-tithe produce mixed with ordinary produce **can be neutralized by a** mere **majority** of ordinary food, and therefore contradicts the ruling of Ḥizkiyah? This implication is the basis of the objection raised above against Ḥizkiyah's ruling. But perhaps this implication is unfounded. [3]**Perhaps** the Mishnah means to say that second tithe **cannot be neutralized at all,** no matter what quantity of permissible food was inadvertently mixed with it! Such an understanding of the Mishnah would lend support to Ḥizkiyah, for he maintains that second tithe can always be redeemed, even when worth less than a perutah. Thus, second tithe is considered something that can be rendered permissible by means other than neutralization — by redemption or by being eaten in Jerusalem — and therefore the rules of neutralization do not apply to it.

לָא מָצֵית אָמְרַתְּ הָכִי [4]The Gemara answers that such an interpretation is untenable: **You cannot say** that the Mishnah intends to imply that second tithe may not be neutralized at all, **for** in this Mishnah, which was stated **regarding terumah** and *bikkurim*, only **the stringent aspects of terumah are mentioned** — those aspects concerning which terumah and *bikkurim* are treated more stringently than second tithe — [5]**but not the** more **lenient aspects of terumah.** We cannot say that this Mishnah maintains that the rules of neutralization are

RASHI

דלגבי תרומה – משנה זו במסכת בכורים (פרק ב משנה א) שנויה, הלכך חשיבותא דידה קא מני ואזיל ולאו קולי דידה, שהרי היא עולה ומעשר אינו עולה.

NOTES

the amount of the prohibited food. If the prohibited food in question is terumah, a hundred times the terumah is required. If the foods are not of the same kind, there must be sufficient permitted food so that the taste of the forbidden food cannot be noticed. If, on the other hand, the food in question is solid, and the pieces are large enough that they do not actually combine, a simple majority is sufficient. Terumah, howeverj, is not neutralized unless it is outnumbered a hundred to one. Our Gemara contrasting terumah to second tithe is referring to this case of solid objects. Therefore, if second tithe cannot be rendered permitted by redemption it should be neutralized by a simple majority, whereas terumah would require a proportion of a hundred to one.

דָּבָר שֶׁיֵּשׁ לוֹ מַתִּירִין A thing that can become permitted. There are two basic explanations given for this ruling: (1) Neutralization should not be relied upon when there are other ways of making the mixture permitted. (2) Neutralization is a function of the confrontation between Halakhic opposites. When forbidden objects mix with permissible objects they "confront" one another. If the permissible food is of sufficient quantity it confronts and neutralizes the forbidden food. If there is no confrontation, the process of neutralization does not occur. In the use of something that can become permitted, there is no confrontation, because an object with the potential to become permissible is not defined objectively as forbidden food. Consequently, it cannot become neutralized (*Ran*).

הֲוָה לֵיהּ דָּבָר שֶׁיֵּשׁ לוֹ מַתִּירִין It is a thing that can become permitted. It is clear from the Mishnah cited here that terumah is not considered "a thing that can become permitted," because terumah can be neutralized by one

HALAKHAH

דָּבָר שֶׁיֵּשׁ לוֹ מַתִּירִין A thing that can become permitted. "Forbidden food that can become permitted cannot be neutralized, no matter how much permissible food is mixed with it. For example, if an egg that was laid on a Festival,

discernible; or (3) where the permitted substance is sixty times the quantity of the prohibited substance; or (4) where the permitted substance is one hundred times the quantity of the prohibited; or (5) where the permitted substance is two hundred times the quantity of the prohibited. Certain prohibited items or substances can never be neutralized, no matter by how much the permitted substances exceed the prohibited (e.g., ḥametz on Pesaḥ).

The neutralization of a prohibited item when mixed with a permitted item can only take effect if the mixture was accidentally created; one may not intentionally effect such a neutralization. A prohibited item can also be neutralized when it loses its importance. For example, a forbidden food may become permitted when it is no longer fit for consumption.

CONCEPTS

דָּבָר שֶׁיֵּשׁ לוֹ מַתִּירִין An object that is prohibited but whose prohibition can or will lapse at some future time. For example, an egg laid on the Sabbath, which may not be moved on that day, will become permitted to be moved once the Sabbath is over. Similarly, food which may not be eaten at present because of a vow may become permitted by having the vow annulled. Since the prohibition in these and many other cases can or will ultimately lapse, it is treated with greater stringency while it is in effect. Thus, if such an object is mixed with permitted substances, it cannot be neutralized, however great the amount of permitted substances involved, as long as the prohibition remains in effect.

TRANSLATION AND COMMENTARY

more stringent in the case of second tithe than in the case of terumah and *bikkurim*, because such an interpretation runs counter to the basic structure of the Mishnah, which lists precisely those instances in which terumah and *bikkurim* are subject to more stringent laws than is second tithe. Thus the initial inference we drew from the Mishnah — that the rules of neutralization which apply to second tithe are more lenient than those which apply to terumah and *bikkurim* — appears well founded, and the objection raised against the ruling of Ḥizkiyah remains unanswered.

וְהָא קָא תָּנֵי [1]In an effort to sustain Ḥizkiyah's position, the Gemara now questions its last assumption — that the Mishnah only mentions those areas of the Halakhah in which terumah is treated more stringently than second tithe: **But** the Mishnah **states: "And** terumah and *bikkurim* **are the property of the priest,"** and hence may be disposed of by the priest as his personal property — unlike second tithe, which is not considered its owner's personal property, but the property of God. Thus we see that the Mishnah also mentions aspects of the law in which terumah is treated more leniently than second tithe! It is, therefore, also possible that with regard to neutralization the law governing terumah is more lenient than that governing second tithe, and that second tithe can never be neutralized, for the reason explained above. If this is so, the objection to Ḥizkiyah's ruling is removed.

לָא סָלְקָא דַּעְתָּךְ [2]Nevertheless, the Gemara refuses to concede that second tithe cannot be neutralized at all: **This cannot enter your mind,** says the Gemara, **for** the following **has been taught explicitly** in a Baraita: **"Second-tithe** produce inadvertently mixed with ordinary produce **is neutralized by a** simple **majority** of the ordinary produce. [3]**And of which second tithe did** the Sages **say this?** [4]**Of tithe that is not worth a perutah, or which entered Jerusalem and left,"** as the Gemara explains in greater detail below.

וְאִם אִיתָא לְדִחִזְקִיָּה [5]Since it has now been established that the Mishnah does indeed imply that, when mixed with ordinary produce, second-tithe produce worth less than a perutah is neutralized if the other produce constitutes a majority of the mixture, the Gemara's original objection against Ḥizkiyah remains: **If Ḥizkiyah's ruling is correct,** and it is possible to redeem second-tithe produce worth less than a perutah with first money that was previously used to redeem other second-tithe produce, [6]then **let** the owner of this

[1]וְהָא קָא תָּנֵי: "וְהֵן נִכְסֵי כֹהֵן"! [2]לָא סָלְקָא דַּעְתָּךְ, דְּתַנְיָא בְּהֶדְיָא: "מַעֲשֵׂר שֵׁנִי בָּטֵיל בְּרוּבָּא. [3]וּבְאֵיזֶה מַעֲשֵׂר שֵׁנִי אָמְרוּ? [4]בְּמַעֲשֵׂר שֶׁאֵין בּוֹ שָׁוֶה פְּרוּטָה, וְשֶׁנִּכְנָס לִירוּשָׁלַיִם וְיָצָא". [5]וְאִם אִיתָא לְדִחִזְקִיָּה, [6]לִיעֲבַד

LITERAL TRANSLATION

[1]But surely it teaches: "And they are the property of the priest"!

[2]This cannot enter your mind, for it has been taught explicitly: "Second tithe is annulled in a majority. [3]And of which second tithe did they say [this]? [4]Of tithe that is not worth a perutah, and which entered Jerusalem and went out."

[5]But if Ḥizkiyah's [ruling] is [correct], [6]let him do

RASHI

לא סלקא דעתך – דלא בטיל כלל, אלא ודאי בטיל ברוב קאמר. **ושנכנס לירושלים ויצא** – לקמן מפרש דלית ליה תקנתא, לא באכילה ולא בחילול.

BACKGROUND

וְאִם אִיתָא לְדִחִזְקִיָּה But if Ḥizkiyah's ruling is correct. Second tithe cannot usually be neutralized, since the option of redemption exists. Therefore, the Gemara claims that if we do not accept Ḥizkiyah's ruling, the Mishnah can be explained as referring to a case in which the second tithe was worth less than a perutah. However, even if we reject Ḥizkiyah's view, there still exists the option of transporting the fruit in question to Jerusalem, where it is permissible to eat second tithe.

Rashi explains that we are discussing a situation in which the fruit is ritually impure, and therefore cannot be eaten in Jerusalem.

Tosafot claims that we are discussing a situation in which the fruit was a great distance from Jerusalem. Since transporting all the fruit entails great difficulty, it is not considered a viable option.

This answer seems to assume that neutralization is not relied upon when another viable option exists.

NOTES

hundred times as much permissible food. The commentators object, however, that even terumah can be rendered permissible if the person who separated it has his statement declaring it terumah revoked.

Tosafot answers that since there is no obligation to revoke one's terumah (and indeed, this may even be prohibited; *Meiri*), terumah is not considered something that can become permitted (see also *Rosh*, *Agudah*, *Ritva* and others).

Other commentators ask why second tithe is not considered potentially permissible food, since it need not be redeemed if eaten in Jerusalem. *Ramban*, *Rashba* and others answer that since bringing the tithe to Jerusalem may entail considerable effort and expense — which people are not necessarily willing to undertake — second tithe is not considered potentially permissible either.

וּבְאֵיזֶה מַעֲשֵׂר שֵׁנִי אָמְרוּ And of which second tithe did they say this? At first glance, it may seem strange that the Mishnah makes a blanket statement that second tithe is treated more leniently with regard to neutralization than is terumah, when in fact in most cases the opposite is true. It is only in this specific instance that second tithe is neutralized in a majority; it is usually not neutralized at all. Upon closer analysis the Mishnah is seen to be accurate. In order to contrast neutralization of second tithe with that of terumah, neutralization of second tithe must be isolated from external factors. Therefore, a case is constructed in which there is no other way to make the second tithe permissible. Thus the comparison between neutralization of terumah and neutralization of second tithe is appropriate.

HALAKHAH

a day when it is forbidden to be eaten, became mixed up with even a thousand eggs, none of the eggs can be eaten on the Festival because they will all be permitted in any case the day after." (*Shulḥan Arukh, Yoreh De'ah* 102:1.)

TRANSLATION AND COMMENTARY

second-tithe produce that has become mixed with ordinary food **do as Ḥizkiyah said, and let him redeem it with** such "**first money.**" Since the mixture will be permitted once the second tithe contained in it is redeemed, the law should be that second-tithe produce cannot be neutralized, and this runs counter to the implication of the Mishnah!

דְּלָא פָּרֵיק [1]The Gemara answers that this is not a conclusive objection against Ḥizkiyah. Although second tithe is generally in the category of forbidden food that can be rendered permitted through redemption — even in the case of second tithe worth less than a perutah — nevertheless the option of redemption is not always available. The case may be one **where** the owner of the second tithe worth less than a perutah has **not** previously **redeemed** other second-tithe produce, and hence has no "first money" available with which to redeem the second tithe worth less than a perutah. In such a case, there is no other means by which the mixture of second tithe and ordinary food can be permitted, and the second-tithe produce may thus be neutralized by a greater quantity of ordinary food.

וְנֵיתֵי מַעֲשֵׂר דְּאִית לֵיהּ [2]The Gemara now objects that even in the absence of previously used "first money," there is another way to redeem the second-tithe produce worth less than a perutah: **Let** the owner of the second-tithe produce worth less than a perutah that has been inadvertently mixed with ordinary produce **bring** another half-perutah's worth of second **tithe that he has** in his possession **and combine them,** and then redeem the two together with a single perutah! Once again, since the mixture can be rendered permitted by redeeming the second tithe, the law should be that the second tithe cannot be neutralized, and the objection against Ḥizkiyah's ruling remains.

דְּאוֹרַיְיתָא וּדְרַבָּנַן לָא מִצְטָרְפִי [3]The Gemara answers that combining the mixture containing the half-perutah's worth of second tithe with other second-tithe produce is not an option, for the half-perutah's worth of second tithe in the mixture cannot be combined with another half-perutah's worth of second-tithe produce for the purposes of redemption. For a half-perutah's worth of **second tithe according to Torah law and** a half-perutah's worth of **second tithe according to Rabbinic law cannot be combined** in order to be redeemed with a single perutah. According to Torah law, second tithe is governed by the standard rules of neutralization, according to which a forbidden food is neutralized by a simple majority of permissible food. It was the Rabbis who said that a forbidden mixture may not be rendered permitted through neutralization if it can be

לֵיהּ לְדִחִזְקִיָּה, וְנֵיחַל לֵיהּ עַל מָעוֹת הָרִאשׁוֹנוֹת!

[1]דְּלָא פָּרֵיק.

[2]וְנֵיתֵי מַעֲשֵׂר דְּאִית לֵיהּ, וְנִצְטָרְפִינְהוּ!

[3]דְּאוֹרַיְיתָא וּדְרַבָּנַן לָא מִצְטָרְפִי.

LITERAL TRANSLATION

as Ḥizkiyah [said], and let him redeem it with the first money!

[1]Where he has not redeemed.

[2]Then let him bring tithe that he has, and combine them!

[3][Second tithe] according to Torah law and [second tithe] according to Rabbinic law are not combined.

RASHI

דלא פריק – לא פדה מעשר עד הנה, שיהו מעות מעשר בידו. **וניתי מעשר** – שוה חצי פרוטה. **ונצרף** – יביאנו אצל המעורב ויאמר: "המעורב וזה מחוללים על פרוטה זו", ואשתכח דיש לו מתירין. **דאורייתא ודרבנן לא מצטרפי** – לתפוס פרוטה זו בקדושת מעשר, שהמעורב, מן התורה, בטל ברוב, דכתיב (שמות כג) "אחרי רבים להטות", ורבנן הוא דאמרו היכא דיש לו מתירין לא ליבטול, הלכך אין איסור מעשר בזה אלא מדרבנן, הילכך אין מצטרף עם זה לתפוס פדיונו, נמצא שוה חצי פרוטה שהביא נאכל בלא חילול, אבל לחזקיה – מעות הראשונות כבר נתפסו.

NOTES

וְנֵיתֵי מַעֲשֵׂר דְּאִית לֵיהּ **Then let him bring tithe that he has.** It would appear that although the Gemara has successfully defended Ḥizkiyah, it continues to question the Mishnah in *Bikkurim*. These questions, however, are independent of Ḥizkiyah's ruling. *Ramban*, followed in our commentary, suggests that the Gemara's questions are still based on Ḥizkiyah's ruling. He explains that had it not been for Ḥizkiyah's ruling, we would have assumed that second tithe worth less than a perutah cannot be redeemed, since it lacks the normal sanctity of second tithe. All the succeeding questions posed by the Gemara assume, based on Ḥizkiyah, that such second tithe can be redeemed if the sum total of second tithe can be made to reach the value of a perutah. The questions, therefore, do not focus on the Mishnah, but on Ḥizkiyah.

דְּאוֹרַיְיתָא וּדְרַבָּנַן **According to Torah law and according to Rabbinic law.** The commentators differ as to why such second tithe need only be redeemed by Rabbinic law. *Rashi*, followed by our commentary, explains that second tithe mixed with a majority of ordinary food is neutralized according to Torah law, and hence need be redeemed only by Rabbinic law. *Ra'avad*, however, explains that according to Torah law, less than a perutah's worth of second tithe need not be redeemed, and may therefore be eaten outside Jerusalem. Only by Rabbinic law must such produce be redeemed.

וּדְרַבָּנַן **And second tithe according to Rabbinic law.** Most opinions agree that according to Torah law even objects that can become permitted are capable of being neutralized. Therefore, in our case, the fruit in question is considered

TRANSLATION AND COMMENTARY

rendered permitted through some other means — in this case, redemption. Therefore, according to Torah law, the half-perutah's worth of second tithe contained in the mixture is neutralized by the majority of ordinary food, and it is only by Rabbinic law that the second tithe retains its identity, thereby requiring redemption in order to be eaten outside Jerusalem. But the unmixed half-perutah's worth of second tithe is in a different category. If it is to be redeemed, it must be redeemed even according to Torah law. Now, the half-perutah of second tithe in the mixture — which requires redemption only by Rabbinic law — cannot combine with the half-perutah that requires redemption by Torah law in order to make up the minimum amount of a perutah needed to effect second-tithe redemption according to Torah law. If such an act of redemption were carried out, it would be ineffective and would lead to the prohibited eating of unredeemed second-tithe produce outside Jerusalem. Now since the second-tithe produce mixed with the ordinary food cannot be redeemed, it can be neutralized by a simple majority of ordinary food. This poses no contradiction, however, to the ruling of Ḥizkiyah, who says that second tithe worth less than a perutah can be redeemed with coins that have already been used to redeem other second-tithe produce.

וְנֵיתֵי דְּמַאי [1]The Gemara again objects: If the owner of the second-tithe produce, which is worth less than a perutah and is mixed with other produce, cannot combine the half-perutah's worth of second tithe found in the mixture with another half-perutah's worth of second-tithe produce because that other second-tithe produce requires redemption by Torah law, let him assemble a different combination that in its entirety requires redemption only by Rabbinic law. **Let him bring doubtfully tithed produce** known as *demai* — produce purchased from a person who we suspect may not have separated the various tithes, and from which the buyer must separate tithes by Rabbinic decree. Since the requirement to tithe *demai* is only Rabbinic in origin, it is only by Rabbinic law that second tithe separated from *demai* needs to be redeemed. In our case, then, rather than relying on neutralization by a majority of permissible food, let the owner of the second-tithe produce worth half a perutah contained in the mixture (which only requires redemption by Rabbinic law) combine it with another half-perutah of second-tithe produce separated from *demai* (which also requires redemption only by Rabbinic law), and redeem the two together with a single perutah. Once again, if this suggestion is accepted, the objection against Ḥizkiyah's ruling remains.

דִּלְמָא אָתֵי לְאַתּוּיֵי וַדַּאי [2]The Gemara answers: This solution is forbidden by Rabbinic decree, **lest a person bring produce that is definitely second tithe** and combine a half-perutah of such second-tithe produce with the half-perutah of second-tithe produce found in the mixture, which must only be redeemed by Rabbinic law. Thus, even according to Ḥizkiyah, a situation exists where it is impossible to redeem second tithe worth less than a perutah. In such circumstances, neutralization is the only way to render the tithe permissible outside Jerusalem.

וְנֵיתֵי שְׁתֵּי פְּרוּטוֹת [3]The Gemara now argues that, according to Ḥizkiyah, there is still a way in which the second tithe in the mixture could be redeemed: **Let him bring two perutot and with them redeem** second **tithe**

[1]וְנֵיתֵי דְּמַאי!
[2]דִּלְמָא אָתֵי לְאַתּוּיֵי וַדַּאי.
[3]וְנֵיתֵי שְׁתֵּי פְּרוּטוֹת וּנְחַלֵּל עֲלַיְיהוּ מַעֲשֵׂר בִּפְרוּטָה וּמֶחֱצָה,

LITERAL TRANSLATION

[1]Then let him bring doubtfully tithed produce!
[2]Perhaps he will come to bring definite [second tithe].
[3]Then let him bring two perutot and let him redeem with them tithe worth a perutah and-a-half,

RASHI

וניתי — חצי שוה פרוטה דמעשר שני של דמאי הלקוח מעם הארץ, דאיסורו ופדיונו דרבנן, דמדאורייתא כל אדם נאמן על המעשרות. **דלמא אתי לאתויי ודאי** — ואז נמצא שוה חצי פרוטה שאינו מעורב נאכל בלא חילול. **וניתי שתי פרוטות** — נחושת.

CONCEPTS

דְּמַאי ***Demai*, doubtfully tithed produce.** Produce purchased from a person who was not known to be scrupulously observant of the laws of tithes (*Am ha'aretz* — עַם הָאָרֶץ). According to Torah law, *all* produce is assumed to have been tithed, since most people do tithe their produce properly (even those who are not known to be observant); thus, even produce purchased from an *am ha'aretz* may be eaten without being tithed, according to Torah law. However, since there was a small percentage of people who did not tithe their produce properly, the Rabbis decreed that produce purchased from an *am ha'aretz* could only be eaten after terumah and first and second tithes had been separated from it. The laws pertaining to *demai* — which is treated less stringently than ordinary untithed produce in other respects as well — are set forth in the Mishnah tractate *Demai*.

NOTES

second tithe only according to Rabbinic law, for according to Torah law it is neutralized by a simple majority. *Ra'avad* offers an alternate explanation. He claims that according to Torah law, second tithe worth less than a perutah does not require redemption, and may be eaten outside Jerusalem. It is only Rabbinic law that prohibits the eating of such second tithe outside Jerusalem.

Rabbi Ḥayyim of Brisk explains that eating second tithe outside Jerusalem is prohibited because it frustrates the positive commandment of redeeming second tithe and bringing it to Jerusalem. If the second tithe is worth less than a perutah, this positive commandment is inapplicable since such second tithe cannot be redeemed. Consequently, according to Torah law such second tithe may be eaten outside Jerusalem. It would appear from *Ra'avad,* however, that second tithe worth less than a perutah does not have the same degree of sanctity as ordinary second tithe.

[1]וּנְחַלֵּל הַאי עַל הֵיאָךְ יְתֵירָא! [2]מִי סָבְרַתְּ פְּרוּטָה וּמֶחֱצָה תָּפְסָה שְׁתֵּי פְּרוּטוֹת? [3]לָא. פְּרוּטָה תָּפְסָה פְּרוּטָה, וַחֲצִי פְּרוּטָה לָא תָּפְסָה. [4]הֲדַר הָוְיָא לֵיהּ דְּאוֹרַיְיתָא וּדְרַבָּנַן, [5]וּדְאוֹרַיְיתָא וּדְרַבָּנַן לָא מִצְטָרְפִי.
[6]וְנֵיתֵי אִיסָּר!
[7]דִּלְמָא אָתֵי לְאַתוּיֵי פְּרוּטוֹת.

LITERAL TRANSLATION

[1]and let him redeem this with that remainder! [2]Do you think that a perutah-and-a-half sanctifies (lit., "seizes") two perutot? [3]No. The perutah sanctifies a perutah, but the half-perutah does not sanctify. [4]It returns to being [second tithe] according to Torah law and [second tithe] according to Rabbinic law, [5]and [second tithe] according to Torah law and [second tithe] according to Rabbinic law are not combined.
[6]Then let him bring an isar!
[7]Perhaps he will come to bring perutot.

TRANSLATION AND COMMENTARY

worth only **a perutah-and-a-half,** [1]**and then he can redeem** the half-perutah of second tithe found in the mixture **with the remainder** — the half-perutah left over from redeeming the second tithe worth a perutah-and-a-half! If the second tithe in the mixture can be redeemed in this way, the law should be that it cannot be neutralized. We return, then, to our initial question against Ḥizkiyah: Why does the Mishnah imply that the tithe can be neutralized?

מִי סָבְרַתְּ [2]The Gemara rejects this argument: **Do you think that a perutah-and-a-half** worth of second tithe acts as a single unit and **takes effect on two perutot**, rendering sacred the entire first perutah and half of the second perutah, thereby leaving a half-perutah available for future redemption of a half-perutah's worth of second tithe? [3]**No. One perutah's** worth of second-tithe produce **takes effect on the** first **perutah** and consecrates it, **but** the remaining **half-perutah's** worth of second tithe **does not take effect** at all on the remaining perutah of redemption money. Thus the second perutah remains unused and unconsecrated, and is not regarded as "first money" for the purposes of redeeming a half-perutah's worth of second tithe. And if you should argue that the half-perutah of second-tithe produce found in the mixture should combine with the other half-perutah of second tithe, [4]this **again would be considered** a combination of **second tithe according to Torah law** — the half perutah's worth of second-tithe produce, **and second tithe according to Rabbinic law** — the second tithe found in the mixture, [5]**and second tithe according to Torah law cannot be combined with second tithe according to Rabbinic law,** as explained above. Thus, the second tithe found in the mixture cannot be redeemed in this way either. As a result, even according to Ḥizkiyah, second tithe cannot always be rendered permissible by means of redemption, and the rules of neutralization apply.

וְנֵיתֵי אִיסָּר [6]The Gemara now makes a final suggestion as to how, according to Ḥizkiyah, second tithe worth less than a perutah and found in a mixture may be redeemed: **Then let him bring an isar** — a single coin worth eight perutot — and use it to redeem a quantity of second-tithe somewhat less than the full value of the isar. For even though one-and-a-half perutot's worth of second tithe cannot consecrate two separate perutot, a quantity of second-tithe produce less than the value of the coin being used for redemption can consecrate the single coin of larger denomination, and the remainder (the "first money") may then be used to redeem the second-tithe produce found in the mixture! And if the second tithe *can* be redeemed, the law should be that it cannot be neutralized.

דִּלְמָא אָתֵי לְאַתוּיֵי פְּרוּטוֹת [7]The Gemara answers: This solution is forbidden by Rabbinic decree, **lest a person bring** separate **perutot** and attempt to redeem one-and-a-half perutot's worth of second tithe with them (which is impossible, as explained above). Thus, there is no way to redeem the mixture containing half a perutah's worth of second tithe. Therefore even according to Ḥizkiyah, such second-tithe produce can be

RASHI

ויחלל עליהן מעשר שוה פרוטה ומחצה – ונחלליה להאי מעורב על היאך חצי פרוטה יתירא, דהויא ליה כדחזקיה. **מי סברת שוה פרוטה ומחצה** – מעשר. **תפסה שתי פרוטות** – בקדושה, דנמצי היאך לאיצטרופי בהדייהו שכבר נתפסו. **פרוטה תפסה שוה פרוטה** – מן המעשר. **חצי פרוטה** – הנותר במעשר. **לא תפסה** – לפרוטה שניה, ואם תאמר המעורב בו יצטרף להשלים! הדר הוה ליה דאורייתא ודרבנן. ואם באת לומר: דחזקיה נמי היכי משכחת שיש עודף, על ידי מי נתפס? משכחת ליה במחלל מעשר בסלע שלם, או בשקל או באיסר, שאפילו לא היה המעשר שוה אלא שלש פרוטות, נתפס כל האיסר. **וניתי איסר שלם** – ויחלל עליו מעשר בפחות מדמיו. **גזירה דלמא אתי לאתויי שתי פרוטות** – ומעשר בפרוטה ומחצה, ונמצא שוה חצי פרוטה נאכל בלא חלול, הלכך טוב לו שיבטל ברוב.

NOTES

דִּלְמָא אָתֵי לְאַתוּיֵי פְּרוּטוֹת **Perhaps he will come to bring perutot.** *Tosafot* explains that the Rabbis issued a decree in this case forbidding redemption by means of an isar. Therefore, the option of redemption is non-existent and the second tithe is not considered something that can be permitted. According to *Ramban,* there was no such

TRANSLATION AND COMMENTARY

neutralized by a majority, as the Mishnah implies. There is thus no conclusive proof from the Mishnah against the ruling of Ḥizkiyah.

וְשֶׁנִּכְנַס לִירוּשָׁלַיִם וְיָצָא [1]The Gemara now turns to the Baraita's second case of second tithe mixed with ordinary food that is neutralized by a simple majority of the permissible food — second tithe which entered Jerusalem and later left. Here too the Gemara must explain why there is no other means by which such second tithe can be permitted, for if it could be permitted through any other means, the second tithe could not be neutralized, no matter how great the amount of ordinary food in the mixture. The Baraita stated that second-tithe produce **"which entered Jerusalem but** then **left"** is neutralized by a simple majority of ordinary produce. [2] **Why,** the Gemara asks, is such second tithe permitted after neutralization by a majority of permissible food? [3]**Let** the owner **bring** the mixture **back into** Jerusalem and eat it there!

בְּשֶׁנִּטְמָא [4]The Gemara answers: The Baraita is referring to a case **where** the second tithe **had become ritually** impure, and therefore can no longer be eaten even in Jerusalem.

וְנִפְרְקֵיהּ [5]In response to this answer the Gemara objects that such second tithe can still be permitted by means other than neutralization, and therefore the law should be that it cannot be neutralized: **Let him redeem** the second-tithe produce, **for Rabbi Elazar said:** [6]**"From where do we know that second-tithe** produce **that has become ritually impure may be redeemed** [53B] **even in Jerusalem** itself, where ritually pure tithe cannot be redeemed? [7]**For it is said** in those verses where the Torah describes the circumstances under which second-tithe produce may be redeemed (Deuteronomy 14:24-25): 'And if the way be too long for you **so that you are unable to carry it** [שְׂאֵתוֹ] ... then you shall turn it into money,' [8]**and** there the word **'carry'** (*se'eto* — שְׂאֵתוֹ) **refers to eating,** a use of the word *se'eto* found elsewhere, [9]**as it is said** (Genesis 43:34): **'And he** [Joseph] **took portions** [*masot* — מַשְׂאֹת — derived from the same root as *se'eto*] to them **from before him,'** where the word 'portions' refers to portions of food." Thus Rabbi Elazar interprets the verses from Deuteronomy about the laws of tithe-redemption as follows: If you are too far away from Jerusalem to bring the second tithe to consume it in the city, you may redeem it; and if you have brought the second tithe to Jerusalem but cannot eat it because it is ritually impure, you may redeem it even in Jerusalem. Now, if second tithe that is ritually impure can always be redeemed, why did the Baraita say that ritually impure second tithe that

LITERAL TRANSLATION

[1]"And which entered Jerusalem and went out." [2]But why? [3]Let him bring it back in again!

[4]Where it had become ritually impure.

[5]Then let him redeem it, for Rabbi Elazar said: [6]"From where [do we know] that second tithe that has become ritually impure may be redeemed [53B] even in Jerusalem? [7]As it is said: 'So that you are unable to carry it.' [8]And 'carry' only [means] eating, [9]as it is said: 'And he took portions from before him.'"

[1]"וְשֶׁנִּכְנַס לִירוּשָׁלַיִם וְיָצָא".
[2]וְאַמַּאי? [3]וְלִיהֲדַר וּנְעַיְּילֵיהּ!
[4]בְּשֶׁנִּטְמָא.
[5]וְנִפְרְקֵיהּ, דְּאָמַר רַבִּי אֶלְעָזָר:
[6]"מִנַּיִן לְמַעֲשֵׂר שֵׁנִי שֶׁנִּטְמָא
שֶׁפּוֹדִין אוֹתוֹ [53B] אֲפִילּוּ
בִּירוּשָׁלַיִם? [7]שֶׁנֶּאֱמַר: 'כִּי לֹא
תוּכַל שְׂאֵתוֹ'. [8]וְאֵין 'שְׂאֵת' אֶלָּא
אֲכִילָה, [9]שֶׁנֶּאֱמַר: 'וַיִּשָּׂא מַשְׂאֹת
מֵאֵת פָּנָיו'"!

RASHI

וליעייליה — עם תערובתו, ויאכלנו בירושלים. **וניפרקיה** — קא סלקא דעתך ביש בו שוה פרוטה נמי קאמר. **ואפילו בירושלים** — שאין מעשר טהור נפדה שם, דכתיב (דברים יד) "כי ירחק ממך [וגו'] ונתת בכסף" ולא כשהיה בירושלים.

BACKGROUND

מַעֲשֵׂר שֵׁנִי שֶׁנִּטְמָא Second tithe that became ritually impure. According to Torah law, second tithe must be eaten in Jerusalem in a state of ritual purity. Hence it may not be eaten if it became ritually impure. However, ritually impure second tithe may be redeemed by exchanging it for money, after which it may be eaten like any other ritually impure produce.

וְאֵין שְׂאֵת אֶלָּא אֲכִילָה And "carry" only means eating. The verb used here — לשאת — has various meanings, including "to carry," "to bear," "to endure." Here the Gemara interprets this term in the sense of "eating," because when the Torah speaks of being "unable to carry" second-tithe produce, it presumably refers to all obstacles to eating the produce in Jerusalem, whether physical (e.g., because the produce is too heavy) or of another nature (e.g., because it is ritually impure).

NOTES

Rabbinic decree, and redemption by means of an isar is in fact permitted. However, since there is the danger that one may use individual perutot, the Rabbis did not allow that the redemption take place by means of an isar. Therefore the second tithe in our case is not available for redemption, and is consequently not considered something that can be permitted by any means other than neutralization.

וְאֵין שְׂאֵת אֶלָּא אֲכִילָה And "carry" only means eating. The commentators object to the Gemara's use of Deuteronomy 14:24 as a proof text, since that verse clearly speaks of tithe outside Jerusalem ("And if the way be too long for you," etc.). *Rashi* on *Sanhedrin* 112b answers that the two clauses which make up this verse can be understood independently of each other. In other words, "and if the way be too long for you" describes one situation, and "so that you are unable to carry [= eat] it" (i.e., because it is ritually impure) describes another. In both cases the tithe may be redeemed.

HALAKHAH

מַעֲשֵׂר שֵׁנִי שֶׁנִּטְמָא Second tithe that became ritually impure. "If second tithe became ritually impure (even in Jerusalem), it should be redeemed. The redemption money must be used to buy food, which must be eaten in a state of ritual purity, as if it were second tithe, and it may then be eaten even outside Jerusalem." (*Rambam, Sefer Zeraim, Hilkhot Ma'aser Sheni* 2:12, 3:3.)

LITERAL TRANSLATION

[1] Rather, [it refers to] what was bought with second-tithe money.

[2] What was bought with second-tithe money let him also redeem it, [3] as we have learned: "That which was bought with second-tithe money which became ritually impure may be redeemed."

[4] [It is] according to Rabbi Yehudah, who said: "It must be buried."

[5] If [it is according to] Rabbi Yehudah, why does it specify "went out"? [6] Even if it did not go out also!

[1] אֶלָּא, בְּלָקוּחַ בְּכֶסֶף מַעֲשֵׂר שֵׁנִי.

[2] לָקוּחַ בְּכֶסֶף מַעֲשֵׂר נַמִי לִיפְרְקֵיהּ, [3] דִּתְנַן: "הַלָּקוּחַ בְּכֶסֶף מַעֲשֵׂר שֵׁנִי שֶׁנִּטְמָא יִפָּדֶה".

[4] כְּרַבִּי יְהוּדָה, דְּאָמַר: "יִקָּבֵר".

[5] אִי רַבִּי יְהוּדָה, מַאי אִירְיָא "יָצָא"? [6] אֲפִילּוּ לֹא יָצָא נַמִי!

RASHI

בלקוח – מעשר זה, ולא הוא עצמו היה מעשר, אלא נרכי סעודה שלקח בירושלים בכסף מעשר. יקבר – דקא סבר: לא אלים למיתפס פדיונו.

TRANSLATION AND COMMENTARY

entered Jerusalem and later went out is neutralized by a majority of permissible food? Let the owner make it permissible by redeeming it!

אֶלָּא [1] The Gemara answers by suggesting another situation in which, as the Baraita says, second tithe that entered and left Jerusalem may become neutralized in a larger quantity of permitted food. **Rather,** says the Gemara, the Baraita **is referring** not to original second-tithe produce, but **to** foodstuffs **bought with second-tithe money** for the purpose of being consumed in Jerusalem, and which subsequently became ritually impure. Since it is now ritually impure, it may not be returned to Jerusalem to be eaten, and since it is produce purchased with second-tithe money rather than actual second-tithe produce, it cannot be redeemed.

לָקוּחַ בְּכֶסֶף מַעֲשֵׂר נַמִי לִיפְרְקֵיהּ [2] The Gemara now challenges this last assumption: On what basis do we assume that produce purchased with second-tithe money and which subsequently became ritually impure may not be redeemed? Let the owner **redeem** the foodstuffs that he has **bought with second-tithe money,** [3] **as we learned** elsewhere in the Mishnah (*Ma'aser Sheni* 3:10): "Foodstuffs **bought with second-tithe money and which became ritually impure may be redeemed"!** And if they can be redeemed, why is it possible for them to be neutralized?

כְּרַבִּי יְהוּדָה [4] The Gemara answers: The Baraita's ruling, which implies that such foodstuffs may not be redeemed, **is in accordance with** the viewpoint of **Rabbi Yehudah, who said** in the same Mishnah: "Foodstuffs bought with second-tithe money and which became ritually impure **must be buried,**" and cannot be redeemed. Therefore, if such foodstuffs inadvertently became mixed with ordinary food, the only means available for rendering the mixture fit for consumption is by neutralization. They are neutralized in a mixture where the ordinary food comprises the majority, for otherwise they may neither be eaten nor redeemed.

אִי רַבִּי יְהוּדָה [5] The Gemara is still not satisfied with this interpretation: **If** the Baraita indeed deals with foodstuffs bought with second-tithe money, and is in accordance with the viewpoint of **Rabbi Yehudah, why does it speak of** a case in which the foodstuffs **"went out"** from Jerusalem? [6] The same law should apply **even if** the foodstuffs **did not leave** Jerusalem, for Rabbi Yehudah is of the opinion that foodstuffs bought with second-tithe money and which became ritually impure must be buried no matter where they are! We remain, therefore, with our original question: What circumstances was the Baraita describing when it ruled that second-tithe produce that had entered and left Jerusalem could be neutralized by a majority of permitted food?

NOTES

הַלָּקוּחַ בְּכֶסֶף מַעֲשֵׂר יִקָּבֵר **Something that was bought with second-tithe money must be buried.** The Mishnah (*Ma'aser Sheni* 3:10) has already taken note of the paradox inherent in Rabbi Yehudah's view: According to that Sage, second tithe that has become ritually impure can be redeemed, but food bought with second-tithe money (which, theoretically, should be treated less strictly) cannot!

Some authorities answer (cf. *Zevaḥim* 49a) that since food bought with second-tithe money is not as sacred as actual second tithe, it cannot be redeemed as easily. *Tosafot,* however, suggests (following Sifrei and other sources) that Rabbi Yehudah's distinction between second tithe and food bought with second-tithe money is based on a Midrashic interpretation of the Biblical text which speaks of second tithe, and not food bought with second-tithe money, rather than on logical argumentation.

HALAKHAH

הַלָּקוּחַ בְּכֶסֶף מַעֲשֵׂר שֵׁנִי שֶׁנִּטְמָא **Something that was bought with second-tithe money and which became ritually impure.** "Produce purchased with second-tithe money may not be redeemed outside Jerusalem unless it was rendered ritually impure by a primary source of ritual impurity (lit., 'a father of ritual impurity' — אַב הַטּוּמְאָה, for example, a dead animal). Instead, it must be brought to Jerusalem and eaten there. In this respect, produce purchased with second-tithe money is treated more stringently than second tithe itself." (*Rambam, Sefer Zeraim, Hilkhot Ma'aser Sheni* 7:1-2.)

TRANSLATION AND COMMENTARY

אֶלָּא [1]The Gemara answers by rejecting this interpretation of the Baraita and suggesting a new one: **Rather, in fact,** the Baraita **is referring to ritually pure second tithe** (whether actual second-tithe produce or foodstuffs purchased with second-tithe money) which entered and left Jerusalem. In order to understand why the Baraita stated that such second-tithe produce can be neutralized by a majority of permitted food, we must first understand **what was meant by** the statement that the produce **"went out"** from Jerusalem. [2]The Gemara explains that this does not mean that the produce actually left Jerusalem, but rather **that the partitions** — the walls of Jerusalem — **fell.** The Baraita refers to a particular case where the walls of Jerusalem fell after the produce had entered the city. Now, the law is that once second tithe has entered the walls of Jerusalem it may no longer be redeemed, since it is "absorbed," as it were, by the walls, and must therefore be eaten in Jerusalem. However, if the walls of Jerusalem fall, the second tithe may no longer be eaten, since second tithe may only be eaten within the walls of Jerusalem. Therefore, if such produce became inadvertently mixed with ordinary food, it is neutralized by a majority of the permitted food, for the second-tithe produce may otherwise neither be eaten nor redeemed.

וְהָאָמַר רָבָא [3]The Gemara raises an objection: **But surely Rava** said: The rule about **partitions for eating** — that second tithe may only be eaten within the walls of Jerusalem — **applies by Torah law,** [4]but the rule about **partitions for absorption** — that second tithe may no longer be redeemed after it has entered the city— **applies** only **by Rabbinic law.** Neutralization was not the only way to render such produce fit for consumption. It is true that Torah law requires that second tithe be eaten only within the walls of Jerusalem, based on the verse (Deuteronomy 12:18) which says: "But you must eat them before the Lord your God," and this is understood as a reference to the city of Jerusalem. But the rule that second tithe that has entered Jerusalem is "absorbed," as it were, by the walls and hence may no longer be redeemed even after it has left the city, applies only by Rabbinic decree. [5]Based on Rava's statement, the Gemara now argues: It stands to reason that **the Rabbis** only **decreed** that the walls of Jerusalem should "absorb" second tithe brought into the city in a case **where the walls are** still **standing** and the tithe was taken out of the city. [6]But **if** the walls of the city **are no** longer **standing, the Rabbis** presumably **did not** issue such a **decree!** Thus, once the walls of Jerusalem came down, the Rabbinic decree forbidding the redemption of second tithe that had entered and then left the city should no longer apply. And since the tithe can be redeemed, why does the Baraita rule that second tithe which entered and left Jerusalem can be neutralized by a majority of permitted food?

לָא פְּלוּג רַבָּנַן [7]Despite this objection, the Gemara continues to maintain that the Baraita is referring to second tithe that entered and left Jerusalem. The Rabbis did indeed apply the decree that once second tithe has entered Jerusalem it can no longer be redeemed, even if the walls of the city subsequently fell. The Gemara explains: **The Rabbis did not differentiate between** a case **where the walls** of Jerusalem **are standing** when the second tithe was removed from the city **and** a case **where the walls are no** longer **standing.** The Rabbinic decree that the walls of Jerusalem "absorb" second tithe which enters the city was an all-embracing enactment which applies whether the walls are still standing or not. Thus the interpretation according to

[1]אֶלָּא, לְעוֹלָם בְּטָהוֹר. וּמַאי ״יָצָא״? [2]דִּנְפוּל מְחִיצוֹת.
[3]וְהָאָמַר רָבָא: מְחִיצָה לֶאֱכוֹל דְּאוֹרַיְיתָא; [4]מְחִיצוֹת לִקְלוֹט דְּרַבָּנַן. [5]וְכִי גָּזְרוּ דְּרַבָּנַן, כִּי אִיתְנְהוּ לִמְחִיצוֹת; [6]כִּי לֵיתְנְהוּ לִמְחִיצוֹת, לָא גָּזְרוּ רַבָּנַן!
[7]לָא פְּלוּג רַבָּנַן בֵּין אִיתְנְהוּ לִמְחִיצוֹת בֵּין לֵיתְנְהוּ לִמְחִיצוֹת.

LITERAL TRANSLATION

[1]Rather, in fact, [it refers] to ritually pure [tithe]. And what does "went out" [mean]? [2]That the partitions had fallen.

[3]But surely Rava said: Partitions for eating [apply] by Torah law; [4]partitions for absorption [apply] by Rabbinic law. [5]And when the Rabbis decreed, [it was] when the partitions exist; [6][but] when the partitions do not exist, the Rabbis did not decree!

[7]The Rabbis did not differentiate between when partitions exist and when partitions do not exist.

RASHI

אלא לעולם בטהור — בין מעשר בין לקוח, ודקאמר נעייליה וניכליה. **מאי יצא** — נמי דקאמר — דנפול מחיצות חומת ירושלים, ושוב אין מעשר נאכל שם עד שיעמדו מחיצות, דבעינן ״לפני ה׳ תאכלנו״ (דברים יב), ובפדייה נמי לא, דקלטוהו מחיצות מלפדותו עוד משנכנס לתוכו. **והאמר רבא** — במסכת מכות (כ,א). **מחיצה לאכול דאורייתא מחיצה לקלוט דרבנן** — מחיצה שנאמרה בתורה לא הוזכרה אלא לאכול בתוכה, ושאמרו במשנה מחיצות קולטות אותם מלפדות עוד אם יצא, דרבנן היא. **וכי גזור רבנן כו׳** — לאו רבא קאמר לה אלא המקשה קאמר: מדאמר רבא קליטת מחיצות מדרבנן בעלמא היא, והשתא דנפול מחיצות ליתא לההיא גזירה, דכי גזור רבנן — היכא דאיתנהו, וזה הוציא את המעשר לחוץ. אבל כי ליתנהו — לא גזור, הלכך ניפרקיה ואמאי בטלי? **ומשני לא פלוג רבנן** — בין יוצא מתוכן לנפלו, דקליטת מחיצות גזרו בסתם, בין איתנהו בין ליתנהו.

BACKGROUND

מְחִיצוֹת Partitions. The Torah states (Deuteronomy 14:25) that second tithe must be brought "to *the place* which the Lord your God shall choose" (i.e., Jerusalem). Thus it appears that the Torah is referring to a specific and well-defined area — namely, the area within the ancient walls of Jerusalem. Hence, if the ancient walls of Jerusalem are destroyed, there is no longer any well-defined "place" to which the second tithe may be brought.

TRANSLATION AND COMMENTARY

which the Baraita deals with second tithe that entered the city, the walls of which subsequently fell, may be accepted.

רַב הוּנָא בַּר יְהוּדָה [1]The Gemara now returns to the objection that was raised against the position of Ḥizkiyah from the first part of the Baraita (see above, 53a), and suggests a new solution. The Baraita had listed second tithe worth less than a perutah as an example of second tithe that could be neutralized by a majority of permitted food. As was pointed out above, this seems to contradict the ruling of Ḥizkiyah that second tithe worth less than a perutah may be rendered fit for consumption outside Jerusalem by redeeming it with money that had already been used to redeem other second tithe. For if Ḥizkiyah is correct in stating that second-tithe produce worth less than a perutah can be rendered permissible by means other than neutralization, then neutralization, which is a remedy of last resort, should not be available. **Rav Huna bar Yehudah said in the name of Rav Sheshet:** The Baraita does not, as we had previously understood it, list two separate cases in which second tithe may be neutralized by a majority of permitted food — i.e., (1) second tithe worth less than a perutah, and (2) second tithe that left Jerusalem. [2]Rather, the Baraita **speaks of** only **a single case: Second tithe** that **is not worth a perutah which entered Jerusalem and** went out. Such produce can be neutralized by a majority of permitted food, since it can otherwise be neither eaten nor redeemed. In such a case even Ḥizkiyah would agree that since the second tithe had already entered Jerusalem, it could no longer be redeemed. Thus the only possible means whereby the produce could be rendered permissible would be, as the Baraita stated, neutralization by a majority.

אַמַּאי [3]The Gemara now raises the same questions that it had raised against the previous interpretations: **Why** is such tithe neutralized by a majority of permitted food? **Let** the owner **bring** the mixture **back into** Jerusalem **and eat it** there!

דִּנְפוּל מְחִיצוֹת [4]Once again the Gemara answers: According to the interpretation offered by Rav Huna bar Yehudah, the Baraita refers not to a case in which the second tithe actually left the city, but rather to a case **where the walls** of Jerusalem **fell,** and hence the tithe may no longer be eaten even in Jerusalem.

וְנִפְרְקֵיהּ [5]The Gemara objects once again: Granted that the tithe may not be eaten, but **let** the owner **redeem it!** [6]**Surely Rava said:** The rule about **partitions for eating** — that second tithe may only be eaten within the walls of Jerusalem — **applies by Torah law,** but the rule about **partitions for absorption** — that second tithe may no longer be redeemed after it has entered the city — applies only **by Rabbinic law,** as explained above. [7]Now it stands to reason that **the Rabbis** issued their **decree** that the walls of Jerusalem "absorb" second tithe brought into the city only with respect to a case **where the walls** of Jerusalem **are** still **standing** and the second tithe was removed from the city. [8]But **if** the walls of the city **are no** longer **standing, the Rabbis** presumably **did not** issue such a **decree!** Thus, the Rabbinic decree forbidding the redemption of produce after it had

[1]רַב הוּנָא בַּר יְהוּדָה אֲמַר רַב שֵׁשֶׁת: [2]חֲדָא קָתָנֵי: ״מַעֲשֵׂר שֵׁנִי שֶׁאֵין בּוֹ שָׁוֶה פְּרוּטָה שֶׁנִּכְנָס לִירוּשָׁלַיִם וְיָצָא״.
[3]אַמַּאי? וְנִיהֲדַר וּנְעַיְּילֵיהּ וְנֵיכְלֵיהּ!
[4]דִּנְפוּל מְחִיצוֹת.
[5]וְנִפְרְקֵיהּ! [6]הָאָמַר רָבָא: מְחִיצָה לֶאֱכוֹל דְּאוֹרַיְיתָא; מְחִיצָה לִקְלוֹט דְּרַבָּנַן. [7]וְכִי גָּזְרוּ רַבָּנַן, כִּי אִיתְנְהוּ לִמְחִיצוֹת; [8]כִּי לֵיתְנְהוּ לִמְחִיצוֹת, לָא גָּזְרוּ רַבָּנַן!

LITERAL TRANSLATION

[1]Rav Huna bar Yehudah said in the name of Rav Sheshet: [2]It teaches one [case]: "Second tithe that is not worth a perutah which entered Jerusalem and went out."

[3]Why? Let him bring it back in again and eat it!

[4]When the partitions had fallen.

[5]Then let him redeem it! [6]Surely Rava said: Partitions for eating [apply] by Torah law; partitions for absorption [apply] by Rabbinic law. [7]And when the Rabbis decreed, [it was] when the partitions exist; [8][but when] the partitions do not exist, the Rabbis did not decree!

RASHI

רב הונא ברבי יהודה אמר — הא דאותבת לחזקיה מרישא דקתני "כאיזה מעשר אמרו שאין בו שוה פרוטה" וקשיא לך ליעבד כחזקיה — לא קשיא. **חדא קתני אין בו שוה פרוטה שנכנס לירושלים ויצא** — דקליטת מחיצות מעכבת מלחללו עוד על מעות הראשונות. **וניהדר ונעייליה וניכליה** — בירושלים עם תערובתו. **דנפול מחיצות** — והיינו "יצא" דקתני.

SAGES

רַב הוּנָא בַּר יְהוּדָה **Rav Huna bar Yehudah.** A Babylonian Amora of the fourth generation, Rav Huna bar Yehudah transmits Halakhic rulings in the names of Rav Sheshet and Rav Naḥman. He was a colleague of Rava.

BACKGROUND

מַעֲשֵׂר שֵׁנִי שֶׁאֵין בּוֹ שָׁוֶה פְּרוּטָה **Second tithe that is not worth a perutah.** According to the Halakhah, a perutah is the smallest significant unit of currency; anything worth less is regarded as if it is worthless. Hence it is impossible to redeem second tithe worth less than a perutah: It cannot be redeemed with a coin worth less than a perutah, since such a coin is not considered money. Nor can it be redeemed with a coin worth more than a perutah, since the produce itself is not considered valuable enough to be redeemed.

HALAKHAH

מַעֲשֵׂר שֵׁנִי שֶׁאֵין בּוֹ שָׁוֶה פְּרוּטָה **Second tithe that is not worth a perutah.** "If second tithe entered Jerusalem and later left the city, and afterwards the walls of Jerusalem fell, the second tithe may neither be returned to the city nor redeemed, since the walls are no longer standing. Hence, even second tithe worth less than a perutah is neutralized

TRANSLATION AND COMMENTARY

entered Jerusalem and then left it should not apply if the walls are no longer standing! And if the second tithe *can* be redeemed, the law should be that it cannot be neutralized!

לָא פְּלוּג רַבָּנַן [1]The Gemara replies: **The Rabbis did not differentiate** between a case in which the walls of Jerusalem are standing when the second tithe was removed from the city and a case in which the walls are no longer standing; in either case the produce may not be redeemed. Having decreed that the walls of Jerusalem "absorb," as it were, the second tithe, thus prohibiting its redemption, the Rabbis did not see fit to alter their decree to take into account the unlikely case where the walls of Jerusalem fell.

אִי הָכִי [2]The Gemara raises one final objection: **If so,** if the Baraita refers to a case where the walls of the city fell down, **why did it specifically mention** a case where the second tithe in the mixture **"is not worth a perutah"?** [3]**Even if it *is*** worth a perutah, the same rules should apply, because any second tithe that entered Jerusalem while the walls were still standing may be neither eaten nor redeemed after the walls have fallen. Hence, even if the second tithe in the mixture is worth a perutah or more, it should be neutralized by a majority of permitted food!

לָא מִיבָּעְיָא קָאָמַר [4]The Gemara now agrees that this law would indeed apply even if the tithe was worth a perutah or more, but answers that the Baraita specifically brought the case of second tithe worth less than a perutah because it **is speaking in the style of "there is no need."** The Baraita intentionally chose to discuss a problematic case, where one might have thought that a different ruling would apply, rather than the simpler case in which "there is no need" to state the law. The Gemara now explains why second tithe worth less than a perutah presents a problem, using the "no-need" form of presentation: [5]**There is no need to state where** the second tithe **is worth a perutah** and can unquestionably be redeemed before it enters Jerusalem, **that** when it enters the city, **the walls** of the city **"absorb" it** so that it may no longer be redeemed even if the walls subsequently fall. [6]**But** in a case **where** the second tithe **is not** worth a perutah — in which case the only way of redeeming it is the method suggested earlier by Ḥizkiyah — **one might say** that since in any case such tithe can only be redeemed with a coin that has previously been used for the redemption of second tithe, the Rabbis did not issue a decree to remedy this unusual situation, and therefore **the walls** of Jerusalem **do not "absorb" it.** [7]Therefore the Baraita **teaches us** that this is not so, and that even second tithe worth less than a perutah may not be redeemed after it has entered Jerusalem, even if it subsequently left the city or the walls of the city fell. In such a case even Ḥizkiyah would agree that the second tithe is unredeemable by any method. That being the case, the Baraita's statement that such second tithe can be neutralized by a majority of permitted food presents no difficulty to Ḥizkiyah.

תָּנוּ רַבָּנַן [8]The Gemara now seeks the source for the rule that underlies much of the previous discussion — that second tithe worth less than a perutah cannot be redeemed in the ordinary manner: **Our Rabbis taught** in a Baraita: "The Torah states (Leviticus 27:31): 'And **if a man will surely redeem some of his tithe,** he shall add to it the fifth part of it.' [9]The law stated in this verse applies only to ***some of*** his **tithes, but not** to **all of**

[1]לָא פְּלוּג רַבָּנַן. [2]אִי הָכִי, מַאי אִירְיָא אֵין בּוֹ שָׁוֶה פְּרוּטָה? [3]אֲפִילּוּ יֵשׁ בּוֹ נָמֵי! [4]״לָא מִיבָּעְיָא״ קָאָמַר: [5]לָא מִיבָּעְיָא יֵשׁ בּוֹ דְּקָלְטָן לֵיהּ מְחִיצוֹת; [6]אֲבָל אֵין בּוֹ, אֵימָא לָא קָלְטוּ לֵיהּ מְחִיצוֹת. [7]קָא מַשְׁמַע לָן. [8]תָּנוּ רַבָּנַן: ״׳אִם גָּאֹל יִגְאַל אִישׁ מִמַּעַשְׂרוֹ׳. [9]׳מִמַּעַשְׂרוֹ׳ וְלֹא כָּל

LITERAL TRANSLATION

[1]The Rabbis did not differentiate.

[2]If so, why does it specify [that] it is not worth a perutah? [3]Even if it is, [this is] also [the case]!

[4]He is speaking [in the style of] "there is no need."

[5]There is no need [to state] where it is [worth a perutah] that the partitions absorb it; [6]but where it is not, [one might] say [that] the partitions do not absorb it. [7][Therefore] it tells us [otherwise].

[8]Our Rabbis taught: "'If a man will surely redeem some of his tithe.' [9]'Some of his tithe,' but not all

RASHI

אפילו יש בו שוה פרוטה — נמי לאו בר אכילה ולאו בר חילול הוא ואמאי תני ״באיזה מעשר אמרו, בשאין בו שוה פרוטה״ כו׳. **לא מבעיא יש בו** — דכיון דבר פדייה הוא, חיילא עליו קליטת מחיצות דרבנן, ולא מיפרוק תו. אבל אין בו, אימא בכהאי גוונא לא לגזור רבנן קליטת מחיצות לפדייה, דמילתא דלא שכיח היא לחללו על מעות הראשונות, וניעבד ליה כדחזקיה — קא משמע לן.

HALAKHAH

if it became mixed up by accident with a greater quantity of permitted food, since it cannot be rendered permissible in any other way," following Rav Huna bar Yehudah's interpretation of the Baraita. (*Rambam, Sefer Zeraim, Hilkhot Ma'aser Sheni* 6:16.)

מַעַשְׂרוֹ, [1]פְּרָט לְמַעֲשֵׂר שֵׁנִי שֶׁאֵין בּוֹ שָׁוֶה פְּרוּטָה״.
[2]אִיתְּמַר: [3]רַב אַמִי אָמַר: אֵין בּוֹ. [4]רַב אַסִי אָמַר: אֵין בְּחוּמְשׁוֹ. [5]רַבִּי יוֹחָנָן אָמַר: אֵין בּוֹ. [6]רַבִּי שִׁמְעוֹן בֶּן לָקִישׁ אָמַר: אֵין בְּחוּמְשׁוֹ.
[7]מֵיתִיבֵי: ״מַעֲשֵׂר שֵׁנִי שֶׁאֵין בּוֹ שָׁוֶה פְּרוּטָה, [8]דַּיּוֹ שֶׁיֹּאמַר: ׳הוּא וְחוּמְשׁוֹ מְחוּלָּל עַל מָעוֹת רִאשׁוֹנוֹת׳״. [9]בִּשְׁלָמָא לְמַאן דְּאָמַר אֵין בְּחוּמְשׁוֹ, [10]הַיְינוּ דְּקָתָנֵי: ״דַּיּוֹ״; דְּאַף עַל גַּב

LITERAL TRANSLATION

of his tithe, [1]to the exclusion of second tithe that is not worth a perutah."

[2]It was stated: [3]Rav Ammi said: *It* is not worth [a perutah]. [4]Rav Assi said: Its *fifth* is not worth [a perutah]. [5]Rabbi Yoḥanan said: *It* is not worth [a perutah]. [6]Rabbi Shimon ben Lakish said: Its *fifth* is not worth [a perutah].

[7]They raised an objection: "[Regarding] second tithe that is not worth a perutah, [8]it is sufficient that he says: 'It and its fifth is redeemed with the first money.'" [9]Granted according to the one who says [that] its fifth is not worth [a perutah], [10]this is why it teaches: "It is sufficient," for even though

TRANSLATION AND COMMENTARY

his tithes. Since the verse speaks of a person who redeems *'some* of' his tithe rather than one who redeems 'his tithe,' we may infer that the laws of redemption apply only to certain types of tithe, and not to others. [1]From this we may conclude that the verse **excludes second tithe worth less than a perutah** from the laws of redemption."

אִיתְּמַר [2]**It was stated** that the Amoraim disagreed about the interpretation of this Baraita: [3]**Rav Ammi said:** The Baraita excludes from the laws of redemption only second tithe that **is not** itself **worth a perutah**. [4]But **Rav Assi said:** Even if the second tithe itself is worth a perutah or more, it may still not be redeemed if **the fifth of the tithe** that must be added when the owner himself redeems his tithe **is not worth a perutah**. According to Rav Assi, since the verse relates to the law of the fifth that must be added to the value of redeemed produce by anyone redeeming his own second tithe, the exclusion implied by the words "some of his tithe" must be understood as referring to that added fifth. Therefore, the laws of redemption apply only if the fifth that must be added is itself worth at least a perutah. [5]The Gemara also notes a parallel difference of opinion between Rabbi Yoḥanan and Rabbi Shimon ben Lakish on the same issue: **Rabbi Yoḥanan said:** The Baraita excludes from the laws of redemption second tithe that **is not** itself **worth a perutah.** [6]**Rabbi Shimon ben Lakish said:** It excludes from the laws of redemption second tithe **one-fifth of which is not worth a perutah.**

מֵיתִיבֵי [7]**An objection** similar to the ruling of Ḥizkiyah cited above (52b) **was raised** to the viewpoint of Rav Ammi and Rabbi Yoḥanan from the following Baraita: "If a person wishes to redeem **second-tithe** produce that **is not worth a perutah,** and has in his possession a coin that has already been used to redeem other second-tithe produce, [8]**it is sufficient if he says: This** tithe **and** the **fifth of its** value which I must add in order to redeem it **are** hereby **redeemed with** that **first money** I used earlier to redeem other second-tithe produce." The Gemara proceeds to clarify the basis of the objection: The words "it is sufficient" suggest that there might have been a different, more elaborate way to redeem the second tithe, which the Baraita ignores as being unnecessary. [9]Now, argues the Gemara, this Baraita **presents no problem according to the** authorities **who say** that second-tithe produce **the** extra **fifth of which is not worth a perutah** is excluded from the laws of redemption, [10]and **the reason why** the Baraita just cited **states "it is sufficient"** is as follows: Since the second tithe itself is worth a perutah, we might have thought that the tithe must be redeemed by

RASHI

פרט לשאין בו שוה פרוטה — שאינו בכלל גאולה, ולימדך שאינה תופסת פרוטה. **רב אמי אמר אין בו שוה פרוטה** — שנינו, אבל אם יש בו שוה פרוטה — בר גאולה הוא, ותופס פדיונו. **ורב אסי אמר אין בחומשו שוה פרוטה** — שנינו דלאו בר גאולה הוא עד שיהא בו שוה ארבע פרוטות, כדי שיהא ראוי לתוספת חומש דכתיב בהאי קרא. **דיו שיאמר כו׳** — כדחזקיה, ולא אמרינן ימתין עד שיעלנו לירושלים או ימתין עד שיצרפנו עם אחר, דכיון דבחומשיה ליכא [פרוטה], לא קחשיב ודיו בכך.

NOTES

אֵין בְּחוּמְשׁוֹ שָׁוֶה פְּרוּטָה **If a fifth of the second tithe is not worth a perutah.** *Rashi*, followed by our commentary, explains that if the tithe (or a fifth of it) is worth less than a perutah, it cannot be redeemed at all. However, *Rambam* (following the Jerusalem Talmud) apparently understood the Gemara differently. According to him, any amount of second tithe can be redeemed, no matter how little it is worth, and the Gemara's question is whether an extra fifth must be added when redeeming second tithe worth less than a perutah. Still another explanation is offered by *Ra'avad*, who

HALAKHAH

אֵין בְּחוּמְשׁוֹ שָׁוֶה פְּרוּטָה **If a fifth of the second tithe is not worth a perutah.** "Second tithe, a fifth of which is worth less than a perutah, may be redeemed by the owner without adding an additional fifth." (*Rambam, Sefer Zeraim, Hilkhot Ma'aser Sheni* 5:4.)

TRANSLATION AND COMMENTARY

itself with a perutah. Therefore the Baraita comes to teach that **even though** the second tithe **itself is worth a perutah**, [1] **since a fifth of it is not worth a perutah,** it need only be redeemed by means of a coin that had been previously used for tithe redemption. Thus according to the opinion that the Baraita is referring to second tithe a fifth of which is itself worth a perutah, the Baraita **is well** understood. [2] **But according to the** authorities **who say** that the Baraita is referring to second tithe which **is** itself **not worth a perutah**, **what** did the Baraita mean when it said that **"it is sufficient"** that he redeem the tithe with money previously used for redemption of second tithe? How else could he have redeemed the tithe, for surely second tithe worth less than a perutah can only be redeemed by means of a coin that has previously been used for tithe redemption?

קַשְׁיָא [3] Accordingly, the Gemara concludes that it **is difficult** to subscribe to the position of Rav Ammi and Rabbi Yoḥanan, who maintain that the Torah excludes from the laws of redemption only second tithe which is itself worth less than a perutah.

אִיבַּעֲיָא לְהוּ [4] **The** following **question arose** in discussion between the Sages regarding the **fifth** that a person must add when he redeems his own second tithe (and certain other objects, see below): Is it **calculated from the inside or from the outside?** A fifth calculated "from the inside" is a fifth of the value of the article being redeemed. Thus, for example, a fifth "from the inside" of an item worth twenty zuz is four zuz. By contrast, a fifth calculated "from the outside" is a fifth of the total redemption money, i.e., the value of the article itself plus the extra fifth. Thus, a fifth "from the outside" of an item worth twenty zuz is five zuz.

אָמַר רָבִינָא [5] The Gemara now attempts to resolve this question by comparing the redemption of second tithe to the seemingly analogous case in which dedicated property is publicly auctioned in order to restore it to secular use. In such a case, if the person redeeming the property dedicated to the Temple is the same one who dedicated it to the Temple in the first place, he must add a fifth to the redemption price — like the redeemer of second tithe. **Ravina said: Come** and **hear** the following Mishnah (*Arakhin* 8:2), which discusses the laws of redeeming property consecrated to the Temple: [6] **"If** at the public auction **the** original **owner** of property dedicated to the Temple **says** that he is willing to pay **twenty** sela'im to redeem that

LITERAL TRANSLATION

it itself is worth [a perutah], [1] since its fifth is not worth [a perutah], it is well. [2] But according to the one who says [that] *it* is not worth [a perutah], what is "it is sufficient"?

[3] [This is] difficult.

[4] A question was raised (lit., "it was asked of them"): Is the fifth [calculated] from the inside or is the fifth [calculated] from the outside?

[5] Ravina said: Come [and] hear: [6] "[If] the owners say, 'For twenty,'

דִּבְדִידֵיהּ אִית בֵּיהּ, [1] כֵּיוָן דִּבְחוּמְשֵׁיהּ לֵיכָּא, שַׁפִּיר. [2] אֶלָּא לְמַאן דְּאָמַר אֵין בּוֹ, מַאי "דַּיּוֹ"?

[3] קַשְׁיָא.

[4] אִיבַּעֲיָא לְהוּ: חוּמְשָׁא מִלְּגָיו אוֹ חוּמְשָׁא מִלְּבַר?

[5] אָמַר רָבִינָא: תָּא שְׁמַע: [6] "הַבְּעָלִים אוֹמְרִים, 'בְּעֶשְׂרִים',

RASHI

אלא למאן דאמר אין בו מאי דיו — מאי רבותיה דאצטריך למתני דיו? ליתני אומר הוא וחומשו כו'. **חומשא מלגיו** — על שוה עשרים זוז מוסיף ארבע, שהן חומשו של קרן. **או חומשא מלבר** — על ארבעה רבעים מוסיף החמישית מן החוץ, דהוו להו לעשרים זוז חמשא זוזי. **הבעלים אומרים בעשרים** — גבי מקדיש ופודה הקדשו תנן לה במסכת ערכין (כז,א).

BACKGROUND

מִלְּגָיו וּמִלְּבַר From the inside or from the outside. The question of whether a given sum should be calculated "from the inside" or "from the outside" arises whenever one is required to pay a certain percentage of the principal (e.g., the extra fifth added for inadvertent use of sacred property and terumah) together with the principal itself. This question arises because neither the Torah nor the Rabbis used a consistent style when they spoke of such percentages.

NOTES

suggests that second tithe worth less than a perutah need not be redeemed at all, and may therefore be eaten outside Jerusalem according to Torah law.

קַשְׁיָא This is difficult. The commentators ask why the Gemara uses the term קַשְׁיָא — "this is difficult" — rather than יוּבְתָּא "this is a valid refutation" — since the objection here seems decisive. Indeed, Rabbi Yoḥanan's view is not accepted by later authorities.

Some authorities answer that the Gemara's objection was not considered decisive, because elsewhere there seems to be Tannaitic support for Rabbi Yoḥanan's view. Specifically, in *Arakhin* 27a we find a difference of opinion between Tannaim as to whether property dedicated to the Temple and worth less than a perutah can be redeemed. Thus, Rabbi Yoḥanan may hold the same opinion as the Tanna who maintains that property dedicated to the Temple and worth less than a perutah cannot be redeemed, and the same presumably holds true of second tithe (*Nefesh Ḥayyah, Halakhah LeMoshe*).

חוּמְשָׁא מִלְּגָיו מִלְּבַר Calculating the fifth from the inside and from the outside. The commentators ask how the Gemara could not have known whether this fifth is

HALAKHAH

הַבְּעָלִים אוֹמְרִים בְּעֶשְׂרִים If the owners say, For twenty. "If a person who has dedicated property to the Temple offers to redeem it for twenty zuz, and others are willing to pay the same amount, the owner takes precedence, since he has

וְכָל אָדָם ׳בְּעֶשְׂרִים׳, [1]הַבְּעָלִים קוֹדְמִין, מִפְּנֵי שֶׁמּוֹסִיפִין חוֹמֶשׁ. [2]אָמַר אֶחָד: ׳הֲרֵי עָלַי בְּעֶשְׂרִים וְאֶחָד׳, [54A] הַבְּעָלִים נוֹתְנִין עֶשְׂרִים וְשֵׁשׁ. [3]׳עֶשְׂרִים וּשְׁנַיִם׳, הַבְּעָלִים נוֹתְנִין עֶשְׂרִים וְשֶׁבַע. [4]׳בְּעֶשְׂרִים וְשָׁלֹשׁ׳, הַבְּעָלִים נוֹתְנִין עֶשְׂרִים וּשְׁמוֹנֶה. [5]׳בְּעֶשְׂרִים וְאַרְבַּע׳, הַבְּעָלִים נוֹתְנִין עֶשְׂרִים וְתֵשַׁע. [6]׳עֶשְׂרִים וְחָמֵשׁ׳, הַבְּעָלִים נוֹתְנִין שְׁלֹשִׁים,

LITERAL TRANSLATION

and everybody [says], 'For twenty,' [1]the owners take precedence, because they add a fifth. [2][If] one person said, 'I [take it] upon myself for twenty-one,' [54A] the owners give twenty-six. [3]'[For] twenty-two,' the owners give twenty-seven. [4]'For twenty-three,' the owners give twenty-eight. [5]'For twenty-four,' the owners give twenty-nine. [6]'[For] twenty-five,' the owners give thirty,

TRANSLATION AND COMMENTARY

property, **and everybody** else who is present at the auction and is interested in redeeming the property **says** that he is prepared to match the owner's offer of **twenty**, [1]**the owner takes precedence, because he,** unlike the other bidders, must **add** an extra **fifth.** Since the owner is required to pay an extra fifth if he himself redeems the consecrated property, whereas another person would only have to pay its actual value (see Leviticus 27:19), the owner takes precedence, because the Temple treasury profits thereby." Of interest to our discussion here is whether this fifth is calculated as an "inside" fifth — twenty percent of the value of the property — or as an "outside" fifth — twenty percent of the combined value of the property and the extra "fifth." [2]This issue is elucidated by the next Mishnah (*Arakhin* 8:3), which states: **"If someone** other than the owner **says, 'I am willing** to pay **twenty-one** sela'im for that property for which the owner offered twenty,' [54A] **the owner** once again takes precedence, but now he must **pay twenty-six** sela'im." Even though the other person offered more for the property than did the owner, the right to redeem is given to the owner, for he is required to add a fifth, and his offer of twenty — plus the required fifth — is still more than the other bidder's offer of twenty-one. But the owner is still required to match the offer of twenty-one, because Temple property may be sold only to the highest bidder, and the extra fifth is not reckoned as part of the offer price. The result is that the owner must pay twenty-six: twenty on account of his original offer, one to match the higher price offered by the other bidder, and five more as the additional fifth of his original offer. Now since the Mishnah calculates the additional fifth of the owner's original offer of twenty as five (and not four), it is clear that the additional fifth required by the Torah is calculated as an "outside" fifth — a fifth of twenty-five — and not as an "inside" fifth — a fifth of twenty. The Mishnah now demonstrates this rule (and its limits) by several more examples: [3]"Similarly, if the other person offered to pay **twenty-two** sela'im to redeem the property, **the owner** must **pay twenty-seven,** twenty-five for the principal and the added fifth, and the extra two to match the other person's offer. [4]Likewise, if the other person offered **twenty-three** sela'im, **the owner** must **pay twenty-eight,** [5]and if the other person offered **twenty-four, the owner** must **pay twenty-nine.** [6]If the other person offered **twenty-five** sela'im, **the owner** must **pay thirty,** twenty-five for the principal and the added fifth, plus five to match the other person's offer. In all these cases, the additional fifth that the owner must pay is calculated on the basis of his original offer,

RASHI

מפני שמוסיפין חומש — ועשרים שלהן הוו עשרים וחמשה, דאילו שאר כל אדם לא יוסיף חומש. **הבעלים נותנין** — על כרחן עשרים ושש. שאי אפשר לתת לזה באחד ועשרים, שנמצא הקדש נפסד בחמשה סלעים. ולבעלים נמי לא פחתינן מן הקרן שמצאה איש אחר, הלכך נותנין עשרים ואחד לקרן וחמשה לתוספת חומש. ועל עילויו של זה שהעלה בדמיו סלע אין מוסיף חומש, אלא על קרן שמצאה הוא. **עשרים וחמש הבעלים נותנין שלשים** — והתם (ערכין כז,ב) פריך: ונימא לגיזבר אתא גברא במריקאי הרי בא אחר תחתינו, שחפץ ליתן כמה שעולה קרן וחומש שאמרתי, ואין הקדש נפסד ולמה נכוף את זה לתת שלשים? וסיום המשנה: אמר אחד הרי הוא שלי בעשרים ושש — אומר: הגעתיך.

NOTES

calculated "inside" or "outside," as it seems inconceivable that the Sages of the Gemara were unaware of the Mishnah cited here by Ravina. These authorities answer that this Mishnah speaks only of the fifth added when redeeming property dedicated to the Temple. But we might have thought that the fifth added when redeeming second tithe is calculated differently (*Magen Gibborim*, *Imrei Zutrei*). But since Ravina drew a comparison between these different kinds of fifths, we may infer that all fifths are calculated "from the outside" (*Pnei Yehoshua*).

HALAKHAH

to pay an extra fifth, and thus he pays a total of twenty-five zuz. If others are willing to pay more than the owner, the owner still takes precedence, as long as the others do not offer more than twenty-five zuz." (*Rambam, Sefer Hafla'ah, Hilkhot Arakhin* 8:5.) These laws do not, however, apply when redeeming second tithe: "When redeeming second tithe, whoever offers more for the tithe itself is permitted to redeem the tithe, even if the owner would end up paying more as a result of adding the extra fifth." (Ibid., *Sefer Zeraim, Hilkhot Ma'aser Sheni* 5:7.)

TRANSLATION AND COMMENTARY

[1]but the owner **need not add** to his payment **a fifth of the higher valuation** offered **by the other person."** [2]Now, since this Mishnah assumes that five is considered a "fifth" of twenty, we may **conclude from this** that **the fifth is** calculated **from the outside,** and is equal to one-fourth of the value of the property itself. [3]The Gemara sums up: **Conclude from here** that this is indeed so. And since the rules concerning the redemption of second tithe are assumed to parallel those concerning the redemption of consecrated property, the fifth that must be added when a person redeems his own second tithe must also be calculated from the outside.

כְּתַנָּאֵי [4]The Gemara now notes that **this** question as to how to calculate the payment of the additional fifth can be traced back to **a difference of opinion** between **Tannaim.** For we have learned in a Baraita: "The Torah states (Leviticus 27:27) that if a non-kosher animal consecrated to the Temple is redeemed by its original owner, [5]**'he shall add to it a fifth part of it,' so that it** together **with its fifth are** equal in value to **five** of these 'fifths.' [6]**These are the words of Rabbi Yoshiyah.** According to Rabbi Yoshiyah, the fifth is calculated by dividing the principal into four parts and then adding a part equal to one of these four parts. Thus the additional 'fifth' raises the redemption price to five-fourths of the value of the principal. Rabbi Yoshiyah's 'fifth' is clearly an 'outside fifth.' [7]But **Rabbi Yonatan says: 'A fifth part of it' means a fifth of the principal** i.e., an 'inside fifth.'"

אִיבַּעֲיָא לְהוּ [8]The Gemara now raises another question regarding the fifth that must be added when an owner of produce redeems his own second tithe: **The following problem arose** in discussion among the Sages: **Is the fifth indispensable, or is it not indispensable?** There is no question that the owner of second-tithe produce who wishes to redeem it must pay the additional fifth. But what if he failed to pay it? Is his defective redemption payment valid, so that the produce may now be eaten outside Jerusalem? Or is the redemption absolutely invalid? The Gemara analyzes the various aspects of this issue by means of an example: When a person redeems second tithe worth four zuz by paying five zuz (four zuz for the principal and an added zuz as the "outside fifth"), how is the redemption actually effected? [9]**Do** we say that **he** actually **redeems** his tithe worth **four** zuz **with** the **four** zuz of the redemption money, **and** then **adds the fifth** zuz **separately**, as it were, i.e., independent of the redemption price? If this is the case, the redemption is effected by paying the value of the principal alone, and the extra fifth is not really considered part of the redemption money. **Thus** we can conclude that **the** extra **fifth is not indispensable** for the redemption of the second tithe. [10]On the other hand, **perhaps** we should understand the mechanics of the tithe-redemption process differently: The added fifth is an integral part of the redemption money, so that the owner in fact **redeems** tithe worth **four** zuz **with** all **five** zuz of the redemption money. Thus we can conclude that adding the **fifth is indispensable** for the redemption of the second tithe.

[1]לְפִי שֶׁאֵין מוֹסִיפִין חוֹמֶשׁ עַל עִילּוּי שֶׁל זֶה״. [2]שְׁמַע מִינָּהּ חוּמְשָׁא מִלְּבַר. [3]שְׁמַע מִינָּהּ.
[4]כְּתַנָּאֵי: [5]״׳וְיָסַף חֲמִשְׁתוֹ עָלָיו׳, שֶׁיְּהֵא הוּא וְחוּמְשׁוֹ חֲמִשָּׁה. [6]דִּבְרֵי רַבִּי יֹאשִׁיָּה. [7]רַבִּי יוֹנָתָן אוֹמֵר: ׳חֲמִישִׁיתוֹ׳ חוּמְשׁוֹ שֶׁל קֶרֶן״.
[8]אִיבַּעֲיָא לְהוּ: חוֹמֶשׁ מְעַכֵּב, אוֹ אֵינוֹ מְעַכֵּב? [9]אַרְבָּעָה בְּאַרְבָּעָה פָּרֵיק, וְאַכְּנַפְשֵׁיהּ מוֹסִיף חוֹמֶשׁ, אַלְמָא חוֹמֶשׁ לָא מְעַכֵּב? [10]אוֹ דִּלְמָא אַרְבָּעָה בַּחֲמִשָּׁה פָּרֵיק, וְחוֹמֶשׁ מְעַכֵּב?

LITERAL TRANSLATION

[1]because a fifth is not added on to the [higher] valuation of this person." [2]Conclude from this [that] the fifth is [calculated] from the outside. [3]Conclude from this.

[4][This is] like [a dispute of] Tannaim: [5]"'And he shall add to it a fifth part of it,' so that it and its fifth shall be five. [6][These are] the words of Rabbi Yoshiyah. [7]Rabbi Yonatan says: 'A fifth part of it' [means] a fifth of the principal."

[8]A question was raised: Is the fifth indispensable, or is it not indispensable? [9]Does he redeem four with four, and add a fifth separately, [and] thus a fifth is not indispensable? [10]Or, perhaps, he redeems four with five, and a fifth *is* indispensable?

RASHI

שמע מינה חומשא מלבר — מדקתני חומש על עשרים סלעים חמש סלעים, הרי חומש מן החוץ. **הוא וחומשו חמשה** — היינו חומש מלבר, שהוא רביע של קרן. **חומש מעכב** — אכילה חוץ לחומה, עד שיתן החומש. **אכנפשיה** — מאליו, אינו בכלל הפדיון, שארבעה הזוזים פדו מעשר שהוא כנגדם. **או דלמא ארבעה בחמשה פריק** — כך הוא גזירת הכתוב שהחומש מן הפדיון הוא, ואין שוה ארבעה נפדין בפחות מחמשה.

TERMINOLOGY

כְּתַנָּאֵי Like the Tannaim. When an Amoraic controversy is shown to parallel a Tannaitic dispute, the Talmud states: "This Amoraic controversy is like the dispute of the Tannaim." When the Gemara uses this expression without qualification (i.e., without preceding it with the word לֵימָא — "shall we say"), the identification of the Amoraic controversy with an earlier Tannaitic controversy is usually accepted.

SAGES

רַבִּי יֹאשִׁיָּה Rabbi Yoshiyah. Also known as Rabbi Yoshiyah Rabbah (the Great), to distinguish him from the Amora of the same name, Rabbi Yoshiyah was a Tanna who lived in the generation prior to the completion of the Mishnah. He came from the city of Hutzal in Babylonia and emigrated to Eretz Israel to study with Rabbi Yishmael. He and his colleague Rabbi Yonatan were Rabbi Yishmael's closest disciples. He generally appears in the Talmud in association with Rabbi Yonatan, with whom he disagrees about certain basic issues of Halakhic Midrash. He seems to have returned to Babylonia to study with Rabbi Yehudah ben Betera. Rabbi Aḥai, Rabbi Yoshiyah's son, was also an important Sage, and also lived in Hutzal.

רַבִּי יוֹנָתָן Rabbi Yonatan. A Tanna who lived in the generation prior to the completion of the Mishnah, Rabbi Yonatan was a disciple of Rabbi Yishmael and a colleague of Rabbi Yoshiyah, with whom he differed on many issues of Halakhic Midrash. It is likely that he emigrated from Eretz Israel to Babylonia, and this may be the reason why his name does not appear in the Mishnah.

BACKGROUND

חוֹמֶשׁ מְעַכֵּב Is the fifth indispensable? Whether or not the extra fifth is indispensable depends on how this payment is considered from a Halakhic point of view. If the fifth is considered a fine rather than an integral part of what a person owes, the

HALAKHAH

חוּמְשָׁא מִלְּבַר The fifth is calculated from the outside. "Someone who redeems his own second tithe must add 'one-fifth calculated from the outside,' i.e., a quarter. Thus, tithe worth four zuz is redeemed with five zuz," following the conclusion of the Gemara. (*Rambam, Sefer Zeraim, Hilkhot Ma'aser Sheni* 5:1.)

redemption is valid even if the person did not pay the extra fifth. However, if the fifth is considered an integral part of what one owes, redemption takes effect only if the extra fifth has been paid.

CONCEPTS

דְּמַאי ***Demai.*** Produce (or food made from produce) which was purchased from a person who may not have separated the various tithes as required by law. The literal meaning of the word דְּמַאי is "suspicion," i.e., produce about which there is a suspicion that tithes were not properly taken from it. In the Second Temple period, the Sages decreed that such produce should be considered as being of doubtful status, even though the owner claimed that he had separated the tithes, and that the buyer of such produce must tithe it himself. Nevertheless, since it was probable that the produce was in fact tithed, certain leniency was permitted concerning the use of *demai* for food and for other purposes.

בִּיעוּר מַעַשְׂרוֹת **The removal of tithes.** The obligation once in three years to complete the giving of all agricultural dues by the day before Passover in the fourth and seventh years of the seven-year agricultural cycle. In Temple times, on the afternoon of the seventh day of Passover in these years, a special recital of verses of thanksgiving and praise took place (see Deuteronomy 26:12-15).

LITERAL TRANSLATION

[1]Ravina said: Come [and] hear: [2]"*Demai* does not have a fifth, and it does not have [tithe-]removal." [3]But it does have [redemption of] the principal. [4]What is the reason? [5]The principal, which is indispensable for [tithe by] Torah law, applies to [*demai* by] Rabbinic law. [6]The fifth, which is not indispensable for [tithe by] Torah law, does not apply to [*demai* by] Rabbinic law. [7]Shall we say it is like [the following dispute between] Tannaim: [8]"[If] he gave the principal but did not give the fifth, Rabbi Eliezer says: He may eat [it].

[1]אֲמַר רָבִינָא: תָּא שְׁמַע: [2]"הַדְּמַאי אֵין לוֹ חוֹמֶשׁ, וְאֵין לוֹ בִּיעוּר". [3]הָא קֶרֶן יֵשׁ לוֹ. [4]מַאי טַעְמָא? [5]קֶרֶן, דִּמְעַכֵּב בִּדְאוֹרַיְיתָא, אִיתָא בִּדְרַבָּנַן. [6]חוֹמֶשׁ, דְּלָא מְעַכֵּב בִּדְאוֹרַיְיתָא, לֵיתָא בִּדְרַבָּנַן. [7]לֵימָא כְּתַנָּאֵי: [8]"נָתַן אֶת הַקֶּרֶן וְלֹא נָתַן אֶת הַחוֹמֶשׁ, רַבִּי אֱלִיעֶזֶר אוֹמֵר: יֹאכַל.

RASHI

הדמאי — מעשר שני של דמאי שחייבו חכמים להפריש הלוקח מעם הארץ. **אין לו חומש** — אם פודהו בעליו. **ואין לו ביעור** — בשנה שלישית שנצטוו ישראל לבער כל מעשרותיהם מן הבית, ולתת למי שהם רוצים כדכתיב (דברים יד) מקצה שלש שנים וגו'. **הא קרן יש לו** — דכל זמן שלא פדאו אסור לאוכלו חוץ לחומה. **מאי טעמא** — אין לו חומש ויש לו קרן. **דמעכב מדאורייתא** — במעשר דאורייתא. **איתיה בדרבנן** — במעשר דמאי דרבנן.

TRANSLATION AND COMMENTARY

אֲמַר רָבִינָא [1]In answer to this question, **Ravina said: Come and hear** the following Mishnah (*Demai* 1:2), which lists some of the laws pertaining to *demai* — produce purchased from a person who is suspected of not observing the laws of tithing, and from which the Rabbis decreed that certain tithes (including second tithe) must be separated. Since most people do observe the laws of tithing, and it is only by Rabbinic decree that tithes must be separated from *demai*, certain leniencies are allowed with regard to second tithe separated from *demai*. [2]The Mishnah states: "Unlike ordinary second tithe, second tithe separated from **demai does not require** the addition of **a fifth.** A person need not add an extra fifth when redeeming second tithe which he has separated from *demai*. Likewise, second tithe separated from *demai* **is not subject to** the laws of **tithe-removal**. A person need not destroy second-tithe produce that is left in his possession during the fourth and seventh year of the Sabbatical cycle."

הָא קֶרֶן יֵשׁ לוֹ [3]The Gemara now explains how this Mishnah pertains to the question of whether or not the added fifth is indispensable for tithe redemption: The Mishnah states that the extra fifth is not required when second tithe separated from *demai* is redeemed. **But** it is clear that even second tithe separated from *demai* **requires redemption of the principal** before it can be eaten outside Jerusalem. [4]Now, **what is the reason** for the Mishnah's distinction between the additional fifth and the principal when second tithe separated from *demai* is redeemed? [5]It can only be because redemption **of the principal of** ordinary second **tithe, which is indispensable by Torah law, is** also **necessary** when redeeming second tithe separated from produce requiring tithing only **by Rabbinic decree,** i.e., *demai*. [6]By contrast, the addition of the **fifth to** ordinary second **tithe, which is not indispensable by Torah law, is not required** when redeeming second tithe separated from produce requiring tithing only **by Rabbinic decree,** i.e., *demai*. Thus, from the fact that the Mishnah did not require a person redeeming second tithe separated from *demai* to add a fifth we may conclude that the extra fifth is not indispensable for the redemption of ordinary second tithe.

לֵימָא כְּתַנָּאֵי [7]The Gemara now suggests: **Perhaps we should say that this** question of the indispensability of the extra fifth **is the subject of the following Tannaitic dispute.** [8]For we learned in a Tosefta (*Ma'aser Sheni* 4:6): "**If** a person has **paid the principal** when redeeming his second tithe **but has not** yet **paid the** extra **fifth,**

HALAKHAH

דְּמַאי אֵין לוֹ חוֹמֶשׁ ***Demai* does not have a fifth.** "An extra fifth is not added when redeeming second tithe which has been separated from *demai*." (*Rambam, Sefer Zeraim, Hilkhot Ma'aser Sheni* 5:4.)

דְּמַאי אֵין לוֹ בִּיעוּר ***Demai* does not have tithe-removal.** "Second tithe separated from *demai* which was left in one's possession until the fourth or seventh year of the Sabbatical cycle need not be removed, unlike other second tithe." (Ibid., 11:8.)

חוֹמֶשׁ מְעַכֵּב אוֹ אֵינוֹ מְעַכֵּב **Is the fifth indispensable or not?** "If a person redeems his own second tithe without adding a fifth, the redemption is valid according to Torah law. However, the Rabbis decreed that the produce should not be eaten, even on the Sabbath, until the extra fifth is added, in case the owner fails to separate the extra fifth," following Rabbi Yehoshua. (Ibid., 5:12.)

קֶרֶן יֵשׁ לוֹ **But it does have redemption of the principal.** "Second tithe separated from *demai* must be taken to Jerusalem, and may not be taken out of the city. Even if the produce left Jerusalem at a later date, it must be returned to Jerusalem and eaten there." (Ibid., 2:9.)

¹רַבִּי יְהוֹשֻׁעַ אוֹמֵר: לֹא יֹאכַל. ²אָמַר רַבִּי: נִרְאִין דִּבְרֵי רַבִּי אֱלִיעֶזֶר בַּשַּׁבָּת, ³וְדִבְרֵי רַבִּי יְהוֹשֻׁעַ בַּחוֹל״. ⁴מִדַּאֲמַר ״נִרְאִין דִּבְרֵי רַבִּי אֱלִיעֶזֶר בַּשַּׁבָּת״, ⁵מִכְּלָל דִּפְלִיגִי אֲפִילּוּ בַּחוֹל. ⁶מִדַּאֲמַר ״נִרְאִין דִּבְרֵי רַבִּי יְהוֹשֻׁעַ בַּחוֹל״, ⁷מִכְּלָל דִּפְלִיגִי אֲפִילּוּ בַּשַּׁבָּת. ⁸מַאי לָאו בְּהָא סְבָרָא קָמִיפַּלְגִי, ⁹דְּרַבִּי אֱלִיעֶזֶר סָבַר חוֹמֶשׁ לָא מְעַכֵּב, ¹⁰וְרַבִּי יְהוֹשֻׁעַ סָבַר חוֹמֶשׁ מְעַכֵּב.
¹¹אֲמַר רַב פַּפָּא: לָא. דְּכוּלֵּי עָלְמָא חוֹמֶשׁ לָא מְעַכֵּב, ¹²וְהָכָא בְּחָיְישִׁינַן לִפְשִׁיעוּתָא קָמִיפַּלְגִי.

LITERAL TRANSLATION

¹Rabbi Yehoshua says: He may not eat [it]. ²Rabbi [Yehudah HaNasi] said: The words of Rabbi Eliezer appear [correct] with regard to the Sabbath, ³and the words of Rabbi Yehoshua with regard to weekdays." ⁴Since he said "the words of Rabbi Eliezer appear [correct] with regard to the Sabbath," ⁵[this proves] by implication that they disagree even with regard to weekdays. ⁶Since he said "the words of Rabbi Yehoshua appear [correct] with regard to weekdays," ⁷[this proves] by implication that they disagree even with regard to the Sabbath. ⁸Is it not [that] they disagree about this idea, ⁹for Rabbi Eliezer maintains [that] the fifth is not indispensable, ¹⁰and Rabbi Yehoshua maintains [that] the fifth is indispensable.
¹¹Rav Pappa said: No. For all (lit., "the whole world") [agree that] the fifth is not indispensable, ¹²but here they disagree about [whether] we are concerned about neglect.

TRANSLATION AND COMMENTARY

Rabbi Eliezer says: He may eat the tithe outside Jerusalem. ¹But **Rabbi Yehoshua says: He may not eat** such produce outside the city. ²In deciding between these two opinions, **Rabbi Yehudah HaNasi said: The** more lenient **viewpoint of Rabbi Eliezer appears correct with regard to the Sabbath**. Otherwise, people who have not yet paid the additional fifth may not have enough food to eat on the Sabbath and will therefore be unable to enjoy the day. ³However, **the** more stringent **viewpoint of Rabbi Yehoshua** should be followed **with regard to weekdays**, when enjoyment of the day is not a factor." ⁴Now, **since** Rabbi Yehudah HaNasi **said** that **"Rabbi Eliezer's viewpoint appears correct** only **with regard to the Sabbath,"** but may not be followed during the rest of the week, ⁵**this proves by implication that** Rabbi Eliezer and Rabbi Yehoshua **disagree** about what the law should be **even with regard to weekdays.** ⁶Likewise, **since** Rabbi Yehudah HaNasi **said** that **"Rabbi Yehoshua's viewpoint appears correct with regard to weekdays,"** but need not be followed on the Sabbath, ⁷**this proves by implication that** Rabbi Eliezer and Rabbi Yehoshua **disagree** about what the law should be **even** with regard to **the Sabbath.** Rabbi Eliezer is of the opinion that even though the extra fifth has not yet been paid, second tithe may be eaten outside Jerusalem even during the week, and Rabbi Yehoshua is of the opinion that the second tithe may not be eaten even on the Sabbath until the extra fifth has been paid. ⁸The Gemara now offers a suggestion as to how to undertand this dispute: **Is it not** reasonable to assume **that** Rabbi Eliezer and Rabbi Yehoshua **disagree about this issue:** ⁹**Rabbi Eliezer maintains that** payment of **the fifth is not indispensable,** so that we permit the redeemed second tithe to be eaten on the Sabbath even if the additional fifth has not been paid, ¹⁰whereas **Rabbi Yehoshua maintains** that payment of **the fifth is indispensable,** and hence the tithe may never be eaten until the fifth is paid?

אֲמַר רַב פַּפָּא ¹¹**Rav Pappa said: No.** This Tosefta is inconclusive, because the dispute between the Tannaim can be explained differently. It can be argued that **all** the Tannaim, including Rabbi Yehoshua, agree **that** by Torah law payment of **the fifth is not indispensable,** ¹²**but here** Rabbi Eliezer and Rabbi Yehoshua **disagree** about **whether we are concerned about willful failure to pay.** It is possible that if the owner of the redeemed produce is permitted to eat it without first paying the additional fifth, he will postpone

RASHI

בשבת – מפני כבוד שבת לא יעכב מלאכול בשביל חומש. **מדקאמר רבי נראין דברי רבי אליעזר בשבת** – אבל בחול אינו רואה את דבריו. **מכלל דאיהו אפילו בחול** – אמר יאכל, ובמעשר ודאי קאמר. **דכולי עלמא חומש לא מעכב** – שיהא האוכלו לוקה עליו משום ״לא תוכל לאכול בשעריך״ (דברים יב). **והכא בחוששין לפשיעותא** – הא דקאמר רבי יהושע לא יאכל, מדרבנן קאמר, שמא יפשע ויתיאש, ולא יתן חומש עוד.

NOTES

שַׁבָּת וְחוֹמֶשׁ מְעַכֵּב The Sabbath and the indispensability of the extra fifth. *Rabbi Zvi Ḥayyot* suggests that the fifth may be indispensable according to Torah law, but the Rabbis may have dispensed with this requirement with respect to the Sabbath, to make that day more enjoyable. But he rejects this tentative suggestion, and reasons that if paying an extra fifth were necessary according to Torah law, then tithe redemption would not take effect at all unless the fifth were paid. Thus it follows that eating "redeemed" tithe without paying the extra fifth would be prohibited by Torah law, and such a Torah prohibition could not be abrogated by the Rabbis.

SAGES

רַבִּי יְהוֹשֻׁעַ Rabbi Yehoshua. This is Rabbi Yehoshua ben Ḥananyah the Levite, one of the leading Sages of the generation following the destruction of the Second Temple. Rabbi Yehoshua had served in the Temple as a singer and, after the destruction, was one of the students who went to Yavneh with their outstanding teacher, Rabban Yoḥanan ben Zakkai. Unlike his colleague Rabbi Eliezer, Rabbi Yehoshua maintained the system of his teacher and of Bet Hillel.

Although Rabbi Yehoshua played an important part in the leadership of the people (for he was apparently a senior judge), he earned a meager living from hard and unremunerative work. After renewing his close ties with the house of the Nasi (the president of the Sanhedrin), he was apparently supported by Rabban Gamliel, who used to give him the tithe belonging to the Levites.

Rabbi Yehoshua was famous among both Jews and non-Jews as an extraordinary scholar, possessing wide knowledge not only of Torah but of secular studies. He was a celebrated preacher.

Continuing the method of his teacher, Rabban Yoḥanan ben Zakkai, Rabbi Yehoshua was a moderate person and tried to deter the people from rebellion against the Roman regime. For a while he had close relations with the emperor's house and was highly regarded there, as he had been sent to Rome with several national delegations.

While Rabbi Yehoshua was modest and humble, he was very firm in his views and principles, and did not make concessions even when difficult personal controversies developed. However, in other matters he accepted authority, and in general had a humorous, realistic temperament.

All the Sages of the following generation were his students, and in most of the controversies with the Sages of his own generation, the Halakhah followed his view. His system became the path taken by the Halakhah. Ḥananyah, his nephew, was his outstanding student.

TERMINOLOGY

...נִרְאִין... נִרְאִין The words of Rabbi X appear correct ... the words of Rabbi Y appear correct.... This expression is used when a scholar adopts a middle position between two conflicting viewpoints, because he accepts part of each view without accepting either in its entirety. Legal rulings introduced by the term נִרְאִין are generally not decisive.

LITERAL TRANSLATION

[1]One maintains [that] we are concerned about neglect, [2]but the other maintains [that] we are not concerned about neglect.

[3]Rabbi Yoḥanan said: All agree regarding consecrated property that he has redeemed it, [4]because the treasurers demand it in the marketplace.

[5]But do they not disagree about consecrated property? [6]But surely it has been taught: "[If] he gave the principal but did not give him the fifth, [7]Rabbi Eliezer says: He has redeemed [it], but the Sages say: He has not redeemed [it]. [8]Rabbi [Yehudah HaNasi] said: The words of Rabbi Eliezer appear [correct] with regard to consecrated property, [9]and the words of the Sages with regard to tithe." [10]Since he said "the words of Rabbi Eliezer appear [correct] with regard to consecrated property,"

[1]מָר סָבַר חָיְישִׁינַן לִפְשִׁיעוּתָא, [2]וּמָר סָבַר לָא חָיְישִׁינַן לִפְשִׁיעוּתָא.

[3]אָמַר רַבִּי יוֹחָנָן: הַכֹּל מוֹדִים בְּהֶקְדֵּשׁ שֶׁחִילֵּל, [4]הוֹאִיל וְגִזְבָּרִין תּוֹבְעִין אוֹתוֹ בַּשּׁוּק.

[5]וּבְהֶקְדֵּשׁ לָא פְּלִיגִי? [6]וְהָתַנְיָא: "נָתַן אֶת הַקֶּרֶן וְלֹא נָתַן לוֹ אֶת הַחוֹמֶשׁ, [7]רַבִּי אֱלִיעֶזֶר אוֹמֵר: חִילֵּל, וַחֲכָמִים אוֹמְרִים: לֹא חִילֵּל. [8]אָמַר רַבִּי: נִרְאִין דִּבְרֵי רַבִּי אֱלִיעֶזֶר בְּהֶקְדֵּשׁ, [9]וְדִבְרֵי חֲכָמִים בְּמַעֲשֵׂר". [10]מִדְּאָמַר "נִרְאִין דִּבְרֵי רַבִּי אֱלִיעֶזֶר בְּהֶקְדֵּשׁ",

RASHI

הואיל וגזברין תובעין אותו – את החומש, וליכא למיחש לפשיעותא. **נראין דברי רבי אליעזר בהקדש** – הואיל וגזברין תובעין אותו.

TRANSLATION AND COMMENTARY

paying it indefinitely, and thus transgress a commandment of the Torah. [1]**One** Tanna — Rabbi Yehoshua — **maintains that we are concerned about willful failure to pay.** Therefore, according to Rabbi Yehoshua, the additional fifth must be paid at the time of redemption; until it is paid the produce, though validly redeemed, cannot be eaten. [2]**But the other** Tanna — Rabbi Eliezer — **maintains that we are not concerned about willful failure to pay.** Hence the owner is permitted to eat the redeemed second tithe even if he has not yet paid the extra fifth, since we trust that he will pay it later.

אָמַר רַבִּי יוֹחָנָן [3]**Rabbi Yoḥanan** now seeks to limit the difference of opinion between Rabbi Eliezer and Rabbi Yehoshua to the specific case of the redemption of second-tithe produce. He **said:** Even though Rabbi Eliezer and Rabbi Yehoshua disagree as to whether the redemption of second tithe is valid if the owner has not paid the extra fifth, **both agree regarding** the redemption of **consecrated property** that if a person has paid only the principal without the extra fifth, the property **is** immediately **redeemed**. In the case of redemption of consecrated property — where, like the case of second tithe, an extra fifth must be added — we are not concerned that the redeemer may fail to pay the additional fifth. [4]This is **because the** Temple **treasurers will demand** the extra fifth from the owner **in the marketplace**. The Temple treasury has an effective collection system. By contrast, there is no system available to make sure that an owner who redeems his second-tithe produce will pay the additional fifth. The only way to guarantee payment is to insist that the entire redemption price — principal plus additional fifth — be paid at the time of redemption.

וּבְהֶקְדֵּשׁ לָא פְּלִיגִי [5]The Gemara raises an objection: **But** is it really true that **there is no disagreement** that **consecrated property** is regarded as redeemed even before the extra fifth is paid? [6]**Surely it has been taught** differently in a Baraita: **"If** a person has **paid the principal** in redeeming consecrated property **but has not** yet paid **the** extra **fifth,** [7]**Rabbi Eliezer says** that the property **is** nevertheless **redeemed, but the Sages say** that in such a case, the property **is not redeemed.** [8]In deciding between these two opinions, **Rabbi Yehudah HaNasi said: The** more lenient **viewpoint of Rabbi Eliezer appears correct with regard to consecrated property,** [9]**but the** more stringent **viewpoint of the Sages** should be followed **with regard to** second **tithe."** [10]Now, **since** Rabbi Yehudah HaNasi **said** that **"Rabbi Eliezer's viewpoint appears correct** only **with regard**

HALAKHAH

קֳדָשִׁים שֶׁלֹּא נָתַן חוֹמֶשׁ Redeeming sacred property without adding a fifth. "If a person redeems property that has been consecrated to the Temple but does not add an extra fifth, the redemption procedure is valid according to Torah law, since the extra fifth is not indispensable. However, it is prohibited by Rabbinic decree to benefit from redeemed property without paying the extra fifth. Nevertheless, the Rabbis ruled that food that had been redeemed without paying an extra fifth could be eaten on the Sabbath, both to ensure that the Sabbath would be enjoyable, and because the Temple treasurers would be sure to collect the extra fifth," following Rabbi Yoḥanan. (*Rambam, Sefer Hafla'ah, Hilkhot Arakhin* 7:3.)

[1] מִכְּלָל דִּפָלֵיג אֲפִילּוּ בְּמַעֲשֵׂר. [2] מִדְּקָאָמַר "נִרְאִין דִּבְרֵי חֲכָמִים בְּמַעֲשֵׂר", [3] מִכְּלָל דְּאִינְהוּ פְּלִיגִי אֲפִילּוּ בְּהֶקְדֵּשׁ.

[4] אֶלָּא, אִי אִתְּמַר הָכִי אִתְּמַר: [5] אָמַר רַבִּי יוֹחָנָן: הַכֹּל מוֹדִים בַּשַּׁבָּת בְּהֶקְדֵּשׁ שֶׁחִילֵּל. [6] חֲדָא, דִּכְתִיב: "וְקָרָאתָ לַשַּׁבָּת עֹנֶג"; [7] וְעוֹד, הוֹאִיל וְגִזְבָּרִין תּוֹבְעִין אוֹתוֹ בַּשּׁוּק.

[8] אָמַר רָמִי בַּר חָמָא: הֲרֵי אָמְרוּ: הֶקְדֵּשׁ אֵינוֹ מִתְחַלֵּל עַל הַקַּרְקַע, [9] דְּרַחֲמָנָא אָמַר: "וְנָתַן

LITERAL TRANSLATION

[1] [this proves] by implication that he disagrees even with regard to tithe. [2] Since he said "the words of the Sages appear correct with regard to tithe," [3] [this proves] by implication that they disagree even with regard to consecrated property.

[4] Rather, if it was said, it was said as follows: [5] Rabbi Yoḥanan said: All agree as to the Sabbath with regard to consecrated property that he has redeemed [it]. [6] Firstly, because it is written: "And you shall call the Sabbath a delight"; [7] and furthermore, because the treasurers demand it in the marketplace.

[8] Rami bar Ḥama said: Now [the Sages] said: Consecrated property is not redeemed by means of land, [9] for the Torah (lit., "the Merciful One") said: "And he shall give

TRANSLATION AND COMMENTARY

to consecrated property," but may not be followed with regard to second tithe, [1] **this proves by implication that** Rabbi Eliezer himself **disagrees even with regard to** the redemption of second **tithe**, and not just about redeeming consecrated property, and maintains that second tithe may be regarded as redeemed even before the additional fifth has been paid. [2] Likewise, **since** Rabbi Yehudah HaNasi **said** that **the viewpoint of the Sages appears correct with regard to tithe,** but need not be followed with regard to consecrated property, [3] **this proves by implication that** Rabbi Eliezer and the Sages **disagree even with regard to consecrated property,** and not just about tithe redemption. Rabbi Eliezer maintains that even though the extra fifth has not yet been paid, both the second tithe and the consecrated property are redeemed, whereas the Sages maintain that if the extra fifth has not yet been paid, neither the second tithe nor the consecrated property are redeemed. This contradicts Rabbi Yoḥanan's statement that the Tannaim agreed unanimously that consecrated property is redeemed even before the payment of the additional fifth has been made.

אֶלָּא [4] To resolve this difficulty, the Gemara amends Rabbi Yoḥanan's statement: **Rather, if such a statement was made, it was made as follows:** [5] **Rabbi Yoḥanan said:** The Tannaim disagree as to whether the failure to pay the additional fifth delays redemption both in the case of second tithe and in the case of consecrated property. Nevertheless, **all agree that consecrated property that was redeemed** without payment of the additional fifth may be used on the Sabbath. There are two reasons for adopting a lenient attitude in this particular case: [6] **First,** the permission to use the property enhances the enjoyment of the Sabbath, **as it is written** (Isaiah 58:13): **"And you shall call the Sabbath a delight."** [7] **Furthermore, since the** Temple **treasurers** will **demand** the extra fifth **from** the owner **in the marketplace** and will be sure to collect it from him, there is no reason to be concerned that the extra fifth will be forever lost to the Temple treasury. But in all other cases involving consecrated property and second tithe, Rabbi Eliezer and Rabbi Yehoshua disagree as to whether failure to pay the additional fifth invalidates the redemption.

אָמַר רָמִי בַּר חָמָא [8] The Gemara now continues with a series of questions, attempting to determine whether certain laws of redemption that apply to payment of the principal apply as well to payment of the added fifth. **Rami bar Ḥama said: Now the Sages said** that **consecrated property cannot be redeemed by means of land,** [9] **for the Torah states** that a person who redeems a field that was consecrated to the Temple "**shall give**

RASHI

הרי אמרו — במסכת בכורות בפרק בתרא (נא,א). ונתן הכסף — "ואם המקדיש יגאל" וגו' ... "ויסף חמישית כסף ערכך עליו והיה לו".

CONCEPTS

הֶקְדֵּשׁ וּמַעֲשֵׂר שֵׁנִי Consecrated property and second tithe. Property which has been consecrated to the Temple and thereby designated for Temple use is known as *hekdesh* — "consecrated property." Such items belong to the Temple, and the Temple treasurers are responsible for ensuring that they are used appropriately. If necessary, *hekdesh* may be sold, after which the money obtained can be used as the Temple treasurers see fit.

In certain respects, the laws of second tithe parallel those of consecrated property. First of all, the use of second tithe is restricted. The owner may only eat it (or buy food with the money used to redeem it) in Jerusalem. Moreover, the owner must add an extra fifth when redeeming it, just as he must when redeeming *hekdesh*. However, second tithe differs from *hekdesh* in that it is the property of the person who separated it. Hence it is impossible to determine whether it was used (or redeemed) as required by law. By contrast, the Temple treasurers will make sure that *hekdesh* is used properly, and that if it is redeemed due payment is made.

TERMINOLOGY

אֶלָּא אִי אִתְּמַר הָכִי אִתְּמַר Rather, if it was said, it was said as follows. Sometimes, when an objection has been raised against an Amoraic statement, the Talmud resolves this objection by suggesting that the Amora's remark was reported incorrectly, and hence must be amended: "If such a statement was made, it was made in the following form."

NOTES

וְנָתַן הַכֶּסֶף וְקָם לוֹ And he shall give the money and it shall become his property. *Tosafot* (*Shabbat* 128a) notes that no such verse exists. Indeed, as *Rashi* points out, the Gemara here is referring to Leviticus 27:19: "And if he that sanctified the field will redeem it, then he shall add the fifth part of the money of the estimation to it, and it shall become his property." However, the Gemara often cites Biblical verses in abbreviated form, or in paraphrase, to emphasize the relevant point. In other texts of the Talmud, however, Leviticus 27:19 is quoted verbatim (cf. *Ḥiddushim Ha-Meyuḥasim LeRitva*.)

Some commentators ask how the Gemara was able to infer from this verse that land cannot be used to redeem consecrated property, for elsewhere the Gemara rules (based on this verse) that consecrated property may be redeemed with movables of any kind, and not only with money.

Tosafot answers that this ruling was based on a "generalization-specification-generalization" exegesis of the Biblical text (see below, 57b), by means of which it was inferred that anything that resembles money — i.e., movables — may be used to redeem consecrated property. However, land is fundamentally different from money, and therefore may not be used.

TRANSLATION AND COMMENTARY

the money and it shall become his property" (a paraphrase of Leviticus 27:19). Since the verse speaks of giving *money*, i.e., coins, we must conclude that consecrated property cannot be redeemed by offering the Temple treasury land of equivalent value. Now the question arises: Does the requirement to use only money apply to the added fifth that must be paid when the owner of consecrated property redeems his own land, or [1]**can** that extra **fifth be paid by using land** rather than money?

תְּרוּמָה אֵינָהּ מִשְׁתַּלֶּמֶת אֶלָּא מִן הַחוּלִּין [2]A similar question arises in connection with terumah: If a non-priest inadvertently partakes of terumah, he must pay a priest the value of the terumah plus a fifth. Now, the law is that if the non-priest ate the terumah, he cannot compensate by giving the priest money, clothing or the like, because the inadvertent eating of **terumah can only be compensated for by** giving a priest **unconsecrated food** that has already been tithed and which, once given to the priest as compensation, will assume all the sanctity of terumah. [3]This is derived from the verse in **the Torah** which **states** (Leviticus 22:14): "And if a man eats of a holy thing — i.e., terumah — unwittingly, he shall add the fifth part of it to it, **and he shall give the holy thing to the** priest." [4]The Gemara interprets the expression "the holy thing" as meaning the priest must be compensated with **something** that is **fit to become holy,** i.e., produce capable of becoming terumah. The question now arises: Does that same law apply to the added fifth that the non-priest must pay if he inadvertently partakes of terumah, or [5]**can** that extra **fifth be paid with something other than unconsecrated food,** i.e. money or something else of monetary value?

מַעֲשֵׂר אֵין מִתְחַלֵּל עַל הָאֲסִימוֹן [6]The Gemara now raises one final question: As explained earlier in this chapter (47b), second-**tithe** produce **cannot be redeemed by means of an *asimon*** — an unminted coin — [7]**because the Torah states** in connection with the money used for the redemption of second tithe (Deuteronomy 14:25): **"And you shall bind up the money in your hand,"** [8]**which** is interpreted by Rabbi Akiva as **including any** coin **that bears an impression,** since the Hebrew word "and you shall bind up" (וְצַרְתָּ) is understood as though it meant "and you shall stamp." Thus we learn that, according to Rabbi Akiva, only

הַכֶּסֶף וְקָם לוֹ״. [1]חוּמְשׁוֹ מַהוּ שֶׁיִּתְחַלֵּל עַל הַקַּרְקַע? [2]תְּרוּמָה אֵינָהּ מִשְׁתַּלֶּמֶת אֶלָּא מִן הַחוּלִּין, [3]דְּרַחֲמָנָא אָמַר: ״וְנָתַן לַכֹּהֵן אֶת הַקֹּדֶשׁ״ — [4]דָּבָר הָרָאוּי לִהְיוֹת קֹדֶשׁ. [5]חוּמְשָׁהּ מַהוּ שֶׁיִּשְׁתַּלֵּם שֶׁלֹּא מִן הַחוּלִּין? [6]מַעֲשֵׂר אֵין מִתְחַלֵּל עַל הָאֲסִימוֹן, [7]דְּרַחֲמָנָא אָמַר: ״וְצַרְתָּ הַכֶּסֶף בְּיָדְךָ״, [8]לְרַבּוֹת כָּל דָּבָר שֶׁיֵּשׁ עָלָיו צוּרָה.

LITERAL TRANSLATION

the money and it shall become his property." [1]Can its fifth be redeemed by means of land?

[2]Terumah cannot be repaid except from unconsecrated food, [3]for the Torah said: "And he shall give the holy thing to the priest" — [4]something that is fit to become holy. [5]Can its fifth be repaid not from unconsecrated food?

[6]Tithe is not redeemed by means of an *asimon*, [7]for the Torah said: "And you shall bind up the money in your hand," [8]to include everything that has an impression on it.

RASHI

תרומה — זר האוכלה בשוגג. **אינה משתלמת** — מעות, אלא פירות חולין. שהתשלומין נעשין תרומה כדכתיב בו "את הקודש" — מה שהוא נותן לו נעשה קודש, אלמא מידי דחזי להכי בעינן. **שלא מן החולין** — מעות או בגדים שוה כסף. **עליו** — בכולהו חומשין כתיב "יוסף עליו".

BACKGROUND

תְּרוּמָה אֵינָהּ מִשְׁתַּלֶּמֶת אֶלָּא מִן הַחוּלִּין Terumah cannot be repaid except from unconsecrated food. A non-priest who stole terumah from a priest (or ate terumah unwittingly) must compensate the priest for the principal and pay him an extra fifth. This fifth may not be paid with terumah even if it belongs to the non-priest, but only with produce that has already been tithed (חוּלִּין). Since tithed produce costs more than terumah — in line with the laws of supply and demand, the demand for terumah is limited, because only priests are permitted to eat it — the requirement to pay the fifth from tithed produce serves as an additional penalty for nonpriests who benefit illegally from terumah.

NOTES

תְּרוּמָה אֵינָהּ מִשְׁתַּלֶּמֶת אֶלָּא מִן הַחוּלִּין Terumah cannot be repaid except from unconsecrated food. *Rashi* and others, followed by our commentary, maintain that compensation for terumah may be paid from all types of produce, but not with money. *Ra'avad*, however, maintains that food that is exempt from tithes (e.g., gleanings from the field left for the poor) cannot be given as compensation for terumah.

HALAKHAH

פִּדְיוֹן הֶקְדֵּשׁ וְחוּמְשׁוֹ Redeeming property consecrated to the Temple and adding a fifth. "Property consecrated to the Temple can be redeemed only by means of money or movable property, but not with land or monetary notes. Likewise, the extra fifth added by the owner when redeeming such property must be paid with money or movables. The added fifth is treated as consecrated property in all respects," following Rava. (*Rambam, Sefer Hafla'ah, Hilkhot Arukhin* 7:1-2.)

תְּרוּמָה וְחוּמְשָׁהּ Terumah and its fifth. "If someone who is not a priest inadvertently ate terumah, he must repay the owner with produce that has previously been tithed, and must pay an extra fifth. This extra fifth must also be paid with previously tithed produce." (Ibid., *Sefer Zeraim, Hilkhot Terumot* 10:1, 18, 23.)

מַעֲשֵׂר שֵׁנִי וְחוּמְשׁוֹ Second tithe and its fifth. "Second tithe, and the additional fifth paid when the owner redeems it, can only be redeemed with minted coins." (Ibid., (*Hilkhot Ma'aser Sheni* 4:9.)

LITERAL TRANSLATION

[1]Can its fifth be redeemed with an *asimon?*
[2]The matter rolled on and reached Rava. [3]He said to them: The verse says "to it" [4]to include its fifth as itself.

[5]Ravina said: We too have also learned [thus]: [6]"Someone who steals terumah but did not eat it repays double the value of the terumah. [7][If] he ate it, he pays two principals and a fifth, [8]one principal and a fifth from unconsecrated produce, and one principal [based on] the value of the terumah." [54B] [9]Conclude from this [that] its fifth is as itself. [10]Conclude from this.

[1]חוּמְשׁוֹ מַהוּ שֶׁיִּתְחַלֵּל עַל הָאֲסִימוֹן?

[2]אִתְגַּלְגַּל מִלְּתָא וּמְטָא לְקַמֵּיהּ דְּרָבָא. [3]אֲמַר לְהוּ: אָמַר קְרָא, "עָלָיו", [4]לְרַבּוֹת חוּמְשׁוֹ כְּמוֹתוֹ.

[5]אָמַר רָבִינָא: אַף אֲנַן נַמִי תְּנֵינָא: [6]"הַגּוֹנֵב תְּרוּמָה וְלֹא אֲכָלָהּ מְשַׁלֵּם תַּשְׁלוּמֵי כֶפֶל דְּמֵי תְרוּמָה. [7]אֲכָלָהּ, מְשַׁלֵּם שְׁנֵי קְרָנִים וְחוֹמֶשׁ, [8]קֶרֶן וְחוֹמֶשׁ מִן הַחוּלִּין, וְהַקֶּרֶן דְּמֵי תְרוּמָה". [54B] [9]שְׁמַע מִינָּהּ חוּמְשׁוֹ כְּמוֹתוֹ. [10]שְׁמַע מִינָּהּ.

TRANSLATION AND COMMENTARY

minted coins which bear impressions may be used to redeem second tithe. Accordingly, the question arises: Does this law also apply to the fifth that a person must add when redeeming his own tithe, or [1]**can** that extra **fifth be paid with an** *asimon?*

אִתְגַּלְגַּל מִלְּתָא [2]Since Rami bar Ḥama was unable to answer these questions, **the matter was left unresolved until it came to** the attention of **Rava**, [3]who **said to** the Sages: In all three cases — consecrated property (Leviticus 27:19), terumah (Leviticus 22:14), and second tithe (Leviticus 27:31) — **the verse** states that the fifth should be added **"to it"** (i.e., to the principal), [4]**which teaches that** in each case **its fifth is** treated **like** the principal itself. In other words, all the laws that apply to payment of the principal also apply to payment of the additional fifth.

אָמַר רָבִינָא [5]**Ravina said: We have learned a similar rule** in the following Mishnah (*Terumot* 6:4): [6]**"If a person stole terumah but did not eat it, he makes a double repayment**, i.e., he repays twice the value of the terumah he stole. In this he is like any other thief, who must restore the article he stole and as a penalty must also pay the value of the stolen article. Now, since a thief must make the double repayment according to the value of the stolen article, a person who steals terumah pays according to **the value of terumah,** which is considerably less than the value of ordinary food, since fewer people — only priests in a state of ritual purity — are interested in receiving it. [7]"But **if** the thief inadvertently **ate** the terumah after he stole it, **he pays twice the principal and a fifth,** calculated as follows: [8]**One principal and a fifth** is paid in kind **with** unconsecrated **food,** as is the case where any non-priest unwittingly ate terumah, **and one principal** — i.e., the penalty for theft — is paid in money according to **the value of terumah,"** as explained above. [54B] [9]Thus, since the Mishnah states that both the principal and the additional fifth paid by a non-priest who inadvertently ate terumah must be paid from unconsecrated produce, we may **conclude from this** that payment of the additional **fifth is** treated **like** payment of the principal itself. [10]The Gemara sums up: **Conclude from here** that this is indeed so.

RASHI

ולא אכלה — דהיא חוזרת בעין. **משלם את הכפל** — של קנס גניבה במעות. **דמי תרומה** — כמה שהיא שוה לימכר בשוק, ודמיה פחותין מדמי חולין, שאינה ראויה אלא לכהנים, ואינה ראויה בימי טומאתו, ואם מטמאה אסורה באכילה — לפיכך דמיה מועטים, והיינו דקאמר דמי תרומה. **אכלה** — בשוגג, דלא ידע שהיא תרומה. **שני קרנין** — אחד לקרן ואחד לכפל, וחומש בשביל אכילתה. **מן החולין** — פירות מתוקנין. **והקרן** — השני, שהוא בא מחמת כפל של קנס גניבה — משלם נמי דמי תרומה, כלומר: מעות כמו שנמכרת תרומה בשוק. **שמע מינה חומשו כמותו** — דמשתלם פירות ולא מעות.

TERMINOLOGY

אַף אֲנַן נַמִי תְּנֵינָא We too have also learned [thus]. This term introduces a quotation from a Mishnah or a Baraita corroborating the previous Amoraic statement.

NOTES

חוּמְשׁוֹ כְּמוֹתוֹ **Its fifth as itself.** All agree that the fifth is not treated exactly like the principal. Thus, a fifth must be added to the principal when redeeming second tithe, but an extra fifth is not necessary when redeeming the first fifth. However, the fifth resembles the principal in that both must be paid from the same type of property (*Rashba*, *Ran*).

HALAKHAH

הַגּוֹנֵב תְּרוּמָה **Someone who steals terumah.** "If a person stole terumah but did not eat it, he must make a double repayment to the owner, like any other thief. The principal is repaid from produce that has already been tithed, while the additional repayment made by a thief (ordinarily worth the value of the stolen item) is assessed according to the market value of terumah. However, if a person stole terumah and ate it without realizing that it was terumah, he must compensate the owner for the principal and pay an extra fifth. Both these acts of compensation are made from tithed produce. He must also make a second payment of the principal as punishment for the theft, and this is assessed according to the market value of terumah." (Ibid., *Hilkhot Terumah* 10:23.)

¹אֲמַר רָבָא: גַּבֵּי גֵּזֶל כְּתִיב: ״וַחֲמִשְׁתָיו יֹסֵף עָלָיו״. ²וּתְנַן: ״נָתַן לוֹ אֶת הַקֶּרֶן וְנִשְׁבַּע לוֹ עַל הַחוֹמֶשׁ, ³הֲרֵי זֶה מוֹסִיף חוֹמֶשׁ עַל חוֹמֶשׁ עַד שֶׁיִּתְמַעֵט הַקֶּרֶן פָּחוֹת מִשָּׁוֶה פְּרוּטָה״.
⁴גַּבֵּי תְּרוּמָה כְּתִיב: ״אִישׁ כִּי יֹאכַל קֹדֶשׁ בִּשְׁגָגָה, וְיָסַף חֲמִשִׁיתוֹ עָלָיו״. ⁵וּתְנַן: ״הָאוֹכֵל תְּרוּמָה בְּשׁוֹגֵג מְשַׁלֵּם קֶרֶן

LITERAL TRANSLATION

[1]Rava said: With regard to robbery it is written: "And its fifths he shall add to it." [2]And we have learned: "[If] he gave him the principal and swore to him about the fifth, [3]then he adds a fifth to the fifth until the principal becomes less than a perutah's worth."
[4]With regard to terumah it is written: "And if a man eats of the holy thing unwittingly, he shall add its fifth to it." [5]And we have learned: "Someone who unwittingly eats terumah pays the principal

TRANSLATION AND COMMENTARY

אֲמַר רָבָא [1]In the course of the Gemara's inquiry into the nature of the payment of the additional fifth, we have been introduced to a number of situations in which payment of an additional fifth is imposed — redemption of second tithe, redemption of consecrated property, and compensation by a non-priest for inadvertently eating terumah. The Gemara now proceeds further in its inquiry into the laws of the additional fifth, and raises the question of whether the additional fifth may itself become the basis for imposing payment of *another* fifth. **Rava said:** The law is that if a person takes a false oath to deny a debt, and later admits that he swore falsely, he must repay the debt and pay the injured party an additional fifth. Now, **with regard to** such a case, which comes under the category of **robbery, it is written** in the Torah (Leviticus 5:23-24): "He shall restore that which he took violently away ... **and he shall add its *fifths* to it.**" The plural form "its fifths" (וַחֲמִשְׁתָיו) implies that it is possible to pay more than one penalty of an additional fifth for a single robbery, as the Gemara proceeds to explain: [2]**We have learned** in the following Mishnah (*Bava Kamma* 9:7): "If a person denied under oath and then later admitted owing somebody money, and then **paid** the other party **the principal,** but **denied under oath** that he still owed the extra **fifth,** this denial of the extra fifth is treated as if it were a denial of a new claim. [3]Hence, if he later admits that his second oath was untrue, **he must** repay the fifth — which is now regarded as the principal in a new case — and **pay an** additional **fifth of the** original **fifth.** If he now denies the second fifth under oath, he will later have to pay an additional fifth of that second fifth, and this can continue **until the principal**, i.e., the money which he most recently denied owing, **is worth less than a perutah,** and anything worth less than a perutah is considered Halakhically worthless." Thus we see that a person may be required to pay a fifth of the first fifth, and then a fifth of that fifth, and so on, if he continues to swear falsely and then confesses to not having paid the additional fifth.

גַּבֵּי תְּרוּמָה כְּתִיב [4]A similar rule exists **with regard to** a non-priest who inadvertently ate **terumah. It is written** in the Torah (Leviticus 22:14): **"And if a man eats of the holy thing** [i.e., terumah] **unintentionally, he shall add its fifth to it."** In the light of the case of robbery discussed above where the expression "its fifths" was used, we might have understood that in the case of terumah only a single fifth need be paid, because here the expression "its fifth" was used. [5]But **we have learned** in the Mishnah (*Terumot* 6:1): **"If** a non-priest **ate terumah**

RASHI

גבי גזל כתיב — גבי אשם גזילות כתיב, אם גזל וכפר ונשבע לשקר "חמישיתיו" — חמישיות הרבה. **ותנן** — נמי זימנין דאיכא טובא. **נתן לו את הקרן** — לאחר שנשבע והודה ונתחייב קרן וחומש, ונשבע לו על החומש, שחזר וכפר את החומש ואמר נתתיו לך, ונשבע והודה, הרי זה מוסיף חומש על חומש שכפר. וכן אם חזר ונתן לו חומש ראשון שנשבע עליו, וחזר וכפר ונשבע על חומש שני והודה, מוסיף חומש על חומש שני, וכן לעולם. **עד שיתמעט הקרן** — חומש שהוא מחוייב כבר וחוזר וכופרו קרוי קרן, עד שתהא כפירת שבועתו בפחות משוה פרוטה. **גבי תרומה** — אוכל תרומה בשוגג. **כתיב חמישיתו** — דלא משמע אלא חד חומש, ואפילו הכי תנן בה חומשא דחומשא, כגון אם נתן קרן וחומש מן החולין כמשפטו, ונעשו התשלומין תרומה, וחזר ואכל אותו חומש — משלם אותו וחומשו.

HALAKHAH

הַכּוֹפֵר בְּחוֹמֶשׁ גְּזֵילָה **Someone who denies owing the additional fifth for something which he robbed.** "If a person committed robbery, swore falsely in denying the claim, confessed and repaid the owner for the principal but not the extra fifth, and then swore that he had already paid the fifth, this fifth is treated like the principal in all respects. Thus, the robber must pay the original owner both the extra fifth and a fifth of this fifth. Likewise, if the robber swore falsely that he had already paid a fifth of the fifth, he must pay an additional fifth of what he denied, until the amount of money denied is less than a perutah." (*Rambam, Sefer Kinyan, Hilkhot Gezelah* 7:12.)

קֶרֶן וְחוֹמֶשׁ בִּתְרוּמָה **The principal and the fifth in the case of terumah.** "If a non-priest unintentionally ate terumah (or drank it or anointed himself with it, assuming that such terumah is normally used for such purposes), he repays the principal and an additional fifth, whether the terumah was ritually pure or not." (Ibid., *Sefer Zeraim, Hilkhot Terumot* 10:2.)

וְחוּמֶשׁ. [1] אֶחָד הָאוֹכֵל וְאֶחָד הַשּׁוֹתֶה וְאֶחָד הַסָּךְ, אֶחָד תְּרוּמָה טְהוֹרָה וְאֶחָד תְּרוּמָה טְמֵאָה, [2] מְשַׁלֵּם חוּמְשָׁהּ וְחוּמְשָׁא דְחוּמְשָׁא״.

[3] וְאִילּוּ גַּבֵּי מַעֲשֵׂר, לָא מִכְתַּב כְּתִיב וְלָא מִיתְנָא תְּנָא, וְלָא אִיבַּעוּיֵי אִיבַּעְיָא לַן.

[4] גַּבֵּי הֶקְדֵּשׁ כְּתִיב: ״וְאִם הַמַּקְדִּישׁ יִגְאַל אֶת בֵּיתוֹ, וְיָסַף חֲמִישִׁית כֶּסֶף עֶרְכְּךָ״.

LITERAL TRANSLATION

and a fifth. [1] Both someone who eats and someone who drinks and someone who anoints [with] both ritually pure terumah and ritually impure terumah, [2] he pays a fifth and a fifth of the fifth."

[3] But with regard to tithe, it is neither written nor taught, nor was the question asked by us.

[4] With regard to consecrated property it is written: "And if he that sanctified it will redeem his house, then he shall add a fifth of the money of your estimation."

TRANSLATION AND COMMENTARY

unintentionally, he pays the principal and an additional **fifth.** [1] And it makes no difference **whether he ate** it **or drank** it (e.g., if it was wine) **or anointed** himself **with it** (e.g., if it was olive oil), nor does it make any difference **whether the terumah** he ate or drank **was ritually pure or not.** [2] In all such cases, the person who consumed the terumah must restore it to the priest in kind, and **he must pay** an additional **fifth of** the entire amount — all of which assumes the status of terumah. If he unwittingly eats the extra fifth that he designated for the priest, he must now reimburse the priest for that original fifth and pay in addition **a fifth of that fifth.**"

וְאִילּוּ גַּבֵּי מַעֲשֵׂר [3] However, Rava continued, **with regard to** the payment of the additional fifth that the Torah imposes when a person redeems his own second **tithe**, **it is neither written** in the Torah that he must add a fifth of the fifth if he later redeems the first fifth with different money, **nor** was such a law **taught** in the Mishnah or in a Baraita, **nor was** any question about the matter **asked** by the Amoraim, as it is obvious that a fifth of the first fifth need not be paid in such a case.

גַּבֵּי הֶקְדֵּשׁ כְּתִיב [4] Now Rava comes to the case about which he has doubts as to whether a fifth can generate obligations to pay further fifths: **With regard to consecrated property, it is written** in the Torah (Leviticus 27:15): **"And if he that sanctified it will redeem his house, then he shall add a fifth of the money of your**

RASHI

ואחד הסך — שמן של תרומה. דסיכה כשתייה, ושתייה כאכילה. דאמרינן בפרק בתרא [דיומא] (עו,א): שתייה כאכילה מ״ואכלת לפני ה׳ וגו׳״ וכתיב ביה ״תירושך״. וסיכה כשתייה, דכתיב ״ותבא כמים בקרבו וכשמן בעצמותיו״. אבל אם ביערה על ידי דבר אחר, אינו משלם חומש, ד״איש כי יאכל קדש״ כתיב, פרט למזיק את התרומה על ידי דבר שאינה אכילה. **גבי מעשר** — גבי פדיון מעשר שני דכתיב ביה נמי ״וחמישיתו יוסף עליו״. **לא מכתב כתיב ביה** — משמעות דחמישיות הרבה. **ולא מיתנא תנא ביה** — חומשא דחומשא, כגון אם חזר וחילל את החומש הראשון. **ולא איבעויי מיבעיא לן** — אם מוסיף חומש על חומש אם לא, דפשיטא לן דלא מוסיף, דלא אשכחן ביה רמז בקרא כדאשכחן בתרומה רמז פורתא, כדבעינן למימר קמן, דבתרומה כתיב ״ויסף חמישיתו״ ולא כתיב ״יסף״ כדגבי מעשר, ולשון ״ויסף״ — משמע שתי תוספות, יוסיף וחוזר ויוסיף. אבל ״יסף״ — חדא משמע. **גבי הקדש** — הפודה את הקדשו כתיב ״ואם המקדיש יגאל ויסף חמישית כסף ערכך״.

NOTES

וְלָא אִיבַּעוּיֵי אִיבַּעְיָא **Nor was any question asked.** *Torat Ḥayyim* explains that "no question was asked" about the cases of robbery and terumah, since it is clear from both the Biblical text and from the Mishnayot that an extra fifth must be added in such cases. Likewise, "no question was asked" about second tithe, since neither the Biblical text nor the Rabbinic sources give the slightest indication that an extra fifth is to be added in this case. Thus the Gemara notes that "no question was asked" about these cases, as an introduction to the question which follows regarding consecrated property.

גַּבֵּי הֶקְדֵּשׁ **With regard to consecrated property.** The commentators (*Ramban*, *Ritva*, *Ran* and others) explain that the Gemara's question applies only to land, or to fields, courtyards, and houses that were consecrated, but not to movables. For it is obvious that an extra fifth must be added when redeeming movables, since the same expression is used in connection with the redemption of movables and the redemption of terumah (see Leviticus 27:13, and the Gemara's discussion below).

HALAKHAH

חוֹמֶשׁ תְּרוּמָה וחוּמְשׁוֹ **The additional fifth in the case of terumah and a fifth of it.** "If a non-priest unintentionally ate the fifth that he had designated as compensation for the priest (after having eaten terumah unwittingly), he must repay the additional fifth to the priest, as well as a fifth of this fifth, since the first fifth is treated as if it were the principal." (*Rambam, Sefer Zeraim, Hilkhot Terumot* 10:15.)

חוֹמֶשׁ חוּמְשׁוֹ שֶׁל מַעֲשֵׂר **A fifth of a fifth in the case of second tithe.** "If a person redeemed his own second tithe and added a fifth, and now wishes to redeem the redemption money, he need only add a fifth to the original principal, but not a fifth of the first fifth, since neither the Torah nor the Mishnah nor Baraitot mention anything about paying an extra fifth in this case." (Ibid., *Hilkhot Ma'aser Sheni* 5:3.)

TRANSLATION AND COMMENTARY

estimation to it." [1] **And we have learned** in the Mishnah (below, 55b): **"Someone who redeems property** that he himself **consecrated** must **add a fifth** of the value of the property." [2] Now, from this Mishnah **we learn** that when redeeming his own property, the owner must add **a fifth.** But **we do not learn** anything from this Mishnah about the redemption of that first fifth. We do not know whether the owner who now wishes to redeem the additional fifth he paid to the Temple treasury as part of the redemption price of his property must add **a fifth of that fifth** or not. [3] Hence, the question arises: **What is the law** in such a case?

גַּבֵּי תְּרוּמָה כְּתִיב [4] The Gemara now analyzes this question by considering possible sources for the law requiring the payment of a fifth of a fifth in a case where a person inadvertently ate a fifth that had been consecrated as terumah and was part of the compensation paid by a non-priest for inadvertently eating terumah. It seeks to find out whether these sources are instructive as well with regard to consecrated property: If the reason that a non-priest must pay a fifth of the first fifth in the case of terumah is that **with regard to terumah it is written** (Leviticus 22:14): **"And he shall add,"** [5] then so too **with regard to consecrated property, it is also written** (Leviticus 27:15): **"And he shall add."** According to this interpretation, the non-priest must pay a fifth of the first fifth in the case of terumah because the Torah states *"and* he shall add," the conjunction "and" serving as an extending particle implying that he shall add *and* then he shall add again. Now, since the same expression is used in connection with the redemption of consecrated property, we may infer that there, too, one must add a fifth of the first fifth. [6] On the other hand, **perhaps** the reason that a person pays a fifth of the first fifth in the case of terumah is different: **With regard to terumah it is written: "And he shall add."** [7] Now, **if you remove the letter** ***vav*** **from** the word **"and he shall add"** (*veyasaf* — וְיָסַף) **and you attach it to** the word **"its fifth"** (*ḥamishito* — חֲמִשִׁיתוֹ) this word **becomes "its fifths"** (*ḥamishitav* — חֲמִשִׁתָיו). The Talmud frequently interprets Biblical verses by recourse to letter-transposition. Thus it is possible that the reason why a person must pay a fifth of a fifth in the case of terumah is not that the Torah uses the expression *"and* he shall add," as explained previously, but that by means of letter-transposition the word "its fifth" is transformed into "its *fifths.*" For if we remove the *vav* ("ו" — "and") from the word "and he shall add" (וְיָסַף) and place it next to the letter *vav* that is the last

[1] וּתְנַן: ״הַפּוֹדֶה אֶת הֶקְדֵּשׁוֹ מוֹסִיף חוֹמֶשׁ״. [2] חוּמְשָׁא תְּנַן. חוּמְשָׁא דְּחוּמְשָׁא לָא תְּנַן. [3] מַאי?

[4] גַּבֵּי תְּרוּמָה כְּתִיב: ״וְיָסַף״; [6] גַּבֵּי קֹדֶשׁ נַמִי הָא כְּתִיב: ״וְיָסַף״. [17] אוֹ דִּלְמָא, גַּבֵּי תְּרוּמָה כְּתִיב: ״וְיָסַף״. [7] אִי שָׁקְלַתְּ לֵיהּ לְוָי״ו דְּ״וְיָסַף״ וְשָׁדֵית לֵיהּ עַל ״חֲמִשִׁיתוֹ״, הֲוָה לֵיהּ ״חֲמִישִׁיתָיו״.

LITERAL TRANSLATION

[1] And we have learned: "Someone who redeems his consecrated property adds a fifth." [2] A fifth we have learned. A fifth of the fifth we have not learned. [3] What [is the law]?

[4] With regard to terumah it is written: "And he shall add"; [5] with regard to consecrated property surely it is also written: "And he shall add." [6] Or perhaps, with regard to terumah it is written: "And he shall add." [7] If you remove the [letter] *vav* from "and he shall add" and you attach it to "its fifth," it becomes "its fifths."

RASHI

הכי גרסינן: ותנן הפודה את הקדשו מוסיף חומש — ובמתניתין דפירקין הוא, ולא גרסינן הנהנה מן ההקדש שוה פרוטה כו׳ — דההיא במעילה קא מיירי, וגבי מעילה לא כתיב "ויסף" אלא "יסף", ולא כתיב "חמישית" אלא "חמישיתו ואת אשר חטא מן הקדש ישלם וגו׳". **מאי** — אם חזר וחילל את החומש, מהו שיוסיף חומש? מי אמרינן: האי דגבי תרומה, אף על גב דלא כתיב "חמישיתיו" — תנן בה חומשא דחומשא, משום דכתיב "ויסף" דמשמע שתי תוספות. אי טעמא משום משמעותא הוא, הכא נמי כתיב "ויסף" וחייב להוסיף. **או דלמא** — טעמא דתרומה לאו משום משמעותא הוא, אלא משום דקיימא לן גורעין ומוסיפין ודורשין. הלכך, "ויסף" דגבי תרומה, כי שקלת לה וא"ו ד"ויסף" ותיקרי ביה "יסף חמישיתו", ושדית ליה בסוף חמישיתיו — אתקרי חמישיתיו בשני ווין, ונשתמע חמישיות הרבה. אבל הכא, גבי הקדש דלא כתיב אלא חמישית, אף על גב דשקלת כו׳. ואם תאמר: נישדייה באמצע תיבה ונקרי חמישיות כסף ערכך! לא אשכחן גורעין ומוסיפין להפסיק את התיבה, אלא או בראשה או בסופה, כדאמרינן בסדר יומא (מח,א): "ולקח מדם הפר" — דם מהפר יקבלנו.

NOTES

אִי שָׁקְלַתְּ לֵיהּ לְוָי״ו If you remove the letter *vav*. This hermeneutic technique, which is found in other places in the Gemara as well, is known as גּוֹרְעִים וּמוֹסִיפִים וְדוֹרְשִׁים — "removing and adding and interpreting."

Rashi asks why a similar deduction could not have been drawn from the words וְיָסַף חֲמִישִׁית used in connection with second tithe. Specifically, the letter *vav* at the beginning of וְיָסַף could have been placed between the last two letters of חֲמִישִׁית, yielding חֲמִישִׁיוֹת — "fifths."

Rashi answers that letter transposition is only performed when the letters are moved to the beginning or end of a word. Other commentators, however, challenge this explanation, noting that there are cases in which letters are transposed to the middle of a word (see, for example, *Bekhorot* 44b). Accordingly, *Ritva* suggests that letter-transposition is only performed when the resulting word is

TRANSLATION AND COMMENTARY

letter of the next word, "its fifth" (חֲמִישִׁיתוֹ), this word then becomes "its *fifths*" (חֲמִשִׁיתָוו = חֲמִישִׁיתָיו), implying that a person sometimes pays more than one additional fifth. [1]But **with regard to consecrated property it is written: "And he shall add a fifth,"** and here letter-transposition cannot generate the word "fifths" because the word for "fifth" used in the context of consecrated property (חֲמִישִׁית) does not already have a *vav* as its last letter. (The device of letter-transposition — if used at all — is only used by joining the first or last letter of a word to the first or last letter of the word next to it.) Adding the *vav* from the word "and he shall add" (וְיָסַף) would not therefore transform it into the plural form, as the Gemara now explains: [2]For **even if you remove the letter** *vav* ("ו") **of "and he shall add"** (וְיָסַף) **and you attach it to the** end of the word **"a fifth"** (חֲמִישִׁית), **in the end it only becomes "its fifth"** (חֲמִשְׁתוֹ — singular), but not "its fifths." Thus, the case of terumah is not instructive as to whether a person has to add a fifth to a fifth in the case of consecrated property.

וְתֵיפּוֹק לֵיהּ [3]In an attempt to solve Rava's question, the Gemara suggests: Why **can he not derive** the answer to this question **from the fact that** the first fifth **is** merely **second**-degree *hekdesh* — consecrated property. Property consecrated to the Temple may have "original" or "derivative" sanctity, depending on the circumstances of its transfer to the Temple treasury. Property originally dedicated for Temple use enjoys original sanctity. Property transferred to the Temple treasury in order to redeem previously consecrated property — including property transferred as payment of the additional fifth — has only secondary or derivative sanctity, its sanctity being "derived" from the consecrated property it redeemed. [4]Now, the rule is, as **Rabbi Yehoshua ben Levi said**, basing himself on an inference from the Biblical text (see below), that **a person** must **add a fifth** when redeeming **first**-degree ***hekdesh*** — property consecrated directly to the Temple — but **he** need **not add a fifth** when redeeming **second**-degree ***hekdesh*** — property used to redeem property previously consecrated directly to the Temple! Since the sanctity of the additional fifth is not original but is only derived from the property that had originally been consecrated, it too should not require the payment of an additional fifth when it is redeemed. Can we not, then, solve Rava's question on the basis of Rabbi Yehoshua ben Levi's rule?

אֲמַר לֵיהּ רַב פַּפִּי לְרָבִינָא [5]However, the Gemara rejects this proof: **Rav Pappi said to Ravina**: **Rava said as follows:** The assumption that the additional fifth is to be regarded as "second *hekdesh*" is not well-founded. It is true that the principal of the redemption money paid to redeem consecrated property must be regarded as second *hekdesh* because it is a replacement for property which was originally consecrated. However, **the fifth**

[1]גַּבֵּי הֶקְדֵּשׁ כְּתִיב: "וְיָסַף חֲמִישִׁית". [2]אַף עַל גַּב דְּכִי שָׁקְלַתְּ לֵיהּ לְוָי"ו דְּ"וְיָסַף" וְשָׁדֵית לֵיהּ עַל "חֲמִישִׁית", סוֹף סוֹף הֲוָה לֵיהּ "חֲמִשְׁתוֹ". [3]וְתֵיפּוֹק לֵיהּ דַּהֲוָה לֵיהּ הֶקְדֵּשׁ שֵׁנִי, [4]וְאָמַר רַבִּי יְהוֹשֻׁעַ בֶּן לֵוִי: אַהֶקְדֵּשׁ רִאשׁוֹן מוֹסִיף חוֹמֶשׁ. עַל הֶקְדֵּשׁ שֵׁנִי אֵין מוֹסִיף חוֹמֶשׁ! [5]אֲמַר לֵיהּ רַב פַּפִּי לְרָבִינָא: הָכִי אֲמַר רָבָא: חוֹמֶשׁ

LITERAL TRANSLATION

[1]With regard to consecrated property it is written: "And he shall add a fifth." [2]Even if you remove the [letter] *vav* of "and he shall add" and you attach it to "a fifth," in the end it [only] becomes "its fifth."

[3]Then let him derive it [from the fact] that it is second *hekdesh*, [4]and Rabbi Yehoshua ben Levi said: To first *hekdesh*, he adds a fifth. To second *hekdesh*, he does not add a fifth!

[5]Rav Pappi said to Ravina: Thus did Rava say: The fifth

RASHI

תיפוק ליה כו׳ — מאי קמבעיא ליה לרבא? תיפוק ליה דאם חזר וחילל את החומש הראשון אין מוסיף חומש, דהוה ליה הקדש שני, אפילו חזר וחילל קרן עצמו שהתפיס תחת הראשון, אין מוסיף חומש. **ואמר רבי יהושע בן לוי כו׳** — ויליף לה מקרא בשמעתא. **חומש בתחלת הקדש דמי** — שהרי מאליו ניתוסף, ולא נתפס תחת הראשון. הלכך, בעיין מטעם דהקדש שני לא תיפשוט ליה, משום הכי מספקא ליה.

SAGES

רַבִּי יְהוֹשֻׁעַ בֶּן לֵוִי Rabbi Yehoshua ben Levi. One of the greatest of the Amoraim of the first generation in Eretz Israel, Rabbi Yehoshua ben Levi was, according to some opinions, the son of Levi ben Sisi, one of the great students of Rabbi Yehudah HaNasi, and it seems that Rabbi Yehoshua ben Levi was himself one of Rabbi Yehudah HaNasi's younger students. Many Halakhic disputes are recorded between him and Rabbi Yoḥanan, who was apparently younger than him and a student and colleague of his. In general the Halakhah follows Rabbi Yehoshua ben Levi, even against Rabbi Yoḥanan, whose authority was very great.

Rabbi Yehoshua ben Levi was also one of the great teachers of Aggadah, and many very important stories are related in his name. Because of the great respect in which he was held, Aggadic statements in his name are presented at the end of the six orders of the Mishnah.

A great deal is told of his piety and sanctity, and he is regarded as one of the most righteous men of all generations. Among other things, it is told that he would sit with the most dangerously infected lepers and study Torah. He was famous as a worker of miracles, to whom Elijah the Prophet appeared, and his prayers were always accepted. According to tradition he is one of those over whom the Angel of Death had no dominion, and he entered the Garden of Eden alive.

He taught many students. All the Sages of the succeeding generation were his students to some degree, and quote Torah teachings in his name. His son, Rabbi Yosef, was also a Sage, and married into the Nasi's family.

NOTES

found in the same form elsewhere in the Torah, whereas the word (חֲמִישִׁיּוֹת "fifths") does not appear anywhere else in the Torah (see also *Tosafot, Sanhedrin* 4b).

HALAKHAH

חוּמְשׁוֹ שֶׁל הֶקְדֵּשׁ A fifth in the case of *hekdesh*. "Anyone who redeems property that he himself consecrated to the Temple must add a fifth to the value of the principal. This fifth is treated as if it were the principal; hence, if the owner wishes to redeem it, he must add a fifth to it when doing so." (*Rambam, Sefer Hafla'ah, Hilkhot Arakhin* 7:2.)

הֶקְדֵּשׁ רִאשׁוֹן וְשֵׁנִי Original and second *hekdesh*. "An additional fifth is added only when redeeming original *hekdesh*, i.e., property that a person had consecrated directly to the Temple. However, if a person redeemed *hekdesh* with something else (e.g., one animal with another), he need not add an extra fifth when redeeming the animal," following Rabbi Yehoshua ben Levi. (Ibid., 7:4-5.)

SAGES

רַב טַבְיוֹמִי Rav Tavyomi. A fifth-generation Babylonian Amora, Rav Tavyomi was a disciple of Abaye and Rava, many of whose legal traditions he transmitted.

BACKGROUND

מַקְדִּישׁ וּמַתְפִּיס Consecration and transferring sanctity. Property is ordinarily consecrated by donating it to the Temple. However, property may also be sanctified through "transfer of sanctity" (הַתְפָּסָה), i.e., by substituting a non-consecrated object for a consecrated one. To be sure, this is prohibited in certain cases — for example, if a non-consecrated animal is exchanged for a sacrificial animal (תְּמוּרָה, see Leviticus 27:33) — but generally substitution is considered a valid way of redeeming consecrated property and rendering another object sacred in its place.

TERMINOLOGY

תָּנֵי תַּנָּא קַמֵּיהּ דְּ.... The Tanna taught [a Baraita] before.... This expression describes the situation in which a Baraita was recited in the presence of the head of the Academy, and the latter offered his comments on it.

TRANSLATION AND COMMENTARY

is considered like first *hekdesh*. Even though the additional fifth was not originally consecrated to the Temple, it is treated as first *hekdesh* because it was not given in exchange for property previously consecrated. Rather, it was given as a supplement to the money paid to redeem the original consecrated property. Hence our question cannot be resolved on the basis of Rabbi Yehoshua ben Levi's principle.

מַאי הֲוָה עֲלָהּ [1]Accordingly, the Gemara asks: **What was the conclusion of this** matter? How in the end was the question resolved?

אֲמַר רַב טַבְיוֹמִי מִשְּׁמֵיהּ דְּאַבַּיֵי [2]**Rav Tavyomi said in the name of Abaye: The verse** (Leviticus 27:15) **says:** "And if he that sanctified it will redeem his house, **he shall add a fifth of the money of your estimation** to it." Now, since the verse mentions "a fifth" and "the money of the estimation" (i.e., the assessed value paid to redeem the principal) together, [3]we may assume that the Torah **draws an analogy between "his fifth" and "the money of his estimation,"** as follows: [4]**Just as** a person must **add a fifth to "the money of estimation"** when redeeming property that he has initially consecrated, **so too he** must **add a fifth to the money of the fifth** when in turn he wants to redeem it.

גּוּפָא [5]**Returning to the statement quoted above,** the Gemara now proceeds to analyze it: **Rabbi Yehoshua ben Levi said: A person** must **add a fifth** when redeeming **first**-degree ***hekdesh***, but **he** need **not add a fifth** when redeeming **second**-degree ***hekdesh***. [6]**Rava asked: What is Rabbi Yehoshua ben Levi's reason** for this distinction? [7]Rava now suggests that Rabbi Yehoshua ben Levi based his opinion on **the verse** (Leviticus 27:15) that states: **"And if he** that sanctified it will **redeem his house,** he shall add a fifth." [8]Since the Torah uses the expression "he that sanctified," we may infer that the obligation to add a fifth mentioned in this verse applies only to a person **who** actually **sanctified** property to the Temple, thereby rendering it "first-degree *hekdesh*," **and not to** a person **who** merely **transferred sanctity** to something else by redeeming something that had already been consecrated directly to the Temple, thereby creating "second-degree *hekdesh*."

תָּנֵי תַּנָּא [9]The Gemara now relates that **a Tanna** — a reciter of Baraitot — **recited** the following Baraita **before Rabbi Elazar:** "The verse (Leviticus 27:27) states: **'And if it be of the unclean animal, he shall redeem it according to your estimation.'** [10]From here we may draw an analogy to other cases: **Just as an unclean animal**

כִּתְחִילַּת הֶקְדֵּשׁ דָּמֵי.
[1]מַאי הֲוָה עֲלָהּ?
[2]אֲמַר רַב טַבְיוֹמִי מִשְּׁמֵיהּ דְּאַבַּיֵי: אֲמַר קְרָא: "וְיָסַף חֲמִישִׁית כֶּסֶף עֶרְכְּךָ". [3]מַקִּישׁ חוּמְשׁוֹ לְכֶסֶף עֶרְכּוֹ. [4]מַה כֶּסֶף עֶרְכּוֹ מוֹסִיף חוֹמֶשׁ, אַף כֶּסֶף חוּמְשׁוֹ נַמִי מוֹסִיף חוֹמֶשׁ.
[5]גּוּפָא: "אָמַר רַבִּי יְהוֹשֻׁעַ בֶּן לֵוִי: עַל הֶקְדֵּשׁ רִאשׁוֹן מוֹסִיף חוֹמֶשׁ, וְעַל הֶקְדֵּשׁ שֵׁנִי אֵין מוֹסִיף חוֹמֶשׁ". [6]אָמַר רָבָא: מַאי טַעְמָא דְּרַבִּי יְהוֹשֻׁעַ בֶּן לֵוִי? [7]אָמַר קְרָא: "וְאִם הַמַּקְדִּישׁ יִגְאַל אֶת בֵּיתוֹ". [8]הַמַּקְדִּישׁ וְלֹא הַמַּתְפִּיס.
[9]תָּנֵי תַּנָּא קַמֵּיהּ דְּרַבִּי אֶלְעָזָר: "'וְאִם בַּבְּהֵמָה הַטְּמֵאָה וּפָדָה בְעֶרְכֶּךָ'. [10]מַה בְּהֵמָה טְמֵאָה

LITERAL TRANSLATION

is like original *hekdesh*.

[1]What was the conclusion (lit., "what was there") about it?

[2]Rav Tavyomi said in the name of Abaye: The verse says: "And he shall add a fifth of the money of your estimation." [3]It compares his fifth to the money of his estimation. [4]Just as he adds a fifth [to] the money of his estimation, so too he adds a fifth [to] the money of his fifth.

[5]Returning to the statement quoted above (lit., "the thing itself"): "Rabbi Yehoshua ben Levi said: To first *hekdesh*, he adds a fifth, but to second *hekdesh* he does not add a fifth." [6]Rava said: What is the reason of Rabbi Yehoshua ben Levi? [7]The verse says: "And if he that sanctified it will redeem his house." [8]He that sanctified but not he that caused [sanctity] to take hold.

[9]A Tanna taught before Rabbi Elazar: "'And if it be of the unclean animal, he shall redeem it according to your estimation.' [10]Just as an unclean animal

RASHI

המתפיס — זה תחת הראשון, שהשני נתפס בקדושה של אחר ולא מחמת עצמה באה לו. **ואם בבהמה הטמאה** — הוה ליה למכתב "ואם בהמה טמאה כו'", "ואם בבהמה" מאי היא? אלא הכי קאמר: בהקדשות שהן כבהמה טמאה קאמר לך קרא "ויסף חמישיתו". **מה בהמה טמאה תחלתה הקדש** — ולקמיה פריך: מי לא משכחת לה נמי שתהא הקדש שני, שיתפיסנה לבדק הבית תחת בדק הבית אחר?

HALAKHAH

חוֹמֶשׁ כִּתְחִילַּת הֶקְדֵּשׁ A fifth is treated as if it were original *hekdesh*. "The fifth that a person adds when redeeming property consecrated to the Temple is treated as if it too had been directly consecrated to the Temple. Thus, a person who committed *me'ilah* by making personal use of the fifth must pay a fifth of it to the Temple treasury in addition to the principal." (*Rambam, Sefer Avodah, Hilkhot Me'ilah* 1:5.)

מְיוּחֶדֶת שֶׁתְּחִילָּתָהּ הֶקְדֵּשׁ וְכוּלָּהּ לַשָּׁמַיִם, וּמוֹעֲלִין בָּהּ, [1]אַף כֹּל שֶׁתְּחִילָּתָהּ הֶקְדֵּשׁ וְכוּלָּהּ לַשָּׁמַיִם מוֹעֲלִין בָּהּ״. [2]אֲמַר לֵיהּ רַבִּי אֶלְעָזָר לְתַנָּא: [3]בִּשְׁלָמָא ״כּוּלָּהּ לַשָּׁמַיִם״ לְמַעוּטֵי קָדָשִׁים קַלִּים. [4]כֵּיוָן דְּאִית לְהוּ לַבְּעָלִים בְּגַוַּיְיהוּ, לֵית בְּהוּ מְעִילָה. [5]אֶלָּא ״תְּחִילַּת הֶקְדֵּשׁ״ לְמַעוּטֵי מַאי? [6]תְּחִילַּת הֶקְדֵּשׁ הוּא דְּאִית בֵּיהּ מְעִילָה, סוֹף הֶקְדֵּשׁ לֵית בֵּיהּ מְעִילָה?! [7]דִּלְמָא לְעִנְיַן חוֹמֶשׁ קָאָמְרַתְּ, וּכְרַבִּי יְהוֹשֻׁעַ בֶּן לֵוִי?

LITERAL TRANSLATION

is special [in] that it is original *hekdesh* and all of it [belongs] to Heaven, and it is subject to *me'ilah* (lit., 'one commits *me'ilah* with it'), [1]so everything that is original *hekdesh* and all of it [belongs] to Heaven is subject to *me'ilah*."

[2]Rabbi Elazar said to the Tanna: [3]Granted that "all of it [belongs] to Heaven" is to exclude sacrifices of lesser holiness. [4]Since their owners have [a part] of them, they are not subject to *me'ilah*. [5]But what does "original *hekdesh*" exclude? [6]Is it original *hekdesh* that is subject to *me'ilah*, [whereas] final *hekdesh* is not subject to *me'ilah*?! [7]Perhaps you said [this] in connection with the fifth, and in accordance with Rabbi Yehoshua ben Levi?

RASHI

וכולה לשמים — שאין לבעלים בה כלום, דסתם הקדש בהמה טמאה לבדק הבית היא. **ומועלין בה** — השתא קא סלקא דעתך דמעילה ממש קאמר, ולא אפשר ליה לאוקומא הכי, חדא: דקרא לא במעילה משתעי, ועוד: דאפילו לית גבה כל הני — שייכא מעילה לענין הקדש. **דלמא לענין חומש קאמרת** — הך מעילה לאו מעילה ממש קאמר, ולא בנהנה מן ההקדש אלא בחומש קאמר. ובבא לפדות הקדש קאמר. וקרי לחומש מעילה, משום דבמעילה נמי שייך חומש, ולמעוטי הקדש שני אתא וכדרבי יהושע בן לוי.

TRANSLATION AND COMMENTARY

is special in that it is original *hekdesh* (as the Gemara explains below) **and belongs entirely to Heaven,** as the owner will derive no benefit from it after it is consecrated, **and it is subject to** *me'ilah* — a person who unwittingly makes personal use of it must bring a guilt-offering — [1]**so everything that is original *hekdesh* and belongs entirely to Heaven is subject to *me'ilah*."**

אֲמַר לֵיהּ רַבִּי אֶלְעָזָר לְתַנָּא [2]This Baraita appeared to Rabbi Elazar to contain some inherent difficulties. **Rabbi Elazar said to the Tanna:** According to the simple reading of this Baraita, there are two conditions for the imposition of liability for a guilt-offering. The consecrated property must belong entirely to Heaven and it must be original *hekdesh*. It is important to know what practical consequences are implied by these conditions. [3]**Granted** that the expression **"belongs entirely to Heaven"** comes to **exclude sacrifices of lesser sanctity,** parts of which may be eaten by the people who bring them (e.g., peace-offerings) and not just by a priest. [4]**Since the owner has a part in** these sacrifices of lesser sanctity — they are not dedicated exclusively to the priests and to the altar — a person who unwittingly eats from them **is not required** to bring **a guilt**-offering. [5]**But what is** intended to be **excluded** by the condition that liability for a guilt-offering applies only to cases involving the unintentional misappropriation of **original *hekdesh*?** At this point, the Gemara introduces some new terminology. We are already familiar with the concepts of "original" *hekdesh* and "second" *hekdesh*. The Gemara now begins to speak of "final" *hekdesh* and "middle" *hekdesh*. "Final" *hekdesh* refers to those Temple assets that will ultimately be used by the Temple, such as a kosher animal that will be offered as a sacrifice. "Middle" *hekdesh* appears to have the same meaning as "second" *hekdesh*. The Gemara has asked how we are to understand the condition that a guilt-offering is brought only if "original" *hekdesh* was inadvertently misappropriated. [6]Can we reasonably understand this to mean that only **original *hekdesh*** — property directly consecrated to the Temple, even if it is not fit for Temple use (e.g., an unclean animal) — **is subject to *me'ilah*, whereas "final" *hekdesh*** — property that *is* suitable for Temple use (e.g., a kosher animal which may be offered as a sacrifice) — **is not subject to *me'ilah*?!** This interpretation of the Baraita is obviously absurd, for "final" *hekdesh* must certainly be consecrated property to which the laws of *me'ilah* apply. In the light of this, Rabbi Elazar suggests to the Tanna that the Baraita he recited should not be understood as referring to a guilt-offering: [7]**Perhaps you taught** the Baraita **in connection with a fifth, and in accordance with Rabbi Yehoshua ben Levi.** Perhaps the Baraita is not referring to *me'ilah* at all, as indeed the verse which it cites deals with the redemption of consecrated property and not with *me'ilah*. Rather, the Baraita teaches that the requirement to add an extra fifth when a person redeems property that he himself consecrated to the Temple applies only to the

CONCEPTS

מְעִילָה ***Me'ilah.*** The unlawful use of consecrated property. Anyone who benefits from consecrated property or damages it through use is guilty of *me'ilah*. Intentional *me'ilah* is punishable by death at the hands of Heaven, according to some authorities, and by lashes according to others. One who commits *me'ilah* unintentionally, or even under duress, must repay the Temple for the loss he caused or for the benefit he gained, plus a fine of one-fifth of the value of such loss or benefit. He must also bring a special sacrifice, אָשָׁם מְעִילוֹת — a "guilt-offering for trespass." (See Leviticus 5:15-16.) The laws of *me'ilah* apply to all types of consecrated property, whether sacrifices, money or objects donated to the Temple. *Me'ilah* is a special case in that the principle of אֵין שָׁלִיחַ לִדְבַר עֲבֵירָה — "there is no agent for transgression" — does not apply to it. Usually, if someone commits a transgression at the behest of someone else, only the person who actually committed the act is liable to punishment, and not the person who sent him. In the case of *me'ilah*, however, if an agent is sent by someone else to make use of consecrated property, the sender is the one who transgresses.

קָדָשִׁים קַלִּים **Sacrifices of lesser holiness.** In this category are the various types of individual peace-offerings (שְׁלָמִים), the thanks-offering (תּוֹדָה), the Nazirite's ram (אֵיל נָזִיר), firstborn animals (בְּכוֹר), the animal tithes (מַעְשַׂר בְּהֵמָה), and the Paschal sacrifice (פֶּסַח). These sacrifices may be slaughtered anywhere in the Temple courtyard. With the exception of the thanks-offering, the Nazirite's ram and the Paschal sacrifice, they may be eaten during a period of two days and the intervening night from the time they were sacrificed. They may be eaten by priests, their wives, children, servants and, with the exception of firstborn animals, by the people bringing the sacrifices, and by any ritually pure, circumcised person they invite.

There is no need to consume

NOTES

מַה בְּהֵמָה טְמֵאָה ... מוֹעֲלִין בָּהּ **Just as an unclean animal is subject to *me'ilah*.** *Rashi* interprets the phrase "is subject to *me'ilah*" as meaning: "is subject to an additional fifth." This explanation is clearly forced, as it does not accord with the them within the Temple, precincts, but they must be eaten within the walls of Jerusalem. The prohibition against misappropriation (מְעִילָה) applies only to those portions designated to be burned on the altar (אֵימוּרִים), and only after the blood has been sprinkled on the altar (זְרִיקָה).

SAGES

רַב אַחָא מִדִּיפְתִּי Rav Aḥa of Difti. A Babylonian Amora of the sixth and seventh generations. See *Bava Metzia*, Part I, p. 56.

TRANSLATION AND COMMENTARY

second *hekdesh*. The Baraita uses the expression "is subject to *me'ilah*," even though it is referring to a fifth, because one who is guilty of *me'ilah* is also required to add a fifth when he reimburses the Temple treasury. Thus, according to this explanation, the Baraita teaches that only a person who redeems original *hekdesh* must add the extra fifth, but one who redeems second *hekdesh* must pay only the principal, as Rabbi Yehoshua ben Levi ruled.

אֲמַר לֵיהּ [1]The Tanna **said to** Rabbi Elazar: **Yes, this is** indeed **what I meant** when I recited the Baraita.

אֲמַר לֵיהּ רַב אַשִׁי לְרָבִינָא [2]Rabbi Elazar interprets the Baraita as referring to the fifth that must be added when redeeming consecrated property, and concludes that the Baraita presents the position of Rabbi Yehoshua ben Levi. Accordingly, when the Baraita states that the additional fifth must be paid only when redeeming property similar to an unclean animal, which is original *hekdesh*, it means to exempt the redemption of second *hekdesh* from payment of the additional fifth. **Rav Ashi** questioned this conclusion and **said to Ravina: Is an unclean animal** only **subject to** original ***hekdesh***, [55A] but **not subject to middle *hekdesh*?** It is true that an unclean animal cannot become final *hekdesh*, as it is not fit for use as a sacrifice. However, it can become second *hekdesh*, or to use the Gemara's new terminology "middle *hekdesh*." That is to say , an unclean animal may be presented to the Temple treasury as the redemption payment for previously consecrated property. Now, if it is true, as we said above, that all property similar to an unclean animal requires a fifth to be added to its redemption payment, and if it is also true that an unclean animal may be subject to second or middle *hekdesh*, it should follow that a person who redeems second *hekdesh* should be required to pay the additional fifth. But, says Rav Ashi, this conclusion conflicts with the ruling of Rabbi Yehoshua ben Levi, who states that in the redemption of second *hekdesh*, the additional fifth is not required!

אֲמַר לֵיהּ [3]Ravina **said to** Rav Ashi: Perhaps you are correct in saying that an unclean animal can attain the status of middle *hekdesh*. But **since** an unclean animal **is not subject to final *hekdesh***, as it can neither be offered as a sacrifice nor used by the Temple in its present form without being redeemed, whenever second-degree *hekdesh* is redeemed there is no need to add the extra fifth.

אֲמַר לֵיהּ רַב אַחָא מִדִּיפְתִּי [4]**Rav Aḥa of Difti** found this explanation unconvincing. He **said to Ravina: But** an unclean animal **is subject to middle *hekdesh*, so** whenever a person wishes to redeem second-degree *hekdesh* **he should have to add a fifth too!** You must agree, says Rav Aḥa of Difti, that an unclean animal is subject to second or middle *hekdesh*. Where is the flaw in Rav Ashi's reasoning that whoever redeems second *hekdesh* must pay the additional fifth?

אֲמַר לֵיהּ [5]Ravina **answered** Rav Aḥa's objection: Middle *hekdesh* **is** in this respect **considered like final**

[1]אֲמַר לֵיהּ: אִין, הָכִי קָאָמִינָא.
[2]אֲמַר לֵיהּ רַב אַשִׁי לְרָבִינָא: בְּהֵמָה טְמֵאָה בִּתְחִילַּת הֶקְדֵּשׁ אִיתָא, [55A] בְּאֶמְצַע הֶקְדֵּשׁ לֵיתָא?
[3]אֲמַר לֵיהּ: לְפִי שֶׁאֵינָהּ בְּסוֹף הֶקְדֵּשׁ.
[4]אֲמַר לֵיהּ רַב אַחָא מִדִּיפְתִּי לְרָבִינָא: בְּאֶמְצַע הֶקְדֵּשׁ מִיהָא אִיתָא, וְלוֹסִיף נַמִי חוֹמֶשׁ!
[5]אֲמַר לֵיהּ: הֲרֵי הוּא כְּסוֹף הֶקְדֵּשׁ. מַה סוֹף הֶקְדֵּשׁ אֵינוֹ

LITERAL TRANSLATION

[1]He said to him: Yes, this is what I meant (lit., "said").

[2]Rav Ashi said to Ravina: Is an unclean animal subject to original *hekdesh*, [55A] [but] not subject to middle *hekdesh*?

[3]He said to him: Because it is not subject to final *hekdesh*.

[4]Rav Aḥa of Difti said to Ravina: Nevertheless it is subject to middle *hekdesh*, so let him also add a fifth!

[5]He said to him: It is like final *hekdesh*. Just as [for] final *hekdesh* he does not

RASHI

באמצע הקדש ליתא — נהי דבסוף הקדש לא משכחת לה, משום דלאו למזבח חזיא, ולא לשקעה בבנין. מיהו, בהקדש שני משכחת לה, שמתפיסה תחת אחר, וחוזר ופודה אותה. **לפי שאינה בסוף הקדש** — ומשום הכי אימעיט אמצע הקדש מינה, כדמפרש ואזיל. (סוף הקדש אמצע הקדש) מדמינן לסוף הקדש. **מה סוף הקדש** — נפקא לן מינה דממעט מחומש.

NOTES

plain meaning of the text. *Rabbenu Tam* therefore explains that the phrase "is subject to *me'ilah*" is part of the conditional clause of the sentence, and denotes a (third) condition that must be fulfilled in order for something to require an extra fifth. Thus the Gemara's statement must be interpreted elliptically, as follows: "Just as an unclean animal is special in that it is original *hekdesh*, belongs entirely to Heaven, is subject to *me'ilah* and must have a fifth added, so everything that is original *hekdesh* ... and is subject to *me'ilah* must have an extra fifth added." Indeed, this way of understanding the text is explicitly supported by the parallel Baraita in the Sifra (*Ramban*, *Ritva* and *Rosh*; *Ra'avad*, however, explains the Gemara differently).

מוֹסִיף חוֹמֶשׁ, אַף אֶמְצַע הֶקְדֵּשׁ אֵינוֹ מוֹסִיף חוֹמֶשׁ.
[1]אֲמַר לֵיהּ רַב זוּטְרָא בְּרֵיהּ דְּרַב מָרִי לְרָבִינָא: מַאי חָזֵית דִּמְדַמֵּית לֵיהּ לְסוֹף הֶקְדֵּשׁ? [2]נְדַמְיֵיהּ לִתְחִילַּת הֶקְדֵּשׁ! [3]אֲמַר לֵיהּ: מִסְתַּבְּרָא לְסוֹף הֶקְדֵּשׁ הֲוָה לֵיהּ לְדַמּוּיֵי, [4]שֶׁכֵּן נִתְפָּס מִנִּתְפָּס.
[5]אַדְּרַבָּה, לִתְחִילַּת הֶקְדֵּשׁ הֲוָה לֵיהּ לְדַמּוּיֵי, [6]שֶׁכֵּן דָּבָר שֶׁיֵּשׁ אַחֲרָיו קְדוּשָּׁה מִדָּבָר שֶׁיֵּשׁ אַחֲרָיו קְדוּשָּׁה!
[7]כְּדַאֲמַר רָבָא: ״הָעֹלָה״ עוֹלָה רִאשׁוֹנָה. [8]הָכִי נַמִי ״הַטְּמֵאָה״

LITERAL TRANSLATION

add a fifth, so too [for] middle *hekdesh* he does not add a fifth.

[1]Rav Zutra the son of Rav Mari said to Ravina: What do you see that you compare it to final *hekdesh*? [2]Compare it to original *hekdesh*! [3]He said to him: It stands to reason that one should compare it to final *hekdesh*, [4]for then [we deduce] transferred [sanctity] from transferred [sanctity].

[5]On the contrary, one should compare it to original *hekdesh*, [6]for then [we deduce] something that has sanctity after it from something that has sanctity after it!

[7]As Rava said: *"The* burnt-offering" means the *first* burnt offering. [8]So too *"the* unclean [animal]"

RASHI

אף אמצע הקדש כו׳ — וסוף הקדש ודאי בלא מיעוטא דקרא נמי לא שייך ביה חומש, דהא לא פריק ליה. מיהו, אהני מיעוטא דקרא לדמויי ליה אמצע הקדש, דבלאו מיעוטא לא מצית למיגמר אמצע הקדש מסוף הקדש, דהתם משום דלא שייכא ביה חומש הוא. כדאמר רבא כו׳ — כלומר, בהדיא אימעיט אמצע הקדש מינה, כדאמר רבא בסדר יומא (לד,א). העולה — דכתיב גבי סדר המערכה ״ובער עליה הכהן עצים בבקר בבקר וערך עליה העולה״, ה׳ יתירה דריש שתהא היא ראשונה, שלא יהא הקטר קודם לתמיד של שחר.

TRANSLATION AND COMMENTARY

***hekdesh*. Just as in the case of final *hekdesh* one does not add a fifth** — since unclean animals are not subject to final *hekdesh*, as explained above, **so too in the case of middle *hekdesh* one does not add a fifth.**

אֲמַר לֵיהּ [1]**Rav Zutra the son of Rav Mari** questioned the comparison between final and middle *hekdesh*, and **said to Ravina: Why do you see** fit to **compare** middle *hekdesh* **to final *hekdesh***, and therefore conclude that it is not necessary to add a fifth when redeeming middle *hekdesh*? [2]You can just as well **compare** middle *hekdesh* **to original *hekdesh*,** and say that the redemption of middle *hekdesh* requires the extra fifth just as does the redemption of original *hekdesh*!

אֲמַר לֵיהּ [3]Ravina **answered** Rav Mari's question: **It stands to reason that** middle *hekdesh* **should be compared to final *hekdesh*,** [4]**for** by doing so we infer one type of **transferred sanctity** — middle *hekdesh* — which is considered "transferred sanctity" because it acquired its sanctity by being used to redeem original *hekdesh* **from** another type of **transferred** sanctity — from final *hekdesh* — which is considered "transferred sanctity" because the animal that will ultimately be used as a sacrifice may itself have been contributed to the Temple in order to redeem some other consecrated property. Since both middle and final *hekdesh* share the attribute of "transferred sanctity," it is reasonable to assume that the same laws should apply in both cases.

אַדְּרַבָּה [5]The Gemara objects: **On the contrary,** middle *hekdesh* **should be compared to original *hekdesh*,** [6]**for** by doing so we infer **something with sanctity following it** — middle *hekdesh* — **from something else with sanctity following it** — original *hekdesh*. Original and middle *hekdesh* are both capable of being "followed by sanctity." In other words, both these types of *hekdesh* may be redeemed, and their sanctity "follows" — i.e., is transferred to — the property with which they are redeemed. This is not the case with final *hekdesh* which, being used for the Temple service, is forbidden to be redeemed. Since both original and middle *hekdesh* are "followed by sanctity," it is reasonable that their redemption should be governed by similar rules. Specifically, in both cases their redemption should be subject to payment of the additional fifth. This contradicts the ruling of Rabbi Yehoshua ben Levi.

כְּדַאֲמַר רָבָא [7]The Gemara answers that we can prove that middle *hekdesh* should be compared to final *hekdesh* on the basis of what **Rava said** elsewhere in connection with the verse (Leviticus 6:5), which states: "And he shall lay the burnt-offering in order upon it [the fire]." Rava said that the expression ***"the* burnt-offering"** — the daily burnt-offering brought in the Temple (Numbers 28:1ff.) — implies that this offering must be **the *first* burnt-offering** of the day. Since the Torah speaks of *"the* burnt-offering," using the definite article (which denotes uniqueness and precedence), we can infer that the daily burnt-offering offered in the Temple must be offered before any other sacrifice. [8]**So too**, argues the Gemara, from the use of the definite article in Leviticus 27:27, which in describing the redemption of unclean animals speaks of ***"the* unclean animal,"**

NOTES

הָעֹלָה עוֹלָה רִאשׁוֹנָה ***"The* burnt-offering" means the *first* burnt-offering.** The daily burnt-offering sacrificed in the Temple is called the "first" burnt-offering, either because it is the first sacrifice offered on a daily basis, or because it

SAGES

רַב זוּטְרָא בְּרֵיהּ דְּרַב מָרִי **Rav Zutra the son of Rav Mari.** A fifth-generation Babylonian Amora, Rav (sometimes known as Mar) Zutra was apparently the son of Rav Mari the son of Issur the proselyte, the grandson of the noted Amora Shmuel. Rav Zutra occasionally engaged in Halakhic discussions with Ravina, although he was apparently young at the time, and he considered himself subordinate to Rav Ashi, the leading Amora of that generation.

BACKGROUND

הָעֹלָה עוֹלָה רִאשׁוֹנָה ***"The* burnt-offering" means the *first* burnt-offering.** Use of the definite article in Hebrew often serves to provide additional emphasis, implying that the word so highlighted denotes something unique, and does not merely refer to something discussed previously. Indeed, the definite article is occasionally used this way in other languages as well. However, the exact force of this article varies from place to place, although it is frequently used to indicate that a certain item is the first, the largest, etc.

TRANSLATION AND COMMENTARY

we can infer that the Torah is referring to the *first unclean animal* dedicated to the Temple, i.e., first *hekdesh*, but not to middle *hekdesh* or final *hekdesh*. Thus, we see from here that first *hekdesh* is in a category by itself, and the only comparisons possible are between middle and final *hekdesh*. Our conclusion must therefore be that the redemption of middle *hekdesh* is not subject to payment of the additional fifth.

תַּנְיָא כְּוָתֵיהּ ¹The Gemara notes that a Baraita **was taught in accordance with** the viewpoint of **Rabbi Yehoshua ben Levi.** The Gemara quotes the entire Baraita, although support for Rabbi Yehoshua ben Levi's view appears only in the last clause of the Baraita. The Baraita states as follows: ²"If a person says: 'I am giving **this cow** to the Temple **in place of** another previously **consecrated cow** in order to redeem it,' or: 'I am giving **this garment** to the Temple **in place of** another **consecrated garment** in order to redeem it,' ³**the consecrated property is redeemed** even if the cow or garment designated as the redemption payment is worth less than the consecrated property. ⁴**But the Temple treasury has the upper hand.** If the redemption payment is worth as much as or more than the consecrated property, the Temple treasury keeps it, and need not refund the difference. But if the redemption payment is worth less than the original consecrated property, the redeemer must pay the Temple treasury the difference, even though the redemption takes effect in any case." ⁵The Baraita continues: "If a person appraised the redemption payment before redeeming the *hekdesh* by saying 'I am giving **this cow,** which is **worth five sela'im, in place of a consecrated cow,'** or 'this garment,

LITERAL TRANSLATION

[means] the *first* unclean [animal].
¹It was taught in accordance with Rabbi Yehoshua ben Levi: ²"'This cow instead of a cow of consecrated property,' 'this garment instead of a garment of consecrated property,' ³his consecrated property is redeemed, ⁴but the Temple treasury has the upper hand. ⁵'This cow, at five sela'im, instead of a cow of consecrated property,' 'this garment,

טְמֵאָה רִאשׁוֹנָה.
¹תַּנְיָא כְּוָתֵיהּ דְּרַבִּי יְהוֹשֻׁעַ בֶּן לֵוִי: ²"'פָּרָה זוֹ תַּחַת פָּרָה שֶׁל הֶקְדֵּשׁ', 'טַלִּית זוֹ תַּחַת טַלִּית שֶׁל הֶקְדֵּשׁ', ³הֶקְדֵּשׁוֹ פָּדוּי, ⁴וְיַד הֶקְדֵּשׁ עַל הָעֶלְיוֹנָה. ⁵'פָּרָה זוֹ, בְּחָמֵשׁ סְלָעִים, תַּחַת פָּרָה שֶׁל הֶקְדֵּשׁ', 'טַלִּית זוֹ,

RASHI

הקדשו פדוי – אַף עַל פִּי שֶׁלֹּא שָׁם דָּמִים קְצוּבִין דְּקַיְימָא לָן הֶקְדֵּשׁ שָׁוֶה מָנֶה שֶׁחִילְּלוֹ עַל שָׁוֶה פְּרוּטָה – מְחוּלָּל, וְשָׁרֵי לְאִיתְהֲנוּיֵי מִינֵּיהּ. וּמַיְיהוּ, יַד הֶקְדֵּשׁ עַל הָעֶלְיוֹנָה שָׁאִם דָּמִים הַלָּלוּ יְתֵירִים עַל דְּמֵי הַהֶקְדֵּשׁ – קָנָה הֶקְדֵּשׁ, וְאִם הֶקְדֵּשׁ יָתֵר עֲלֵיהֶם – יִשְׁלִים עַל כָּרְחוֹ. טַלִּית זוֹ בַּחֲמֵשׁ סְלָעִים בּוֹ' הֶקְדֵּשׁוֹ פָּדוּי – אַף עַל פִּי שֶׁאֵינוֹ שָׁוֶה. וְלֹא תֵימָא הוֹאִיל וְשָׂם לָהּ דָּמִים, וְאֵינָהּ שָׁוֶה כַּמָּה שֶׁאָמַר אֵין דְּבָרָיו כְּלוּם, אֶלָּא הֶקְדֵּשׁ פָּדוּי, וְהוּא יַשְׁלִים.

NOTES

was the first sacrifice ever offered (as a dedication ceremony), or because this was the first sacrifice offered by the Jews in the wilderness after they left Egypt (*Tosafot*).

פָּרָה זוֹ תַּחַת פָּרָה שֶׁל הֶקְדֵּשׁ... הֶקְדֵּשׁוֹ פָּדוּי **This cow instead of a cow of consecrated property,"... his consecrated property is redeemed.** *Ra'avad*'s text of the Gemara reads: "His consecrated property is *not* redeemed." According to this reading, redemption of the *hekdesh* does not take effect, because consecrated property can only be redeemed with something whose value has been previously appraised, as the Torah states (Leviticus 27:27): "He shall redeem it *according to your estimation.*" Nevertheless, *hekdesh* still has the upper hand, according to *Ra'avad*, because the Temple keeps the second cow, even though redemption of the first cow did not take effect.

פָּרָה זוֹ בְּחָמֵשׁ סְלָעִים **"This cow at five sela'im."** At first sight, there seems to be no difference between this case and the previous one. In both instances, the *hekdesh* is redeemed (unless *Ra'avad*'s reading in the Gemara is accepted; see previous note). *Rosh* therefore explains that in the first case, the Temple treasury may keep the second cow even if it was worth considerably more than the cow originally consecrated to the Temple, since the person redeeming it did not specify how much the second cow was worth. However, in the second case, the person who redeemed the first cow may invalidate the redemption procedure, since he explicitly stated that the second cow was worth five sela'im, implying that he wanted the redemption to take effect only if the second cow was indeed worth the amount specified.

HALAKHAH

פָּרָה זוֹ תַּחַת פָּרָה שֶׁל הֶקְדֵּשׁ **"This cow instead of a cow of consecrated property."** "*Hekdesh* can be redeemed only after accurately assessing its value. However, if a person redeems *hekdesh* without appraising it first — for example, by stating; 'I am redeeming a cow or garment belonging to *hekdesh* with this cow or garment' — the redemption process nevertheless takes effect. However, *hekdesh* has the upper hand in such cases: If the second cow is worth more than the *hekdesh* cow, the Temple keeps it, and the owner is not entitled to a refund. If the second cow is worth less, the owner must pay the Temple treasury the difference, as well as one-fifth of the principal." (*Rambam, Sefer Hafla'ah,*

Hilkhot Arakhin 7:11.)

פָּרָה זוֹ בְּחָמֵשׁ סְלָעִים **"This cow, at five sela'im."** "If a person appraises something that he has designated as a redemption payment for *hekdesh* — for example, by saying: 'I am giving this cow, which is worth five sela'im, to redeem a cow of *hekdesh*' — he calculates the extra fifth based on the value of the redemption payment that he set, even if it was worth more than the *hekdesh*. For example, if a person appraises the redemption payment at five sela'im, and the *hekdesh* is only worth two-and-a-half, he adds an extra sela as the fifth, rather than half a sela (= a fifth of two-and-a-half sela'im)." (Ibid., 7:11.)

בְּחָמֵשׁ סְלָעִים, תַּחַת טַלִּית שֶׁל הֶקְדֵּשׁ׳, [1] הֶקְדֵּשׁוֹ פָּדוּי. [2] עַל הֶקְדֵּשׁ רִאשׁוֹן מוֹסִיף חוֹמֶשׁ. עַל הֶקְדֵּשׁ שֵׁנִי אֵין מוֹסִיף חוֹמֶשׁ״.

משנה [3] הָאוֹנָאָה אַרְבָּעָה כֶּסֶף.

[4] וְהַטַּעֲנָה שְׁתֵּי כֶּסֶף, וְהַהוֹדָאָה שָׁוֶה פְּרוּטָה.

[5] חָמֵשׁ פְּרוּטוֹת הֵן: הַהוֹדָאָה

LITERAL TRANSLATION

at five sela'im, instead of a garment of consecrated property,' [1] his consecrated property is redeemed. [2] To first *hekdesh* he adds a fifth. To second *hekdesh* he does not add a fifth."

MISHNAH [3] Fraud is four silver [ma'ot].

[4] And a claim is two silver [ma'ot], and an admission is a perutah's worth.

[5] There are five perutot: An admission

TRANSLATION AND COMMENTARY

which is **worth five sela'im, in place of a consecrated garment,'** [1] **the consecrated property is redeemed** even if his assessment of the redemption payment was incorrect, and it is worth less than the *hekdesh*. He must nevertheless make up the difference to the Temple treasury." The Baraita concludes with a statement that applies directly to the issue of whether the additional fifth is imposed on redemption of second or middle *hekdesh*: [2] **"To first *hekdesh* one adds a fifth,** but **to second *hekdesh* one does not add a fifth."** This explicitly supports Rabbi Yehoshua ben Levi's ruling.

MISHNAH הָאוֹנָאָה אַרְבָּעָה כֶּסֶף [3] This Mishnah begins with a repetition of the law mentioned in a previous Mishnah (above, 49b) regarding the legal definition of fraud: **Fraud** is said to occur in a sales transaction when the buyer's overpayment or underpayment with respect to the market value of the merchandise **is four silver ma'ot** per sela (a sela being worth twenty-four ma'ot), i.e., one-sixth of the purchase price.

וְהַטַּעֲנָה שְׁתֵּי כֶּסֶף [4] Having mentioned the legal definition of fraud, the Mishnah now lists certain legal procedures that are available only if a certain minimum amount of money is involved. First, if a person claims that another owes him a specific sum of money, and the defendant admits that he owes part of the sum, the defendant is required to pay the amount he admits owing and to swear that he owes no additional money. Upon taking the oath, the defendant is exempt from paying the amount of money still in dispute. Such an oath is imposed by the courts only if the **claim** lodged by the plaintiff against the defendant **is** of a certain minimum amount, namely, **two silver ma'ot,** and only if the partial **admission** made by the defendant is of a certain minimum amount, namely, **a perutah's worth**. But if less than two ma'ot are claimed or less than one perutah is admitted, the defendant is exempt from paying the amount he denies owing even without taking an oath.

חָמֵשׁ פְּרוּטוֹת הֵן [5] The Mishnah now notes that **there are five** circumstances in which the minimum legal measure set by the Halakhah is a **perutah:** (1) A defendant who makes a partial admission of a claim for money against him is only required to take an oath to support his contention that he does not owe the full sum demanded by the plaintiff, provided his partial **admission** amounts to at least **one perutah,** as explained above.

RASHI

על הקדש שני – אם חזר ופדה את זה.

משנה האונאה ארבעה כסף – למקח סלע, וכדאמרן דהוה ליה שתות.

והטענה שתי כסף – שאין שבועת הדיינין על הטענה פחותה משתי מעות כסף, שיטענו ״שוה שתי כסף יש לי בידך״, וזה יודה לו מהם שוה פרוטה ויכפור השאר, או יודה הכל ויכפור פרוטה.

וההודאה שוה פרוטה – כדפרשינן, להיות הודאה במקצת, ויתחייב שבועה.

NOTES

הָאוֹנָאָה אַרְבָּעָה כֶּסֶף **Fraud is four silver ma'ot.** *Ramban* objects that fraud is not determined on the basis of a fixed sum of money. Rather, "fraud" is calculated as a percentage of how much the merchandise was worth. Some commentators therefore suggest that the Mishnah stated that "fraud is four silver ma'ot" rather than "fraud is one-sixth" for stylistic reasons (i.e., to maintain stylistic unity), since a previous Mishnah (above, 49b) had also stated that "fraud is four silver ma'ot" (*Ritva*).

HALAKHAH

וְהַטַּעֲנָה שְׁתֵּי כֶּסֶף וְהַהוֹדָאָה שָׁוֶה פְּרוּטָה **And a claim is two silver ma'ot, and an admission is a perutah's worth.** "A person who admits to part of a claim lodged against him is required to take an oath affirming that he is telling the truth only if he admits to owing at least a perutah, and denies owing at least two silver ma'ot more than he admitted," following the Mishnah as interpreted by Rav (*Shevuot* 39b). (*Shulḥan Arukh, Ḥoshen Mishpat* 88:1.)

וְהָאִשָּׁה מִתְקַדֶּשֶׁת בְּשָׁוֶה פְּרוּטָה **And a woman is betrothed with a perutah's worth.** "A man who wishes to betroth a woman by giving her money or an object must give her at least a perutah or something worth a perutah." (Ibid., *Even HaEzer* 31:1.)

[1]שָׁוֶה פְּרוּטָה; [1]וְהָאִשָּׁה מִתְקַדֶּשֶׁת בְּשָׁוֶה פְּרוּטָה; [2]וְהַנֶּהֱנֶה בְּשָׁוֶה פְּרוּטָה מִן הַהֶקְדֵּשׁ מָעַל; [3]וְהַמּוֹצֵא שָׁוֶה פְּרוּטָה חַיָּיב לְהַכְרִיז; [4]וְהַגּוֹזֵל אֶת חֲבֵירוֹ שָׁוֶה פְּרוּטָה וְנִשְׁבַּע לוֹ יוֹלִיכֶנּוּ אַחֲרָיו אֲפִילּוּ לְמָדַי.

גמרא [5]תָּנֵינָא חֲדָא זִימְנָא: ״הָאוֹנָאָה אַרְבָּעָה כֶּסֶף מֵעֶשְׂרִים וְאַרְבָּעָה כֶּסֶף לַסֶּלַע — שְׁתוּת לְמִקָּח״! [6]״הַטַּעֲנָה שְׁתֵּי כֶסֶף, וְהַהוֹדָאָה שָׁוֶה פְּרוּטָה״ אִצְטְרִיכָא לֵיהּ. [7]הָא נַמִי תָּנֵינָא: ״שְׁבוּעַת הַדַּיָּינִין, הַטַּעֲנָה שְׁתֵּי כֶסֶף, וְהַהוֹדָאָה שָׁוֶה פְּרוּטָה״! [8]סֵיפָא אִצְטְרִיכָא לֵיהּ, דְּקָתָנֵי: ״חָמֵשׁ פְּרוּטוֹת הֵן״.

LITERAL TRANSLATION

is a perutah's worth; [1]and a woman is betrothed with a perutah's worth; [2]and someone who benefits from a perutah's worth of consecrated property is guilty of *me'ilah*; [3]and someone who finds [something] worth a perutah must announce [it]; [4]and someone who robs his fellow [of something] worth a perutah and swears [falsely] to him must bring it after him even to Media.

GEMARA [5]We have learned it once: "Fraud is four silver [ma'ot] out of twenty-four silver [ma'ot] to a sela — one-sixth of the purchase"!

[6]"A claim is two silver [ma'ot], and an admission is a perutah's worth" was necessary for him.

[7]This too we have learned: "[For] the judges' oath, the claim [is] two silver [ma'ot], and the admission is a perutah's worth"!

[8]He needed the last [clause], which teaches: "There are five perutot."

TRANSLATION AND COMMENTARY

(2) [1]**A woman can be betrothed** by giving her something **worth** at least **a perutah.** (3) [2]**Someone** who unwittingly **benefits from** at least **a perutah's worth of consecrated property is guilty of** *me'ilah* — misappropriation — and must repay the Temple for the benefit gained, add a penalty of one-fifth of the value of the benefit gained, and bring a special sacrifice, a guilt-offering for *me'ilah.* (4) [3]**Someone who finds something worth** at least **a perutah must** publicly **announce** the find, so that the owner will know to come and claim it. (5) [4]**Someone who robs another of something worth** at least **a perutah,** then **takes a false oath** denying the robbery, and later admits his guilt, cannot atone for his offense unless he personally **restores** the goods he took **to** the injured party, **even** if that means going **to** a distant land like **Media** to find him.

GEMARA תָּנֵינָא חֲדָא זִימְנָא [5]The Gemara immediately objects that the beginning of the Mishnah is superfluous: Surely **we have** already **learned** the definition of fraud **once** before in a previous Mishnah. For we learned earlier in this chapter (above, 49b): **"Fraud is** an overpayment or underpayment of **four silver ma'ot out of** the **twenty-four silver ma'ot in a sela,** i.e., **one-sixth of the purchase."** Why was it necessary to repeat this statement in our Mishnah?

הַטַּעֲנָה שְׁתֵּי כֶסֶף [6]The Gemara answers that the first clause of our Mishnah adds nothing to the teaching of the previous Mishnah. It was included only as a prologue to the next clause, which the Tanna **had to mention,** namely: "In order for the court to impose an oath on a defendant in a case of partial admission, **the claim** lodged by the plaintiff **must be** for at least **two silver ma'ot, and** the defendant's **admission must be** of at least **one perutah's worth."**

הָא נַמִי תָּנֵינָא [7]The Gemara now objects that the clause just quoted concerning the minimum amount of disputed debt that can be the subject of an oath need not have been mentioned either, for **that** law **too we have learned** elsewhere in the Mishnah (*Shevu'ot* 6:1): "In order for **the judges' oath** to be imposed, **the claim** lodged by the plaintiff must be for at least **two silver ma'ot, and the** defendant's partial **admission** must be of at least **one perutah's worth"!**

סֵיפָא אִצְטְרִיכָא לֵיהּ [8]The Gemara again replies that this clause was included only as a prologue to what follows, for the Tanna **had to teach the last clause** of the Mishnah, **which states: "There are five perutot,** etc."

TERMINOLOGY

תָּנֵינָא חֲדָא זִימְנָא **We have learned it once.** I.e., we have already learned what was just said elsewhere in a Mishnah or a Baraita. Why was it necessary to repeat the matter here?

סֵיפָא אִצְטְרִיכָא לֵיהּ **He needed the last clause** (lit., "the end"). Only the last clause of the source cited really needed to be mentioned; but since the last clause was mentioned, the first one was also cited.

CONCEPTS

שְׁבוּעַת הַדַּיָּינִין **The judges' oath.** An oath taken by a defendant in a court of law to clear himself of a claim. Such an oath is taken only if the claim is of a certain minimum amount (two silver ma'ot). By Torah law, it is taken only if the defendant admits part of a claim, or if one witness has testified against the defendant, or if the defendant claims to have lost an article placed in his care. By Rabbinic decree, there are many other oaths that may be imposed by a court.

RASHI

המוצא שוה פרוטה כו' — אבל בציר מהכי — לא, כדאמרן (בבא מציעא כז,א) מ"אשר תאבד ממנו", פרט לאבידה שאין בה שוה פרוטה. **ויוליכנו אחריו** — אם הודה שנשבע לשקר, דלא הויא ליה כפרה עד שיחזירנו לידו ממש ולא לשלוחו, כדכתיב (במדבר ה) "ונתן לאשר אשם לו".

HALAKHAH

מְעִילָה בִּפְרוּטָה **Me'ilah of a perutah.** "A person who benefits from a perutah's worth of consecrated property is guilty of *me'ilah*, and must bring a guilt-offering." (*Rambam, Sefer Korbanot, Hilkhot Me'ilah* 1:1.)

וְהַמּוֹצֵא שָׁוֶה פְּרוּטָה **And someone who finds something worth a perutah.** "A person who finds a lost object worth at least a perutah must announce that he has found it." (*Shulḥan Arukh, Ḥoshen Mishpat* 262:1.)

הַגּוֹזֵל וְנִשְׁבַּע **Someone who robs and swears falsely.** "If a person robs another person of property and swears that he did not rob him, and the object taken is worth at least one perutah, the robber, on confessing the crime, must go to the owner personally to return it to him, no matter how far away he lives." (Ibid., 367:1.)

TRANSLATION AND COMMENTARY

חָמֵשׁ פְּרוּטוֹת הֵן כו׳ [1]The Mishnah states that **"there are five** cases which require that the amount involved be at least **one perutah."** At this point the Gemara assumes that the Mishnah intended to present an exhaustive list of these circumstances, and therefore raises the following objection: If the Tanna wishes the list to be comprehensive, **let** him **also teach:** "The minimum amount that constitutes **fraud must be** at least **one perutah."** If the sixth by which the seller overcharged or by which the buyer underpaid amounts to less than a perutah, the person defrauded need not be reimbursed. Only if the fraud amounts to a perutah or more do the *ona'ah* laws apply. If the Mishnah's list is exhaustive, why was this law not included?

אָמַר רַב כָּהֲנָא [2]**Rav Kahana said** in reply: The Mishnah's exclusion of the laws of *ona'ah* from its list of "five perutot" **implies** that **there is no fraud for perutot,** i.e., the laws of *ona'ah* do not apply if the price of the article is less than an isar — the smallest silver coin, worth eight copper perutot. Since the Mishnah did not include the law concerning fraud, we may infer that one is only required to refund the amount overcharged if the price of the article is at least an isar.

וְלֵוִי אָמַר [3]**But Levi said: There is fraud for perutot,** i.e., the laws of *ona'ah* apply even if the overcharge or underpayment is a perutah. [4]**And** this statement by **Levi** corresponds to what he **taught in his** collection of **Baraitot: "There are five** cases where the minimum amount involved must be at least **one perutah:** (1) [5]The minimum amount that constitutes **fraud must be** at least **one perutah.** (2) [6]A defendant who makes a partial admission of a claim for money against him is required to take an oath only if his partial **admission** amounts to at least **one perutah.** (3) [7]**The betrothal of a woman requires** that something worth at least **one perutah** be given to her. (4) [8]**Robbery** must be of property worth at least **one perutah** in order that the robber be required personally to return the goods he took. (5) [9]**A session of the judges is** only convened to adjudicate a claim amounting to at least **one perutah."**

[1]"חָמֵשׁ פְּרוּטוֹת הֵן כו׳". וְלִיתְנֵי נַמִי: "הָאוֹנָאָה פְּרוּטָה".
[2]אָמַר רַב כָּהֲנָא: זֹאת אוֹמֶרֶת אֵין אוֹנָאָה לִפְרוּטוֹת.
[3]וְלֵוִי אָמַר: יֵשׁ אוֹנָאָה לִפְרוּטוֹת. [4]וְכֵן תָּנֵי לֵוִי בְּמַתְנִיתֵיהּ: "חָמֵשׁ פְּרוּטוֹת הֵן: [5]הָאוֹנָאָה פְּרוּטָה; [6]וְהַהוֹדָאָה פְּרוּטָה; [7]וְקִדּוּשֵׁי אִשָּׁה בִּפְרוּטָה; [8]וְגֶזֶל בִּפְרוּטָה; [9]וִישִׁיבַת הַדַּיָּינִין בִּפְרוּטָה".

LITERAL TRANSLATION

[1]"There are five perutot, etc." But let him also teach: "Fraud is a perutah."

[2]Rav Kahana said: This means (lit., "says") [that] there is no fraud for perutot.

[3]But Levi said: There is fraud for perutot. [4]And so Levi taught in his Baraita: "There are five perutot: [5]Fraud is a perutah; [6]and an admission is a perutah; [7]and the betrothal of a woman is with a perutah; [8]and robbery is of a perutah; [9]and a session of the judges is for a perutah."

RASHI

גמרא **וניתני נמי האונאה פרוטה** — כגון אם היה המקח בשש פרוטות. **אין אונאה לפרוטות** — בפחות מאיסר, שהוא מטבע של כסף. **וגזל בפרוטה** — לחייבו קרבן שבועה אם נשבע לשקר, ולהוליכו אחריו. **וישיבת הדיינין בפרוטה** — למי שיש לו עדים, או שחייב מודה ודוחהו מלשלם, ישבו הדיינין ויכופו אותו.

NOTES

וְלִיתְנֵי נַמִי But let him also teach. At first sight, it would appear that the Mishnah should also have stated that land cannot be acquired with less than a perutah. *Ritva,* however, explains that it was not necessary for the Mishnah to mention this, since this law could have been inferred from the Mishnah's ruling that a woman cannot be betrothed with less than a perutah, as in this respect the same laws apply to betrothing women and to buying land.

אֵין אוֹנָאָה לִפְרוּטוֹת There is no fraud for perutot. Various explanations of Rav Kahana's ruling have been suggested by the commentators. *Rashi,* followed by our commentary, explains that the laws of *ona'ah* do not apply unless the merchandise was worth at least one isar (= eight perutot). *Rabbi Aaron HaLevi* maintains that the laws of *ona'ah* apply only if the overcharge itself was worth an isar, while *Rosh* appears to maintain (cf. *Tur* according to *Rif)* that the overcharge must be worth at least a ma'ah (= four isars). Still others suggest that if the overcharge was less than a perutah, the sale is void (since such a small overcharge constitutes a substantial portion of the total sale), although *Ra'avad* rejects this view.

HALAKHAH

אוֹנָאָה לִפְרוּטוֹת Fraud for perutot. "A person who overcharged or underpaid need not return the money he overcharged or underpaid unless it was at least a perutah." This is the viewpoint of *Rambam,* who accepts Rav Kahana's ruling, which is supported by the Mishnah. But *Rosh* maintains that according to Rav Kahana, the laws of *ona'ah* apply only if a person has overcharged or underpaid at least a ma'ah. "Others (*Rema,* following *Tur,* citing *Remah* and *Rosh*) maintain that the laws of *ona'ah* apply even to a perutah." (Ibid., 227:5.)

וִישִׁיבַת הַדַּיָּינִין בִּפְרוּטָה And a session of judges is for a perutah. "The court does not convene to adjudicate a claim worth less than a perutah," following Levi. (Ibid., 6:1.)

[1]וְתַנָּא דִּידַן מַאי טַעְמָא לָא קָתָנֵי יְשִׁיבַת הַדַּיָּינִין? [2]תְּנָא לֵיהּ גָּזֵל. [3]וּמִי לָא תָּנֵי גָּזֵל וְקָתָנֵי אֲבֵידָה? [4]הָנָךְ אִצְטְרִיכָא לֵיהּ: [5]גָּזֵל — ״הַגּוֹזֵל מֵחֲבֵירוֹ שָׁוֶה פְּרוּטָה וְנִשְׁבַּע לוֹ יוֹלִיכֶנּוּ אַחֲרָיו וַאֲפִילּוּ לְמָדַי״. [6]אֲבֵידָה — ״הַמּוֹצֵא אֲבֵידָה שָׁוֶה פְּרוּטָה חַיָּיב לְהַכְרִיז״, וְאַף עַל גַּב דְּזַל. [7]וְלֵוִי מַאי טַעְמָא לָא תָּנֵי אֲבֵידָה בִּפְרוּטָה? [8]תְּנָא לֵיהּ גָּזֵל.

LITERAL TRANSLATION

[1]And what is the reason [that] our Tanna does not teach a session of the judges?
[2]He taught it [in] robbery.
[3]But does he not teach robbery and [also] teach a lost object?
[4]He needed [both of] these:
[5]Robbery — "someone who robs his fellow [of something] worth a perutah and swears [falsely] to him must bring it after him even to Media." [6]A lost object — "someone who finds a lost object worth a perutah must announce [it]," even if it depreciated.
[7]And what is the reason that Levi does not teach [that] a lost object is a perutah?
[8]He taught robbery.

RASHI

תנא גזל — מכיון דתנא גזל בפרוטה — שמע מינה ממונא הוא, וכפינן. הנך אצטריך ליה גזל — לאשמועינן דיוליכנו אחריו. אף על גב דזל — בין מציאה להכרזה.

TRANSLATION AND COMMENTARY

וְתַנָּא דִּידַן [1]Comparing the list of "five perutot" mentioned in our Mishnah with the list taught by Levi, the Gemara asks: **What is the reason that the Tanna** who was the author of our Mishnah **did not mention** the law concerning **"a session of judges"?**

תְּנָא לֵיהּ גָּזֵל [2]The Gemara answers: The Tanna of our Mishnah **taught** that **robbery** must be of property worth at least a perutah. This implies that only something worth a perutah or more is considered "money" that must be returned to its rightful owner. We may infer from this that the judges convene only when they are presented with a claim amounting to at least one perutah. Hence, it was unnecessary for the Tanna to list "a session of judges" separately.

וּמִי לָא תָּנֵי גָּזֵל [3]The Gemara objects to this answer: **But did not** the Tanna of our Mishnah first **mention** the case of **robbery and** then also go on to **mention** the case of **a lost object,** even though both cases illustrate the same principle, that only something worth a perutah is considered "money" which must be returned to its owner? If our Mishnah mentions the case of a lost object separately, despite the fact that it has already mentioned robbery, why should it not also mention "a session of judges"?

הָנָךְ אִצְטְרִיכָא לֵיהּ [4]The Gemara answers: Even though the case of robbery and the case of a lost object are both based on the same principle, the Tanna **had to mention both of these** in order to teach us the unique features of each, as the Gemara now explains: [5]The Mishnah had to mention the law regarding **robbery,** not merely to teach us that the law only applies if the goods taken are worth at least one perutah, but in particular to teach us what follows, that **"someone who robs another person of something worth at least a perutah, and** then **takes a false oath** denying the robbery, and later admits his guilt, cannot atone for his offense unless he personally **brings** the goods he took **to** the injured party, even if that means going **to** a distant land like **Media** to find him." [6]Similarly, the Mishnah had to mention the case of **a lost object** to teach us that **"someone who finds a lost object worth** at least **a perutah** when it was found **must** publicly **announce** the find," **even if it depreciated** in value to less than a perutah before the finder had a chance to make his announcement. Thus the Tanna had to mention the case of robbery and the case of a lost object individually to teach us the special aspects of each. It was unnecessary to mention that the judges do not convene to adjudicate claims amounting to less than a perutah, because that law can be inferred from the case of robbery.

וְלֵוִי מַאי טַעְמָא לָא תָּנֵי [7]The Gemara once again compares the list of "five perutot" listed in our Mishnah with the list taught by Levi, and this time it objects to Levi's list: **What is the reason that Levi did not mention** that **"a lost object** need not be announced unless it **is** worth at least **a perutah"?**

תְּנָא לֵיהּ גָּזֵל [8]The Gemara answers: **He mentioned** the law regarding **robbery,** from which the law concerning a lost object may also be inferred, as the same principle applies in both cases — only something worth a perutah is considered "money" that must be restored to its rightful owner.

HALAKHAH

אֲבֵידָה שֶׁהוּזְלָה **A lost object that depreciated.** "A person who finds a lost object which is worth a perutah at the time it is found must announce that he has found it, even if it depreciates between the time he found it and the time he announces it." (*Shulḥan Arukh, Ḥoshen Mishpat* 262:1.)

BACKGROUND

מָדַי **Media.** Media was located in North Persia, south of the Caspian Sea. In ancient times it was an independent state, and only in the sixth century BCE (during the rule of King Cyrus) did it become the nucleus of the Persian empire.

Media was very far from Eretz Israel, and even though Jews lived there from ancient times, there were no easy communications between Media and centers of Jewish settlement such as Babylonia.

יוֹלִיכֶנּוּ אַחֲרָיו אֲפִילּוּ לְמָדַי **He must bring it after him even to Media.** Most commentators understand this as meaning that the item must be returned to its owner, no matter how far away he lives. Thus "Media" simply denotes a very distant place. However, a tradition ascribed to the *Gra* has it that the Mishnah's mention of Media alludes to the Biblical verse (Isaiah 13:17): "Behold, I will stir up the Medes against them, who shall not regard silver." According to this interpretation, the Mishnah's reference to Media implies that the robber must return the goods even if they are worth little or nothing in their place of origin.

TRANSLATION AND COMMENTARY

¹וּמִי לָא קָתָנֵי גֵּזֶל The Gemara objects: **But did not** Levi first **mention** the case of **robbery and** then go on to **mention** the law concerning **a session of the judges,** even though the same basic principle applies in both cases? Why then did he not also mention the case of a lost object?

יְשִׁיבַת הַדַּיָּינִין אִצְטְרִיכָא לֵיהּ ² The Gemara answers: Levi **had to mention** the law concerning **a session of the judges** in order **to exclude the viewpoint of Rav Ketina. ³For Rav Ketina said: The court meets even** to adjudicate claims **of less than a perutah.** By explicitly mentioning that a court session is held only for a claim amounting to at least one perutah, Levi intended to indicate that the law is not in accordance with Rav Ketina's view.

וְלֵוִי מַאי טַעְמָא לָא קָתָנֵי ⁴ The Gemara now raises another objection to Levi's list: **And what is the reason that,** unlike our Mishnah, **Levi did not mention consecrated property,** i.e., that a person must bring a trespass-offering only if he has benefited from at least one perutah's worth of consecrated property?

LITERAL TRANSLATION

¹But does he not teach robbery and [also] teach a session of the judges?
²He needed a session of the judges, to exclude [the view] of Rav Ketina. ³For Rav Ketina said: The court meets even for less than a perutah's worth.
⁴And what is the reason that Levi does not teach consecrated property?
⁵He deals with secular [property]. He does not deal with holy things.
⁶But our Tanna, who does deal with holy things, should teach [that] tithe is for a perutah!
⁷[It is] according to him who says: Its fifth is not worth a perutah.
⁸But let him teach: The fifth of tithe is a perutah!
⁹He deals with the principal. He does not deal with the fifth.
¹⁰Returning to the statement quoted above (lit., "the thing itself"): Rav Ketina said: The court meets even for less than

---

¹וּמִי לָא קָתָנֵי גֵּזֶל וְקָתָנֵי יְשִׁיבַת הַדַּיָּינִין?
²יְשִׁיבַת הַדַּיָּינִין אִצְטְרִיכָא לֵיהּ, לְאַפּוּקֵי מִדְּרַב קְטִינָא. ³דְּאָמַר רַב קְטִינָא: בֵּית דִּין נִזְקָקִין אֲפִילּוּ לְפָחוֹת מִשְׁוֵה פְּרוּטָה.
⁴וְלֵוִי מַאי טַעְמָא לָא קָתָנֵי הֶקְדֵּשׁ?
⁵בְּחוּלִּין קָמַיְירֵי. בְּקָדָשִׁים לָא קָמַיְירֵי.
⁶אֶלָּא תַּנָּא דִּידָן, דְּקָא מַיְירֵי בְּקָדָשִׁים, נִתְנֵי מַעֲשֵׂר בִּפְרוּטָה!
⁷כְּמַאן דְּאָמַר: אֵין בְּחוּמְשׁוֹ פְּרוּטָה.
⁸וְלִיתְנֵי: חוֹמֶשׁ מַעֲשֵׂר בִּפְרוּטָה!
⁹בְּקַרְנָא קָא מַיְירֵי. בְּחוֹמֶשׁ לָא קָא מַיְירֵי.
¹⁰גּוּפָא: אָמַר רַב קְטִינָא: בֵּית דִּין נִזְקָקִין אֲפִילּוּ לְפָחוֹת

SAGES

רַב קְטִינָא Rav Ketina. A second-generation Babylonian Amora, Rav Ketina lived in Sura and was a disciple of Rav. Very little is known of his personal life, although his teachings are cited by other Babylonian Amoraim of the second and third generations. These teachings include Halakhic and Aggadic dicta, as well as comments regarding ethical matters. The Talmud relates that Rav Ketina was a holy man, and the prophet Elijah and various angels appeared to him in visions.

BACKGROUND

בֵּית דִּין נִזְקָקִין The court meets. As the Mishnah indicates, the perutah is the smallest Halakhically significant unit of currency. Therefore something worth less than a perutah is ordinarily treated as if it is worthless. However, it is clear that even something worth less than a perutah has some (admittedly limited) value, and thus a claim of less than a perutah's worth may be subject to adjudication in certain situations.

RASHI

לִיתְנֵי מַעֲשֵׂר בִּפְרוּטָה — דְּנָלִיר מֵהָכִי לֹא תְפִיס פִּדְיוֹנוֹ.

בְּחוּלִּין קָמַיְירֵי ⁵ The Gemara answers that Levi **deals** only with cases **of secular property. He does not deal with** cases involving **holy things,** i.e., property dedicated to the Temple. Hence there was no reason for him to mention the regulation regarding consecrated property.

אֶלָּא תַּנָּא דִּידָן ⁶ The Gemara now turns its attention back to our Mishnah and asks: But **our Tanna, who does deal with holy things** — as we see from the fact that he mentioned a case involving consecrated property — **should have mentioned** another case in which the minimum amount involved must be a perutah. Why did he not state **that second-tithe** — a form of consecrated property — cannot be redeemed unless it is worth at least **one perutah"!**

כְּמַאן דְּאָמַר ⁷ The Gemara answers that our Mishnah **is in accordance with** the authority **who says** that second tithe cannot be redeemed if the **fifth** that must be added when the owner himself redeems his tithe **is not worth** at least **one perutah.** Thus second tithe can only be redeemed if the tithe itself is worth at least four perutot — so that one-fifth of it is worth one perutah. It could not, therefore, have been included in the list of cases for which the minimum amount required by the Halakhah is one perutah.

וְלִיתְנֵי ⁸ The Gemara again objects: Granted that the Mishnah could not have included second tithe itself on its list, but **let** the Tanna **state: "Second tithe cannot be redeemed unless the** second **tithe's fifth** is worth at least **one perutah"!**

בְּקַרְנָא קָא מַיְירֵי ⁹ The Gemara answers: Our Tanna **deals** only **with** laws concerning **the principal. He does not deal with** laws concerning **the** additional **fifth.** Hence there was no reason for him to mention that the additional fifth must be worth at least one perutah.

גּוּפָא ¹⁰ The Gemara now examines Rav Ketina's statement cited in the course of the previous discussion. **Returning to the statement quoted above:** "Rav Ketina said: The court meets even to adjudicate claims **of less than**

TRANSLATION AND COMMENTARY

a perutah." [1]**Rava raised an objection** to this statement from the following Baraita: "The verse in the Torah (Leviticus 5:16) states: **'"And he shall make amends for the wrong that he has done in the holy thing.'** [55B] From the use of the amplifying particle *et* (אֶת) in this verse, the Torah intended **to include** even **less than a perutah's worth for restoration."** In other words, one must make restitution for misusing consecrated property, even if it is worth less than a perutah.

לְקֹדֶשׁ אִין [2]The Gemara now deduces from this Baraita that the law requiring restitution of less than a perutah applies specifically **to holy things but not to** the property of **a private person.** We may therefore infer from the verse just cited that the Torah holds a person accountable for misdeeds involving less than a perutah only when the Temple treasury is the victim. But in all purely civil disputes the court will entertain claims only if they are for a perutah or more. This contradicts Rav Ketina.

אֶלָּא [3]The Gemara answers by reinterpreting Rav Ketina's statement: **Rather, if** in fact **this statement was made, it was made in the following form:** [4]**Rav Ketina said:** It is true that the court does not convene to adjudicate a case unless it involves a claim of at least a perutah. But **if the court met** to judge an initial claim **worth** at least **a perutah,** the judges will **conclude** the case and render their decision **even** if the claim is now **worth less than a perutah**, for example, where the claim was reduced in the course of the trial. [5]**To begin a lawsuit we** *do* **require** that the claim amount to at least **a perutah,** but **to conclude the lawsuit** and to render a decision **we do not require** that the claim still be worth **a perutah.**

MISHNAH חֲמִשָּׁה חוּמְשִׁין הֵן [6]The previous Mishnah listed five cases in which the Halakhah applies certain rules only if the object or money involved is worth at least a perutah. The present Mishnah lists five cases in which the Halakhah requires that a fifth of the value of an article be added to it: **There are five** situations in which a person who redeems something or pays restitution must add a **fifth** to the principal.

מִשָּׁוֶה פְּרוּטָה. [1]מְתִיב רָבָא: "'וְאֵת אֲשֶׁר חָטָא מִן הַקֹּדֶשׁ' [55B] לְרַבּוֹת פָּחוֹת מִשָּׁוֶה פְּרוּטָה לְהִישָּׁבוֹן".

[2]לְקֹדֶשׁ — אִין. אֲבָל לְהֶדְיוֹט — לָא!

[3]אֶלָּא, אִי אִתְּמַר הָכִי אִתְּמַר: [4]אָמַר רַב קְטִינָא: אִם הוּזְקְקוּ בֵּית דִּין לְשָׁוֶה פְּרוּטָה, גּוֹמְרִין אֲפִילּוּ לְפָחוֹת מִשָּׁוֶה פְּרוּטָה. [5]תְּחִילַּת הַדִּין, בָּעֵינַן פְּרוּטָה. גְּמַר הַדִּין, לָא בָּעֵינַן פְּרוּטָה.

משנה [6]חֲמִשָּׁה חוּמְשִׁין הֵן.

LITERAL TRANSLATION

a perutah's worth. [1]Rava raised an objection: "'And he shall make amends for the wrong that he has done in the holy thing.' [55B] To include less than a perutah's worth for restoration."

[2]To the Sanctuary — yes. But to a private person — no!

[3]Rather, if it was said, it was said as follows: [4]Rav Ketina said: If the court met for a perutah's worth, they conclude even for less than a perutah's worth. [5][For] the beginning of the lawsuit, we need a perutah. [For] the conclusion of the lawsuit, we do not need a perutah.

MISHNAH [6]There are five fifths.

RASHI

לרבות פחות כו׳ — "ואת" דריש, דכל אתין וגמין ריבויין. **אם הוזקקו בית דין לשוה פרוטה** — בין תובע לנתבע. **גומרין אפילו בפחות** — אם חזר השני ותבעו פחות משוה פרוטה קודם שעמדו בית דין משם — נזקקין לו.

BACKGROUND

שָׁוֶה פְּרוּטָה A perutah's worth. The perutah was the smallest coin in circulation. The perutah is considered the smallest monetary unit with any Halakhic significance; anything worth less than a perutah is not regarded as being worth money at all, and none of the commandments concerning money apply to it. Naturally, something worth less than a perutah does have some value, for the value of a perutah can be made up of many tiny objects. However, so long as their total value does not reach that basic amount, one may have moral responsibility for the objects but they are not recognized as having monetary value.

תְּחִילַּת הַדִּין וְסוֹף הַדִּין The beginning of a lawsuit and the end of a lawsuit. "The beginning of a lawsuit" means the initial claim. Thus, if the plaintiff initially demands less than a perutah, his claim is not deemed sufficiently important to warrant the court's attention. However, if he originally claimed more than a perutah, and later one of the litigants (whether the plaintiff or the defendant) admitted to part of a claim, the trial continues, even though the amount of money now in dispute is worth less than a perutah.

LANGUAGE

הֶדְיוֹט Private person. This word is derived from the Greek ἰδιώτης, *idiotes*, meaning "common man, layman, private person."

NOTES

גּוֹמְרִין אֲפִילּוּ לְפָחוֹת מִשָּׁוֶה פְּרוּטָה Concluding a lawsuit for a claim of less than a perutah. *Rashi* explains that the defendant is permitted to lodge a counterclaim against the plaintiff for less than a perutah once the trial has begun but before it has ended. But *Ritva* and others, followed by our commentary, explain that if the value of a claim decreases in the course of the trial, or if the defendant admits to owing part of the money (*Meiri*), the trial goes on, even if the claim now comes to less than a perutah.

חֲמִשָּׁה חוּמְשִׁין Five fifths. Even though none of these laws is directly related to our chapter — in fact, all these cases are discussed elsewhere in the Mishnah — they were included here by way of association. Specifically, since the previous Mishnah spoke of "five perutot," this Mishnah cites another list of five cases in which similar laws apply (*Ritva*).

HALAKHAH

מְעִילָה פָּחוֹת מִשָּׁוֶה פְּרוּטָה *Me'ilah* involving less than a perutah. "If a person derives less than a perutah's worth of benefit from consecrated property (whether he does so intentionally or not), he must compensate the Temple treasury for the principal. But he need not bring an additional fifth or a trespass-offering, and such a person is not punished by flogging." (*Rambam, Sefer Avodah, Hilkhot Me'ilah* 7:8.)

גְּמַר דִּין אֲפִילּוּ בְּפָחוֹת מִשָּׁוֶה פְּרוּטָה Conclusion of a lawsuit for less than a perutah. "If the court convened to adjudicate a case entailing a claim of at least one perutah, and in the course of the session the defendant claims a sum of less than a perutah from the plaintiff, this claim must also be settled." (*Shulḥan Arukh, Ḥoshen Mishpat* 6:1.)

[1] אֵלּוּ הֵן: הָאוֹכֵל תְּרוּמָה, וּתְרוּמַת מַעֲשֵׂר, וּתְרוּמַת מַעֲשֵׂר שֶׁל דְּמַאי, וְהַחַלָּה, וְהַבִּכּוּרִים, מוֹסִיף חוֹמֶשׁ.
[2] וְהַפּוֹדֶה נֶטַע רְבָעִי וּמַעֲשֵׂר שֵׁנִי שֶׁלּוֹ מוֹסִיף חוֹמֶשׁ.
[3] הַפּוֹדֶה אֶת הֶקְדֵּשׁוֹ מוֹסִיף חוֹמֶשׁ.
[4] הַנֶּהֱנֶה שָׁוֶה פְּרוּטָה מִן הַהֶקְדֵּשׁ מוֹסִיף חוֹמֶשׁ.
[5] וְהַגּוֹזֵל אֶת חֲבֵירוֹ שָׁוֶה פְּרוּטָה וְנִשְׁבַּע לוֹ מוֹסִיף חוֹמֶשׁ.

LITERAL TRANSLATION

[1] They are these: Someone who eats terumah, or terumah of tithe, or terumah of tithe from *demai*, or *hallah*, or first-fruits, adds a fifth.

[2] And someone who redeems his own fourth-year produce or his own second tithe adds a fifth.

[3] Someone who redeems his consecrated property adds a fifth.

[4] Someone who benefits a perutah's worth from consecrated property adds a fifth.

[5] And someone who robs his fellow [of something] worth a perutah and swears [falsely] to him adds a fifth.

TRANSLATION AND COMMENTARY

[1] **These** cases **are** classified under the following five main headings: (1) A non-priest **who** inadvertently **eats terumah, or terumah of** first **tithe** given by a Levite to a priest, **or terumah of** first **tithe** separated **from** *demai*, **or hallah**, the portion of dough which must be given to a priest, **or first-fruits,** must repay a priest the value of the priestly gift and **add a fifth** of its value as a fine. Each of these priestly gifts is described by the Torah as a type of terumah. Hence the law requiring a non-priest who inadvertently partakes of terumah to compensate the priest with an additional fifth (Leviticus 22:14) applies to each of these priestly gifts as well. All these cases are regarded by the Mishnah as a single case calling for payment of an additional fifth, because they are all derived from a single source.

וְהַפּוֹדֶה נֶטַע רְבָעִי [2](2) The fruit of a tree is forbidden for the first three years after the tree is planted. From the fifth year onwards, the fruit is permitted. The fruit of the fourth year must either be eaten in Jerusalem or redeemed with money which is then brought to Jerusalem and spent on foodstuffs (Leviticus 19:24). Now, **someone who redeems his own fourth-year produce or** who redeems **his own second tithe** must **add a fifth** to the value of the produce when he redeems it.

הַפּוֹדֶה אֶת הֶקְדֵּשׁוֹ [3](3) **Someone who redeems property which he** himself **has consecrated** to the Temple must **add a fifth** of the value of the consecrated property to the redemption price.

הַנֶּהֱנֶה שָׁוֶה פְּרוּטָה [4](4) **Someone who** unknowingly **derives a perutah's worth of benefit from consecrated property** must **add a fifth** of its value when reimbursing the Temple.

וְהַגּוֹזֵל אֶת חֲבֵירוֹ [5](5) **And someone who robs another person of something worth** at least **a perutah and** then **takes a false oath** denying the robbery, and later admits his guilt, must **add a fifth** of the value of the property when reimbursing its owner.

RASHI

משנה האוכל תרומה – בשוגג, תרומה גדולה. **ותרומת מעשר** – מעשר מן המעשר. **ותרומת מעשר של דמאי** – שהלוקח מעם הארץ צריך להפריש מספק, אבל תרומה גדולה של דמאי – ליכא, דלא חייבוהו חכמים להפריש, כדאמרינן בסוטה (מח,א). לפי שעלא בכל גבול ארץ ישראל וראה שלא היו מפרישין אלא תרומה גדולה בלבד, אלמא זהירין היו בה. **מוסיף חומש** – דכל הני איקרו תרומה: בתרומת מעשר כתיב (במדבר יח) "והרמותם ממנו תרומת ה'", בחלה כתיב (שם טו) "חלה תרימו תרומה", בבכורים כתיב (דברים יב) "ותרומת ידך" ואמר מר: אלו בכורים (מכות יז,א). וכל הני חד נינהו, דמשם אחד הן באין. **נטע רבעי** – מוסיף חומש בפדיונו, דפדיון נטע רבעי "קדש" "קדש" גמר ממעשר, בפרק שני דקדושין (נד,ב): גבי נטע רבעי כתיב "קדש הלולים" וגבי מעשר כתיב "כל מעשר הארץ מזרע הארץ וגו'". והני תרי נמי חד חשיב להו, דמחד קרא נפקי, דחומש בנטע רבעי לא כתיב, אלא ממעשר יליף. **שלו** – דוקא נקט, שאם חילל של אחרים, אין מוסיף חומש, "איש ממעשרו" כתיב (ויקרא כז). **הקדשו** – ולא של אחרים "המקדיש" כתיב. **הנהנה** – בשוגג, דחייב קרבן מעילה וחומש.

NOTES

מוסיף חומש...מוסיף חומש He adds a fifth...he adds a fifth. The Mishnah repeats the words "he adds a fifth" at the end of each clause — rather than listing the different examples and then concluding that "all of the above add a fifth" — because there are more than five cases in which a fifth is added. But since there are only five general categories in which a fifth is added, the Mishnah listed each category separately, concluding each category with the words "he adds a fifth."

HALAKHAH

פִּדְיוֹן מַעֲשֵׂר שֵׁנִי וְנֶטַע רְבָעִי Redeeming second tithe and produce of the fourth year. "A person who redeems his own second tithe or fourth-year produce adds a fifth to the principal." (*Rambam, Sefer Zeraim, Hilkhot Ma'aser Sheni* 5:1, 9:2.)

חוֹמֶשׁ בְּהֶקְדֵּשׁ A fifth for consecrated property. "A person who unintentionally benefits from a perutah's worth or more of consecrated property must repay the Temple treasury for the benefit he derived, add a fifth, and bring a guilt-offering." (Ibid., *Sefer Avodah, Hilkhot Me'ilah* 1:3.)

CONCEPTS

תְּרוּמָה, תְּרוּמָה גְּדוֹלָה Terumah, the great terumah. Whenever the term תְּרוּמָה appears without qualification, it refers to this offering, תְּרוּמָה גְּדוֹלָה. Deuteronomy 18:4 commands that "the first fruit of your corn, of your wine, and of your oil" be given to the priest (see also Numbers 18:12). The Sages extended the scope of this commandment to include all produce. This mitzvah applies only in Eretz Israel. After the בִּכּוּרִים — the first fruits — have been separated, a certain portion of the produce must be set aside for priests. The Torah does not specify the amount of terumah that must be set aside; one may theoretically fulfill one's obligation by giving even a single kernel of grain from an entire crop. The Sages established a measure: one-fortieth for a generous gift, one-fiftieth for an average gift, and one-sixtieth for a miserly gift. A person should not set aside other tithes until he has set aside terumah. This is considered holy and may only be eaten by a priest and his household while they are in a state of ritual purity (see Leviticus 22:9-15). To emphasize that state of ritual purity, the Sages obligated the priests to wash their hands before partaking of terumah. This is the source of נְטִילַת יָדַיִם — "the ritual washing of hands." A ritually impure priest — or a non-priest — who eats terumah is subject to the penalty of death at the hand of Heaven (מִיתָה בִּידֵי שָׁמַיִם). If terumah contracts ritual impurity, it may no longer be eaten and must be burned. Nevertheless, it remains the property of the priest and he may benefit from its being burned. Nowadays, terumah is not given to priests because they have no proof of their priestly lineage. Nevertheless, the obligation to separate terumah remains, though only a small portion of the produce is separated.

חַלָּה Hallah (lit., cake, loaf). The Torah commands the giving of a portion of dough to the priests (Numbers 15:20). This portion is called חַלָּה and is governed by all the rules pertaining to תְּרוּמָה,

the priests' portion of the crop. The Torah does not specify a measure for חַלָּה. The Sages required a private person to give one twenty-fourth of his dough, and a commercial baker one forty-eighth. חַלָּה must be taken from all dough made from any one of the five main types of grain, provided that the quantity of flour is a least a tenth of an *ephah* in volume. If חַלָּה is not taken, the dough is considered untithed produce (טֶבֶל), and may not be eaten. Nowadays, since all Jews have the same status of being ritually impure, חַלָּה is governed by the same laws as ritually impure תְּרוּמָה, and must be burned. Accordingly, the measures mentioned above no longer apply. Only a small portion is separated from the dough and burned, and the rest of the dough may then be used. A blessing is recited for the separation of חַלָּה. חַלָּה is considered one of the mitzvot practiced particularly by women. The laws governing this mitzvah are discussed comprehensively in tractate *Ḥallah*.

CONCEPTS

תְּרוּמַת מַעֲשֵׂר The terumah of the tithe. The Levites are commanded to separate a certain portion of the tithe given to them and to donate it to the priests (Numbers 18:26-32). All the laws applying to תְּרוּמָה also apply to תְּרוּמַת מַעֲשֵׂר. Even today, תְּרוּמַת מַעֲשֵׂר must be separated from produce, though it is in a state of ritual impurity and cannot therefore be used.

גמרא [1]אֲמַר רָבָא: קַשְׁיָא לֵיהּ לְרַבִּי אֶלְעָזָר ״תְּרוּמַת מַעֲשֵׂר שֶׁל דְּמַאי״: [2]וְכִי עָשׂוּ חֲכָמִים חִיזּוּק לְדִבְרֵיהֶם כְּשֶׁל תּוֹרָה?

[3]אֲמַר רַב נַחְמָן אֲמַר שְׁמוּאֵל: הָא מַנִּי? [4]רַבִּי מֵאִיר הִיא, דְּאָמַר: ״עָשׂוּ חֲכָמִים חִיזּוּק לְדִבְרֵיהֶם כְּשֶׁל תּוֹרָה״.

[5]דְּתַנְיָא: ״הַמֵּבִיא גֵּט מִמְּדִינַת הַיָּם, נְתָנוֹ לָהּ, וְלֹא אָמַר לָהּ: ׳בְּפָנַי נִכְתַּב וּבְפָנַי נֶחְתַּם׳,

LITERAL TRANSLATION

GEMARA [1]Rava said: "Terumah of tithe from *demai*" was difficult for Rabbi Elazar: [2]Did the Sages make a reinforcement for their words as [for those] of the Torah?

[3]Rav Naḥman said in the name of Shmuel: Whose is this? [4]It is Rabbi Meir, who said: "The Sages made a reinforcement for their words as [for those] of the Torah."

[5]For it has been taught: "Someone who brings a bill of divorce from a country overseas [and] gave it to [the woman], but did not say to her: 'In my presence it was written and in my presence it was signed,'

RASHI

גמרא קשיא ליה לרבי אלעזר – משנתינו היתה קשה לרבי אלעזר בן פדת. **עשו חכמים חיזוק** – להוסיף על תרומת מעשר של דמאי חומש, שאין הפרשתו אלא מדבריהם. **המביא גט ממדינת הים** – לאשה, שעשאו בעלה שליח להוליכו לגרש הצריכוהו לומר ״בפני נכתב ונחתם״, והתם מפרש לפי שאין בקיאין לשמה ואין עדים מצויין לקיימו.

TRANSLATION AND COMMENTARY

GEMARA אֲמַר רָבָא [1]**Rava said: Rabbi Elazar found** the Mishnah's mention of **"terumah of tithe** separated **from *demai*" difficult** to understand: [2]**Did the Sages reinforce their rulings like they did those of the Torah?** The requirement to tithe *demai* — produce bought from a person suspected of not separating tithes — is of Rabbinic origin. Why then did the Rabbis penalize a person who inadvertently ate terumah set aside by a Levite from tithe separated from *demai* with the same severity as the Torah penalized a person who inadvertently ate definite terumah? In the case of a person who inadvertently ate terumah set aside from tithe separated from *demai*, the Rabbis should only have required payment of the principal, and should have dispensed with the additional fifth.

אֲמַר רַב נַחְמָן [3]**Rav Naḥman answered in the name of Shmuel: Whose** view **does this** Mishnah reflect? [4]That of **Rabbi Meir, who says** that **the Sages** indeed **reinforced their rulings,** and were as stringent about Rabbinic decrees **as** they were about the laws **of the Torah.**

דְּתַנְיָא [5]The Gemara now offers an example unrelated to the laws of tithes to prove that Rabbi Meir consistently maintained that the Rabbis enforced their own enactments as strictly as they enforced Torah laws. **For it has been taught** in a Baraita, concerning a husband living outside Eretz Israel who wishes to divorce his wife residing in Eretz Israel and who sends a messenger to Eretz Israel with a bill of divorce for his wife: "If the messenger **brought the bill of divorce from the overseas country and gave it to the wife, but he did not say to her**: 'This bill of divorce **was written in my presence and signed in my presence,'** as required

NOTES

וְכִי עָשׂוּ חֲכָמִים חִיזּוּק לְדִבְרֵיהֶם Did the Sages make a reinforcement for their words? The Gemara assumes here that the Sages did not ordinarily enact protective measures for their decrees. But in other cases the Rabbis *did* treat their decrees as strictly as Torah law, if not more so. Accordingly, some commentators (*Tosafot*) suggest that only Rabbinic decrees which extend and amplify existing Torah laws are treated as stringently as Torah law. Other authorities (*Tosafot*, *Yevamot* 36b) maintain that the Rabbis were only strict about cases which are frequently encountered. *Meiri* claims that the Rabbis were strict about their own decrees only when people might otherwise tend to be too lenient, or when excessive leniency might lead to considerable damage.

As for the Gemara's suggestion that *demai* should not have been treated so strictly, *Ritva* explains that the laws of *demai* are less stringent than other Rabbinic prohibitions, since most people do tithe their produce as required by law. Indeed, this is why Shmuel answered Rabbi Elazar's objection by citing Rabbi Meir's ruling regarding a bill of divorce delivered in violation of Rabbinic law. The Rabbinic decree requiring an agent to declare that the bill of divorce was written and signed in his presence is itself a preventive measure guarding against a remote contingency, and we may thus infer that Rabbi Meir was strict regarding all Rabbinic laws.

בְּפָנַי נִכְתַּב וּבְפָנַי נֶחְתַּם "It was written and signed in my presence." The Rabbis decreed that a messenger who brings a bill of divorce from the Diaspora to Eretz Israel (or from one country in the Diaspora to another) on behalf of the husband must declare that it was written and signed in his presence. However, no such declaration is necessary if the bill of divorce was sent from one place in Eretz Israel to another (see the beginning of tractate *Gittin*). This decree was issued because it might not be possible to find witnesses in Eretz Israel who could authenticate the signatures on the bill of divorce (in which case the messenger's word suffices), or because scribes in the Diaspora, who were not always learned, might write the bill of divorce in violation of the Halakhah, thereby rendering it invalid.

Precisely what is considered the "Diaspora" for purposes of this law is the subject of a Tannaitic dispute. However, the accepted view is that any place outside the boundaries of Eretz Israel (except Babylonia, which was treated like Eretz Israel for the purposes of this law) is considered the Diaspora, no matter how close it is to Eretz Israel.

LITERAL TRANSLATION

[1]he must divorce [her], and the offspring is a *mamzer*. [2][These are] the words of Rabbi Meir. [3]But the Sages say: The offspring is not a *mamzer*. [4]What should he do? He should take it from her, and again give it to her in the presence of two [witnesses] and he should say to her: 'In my presence it was written and in my presence it was signed.'"

[5]Now, according to Rabbi Meir, because he did not say to her, "In my presence it was written and in my presence it was signed," [6]he must divorce [her] and the offspring is a *mamzer*? [7]Yes. [8]Rabbi Meir [follows] his [own] reasoning, for Rav Hamnuna said in the name of Ulla: [9]Rabbi Meir used to say: If anyone deviates from the formula (lit., "coin") that the Sages coined in bills of divorce, [10]he must divorce her and the offspring is a *mamzer*.

[1]יוֹצִיא, וְהַוָּלָד מַמְזֵר. [2]דִּבְרֵי רַבִּי מֵאִיר. [3]וַחֲכָמִים אוֹמְרִים: אֵין הַוָּלָד מַמְזֵר. [4]כֵּיצַד יַעֲשֶׂה? יִטְּלֶנּוּ מִמֶּנָּה, וְיַחֲזוֹר וְיִתְּנֶנּוּ לָהּ בִּפְנֵי שְׁנַיִם, וְיֹאמַר לָהּ: 'בְּפָנַי נִכְתַּב וּבְפָנַי נֶחְתַּם'".

[5]וּלְרַבִּי מֵאִיר, מִשּׁוּם דְּלָא אֲמַר לָהּ "בְּפָנַי נִכְתַּב וּבְפָנַי נֶחְתַּם", [6]יוֹצִיא וְהַוָּלָד מַמְזֵר? [7]אִין. [8]רַבִּי מֵאִיר לְטַעְמֵיהּ, דְּאָמַר רַב הַמְנוּנָא מִשְּׁמֵיהּ דְּעוּלָּא: [9]אוֹמֵר הָיָה רַבִּי מֵאִיר: כָּל הַמְשַׁנֶּה מִמַּטְבֵּעַ שֶׁטָּבְעוּ חֲכָמִים בְּגִיטִּין, [10]יוֹצִיא וְהַוָּלָד מַמְזֵר.

RASHI

יוציא — מי שנשאה על ידי גט זה.

TRANSLATION AND COMMENTARY

by Rabbinic decree, the divorce is invalid. [1]If the woman relies on such a divorce and remarries, the second husband **must divorce her, and the offspring** of the second marriage **is a** ***mamzer*** (a child born from an adulterous relationship). [2]**These are the words of Rabbi Meir."** There is a Rabbinic requirement that a messenger bringing a bill of divorce from outside Eretz Israel to a woman residing in Eretz Israel must declare that the document was written and signed in his presence. The reason for this requirement is the subject of a difference of opinion between Amoraim at the beginning of tractate *Gittin*. The Gemara there concludes that the declaration is necessary in order to establish the authenticity of the bill of divorce, and to preclude its subsequent denial by the husband. Rabbi Meir maintains that if the messenger fails to make the required declaration, the divorce is invalid; if the woman remarries, the second union is adulterous. [3]The Baraita continues: **"But the Sages** disagree with Rabbi Meir and **say:** The messenger's failure to make the declaration indeed renders the divorce invalid, but if the woman remarries, **the offspring** of that second marriage **is not a** ***mamzer*****."** The Sages adopt this more lenient position because the bill of divorce is in fact valid under Torah law. Its only defect is that the messenger did not comply with a Rabbinic requirement. [4]The Baraita continues: "If the husband's messenger fails to make the proper declaration, **what should he do** to repair the situation? **He should take** the bill of divorce back **from** the woman, **and then give it to her** again **in the presence of two witnesses and say to her:** 'This bill of divorce **was written in my presence and signed in my presence.'"**

וּלְרַבִּי מֵאִיר [5]The Gemara proceeds to prove from this Baraita that Rabbi Meir holds that Rabbinic decrees are enforced as strictly as Torah laws: **Now,** argues the Gemara, is it possible that **according to Rabbi Meir,** just **because** the husband's messenger failed to abide by a Rabbinic enactment and **did not say to** the woman, "This bill of divorce **was written in my presence and signed in my presence,"** [6]the second husband **must divorce** the woman, **and the offspring** of the second marriage **is a** ***mamzer***? Such measures rightly apply to a divorce invalid according to Torah law, but they appear disproportionately harsh when applied to a divorce that is valid by Torah law but was only invalidated by the Rabbis!

אִין [7]The Gemara answers: **Yes,** according to Rabbi Meir such harsh measures are appropriate even in this case, for Rabbi Meir treats a divorce invalid by Rabbinic decree in the same way as if it were invalid according to Torah law. [8]For **Rabbi Meir follows his own reasoning, as Rav Hamnuna said in the name of Ulla:** [9]**Rabbi Meir said: If anyone deviates from the formula instituted by the Sages in connection with bills of divorce** (i.e., the wording and procedures of the bill of divorce as fixed by the Rabbis), the divorce is invalid. [10]Whoever marries a woman so divorced **must divorce her, and their offspring is a** ***mamzer*****.** Thus we see that Rabbi Meir is of the

HALAKHAH

גֵּט שֶׁהַמְּבִיאוֹ לֹא אָמַר בְּפָנַי נִכְתַּב וּבְפָנַי נֶחְתַּם A bill of divorce brought from abroad by someone who did not say: "It was written and signed in my presence." "If someone appointed an agent to bring his wife a bill of divorce from abroad, and the agent gave her the bill of divorce without saying: 'It was written and signed in my presence,' he must take it back and give it to her again in the presence of two witnesses, this time declaring that it was written and signed in his presence," following the view of the Sages. (*Shulhan Arukh, Even HaEzer* 142:7).

CONCEPTS

מַמְזֵר, מַמְזֶרֶת Mamzer, mamzeret. A child born from an incestuous or adulterous relationsip, i.e., a child born from relations between a married woman and a man other than her husband, or between relatives who are forbidden to marry by Torah law, where the participants in such a relationship are subject to excision (כָּרֵת). An exception to this rule is a menstruating woman (נִדָּה), with whom sexual relations are forbidden under penalty of כָּרֵת, but whose child is not a *mamzer*. The offspring of an unmarried couple is not a *mamzer*. A *mamzer* inherits from his natural father and is considered his father's son in all respects. A *mamzer* may only marry a female *mamzer* or a convert to Judaism. Likewise, a *mamzeret* may only marry a *mamzer* or a convert. The offpring of such a union is a *mamzer*.

BACKGROUND

יוֹצִיא, וְהַוָּלָד מַמְזֵר He must divorce her, and their offspring is a *mamzer*. If a woman receives a bill of divorce which is invalid according to Torah law, the resulting divorce is invalid, and the woman remains married. Therefore, if such a woman remarries, her relationship with the second "husband" is considered adulterous, and any children born to her and her new "husband" are *mamzerim*. Such children may only marry other *mamzerim* or proselytes. The second "husband" must immediately terminate his relationship with the woman, in addition to giving her a bill of divorce. Such a bill of divorce is only necessary by Rabbinic decree, since the relationship between the woman and her second "husband" was never a marriage in the first place, according to Torah law.

כָּל הַמְשַׁנֶּה מִמַּטְבֵּעַ שֶׁטָּבְעוּ חֲכָמִים If anyone deviates from the formula that the Sages coined. The Torah (Deuteronomy 24:1ff.) states that a man who divorces his wife must write her a "bill of divorce," although it is not clear precisely what such a bill of divorce must include. However, the Rabbis taught

on the basis of oral tradition that certain elements of the bill of divorce are required by Torah law, and thus a bill of divorce which does not include these elements (or misrepresents them) is null and void.
Other elements of the bill of divorce are required only by Rabbinic decree. Hence failure to comply with these requirements — for example, by dating the bill of divorce according to a calendar not followed in the country where the bill of divorce was written — does not render the bill of divorce invalid, according to most opinions. However, Rabbi Meir maintains that failure to fulfill such requirements renders the bill of divorce — and any divorce performed with it — invalid. Thus we see that Rabbi Meir is of the opinion that Rabbinic decrees have the same force as Torah law, and a person who violates such rulings is subject to the same fines and penalties as one who violates Torah law.

TRANSLATION AND COMMENTARY

opinion that Rabbinic decrees are enforced as stringently as Torah laws. This is why Rabbi Meir requires that a person who inadvertently ate the terumah of first tithe separated from *demai* (a violation of Rabbinic law) should pay the additional fifth, just as if he had eaten terumah separated by a Levite from definitely tithed produce.

מְתִיב רַב שֵׁשֶׁת [1]**Rav Sheshet raised an objection** to the Gemara's assumption that Rabbi Meir is of the opinion that Rabbinic decrees are enforced as stringently as Torah laws. The law is that coins used to redeem second-tithe produce may not themselves be redeemed by other coins or produce. This law is relaxed in the case of *demai*, as we have learned in the following Mishnah (*Demai* 1:2) concerning second tithe which had been separated from *demai*: [2]"**We may redeem** money that has been used to redeem second tithe separated from *demai*. Specifically, **silver** redemption money may be redeemed once again **with** other **silver** coins, **copper** redemption money **with** other **copper** coins, **silver** redemption money **with copper** coins, **and** even **copper** redemption money **with** actual **produce**. And if he then wishes, **he may go back and redeem the produce** with other money and bring that money to Jerusalem. [3]**These are the words of Rabbi Meir.** [4]**But the Sages say:** If he redeemed money with actual produce, **the produce** itself **must be taken up to Jerusalem and eaten** there, for it cannot be exchanged once again for money."

וּמִי מְחַלְּלִינַן כֶּסֶף עַל נְחוֹשֶׁת [5]Rav Sheshet continues laying the foundation for his objection: Rabbi Meir stated that silver coins used to redeem second tithe separated from *demai* — which requires tithing only by Rabbinic ordinance — can be exchanged for copper coins. Now, if it is true that Rabbi Meir is as stringent about Rabbinic ordinances as he is about Torah laws, it should follow that silver coins used to redeem second tithe separated from produce requiring tithing by Torah law may *also* be redeemed with copper coins. **But can we** in fact **redeem** such **silver** redemption money **with copper** coins? [6]**Surely we have learned** in another Mishnah (*Ma'aser Sheni* 2:6): **"If a sela of second-tithe money** (i.e., money already used to redeem second-tithe produce) **and** a sela of ordinary **unconsecrated money were mixed together,** and the owner of the coins wishes to spend the ordinary sela outside Jerusalem, but is unable to distinguish it from the second-tithe money, then he should **bring**

[1]מְתִיב רַב שֵׁשֶׁת: [2]״מְחַלְּלִין אוֹתוֹ, כֶּסֶף עַל כֶּסֶף, נְחוֹשֶׁת עַל נְחוֹשֶׁת, כֶּסֶף עַל נְחוֹשֶׁת, וּנְחוֹשֶׁת עַל הַפֵּירוֹת, וְיַחֲזוֹר וְיִפְדֶּה אֶת הַפֵּירוֹת. [3]דִּבְרֵי רַבִּי מֵאִיר. [4]וַחֲכָמִים אוֹמְרִים: יַעֲלוּ פֵּירוֹת וְיֵאָכְלוּ בִּירוּשָׁלַיִם״.
[5]וּמִי מְחַלְּלִינַן כֶּסֶף עַל נְחוֹשֶׁת? [6]וְהָא תְּנַן: ״סֶלַע שֶׁל מַעֲשֵׂר שֵׁנִי וְשֶׁל חוּלִּין שֶׁנִּתְעָרְבוּ, מֵבִיא

LITERAL TRANSLATION

[1]Rav Sheshet raised an objection: [2]"One may redeem [it], silver for silver, copper for copper, silver for copper, and copper for produce, and one again redeems the produce. [3][These are] the words of Rabbi Meir. [4]But the Sages say: The produce must be taken up and eaten in Jerusalem."

[5]But can we redeem silver for copper? [6]But surely we have learned: "[If] a sela of second-tithe [money] and [a sela of] unconsecrated [money] were mixed together, he brings

RASHI

מחללין אותו — גבי מעשר שני של דמאי קתני לה. **נחושת על הפירות** — ואפילו חוץ לירושלים. **ויחזור ויפדה את הפירות** — ויעלה הכסף לירושלים, דכתיב (דברים יד) ״וצרת הכסף״. **וחכמים אומרים יעלו פירות ויאכלו בירושלים** — ולא הזקיקוהו לכך לחזור ולחללן, ואם רוצה, מעלה הפירות עצמן, דהקילו בו. **ומי מחללינן כו׳** — מסקנא דתיובתא דאותיב רב ששת היא, והכי קאמר: שמעינן לרבי מאיר דמיקל בפדיון דמאי לחללו כסף על כסף, כסף על נחושת. ובמעשר ודאי מי מחללינן כי האי גוונא, אפילו כסף על נחושת דדמי לפדיון? והתנן כו׳. **שנתערבו** — ורוצה ליהנות בשל חולין. **מביא בסלע מעות** — נחושת מביא בדמי סלע ואומר: כל מקום כו׳, נמצאו שתיהן חולין והמעות מעשר.

NOTES

וְיַחֲזוֹר וְיִפְדֶּה אֶת הַפֵּירוֹת **And one again redeems the produce.** *Ritva*, followed in our commentary, explains: He *may* go back and redeem the produce, although he is not required to do so.

HALAKHAH

חִילּוּל מַעֲשֵׂר שֵׁנִי שֶׁל דְּמַאי **Redeeming second tithe of *demai*.** "Money which has been used to redeem second tithe separated from *demai* may itself be redeemed with other money. Specifically, it is permitted to redeem silver redemption money with silver, silver with copper, copper with copper or copper with produce, after which the produce must be brought to Jerusalem and eaten there," following the Sages' view. (*Rambam, Sefer Zeraim, Hilkhot Ma'aser Sheni* 4:8.)

סֶלַע מַעֲשֵׂר שֵׁנִי שֶׁנִּתְעָרֵב בְּחוּלִּין **A sela of second-tithe money which was mixed with unconsecrated money.** "If a silver sela which has been used to redeem second tithe accidentally becomes mixed up with an unconsecrated sela, the owner should bring other coins (even copper coins) worth a sela and declare: 'The second-tithe money, wherever it is, is hereby redeemed with this money.' He then takes the better of the two silver sela'im, and re-redeems the copper coins with it. (Ibid., 6:2.)

TRANSLATION AND COMMENTARY

a sela's worth of copper **coins and say: 'Wherever the sela of second tithe is, it is redeemed with these coins.'** As a result of this redemption, both of the mixed sela'im take on the status of ordinary coins — one has never been second-tithe money and the other, which had been second-tithe money, is now redeemed — and the copper coins now become second-tithe money. [1]**Then he should select the better** of the two sela'im, **and redeem** the copper coins **with it.** Thus the better sela now becomes second-tithe money, while the inferior sela and the copper coins become unconsecrated money again." [56A] [2]It is necessary to redeem the mixed second-tithe silver coins with copper coins rather than silver coins because silver coins may never be redeemed by means of other silver coins. The reason is that the term "redemption" implies that sanctity is being transferred from one type of object to another, different, type. The reason why it is necessary to change the copper coins back into silver is as follows: **"For the Sages said: One may redeem silver with copper out of necessity.** It is only permitted to redeem silver coins with copper ones in cases where it is absolutely necessary, such as when a second-tithe silver coin is mixed up with another silver coin. In other circumstances, a silver coin remains the preferred means of redemption, as it has greater intrinsic value and deteriorates less than copper. [3]Since the exchange of silver coins for copper coins is permitted only when needed, the person performing the redemption **should not leave** the copper coins **this way, but should** again **redeem them with silver."**

קָתָנֵי מִיהַת [4]After this long introduction, Rav Sheshet arrives at the crux of his objection, and demonstrates how this Mishnah contradicts the earlier statement of Rav Naḥman in the name of Shmuel — that Rabbi Meir enforces Rabbinic law as strictly as he does Torah law: **At all events**, says Rav Sheshet, the Mishnah **states:** "It is permitted to **redeem** silver with copper **out of necessity,"** from which we can infer that only

בְּסֶלַע מָעוֹת וְאוֹמֵר: ׳כׇּל מָקוֹם שֶׁיֶּשְׁנָהּ סֶלַע שֶׁל מַעֲשֵׂר שֵׁנִי, מְחוּלֶּלֶת עַל מָעוֹת הַלָּלוּ׳. [1]וּבוֹרֵר אֶת הַיָּפָה שֶׁבָּהֶן, וּמְחַלְּלָן עָלֶיהָ, [56A] [2]מִפְּנֵי שֶׁאָמְרוּ: מְחַלְּלִין אוֹתוֹ כֶּסֶף עַל נְחֹשֶׁת מִדּוֹחַק. [3]לֹא שֶׁיְּקַיֵּים כֵּן, אֶלָּא שֶׁחוֹזֵר וּמְחַלְּלָן עַל הַכֶּסֶף״.

[4]קָתָנֵי מִיהַת: ״מְחַלְּלִין מִדּוֹחַק״.

LITERAL TRANSLATION

for a sela coins and says: 'Wherever the sela of second tithe is, it is redeemed for these coins.' [1]And he selects the better one, and redeems them for it, [56A] [2]for they said: One redeems it, silver for copper, out of constraint. [3]Not that he should leave [it] so, but that he again redeems them for silver."

[4]At all events it teaches: "One redeems out of constraint."

RASHI

ובורר את היפה שבהן — ומחלל עליה המעות הללו, ותהא היא מעשר, והמעות והסלע השני חולין כבראשונה. **מפני שאמרו** — כלומר, לפיכך הזקיקוהו לכל אלה לחללו תחילה במעות, וחוזר ומחלל המעות, ולא אמרו שיטול היפה שבהן ויאמר ״אם זו של מעשר — הרי טוב, ואם זו של חולין — הרי של מעשר מחוללת על זו״, מפני שאמרו: מחללין כסף על נחושת מדוחק, אבל כסף על כסף, לאו דרך חילול הוא ואפילו מדוחק נמי לא. וכיון דאף כסף על נחושת לא התירו אלא בדוחק, הלכך לא שיקיים כן, שבזיון מעשר הוא, ועוד שהפרוטות מחלידות. **קתני מיהת** — גבי מעשר ודאי, מדוחק — אין, שלא מדוחק — לא. וכיון דאמר כסף על נחושת מדוחק אין שלא מדוחק לא, וגבי דמאי תנא מחללין, אלמא לרבי מאיר לא עשו בו חיזוק.

TERMINOLOGY

קָתָנֵי מִיהַת **At all events it teaches...** When, as part of an objection, a lenghty Mishnah or Baraita is cited by the Talmud, but only one part is actually relevant to the objection raised, the Talmud may first cite this Mishnah or Baraita in its entirety and then repeat the relevant section, introducing it with this expression.

NOTES

לֹא שֶׁיְּקַיֵּים כֵּן **Not that he should leave it so.** According to *Rashi*, followed by our commentary, one is required to exchange the copper coins for silver coins in this case. *Meiri*, however, explains that it is not necessary to exchange the copper coins for silver, although this is permitted if one does not wish to bring the copper coins to Jerusalem and spend them there.

מִדּוֹחַק **Out of constraint.** *Rosh* explains the objection here somewhat differently from *Rashi*, whose view is followed in our commentary. According to the *Rosh*, it was not necessary for the Gemara to prove that *demai* is treated more leniently than regular untithed produce, as this is obvious. Rather, the Gemara attempts to show that Rabbi Meir does not treat *demai* as strictly as do the Sages. Specifically, *Rosh* explains the Gemara's objection as follows: From the Mishnah cited here, we see that Rabbi Meir is of the opinion that silver which has been used to redeem *demai* may itself be redeemed with copper, whereas the Sages maintain that this is forbidden. Thus we may infer that Rabbi Meir treats *demai* more leniently than do the Sages.

HALAKHAH

מְחַלְּלִין כֶּסֶף עַל נְחֹשֶׁת מִדּוֹחַק **Silver may be redeemed for copper out of constraint.** "In an emergency, silver coins of second-tithe money may be redeemed with copper coins, which should then be redeemed again with silver coins at the first opportunity." (*Rambam, Sefer Zeraim, Hilkhot Ma'aser Sheni* 4:7.)

SAGES

רַב יוֹסֵף Rav Yosef. Babylonian Amora of the third generation. See *Bava Metzia*, Part II, pp. 118-119.

TRANSLATION AND COMMENTARY

[1]**where it is** absolutely **necessary** may silver be redeemed with copper, but **where it is not necessary,** silver may **not** be redeemed with copper! Thus we see that ordinarily it is not permitted to redeem silver second-tithe money with copper. But we learned in the Mishnah cited above that, according to Rabbi Meir, it *is* permitted to use copper coins to redeem silver coins that had themselves been used to redeem second tithe separated from *demai*. Hence it follows that Rabbi Meir does not treat Rabbinic ordinances as strictly as he does the corresponding Torah laws, and this contradicts the statement of Shmuel above.

אָמַר רַב יוֹסֵף [2]**Rav Yosef said** in reply to this objection: **Although** it is true that **Rabbi Meir is lenient about the redemption** of second tithe separated from *demai*, as Rav Sheshet demonstrated, **he is** nevertheless **strict about the eating** of *demai*, and treats it as if it is forbidden to be eaten by Torah law. Therefore, in this respect we are still justified in ascribing to Rabbi Meir the general viewpoint that Rabbinic law is to be enforced as strictly as Torah law, and we may justifiably attribute to him — as does Shmuel — the ruling found in our Mishnah that a person who eats terumah of first tithe separated from *demai* must add an extra fifth as if it were regular terumah of tithe.

דְּתַנְיָא [3]The Gemara now cites a Baraita to prove that Rabbi Meir is as strict about eating *demai* as he is about eating produce that has definitely never been tithed: **For it has been taught** in a Baraita: "The Sages **did not permit anyone except a wholesaler to sell *demai*.** A wholesaler — even one known for his strict observance of the laws of tithe — who bought *demai* is permitted to resell it without first separating the necessary tithes. Since everyone knows that a wholesaler needs large quantities of merchandise and therefore buys from a variety of suppliers, some of whom may not have tithed their produce, we can be confident that whoever buys produce from a wholesaler will separate the necessary tithes before eating it, and will not rely on the wholesaler's having done so. [4]**But a private person** — known for his strict observance of the laws of tithes — who bought *demai* **must tithe** it before reselling it **in all circumstances,** even if his volume of business is equal to that of a wholesaler, because anyone who buys from a private person known to tithe his produce assumes that the produce he is buying was home-grown and that the tithes have already been removed. [5]**These are the words of Rabbi Meir.** [6]**But the Sages say:** There is no difference between **a wholesaler**

[1]מְדוּחָק, אִין; שֶׁלֹּא מִדּוּחָק, לָא!
[2]אָמַר רַב יוֹסֵף: אַף עַל פִּי שֶׁמֵּיקֵל רַבִּי מֵאִיר בְּפִדְיוֹנוֹ, מַחְמִיר הוּא בַּאֲכִילָתוֹ.
[3]דְּתַנְיָא: "לֹא הִתִּירוּ לִמְכּוֹר דְּמַאי אֶלָּא לְסִיטוֹן בִּלְבַד, [4]וּבַעַל הַבַּיִת בֵּין כָּךְ וּבֵין כָּךְ צָרִיךְ לְעַשֵּׂר. [5]דִּבְרֵי רַבִּי מֵאִיר. [6]וַחֲכָמִים אוֹמְרִים: אֶחָד הַסִּיטוֹן

LITERAL TRANSLATION

[1]Out of constraint, yes; not out of constraint, no!

[2]Rav Yosef said: Although Rabbi Meir is lenient about its redemption, he is strict about its eating.

[3]For it has been taught: "They did not permit [anyone] to sell *demai* except a wholesaler, [4]and a householder must tithe in any case. [5][These are] the words of Rabbi Meir. [6]But the Sages say: Both a wholesaler

RASHI

מחמיר הוא באכילתו – של מעשר שני של דמאי, ומתניתין באכילה קאי. **לא התירו למכור דמאי** – לא התירו לחבר הלוקח דמאי שימכרנו לאחרים עד שיעשר. **אלא לסיטון בלבד** – סיטון חבר לא הצריכוהו לעשר, אלא מוכרו כשהוא דמאי, והלוקחו ממנו יפריש מעשרותיו. שהכל יודעין שהסיטון מכמה עמי הארץ לוקח, שהסיטון מן המשפיעין למכור במדה גסה הוא, דרכו לקנות פירות מרובין ומוכרן לחנוונים. **ובעל הבית** – הלוקח מעם הארץ. **בין כך ובין כך** – בין שבא לחזור ולמכור במדה גסה לחנוונים כסיטון, בין שבא לחזור ולמכור במדה דקה כחנוונים בחנות פרוטה פרוטה – צריך לעשר קודם שימכור, לפי שהלוקח ממנו סבור שהן מפירות ארצו, וכיון שהוא חבר – מחזיקין אותו בחזקת שעישר, ואין מפרישין.

NOTES

לְסִיטוֹן בִּלְבַד Except to a wholesaler. *Rambam* in his commentary on the Mishnah explains that wholesalers are not required to separate tithes when selling *demai*, because they sell large quantities of produce and accordingly earn small profits. Retailers, however, are required to separate tithes when they sell *demai*, because they earn larger profits.

HALAKHAH

מְכִירַת דְּמַאי Selling *demai*. "All who distribute large quantities of produce (e.g., wholesalers) may sell *demai* without tithing it. Instead, the necessary tithes should be separated by the buyer or recipient. But a person who sells small quantities of *demai* must separate the necessary tithes," following the ruling in tractate *Demai*. (*Rambam, Sefer Zeraim, Hilkhot Ma'aser* 11:2.)

TRANSLATION AND COMMENTARY

and a private person in this matter. Anyone who sells substantial quantities of *demai* need not tithe it first, because the purchaser knows that such produce may not have been tithed. Therefore, both a wholesaler and an ordinary person selling *demai* in large quantities **may sell** the *demai* **or send it to his friend or give it to him as a present, and he need not be concerned** that the recipient will eat the produce without first tithing it." Thus we see that Rabbi Meir is strict about the eating of *demai*, being more concerned than the Sages about the possibility that the purchaser will inadvertently eat *demai*.

מְתִיב רָבִינָא [1]**Ravina raised an objection** to Rav Yosef's assertion that Rabbi Meir treats the eating of *demai* as if it were forbidden by Torah law. Ravina's objection is based on a Mishnah (*Demai* 5:3) which states: **"If** a person **buys** several loaves of bread **from a baker** who is not strictly observant of the laws of tithes, so that his bread is considered *demai*, **he may separate tithes from the warm,** fresh loaves **for** the loaves that are **cold,** [2]**or** he may separate tithes from the **cold** loaves **for** those that are **warm** and fresh, **and** he may do so **even** if the various loaves came **from many** different **molds.** [3]**These are the words of Rabbi Meir."** In this statement Rabbi Meir appears to be taking a lenient view in two repects. As a general rule, produce that need not be tithed — having previously been tithed — may not be used as tithe for untithed produce. In the case of the baker who sells bread from a variety of molds, we would generally not permit bread from one mold to be used as tithe for bread from another, because the molds may be from different sources, some requiring tithing and others not. Rabbi Meir appears to be relaxing this rule in the case of *demai*. In addition, by permitting the separation of cold, stale loaves as tithe for warm, fresh loaves, Rabbi Meir appears to be relaxing the rule that inferior produce may not be separated as tithe for superior produce. These two examples of leniency seem inconsistent with our current understanding of Rabbi Meir's view.

וְאֶחָד בַּעַל הַבַּיִת מוֹכֵר וְשׁוֹלֵחַ לַחֲבֵירוֹ, וְנוֹתֵן לוֹ בְּמַתָּנָה, וְאֵינוֹ חוֹשֵׁשׁ".

[1]מְתִיב רָבִינָא: "הַלּוֹקֵחַ מִן הַנַּחְתּוֹם מְעַשֵּׂר מִן הַחַמָּה עַל הַצּוֹנֶנֶת, [2]וּמִן הַצּוֹנֶנֶת עַל הַחַמָּה, וַאֲפִילּוּ מִדְּפוּסִים הַרְבֵּה. [3]דִּבְרֵי רַבִּי מֵאִיר".

LITERAL TRANSLATION

and a householder may sell or send [produce] to his fellow, or give it to him as a gift, and he is not concerned."

[1]Ravina raised an objection: "Someone who buys from a baker tithes from the warm for the cold, [2]and from the cold for the warm, and even from many molds. [3][These are] the words of Rabbi Meir."

RASHI

וחכמים אומרים אחד סיטון ואחד בעל הבית – שבא למכור במדה גסה כדרך המשפיעין וכדרך הסיטונות – מוכר ושולח לחבירו, שחזקה כל המוכרים ונותנין במדה גסה בחזקת שלא עישרו דמאי הם, והלוקח מהם מעשר ואוכל. במסכת דמאי (פרק ב משנה ה) מפרש איזו מדה גסה: ביבש – שלשה קבין, בלח – שוה דינר. **מן הנחתום** – עם הארץ. **מעשר דמאי מן החמה כו'** – ואפילו מן דפוסין הרבה אין הככרות דומות זו לזו, ויש לומר שנחתום הזה לקח ככרות של דפוס זה מאיש אחד, וככרות של דפוס זה מאיש אחר. ועמי הארץ יש מהם שמעשרין ויש מהן שאין מעשרין, ושמא זה לא עישר וזה עישר, והמפריש מזה על זה מפריש מן החיוב על הפטור, ואין שם מעשר חל עליו, ונתן טבל לכהן, או מן הפטור על החיוב, ואין שם מעשר חל עליו, ונמצא שאין שכנגדו מתוקן. לא חיישינן בדמאי להכי, ותלינן למימר מחד גברא זבין. ואי עשו חיזוק כשל תורה, בשלמא מן הצוננת על החמה – אף על פי שהחמה יפה מן הצוננת לא חיישינן, כדרבי אילעאי. אלא מן דפוסים הרבה ניחוש דלמא מפריש מן הפטור כו'. קשיא לא גרסינן, דאביי תרוצי קא מתרץ.

LANGUAGE

נַחְתּוֹם A baker. This word, which appears frequently in the Mishnah, is apparently derived from the Akkadian *nuhatimmu*, meaning "baker." In Rabbinic Hebrew, נַחְתּוֹם means a professional baker, who sells the bread or cakes which he bakes.

BACKGROUND

מְעַשֵּׂר מִן הַחַמָּה עַל הַצּוֹנֶנֶת Tithing from warm bread for cold bread. Warm bread, which has just been removed from the oven, generally tastes better than cold bread, particularly since the cold bread may be a few days old. Now, since warm bread and cold bread may have been baked from different lots of wheat purchased from different people, it is possible that some of the wheat was tithed, while the rest was not.

NOTES

מִן הַחַמָּה עַל הַצּוֹנֶנֶת From the warm for the cold. *Rambam* explains in his commentary for the Mishnah that even if some of the bread is warm and the rest cold, we assume that all the bread was baked from wheat harvested in the same year. Otherwise it would not be possible to separate tithes from one loaf for another, since tithes may not be separated from produce harvested in one year for produce harvested in a different year.

דְּפוּסִים Molds. Professional bakers shaped their dough into loaves with molds rather than with their hands, to ensure that the bread would be uniform in size and shape. It seems that different bakers used distinctive molds as a promotion device for their bread. However, each baker apparently had several such molds, each of which was used for a different lot of wheat (so that they would be able to bake loaves of uniform quality). Thus the wheat from which the different loaves were baked may have come from different suppliers.

HALAKHAH

הַלּוֹקֵחַ מִן הַנַּחְתּוֹם Buying from a baker. "Someone who buys bread from a baker who is not known to observe the tithe laws should not separate tithes from warm bread for cold bread, because the loaves may have been baked by different people, some of whom observe the tithe laws while others do not," following Rabbi Yehudah's view in the Mishnah from tractate *Demai* (5:30), against Rabbi Meir. (Ibid., 14:5.)

TRANSLATION AND COMMENTARY

בִּשְׁלָמָא [1]Ravina now proceeds to analyze this ruling: **No difficulty** is posed by Rabbi Meir's ruling that one may designate a **cold** loaf as tithe **for a warm** loaf. Rabbi Meir's lenient position in this case can be explained as being **in accordance with** the opinion of **Rabbi Il'ai.** Ordinarily, as we have said, it is not permitted to designate inferior produce as tithe or terumah for superior produce (in our case, stale bread for fresh bread), because the verse states (Numbers 18:30) that terumah should be separated from "the best of it." [2]But on this point **Rabbi Il'ai said: From where do we know that if** someone makes a mistake and **separates terumah from inferior** produce for **superior** produce, **his terumah is** nevertheless considered valid **terumah?** [3]**As it is said** (Numbers 18:32): **"And you shall bear no sin by reason of it, when you have set aside the best of it from it,"** which implies that if he designates inferior produce as terumah, he *does* bear a sin.

אִם אֵינוֹ קֹדֶשׁ [4]Rabbi Il'ai now argues: **If** we assume that terumah separated from inferior produce **does not** become a **"holy"** object, i.e., does not acquire the status of terumah, **why is there** any **"bearing of sin"**? If inferior produce cannot become terumah for superior produce, how can the Torah state that a person who separated such produce as terumah bears a sin, when in fact his actions had no legal consequences? [5]Accordingly, **it follows from here that** even though it is forbidden to do so, **if** a person in fact **separates terumah from inferior** produce **for superior** produce, **his terumah is** nevertheless considered valid **terumah**. The upshot of Rabbi Il'ai's statement is that Rabbi Meir's ruling that stale loaves may be offered as terumah or tithe for fresh loaves is not an example of leniency in the laws of tithing when applied to *demai.* It is the generally accepted rule that if inferior produce is offered as terumah for superior produce, the terumah is valid. While it is true that this practice is discouraged in the case of ordinary untithed produce, Rabbi Meir, by permitting such things, is not suggesting a fundamentally different rule for *demai* than that which applies to the tithing of ordinary untithed produce.

אֶלָּא אֲפִילּוּ מִדְּפוּסִים הַרְבֵּה [6]It is the next part of Rabbi Meir's ruling that is more problematic, and forms the basis of Ravina's objection: **But what about the case of** a person who bought bread from a baker **"even from many molds,"** where Rabbi Meir says that bread from one mold may be offered as tithe for bread from another mold? [7]**Let us be concerned** about the possibility **that** the buyer **will designate** produce **which is liable** for tithing **as tithe** for produce **which is exempt, or** that he will designate produce

[1]בִּשְׁלָמָא ״מִן הַצּוֹנֶנֶת עַל הַחַמָּה״, כְּדְרַבִּי אִילְעַאי. [2]דְּאָמַר רַבִּי אִילְעַאי: מִנַּיִן לַתּוֹרֵם מִן הָרָעָה עַל הַיָּפָה שֶׁתְּרוּמָתוֹ תְּרוּמָה? [3]שֶׁנֶּאֱמַר: ״וְלֹא תִשְׂאוּ עָלָיו חֵטְא, בַּהֲרִימְכֶם אֶת חֶלְבּוֹ מִמֶּנּוּ״. [4]אִם אֵינוֹ קֹדֶשׁ, נְשִׂיאַת חֵטְא לָמָּה? [5]מִכָּאן לַתּוֹרֵם מִן הָרָעָה עַל הַיָּפָה שֶׁתְּרוּמָתוֹ תְּרוּמָה. [6]אֶלָּא ״אֲפִילּוּ מִדְּפוּסִים, הַרְבֵּה״ [7]לֵיחוּשׁ דִּלְמָא אָתֵי לְאַפְרוֹשֵׁי מִן הַחִיּוּב עַל הַפָּטוּר

LITERAL TRANSLATION

[1]Granted "from the cold for the warm," [it is] as Rabbi Il'ai, [2]for Rabbi Il'ai said: From where [do we know] that [if] someone separates terumah from the bad for the good, his terumah is terumah? [3]As it is said: "And you shall bear no sin by reason of it, when you have set aside the best of it from it." [4]If it is not holy, why is there "bearing of sin"? [5]From here [we see that if] someone separates terumah from the bad for the good, his terumah is terumah.

[6]But [regarding] "even from many molds," [7]let us be concerned that perhaps he will come to separate from the liable for the exempt,

SAGES

רַבִּי אִילְעַאי Rabbi Il'ai. A famous Palestinian Amora of the third generation, Rabbi Il'ai was a disciple of Rabbi Yoḥanan, and transmitted the teachings of his teacher, of Resh Lakish and of the students of Rabbi Yoḥanan: Rabbi Elazar, Rabbi Ammi and Rabbi Abbahu. Several Sages of the fourth generation were his students.

NOTES

אִם אֵינוֹ קֹדֶשׁ, נְשִׂיאַת חֵטְא לָמָּה? If it is not holy, why is there "bearing of sin"? The commentators object: Perhaps a person who separates terumah from inferior produce should be considered a sinner even if the produce he has separated does not become terumah, since he nevertheless violated Torah law, for the Torah commands us to separate tithes from superior produce! *Tosafot* (*Kiddushin* 46b) resolves this objection by explaining that the Biblical expression "you shall bear no sin" must mean that terumah separated from inferior produce becomes terumah *de facto.* Otherwise this phrase would be superfluous, for it is obvious that one is required to separate tithes from superior produce.

HALAKHAH

הַתּוֹרֵם מִן הָרָעָה עַל הַיָּפָה Someone who separates terumah from the bad for the good. "A person who has produce of varying quality should separate terumah from the better-quality produce. However, if he separates terumah from inferior produce, his terumah is valid," following the ruling of Rabbi Il'ai. (*Rambam, Sefer Zeraim, Hilkhot Terumot* 5:1,3.)

TRANSLATION AND COMMENTARY

which is exempt from being tithed for produce **which is liable!** In order to understand Ravina's objection, some basic principles governing the laws of terumah and tithes must be understood. Produce from which terumah and tithes have not been separated is called *tevel* (טֶבֶל), and may not be eaten by anyone. Once the terumah and tithes have been separated, the produce is no longer *tevel*; the terumah may now be eaten by a priest, the first tithe may now be eaten by the Levite, the second tithe is taken to Jerusalem where it will be eaten, and the remainder of the produce may now be eaten anywhere by the owner. However, if a person designates produce which is liable for tithing (i.e., previously untithed produce) as terumah or tithe for produce which is exempt (i.e., produce already tithed), the portions separated do not assume the status of terumah or tithe, but rather remain *tevel* and may not be eaten. Similarly, if one designated produce which is exempt from tithing (i.e., produce already tithed) as terumah or tithe for previously untithed produce, the produce requiring tithing is still *tevel* and may not be eaten. Now, with regard to the case ruled on by Rabbi Meir, the loaves of *demai* bread baked in different molds may have been baked by different people, some of whom separated the necessary tithes, while others did not. If the buyer designates a loaf which has not yet been tithed as tithe for a loaf which has already been tithed, his tithe is not valid and the loaf remains forbidden as *tevel*. Similarly, if he designates a loaf which has already been tithed as tithe for a loaf which has not yet been tithed, his tithe is not valid, and the second loaf remains untithed and may not be eaten. Accordingly, Ravina raises the objection: If Rav Yosef is correct in his assertion that Rabbi Meir regards the eating of *demai* as seriously as he does the eating of outright *tevel* forbidden by Torah law, how can Rabbi Meir permit a person to tithe loaves of bread purchased from a baker, if they were baked in different molds and we suspect that they were baked by different people, some of whom may have tithed and some of whom may not have tithed?

אֲמַר אַבַּיֵי [1]Before resolving Ravina's objection, Abaye briefly surveys and assesses the other objections and proposed solutions raised in the course of the Gemara's discussion up to this point: **Abaye said: Rabbi Elazar's difficulty** at the beginning of the discussion **was well-founded,** when he asked why the penalty of the additional fifth laid down by the Torah should be applied to a person who eats terumah separated by a Levite from first-tithe *demai* produce. [2]**And Shmuel did not answer him well** when he replied that the Mishnah follows the opinion of Rabbi Meir, who is indeed strict about the enforcement of Rabbinic law, as evidenced by his ruling in the case of a bill of divorce given in violation of a Rabbinic decree. Abaye does not accept Shmuel's comparison between the case of the bill of divorce given in violation of a Rabbinic decree and the case of eating terumah of tithe from *demai*. Rabbi Meir may well have been stricter about the case of a divorce given in violation of Rabbinic law than about *demai*, since the corresponding Torah laws are also stricter. [3]**Rabbi Elazar's difficulty** concerns a case where violation of the corresponding Torah law (i.e., eating produce considered untithed by Torah law) is punishable by **death at the hands of Heaven, but Shmuel answered** Rabbi Elazar's objection by demonstrating that Rabbi Meir is strict in the case of divorce, where violation of the corresponding Torah law (adultery) is punishable by **death at the hands of the court!** [4]Accordingly, Abaye argues that Shmuel's comparison is inappropriate because **death at the hands of the court is perhaps different, as it is stricter** than death at the hands of Heaven — the penalty for the eating of terumah by a non-priest. In other words, since a person who marries a woman who has received an invalid divorce is subject to death at the hands of the court, while a non-priest who eats terumah is only subject to death at the hands of Heaven (which is less severe), Rabbi Meir may only have been stringent in the case of a Rabbinically invalid divorce, but not in the case of one who eats terumah of tithe from *demai*.

וּמִן הַפְּטוּר עַל הַחִיּוּב?! [1]אֲמַר אַבַּיֵי: רַבִּי אֶלְעָזָר שַׁפִּיר קָא קַשְׁיָא לֵיהּ, [2]וּשְׁמוּאֵל לָא שַׁפִּיר קָא מְשַׁנֵּי לֵיהּ. [3]דְּקַשְׁיָא לֵיהּ לְרַבִּי אֶלְעָזָר מִיתָה דְּבִידֵי שָׁמַיִם, וּמְשַׁנֵּי לֵיהּ שְׁמוּאֵל מִיתַת בֵּית דִּין. [4]דִּלְמָא שָׁאנֵי מִיתַת בֵּית דִּין, דַּחֲמִירָא.

LITERAL TRANSLATION

or from the exempt for the liable?! [1]Abaye said: Rabbi Elazar's difficulty is well-founded, [2]and Shmuel does not answer it well. [3]For Rabbi Elazar's difficulty [is about] death at the hands of Heaven, and Shmuel answers it [with] death by the court. [4]Perhaps death by the court is different, for it is [more] severe.

RASHI

אמר אביי רבי אלעזר דקשיא ליה – וכי עשו חיזוק כו׳, שפיר קשיא ליה. **ושמואל דשני** – הא מני רבי מאיר היא, ואייתי ראיה מן ״המביא גט״. **לא שפיר שני ליה** – כדמפרש ואזיל. **דקשיא ליה לרבי אלעזר** – וכי עשו חיזוק בתרומת מעשר של דמאי שהיא קלה, שאפילו תרומה ודאית אינה אלא במיתה בידי שמים זר האוכלה. **ומשני ליה שמואל** – שעשו חיזוק לדבריהם באשת איש, שאיסור תורה שבה מיתה בידי אדם, והיא חמורה.

LITERAL TRANSLATION

[1] And Rav Sheshet does not object well to it, for they are speaking of death, [2] and Rav Sheshet raises an objection [from] a negative commandment, for it is written: "You may not eat within your gates." [3] And according to the objection Rav Sheshet raises, Rav Yosef answers him well.

[4] But [as for] Ravina, rather than raising an objection from a baker, let him support him from a shopkeeper. [5] For we have learned: "Someone who buys from a shopkeeper

[1] וְרַב שֵׁשֶׁת לָא שַׁפִּיר קָא מוֹתִיב לֵיהּ, דְּקָאָמְרִי אִינְהוּ מִיתָה, [2] וּמוֹתִיב רַב שֵׁשֶׁת לָאו, דִּכְתִיב: "לֹא תוּכַל לֶאֱכֹל בִּשְׁעָרֶיךָ". [3] וּלְמַאי דְּמוֹתִיב רַב שֵׁשֶׁת, רַב יוֹסֵף שַׁפִּיר קָא מְשַׁנֵּי לֵיהּ. [4] אֶלָּא רָבִינָא, עַד דְּמוֹתִיב מִנַּחְתּוֹם, לְסַיֵּיעַ לֵיהּ מִפַּלְטֵר. [5] דִּתְנַן: "הַלּוֹקֵחַ מִן הַפַּלְטֵר

RASHI

ורב ששת — דאותביה לשמואל מחילול, שלא עשו בו חיזוק בחילול של דמאי. **לאו שפיר אותביה** — דהא חילול כי לא עביד ליה שפיר — לאו בעלמא הוא ד"לא תוכל לאכול" וגו'. **ולמאי דאותיב רב ששת רב יוסף שפיר שני ליה** — דאף על פי שמיקל רבי מאיר בפדיונו כו'. **פלטר** — הוא לענין ככרות כסיטון לענין תבואה, לוקח ככרות הרבה ומוכר לחנווניס ולנחתומים.

TRANSLATION AND COMMENTARY

וְרַב שֵׁשֶׁת [1] Abaye continues analyzing the different views discussed above: Rav Sheshet cited a Mishnah dealing with the redemption of money previously used to redeem second-tithe produce to prove — against Shmuel — that Rabbi Meir did not consistently enforce Rabbinic law as strictly as Torah law. Abaye argues that **Rav Sheshet did not offer a valid refutation** of Shmuel's argument, **for** both Rabbi Elazar and Shmuel, who initially dealt with the question of Rabbi Meir's attitude towards Rabbinic decrees, **spoke of** cases in which a person who violates the corresponding Torah laws is subject to the **death** penalty either by Heaven or by the court, as explained above. [2] **But Rav Sheshet**, who tried to prove that Rabbi Meir is lenient about Rabbinic decrees, **raised an objection from** a case — redemption of second-tithe money — in which a person who transgresses the corresponding Torah law violates **a negative commandment**, which is not punishable by death. For a person who eats second tithe that has not been properly redeemed violates what **is written** (Deuteronomy 12:17): **"You may not eat** second tithe **within your gates,"** and this prohibition is not punishable by death. Perhaps Rabbi Meir's lenient attitude with respect to a person who redeems second-tithe money of *demai* can be accounted for by the fact that the punishment for eating undisputed second tithe outside Jerusalem is likewise relatively lenient. But in all cases in which the death penalty may be involved — such as the case of our Mishnah and the case of divorce — Rabbi Meir indeed enforces the Rabbinic law stringently and, in the case of our Mishnah, requires that the extra fifth be paid. Thus, says Abaye, Rav Sheshet's objection to Shmuel's explanation is not well-founded. [3] Abaye continues: However, even if we disregard the previous argument and accept the **objection raised by Rav Sheshet, Rav Yosef answered him well.** Rav Yosef pointed out that Rav Sheshet had only demonstrated that Rabbi Meir was lenient about redeeming second tithe separated from *demai*, but Rav Sheshet had proved nothing about Rabbi Meir's position with regard to the eating of *demai*. There Rabbi Meir might be strict, and rule that a person who eats terumah of tithe separated from *demai* must add an extra fifth as if it were terumah of tithe.

אֶלָּא רָבִינָא [4] Abaye now turns to Ravina's objection and analyzes it: **But as for Ravina, rather than raising an objection from** the case of **a baker,** where Rabbi Meir permits tithing from bread in different molds, Ravina **should have found support** for the assertion that Rabbi Meir is in fact strict about *demai* from another Mishnah, which deals with *demai* bread bought **from a shopkeeper.** [5] **For we have learned** in the following Mishnah (*Demai* 5:4): **"Someone who buys** several loaves of bread baked in different molds **from a shopkeeper** who is not known to be strictly observant of the tithe laws, must divide up the loaves according to the different molds

BACKGROUND

נַחְתּוֹם וּפַלְטֵר **Bakers and shopkeepers.** A baker (נַחְתּוֹם) usually had a small bakery where he baked his own bread. Such bakers usually bought flour from different people, and some of this flour might not have been tithed properly. By contrast, a shopkeeper (פַּלְטֵר) sold bread which he purchased from a baker, but did not bake his own bread. These shopkeepers — who ordinarily sold bread to many customers — might have bought their bread from different suppliers, some of whom observed the tithe laws while others did not.

NOTES

מִיתָה וְלָאו **Sins punishable by death versus negative commandments.** The commentators ask: Why did Abaye claim that Rav Sheshet's objection was not well-founded? It stands to reason that Rabbi Meir was more lenient than the Sages regarding *all* Rabbinic decrees, regardless of whether the corresponding Torah prohibitions are ordinary negative commandments or punishable by death!

Tosefot Sens answers that Abaye assumed that only where violation of a given Torah law is punishable by death would Rabbi Meir treat the corresponding Rabbinic prohibition more strictly than did the Sages.

HALAKHAH

הַלּוֹקֵחַ מִן הַפַּלְטֵר **Someone who buys from a shopkeeper.** "Someone who buys bread from a shopkeeper may separate tithes from one loaf for the others, even if they were baked in different molds," following the view of Rabbi Yehudah in the Mishnah in tractate *Demai* (5:4), who disagrees with the view of Rabbi Meir cited in our Gemara. (*Rambam, Sefer Zeraim, Hilkhot Ma'aser* 14:6.)

TRANSLATION AND COMMENTARY

and **designate tithes** separately **for each and every** type of **mold.** [1]**These are the words of Rabbi Meir."** Thus we see that even in the case of *demai*, Rabbi Meir was concerned that the different loaves might have been baked by different bakers, and that the buyer might mistakenly designate produce which must be tithed as tithe for produce which is exempt from tithes, and vice versa.

אֶלָּא מַאי אִית לָךְ לְמֵימַר [2]But what about the ostensible contradiction between the two Mishnayot dealing with bread baked in different molds? **What do you have to say** to resolve this contradiction? [3]Abaye answers: **A shopkeeper buys from two or three** different **people,** [4]whereas **a baker buys from a single person!** A shopkeeper presumably buys his bread from different suppliers, and hence we are concerned about the possibility that the different loaves may have been baked by different people. But a baker who sells bread baked in different molds presumably bought it all from the same source, and for this reason Rabbi Meir permitted the separation of tithes from the different loaves as though all were of equal status. Thus there is no proof from his ruling concerning a baker that Rabbi Meir treats the eating of *demai* leniently, and Ravina's objection is refuted.

רָבָא אָמַר [5]The discussion concludes with Rava's response to Abaye, who had criticized Shmuel's reply to Rabbi Elazar (above, 55b): Abaye had argued that the comparison between a bill of divorce given in violation of a Rabbinic decree and the eating of terumah of tithe separated from *demai* is invalid, because the death sentence for violating the corresponding Torah law in the first case is handed down by the court, whereas in the second case it is decreed and carried out by the hands of Heaven. **Rava said** in response to this: **Shmuel** in fact **answered** Rabbi Elazar **well:** [6]The two cases may indeed be compared, for **the concept of death is general.** In both these cases, a person who violates the corresponding Torah laws is subject to death, and it makes no difference whether the penalty is handed down by the court or decreed by Heaven. Thus Rabbi Meir's strict ruling concerning the bill of divorce given in violation of a Rabbinic decree can fairly be adduced as support for the contention that Rabbi Meir rules that one who eats terumah of tithe separated from *demai* must pay an extra fifth.

MISHNAH אֵלּוּ דְּבָרִים [7]The Mishnah returns to the subject of *ona'ah* (overcharging and underpaying), and lists types of property concerning which the laws of *ona'ah* do not apply: **These are the things which are not subject to** the laws of ***ona'ah***: **Slaves, promissory notes, land and property consecrated** to the Temple. (The Gemara explains below why the laws of *ona'ah* do not apply to such items.)

מְעַשֵּׂר מִן כָּל דְּפוּס וּדְפוּס. [1]דִּבְרֵי רַבִּי מֵאִיר״. [2]אֶלָּא מַאי אִית לָךְ לְמֵימַר? [3]פַּלְטֵר מִתְּרֵי תְּלָתָא גַּבְרָא זָבֵין. [4]נַחְתּוֹם, נַמִי, מֵחַד גַּבְרָא הוּא זָבֵין! [5]רָבָא אֲמַר: שְׁמוּאֵל שַׁפִּיר קָא מְשַׁנֵּי לֵיהּ. [6]שֵׁם מִיתָה בָּעוֹלָם. **מִשְׁנָה** [7]אֵלּוּ דְּבָרִים שֶׁאֵין לָהֶם אוֹנָאָה: הָעֲבָדִים, וְהַשְּׁטָרוֹת, וְהַקַּרְקָעוֹת, וְהַהֶקְדֵּשׁוֹת.

LITERAL TRANSLATION

tithes from each and every mold. [1][These are] the words of Rabbi Meir."

[2]But what do you have to say? [3]A shopkeeper buys from two [or] three men. [4]A baker, too, buys from one man!

[5]Rava said: Shmuel answers it well. [6]The concept (lit., "name") of death in general.

MISHNAH [7]These are things for which there is no *ona'ah*: Slaves, and promissory notes, and land, and consecrated property.

RASHI

מעשר מכל דפוס ודפוס — אלמא חייש דלמא אתי לאפרושי מן החיוב על הפטור. **אלא מאי אית לך למימר** — מאי שנא דחייש על הפלטר — משום דמתרי תלתא זבין. **נחתום נמי** — דלא חייש ליה רבי מאיר לא תקשי לך, דקסבר: נחתום, מתוך שאינו לוקח הרבה ביחד — תלינן למימר מחד גברא זבין, ויש אדם אחד עושה ככרות בדפוסין חלוקין. **משנה אלו דברים שאין להם אונאה** — בגמרא מפרש טעמא. **השטרות** — המוכר שטרות לגבות חוב שבתוכו, ויטלנו לעצמו. **וההקדשות** — גזבר המוכר הקדש, או המוכר עולתו שנפל בו מום.

BACKGROUND

דְּבָרִים שֶׁאֵין לָהֶם אוֹנָאָה **Things for which there is no *ona'ah*.** The commentators differ as to precisely which of the laws of fraud do not apply in such cases. *Ramban* explains that it is prohibited by Torah law to overcharge for such items, even though the sale is not void if one overcharged by more than one-sixth. However, *Tosafot* seems to be of the opinion that it is not prohibited to overcharge when selling such items. Others maintain that overcharging for such items is forbidden as deceitful behavior, even though not prohibited by the regular laws of fraud (*Sma* citing *Maharshal*, *Rashash* and others).

NOTES

נַחְתּוֹם וּפַלְטֵר **Bakers and shopkeepers.** According to *Ritva* (following the Jerusalem Talmud), Rabbi Yehudah's and Rabbi Meir's opinions about bread purchased from bakers and shopkeepers reflect different views as to how such people do business. According to Rabbi Meir, a shopkeeper buys from different suppliers, since he sells large quantities of food, and hence each loaf of bread he sells must be tithed separately. However, a baker buys his flour from a single supplier, since he sells small quantities of food. On the other hand, Rabbi Yehudah is of the opinion that shopkeepers usually have a fixed clientele, so they order bread from a single baker. But a baker, whose sales depend on the demand at any given moment, will buy from whoever happens to be selling flour at the time.

הָעֲבָדִים, וְהַשְּׁטָרוֹת, וְהַקַּרְקָעוֹת **Slaves, promissory notes and land.** Theoretically, land should have been mentioned

HALAKHAH

דְּבָרִים שֶׁאֵין לָהֶם אוֹנָאָה **Things for which there is no *ona'ah*.** "The laws of *ona'ah* do not apply to a person who

LITERAL TRANSLATION

[1]They do not have the double repayment or fourfold and fivefold repayment.

[2]An unpaid bailee does not swear [about them], and a paid bailee does not pay [for them].

[3]Rabbi Shimon says: [56B] [Concerning] sacrifices for which he is responsible,

[1]אֵין לָהֶן תַּשְׁלוּמֵי כֵפֶל וְלֹא תַּשְׁלוּמֵי אַרְבָּעָה וַחֲמִשָּׁה. [2]שׁוֹמֵר חִנָּם אֵינוֹ נִשְׁבַּע, וְנוֹשֵׂא שָׂכָר אֵינוֹ מְשַׁלֵּם. [3]רַבִּי שִׁמְעוֹן אוֹמֵר: [56B] קָדָשִׁים שֶׁהוּא חַיָּיב בְּאַחֲרָיוּתָן,

RASHI

ולא תשלומי ארבעה וחמשה — אם טבח או מכר. ומשום הקדשות אצטריך למיתנייה, דאילו עבדים ושטרות וקרקעות לא שייך למימר, דאילו תשלומי ארבעה וחמשה אינה נוהגת אלא בשור ושה בלבד. **אינו נשבע** — שלא פשע, שלא הזקיקתו תורה לישבע עליהן. **אינו משלם** — אם נגנבו ממנו. **קדשים שחייב באחריותן** — אמר: הרי עלי עולה, והפרישה והוממה ומכרה.

TRANSLATION AND COMMENTARY

אֵין לָהֶן תַּשְׁלוּמֵי כֵפֶל [1]The Mishnah goes on to note that these items of property are unique in other respects as well: **They are not subject to the double repayment or to fourfold and fivefold repayment.** Ordinarily, a thief must repay twice the value of a stolen article, i.e., he must restore the principal to its owner — the article itself or, when the article is unavailable, its value — and he must make an additional payment equal to the value of the article. But if he stole one of the items listed in this Mishnah, he must repay only the principal, and does not make the double repayment. Similarly, someone who steals and then sells or slaughters a sheep is ordinarily obligated to repay its owner four times the value of the sheep, and if the stolen animal is an ox, the restitution required is five times the animal's worth. But if he stole and then sold or slaughtered a sheep or ox that had been consecrated to the Temple, he has to repay only the principal, without making the fourfold or fivefold repayment ordinarily required.

שׁוֹמֵר חִנָּם [2]The Mishnah goes on to mention other unique aspects of the four items listed: An unpaid bailee — a person who accepts an article for safekeeping without remuneration — who claims that the article was lost or stolen while in his care, is not liable for loss of the article, but must ordinarily support his claim with an oath — known as "the oath of the bailees" — that he was not negligent. If, however, he was safeguarding one of the items listed in the Mishnah, **the unpaid bailee need not** take the usual oath of the bailees **concerning them.** A paid bailee — a person who guards an article for a fee — must ordinarily compensate the owner of the article if it is lost or stolen while in his care. If, however, **the paid bailee** was safeguarding one of the items listed in the Mishnah, he **need not compensate** the depositor even in the case of loss or theft.

רַבִּי שִׁמְעוֹן אוֹמֵר [3]**Rabbi Shimon** limits the ruling that consecrated property is not subject to the laws of *ona'ah* and **says:** [56B] **Sacrifices for which** a person **is responsible are subject to** the laws of

NOTES

first, since the laws of *ona'ah* governing the sale of slaves and promissory notes are inferred from those applying to land (see Gemara below). Some commentators explain that slaves and promissory notes were mentioned first because they resemble ordinary movables, to which the laws of *ona'ah* do apply. Thus the Mishnah gave precedence to laws which are less obvious. Others suggest that the Mishnah gave precedence to these laws because they were inferred through Biblical hermeneutics, of which the Tannaim were particularly fond. (*Ritva*, *Tosefot Yom Tov* and others).

קַרְקָעוֹת אֵין לָהֶם אוֹנָאָה Land is not subject to *ona'ah*. Even though this law would not seem to have any logical explanation, as it was deduced through Biblical hermeneutics (see the Gemara's discussion below), the commentators have suggested various rationales. *Rashbam* explains that it is impossible to overcharge for land because there is no limit to what people are willing to pay for it. Others explain that people are willing to waive an overcharge on land after they have paid for it because land lasts forever.

הַקַּרְקָעוֹת אֵין לָהֶן תַּשְׁלוּמֵי כֵפֶל Land is not subject to the double payment. The double payment applies only when the thief steals an object secretly. Where the theft is public it is defined as robbery, and the double payment does not apply. Theft of land would under normal circumstances be

HALAKHAH

overcharges (or underpays) for slaves, promissory notes or property consecrated to the Temple, even if they were worth a thousand zuzim and he sold them for one zuz (or vice-versa). *Rema* writes that some authorities (*Rosh* and *Tur*) maintain that the laws of *ona'ah* do not apply as long as the *ona'ah* is less than or equal to the value of the merchandise. But if a person overcharges by more than the value of the merchandise (e.g., if he charges more than two hundred zuz for something worth one hundred), the laws of *ona'ah* apply even to these things." (*Shulḥan Arukh, Ḥoshen Mishpat* 227:29.)

אֵין לָהֶן תַּשְׁלוּמֵי כֵפֶל They do not have the double repayment. "Someone who steals slaves, promissory notes, land or consecrated property must compensate the owner for the principal, but does not make the double payment." (*Rambam, Sefer Kinyan, Hilkhot Genevah* 2:1,2.)

TRANSLATION AND COMMENTARY

ona'ah. If a person declares: "I undertake to bring a sacrifice to the Temple," he thereby assumes a general responsibility to donate an animal that will be fit for sacrifice. Thus, if the animal he dedicates as a sacrifice is lost or harmed, the owner must bring another, as he must fulfill his obligation to donate a fit animal. Since the owner is personally responsible for the fitness of the animal, it is considered as if he owns it. Accordingly, if an animal develops a blemish that renders it unfit as a sacrifice and the owner is permitted to sell it, the laws of *ona'ah* would apply to the sale in the same way that they apply to other personal property. [1]By contrast, sacrifices **for which** a person **is not responsible are not subject to** the laws of ***ona'ah.*** If a person declares: "This animal is hereby dedicated to the Temple as a sacrifice," the owner is not required to replace it if it is damaged or lost, since he undertook to dedicate only this particular animal. The donor is regarded as having fulfilled his obligation when he gives the animal to the Temple, fit or unfit. This form of language used by the donor renders the animal Temple property from the moment it is dedicated. The animal is regarded as "property for which a person is not responsible," and is not considered as the property of the owner. Hence the laws of *ona'ah* do not apply to its sale.

רַבִּי יְהוּדָה אוֹמֵר [2]**Rabbi Yehudah says: Even** in the case of someone who **sells a Torah scroll, an animal or a pearl, the laws of *ona'ah* do not apply.** (The Gemara explains why below.) [3]The Sages disagreed with Rabbi Yehudah, and **said to** him: The Rabbis **only mentioned those** items listed at the beginning of the Mishnah, i.e., slaves, promissory notes, land and consecrated property. All other types of property are subject to the laws of *ona'ah.*

יֵשׁ לָהֶן אוֹנָאָה. [1]וְשֶׁאֵינוֹ חַיָּיב בְּאַחֲרָיוּתָן, אֵין לָהֶן אוֹנָאָה.
[2]רַבִּי יְהוּדָה אוֹמֵר: אַף הַמּוֹכֵר סֵפֶר תּוֹרָה, בְּהֵמָה, וּמַרְגָּלִית, אֵין לָהֶם אוֹנָאָה. [3]אָמְרוּ לוֹ: לֹא אָמְרוּ אֶלָּא אֶת אֵלּוּ.

LITERAL TRANSLATION

there is *ona'ah* for them. [1]But [concerning sacrifices] for which he is not responsible, there is no *ona'ah* for them.

[2]Rabbi Yehudah says: Even [in the case of] someone who sells a Torah scroll, an animal or a pearl, there is no *ona'ah* for them. [3]They said to him: They did not speak except about these.

RASHI

יש להן אונאה — דכיון דאם מתה או נגנבה חייב באחריותה דידיה היא, ו״לא תונו איש את אחיו״ קרינא ביה. **ושאינו חייב באחריותן** — כגון דאמר הרי זו. **אף המוכר ספר תורה כו׳** — מפרש טעמא בגמרא בברייתא.

NOTES

classified as robbery since the theft is obvious. The exemption of land from double compensation must refer to a theft of land carried out by stealth. This would occur, for example, if a thief secretly moved the border mark of his neighbor's field (*Rambam*).

קָדָשִׁים שֶׁהוּא חַיָּיב בְּאַחֲרָיוּתָן, יֵשׁ לָהֶן אוֹנָאָה **Concerning sacrifices for which he is responsible, there is *ona'ah* for them.** Rabbi Shimon distinguishes between consecrated property for which the original owner is not responsible should it be damaged or lost — considered to be property belonging to the Temple treasury — and consecrated property for which the original owner is responsible, which is treated as property belonging to the original owner. In our Mishnah, Rabbi Shimon applies this distinction only to the laws of *ona'ah*, ruling that consecrated property for which one is responsible is subject to the laws of *ona'ah*. But Rabbi Shimon's distinction applies to the other laws mentioned in our Mishnah as well. Thus, if consecrated property for which one is responsible is stolen, it is subject to the laws of double, fourfold and fivefold payment. Similarly, the ordinary laws of bailees apply when such property is entrusted to a bailee (*Tosefot Yom Tov* and others).

אַף הַמּוֹכֵר סֵפֶר תּוֹרָה **Even someone who sells a Torah scroll.** *Ra'avad* explains that according to Rabbi Yehudah, the laws of fraud do not apply if a person overcharged for a Torah scroll, since there is no limit to its value. However, if the buyer underpaid, the laws of fraud do apply, and the buyer must pay the seller the remainder of the scroll's value. *Meiri*, however, is of the opinion that if the laws of fraud do not apply equally in both directions (as in this case), they do not apply even if one underpaid.

HALAKHAH

שׁוֹמְרִים בְּקַרְקָעוֹת וכו׳ **Bailees to whom land, etc., has been entrusted.** "The various laws pertaining to bailees' obligations do not apply to land, slaves, promissory notes or consecrated property entrusted to them for safekeeping. Specifically, an unpaid bailee need not take an oath that he was not negligent, and a paid bailee (or hirer, or borrower) need not compensate the depositor for loss. Likewise, the bailee is exempt even if he was negligent, although some authorities maintain that he is liable in this case." (*Shulḥan Arukh, Ḥoshen Mishpat* 301:1.) "However, if the depositor is certain of his claim, the bailee must take a Rabbinically imposed oath [שְׁבוּעַת הֶסֵּת] affirming his innocence." (Ibid., 95:1, 301:3.)

BACKGROUND

יָצְאוּ שְׁטָרוֹת וכו׳ Promissory notes are excluded. Even though debts cannot be collected without promissory notes, such notes merely serve as evidence of the transaction described therein. However, they are not intrinsically worth anything except for the paper on which they were written, and hence the laws of fraud do not apply to them.

TRANSLATION AND COMMENTARY

GEMARA מְנָהָנֵי מִילֵּי [1]The Gemara asks: **From where** do we know that the laws of *ona'ah* do not apply to the various items mentioned in the Mishnah? The Gemara answers by citing a Baraita explaining the verse (Leviticus 25:14) in which the Torah prohibits *ona'ah*. [2]**Our Rabbis taught: "'And if you sell something to your neighbor, or buy something from your neighbor's hand,** you shall not wrong every man his brother.'" The Baraita goes on to explain how each of the items mentioned in the Mishnah is excluded by one of the words of the verse: "Since the verse speaks of 'your neighbor's *hand*,' it must refer to **an object that is acquired from hand to hand,** i.e., ordinary movable goods that can be transferred from hand to hand. [3]**Land is** thus **excluded, since it is not movable** property that can be physically transferred from one hand to another. [4]Likewise, non-Jewish **slaves are excluded, since** elsewhere (Leviticus 25:46) **they are compared to land**. In that verse the Torah speaks of slaves as if they were "an inheritance" (i.e., land), implying by this analogy that the same laws apply to both land and slaves. Hence we may infer that just as the laws of *ona'ah* do not apply to land, so too these laws do not apply to slaves. [5]Likewise, **promissory notes are excluded** from the laws of *ona'ah*, for **it is written** in the verse (Leviticus 25:14) concerning *ona'ah*: **'If you sell something** (literally, 'a sale').' From the wording used in the Biblical verse ('sell *a sale*') we can infer that the Torah is describing **something which is itself is sold and which is itself acquired,** i.e., something which has intrinsic value. [6]This **excludes promissory notes,** which have no intrinsic value, **since** the notes **themselves are not sold and** the notes **themselves are not acquired.** [7]The notes **only exist as evidence of** the debts that are recorded **in them.** When a promissory note is transferred from one party to another, it is not the paper itself that is the object of the sale, but rather the evidence contained in the document that the debtor owes money." [8]The Baraita continues by noting that there are cases where promissory notes *are* subject to the laws of *ona'ah*: **"From here** the Rabbis **said: If a person sells his** canceled **promissory notes to a dealer in perfume** as wrapping paper for the perfumes, spices or medicines he is selling, **they are subject to** the laws of ***ona'ah*** if the notes were sold for more than the value of the paper, for in such a case the notes are sold for the value of the paper on which they were written."

גמרא [1]מְנָהָנֵי מִילֵּי? [2]דְּתָנוּ רַבָּנַן: ״׳וְכִי תִמְכְּרוּ מִמְכָּר לַעֲמִיתֶךָ אוֹ קָנֹה מִיַּד עֲמִיתֶךָ׳ — דָּבָר הַנִּקְנֶה מִיָּד לְיָד. [3]יָצְאוּ קַרְקָעוֹת, שֶׁאֵינָן מִטַּלְטְלִים. [4]יָצְאוּ עֲבָדִים, שֶׁהוּקְּשׁוּ לְקַרְקָעוֹת. [5]יָצְאוּ שְׁטָרוֹת דִּכְתִיב: ׳וְכִי תִמְכְּרוּ מִמְכָּר׳ — שֶׁגּוּפוֹ מָכוּר וְגוּפוֹ קָנוּי. [6]יָצְאוּ שְׁטָרוֹת, שֶׁאֵין גּוּפָן מָכוּר וְאֵין גּוּפָן קָנוּי, [7]וְאֵינָן עוֹמְדִין אֶלָּא לִרְאָיָה שֶׁבָּהֶם. [8]מִכָּאן אָמְרוּ: הַמּוֹכֵר שְׁטָרוֹתָיו לְבַשָּׂם, יֵשׁ לָהֶם אוֹנָאָה״.

LITERAL TRANSLATION

GEMARA [1]From where are these things [derived]? [2]For our Rabbis taught: "'And if you sell something to your neighbor or buy something from your neighbor's hand' — an object that is acquired from hand to hand. [3]Land is excluded, since it is not movable. [4]Slaves are excluded, since they were likened to land. [5]Promissory notes are excluded, for it is written: 'And if you sell something' — [something] which is itself sold and which is itself acquired. [6]Promissory notes are excluded, for they are not themselves sold and they are not themselves acquired, [7]and they stand only for the proof that is in them. [8]From here they said: If someone sells his promissory notes to a perfume seller, there is *ona'ah* for them."

RASHI

גמרא דבר הנקנה מיד ליד — הזהיר עליו ב״בל תונו״. **שהוקשו לקרקעות** — [דכתיב] ״והתנחלתם אותם וגו׳״ (ויקרא כה) — הוקשו לאחוזה. **מכאן אמרו** — מדלא אמעוט שטרות אלא משום דאין גופן קנוי ומכור. **המוכר שטרותיו לבשם** — לצור בהם אבקת סממנין, נמצא ממכרן של אלו לצורך תשמיש גופן הוא. **יש להן אונאה** — דגופן קנוי ומכור.

NOTES

יָצְאוּ קַרְקָעוֹת Land is excluded. According to the Baraita, the phrase "from your neighbor's hand" teaches that land is excluded from the laws of *ona'ah*. This is hard to understand in the light of the fact that this verse, which serves as the source for the laws of *ona'ah*, clearly refers to a sale of land (see Leviticus 25:14-17). In his Torah commentary *Ramban* argues that in fact the prohibition of *ona'ah* does apply to land. The phrase "from your neighbor's hand" merely teaches that land is excluded from claims of *ona'ah*. Even though the prohibition of *ona'ah* applies to land, the defrauded party may neither demand a refund nor invalidate the sale when the transaction involves landed property. *Rashi*, on the other hand, seems to understand that land is excluded from all aspects of *ona'ah*, including the prohibition.

[1] פְּשִׁיטָא!
[2] לְאַפּוּקֵי מִדְּרַב כָּהֲנָא, דְּאָמַר: אֵין אוֹנָאָה לִפְרוּטוֹת. [3] קָא מַשְׁמַע לָן: יֵשׁ אוֹנָאָה לִפְרוּטוֹת.
[4] ״הֶקְדֵּשׁוֹת אָמַר קְרָא: ׳אָחִיו׳. אָחִיו וְלֹא הֶקְדֵּשׁ״.
[5] מַתְקִיף לָהּ רַבָּה בַּר מֶמֶל: כָּל הֵיכָא דִּכְתִיב ״יָדוֹ״, יָדוֹ מַמָּשׁ הוּא? [6] אֶלָּא מֵעַתָּה, דִּכְתִיב: ״וַיִּקַּח אֶת כָּל אַרְצוֹ מִיָּדוֹ״, [7] הָכִי נַמִי דְּכָל אַרְעָא בִּידֵיהּ הֲוָה נָקֵיט לָהּ? אֶלָּא,

LITERAL TRANSLATION

[1] It is obvious!

[2] To exclude [the viewpoint of] Rav Kahana who said: There is no *ona'ah* for perutot. [3] It tells us: There is *ona'ah* for perutot.

[4] "[Concerning] consecrated property the verse says: 'His brother.' His brother and not consecrated property."

[5] Rabbah bar Memel objected to this: Wherever it is written "his hand," is it literally his hand? [6] If so (lit., "but from now"), when it is written: "And he took all his land from his hand," [7] so too [is it] that he held all the land in his hand? Rather,

TRANSLATION AND COMMENTARY

פְּשִׁיטָא [1] The Gemara interrupts the quotation from the Baraita at this point and objects: **Surely this is obvious!** If the promissory notes were sold as wrapping paper for more than the value of the paper, there is no reason to imagine that the laws of *ona'ah* should be suspended, for in such a case notes are no different from other movable goods! What need was there to single this case out for special mention?

לְאַפּוּקֵי מִדְּרַב כָּהֲנָא [2] The Gemara answers that it was necessary for the Baraita to state that the laws of *ona'ah* apply in this case in order to **exclude** and reject **the viewpoint of Rav Kahana, who said: There is no fraud for perutot,** i.e., the laws of *ona'ah* do not apply if the overcharge amounted to only a few perutot. (See above, 55a.) [3] By stating that the laws of *ona'ah* apply to promissory notes sold for the value of their paper, the Rabbis **teach us** that **fraud applies** even **to perutot.** The perutah was the smallest copper coin in circulation during the Talmudic period. Rav Kahana was of the opinion that the laws of *ona'ah* did not apply to any sale worth less than an isar, which was equivalent to eight perutot. Since the price of a promissory note sold for the value of its paper is less than an isar, we may infer that, contrary to the opinion of Rav Kahana, the laws of *ona'ah* apply even if the overcharge amounted to only a perutah.

הֶקְדֵּשׁוֹת אָמַר קְרָא [4] The Gemara now continues its quotation from the Baraita: "The laws of *ona'ah* do not apply to **consecrated property.** Since **the verse** (Leviticus 25:14) **says:** 'You shall not wrong every man **his brother,**' we may infer that the laws of *ona'ah* apply only to a person who overcharges or underpays **his brother,** i.e., a private person, **but not** to a person who overcharges or underpays when selling or buying **consecrated property.**"

מַתְקִיף לָהּ רַבָּה בַּר מֶמֶל [5] **Rabbah bar Memel** now **objects to** the exegesis of the Baraita which excludes land from the application of the laws of *ona'ah* because the word "hand" used in the verse is interpreted literally as referring exclusively to movables transferred "from hand to hand." Is it in fact true that **wherever** the expression **"his hand" is written** in the Torah, **it literally** means **his hand?** This is surely not true. [6] For **if so,** how are we to explain the following verse (Numbers 21:26), **where it is written** that Siḥon, king of the Amorites, **"took all** of the king of Moab's **land from his hand"?** [7] Can we say that **even here** the verse means that **he held all the land in his hand?! Rather,** the expression "from his hand" must be interpreted

RASHI

פשיטא — מאי שנא מכל מטלטלי דעלמא? **לפרוטות** — סתם מוכר שטרות לבשם אין שם המקח של איסר ביחד, אלא של פרוטות. **ידו ממש הוא** — דקדייקת לעיל ״מיד עמיתך״ מטלטלים דוקא, הנקחין מיד אל יד.

NOTES

״יָדוֹ״ יָדוֹ מַמָּשׁ Interpreting "his hand" literally. Most Biblical passages containing the expression "his hand" (יָדוֹ) must be interpreted literally. However, there are certain passages which admit of an alternative explanation (i.e., "his possession"), and thus the question arises as to which interpretation is preferable in such cases. The Gemara therefore concludes that "his hand" should be interpreted literally unless there is explicit evidence to the contrary, as in the case of a bill of divorce or theft (*Torat Ḥayyim*).

HALAKHAH

בְּכָל הַמִּטַּלְטְלִין יֵשׁ אוֹנָאָה The laws of fraud apply to all movables. "The laws of fraud apply to all movable goods, even to Torah scrolls and precious stones," following the view of the Sages in our Mishnah. (*Shulḥan Arukh, Ḥoshen Mishpat* 227:15.)

SAGES

רַבָּה בַּר מֶמֶל Rabbah bar Memel. The name of this Sage is actually Rabbi Abba bar Memel, a Palestinian Amora of the second and third generations. See *Bava Metzia*, Part I, p. 229.

CONCEPTS

קַרְפֵּף Enclosure. The origin of this word is unclear. It may be connected to the root קפף or גפף, in the sense of making a partition. At all events, a קַרְפֵּף is a courtyard surrounded by a partition, which one cannot enter without a key. Some authorities hold that a קַרְפֵּף was situated outside the city, and others say that a קַרְפֵּף is actually a rear courtyard adjacent to a house, which is not used all the time but serves as a storage area.

TRANSLATION AND COMMENTARY

as meaning "from the king of Moab's **possession."** Sihon removed all of the Moabite king's land from his possession. [1]**Here too,** when the Torah prohibits *ona'ah* in buying something from "one's neighbor's hand," it may in fact be referring to anything bought **"from** the neighbor's **possession,"** including land. Thus we have no evidence that the laws of *ona'ah* do not apply to land.

וְכָל הֵיכָא דִּכְתִיב [2]But the Gemara refuses to accept Rabbah bar Memel's conclusion that, as used in the Torah, the term "his hand" refers broadly to a person's possession or domain. Is it really true, asks the Gemara, that **wherever** the expression **"his hand" is written** in the Torah, **it does not literally mean his hand?** [3]Surely the opposite **has been taught** in the following Baraita, which discusses the law of double payment made by a thief: "The verse (Exodus 22:3) says: **'If** the theft **is certainly found in his hand** ... he shall restore double.' [4]Now, if we interpret this Biblical text literally, **we only know** that the thief is required to make the double payment if the stolen object was taken by the thief's **hand,** i.e., where the thief acquired the stolen object by physically taking it with his hand. [5]**From where do we derive** the law that the thief is obliged to make the double payment even if the stolen object was acquired by means of his **roof, his courtyard or his enclosure?** From where do we know that if a person wishes to steal something that has entered his property, his property may acquire the object for him through the mode of acquisition known as courtyard-acquisition? [6]**The verse teaches: 'If it is certainly found'** (הִמָּצֵא תִמָּצֵא). Since the Torah uses this expression rather than the normal תִּמָּצֵא ("is found"), we may infer from the use of this emphatic form that the thief is obliged to make the double payment **in all circumstances,** no matter how he acquired the stolen object."

טַעְמָא דִּכְתַב רַחֲמָנָא [7]This Baraita proves, says the Gemara, that the expression "his hand" is usually to be understood literally: **The** only **reason** that the expression "his hand" is not interpreted literally in the case of the thief **is that the Torah wrote: "If it is certainly found,"** the emphatic form teaching us that a thief is obliged to make the double payment irrespective of the way in which the stolen object came into his possession. [8]**If not** for the Torah's use of this special emphatic form, **I would have said** that **wherever** the Torah **uses the expression "his hand," it literally means his hand.** This refutes Rabbah bar Memel's objection.

וְתוּ תַּנְיָא [9]The Gemara now reinforces its refutation of the objection raised by Rabbah bar Memel: **And moreover, it has been taught** in another Baraita, which discusses the manner in which a bill of divorce must be handed to a wife: "The verse (Deuteronomy 24:1) says: **'And he shall give it into her hand'** Now, if we interpret this Biblical text literally, **we only know** that the divorce is valid if the bill of divorce is placed directly into the wife's **hand.** [10]**From where do we derive** the law that the divorce is valid even if the bill of divorce was placed on **her roof, in her courtyard, or in her enclosure? The verse teaches:**

"מֵרְשׁוּתוֹ". [1]הָכָא נַמִי מֵרְשׁוּתוֹ. [2]וְכָל הֵיכָא דִּכְתִיב "יָדוֹ" לָאו יָדוֹ מַמָּשׁ הוּא? [3]וְהָתַנְיָא: "'אִם הִמָּצֵא תִמָּצֵא בְיָדוֹ'. [4]אֵין לִי אֶלָּא יָדוֹ. [5]גַּגּוֹ, חֲצֵירוֹ, וְקַרְפֵּיפוֹ מִנַּיִן? [6]תַּלְמוּד לוֹמַר: 'אִם הִמָּצֵא תִמָּצֵא' — מִכָּל מָקוֹם". [7]טַעְמָא דְּכָתַב רַחֲמָנָא: "אִם הִמָּצֵא תִמָּצֵא". [8]הָא לָאו הָכִי, הֲוָה אָמִינָא: כָּל הֵיכָא דְּכָתַב "יָדוֹ", יָדוֹ מַמָּשׁ הוּא.

[9]וְתוּ, תַּנְיָא: "'וְנָתַן בְּיָדָהּ'. אֵין לִי אֶלָּא יָדָהּ. [10]גַּגָּהּ, חֲצֵירָהּ, וְקַרְפֵּיפָהּ מִנַּיִן? תַּלְמוּד לוֹמַר:

LITERAL TRANSLATION

[it means] "from his possession." [1]Here too [it means] from his possession.

[2]And wherever it is written "his hand," is it not literally his hand? [3]But surely it has been taught: "'If it is certainly found in his hand.' [4][From this] I know (lit., 'have') nothing but his hand. [5]His roof, his courtyard and his enclosure, from where [are they derived]? [6]The verse teaches: 'If it is certainly found' — in all cases (lit., 'anyhow')."

[7]The reason is that the Torah (lit., "the Merciful One") wrote: "If it is certainly found." [8][But] if this were not so, I would have said: Wherever it is written "his hand," [it means] his hand literally.

[9]And moreover, it has been taught: "'And he shall give it into her hand.' [From this] I know (lit., 'have') nothing but her hand. [10]Her roof, her courtyard, and her enclosure, from where [are they derived]? The verse teaches:

RASHI

הכא נמי מרשות – "עמיתך" קאמר, ואפילו קרקעות נמי במשמע. **אין לי** – שיתחייב כפל. **אלא** – בזמן שלקחה בידו. **גגו חצירו [קרפיפו] מנין** – שאם נכנסה שם ונעל בפניה לגנבה, מנין שקנתה לו חצירו ומתחייב כפל? **תלמוד לומר ונתן מכל מקום** – מדלא כתיב ובידה יתננו.

TRANSLATION AND COMMENTARY

'And he shall give it,' and this means **in all circumstances,** no matter how it enters her possession." Since the Torah states: "He shall give it into her hand" (וְנָתַן בְּיָדָהּ), rather than "into her hand he shall give it" (בְּיָדָהּ יִתְּנֶנּוּ), we may infer that the primary emphasis here was on the "giving," and as long as the husband got the bill of divorce into his wife's possession, regardless of whether it entered her hand, her courtyard or enclosure, etc., the divorce is valid.

טַעְמָא דִּכְתַב רַחֲמָנָא [1]The Gemara now proves from this Baraita that ordinarily the expression "hand" used in the Torah should be taken literally: **The** only **reason** that the expression "her hand" is not interpreted literally here **is that the Torah wrote: "And he shall give,"** rather than "into her hand he shall give it," as explained above. [2]**But if not** for the fact that the Torah used this expression, **I would have said** that **wherever** the Torah **uses the expression "his hand," it literally means his hand.** This again refutes Rabbah bar Memel's objection.

אֶלָּא [3]**Hence,** the Gemara concludes, **every** time the expression **"his hand"** appears in the Torah it is to be understood **literally** as **his hand,** unless there is some indication in the verse that the expression should *not* be taken literally. Since the verse prohibiting *ona'ah* describes objects bought "from one's neighbor's hand," it follows that the laws of *ona'ah* apply specifically to movables and not to landed property. As for the verse (Numbers 21:26 — "and he took all the land *from his hand*") used by Rabbah bar Memel to prove that the expression "his hand" ought not to be taken literally, [4]**there** the situation **is different, for** in that case **we cannot** possibly **say** that "hand" should be interpreted literally as it generally is, **but rather** the context demands that it be interpreted as meaning **"in his possession."**

בָּעֵי רַבִּי זֵירָא [5]**Rabbi Zera posed a question** concerning the scope of the laws of *ona'ah*: **Is** a **hiring** (or rental) agreement **subject to** ***ona'ah*** **or is it not subject to** ***ona'ah*?** If a person overcharges or underpays when hiring something, do the laws of *ona'ah* apply or not? [6]The Gemara explains the two sides of the issue: On the one hand, when **the Torah** mentioned the laws of *ona'ah* (Leviticus 25:14, "If you sell something to your neighbor, ... you shall not wrong one another"), **did it mean** that the laws of *ona'ah* should apply only **to a sale, but not to hiring, or is there perhaps no difference** between a sale and a hire, and the laws of *ona'ah* should apply equally to both cases?

'וְנָתַן' — מִכָּל מָקוֹם". [1]טַעְמָא דִּכְתַב רַחֲמָנָא: "וְנָתַן". [2]הָא לָאו הָכִי, הֲוָה אָמִינָא: כָּל הֵיכָא דִּכְתַב "יָדוֹ", יָדוֹ מַמָּשׁ. [3]אֶלָּא, כָּל "יָדוֹ" יָדוֹ מַמָּשׁ הוּא, [4]וְשָׁאנֵי הָתָם, דְּלֵיכָּא לְמֵימַר הָכִי, אֶלָּא "בִּרְשׁוּתוֹ". [5]בָּעֵי רַבִּי זֵירָא: שְׂכִירוּת יֵשׁ לוֹ אוֹנָאָה אוֹ אֵין לוֹ אוֹנָאָה? [6]"מִמְכָּר" אָמַר רַחֲמָנָא, אֲבָל לֹא שְׂכִירוּת, אוֹ דִּלְמָא לָא שְׁנָא?

LITERAL TRANSLATION

'And he shall give' — in all cases." [1]The reason is that the Torah wrote: "And he shall give." [2][But] if this were not so, I would have said: Wherever it is written "his hand," [it means] his hand literally. [3]Rather, every [mention of] "his hand" [means] his hand literally, [4]and there it is different, for this cannot be said, but rather "in his possession." [5]Rabbi Zera asked: Is there *ona'ah* for hiring, or is there no *ona'ah* [for hiring]? [6]Did the Torah say "sale," but not hire, or perhaps there is no difference?

RASHI

ושאני התם — "ויקח את כל ארצו".
יש להם אונאה — אם מכרן.

SAGES

רַבִּי זֵירָא **Rabbi Zera.** A Palestinian Amora of the third generation. See *Bava Metzia,* Part I, p. 60.

NOTES

שְׂכִירוּת יֵשׁ לוֹ אוֹנָאָה **Is hiring subject to *ona'ah?*** According to most Rishonim, Rabbi Zera asked whether the laws of *ona'ah* apply to the rental of movable property. Abaye answered that rentals are governed by the laws of *ona'ah,* because a rental is regarded as a temporary sale. Therefore, since the laws of *ona'ah* apply to sales, they apply to rentals as well. Abaye's position that a rental may be regarded as a temporary sale can be understood in one of two ways: (1) The rented object is itself acquired by the renter for the period of the rental. (2) The use of the rented object is acquired for the period of the rental, but the object itself is not acquired. According to the first explanation — that a rented object is considered as if temporarily bought — it follows that the laws of *ona'ah* do not apply when landed property is rented, for land is excluded from the laws of *ona'ah* even when it is bought (*Ramban*). According to the second explanation — that the use of the rented object is considered as if it were temporarily bought — it is possible that the laws of *ona'ah* do apply to the rental of land, even though they do not apply when land is bought (*Mordekhai*).

The explanation offered above assumes that the laws of *ona'ah* apply only to transactions that can be regarded as sales. *Rabbenu Yehonatan* suggests an alternate explanation rejecting this assumption. According to *Rabbenu Yehonatan,* Rabbi Zera asked whether the laws of *ona'ah* apply to the rental of land. If a rental is *not* regarded as a sale, then the laws of *ona'ah* should apply in the same way that they apply to the rental of movables. But if a rental *is* treated as a temporary sale, then the *ona'ah* laws should not apply, just as they do not apply when land is bought. Some Rishonim seem to understand Rabbi Zera's question as applying not only to the renting of objects, but also to the hiring of

[1]אֲמַר לֵיהּ אַבַּיֵי: מִי כְּתִיב: "מִמְכָּר לְעוֹלָם"? [2]מִמְכָּר סְתָמָא כְּתִיב, וְהַאי נַמִי בְּיוֹמֵיהּ מְכִירָה הִיא.

[3]בָּעֵי רָבָא: חִטִּין וּזְרָעָן בְּקַרְקַע, מַהוּ? [4]יֵשׁ לָהֶם אוֹנָאָה אוֹ אֵין לָהֶם אוֹנָאָה? [5]כְּמַאן דְּשַׁדְיָין בְּכַדָּא דָּמְיָין, וְיֵשׁ לָהֶם אוֹנָאָה, [6]אוֹ דִּלְמָא בָּטְלִינְהוּ עַל גַּב אַרְעָא?

[7]הֵיכִי דָּמֵי? [8]אִילֵימָא דַּאֲמַר אִיהוּ: "שְׁדָאִי בָּהּ שִׁיתָּא", וְאָתוּ סָהֲדֵי וְאָמְרִי דְּלָא שְׁדָא בָּהּ אֶלָּא חֲמִשָּׁה, [9]וְהָאָמַר רָבָא: כָּל דָּבָר שֶׁבְּמִדָּה, וְשֶׁבְּמִשְׁקָל,

LITERAL TRANSLATION

[1]Abaye said to him: Is it written: "Sale forever"? [2]Just "sale" is written, and this too on its day is a sale.

[3]Rava asked: [Regarding] wheat that he planted in the ground, what [is the law]? [4]Is there *ona'ah* for it or is there no *ona'ah* for it? [5]Is it as if it has been put into a jar, and there is *ona'ah* for it, [6]or perhaps he assimilated (lit., "annulled") it by the soil?

[7]How do we visualize the case (lit., "how is it like?")? [8]If we say that he said: "I put in six," and witnesses came and said that he put in only five, [9]surely Rava said: [In] any matter of measure, of weight

TRANSLATION AND COMMENTARY

אֲמַר לֵיהּ אַבַּיֵי [1]**Abaye said to** Rabbi Zera: **Does** the Torah **specify** that the laws of *ona'ah* apply only to **"a permanent sale"?** Clearly it does not. Nowhere does the Torah state that a sale must be for a specific period in order that the laws of *ona'ah* should apply to it. [2]Rather, the Torah **just** uses the word **"sale"** without specifying what kind, **and** to hire something **may also be** considered **a sale,** even if only **for the period** of the rental! During the rental term the hirer may use the object as if it were his own; the only limitation on his ownership is the fact that at the conclusion of the period of rental he must return it. Since a rental is considered "a sale for a limited period," the laws of *ona'ah* should apply to a rental the same way as they apply to a typical sale.

בָּעֵי רָבָא [3]Our Mishnah stated that whereas ordinary movables are subject to the laws of *ona'ah*, land is not. **Rava** asked whether the object of the sale in the following case should be treated like movable property or like land: **What** is the law if someone sells **wheat** which has already been planted **in the ground** but has not yet taken root? [4]**Is** such wheat **subject to** the laws of ***ona'ah*, or is it not subject to** the laws of ***ona'ah*?** The Gemara now explains Rava's query in greater detail, presenting the different sides of the question: If the wheat has already taken root, it should certainly be treated like the land in which it is planted, and be excluded from the laws of *ona'ah*. [5]But if it has not yet taken root, do we say that the wheat **is** considered **as if it has been** merely **put into a jar,** in which case **it is subject to** the laws of ***ona'ah*** like any other movable property? [6]**Or perhaps** immediately upon being planted and even before **it** has taken root the wheat **becomes assimilated to the soil** and, now being regarded as land, is not subject to the laws of *ona'ah*?

הֵיכִי דָּמֵי [7]Before attempting to answer Rava's question, the Gemara asks: **How do we visualize the case?** [8]**If we say** that Rava is asking about a case **where** the seller **said: "I put six** measures of wheat **into the ground," and witnesses came and said that he only** put in **five,** would Rava have had any doubt as to the law? [9]**Surely Rava** himself **said:** In **any** case of overcharge or underpayment resulting from incorrect **measuring, weighing**

RASHI

בטלינהו אגב ארעא — ואין אונאה לקרקעות, ובשלא השרישו קאי. **שדאי** — זרעתי בה שש סאין.

SAGES

רָבָא Rava. A Babylonian Amora of the fourth generation. See *Bava Metzia*, Part II, pp. 9-10.

BACKGROUND

חִטִּין וּזְרָעָן בְּקַרְקַע Wheat that he planted in the ground. Certain laws apply only to the ground or to things connected to the ground, such as houses, trees and plants, but not to movables. Accordingly, the Gemara asks about the Halakhic status of wheat (or other seeds) planted in the ground. On the one hand, such wheat should perhaps be regarded as "connected" to the ground, since it is already located there, and the owner wants to leave it there. On the other hand, since the wheat is not yet literally connected to the ground (since it has not yet taken root), it should perhaps be treated like movables which happen to be located in the ground at a given moment.

כָּל דָּבָר שֶׁבְּמִדָּה, וְשֶׁבְּמִשְׁקָל, וְשֶׁבְּמִנְיָן Any matter of measure, of weight or of number. The value and price of most goods cannot be determined with absolute precision, so the parties to a sale are ordinarily willing to waive a slight overcharge (i.e., less than one-sixth). However, in the case of something sold by measure, weight or number, it is possible to measure the merchandise with precision, so even the slightest deviation may be grounds for voiding the sale.

NOTES

workers. According to this explanation, Abaye answered that hiring a worker is viewed as buying him for the day, as if he were a temporary slave. Since slaves are not subject to the laws of *ona'ah*, the laws of *ona'ah* do not apply when workers are hired (*Rambam*).

חִטִּין וּזְרָעָן בְּקַרְקַע Wheat that he planted in the ground. The commentators differ as to precisely what case the Gemara is referring to here. *Rambam* and *Ra'avad* explain that Rava's question applies to a case in which a person hired a worker to plant the usual amount of wheat in a given area, but the worker planted less. Others, followed by our commentary, suggest that Rava is asking whether the laws of fraud apply if a person sold wheat planted in the ground for a higher (or lower) price than the standard market price (*Rabbenu Ḥananel*, *Rashba*, *Ritva* and others).

דָּבָר שֶׁבְּמִדָּה Things that are measured. Since the buyer specified exactly how much he wanted, it is clear that he is not willing to waive even the slightest overcharge (*Rashi, Menaḥot* 69a).

HALAKHAH

אוֹנָאָה בִּשְׂכִירוּת Fraud in hiring. "The laws of fraud apply to overcharging for the hire of utensils and animals in the same way that they apply to overcharging for a sale (since hire is simply a form of purchase for a limited time.) Hence, if one hires a worker for more or less than the standard wage, the party who was defrauded is not entitled to compensation, since hiring labor is, Halakhically speaking, tantamount to acquiring a slave, and the laws of fraud do not apply to slaves. Likewise, the laws of fraud do not apply to land rental or to the hiring of items attached to the ground." (*Shulḥan Arukh, Ḥoshen Mishpat* 227: 32,33,35.)

TRANSLATION AND COMMENTARY

or counting, the injured party **may withdraw** from the transaction **even** if the overcharge or underpayment amounts to **less than** the amount that constitutes ***ona'ah***. The laws of *ona'ah* from which landed property is excluded are limited to discrepancies between the general market price of the item and the price charged by a particular seller. If, however, the fair market price was charged, but an error was made when measuring, weighing or counting the merchandise or when counting out the money, the resulting mistake must be rectified no matter how small, and no matter how much time has elapsed. Transactions based on a mistake are invalidated not only when they involve movable goods, but also when they involve landed property. Thus, if the parties agreed on six measures of wheat and the seller planted only five, the sale is void. Accordingly, Rava could not possibly have asked about this case, for the answer is obvious.

אֶלָּא דַּאֲמַר אִיהוּ [1]**Rather,** says the Gemara, Rava must have been asking about a case **where** the seller **said: "I planted as** much wheat as **was required,"** i.e., as much as people normally plant in this particular type of land, [2]**but later it became clear that he had not planted as** much as **was required.** A mistaken measurement invalidates a transaction even if it involves land, but a mistake in judgment is treated like a mistake in the price, and is governed by the laws of *ona'ah*. [3]Thus the question arises: In such a case, **is** the wheat **subject to** the laws of ***ona'ah*** **or is it not subject to** the laws of *ona'ah*? [4]**Is** the wheat which has not yet taken root considered **as if it has** merely **been put into a jar,** in which case **it is subject to** the laws of ***ona'ah*** just like any other movable property? [5]**Or perhaps** the moment it is planted and even before **it** has taken root wheat **becomes assimilated to the soil** and, now regarded as land, such wheat is not subject to the laws of *ona'ah*?

וְשֶׁבְּמִנְיָן, אֲפִילּוּ פָּחוֹת מִכְּדֵי אוֹנָאָה, חוֹזֵר.
[1]אֶלָּא, דַּאֲמַר אִיהוּ: ״שְׁדָאִי בָּהּ כִּדְאִבָּעֵי לָהּ״, [2]וְאִיגַּלְּאִי מִילְּתָא דְּלָא שְׁדָא בָּהּ כִּדְאִבָּעֵי לָהּ. [3]יֵשׁ לָהֶם אוֹנָאָה אוֹ אֵין לָהֶם אוֹנָאָה? [4]כְּמַאן דְּשָׁדֵי בְּכַדָּא דָּמְיָין, וְיֵשׁ לָהֶם אוֹנָאָה, [5]אוֹ דִּלְמָא בָּטְלִינְהוּ אַגַּב אַרְעָא?

LITERAL TRANSLATION

or of number, even [if] less than *ona'ah*, he may withdraw (lit., "it returns").

[1]Rather, [the case is] that he said: "I put in as much as was required," [2]and [later] it became clear that he had not put in as much as was required. [3]Is there *ona'ah* for it or is there no *ona'ah* for it? [4]Is it as if it has been put into a jar, and there is *ona'ah* for it, [5]or perhaps he assimilated it by the soil?

RASHI

חוזר — דמקח טעות הוא. דהא בהדיא פירש בחזקת כן, ואינו כן. וכיון שהמקח טעות הוא, אפילו בטיל להו אגב ארעא — חוזר, דנהי דאימעיט קרקעות מדין אונאה — מדין מקח טעות לא אימעיט, שהרי אין זה מכר דאדעתא דהכי לא זבן. **כדבעי לה** — כמה שצריך לקרקע. דמידי דאומדנא דשכיח דטעו הוי כדין אונאה.

NOTES

דָּבָר שֶׁבְּמִדָּה, וְשֶׁבְּמִשְׁקָל, וְשֶׁבְּמִנְיָן Any matter of measure, of weight or of number. The Rishonim disagree about what Rava meant when he said that a mistake resulting from incorrect measuring, weighing or counting "returns" (חוזר). According to *Rashi*, the transaction "returns," i.e., the entire transaction is void. Since an explicit agreement was violated, the transaction becomes null and void. According to *Ri Migash*, on the other hand, the transaction is binding and it is only the discrepancy that "returns." The parties to the transaction must strictly adhere to the agreement reached between them concerning the measure, weight or quantity of the merchandise. If the seller fails to provide the merchandise as promised, the discrepancy must be rectified even if it amounts to less than one-sixth.

Rashbam distinguishes between movables and landed property. A mistake in measuring, weighing or counting in a transaction involving movables nullifies the entire transaction. In a sale involving land, however, both parties prefer that the sale not be invalidated. The sale is therefore binding, and the mistake must be rectified.

שְׁדָאִי בָּהּ כִּדְאִבָּעֵי לָהּ I put in as much as was required. Our commentary follows *Rashi,* who understands that Rava asked about a case in which someone sold wheat which had been planted in the ground but had not yet taken root. The

HALAKHAH

אוֹנָאָה בְּמִדָּה וּבְמִנְיָן Fraud for items that are measured or counted. "If a person sells something by weight, measure or quantity, any shortage or surplus must be refunded no matter how small, and regardless of how much time has passed since the sale took place. *Sma* adds: In cases where this is not possible (e.g., where a person sold land, and it may not be possible to provide land from an adjacent field to make up what is missing), the sale is canceled." (Ibid., 232:1.)

אוֹנָאָה בְּחִטִּין שֶׁזְּרָעָן Fraud for wheat that has been planted. "If a person hired someone to sow land, and he told him: 'I have sown as many seeds as are normally sown in this sort of land,' and witnesses came and testified that he had planted fewer seeds than he should have, it is unclear whether the laws of fraud apply, and hence the defendant is not required to pay the plaintiff, but merely to take a Rabbinically ordained oath." (Ibid., 227:34.)

LITERAL TRANSLATION

[1]Does one take an oath about it, or does one not take an oath about it? [2]Is it as if it has been put into a jar, and one takes an oath about it, [3]or perhaps he assimilated it by the soil, and one does not take an oath about it?

[4]Does the omer permit it, or does the omer not permit it? [5]How do we visualize the case? [6]If it took root, we have learned [it], [and] if it did not

[1]נִשְׁבָּעִין עֲלֵיהֶן, אוֹ אֵין נִשְׁבָּעִין עֲלֵיהֶן? [2]כְּמַאן דְּשַׁדְיָין בְּכַדָּא דָּמְיָין, וְנִשְׁבָּעִין עֲלֵיהֶן, [3]אוֹ דִּלְמָא בָּטְלִינְהוּ אַגַּב אַרְעָא, וְאֵין נִשְׁבָּעִין עֲלֵיהֶן? [4]עוֹמֶר מַתִּירָן, אוֹ אֵין עוֹמֶר מַתִּירָן? [5]הֵיכִי דָּמֵי? [6]אִי דְּאַשְׁרוּשׁ, תָּנֵינָא, אִי דְּלָא

RASHI

נשבעין עליהן – אם הודה במקצת, כגון טענו: פסקת עמי לזרוע שש שמסרתי לך, וזרעת חמש. והוא אומר: זרעתי חמש ומחצה. **עומר מתירן** – קא סלקא דעתך אגידולין דידהו קמיבעיא ליה, ולהכי קמהדר: אי דאשרוש קודם לעומר. **תנינא** – דעומר מתיר את גידוליהן, במסכת מנחות (ע,א), והתם מפרש טעמא. **ואי דלא אשרוש** – בשעת הבאת עומר.

TRANSLATION AND COMMENTARY

נִשְׁבָּעִין עֲלֵיהֶן [1]The Gemara leaves the question open, and proceeds to raise another, related question the answer to which depends on whether such wheat is classified as land or as movable property: **Does a person take an oath about** wheat that has been planted but has not yet taken root, **or does a person not take an oath about it?** According to the Halakhah, if a person claims that another owes him money, and this second person admits that he owes part of the sum but not all of it, the court requires the defendant to pay the amount to which he has admitted liability, and to take an oath that he owes no additional money, after which he is exempt from paying the amount he denies owing. This oath is imposed only if the claim involves movable property; the defendant need not take an oath about claims involving land. Now, if the plaintiff claims that the defendant agreed to plant six measures of wheat for him but planted only four, and therefore owes two, whereas the defendant claims that he in fact planted five measures and owes only one, the question arises: Is the defendant required to take an oath confirming that he does not owe the sixth measure, or not? [2]The Gemara explains the different sides of the question: **Is the** wheat considered **as if it has** merely **been put into a jar,** in which case the defendant **takes an oath about it** as he would in the case of any other movable property? [3]**Or perhaps** the wheat **is** regarded as having become **assimilated to the soil** the moment it was planted, in which case the defendant **does not take an oath about it**, for it is considered like land?

עוֹמֶר מַתִּירָן [4]The Gemara leaves the question unanswered, and proceeds with yet another related question: **Does the omer render** wheat planted in the ground **permissible, or does the omer not render it permissible?** According to Torah law (Leviticus 23:10–14), each year's new crop of grain could not be eaten until the offering of roasted barley flour known as the omer was offered in the Temple on the 16th of Nisan, the day following the first day of Pesaḥ. Once the omer was offered, the grain from the new harvest could be eaten. The question arises as to whether or not the omer allows one to eat grain that has been planted in the ground. The Gemara first understands the question as referring to the produce that will eventually grow from the grain that has been planted, and attempts to clarify the case in which there is a question: [5]**How do we visualize the case?** [6]**If** the grain has already **taken root** before the omer was brought, **we have** already **learned** what the law is, and hence the question is superfluous, **and if** the grain **has not**

NOTES

ona'ah in question involves a discrepancy in the amount of wheat planted, the seller thinking that he had planted the correct amount and afterwards finding out that he had not. This mistake is classified as *ona'ah* rather than as a "matter of measurement, weighing or counting" since the amount of wheat that must be planted is a matter of judgment.

Rabbenu Ḥananel has a slightly different reading of the text: "Rather, the case is that he said: 'I put in as much as was required.' Is it subject to *ona'ah* or not?" According to this reading, the seller in fact planted the correct amount of wheat in the field. However, he overcharged for the wheat, and so a question arises as to whether the planted wheat is considered movable property or land (*Ramban*).

Rambam understands the Gemara as referring not to a sale of planted wheat but to a worker hired to plant the required amount of wheat, and about whom witnesses testify that he failed to do so.

נִשְׁבָּעִין עֲלֵיהֶן **Does one take an oath about it?** Here too the commentators differ as to the precise nature of the case under discussion. In addition to *Rashi*'s explanation, followed in our commentary, we may note that of *Ritva*, who explains that the Gemara's question applies when a person claims that he deposited five measures of wheat (which had been planted in the ground) with someone else, but the bailee admits to receiving only four (which were damaged because he was negligent in caring for them).

Rosh, however, explains that the Gemara's question applies when a person claims that he owns wheat planted in someone else's field, and his claim is corroborated by a single witness. Thus the question arises as to whether the owner of the field must swear that the wheat is his own in order to refute the plaintiff's claim, since a defendant must ordinarily take an oath supporting his position if he is contradicted by a single witness.

TRANSLATION AND COMMENTARY

yet **taken root, we have** also already **learned** what the law is, and again the question is superfluous! [1]For **we have learned** in a Mishnah (*Menaḥot* 70a): **"If** the grain **took root before the omer** was brought, **the omer** offering **permits it** to be harvested and eaten, although the grain did not ripen until after the offering was brought. [2]**But if** the grain did **not** take root before the omer was brought, the grain **is forbidden until** next year, when **the next omer comes."** Thus, if the grain has already taken root, it is permitted, and if not, it is prohibited. In which case, then, is there any question?

לָא [3]The Gemara answers: **No!** Our question is indeed **necessary,** and it was asked in reference to a different case, **in which** the crop **was harvested** before the omer was brought, in which case the harvest should be permitted by the omer offering. But after harvesting the crop, the farmer **planted** the grain **before the omer** was brought. [4]**Then the omer came and passed, but** the grain **had not** yet **taken root before the omer** was brought. In other words, the seeds were planted before the omer offering was brought but took root only after the omer was brought. [57A] Now, the wheat which later grows from these grains may certainly not be eaten until the omer of the next year is brought, for the grains took root after the omer for the previous year was brought, and were not rendered fit by that omer. A question arises, however, when a person plants seeds from grain rendered fit by the omer, and then decides — before the seeds have taken root — to remove them from the soil and eat them. [5]The Gemara explains: **What is the law about removing** the wheat grains before they take root **and eating** them before the next omer is brought? The answer to this question depends on how we regard the planted grain before it has taken root: [6]**Is** the grain which has been planted but has not yet taken root considered **as if it has** merely **been put into a jar,** in which case it is not treated as part of the ground and is movable property no different from grain stored in the house, **and the** previous **omer permits it?** [7]**Or perhaps,** immediately upon being planted and even before **it** has taken root, the grain **becomes assimilated to the soil,** and the seed grains, along with the wheat they will ultimately produce, will be rendered fit only by the omer brought the following year?

אַשְׁרוּשׁ, תָּנֵינָא. [1]דִּתְנַן: ״אִם הִשְׁרִישׁוּ קוֹדֶם לָעוֹמֶר, עוֹמֶר מַתִּירָן, [2]וְאִם לָאו, אֲסוּרִין עַד שֶׁיָּבֹא עוֹמֶר הַבָּא״.

[3]לָא. צְרִיכָא דַּחֲצַדִינְהוּ וּזְרַעִינְהוּ קוֹדֶם לָעוֹמֶר, [4]וַאֲתָא לֵיהּ עוֹמֶר וְחָלֵיף עִילָּוַיְיהוּ, וְלָא אַשְׁרוּשׁ קוֹדֶם לָעוֹמֶר. [57A] [5]מַהוּ לְמִינְקַט וּמֵיכַל מִינַּיְיהוּ? [6]כְּמַאן דְּשַׁדְיָין בְּכַדָּא דָּמֵי, וְשָׁרִינְהוּ עוֹמֶר, [7]אוֹ דִּלְמָא בָּטְלִינְהוּ אַגַּב אַרְעָא?

LITERAL TRANSLATION

take root, we have learned [it]. [1]For we have learned: "If it took root before the omer, the omer permits it, [2]and if not, it is forbidden until the next omer comes."

[3]No. It is necessary where he harvested it and planted it before the omer, [4]and the omer came and passed over it, and it did not take root before the omer. [57A] [5]What [is the law] about taking and eating it? [6]Is it as if it has been put into a jar, and the omer permits it, [7]or perhaps it is assimilated by the soil?

RASHI

תנינא — דאין עומר מתירן. **דחצדינהו** — מן החדש, והיו צריכין שיתירם עומר לאכילה. **וזרעינהו קודם לעומר** — וחלף ליה עומר עלייהו בדלא אשרוש. **מהו למינקט מינייהו ומיכל** — כלומר, אגידולין דידהו לא מבעיא לן, שהרי אפילו התיר עומר של אשתקד את הזרעים קודם שנזרעו וזרעם קודם העומר ולא השרישו, הוו הגידולין אסורין עד שיבא עומר הבא. כי קא מיבעי ליה, לנקוטי מן הזרעים שבקרקע ומיכל לאחר העומר. **ושרינהו עומר** — שהעומר מתיר את התלושין חדשים של שנה זו, ואת גידולין המחוברין שהשרישו. **או דלמא בטלינהו אגב ארעא** — וכקרקע בעלמא דמו, ולא שייך עומר גבייהו למשרינהו.

NOTES

אוֹנָאָה, שְׁבוּעָה, עוֹמֶר **Fraud, oaths and the omer.** The commentators ask why these cases were discussed separately, since they all seem to reflect the same fundamental issue, i.e., is wheat planted in the ground considered like the ground, or not? *Mishḥat Aharon* answers that the law is not necessarily the same in all these cases. Thus wheat planted in the ground may be treated like movable property with regard to the laws of fraud, even though it may be considered like land with regard to the laws of oaths. Accordingly one would not be required to swear about it, since the Torah generally prefers not to impose oaths.

בָּטְלִינְהוּ אַגַּב אַרְעָא **It is assimilated by the soil.** *Nishmat Adam* claims that the Gemara's question about the status

HALAKHAH

אֵיזוֹ תְּבוּאָה מַתִּיר הָעוֹמֶר **What type of produce is permitted by the omer?** "Produce that did not take root before the 16th of Nisan may not be eaten until the next omer is brought. *Shakh* adds: If the produce took root before the omer, even if it was only harvested later, it is permitted by the omer. Some maintain that it takes three days for seeds to take root (*Terumat HaDeshen,* cited by *Shakh*), while others maintain that this takes two weeks." (*Shulḥan Arukh, Yoreh De'ah* 293:3.)

TERMINOLOGY

תֵּיקוּ Let it stand, i.e., the question raised in the previous passage remains unresolved ("standing"), because we do not possess sources enabling us to resolve it, and there is no logical proof tending towards one solution or another. From a theoretical standpoint, therefore, the question remains "standing" in its place. However, in Halakhic decision-making there are various principles as to what action is to be taken in such cases. If the unresolved problem relates to a prohibition found in the Torah, the decision leans towards stringency. If the unresolved problem refers to a Rabbinical decree, the decision leans towards leniency. In matters of civil law, where absolute degrees of stringency or leniency have no place, the decision is to leave the existing situation in place.

SAGES

רַב חָסָא Rav Ḥasa. A Babylonian Amora of the third generation, Rav Ḥasa is mentioned relatively infrequently in the Talmud. Elsewhere, the Gemara relates that after a certain Ḥasa (probably Rav Ḥasa) died by drowning, Rav Naḥman described him as "a great man." Rav Ḥasa's grandson, Rav Ḥama, was also an Amora.

רַבִּי אַמִּי Rabbi Ammi. A Palestinian Amora of the third generation. See *Bava Metzia*, Part II, p. 298.

TRANSLATION AND COMMENTARY

תֵּיקוּ [1]After raising all these questions about the Halakhic status of grain planted in the ground, the Gemara concludes: **Let these questions stand.** All these questions remain unanswered.

אֲמַר רָבָא אָמַר רַב חָסָא [2]The Gemara now returns to the analysis of our Mishnah, and considers another aspect of the exclusion of land, slaves, promissory notes and consecrated property from the laws of *ona'ah*. **Rava said in the name of Rav Ḥasa: Rabbi Ammi posed the** following problem: [3]The various items listed in our Mishnah **are not subject to *ona'ah*.** If a person is overcharged by one-sixth when buying ordinary movables, the sale is valid, but the buyer is entitled to a refund of the overcharge. If the overcharge exceeds one-sixth, the sale is canceled altogether. But if the transaction involved one of the items listed in our Mishnah and the buyer was overcharged by one-sixth, the overcharge need not be refunded, because these items were excluded from the laws of *ona'ah*. In the light of this, the following question arises: What is the law if the transaction involved one of the items listed in our Mishnah and the overcharge exceeded one-sixth? [4]**Are they subject to cancellation of the sale or not?** Are these items excluded from the laws of *ona'ah* only when the overcharge amounts to one-sixth, or even when it amounts to more than one-sixth?

LITERAL TRANSLATION

[1]Let [the questions] stand.

[2]Rava said in the name of Rav Ḥasa: Rabbi Ammi asked: [3]There is no *ona'ah* for them, [4][but] are they subject to cancellation of the sale or not?

[1]תֵּיקוּ.

[2]אֲמַר רָבָא אָמַר רַב חָסָא: בָּעֵי רַבִּי אַמִּי: [3]אוֹנָאָה אֵין לָהֶם, [4]בִּיטּוּל מִקָּח יֵשׁ לָהֶם אוֹ אֵין לָהֶן?

RASHI

בעי רבי אמי אונאה — הא תנן לה במתניתין דאין להו לכל הנך דמתניתין. **ביטול מקח** — יותר משתות. **יש להן או אין להם** — מי אמרינן מ"אל תונו" (ויקרא כה) הוא דאימעוט — והא לאו בכלל אונאה הוא, אלא מקח טעות הוא, או דלמא: כיון דלאו דבר שבמדה הוא, ולא אטעייה בדיבוריה, כשאר דין אונאה הוא.

NOTES

of wheat grains planted in the ground — whether they are considered a part of the ground or not — applies with regard to the Sabbath laws as well. Specifically, if wheat grains planted in the ground are considered part of the ground, picking them on the Sabbath would be prohibited by Torah law. However, most authorities disagree, claiming that the Torah only prohibited detaching produce from the ground if it is growing. Nevertheless, it is forbidden by Rabbinic decree to remove grains of wheat from the ground, since they are *muktzeh* — unfit for Sabbath use — and by Rabbinic decree may not be handled on that day.

בִּיטּוּל מִקָּח Cancellation of the sale. *Rashi* explains the Gemara as discussing a land sale in which the deviation in price exceeds one-sixth. According to this opinion, the conclusion of our Gemara that land is subject to cancellation of the sale contradicts a statement in the Gemara below (108a), which implies that land is not subject to *ona'ah* even when the price is double the actual value.

Many Rishonim are of the opinion that the two passages are in disagreement. Some accept the ruling of our Gemara that sale of land is subject to cancellation, while others reject the conclusion of our Gemara, and rule that sale of land is not subject to cancellation (*Rif*). *Ba'al HaMa'or* claims that the two passages are in agreement. He explains that sale of land is subject to cancellation only when the price is greater than double the value of the land. However, sale of land is not subject to cancellation if the price is exactly double the value, as implied by the Gemara in the later passage. His opinion is based on the Jerusalem Talmud (*Ketubot* 11:4), which limits cancellation of a land sale to cases in which there is an extreme deviation of price. *Ba'al HaMa'or* interprets "extreme deviation" as a price that exceeds double the value. (Cancellation as a result of undercharging occurs when the price is less than half the value.)

Ramban rejects this understanding of the Jerusalem Talmud. According to him, "extreme deviation" is either double the value or double the normal definition of *ona'ah* (i.e., one-third). Thus, according to *Ramban*, the two passages in the Babylonian Talmud are in disagreement, despite the viewpoint of the Jerusalem Talmud.

בִּיטּוּל מִקָּח יֵשׁ לָהֶם אוֹ אֵין לָהֶן Are they subject to cancellation of the sale or not? *Tosafot* (*Bava Batra* 61b) claims that the exclusion of land from *ona'ah* is a Torah law for which no reason is given. Accordingly, the question posed by Rabbi Ammi is whether cancellation of the sale which applies where the *ona'ah* was more severe is included in this decree. *Rashi* explains that this matter depends on whether severe *ona'ah* is canceled because the laws of *ona'ah* prescribe cancellation in such a case, or because it is considered a sale based on a mistake. If cancellation is based on the laws of *ona'ah*, land which is excluded from these laws would likewise be excluded from cancellation. But if the transaction is considered a sale based on a mistake, such a transaction involving land would be canceled. It is also possible to claim that if the *ona'ah* merely exceeds one-sixth, the cancellation is based on the laws of *ona'ah*. But if the price is double the value, it is considered a sale based on a mistake.

Rashbam (*Bava Batra* 61b) maintains that there is a reason why land is excluded from *ona'ah*. He claims that the objective value of real estate does not necessarily correspond to the market value. This can be understood if one considers the stability and permanence of land ownership. Therefore the objective value of real estate cannot be limited by transient market trends. Consequently, a deviation from the market value does not necessarily constitute *ona'ah*. According to this opinion, Rabbi Ammi questioned whether there is a limit to the extent by which we consider the objective value of real estate to deviate from the market value. If there is such a limit, a price beyond this point would be considered *ona'ah*, and would not be included in the exemption that applies to land.

¹אֲמַר רַב נַחְמָן: הֲדַר אֲמַר רַב חָסָא פָּשֵׁיט רַבִּי אַמִי: ²אוֹנָאָה אֵין לָהֶם, בִּיטּוּל מִקָּח יֵשׁ לָהֶם. ³רַבִּי יוֹנָה אֲמַר אַהֶקְדֵּשׁוֹת, רַבִּי יִרְמְיָה אֲמַר אַקַּרְקָעוֹת, ⁴וְתַרְוַיְיהוּ מִשְּׁמֵיהּ דְּרַבִּי יוֹחָנָן אָמְרוּ: ⁵אוֹנָאָה אֵין לָהֶם, בִּיטּוּל מִקָּח יֵשׁ לָהֶן. ⁶מַאן דַּאֲמַר אַהֶקְדֵּשׁוֹת, כָּל שֶׁכֵּן אַקַּרְקָעוֹת. ⁷מַאן דַּאֲמַר אַקַּרְקָעוֹת, אֲבָל אַהֶקְדֵּשׁוֹת לָא, כִּדְשְׁמוּאֵל. ⁸דְּאָמַר שְׁמוּאֵל:

LITERAL TRANSLATION

[1]Rav Naḥman said: Rav Ḥasa later said [that] Rabbi Ammi solved it: [2]There is no *ona'ah* for them, [but] they are subject to cancellation of the sale. [3]Rabbi Yonah said with regard to consecrated property [and] Rabbi Yirmeyah said with regard to land, [4]and both of them said in the name of Rabbi Yoḥanan: [5]There is no *ona'ah* for them, [but] they are subject to cancellation of the sale. [6]He who says [this] with regard to consecrated property, how much more so [would he say this] with regard to land. [7]He who says [this] with regard to land [would] not [say this] with regard to consecrated property, in accordance with Shmuel. [8]For Shmuel said:

TRANSLATION AND COMMENTARY

אֲמַר רַב נַחְמָן [1]**Rav Naḥman reported** that **Rav Ḥasa subsequently said that Rav Ammi solved** his problem as follows: [2]The items listed in the Mishnah **are not subject to** the laws of ***ona'ah***, and therefore *ona'ah* of exactly one-sixth need not be remedied. But **they are subject to cancellation of the sale** if the *ona'ah* amounts to more than one-sixth.

רַבִּי יוֹנָה [3]The Gemara now cites opinions — unrelated to the traditions cited previously in the name of Rabbi Ammi — of two other Amoraim as to when a sale of the items mentioned in our Mishnah is canceled. **Rabbi Yonah made** the following **statement with regard to consecrated property, and Rabbi Yirmeyah made** it **with regard to land,** [4]**and both** Rabbi Yonah and Rabbi Yirmeyah **made their statements in the name of Rabbi Yoḥanan:** [5]These items — consecrated property according to Rabbi Yonah, and land according to Rabbi Yirmeyah — **are not subject to** the laws of ***ona'ah*** if the overcharge is exactly one-sixth, but **they are subject to cancellation of the sale** if the overcharge is more than one-sixth.

מַאן דַּאֲמַר אַהֶקְדֵּשׁוֹת [6]The Gemara now analyzes the relationship between the opinions expressed by Rabbi Yonah and Rabbi Yirmeyah: **The authority** (Rabbi Yonah) **who says** that Rabbi Yoḥanan's ruling **applies to consecrated property maintains that it would apply even more so to land.** [7]But **the authority** (Rabbi Yirmeyah) **who says** that Rabbi Yoḥanan's ruling **applies to land** may well be of the opinion that it does **not** apply **to consecrated property, in accordance with** the viewpoint of **Shmuel.** Even if it is true that an overcharge exceeding one-sixth may result in the cancellation of the sale of land, a sale of consecrated property may still be valid even if the property is sold for substantially more or less than it is actually worth, since special laws apply to consecrated property, [8]**as Shmuel said:**

RASHI

רבי יונה ורבי ירמיה – מילתא באפי נפשייהו אמרי, ולאו אדרבי אמי קיימי, אלא רבי [ירמיה] אקרקעות ורבי [יונה] אהקדשות אמרי משמיה דרבי יוחנן: אונאה אין להם, ביטול מקח יש להן. **מאן דאמר אהקדשות** – אמרה רבי יוחנן. **כל שכן** – דאקרקעות נמי אמר, דכיון דאשמועינן דביטול מקח לאו בכלל אונאה הוא, מהיכא אימעיט? אי דהקדשות קחשיב ליה מקח טעות, אף על גב דליכא טעות כלפי שמיא – ואפילו הכי אמרינן ביטול מקח – כל שכן דלגבי חבריה, דאיכא למימר טעה ואדעתא דהכי לא אקנייה, כל שכן דהדר. **מאן דאמר אקרקעות** – אמרה. **אבל אהקדשות לא** – דאילו גבי הדיוט אמרינן טעה, ואדעתא דהכי לא אקני, אבל אהקדש, ליכא למימר הכי וכיון דליתנהו בדין אונאה – טעות נמי לא אמרינן בהו, כדשמואל.

SAGES

רַבִּי יוֹנָה **Rabbi Yonah.** Rabbi Yonah was one of the leading Amoraim in Eretz Israel during the fourth generation. He was an outstanding disciple of two of Rabbi Yoḥanan's younger students, Rabbi Il'ai and Rabbi Zera, and a student-colleague of Rabbi Yirmeyah.

Many of Rabbi Yonah's teachings appear in the Jerusalem Talmud, and he was apparently one of the leading scholars of his time. Many Amoraim of the following generation were his students. Rabbi Yonah was one of the last Amoraim from Eretz Israel to be cited in the Babylonian Talmud.

Rabbi Yonah was renowned for his piety, and the Talmud mentions various miracles performed for him. He was also highly respected by the non-Jewish leaders of his time.

Rabbi Yonah's son, Rav Mana, was also his outstanding disciple, and one of the leading Amoraim in Eretz Israel during the next generation.

רַבִּי יִרְמְיָה **Rabbi Yirmeyah.** A Babylonian Amora of the third and fourth generations. See *Bava Metzia*, Part II, p. 5.

NOTES

אֲבָל אַהֶקְדֵּשׁוֹת לָא **Would not say this with regard to consecrated property.** The distinction between land and consecrated property requires explanation. According to *Rashi*, cancellation of the sale applies to land because the sale was based on a mistake. Consent to the transaction is consequently meaningless since it was given mistakenly. *Rashi* claims that this is inapplicable to consecrated property, since there can be no mistake or misrepresentation when dedicating property to God. An alternative distinction between land and consecrated property can be suggested. In the case of land the transaction is a sale — the transfer of merchandise for its value in currency. When the value deviates seriously from the currency, the transaction is not considered a sale and is subsequently void. With respect to consecrated property, the act is one of redemption, or the transfer of sanctity from one object to another. Therefore this act can remain binding despite the discrepancy between the value of the objects.

HALAKHAH

בִּיטּוּל מִקָּח בְּקַרְקָעוֹת **Cancellation of a sale with regard to land.** "If a person overcharges for any of the items mentioned in our Mishnah, to which the laws of *ona'ah* do not apply, the sale is valid, not matter how much he overcharged. *Rema*, however, cites other authorities (*Tur*, following *Rabbenu Tam* and *Rosh*), who maintain that if a person charges twice the actual value of the item or more, the sale is invalid." (*Shulḥan Arukh, Ḥoshen Mishpat* 227:29.)

BACKGROUND

מָנֶה וּפְרוּטָה Maneh and perutah. Shmuel used this example because the maneh was the coin with the highest denomination, and the perutah was the coin with the least value of all. As noted in the Talmud, there was not always a fixed relationship between silver and copper coins, but on an average the value of a maneh was reckoned as 19,200 perutot, so someone who pays a perutah for something worth a maneh has undervalued it by a factor of nearly 20,000.

TRANSLATION AND COMMENTARY

Consecrated property worth a maneh (one hundred zuz) **which was redeemed with something worth** only **a perutah is** nevertheless **redeemed,** even though the Temple treasury was underpaid by far more than one-sixth. From Shmuel's statement we learn that the laws governing the redemption or sale of consecrated property cannot be applied to the sale of other types of property, particularly in cases where the Temple treasury is the victim of underpayment that in other circumstances would be regarded as *ona'ah*. Thus Rabbi Yirmeyah's opinion that a sale of land involving an overcharge of more than one-sixth is canceled cannot be extended to apply to the sale of consecrated property.

תְּנַן הָתָם [1]**We have learned elsewhere** in a Mishnah (*Temurah* 26b): **"If** a person redeems a **consecrated animal which was blemished** — and hence unfit to be offered as a sacrifice — by presenting to the Temple another animal worth less than the blemished one, the consecrated animal **becomes *hullin*,** i.e., loses its sanctity, [2]**and it is necessary to assess its worth.** The Temple treasury must be paid the difference between the value of the blemished animal and the value of the animal presented as its replacement."

אָמַר רַבִּי יוֹחָנָן [3]Rabbi Yoḥanan and Resh Lakish disagree in their understanding of this Mishnah. **Rabbi Yoḥanan said:** When the Mishnah states: **"It becomes *hullin*,"** this means **according to Torah law,** [4]**but** when it

הֶקְדֵּשׁ שָׁוֶה מָנֶה שֶׁחִילְּלוֹ עַל שָׁוֶה פְּרוּטָה מְחוּלָּל.

[1]תְּנַן הָתָם: ״אִם הָיָה קוֹדֶשׁ בַּעַל מוּם, יָצָא לְחוּלִּין, [2]וְצָרִיךְ לַעֲשׂוֹת לוֹ דָּמִים״.

[3]אָמַר רַבִּי יוֹחָנָן: ״יָצָא לְחוּלִּין״ דְּבַר תּוֹרָה, [4]״וְצָרִיךְ לַעֲשׂוֹת לוֹ

LITERAL TRANSLATION

Consecrated property worth a maneh which he redeemed for a perutah's worth is redeemed.

[1]We have learned there: "If the consecrated [animal] was blemished, it becomes *hullin*, [2]and it is necessary to make a valuation for it."

[3]Rabbi Yoḥanan said: "It becomes *hullin*" by Torah law, [4]"and it is necessary to make

RASHI

מחולל – כדאמרן דאימעוט מאונאה, וטעות נמי ליכא בהו, דמאן טעה. **תנן התם** – במסכת תמורה (כו,ב). **אם היה קודש בעל מום** – רישא דמתניתין הכי: האומר הרי זו תחת זו, זו תמורת זו, זו חלופי זו – הרי זו תמורה. זו מחוללת על זו – לא אמר כלום, שאין קרבן תמים מתחלל. ואם היה קודש בעל מום – יצא לחולין, וצריך לעשות לו דמים. אם אין זו של חולין יפה כשל הקדש מוסיף עליה מעותיו עד כדי דמי הקדש. **יצא לחולין דבר תורה** – ואפילו אין זו יפה כמותה, כדאמר דאמעיט באונאה.

NOTES

הֶקְדֵּשׁ שָׁוֶה מָנֶה שֶׁחִילְּלוֹ עַל שָׁוֶה פְּרוּטָה Consecrated property worth a maneh which he redeemed for a perutah's worth. The reasoning behind this ruling may be explained as follows: Once one pays even a perutah to redeem sacred property, the redemption money acquires the sanctity of the consecrated object (which in turn loses its sanctity, even if it was worth considerably more than a perutah). The same holds true for the laws of *me'ilah*: As soon as one derives a perutah's worth of benefit from sacred property, it loses its sanctity and becomes *hullin*, even if it is worth substantially more than a perutah (*Tosefot Rid*; *Tosafot*, however, disagrees).

וְצָרִיךְ לַעֲשׂוֹת לוֹ דָּמִים And it is necessary to make a valuation for it. The commentators ask how the animal becomes *hullin*, since the owner is required to pay additional redemption money. *Tosafot* in tractate *Temurah* explains that the animal becomes *hullin* only after its value is paid in full to the Temple treasury. Even though it is obvious that an animal becomes *hullin* after it has been redeemed in full, and thus it would appear unnecessary for the Mishnah to include such a ruling, this law was included for stylistic reasons: Since the first clause of the Mishnah treats of cases in which one of the animals becomes sacred, the latter clause discusses cases in which one of the animals eventually becomes *hullin*.

Another explanation is offered by *Ramban*, who suggests that the animal becomes *hullin* immediately, even though its original owner still owes money to the Temple treasury, because he will presumably pay the Temple the money he owes. By contrast, if one overcharged too much on a sale to an ordinary person, the sale is void, since we cannot be certain that the seller will ultimately reimburse the buyer.

Still another explanation is suggested by *Tosafot*, who maintains that only that portion of the animal for which one paid becomes *hullin*; the rest of the animal retains its sanctity.

HALAKHAH

הֶקְדֵּשׁ שֶׁחִילְּלוֹ עַל שָׁוֶה פְּרוּטָה Consecrated property which he redeemed for a perutah's worth. "Consecrated property should be redeemed for its full value. However, if a person redeems it for less (even if he redeems something worth a hundred dinarim for a single perutah), the redemption is valid, and the sacred object loses its sanctity. But the Rabbis decreed that a person who does this must pay the Temple treasury the difference between the value of the redemption and the value of the consecrated item." (*Rambam*, *Sefer Hafla'ah*, *Hilkhot Arakhin* 7:8.)

יָצָא לְחוּלִּין, וְצָרִיךְ לַעֲשׂוֹת לוֹ דָּמִים It goes out to *hullin* and it is necessary to make a valuation for it. "If a person has

דָּמִים״ מִדִּבְרֵיהֶם. [1]וְרֵישׁ לָקִישׁ אָמַר: אַף ״צָרִיךְ לַעֲשׂוֹת לוֹ דָּמִים״ מִן הַתּוֹרָה.

[2]בְּמַאי עָסְקִינַן? [3]אִילֵימָא: בִּכְדֵי אוֹנָאָה, בְּהָא לֵימָא רֵישׁ לָקִישׁ: [4]צָרִיךְ לַעֲשׂוֹת לוֹ דָּמִים דְּבַר תּוֹרָה? [5]וְהָתְנַן: ״אֵלּוּ דְּבָרִים שֶׁאֵין לָהֶם אוֹנָאָה: [6]הַקַּרְקָעוֹת, וְהָעֲבָדִים, וְהַשְּׁטָרוֹת, וְהַהֶקְדֵּשׁוֹת״!

[7]אֶלָּא, בִּיטּוּל מִקָּח.

[8]בְּהָא לֵימָא רַבִּי יוֹחָנָן: צָרִיךְ לַעֲשׂוֹת לוֹ דָּמִים מִדִּבְרֵיהֶם? [9]וְהָאָמַר רַבִּי יוֹנָה אַהֶקְדֵּשׁוֹת, וְרַבִּי יִרְמְיָה אָמַר אַקַּרְקָעוֹת,

LITERAL TRANSLATION

a valuation for it" by Rabbinic decree (lit., "from their words"). [1]But Resh Lakish said: "It is necessary to make a valuation for it" also by Torah law.

[2]With what are we dealing? [3]If we say: At the rate of *ona'ah*, in this [case] would Resh Lakish say: [4]Is it necessary to make a valuation for it by Torah law? [5]But surely we have learned: "These are things for which there is no *ona'ah*: [6]Land, and slaves, and promissory notes, and consecrated property"!

[7]Rather, cancellation of the sale.

[8]In this [case] would Rabbi Yoḥanan say: It is necessary to make a valuation for it by Rabbinic decree? [9]But surely Rabbi Yonah said with regard to consecrated property, and Rabbi Yirmeyah said with regard to land,

TRANSLATION AND COMMENTARY

states: **"It is necessary to make a valuation of it,"** this means only **by Rabbinic decree.** In other words, according to Torah law the consecrated animal is redeemed even if the redemption price was far less than what the consecrated animal was actually worth; but the Rabbis decreed that the Temple treasury must be paid its full value. [1]**But Resh Lakish said:** The expression used by the Mishnah: **"It is necessary to make a valuation of it," applies also according to Torah law;** it is by Torah law that the Temple treasury must be paid the consecrated animal's full value.

בְּמַאי עָסְקִינַן [2]The Gemara now seeks to understand the circumstances that could give rise to the Mishnah's ruling, and asks: **With what** situation **are we dealing** in this Mishnah? [3]**If we say** that the Mishnah is dealing with a case in which the person who redeemed the consecrated animal offered another animal worth exactly one-sixth less than the value of the consecrated animal, thus underpaying the Temple treasury by **the rate of *ona'ah*** which must ordinarily be refunded, **would Resh Lakish say** that [4]**in such a case it is necessary to make a valuation of** the blemished animal and pay the difference to the Temple treasury even **according to Torah law?** If the Temple treasury was underpaid by one-sixth, there should be no reason to compensate the Temple for the difference between the consecrated animal's true value and the value of the replacement, as the Gemara explains: [5]**Surely we have learned** in our Mishnah: **"These are the things which are not subject to** the laws of ***ona'ah*: [6]Land, and slaves, and promissory notes, and consecrated property"!** Thus we see that the requirement to compensate for *ona'ah* does not apply to consecrated property, and hence there should be no reason to make up the difference to the Temple!

אֶלָּא, בִּיטּוּל מִקָּח [7]**On the other hand,** the Mishnah may be referring to a case in which the Temple treasury was underpaid by more than one-sixth of the animal's value, which is ordinarily grounds for **cancellation of the sale.** In such a case, the consecrated animal becomes *ḥullin*, and the difference in value between it and the animal designated as its replacement must later be paid to the Temple treasury — by Rabbinic decree according to Rabbi Yoḥanan, and by Torah law according to Resh Lakish.

בְּהָא לֵימָא רַבִּי יוֹחָנָן [8]But this explanation given by the Gemara is also problematic: If the Temple treasury was underpaid by more than one-sixth, **would Rabbi Yoḥanan say** that **in such a case it is only necessary to make a valuation of** the animal **by Rabbinic decree?** [9]**Surely Rabbi Yonah made** the following **statement with regard to consecrated property, and Rabbi Yirmeyah made** it **with regard to land,**

TERMINOLOGY

בְּמַאי עָסְקִינַן With what are we dealing? This term introduces an investigation of the particular circumstances of a case mentioned in a Mishnah. It is often followed by a suggestion or suggestions which are at once rejected: ...אִילֵימָא — "Shall we say...? No," or ...אִי... אִי — "If the case is X, then this problem arises, whereas if the case is Y, another problem arises."

RASHI

אף צריך לעשות לו דמים דבר תורה — דגבי הקדשות ״ערכך״ כתיבא בכולהו, וקסבר: ״ערכך״ — שוויו משמע. ורבי יוחנן סבר: ״ערכך״ — כל דמים שיערכוהו משמע ליה, אם זול אם יוקר. **והאמר רבי יונה אהקדשות כו׳** — לרבי יונה קשיא דרבי יוחנן אדרבי יוחנן.

HALAKHAH

two animals, one of which is consecrated but has a blemish rendering it unfit for sacrificial use, while the other is *ḥullin*, and he declares that the non-consecrated animal is to be substituted for the consecrated animal, the consecrated animal becomes *ḥullin*." (Ibid., *Sefer Korbanot, Hilkhot Temurah* 2:2.) "If the consecrated animal is worth more than the non-consecrated animal, he is required (by Rabbinic decree) to pay the Temple treasury the difference between the value of the non-consecrated animal and the value of the consecrated animal." (Ibid., *Sefer Hafla'ah, Hilkhot Arakhin* 7:8.)

TERMINOLOGY

אֵיפוֹךְ Reverse! Sometimes, when certain opinions are attributed to a pair of Sages in one context, and the opposite opinions are attributed to these Sages in another context, the Talmud may attempt to resolve the contradiction by suggesting that the viewpoints attributed to these Sages be "reversed." Subsequently, however, the Gemara may reject this suggestion, saying: לְעוֹלָם לָא תֵּיפוֹךְ — "in fact do not reverse the opinions, but instead explain as follows...."

[1]וְתַרְוַיְיהוּ מִשְּׁמֵיהּ דְּרַבִּי יוֹחָנָן אָמְרִי: אוֹנָאָה אֵין לָהֶם, בִּיטּוּל מִקָּח יֵשׁ לָהֶם!

[2]לְעוֹלָם, בְּבִיטּוּל מִקָּח, [3]וְאֵיפוּךְ דְּרַבִּי יוֹחָנָן לְרֵישׁ לָקִישׁ, וּדְרֵישׁ לָקִישׁ לְרַבִּי יוֹחָנָן.

[4]בְּמַאי קָמִיפַּלְגִי? [5]בְּדִשְׁמוּאֵל. דְּאָמַר שְׁמוּאֵל: הֶקְדֵּשׁ שָׁוֶה מָנֶה שֶׁחִילְּלוֹ עַל שָׁוֶה פְּרוּטָה מְחוּלָּל. [6]מָר אִית לֵיהּ דִּשְׁמוּאֵל, וּמָר לֵית לֵיהּ דִּשְׁמוּאֵל.

LITERAL TRANSLATION

[1]and both of them said in the name of Rabbi Yoḥanan: There is no *ona'ah* for them, [but] they are subject to cancellation of the sale!

[2]In fact, [it refers to] cancellation of the sale, and reverse [the opinion] of Rabbi Yoḥanan with that of Resh Lakish, [3]and that of Resh Lakish with that of Rabbi Yoḥanan.

[4]About what do they disagree? About Shmuel's [statement]. [5]For Shmuel said: Consecrated property worth a maneh which he redeemed for a perutah's worth is redeemed. [6]One Sage accepts Shmuel's [ruling], and the other Sage does not accept Shmuel's [ruling].

TRANSLATION AND COMMENTARY

[1]**and both** Rabbi Yonah and Rabbi Yirmeyah **made their statements in the name of Rabbi Yoḥanan:** These items — consecrated property according to Rabbi Yonah, and land according to Rabbi Yirmeyah — **are not subject to** the laws of ***ona'ah*** if the overcharge was exactly one-sixth, but **they are subject to cancellation of the sale** if the overcharge was more than one-sixth! According to the statement of Rabbi Yonah, Rabbi Yoḥanan ruled that a sale, i.e., a redemption, of consecrated property is canceled if the Temple was underpaid by more than one-sixth, and this implies that the cancellation is required by Torah law. How then can Rabbi Yoḥanan also have ruled that if a person redeems a consecrated animal and underpays by more than one-sixth, it is only by Rabbinic decree that he must compensate the Temple treasury? These two rulings appear contradictory.

לְעוֹלָם בְּבִיטּוּל מִקָּח [2]The Gemara answers: **In fact,** the Mishnah in tractate *Temurah* is referring to a case in which the underpayment was by more than one-sixth of the consecrated animal's value, and which would ordinarily permit **cancellation of the sale.** [3]**And** as for the Gemara's objection above, it may be resolved as follows: According to Rabbi Yonah, we must **reverse Rabbi Yoḥanan's opinion with that of Resh Lakish, and Resh Lakish's with that of Rabbi Yoḥanan.** If we reverse the attribution of the two opinions, and assume that it is Rabbi Yoḥanan who maintains that by Torah law the difference must be made up, whereas Resh Lakish maintains that it is only by Rabbinic decree that the difference must be made up, then there is no problem. The Mishnah can then be explained as referring to a case in which the Temple treasury was underpaid by more than one-sixth. In such a case, Rabbi Yoḥanan maintains that it is by Torah law that the difference must be made up, and this conforms with his own opinion (as reported by Rabbi Yonah) that even a sale of consecrated property is canceled if the Temple treasury was underpaid by more than one-sixth.

בְּמַאי קָמִיפַּלְגִי [4]The Gemara now attempts to understand the basis of the difference of opinion between Rabbi Yoḥanan and Resh Lakish as to whether Torah law or Rabbinic decree requires that the difference in value be paid to the Temple treasury, and asks: **About what** issue **do** Rabbi Yoḥanan and Resh Lakish **disagree?** [5]The Gemara answers: They differ **about** the viewpoint of **Shmuel**, which Resh Lakish accepts and Rabbi Yoḥanan rejects. **For Shmuel said: Consecrated property worth a maneh** (one hundred zuz) **which was redeemed with something worth** only **a perutah is** nevertheless **redeemed,** even though the Temple treasury was underpaid by far more than one-sixth. [6]**One** Sage, Resh Lakish, **accepts Shmuel's ruling, and the other,** Rabbi Yoḥanan, **does not accept Shmuel's ruling.** According to Shmuel, the redemption of consecrated property is valid no matter how little is paid for it. From this, in accordance with the view now attributed to Resh Lakish, it follows that it is only by Rabbinic decree that a person who redeems a blemished consecrated animal with an animal of lesser value is required to make good the difference. However, if Shmuel's view is not accepted, it follows — in accordance with the view now attributed to Rabbi Yoḥanan — that Torah law requires that the difference be paid to the Temple treasury.

RASHI

ואיפוך — אליבא דרבי יונה. אבל אליבא דרבי ירמיה לא תיפוך, דהא לרבי ירמיה אליבא דרבי יוחנן הקדשות אין להם בטול מקח. דמאן דאמר אקרקעות — אבל אהקדשות לא, כדשמואל. והכי נמי איתא בתמורה לרבי יונה איפוך, וקמיפלגי ריש לקיש ורבי יוחנן, מאן דאמר אין להן ביטול מקח — אית ליה דשמואל, דכיון דאימעיט מאונאה — לא שנא שתות לא שנא יתר משתות, דאילו גבי הדיוט אמרינן טעה אבל בהקדש ליכא למימר טעות. **ומר לית ליה דשמואל** — קסבר: כיון דאיכא יתר משתות, לאו דרך מקח הוא, וכיון דלגבי מקח לאו מידי הוא, גבי חילול נמי לאו מידי עבד.

TRANSLATION AND COMMENTARY

אִיבָּעֵית אֵימָא [1]The Gemara now offers an alternative explanation of the difference of opinion between Rabbi Yoḥanan and Resh Lakish: **If you wish, you can explain** their dispute as follows: **All** authorities — both Rabbi Yoḥanan and Resh Lakish — **agree with** the basic principle expressed in **Shmuel's ruling,** [2]**but here they disagree about** the application of that principle. [3]**One Sage,** Resh Lakish, **maintains** that one should not set out to redeem consecrated property for less than its value, but that **if** one **does redeem** consecrated property for less than its true value the redemption **is valid.** Nevertheless, as an **initial,** deliberate act one may **not** redeem consecrated property by paying less for it than it is worth. And since, *ab initio*, one must pay the Temple treasury the full value of the consecrated property, a person who paid less is required by Torah law to make up the difference. [4]**And the other Sage,** Rabbi Yoḥanan, **maintains** that one may redeem consecrated property for less than its true value **even *ab initio.*** Hence there is no need by Torah law to compensate the Temple for the difference between the consecrated animal's value and the value of the animal offered as its redemption price. Accordingly, it is only by Rabbinic decree that this difference must be made up.

אִיבָּעֵית אֵימָא [5]The Gemara now suggests an alternative explanation of the Mishnah in *Temurah*, which has been explained above as referring to a case in which a person redeemed a blemished consecrated animal and underpaid by more than one-sixth of the animal's value: **If you wish,** you can **say** that the Mishnah should be understood as follows: **In fact,** it is referring to a case in which the person who redeemed the animal underpaid by exactly one-sixth of its value, i.e., **the rate of *ona'ah*** for which the injured party must ordinarily be compensated. [6]**And** there is **no** need to **reverse** the opinions of Rabbi Yoḥanan and Resh Lakish, for, as originally stated, it is Resh Lakish who maintains that the difference between the value of the consecrated animal and the value of the animal offered as the redemption price must be made up according to Torah law, and it is Rabbi Yoḥanan who maintains that this is only necessary by Rabbinic decree. When this explanation was first suggested above, it was asked how Resh Lakish could maintain that Torah law requires that the difference be made up, when our Mishnah states that consecrated property is not subject to the laws of *ona'ah*. The Gemara resolves this question by suggesting a new explanation of the dispute between Rabbi Yoḥanan and Resh Lakish: [7]Resh Lakish and Rabbi Yoḥanan **disagree about a statement of Rav Ḥisda**, which Resh Lakish accepts and Rabbi Yoḥanan rejects. [8]**For Rav Ḥisda said: What is the meaning of**

[1]אִיבָּעֵית אֵימָא: דְּכוּלֵּי עָלְמָא אִית לְהוּ דִּשְׁמוּאֵל, [2]וְהָכָא בְּהָא קָמִיפַּלְגִי: [3]מָר סָבַר: שֶׁחִילְּלוֹ — אִין; לְכַתְּחִילָּה — לָא. [4]וּמָר סָבַר: אֲפִילּוּ לְכַתְּחִלָּה. [5]אִיבָּעֵית אֵימָא: לְעוֹלָם בִּכְדֵי אוֹנָאָה, [6]וְלָא תֵּיפּוּךְ. [7]וּבִדְרַב חִסְדָּא קָמִיפַּלְגִי, [8]דַּאֲמַר: מַאי

LITERAL TRANSLATION

[1]If you wish, say: All agree with Shmuel's [ruling], [2]but here they disagree about this: [3]One Sage maintains: If he redeemed it — yes; from the outset — no. [4]And the other Sage maintains: Even from the outset.

[5]If you wish, say: In fact, [it refers to a case] at the rate of *ona'ah*, [6]and do not reverse. [7]And they disagree about [the statement] of Rav Ḥisda, [8]who said: What does

RASHI

שחיללו אין – דהא אימעיט מאונאה, לא שנא גדולה ולא שנא קטנה. **לכתחילה לא** – ודבר תורה, ד"ערכך" – שוויו משמע. **ומר סבר אפילו לכתחילה** – "ערכך" כל דהו משמע, הלכך לאפקועי איסוריה ואפילו מדרבנן, שרי, ומיהו לאחר זמן ישלם. **לעולם בבדי אונאה** – וקאמר דבר תורה, ואפילו בכדי אונאה צריך לעשות דמים דבר תורה. **ולא תיפוך** – דאי מפכת לה, קשיא דרבי יוחנן אדרבי יוחנן. דאילו לדידיה לא מצי לתרוצי אין להן אונאה, דמתניתין כרב חסדא דפחות מכדי אונאה חוזר, מדאמר רבי יוחנן: אונאה – אין להן, ביטול מקח – יש להן. מכלל ד"אונאה אין להן" דקאמר, אין מחזירין להן אונאה הוא. אבל ריש לקיש, כי מותבת ליה ממתניתא, מוקי לה כרב חסדא. **מאי אין להן אונאה** – דגבי הקדשות דאפילו פחות מכדי אונאה חוזר.

TERMINOLOGY

אִיבָּעֵית אֵימָא If you wish, say.... This expression is used to introduce an additional answer to a question previously asked, or an additional explanation of a problem previously raised.

NOTES

חִלּוּל הֶקְדֵּשׁ לְכַתְּחִילָּה Redeeming sacred property from the outset for less than it is worth. The commentators ask: How is it permitted to redeem sacred property for less than its value, when the Torah explicitly states that consecrated property must be "appraised" before being redeemed (see Leviticus 27:12)? Moreover, from other passages in the Gemara (see, for example, *Sanhedrin* 88a), it is clear that consecrated property must be appraised by at least ten people, and if not, the redemption is null and void.

Tosafot answers that the Torah's ruling that sacred property must be appraised before being redeemed applies only if the Temple treasurer sells or redeems it; but a private person is not required to appraise sacred property before redeeming it. Others distinguish between cases in which the owner intended to redeem sacred property for its true value — in which case the item must be appraised — and cases in which the owner wanted to redeem it for less than it is worth. In such cases the redemption is valid even if the item was not appraised (*Rashba*, *Ritva*, *Ran* and others).

TRANSLATION AND COMMENTARY

the Mishnah's statement that "there is no *ona'ah* for **consecrated property"?** It does not mean that consecrated property is in no way subject to the laws of *ona'ah* — so that an overcharge or underpayment is never returned, as we previously understood — [1]but rather that consecrated property **is not subject to the** standard **laws of *ona'ah*.** That is to say, [57B] **even** if the overcharge committed against the Temple treasury was **less than the** minimum **rate of *ona'ah*** which ordinarily entitles the injured party to a remedy (one-sixth), the Temple treasury may nevertheless **withdraw** from the transaction. Rav Ḥisda's statement introduces a radically different interpretation of our Mishnah's ruling that transactions involving consecrated property are not subject to the laws of *ona'ah*. Until this point in the discussion, the Gemara understood the Mishnah to be *limiting* the application of the laws of *ona'ah* in the case of consecrated property, and to be saying that the protection afforded by these laws is not extended to transactions involving consecrated property. Rav Ḥisda claims that the opposite is true: The Mishnah is *expanding* the application of the laws of *ona'ah* in the case of consecrated property to the extent that overcharging by even the slightest amount is illegal. Resh Lakish accepts the view of Rav Ḥisda, and therefore rules that when a person redeems a consecrated animal, he is required by Torah law to make up *any* difference between the value of the consecrated animal and that of the animal offered as the redemption price. Rabbi Yoḥanan rejects the view of Rav Ḥisda, and rules that by Torah law the difference need not be made up.

מֵיתִיבֵי [2]The Gemara now **raises an objection** to Rav Ḥisda's understanding of the Mishnah from another Baraita, which states: "The prohibitions against charging **interest and** against ***ona'ah* apply to** transactions between **lay people, but there is no** prohibition against charging **interest or** against ***ona'ah*** in transactions involving **consecrated property"!** Thus this Baraita states that if a person overcharged or underpaid for Temple property, the overcharge or underpayment need not be refunded. This contradicts Rav Ḥisda's understanding of our Mishnah, according to which even the slightest *ona'ah* in the sale of consecrated property entitles the injured party to a remedy!

מִי אַלִּימָא מִמַּתְנִיתִין [3]The Gemara replies: **Is this** Baraita **any stronger than our Mishnah, which we explained as meaning "subject to the** standard **laws of *ona'ah*"?** Rav Ḥisda's interpretation of the Mishnah is valid for the Baraita as well. Just as we explained the Mishnah's statement that "there is no *ona'ah* for consecrated property" as meaning that the standard laws of *ona'ah* do not apply to it, and hence even the slightest

"אֵין לָהֶם אוֹנָאָה"? [1]אֵינָן בְּתוֹרַת אוֹנָאָה, [57B] דַּאֲפִילּוּ פָּחוֹת מִכְּדֵי אוֹנָאָה חוֹזֵר.
[2]מֵיתִיבֵי: "רִבִּית וְאוֹנָאָה לְהֶדְיוֹט, וְאֵין רִבִּית וְאוֹנָאָה לַהֶקְדֵּשׁ"!
[3]מִי אַלִּימָא מִמַּתְנִיתִין, דְּאוֹקִימְנָא "בְּתוֹרַת אוֹנָאָה"?

LITERAL TRANSLATION

"there is no *ona'ah* for them" [mean]? [1]They are not within the law of *ona'ah*, [57B] for even less than the rate of *ona'ah* returns.

[2]They raised an objection: "There is interest and *ona'ah* for a lay person, but there is no interest or *ona'ah* for consecrated property"!

[3]Is this stronger than our Mishnah, which we explained [as meaning] "within the law of *ona'ah*"?

RASHI

ואין רבית ואונאה להקדש — אין איסור אונאה ואיסור רבית נוהג בהקדש. ולקמיה מפרש היכי דמי רבית דהקדש.

BACKGROUND

רִבִּית וְאוֹנָאָה לְהֶדְיוֹט Interest and fraud for ordinary people. When discussing the laws of fraud and interest, the Torah uses the expression "your neighbor" (רֵעֲךָ), and thus the inference is drawn that these laws apply only if both parties are lay people. But they do not apply where one of the parties is the Temple treasury. To be sure, there are certain cases in which the fraud and interest laws governing Temple property may be stricter than those which apply to ordinary property, because benefiting from consecrated property is forbidden as *me'ilah* (which, however, is an independent prohibition, having nothing to do with the laws of fraud and interest).

NOTES

אֵינָן בְּתוֹרַת אוֹנָאָה They are not within the law of *ona'ah*. The commentators have suggested various rationales for this viewpoint. *Ra'avad* suggests that since the Torah explicitly states that consecrated property must be appraised before being redeemed, even the slightest overcharge or underpayment is unacceptable and must be refunded. *Rosh* explains that an overcharge or underpayment involving consecrated property must be refunded because such property does not have a human owner who can waive the difference.

פָּחוֹת מִכְּדֵי אוֹנָאָה חוֹזֵר Less than the rate of *ona'ah* returns. The Rishonim offer several explanations for Rav Hisda's ruling that with regard to consecrated property even the slightest overcharge must be returned. *Rosh* suggests that, according to Rav Ḥisda, rather than excluding consecrated property from the laws of *ona'ah* (above, 56b), the term "his brother" teaches that the laws of *ona'ah* regarding consecrated property are even *more* stringent, for in such a case the *ona'ah* must always be returned no matter how slight. *Rosh* argues that this distinction between consecrated property and ordinary property has a logical basis. Ordinarily, *ona'ah* amounting to less than one-sixth need not be returned, because such an insignificant amount is waived. In the case of consecrated property, however, there can be no waiver, so even "insignificant" *ona'ah* must be returned.

Ra'avad suggests that, according to Rav Ḥisda, the Torah's requirement that consecrated land be evaluated by ten people before it is redeemed implies that even a tiny discrepancy must be corrected.

LITERAL TRANSLATION

[1] הָכִי נַמִי, רִבִּית וְדִין אוֹנָאָה לְהֶדְיוֹט, [2] וְאֵין רִבִּית וְדִין אוֹנָאָה לַהֶקְדֵּשׁ.
[3] אִי הָכִי, הַיְינוּ דְּקָתָנֵי סֵיפָא: [4] "זֶה חוֹמֶר בְּהֶדְיוֹט מִבְּהֶקְדֵּשׁ"?
[5] אַרִבִּית.
[6] לִיתְנֵי נַמִי: "זֶה חוֹמֶר בְּהֶקְדֵּשׁ מִבְּהֶדְיוֹט", אַאוֹנָאָה!
[7] הָכִי הָשְׁתָּא? [8] בִּשְׁלָמָא "זֶה חוֹמֶר בְּהֶדְיוֹט מִבְּהֶקְדֵּשׁ" —

[1] Here too, there is interest and the law of *ona'ah* for a lay person, [2] but there is no interest and no law of *ona'ah* for consecrated property.
[3] If so, [what] is this that the last clause teaches: [4] "This is more stringent for a lay person than for consecrated property"?
[5] [It refers] to interest.
[6] Let it also teach: "This is more stringent for consecrated property than for a lay person," [referring] to *ona'ah*!
[7] How can you compare? [8] Granted "this is more stringent for a lay person than for consecrated property" —

RASHI

דין אונאה להדיוט – שתות. **ואין דין אונאה להקדש** – דאפילו פחות מכדי אונאה, חוזר. **היינו דקתני כו'** – בתמיה, והא חומרא דהקדש הוא! ומשני: כי קתני חומר דהדיוט ארבית קאי. **אאונאה** – ומשום אונאה ליתני נמי זה חומר בהקדש.

TRANSLATION AND COMMENTARY

overcharge must be refunded, [1] **so too** the Baraita can be similarly explained: **The** prohibition against taking **interest and the laws of *ona'ah*** apply **to** transactions between **lay people,** [2] **but the** prohibition against taking **interest and the** standard **laws of *ona'ah* do not** apply **to** transactions involving **consecrated property,** in which even the slightest overcharge must be refunded.

אִי הָכִי [3] The Gemara objects: **If so, what** does **the last clause** of the Baraita **teach?** How are we to understand the final clause of the Baraita just quoted, which states: [4] **"This** ruling — that the prohibition against taking interest and the laws of *ona'ah* apply to lay people but not to the Temple treasurer — **is more stringent for a lay person than for consecrated property"!** This statement clearly shows that the purpose of the Baraita is to relax the application of the laws of *ona'ah* and of usury in transactions involving consecrated property. This conforms with our initial understanding of the Mishnah, but clearly contradicts Rav Ḥisda's interpretation.

אַרִבִּית [5] The Gemara answers: The Baraita's statement that transactions between lay people are treated more strictly than are transactions to which the Temple treasury is a party **refers** only **to** the application of the laws of **interest,** which are applied to lay people but not to the Temple treasury. But *ona'ah* involving consecrated property is in fact treated more strictly than *ona'ah* involving lay people, as Rav Ḥisda ruled.

לִיתְנֵי נַמִי [6] The Gemara objects: If Rav Ḥisda is correct, why does the Baraita make only a partial statement of the relative strictness of the laws of interest and of *ona'ah* as they apply to consecrated property? To say that the laws of interest are more strictly applied to lay people than to the Temple treasury tells only half the story! **Let** the Baraita **also state:** "The laws of *ona'ah* **are more stricly applied to** transactions involving **consecrated property than to** transactions between **lay people"!** If the laws of *ona'ah* applying to consecrated property are indeed more strict than those applying to lay people, the Baraita should have said so.

הָכִי הָשְׁתָּא [7] The Gemara answers: **How can you compare** the two cases? Is it really necessary to draw a comparison between the application of the laws of *ona'ah* and the application of the laws of interest in the sale of consecrated property? [8] **Granted** that the Baraita should wish to point out that the prohibition against interest is **more strictly applied** to transactions between **lay people than to** transactions involving **consecrated property,**

TERMINOLOGY

לִיתְנֵי נַמִי And let it also teach.... An expression used by the Gemara to introduce a case that should have been included among those dealt with by the Mishnah: "Since the Mishnah is dealing with a whole series of cases, should it not have added the following one as well?"

הָכִי הָשְׁתָּא How can you compare? The Talmud uses this expression in rejecting a comparison suggested previously: "How can you compare? There, in case A, the circumstances are of type X, whereas here, in case B, the circumstances are different!"

NOTES

זֶה חוֹמֶר בְּהֶדְיוֹט מִבְּהֶקְדֵּשׁ This is more stringent for a lay person than for consecrated property. *Shittah Mekubbetzet* explains that the laws which apply to consecrated property are usually stricter than those which apply to lay people. Here, though, we see that it is prohibited to pay or to charge interest to a lay person, even though it is permitted to pay interest to the Temple treasury.

זֶה חוֹמֶר בְּהֶדְיוֹט מִבְּהֶקְדֵּשׁ וְתוּ לָא This is more stringent for a lay person than for consecrated property, and there is nothing more. The Gemara implies that the only case in which the property of a lay person is treated more stringently than consecrated property is with regard to the laws of interest. But, as the Rishonim point out, our Mishnah (above, 56a) mentions other areas in which the laws applying to lay people are more stringent than those applying to consecrated property. For example, the double repayment made by a thief applies to the property of a lay person, but not to consecrated property. Paid and unpaid bailees are liable for the loss of property belonging to a lay person, but not for the loss of consecrated property. How then can the Gemara claim that interest is the only area of greater stringency regarding a lay person?

Some Rishonim amend the text and omit the phrase "and there is nothing more." Accordingly, the Gemara's argument is that a case in which the law regarding a lay person is more stringent is a novelty and therefore deserves special mention. Cases in which the law regarding consecrated property is more stringent than the law applying to a lay

SAGES

רַב הוֹשַׁעְיָא Rav Hoshaya (or Oshaya, אוֹשַׁעְיָא). A Babylonian Amora of the third generation. See *Bava Metzia*, Part II, p. 352.

TRANSLATION AND COMMENTARY

for there are **no other** examples where secular property is treated more strictly than consecrated property. [1]**But in the case of consecrated property,** would telling us that the laws of *ona'ah* are strictly applied in cases involving the sale of consecrated property exhaust the list of examples of cases in which consecrated property is dealt with more strictly than is secular property? [2]**Is "this a greater stringency" and is there nothing else?** It is well known that there are many stringencies that apply to consecrated property but not to secular property. Hence stating that "this is a greater stringency" would be of little interest. Thus the Baraita does not contradict Rav Ḥisda. It can in fact be explained in the same way that Rav Ḥisda would explain the Mishnah.

רִבִּית דְּהֶקְדֵּשׁ [3]The Baraita cited in the course of the previous discussion stated that there is no prohibition against interest in the case of consecrated property. The Gemara now wishes to clarify this ruling: **How is interest on consecrated property to be visualized?** [4]**If we say** that the Baraita is referring to a typical loan, in which, for example, **the Temple treasurer lent** a private person **one hundred zuz** of Temple funds on condition that the borrower return **one hundred and twenty** zuz (the original loan together with an additional twenty zuz of interest), and the Baraita is informing us that in such a case the Temple treasury is permitted to collect the interest, **the** Temple **treasurer committed *me'ilah*** by lending the money, because by lending the money to a lay person he has deprived the Temple treasury of funds and has not received anything in their place. [5]**And** the law is that **if the** Temple **treasurer commits *me'ilah*, the money** he has disbursed immediately loses its sanctity and **becomes *ḥullin*** (unconsecrated property), after which **it is like** the property **of a lay person**, to which the prohibition against the taking of interest should apply. Thus the Baraita cannot be referring to an ordinary loan of Temple funds.

אָמַר רַב הוֹשַׁעְיָא [6]**Rav Hoshaya** suggested a solution to this problem and said: **With what** case **are we dealing here** in the Baraita? [7]We are not dealing with the case of a loan, but with a case **in which** a lay person was advanced money from Temple funds to supply fine flour at a later date for the meal-offerings in the Temple.

וְתוּ לָא. [1]אֶלָּא הֶקְדֵּשׁ, [2]"זֶה חוּמֶר" וְתוּ לָא? [3]רִבִּית דְּהֶקְדֵּשׁ הֵיכִי דָּמֵי? [4]אִילֵימָא דְּאוֹזְפֵיהּ גִּזְבָּר מֵאָה בְּמֵאָה וְעֶשְׂרִים, וַהֲלֹא מָעַל הַגִּזְבָּר, [5]וְכֵיוָן שֶׁמָּעַל הַגִּזְבָּר יָצְאוּ מְעוֹתָיו לַחוּלִּין וְהָווּ לְהוּ דְּהֶדְיוֹט?! [6]אָמַר רַב הוֹשַׁעְיָא: הָכָא בְּמַאי עָסְקִינַן? [7]כְּגוֹן שֶׁקִּיבֵּל עָלָיו

LITERAL TRANSLATION

and [there is] nothing more. [1]But [in the case of] consecrated property, [2]is "this more stringent" and [is there] nothing more?

[3]How is interest on consecrated property to be visualized? [4]If we say that the [Temple] treasurer lent one hundred for one hundred and twenty, did not the treasurer commit *me'ilah*, [5]and since the treasurer committed *me'ilah* his money became *ḥullin* and became that of a lay person?!

[6]Rav Hoshaya said: With what are we dealing here? [7]Where, for example, he took upon himself

RASHI

אלא הקדש זה חומר ותו לא — בתמיה. **דאוזיף** — שהלוה להדיוט. **והלא מעל** — שהוציא מעות הקדש לחולין ולא הכניס תחתיהן להקדש כלום. ושוגג הוא אצלו, כסבור שמותר משום שכר הקדש. **והוו ליה דהדיוט** — של גזבר, שהרי עליו לשלם להקדש קרן וחומש. **הכא במאי עסקינן** — האי דקתני "אין רבית להקדש" — לאו בהלואה קאי, אלא בהדיוט שקיבל מעות מן הלשכה מן הגזבר לספק סלתות כל השנה למנחות של צבור ארבע סאין בסלע, והוקרו ועמדו משלש סאין בסלע. דאילו הדיוט אסור לפסוק על פירות עד שיצא השער, וכאן אפילו לא יצא השער עדיין לארבע, פוסקין.

NOTES

person are not unusual, and therefore need not be mentioned (*Tosafot*).

Rosh explains the Gemara according to our text. When the Baraita states that "this is more stringent for a lay person than for consecrated property," implying that "this" — the laws of interest — is the only such case, it is referring only to cases that occur frequently. The laws mentioned in the Mishnah are only infrequently applied, for they apply only when property is stolen or lost.

Ritzbash interprets the Gemara differently, and thus avoids the entire question. According to him, the Gemara is not discussing cases in which there is a greater stringency for a lay person. Rather, the Gemara is discussing prohibitions that apply to lay people but not to consecrated property. The only such prohibition is that of interest.

רִבִּית דְּהֶקְדֵּשׁ הֵיכִי דָּמֵי How is interest on consecrated property to be visualized? The Gemara seeks a case in which the Baraita's ruling that there is no prohibition against interest with respect to consecrated property would apply. One might have thought that the Gemara would suggest the simple case of an ordinary person lending money to the Temple treasury at interest. *Ritzbash* explains why the Baraita cannot be referring to such a case. The Temple treasurer would be unable to pay the interest in such a case even if the prohibition against paying interest did not apply. The treasurer would be barred from using Temple funds to pay the interest because such money is consecrated and would remain unredeemed, since there is nothing that would become consecrated in its place.

כְּגוֹן שֶׁקִּיבֵּל עָלָיו Where, for example, he took upon himself. The Gemara rejected the possibility that the Baraita is referring to an ordinary case of interest, arguing that the

לְסַפֵּק סְלָתוֹת מֵאַרְבַּע, וְעָמְדוּ מִשָּׁלֹשׁ, [1]כִּדְתַנְיָא: ״הַמְקַבֵּל עָלָיו לְסַפֵּק סְלָתוֹת מֵאַרְבַּע וְעָמְדוּ מִשָּׁלֹשׁ, מְסַפֵּק מֵאַרְבַּע. [2]מִשָּׁלֹשׁ וְעָמְדוּ מֵאַרְבַּע, מְסַפֵּק מֵאַרְבַּע, שֶׁיַּד הֶקְדֵּשׁ עַל הָעֶלְיוֹנָה״.

[3]רַב פַּפָּא אָמַר: הָכָא בְּאַבְנֵי בִנְיָן

LITERAL TRANSLATION

to supply fine flour for four, and it stood at three, [1]as it was taught: "Someone who takes upon himself to supply fine flour for four and it stood at three, he supplies [it] for four. [2]For three and it stood at four, he supplies [it] for four, for *hekdesh* has the upper hand."

[3]Rav Pappa said: Here we are dealing with building stones

RASHI

רב פפא אמר – לעולם בהלואה, דאוזיף מאה במאה ועשרין. ודקשיא לך הלא מעל. **באבני בנין** – עסקינן, שהלוה הגזבר מהן להדיוט, דאין בהן מעילה ואין על הגזבר לשלם, אלא שליח בעלמא הוא.

TRANSLATION AND COMMENTARY

If, for example, **he undertakes to supply fine flour** at the price of **four** se'ahs of flour per sela, **and** later the price of flour rises and **stands at three** se'ahs per sela, the supplier must sell the flour to the Temple at the price originally agreed upon. Ordinarily, it is forbidden to pay in advance for merchandise that is not currently available, and whose market price has not yet been set. This is forbidden because if the price of the merchandise rises between the contract date and the date of delivery the buyer will, in effect, receive a discount for having paid in advance, which by Rabbinic decree is tantamount to charging interest. But a person is permitted to sell merchandise to the Temple at a pre-determined price even though the real price per unit may turn out to be higher. [1]The Gemara provides further support for Rav Hoshaya's suggested solution: **For it was taught** in another Baraita: **"If** a person **undertakes to supply fine flour** to the Temple **at four** se'ahs per sela **and** the price later **stands at three** se'ah per sela, **he** must **supply** the flour **at four** se'ahs per sela, as he originally promised, even though the Temple thereby receives a discount for having paid in advance." [2]This Baraita continues to discuss the laws which apply in the opposite case as well: "If a person undertakes to supply fine flour **at three** se'ahs per sela **and** the price later **stands at four** se'ahs per sela, **he must supply** the flour **at four** se'ahs per sela, even though he initially specified a higher price per unit. **For *hekdesh*** — i.e., the Temple treasury — always **has the upper hand** whenever there is a change in prices."

רַב פַּפָּא אָמַר [3]Rav Pappa offered a different explanation of the Baraita's statement that the prohibition against interest does not apply to consecrated property. In his opinion, contrary to that of Rav Hoshaya, the case is one of a loan. **Rav Pappa explains: Here we are dealing with building stones** which were

BACKGROUND

קִיבֵּל עָלָיו לְסַפֵּק סְלָתוֹת He took upon himself to supply fine flour. Large quantities of fine flour, oil and wine were used in the Temple, since many types of offerings were brought from these products. As indicated in the discussion here, special laws applied when such commodities were purchased for Temple use. For example, the Temple treasury always had the upper hand in such transactions. Accordingly, it stands to reason that people undertook to supply such items to the Temple (even if doing so caused them a slight loss) because it was considered religiously praiseworthy to do so. Moreover, since only the finest-quality merchandise was used in the Temple, the merchants who supplied these goods gained prestige and honor by doing so.

NOTES

treasurer would have committed *me'ilah* if he disbursed Temple funds without immediately replacing them by transferring their sanctity to some other funds or property. How does Rav Hoshaya counter this argument when he suggests that the Baraita is referring to a case in which the treasurer paid for merchandise in advance?

One approach taken by the Rishonim is to construct a case in which the Temple funds are immediately replaced. *Ra'avad*, for example, explains that collateral was left with the treasurer in order to replace the Temple funds. *Ran* suggests that at the time the money was advanced, the flour supplier already had sufficient merchandise in stock with which the Temple funds could be redeemed.

A second approach is to construct a case in which the Temple funds need not be replaced. *Tosafot*, for example, explains that the Baraita is referring to a case in which a private donor paid the supplier in advance with unconsecrated money. Others suggest that the supplier himself agreed to donate the flour. Accordingly, Temple funds were not involved, and hence there was nothing to replace (*Ramban*). *Rosh* understands that Temple funds were indeed used, but nevertheless they need not be replaced. In order that it be possible to purchase items required by the Temple, the Rabbis decided that Temple funds used for such purposes would never be consecrated.

לְסַפֵּק סְלָתוֹת מֵאַרְבַּע וְעָמְדוּ מִשָּׁלֹשׁ To supply fine flour for four, and it stood at three. Rav Hoshaya explains the Baraita which excludes consecrated property from the prohibition against interest as referring to a case of interest forbidden only by Rabbinic decree. If this exemption is based on a Biblical verse, as most Rishonim maintain, why does Rav Hoshaya not explain the Baraita as referring to interest forbidden by Torah law?

Ramban answers that Rav Hoshaya wished to explain the Baraita in such a way that it can also be referring to interest that is only Rabbinically forbidden. The Biblical verse excluding consecrated property from the laws of interest must of course refer to interest prohibited by Torah law. *Ramban* suggests that it refers to a case in which a person accepted a monetary obligation to the Temple treasury, and later the date of payment was extended on condition that interest be added to the donation. *Ramban* cites another opinion, according to which Rav Hoshaya is referring to a case of interest forbidden by the Torah, i.e., a case in which a donor assumed the obligation to supply a sela's worth of flour and the price of flour subsequently rose.

Meiri argues that, according to Rav Hoshaya, the Torah does not exclude consecrated property from the laws of interest. Accordingly, Rav Hoshaya had to choose an example of interest forbidden only by Rabbinic decree.

הַמְסוּרוֹת לַגִּזְבָּר עָסְקִינַן, כְּדִשְׁמוּאֵל. [1]דְּאָמַר שְׁמוּאֵל: בּוֹנִין בַּחוֹל, וְאַחַר כָּךְ מַקְדִּישִׁין. [2]"אֵין בָּהֶן תַּשְׁלוּמֵי כֵפֶל וכו'". [3]מְנָהָנֵי מִילֵּי? [4]דְּתָנוּ רַבָּנַן: "'עַל כָּל דְּבַר פֶּשַׁע' — כְּלָל. [5]'עַל שׁוֹר, עַל חֲמוֹר, עַל שֶׂה, עַל שַׂלְמָה' — פְּרָט. [6]'עַל כָּל אֲבֵדָה אֲשֶׁר יֹאמַר' — חָזַר וְכָלַל. [7]כְּלָל וּפְרָט וּכְלָל

TRANSLATION AND COMMENTARY

entrusted to the Temple treasurer for use in the Temple, but were not yet consecrated. The Baraita rules that in the light of the fact that the stones have already been designated for use in the Temple, they may be lent out in exchange for more than their worth without violating the proscription against interest. Unlike a loan of consecrated money to a lay person, lending the stones does not constitute *me'ilah* because the stones have not yet been consecrated to the Temple. [1]The Baraita's ruling is **in accordance with Shmuel's opinion, for Shmuel said: We build** the Temple **with unconsecrated** building materials **and** only **consecrate** it **later** after construction is completed, because if the workmen use consecrated materials, they may inadvertently derive personal benefit from them, thereby committing *me'ilah*. Thus, when the treasurer lends the stones, he is not guilty of *me'ilah* because the stones are still unconsecrated, yet the ordinary prohibition against taking interest does not apply because the stones have already been designated for Temple use.

אֵין בָּהֶן תַּשְׁלוּמֵי כֵפֶל וכו' [2]The Gemara now turns back to our Mishnah and seeks the Biblical source for the laws recorded there. The Mishnah states that if slaves, promissory notes, land or consecrated property are stolen, **"they are not subject to the double repayment"** normally imposed on a thief. [3]The Gemara asks: **From where is this** law **derived?** [4]The Gemara answers by citing a Baraita: **For our Rabbis taught** in explaining the verse (Exodus 22:8) "For every matter of trespass, whether it be for ox, for ass, for sheep, for raiment or for any manner of lost thing ... he shall pay double," one of the verses from which the law of double repayment is learned: "The expression **'for every matter of trespass' is a generalization.** [5]The expression **'for ox, for ass, for sheep, for raiment' is a specification,** as specific types of stolen items are listed. [6]The expression 'for any manner of lost thing of **which one says' is a further generalization.** [7]Now, one of the principles of Rabbinic hermeneutics is that if a Biblical verse is formulated as **a generalization** followed by a **specification** followed by another **generalization,**

LITERAL TRANSLATION

entrusted to the [Temple] treasurer, in accordance with [the opinion] of Shmuel. [1]For Shmuel said: One builds with unconsecrated [property], and afterwards one consecrates [it].

[2]"They do not have the double repayment, etc." [3]From where are these things [derived]? [4]For our Rabbis taught: "'For every matter of trespass' — [this is] a generalization. [5]'For ox, for ass, for sheep, for raiment' — [this is] a specification. [6]'For any matter of lost thing of which one says' — it again generalizes. [7][In the case of] a generalization, specification, and generalization

RASHI

דאמר שמואל בונין בחול — כשהן בונין בנייני הקדש לא היו קונין האבנים והטיט ממעות הקדש, כדי שלא יבואו האומנין והעם לידי מעילה אם ישבו עליהם, או אם יהנו מהם. אלא לוקחין בהקפה, והרי הן חול עד שיבנו בחומה. ומשהן בנויות בחומה נותנין מעות הקדש, ולוקחין אותן, והוא הקדשן. או אם התנדב אדם אבנים, נותנן לגנאי ואינו קורא שם הקדש עליהן עד שיתננו בבנין, הלכך לא מעל הגזבר. **על כל דבר פשע** — סיפיה דקרא משתעי בטוען טענת גנב, או בגנב עצמו.

NOTES

בּוֹנִין בַּחוֹל One builds with unconsecrated property. The Temple was not built with consecrated property because it was feared that the workmen might inadvertently derive personal benefit from the building materials, thereby committing *me'ilah*. *Tosafot* (*Me'ilah* 14a), however, suggests another explanation. Since people paid for the Temple construction with money which had already been consecrated to the Temple, the workmen could not accept such money in payment for their services, since they would commit *me'ilah* by doing so. Rather, the money had to be redeemed by using it to pay for the building stones, after which these stones acquired the money's sanctity. Then the money, which was no longer sacred, could be used to pay the workers.

HALAKHAH

בּוֹנִין בַּחוֹל, וְאַחַר כָּךְ מַקְדִּישִׁין One builds with unconsecrated property and afterwards one consecrates it. "The Temple is not built from property that has already been consecrated, since the construction workers may inadvertently derive personal benefit from it and thereby commit *me'ilah*. Instead, the Temple is built from unconsecrated materials, which are consecrated only after the construction work is finished." (*Rambam, Sefer Avodah, Hilkhot Me'ilah* 8:4.)

BACKGROUND

בְּאַבְנֵי בִנְיָן הַמְסוּרוֹת לַגִּזְבָּר Building stones entrusted to the Temple treasurer. Since the prohibition against committing *me'ilah* is exceptionally severe, the Temple treasurers often preferred to perform certain types of Temple business with ordinary money (*ḥullin*), so as to avoid committing *me'ilah* inadvertently. However, after successfully concluding these transactions, they would consecrate the *ḥullin* money to the Temple, rendering it *hekdesh*. Thus we see that the Temple treasurers were responsible not only for money consecrated to the Temple, but also for *ḥullin* money.

CONCEPTS

כְּלָל וּפְרָט וּכְלָל The rule of generalization-specification-generalization. This is one of Rabbi Yishmael's thirteen principles of Biblical hermeneutics. It applies when a Biblical verse (or, according to some opinions, several verses, even if they are at a distance from one another) contains a general expression followed by a specific example (or examples), followed by another general expression. This combined use of generalizations and specifications presumably indicated that the specific instance in the middle should be taken as an archetypical example of a broader category in which the law in question applies. The law under consideration is assumed to apply in all cases which bear some essential similarity to the specific example. Thus, for example, the specific examples mentioned in our verse (Exodus 22:8) are all movables with intrinsic value, so the laws of the double repayment are assumed to apply to all such items.

TRANSLATION AND COMMENTARY

we may deduce that the verse refers only to cases **similar to** those mentioned in **the specification."** In such verses, we assume that the Torah generalized at the beginning and at the end, while mentioning a specific case or cases in the middle, to teach us that the law under discussion applies only to cases which bear some resemblance to the one(s) specified in the middle. [1]The Baraita now identifies the rules that are to be derived from the specific examples cited in the verse: "**Just as the** items **specified** in our verse — an ox, an ass, a sheep and raiment — **are clearly defined** as **movable and intrinsically valuable objects,** [2]**so too** we may infer that a thief must make the double repayment for **anything** he steals, provided it **is movable and intrinsically valuable.** [3]Thus **land is excluded** from the law of double repayment, **since it is not movable** property. [4]**Slaves are excluded, since they were likened to land** (cf. above, 56b). [5]**Promissory notes are excluded, for even though they are** classified as **movables, they are not themselves intrinsically valuable,** as they merely serve as evidence of a loan. [6]And **consecrated property** is excluded because **the** same **verse** (Exodus 22:8) **says**: 'he shall pay double to **his neighbor,**' which implies that the law of double repayment applies only in the case of a thief who steals the property of **his neighbor, and not** in the case of **consecrated property.**"

וְלֹא תַּשְׁלוּמֵי אַרְבָּעָה וַחֲמִשָּׁה וכו׳ [7]The next clause of the Mishnah states that if a thief steals and then sells or slaughters a sheep or ox consecrated to the Temple, he has to return only the principal, because consecrated property "is not subject to the law of **fourfold and fivefold repayment"** — the penalty for a thief who sells or slaughters a stolen sheep (fourfold repayment) or an ox (fivefold repayment). [8]The Gemara asks: **What is the reason** that consecrated property is treated differently from secular property in this regard? [9]The Gemara explains: Because **the Torah said** that a person who steals a sheep or ox and then sells or slaughters it must make **fourfold and fivefold repayment, but not threefold and fourfold repayment.** The fourfold and fivefold repayment made in such cases is made up of the double repayment paid by all thieves, plus an extra two (in the case of a sheep) or three (in the case of an ox) times the animal's value — a total of four or five times the animal's value. Thus, items for which a thief does not make the double repayment — for example, consecrated property — must be exempt from fourfold and fivefold repayment as well, because the Torah only specifies paying *four or five* times the principal — that is, the principal, an amount equal to the principal making up the double repayment, and a further two or three times the animal's worth — but not

LITERAL TRANSLATION

you only deduce what is similar to the specification. [1]Just as the specification is explicit — something that is movable and is itself [worth] money — [2]so too anything that is movable and is itself [worth] money. [3]Land is excluded, since it is not movable. [4]Slaves are excluded, since they were likened to land. [5]Promissory notes are excluded, for even though they are movables, they are not themselves [worth] money. [6][Concerning] consecrated property, the verse says: 'His neighbor.' His neighbor and not consecrated property."

[7]"Nor fourfold and fivefold repayment, etc." [8]What is the reason? [9]The Torah (lit., "the Merciful One") said fourfold and fivefold repayment, and not threefold and fourfold repayment.

אִי אַתָּה דָּן אֶלָּא כְּעֵין הַפְּרָט. [1]מַה הַפְּרָט מְפוֹרָשׁ — דָּבָר הַמִּטַּלְטֵל וְגוּפוֹ מָמוֹן — [2]אַף כָּל דָּבָר הַמִּטַּלְטֵל וְגוּפוֹ מָמוֹן. [3]יָצְאוּ קַרְקָעוֹת, שֶׁאֵינָן מִטַּלְטְלִין. [4]יָצְאוּ עֲבָדִים, שֶׁהוּקְּשׁוּ לְקַרְקָעוֹת. [5]יָצְאוּ שְׁטָרוֹת, שֶׁאַף עַל פִּי שֶׁמִּטַּלְטְלִין, אֵין גּוּפָן מָמוֹן. [6]הֶקְדֵּשׁוֹת, אָמַר קְרָא: ׳רֵעֵהוּ׳. רֵעֵהוּ וְלֹא הֶקְדֵּשׁ״.

[7]״וְלֹא תַּשְׁלוּמֵי אַרְבָּעָה וַחֲמִשָּׁה וכו׳״. [8]מַאי טַעְמָא? [9]תַּשְׁלוּמֵי אַרְבָּעָה וַחֲמִשָּׁה אָמַר רַחֲמָנָא, וְלֹא תַּשְׁלוּמֵי שְׁלֹשָׁה וְאַרְבָּעָה.

RASHI

ולא תשלומי שלשה וארבעה — שלשה לשה וארבעה לשור, דכיון דאימעיט מכפל בגר להו חדא, שהכפל בטובח ומוכר בכלל תשלומי ארבעה וחמשה.

NOTES

יָצְאוּ שְׁטָרוֹת Promissory notes are excluded from the double repayment. *Tosafot* (*Bava Kamma* 62b) asks why it was necessary to adduce a Biblical proof text to exclude promissory notes from the double repayment. According to Torah law, even if a person intentionally destroys a promissory note belonging to another person, he need not reimburse the owner, since the note has no intrinsic value. Why then might we have thought that a person who steals a promissory note must make the double repayment?

Tosafot answers that since a person who steals a promissory note must return it if it is still intact, one might think that he must also make the double repayment in such a case.

[1]״שׁוֹמֵר חִנָּם אֵינוֹ נִשְׁבָּע וכו׳״. [2]מְנָהָנֵי מִילֵּי? [3]דְּתָנוּ רַבָּנַן: ״׳כִּי יִתֵּן אִישׁ אֶל רֵעֵהוּ׳ — כְּלָל. [4]׳כֶּסֶף אוֹ כֵלִים׳ — פְּרָט. [5]׳וְגֻנַּב מִבֵּית הָאִישׁ׳ — חָזַר וְכָלַל. [6]כְּלָל וּפְרָט וּכְלָל אִי אַתָּה דָּן אֶלָּא כְּעֵין הַפְּרָט. [7]מַה הַפְּרָט מְפוֹרָשׁ — דָּבָר הַמִּטַּלְטֵל וְגוּפוֹ מָמוֹן — אַף כָּל דָּבָר הַמִּטַּלְטֵל וְגוּפוֹ מָמוֹן. [8]יָצְאוּ קַרְקָעוֹת, שֶׁאֵינָן מִטַּלְטְלִין. [9]יָצְאוּ עֲבָדִים, שֶׁהוּקְּשׁוּ לְקַרְקָעוֹת. [10]יָצְאוּ שְׁטָרוֹת, שֶׁאַף עַל פִּי שֶׁמִּטַּלְטְלִין, אֵין גּוּפָן מָמוֹן. [11]הֶקְדֵּשׁוֹת, אָמַר קְרָא: ׳רֵעֵהוּ׳. רֵעֵהוּ וְלֹא שֶׁל הֶקְדֵּשׁ״.

LITERAL TRANSLATION

[1]"An unpaid bailee does not swear, etc." [2]From where are these things [derived]? [3]For our Rabbis taught: "'If a man shall deliver to his neighbor' — [this is] a generalization. [4]'Money or utensils' — [this is] a specification. [5]'And it is stolen from the man's house' — it again generalizes. [6][In the case of] a generalization, specification, and generalization you only deduce what is similar to the specification. [7]Just as the specification is explicit — something that is movable and is itself [worth] money — so too anything that is movable and is itself [worth] money. [8]Land is excluded, since it is not movable. [9]Slaves are excluded, since they were likened to land. [10]Promissory notes are excluded, for even though they are movables, they are not not themselves [worth] money. [11][Concerning] consecrated property, the verse says: 'His neighbor.' His neighbor and not consecrated property."

TRANSLATION AND COMMENTARY

three or four times the principal (i.e. the principal, plus a further two or three times the animal's value). The fact that the Torah makes no mention of "threefold and fourfold repayment" teaches us that the laws of double repayment and fourfold or fivefold repayment are linked. There can never be a case in which fourfold or fivefold repayment does not include double repayment. Thus, if a thief who steals consecrated property is exempt from the double repayment, he must also be exempt from fourfold and fivefold repayment if the theft is of a sheep or an ox.

שׁוֹמֵר חִנָּם אֵינוֹ נִשְׁבָּע וכו׳ [1]The Gemara continues by explaining the next clause in the Mishnah, which states that **"an unpaid bailee** to whom slaves, promissory notes, land or consecrated property were entrusted for safekeeping but were later lost or stolen **does not swear** the oath of the bailees that is usually required in order to exempt the unpaid bailee from compensating the owner. [2]The Gemara asks: **From where is this** law **derived?** [3]The Gemara answers by citing a Baraita: **For our Rabbis taught** in explaining the verses (Exodus 22:6-7) which deal with the unpaid bailee's oath: "If a man shall deliver to his neighbor money or utensils to keep and it is stolen from the man's house ... then the master of the house shall be brought to the judges" to take an oath: "The expression **'if a man shall deliver to his neighbor' is a generalization,** as no particular type of deposit is specified in this clause. [4]The expression **'money or utensils' is a specification**, as specific types of deposit are mentioned. [5]The expression **'and it is stolen from the man's house' is a further generalization,** for no specific type of deposit is mentioned here. [6]Now, when a Biblical verse is formulated as **a generalization,** followed by a **specification,** followed by another **generalization,** the rule is that **we may deduce** that the verse refers only to cases **similar to** those mentioned in the **specification,** as explained above. [7]Accordingly we may infer that **just as the** items **specified** in our verse — money and utensils — **are clearly defined** as **movable and intrinsically valuable objects, so too** we may infer that an unpaid bailee is required to swear about **any** deposit in his care which was lost or stolen provided that **it is movable and intrinsically** valuable. [8]Thus **land is excluded, since it is not movable** property. [9]**Slaves are excluded, since they were likened to land.** [10]**Promissory notes are excluded, for even though they are** classified as **movables, they are not themselves intrinsically valuable,** as they merely serve as evidence of loan. [11]And **as for consecrated property, the verse says:** 'If a man shall deliver to **his neighbor,**' which implies that the law regarding the bailee's oath applies only to a deposit which a person received from **his neighbor, and not** to **consecrated property."**

RASHI

וכי יתן וגו׳ — לקמן ב״השואל״ (צד,ב) אמרינן: פרשה ראשונה נאמרה בשומר חנם, שניה בשומר שכר. וכתוב בפרשה ראשונה ״ונקרב בעל הבית וגו׳״ ואוקימנא לשבועה ב״המפקיד״ (בבא מציעא מא,א).

NOTES

שְׁבוּעָה בְּהֶקְדֵּשׁ וְקַרְקָעוֹת **Swearing about land and consecrated property.** The Rishonim disagree as to whether a bailee who was negligent about guarding land or consecrated property must reimburse the depositor. Some authorities maintain that negligence is considered tantamount to intentional damage, and hence the bailee must reimburse the depositor (*Rashi, Ra'avad, Rambam*). Others, however, maintain that land and consecrated property are totally excluded from the laws applying to bailees, so the bailee is exempt in this case (*Tosafot*, and see also *Ramban* and *Rashba*).

[1]״נוֹשֵׂא שָׂכָר אֵינוֹ מְשַׁלֵּם וכו׳״. [2]מְנָהָנֵי מִילֵּי? [3]דְּתָנוּ רַבָּנַן: ״׳כִּי יִתֵּן אִישׁ אֶל רֵעֵהוּ׳ — כְּלָל, [4]׳חֲמוֹר אוֹ שׁוֹר אוֹ שֶׂה׳ — פְּרָט. [5]׳וְכָל בְּהֵמָה לִשְׁמוֹר׳ — חָזַר וְכָלַל. [6]כְּלָל וּפְרָט וּכְלָל אִי אַתָּה דָּן אֶלָּא כְּעֵין הַפְּרָט. [7]מַה הַפְּרָט מְפוֹרָשׁ — דָּבָר הַמִּטַּלְטֵל וְגוּפוֹ מָמוֹן — אַף כָּל דָּבָר הַמִּטַּלְטֵל וְגוּפוֹ מָמוֹן. [8]יָצְאוּ קַרְקָעוֹת, שֶׁאֵינָן מִטַּלְטְלִין. [9]יָצְאוּ עֲבָדִים, שֶׁהוּקְּשׁוּ לְקַרְקָעוֹת. [10]יָצְאוּ שְׁטָרוֹת, שֶׁאַף עַל פִּי שֶׁמִּטַּלְטְלִין, אֵין גּוּפָן מָמוֹן. [11]הֶקְדֵּשׁוֹת, אָמַר קְרָא: ׳רֵעֵהוּ׳. רֵעֵהוּ וְלֹא שֶׁל הֶקְדֵּשׁ״. [12]״שׁוֹמֵר חִנָּם אֵינוֹ נִשְׁבָּע וכו׳״. [13]וּרְמִינְהוּ: [14]״בְּנֵי הָעִיר שֶׁשָּׁלְחוּ

LITERAL TRANSLATION

[1]"A paid bailee does not pay, etc." [2]From where are these things [derived]? [3]For our Rabbis taught: "'If a man shall deliver to his neighbor' — [this is] a generalization. [4]'An ass or an ox or a sheep' — [this is] a specification. [5]'Or any animal to keep' — it again generalizes. [6][In the case of] a generalization, specification, and generalization you deduce only what is similar to the specification. [7]Just as the specification is explicit — something that is movable and is itself [worth] money — so too anything that is movable and is itself [worth] money. [8]Land is excluded, since it is not movable. [9]Slaves are excluded, since they were likened to land. [10]Promissory notes are excluded, for even though they are movables, they are not themselves [worth] money. [11][Concerning] consecrated property the verse says: 'His neighbor.' His neighbor and not consecrated property."

[12]"An unpaid bailee does not swear, etc." [13]A contradiction was raised (lit., "cast them together"): [14]"If townspeople sent

TRANSLATION AND COMMENTARY

נוֹשֵׂא שָׂכָר אֵינוֹ מְשַׁלֵּם וכו׳ [1]The next clause of the Mishnah states that **"a paid bailee** to whom slaves, promissory notes, land or consecrated property has been entrusted for safekeeping **does not pay"** if they are lost or stolen. [2]The Gemara asks: **From where is this** law **derived?** [3]The Gemara answers by citing a Baraita: **For our Rabbis taught** in explaining the verses (Exodus 22:9-11) which state that a paid bailee must pay the depositor if the deposit was lost or stolen while in the bailee's care: "The expression with which the verse begins — **'if a man shall deliver to his neighbor' — is a generalization,** since no particular type of deposit is specified. [4]The expression **'an ass or an ox or a sheep' is a specification.** [5]The expression **'or any animal to keep' is a further generalization.** [6]And in the case of **a generalization** followed by a **specification** followed by another **generalization,** the rule is that **we may deduce** that the verse refers only to cases **similar to** those mentioned in **the specification.** [7]Accordingly we may infer that **just as the** items **specified** in our verse — an ass, an ox or a sheep — **are clearly defined** as **movable and intrinsically valuable objects, so too** must a paid bailee reimburse the depositor for **any** deposit lost or stolen while in his care provided that **it is movable and intrinsically valuable.** [8]Thus **land is excluded, since it is not movable property.** [9]**Slaves are excluded, since they were likened to land.** [10]**Promissory notes are excluded, for even though they are** classified as **movables, they are not themselves intrinsically valuable.** [11]And **as for consecrated property, the verse says 'his neighbor,'** which implies that the paid bailee must only pay if he received property from **his neighbor, and not consecrated property** from the Temple."

שׁוֹמֵר חִנָּם אֵינוֹ נִשְׁבָּע וכו׳ [12]Having presented the sources for the various laws mentioned in the Mishnah, the Gemara now proceeds to analyze these laws in greater detail: We learned in the Mishnah: **"An unpaid bailee** to whom slaves, promissory notes, land or consecrated property has been entrusted **does not swear** the usual oath of the bailees." [13]**A contradiction was raised** between our Mishnah — which says that an unpaid bailee to whom consecrated property was entrusted need not take the bailee's oath if the property was lost or stolen — and another Mishnah (*Shekalim* 2:1), which seems to say otherwise: Every adult male was required to contribute a half-shekel to the Temple each year during the month of Adar. The money was used to cover the expenses of the Temple, which included buying communal sacrifices and paying for maintenance and repairs of the Temple and the walls of Jerusalem. The money was kept in a special chamber in the Temple complex which served as the Temple treasury. Three times a year part of the money was set aside and put into three special containers. These funds, known as *terumat halishkah* (תְּרוּמַת הַלִּשְׁכָּה), were used for the purchase of the communal sacrifices. [14]The Mishnah in *Shekalim* states: **"If townspeople sent**

BACKGROUND

בְּנֵי הָעִיר שֶׁשָּׁלְחוּ אֶת שִׁקְלֵיהֶן **If townspeople sent their shekalim.** The fiscal year in the Temple began on the first of Nisan. Accordingly, every adult male was required to send half a Temple shekel (worth four ordinary dinarim) to the Temple each year during the month of Adar (the month before Nisan). This money was used to buy communal sacrifices and other Temple necessities. These half-shekalim were collected in each city (beginning on the fifteenth of Adar) by money changers specially appointed to do so, after which the money was sent to the Temple.

NOTES

״וְכָל בְּהֵמָה לִשְׁמוֹר״ — חָזַר וְכָלַל **"Or any animal to keep" — it again generalizes.** *Rabbi Ovadyah of Bertinoro* apparently had a slightly different text here, namely: "'An ass or an ox or a sheep or any animal' — this is a specification. 'To keep' — it again generalizes." (See *Rashash*, who discusses the matter at length.)

אֶת שִׁקְלֵיהֶן וְנִגְנְבוּ אוֹ שֶׁאָבְדוּ, [1]אִם מִשֶּׁנִּתְרְמָה הַתְּרוּמָה, [58A] נִשְׁבָּעִין לַגִּזְבָּרִין. [2]וְאִם לָאו, נִשְׁבָּעִין לִבְנֵי הָעִיר, וּבְנֵי הָעִיר שׁוֹקְלִין אֲחֵרִים תַּחְתֵּיהֶן. [3]נִמְצְאוּ אוֹ שֶׁהֶחֱזִירוּם הַגַּנָּבִים, אֵלּוּ וְאֵלּוּ שְׁקָלִים הֵם, וְאֵין עוֹלִין לָהֶם לַשָּׁנָה הַבָּאָה״!

LITERAL TRANSLATION

their shekalim, and they were stolen or lost, [1]if [this happened] after the allocation was set aside, [58A] they swear to the treasurers. [2]But if not, they swear to the townspeople, and the townspeople contribute other shekalim in their place. [3][If] they were found or if the thieves returned them, both (lit., 'these and those') are shekalim, and they do not count for them the next year"!

RASHI

נשבעים לגזברים — שלא פשעו בהן. שהן בעלי הדין, דמכיון שתרמו את הלשכה, אין אחריות אבידה על הבעלים אלא על ההקדש, כדאמרינן לקמן: תורמין על האבוד, שיהא חלק בקופות הללו למי ששלח שקלו ואבד, ואינו יודע עכשיו שאבד. **ואם לאו** — שנודע להם מקודם לכן שוב אין תורמין עליהם אלא על מנת שישלחו להם אחרים תחתיהם, לפיכך בני העיר הן בעלי הדין של שלוחים. **נמצאו** — קאי אאבדו. **שהחזירום** — קאי א״נגנבו״. **אלו ואלו שקלים הם** — דכיון דקדוש — קדוש.

TRANSLATION AND COMMENTARY

their shekalim to the Temple by messenger **and** the shekalim **were stolen or lost** on the way to Jerusalem, the decision as to whether or not the townspeople must replace the missing shekalim depends on when they were lost or stolen. [1]**If** the shekalim were lost or stolen **after the allocation** for communal sacrifices **was set aside** from the funds which had already reached the Temple treasury, [58A] then the Temple treasury suffers the loss. The funds known as *terumat halishkah* are considered as having been set aside on behalf of all the money that has been collected, even if it has not yet arrived at the Temple. Therefore, once *terumat halishkah* has been set aside, even those shekalim that have not yet arrived in Jerusalem are considered as funds belonging to the Temple treasury, and the responsibility for their loss passes from the townspeople to the Temple. In such a case the messengers are regarded as acting on behalf of the Temple, and not on behalf of the townspeople, and must give an accounting of the lost shekalim to the Temple treasurer. Thus the messengers **must swear to the** Temple **treasurers** that they took proper care of the shekalim. Having taken the oath, they are free of any liability to the Temple. But **if not** — if the messengers lost the money before *terumat halishkah* was set aside in the Temple treasury — the shekalim are treated as if they are still in the townspeople's possession, and the townspeople remain responsible for the loss. [2]In such circumstances, the messengers must **swear to the townspeople** who sent the shekalim that they took proper care of the money, **and** then **the townspeople must contribute other shekalim in place of those** which were lost or stolen. [3]**If** the original shekalim **were found or if the thieves returned them** after the townspeople contributed the second set of shekalim, **both** the original shekalim and the replacement set **are** considered consecrated **shekalim**. Since both sets of shekalim were designated for Temple use, both must be given to the Temple treasury. **And** even though the townspeople ultimately contribute two sets of shekalim, the additional set **does not count towards the next year's** obligation, since the money was already designated for use in the current year." Now, the Gemara is assuming that the messengers bringing the shekalim to Jerusalem are unpaid bailees, but the Mishnah in tractate *Shekalim* says that the messengers are required to take an oath affirming that they took proper care of the shekalim, even though they are consecrated property. This contradicts our Mishnah, which states that an unpaid bailee is not required to take an oath about consecrated property!

HALAKHAH

בְּנֵי הָעִיר שֶׁשָּׁלְחוּ אֶת שִׁקְלֵיהֶן **Townspeople who sent their shekalim.** "If townspeople sent their shekalim to the Temple by messenger, and the money was lost or stolen, the messenger, if unpaid for his services, must swear that he took proper care of the shekalim. He does not then have to compensate the townspeople for the loss. The townspeople, however, must send new shekalim to the Temple in place of the lost money.

"The messenger is required to take an oath even if the townspeople are willing to exempt him from doing so, since this oath was imposed by Rabbinic decree. If the original shekalim are found after the messenger has taken his oath, both they and the replacement shekalim are to be treated as consecrated, and do not count towards next year's shekalim. The original shekalim are considered as this year's shekalim, while the replacement shekalim are counted with last year's.

"If the townspeople paid the messenger to bring the shekalim to the Temple, and the money was lost or stolen under circumstances beyond the messenger's control after the allocation of *terumat halishkah* was made from the Temple treasury, the messenger must swear to the Temple

LITERAL TRANSLATION

[1] Shmuel said: Here we are dealing with a paid bailee, and they swear in order to receive their wages.

[2] If so, "they swear to the treasurers"? It should [say]: "To the townspeople"!

[3] Rabbah said: They swear to the townspeople in the presence of the treasurers, so that they will not suspect them, [4] or also so that they will not call them negligent.

[5] But surely it says: "If they were stolen or lost," and a paid bailee is liable for theft and loss. [6] And here too, even granted that they do not pay, they should at least lose their wages!

[1] אָמַר שְׁמוּאֵל: הָכָא בְּנוֹשֵׂא שָׂכָר עָסְקִינַן, וְנִשְׁבָּעִין לִיטּוֹל שְׂכָרָן.

[2] אִי הָכִי, "נִשְׁבָּעִין לַגִּזְבָּרִין"? "לִבְנֵי הָעִיר" מִבָּעֵי לֵיהּ!

[3] אָמַר רַבָּה: נִשְׁבָּעִין לִבְנֵי הָעִיר בְּמַעֲמַד גִּזְבָּרִין, כִּי הֵיכִי דְּלָא נַחְשְׁדִינְהוּ, [4] וְאִי נַמִי כִּי הֵיכִי דְּלָא לִקְרוּ לְהוּ פּוֹשְׁעִים.

[5] וְהָא "נִגְנְבוּ אוֹ שֶׁאָבְדוּ" קָתָנֵי, וְשׁוֹמֵר שָׂכָר בִּגְנֵיבָה וַאֲבֵידָה חִיּוּבֵי מִיחַיַּיב. [6] וְהָכָא נַמִי, נְהִי דְּשַׁלּוּמֵי לָא מְשַׁלְּמֵי, אַגְרַיְיהוּ מִיהָא לִפְסִיד!

RASHI

הכא בנושא שכר עסקינן — כלומר, שבועה זו לא ליפטר מתשלומין היא, דלאו שומר חנם נשבע על הפשיעה ולא נושא שכר משלם גניבה ואבידה, כי מתניתין. ושבועה זו — כדי ליטול שכרן נשבעין שאינן ברשותן, וגובין שכרן מן בני העיר. ולקמיה פריך: והא כיון דשומר שכר — יש עליו לשומרו מגניבה ואבידה ולא שמר — לא השלים עבודתו, אין לו ליטול שכר! **נשבעים לגזברים** — בתמיה, והלא אין שכרן אלא על בני העיר. **נשבעים לבני העיר** — ליטול שכרן, ובמעמד הגזברים — מפני שההפסד על ההקדש. **והכא נמי נהי דשלומי לא משלמי** — דאימעיט הקדשות מתשלומי שומרים. **אגרייהו מיהא לפסיד** — שהרי נשתעבדו לשומרן מגניבה ואבידה, ועל מנת כן היו נוטלין שכר, והרי לא השלימו מלאכתן.

TRANSLATION AND COMMENTARY

אָמַר שְׁמוּאֵל [1] **Shmuel** attempted to resolve the contradiction and **said:** The oath referred to in the Mishnah in tractate *Shekalim* is not the oath referred to in the Torah that an unpaid bailee takes to free himself from liability for the loss or theft of a deposit. Such an oath need not be taken with respect to the loss of consecrated property, as we learned in our Mishnah. The Mishnah in *Shekalim* deals with an entirely different situation: **Here,** in the Mishnah in *Shekalim*, **we are dealing with paid bailees, and** the messengers must **swear** in order **to receive their wages** from the townspeople. The messengers are entitled to payment only if they discharged their duty as stipulated. Since the loss of the shekalim entrusted to them raises a question as to whether they performed their duty properly, the messengers must affirm under oath that they cared for the money properly and are entitled to their wages.

אִי הָכִי [2] The Gemara objects: **If so,** if this explanation is correct, why does the Mishnah say: "The messengers **swear to the** Temple **treasurers**"? If the messengers must take an oath in order to collect their wages, the Mishnah **should** have **said** that they swear **"to the townspeople,"** since it is the townspeople who must pay them their wages, not the Temple treasurers!

אָמַר רַבָּה [3] **Rabbah answered** this question by saying that the Mishnah's meaning is as follows: The messengers **swear to the townspeople in the presence of the** Temple **treasurers** that they took proper care of the money, **so** that the treasurers **will not suspect** the townspeople of failing to contribute their shekalim, [4] **or,** alternatively, **so** that the treasurers **will not claim that** the messengers were **negligent** in their care of the money. However, the ultimate purpose of the oath is to entitle the messengers to claim their wages from the townspeople.

וְהָא נִגְנְבוּ אוֹ שֶׁאָבְדוּ קָתָנֵי [5] The Gemara raises another objection: **But surely** the Mishnah in *Shekalim* **speaks** about a case in which the shekalim **"were stolen or lost." Now, a paid bailee is** ordinarily **liable for theft and loss**, except, as pointed out in our Mishnah, when the property being guarded is consecrated property. [6] This being the case, **here too,** where the shekalim are consecrated property, **even though** the messengers **do not have to reimburse** the townspeople for the shekalim if they were lost or stolen, **they should at least forfeit their wages.** Since the messengers did not complete the task for which they were hired, they should not be entitled to their wages even if they swear that they cared for the money properly! If the Mishnah in *Shekalim* cannot be understood as referring to a paid bailee, the apparent contradiction remains between that Mishnah and our Mishnah.

HALAKHAH

treasurers that he took proper care of the money, and then the townspeople do not have to send other shekalim. But if the shekalim were lost before the allocation was made, the messenger must swear to the townspeople, after which they must send replacement shekalim to the Temple." (*Rambam, Sefer Zemanim, Hilkhot Shekalim* 3:8-9.)

BACKGROUND

בִּלְסְטִים מְזוּיָּין **By an armed robber.** A thief is someone who steals in secret and does not wish to be seen by anyone. For that reason, normal precautions are useful against his depredations. However, an armed robber (לִסְטִים מְזוּיָּין) does not refrain from violence, and for that reason, when he robs someone, it is regarded as an unavoidable loss.

TERMINOLOGY

הָתֵינָח **This may rest,** or **granted.** This is a formula used to introduce a question: "Granted in case A, but what about case B?"

[1]אָמַר רַבָּה: ״נִגְנְבוּ״ בְּלִסְטִים מְזוּיָּין; [2]״אָבְדוּ״ שֶׁטָּבְעָה סְפִינָתוֹ בַּיָּם.

[3]רַבִּי יוֹחָנָן אָמַר: הָא מַנִּי? [4]רַבִּי שִׁמְעוֹן הִיא, דְּאָמַר: ״קָדָשִׁים שֶׁחַיָּיב בְּאַחֲרָיוּתָן, יֵשׁ לָהֶן אוֹנָאָה, וְנִשְׁבָּעִין עֲלֵיהֶם״.

[5]הָתֵינָח עַד שֶׁלֹּא נִתְרְמָה הַתְּרוּמָה. [6]מִשֶּׁנִּתְרְמָה הַתְּרוּמָה, קָדָשִׁים שֶׁאֵינוֹ חַיָּיב בְּאַחֲרָיוּתָן נִינְהוּ. [7]דְּתַנְיָא:

LITERAL TRANSLATION

[1]Rabbah said: "They were stolen" [means stolen] by an armed robber; [2]"they were lost" [means] that his ship sank in the sea.

[3]Rabbi Yoḥanan said: Whose is this? [4]It is Rabbi Shimon, who said: "[Concerning] consecrated property for which he is responsible, there is *ona'ah* for them, and oaths are sworn about them."

[5]This is well as long as the allocation has not been made. [6][But] after the allocation has been made, they are consecrated property for which he is not responsible. [7]For it has been taught:

RASHI

בלסטים מזוין — דאונס הוי, ולשמירה זו לא קבלו עליהם. **הא מני רבי שמעון היא** — במסכת שבועות (מב,ב). **יש להן אונאה** — בכדי גרס לה, ומאן דגרים לה — לא ידע שאמר רבי שמעון בהדיא לגבי שבועה, והוצרך ללמדה ממשנתנו. **שחייב באחריות** — שהמפקיד חייב באחריות. הלכך, כדידיה דמי לרבי שמעון. והכא נמי חייבין כל בני העיר לשקול אחרים תחתיהן.

TRANSLATION AND COMMENTARY

אָמַר רַבָּה [1]**Rabbah answered** this objection: When the Mishnah in *Shekalim* says that the shekalim **"were stolen,"** it means that they were stolen **by armed robbers.** Since a paid bailee is not required to protect the deposit entrusted to him from situations beyond his control, the messengers may collect their wages. Theft by armed robbers is considered an accident beyond the bailee's control. [2]Similarly, when the Mishnah says that the shekalim **"were lost,"** it refers to a case **where** the money was in a **ship** which **sank at sea,** which is also a case of accident, for which a paid bailee is not liable. Hence he may collect his wages. Thus we see that the Mishnah in *Shekalim* may properly be understood as referring to a paid bailee who is entitled to his wages despite the fact that the deposit entrusted to him was lost or stolen.

רַבִּי יוֹחָנָן אָמַר [3]**Rabbi Yoḥanan** now **suggests** an alternative solution to the contradiction between our Mishnah and the Mishnah in *Shekalim*: In fact, both Mishnayot are referring to unpaid bailees, and in the case of the messengers in the Mishnah in *Shekalim,* the oath that must be taken is the standard bailee's oath needed to free the messengers from liability for the loss or theft of the shekalim. The contradiction between the two Mishnayot, does exist, but the Mishnah in *Shekalim* does not follow the view of our Mishnah that consecrated property is not subject to the bailee's oath. **Whose** view then **does** the Mishnah in *Shekalim* reflect? [4]That of **Rabbi Shimon, who said** in our own Mishnah: **"Sacrifices for which** a person **is responsible are subject to** the laws of ***ona'ah,"*** **and**, similarly, in another Mishnah (*Shevuot* 6:5) he said: **"Oaths are taken about them."** According to Rabbi Shimon, consecrated property for which a person is responsible is treated like any other property, and an unpaid bailee to whom such property was entrusted must take an oath that he cared for it properly, if it is lost or stolen. Since the donors of the shekalim to the Temple treasury are responsible for them and must replace them if they are lost or stolen, the messengers to whom the shekalim were entrusted can free themselves from liability only by swearing that they took proper care of the money.

הָתֵינָח [5]The Gemara now objects to Rabbi Yoḥanan's solution as leading to an injustice to the bailee. We said earlier that if the shekalim were lost or stolen after the allocation of funds (*terumat halishkah*) was made in the Temple, the townspeople were exempt from having to replace their contribution to the Temple. In such a situation the messengers should be exempt from taking an oath. Rabbi Yoḥanan's explanation is **well-founded as long as the allocation has not** yet **been made** by the Temple treasury of the funds that have already reached it. It is then understandable that the messengers must swear about the shekalim. If the shekalim were lost or stolen before the allocation was made, the townspeople are still responsible for their shekalim and must replace them. In such a case, the shekalim are indeed considered consecrated property for which one is responsible, and therefore according to Rabbi Shimon the messengers must take an oath about them. [6]**But after the allocation has been made** the townspeople are no longer required to replace the missing shekalim. **The shekalim** should then **be** considered **consecrated property for which** the townspeople are **no** longer **responsible**. Why then should their messengers be held in any way liable for their loss? [7]**For it has been taught** in a Baraita:

[1]״תּוֹרְמִין עַל הָאָבוּד, וְעַל הַגָּבוּי, וְעַל הֶעָתִיד לִגָּבוֹת״! [2]אֶלָּא אָמַר רַבִּי אֶלְעָזָר: שְׁבוּעָה זוֹ תַּקָּנַת חֲכָמִים הִיא, שֶׁלֹּא יְהוּ בְּנֵי אָדָם מְזַלְזְלִים בַּהֶקְדֵּשׁוֹת. [3]״נוֹשֵׂא שָׂכָר אֵינוֹ מְשַׁלֵּם״. [4]רָמֵי לֵיהּ רַב יוֹסֵף בַּר חָמָא לְרַבָּה: [5]תְּנַן: ״נוֹשֵׂא שָׂכָר אֵינוֹ

LITERAL TRANSLATION

[1]"Allocation is made for what was lost, and for what was collected, and for what is yet to be collected"! [2]Rather, Rabbi Elazar said: This oath was a decree of the Sages, so that people should not treat consecrated property lightly. [3]"A paid bailee does not pay [for them]." [4]Rav Yosef bar Ḥama pointed out a contradiction to Rabbah: We have learned: "A paid bailee does not

TRANSLATION AND COMMENTARY

[1]"**Allocation** of *terumat halishkah* **is made for** money that **was lost, for** money **that was collected, and for** money that **is yet to be collected."** The function of *terumat halishkah* was to assure the participation of the entire nation in the communal sacrifices brought as part of the Temple service. Thus, when the Temple treasurers set aside *terumat halishkah*, they did so even on behalf of the people whose shekalim were stolen or lost after they were given to the Temple treasurers. Likewise, they set it aside on behalf of people whose shekalim were already collected and are now on the way to Jerusalem, even if they are subsequently lost. Moreover, they even set it aside on behalf of people who have not yet contributed their shekalim, but will do so in the future. All these people are considered as having a part in the communal sacrifices purchased with *terumat halishkah*. Since *terumat halishkah* is set aside on behalf of the shekalim that have already been collected, even if they are subsequently lost, it follows that the townspeople who sent their shekalim by messenger are no longer responsible for them after *terumat halishkah* has been set aside. Why then must the messengers take the bailee's oath if the shekalim were lost after *terumat halishkah* was set aside, for even Rabbi Shimon admits that an oath need not be taken for consecrated property for which one is not responsible? Thus we see that Rabbi Yoḥanan's solution to the contradiction between our Mishnah and the Mishnah in *Shekalim* cannot be correct.

אֶלָּא אָמַר רַבִּי אֶלְעָזָר [2]**Rather,** the solution to the contradiction lies in what **Rabbi Elazar** said: **The oath** demanded of the messenger by the Mishnah in *Shekalim* **was** instituted as **a Rabbinic decree, so that people should not treat consecrated property lightly.** The contradiction between the two Mishnayot can thus be resolved as follows: Our Mishnah deals only with the bailee's oath required by Torah law, and by Torah law an unpaid bailee is indeed exempt from taking this oath when the deposit is consecrated property. However, the Rabbis decreed that an unpaid bailee must swear even about the loss of consecrated property, to ensure that bailees take proper care of consecrated property entrusted to them.

נוֹשֵׂא שָׂכָר אֵינוֹ מְשַׁלֵּם [3]The Gemara now considers the next clause of our Mishnah, which states: "Although he is liable for the loss or theft of property entrusted to him, **a paid bailee does not pay** for the loss or theft of land, slaves, promissory notes or consecrated property." [4]**Rav Yosef bar Ḥama pointed out to Rabbah a contradiction** between two Tannaitic rulings: On the one hand, [5]**we have learned** in our Mishnah: **"A paid bailee does not**

RASHI

תורמין על האבוד — כשהיו ממלאים שלש קופות מכסף הלשכה והיא תרומה ליקח מכסף הקופות כל קרבנות צבור, ותורמין אותן על מנת שיהו שלש קופות ראש, ותרומה לשיריים, שיהו אותן שהביאו שקלים הנשארים בלשכה זוכים בתרומת הקופה להיות הקרבנות גם עליהם. ותורמין אותן אף על פי ששלח שקלו ואבד לו ואין ידוע לו. **ועל הגבוי** — ועודנו בדרך. **ועל העתיד לגבות** — מי שנאנס ולא שלח שקלו באדר היה משלחו כל השנה כולה, ונותנין בשופר שכתוב עליו תקלין חדתין. והלשכה היתה נתרמה שלש פעמים בשנה; בפרוס הפסח ובפרוס עצרת, ובפרוס החג, וכשמגיע זמן לתרום נותנין מעות השופר בלשכה, ותורמין. וכשתורמין תרומה ראשונה מתנין אף על העתיד לגבות, וגם בשניה ובשלישית. והמביא אחר שנתרמה השלישית נותנו לשופר ששמו תיקלין עתיקין, ונופל לשירי הלשכה ומהן באין חומת העיר ומגדלותיה. **אלא אמר רבי אלעזר** — לעולם שבועה זו ליפטר מן התשלומין היא, ובשומר חנם. ודקשיא לך מתניתין דאורייתא פטור לגמרי ורבנן הוא דתקון לה שלא יזלזלו בהקדשות בשמירתן.

SAGES

רַב יוֹסֵף בַּר חָמָא **Rav Yosef bar Ḥama.** A third-generation Babylonian Amora, Rav Yosef bar Ḥama lived in Meḥoza, and was apparently the leading Sage of that city. He studied with Rav Sheshet and Rav Naḥman, and engaged in Halakhic discussions with Rabbah and Rabbi Zera. Rav Yosef's son, Rava (generally referred to without a patronymic), was one of the leading Amoraim of the next generation.

NOTES

תּוֹרְמִין עַל הָאָבוּד **Allocation is made for what was lost....** The commentators disagree as to the circumstances referred to by the Baraita. *Rashi* maintains that the Baraita speaks of a case in which the money was lost before the messengers arrived at the Temple. *Tosafot*, however, explains that the money was lost after the Temple treasurers received it. These commentators also seem to disagree about what is meant by money "that is yet to be collected." According to *Tosafot*, the Baraita refers to money which will eventually reach the Temple, whereas *Rashi* seems to be of the opinion that even money that never reaches the Temple is included. Some authorities explain that, according to *Rashi*, the donor does not fulfill his obligation to the Temple unless he replaces the lost shekalim; however, the Baraita means that the donor has a share in the communal sacrifices even if his money never reached the Temple.

BACKGROUND

שְׂכִיר שַׁבָּת, שְׂכִיר חֹדֶשׁ Hired by the week, hired by the month. Some authorities ask why the Gemara had to mention cases in which a person was hired for more than a week. If someone hired for a week may collect pay for the Sabbath, this should certainly be permitted if he was hired for a longer period! *Magen Gibborim* answers that the Baraita teaches us that no matter how long the period of hire, the worker may only collect Sabbath pay if the employer explicitly stated that he was being paid for the entire period of employment. However, if the employer stated that he was paying the worker on a daily basis, the employee may not collect Sabbath pay, even if he was hired for a very long period of time.

TRANSLATION AND COMMENTARY

pay if consecrated property entrusted to his care was lost or stolen." [1]But **the following contradiction** can be raised against our Mishnah from a Baraita, which states: **"If** the Temple treasurer **hires a worker** on a daily basis **to guard the Red Heifer** so that it is not disqualified for ritual use — the ashes of the Red Heifer were mixed with water and employed to purify people who had become ritually impure through contact with a corpse — or **to guard the children** who drew the water used in the Red Heifer purification ceremony — these children had to be protected from exposure to ritual impurity — **or to guard the seeds** of barley from which the omer-offering was brought (see above, 56b), **he does not give** the worker **wages for the Sabbath,** since it is ordinarily prohibited to pay an employee for work done on the Sabbath even if this "work" does not entail violation of the Sabbath laws. [2]**Therefore** the worker hired to guard the Red Heifer, the children, or the seeds **is not liable for** damage to them which occurred on **the Sabbath,** since he is not paid to guard them on that day. [3]But **if** the worker **was hired** to guard the Red Heifer, the children, or the seeds **by the week, by the month, by the year, or by the septennial period** (the seven years from one Sabbatical year to the next), **he receives wages for** the Sabbath. It is only forbidden to pay for services rendered on the Sabbath if the employer explicitly designated the wages as payment for Sabbath work, but not if the payment was part of a salary paid for a longer period of time — for example, a week, a month, etc. [4]**Therefore** the worker is **liable for** damage to what was entrusted to him, if the damage occurred on **the Sabbath."** The Gemara now explains how this Baraita contradicts our Mishnah: The Baraita refers to a worker hired to guard the Red Heifer and the barley seeds from which the omer-offering was to be brought, both of which are consecrated property. And the Baraita speaks of a case in which a paid bailee is "liable for damage that occurs on the Sabbath." [5]**Does not** the imposition of liability stated in this Baraita mean that the paid bailee **must pay** the Temple treasury if the consecrated property is lost or stolen? Thus it would appear that a paid bailee responsible for consecrated property *is* required to compensate the depositor, and this contradicts our Mishnah!

מְשַׁלֵּם". [1]וּרְמִינְהוּ: "הַשּׂוֹכֵר אֶת הַפּוֹעֵל לִשְׁמוֹר אֶת הַפָּרָה, לִשְׁמוֹר אֶת הַתִּינוֹק, לִשְׁמוֹר אֶת הַזְּרָעִים, אֵין נוֹתְנִים לוֹ שְׂכַר שַׁבָּת. [2]לְפִיכָךְ אֵין אַחֲרָיוּת שַׁבָּת עָלָיו. [3]הָיָה שְׂכִיר שַׁבָּת, שְׂכִיר חֹדֶשׁ, שְׂכִיר שָׁנָה, שְׂכִיר שָׁבוּעַ, נוֹתְנִין לוֹ שְׂכַר שַׁבָּת. [4]לְפִיכָךְ אַחֲרָיוּת שַׁבָּת עָלָיו". [5]מַאי לָאו לְשַׁלֵּם?!

LITERAL TRANSLATION

pay [for them]." [1]But [the following] contradiction can be raised: "Someone who hires a worker to guard the [Red] Heifer, to guard the child, [or] to guard the seeds, one does not give him wages for the Sabbath. [2]Therefore the responsibility for the Sabbath is not upon him. [3]If he was hired by the week, hired by the month, hired by the year, hired by the septennial period, one gives him wages for the Sabbath. [4]Therefore, the responsibility for the Sabbath is upon him." [5]Is it not to pay?!

RASHI

השוכר את הפועלים — גזבר של הקדש ששכר פועלים משל הקדש. **לשמור את הפרה** — אדומה, שלקחוה ושומרין אותה שלא תיפסל בעליית עול, או במום. **לשמור את התינוקות** — שלא יטמאו. שהיו מגדלין אותן לפרה בחצירות הבנויות בסלעים, ותחתיהן חלל, כדאמרינן בסוכה ב"הישן תחת המטה" (כא,א). לפי שעשו מעלה בכהן השורף את הפרה שתהא פרישתו בטהרה, ואין אחיו הכהנים נוגעין בו כל שבעה, כדאמרינן בסדר יומא (ח,ב), והתינוקות הללו שלא נטמאו מעולם ממלאים מים למקדשין, ומזין עליו כל שבעה. **ולשמור הזרעים** — שדה המנכרת וזרועה לעומר קודם לפסח שבעים יום, כדאמרינן במנחות (פה,א). אי נמי בשביעית, ספיחים לעומר ושתי הלחם. **אין נותנין לו שכר שבת** — אם שכיר יום הוא. **לפיכך אין אחריות שבת עליו** — אם אירע בהן קלקול בשבת, אין חייב לשלם. **שכיר שבת** — שבוע. **שכיר שבוע** — שמיטה שלימה. **נותנין לו שכר שבת** — שנבלע בשכר שאר הימים, ואינו מפורש לשבת.

NOTES

הַשּׂוֹכֵר אֶת הַפּוֹעֵל Someone who hires a worker. *Rashi*, followed by our commentary, explains that the worker was charged with guarding sacred property. Thus the Gemara asks why a bailee reponsible for such items is liable if they are damaged. However, *Rabbenu Ḥananel* and most other commentators (*Ramban*, *Rashba*, *Rosh* and others) maintain that the "heifer, child, etc." were not sacred property. Rather, the Gemara's objection was based on the case of "guarding seeds." Since the seeds were presumably planted, they are considered part of the ground, and the bailee should not be liable for land entrusted to his care.

HALAKHAH

שְׁמִירָה בְּשַׁבָּת Guarding property on the Sabbath. "A person who is paid on a daily basis to guard someone else's property is not paid for the Sabbath. Hence he is not liable for losses that occur then. However, if the guard is paid on a weekly (monthly, yearly, etc.) basis, he may collect wages for services rendered on the Sabbath (since these wages are included in the total payment), and hence he is liable for losses that occur on the Sabbath. In such cases the employer should not explicitly state that he is paying the guard for the Sabbath. He should include the Sabbath wages in the total payment without any explicit declaration." (*Shulḥan Arukh*, *Oraḥ Ḥayyim* 306:4.)

TRANSLATION AND COMMENTARY

לא לְהַפְסִיד שְׂכָרוֹ [1]Rabbah answers: **No.** The liability mentioned in this Baraita refers to the bailee's **loss of his wages.** If the bailee does not take proper care of the property entrusted to his care, he loses his wages, since he did not discharge his duty. There is, however, no suggestion in the Baraita that the bailee should be held liable to compensate the Temple treasury for damage caused to what was entrusted to him.

אִי הָכִי [2]Rav Yosef bar Ḥama objects: **If so,** if the term "liability" used in the Baraita is understood as being limited to the forfeiture of wages, then **in the first clause** of the Baraita, **which states** that the worker **"is not liable for the Sabbath"** if he is paid on a daily basis, **here too** "liable" should refer to **losing one's wages!** If "liability" in the last clause of the Baraita refers to loss of wages, the same should also apply to the first clause. This clause would then mean that a worker paid on a daily basis — who is not "liable" — does not lose his wages for the Sabbath. [3]Rav Yosef bar Ḥama argues that such an interpretation is impossible: If the worker is paid on a daily basis, **does he** ever **receive wages for the Sabbath**? [4]Surely the first clause of the Baraita specifically **states:** "Such a worker **is *not* given wages for the Sabbath"!** Accordingly, the "liability" mentioned in the Baraita cannot refer to loss of wages, but must refer to liability for loss or theft of the deposit! Therefore the contradiction between the Baraita, according to which a paid bailee of consecrated property is liable for loss or theft, and our Mishnah, according to which the paid bailee is free from liability in such a case, still stands.

אִשְׁתִּיק [5]Unable to answer Rav Yosef bar Ḥama's objection, Rabbah **was silent.** Later he **said to** Rav Yosef bar Ḥama: **Did you hear anything about this** that might resolve the contradiction between our Mishnah and the Baraita?

אֲמַר לֵיהּ [6]Rav Yosef bar Ḥama **said to** Rabbah: **Rav Sheshet said as follows:** The Baraita does indeed refer to ity for loss or theft of the deposit, and not to losing one's wages. Ordinarily, the bailee is free from such liability when the deposit is consecrated property, as stated in our Mishnah. In the case of the Baraita, however, he *is* liable for the loss or theft of the consecrated property, because the Baraita is referring to a case **where** the bailee formally **obligated himself** to pay for such a loss. A person can take upon himself responsibilities from which he would otherwise be free by means of *kinyan sudar* — the symbolic transfer of a kerchief. The Baraita is referring to a case in which a paid bailee of consecrated property assumed responsibilities from which he would otherwise have been exempt.

[1]לֹא. לְהַפְסִיד שְׂכָרוֹ.

[2]אִי הָכִי, רֵישָׁא דְּקָתָנֵי: "אֵין אַחֲרָיוּת שַׁבָּת עָלָיו" הָכִי נַמִי דִּלְהַפְסִיד שְׂכָרוֹ? [3]וּמִי אִית לֵיהּ שְׂכַר שַׁבָּת? [4]וְהָא קָתָנֵי: "אֵין נוֹתְנִין לוֹ שְׂכַר שַׁבָּת"!

[5]אִשְׁתִּיק. אֲמַר לֵיהּ: מִידֵי שְׁמִיעַ לָךְ בְּהָא?

[6]אֲמַר לֵיהּ: הָכִי אָמַר רַב שֵׁשֶׁת: בְּשֶׁקְּנוּ מִיָּדוֹ.

LITERAL TRANSLATION

[1]No. [It is] to lose his wages.

[2]If so, [does] the first clause, which states: "The responsibility for the Sabbath is not upon him" [mean] here, too, to lose his wages? [3]But does he have wages for the Sabbath? [4]Surely it states: "One does not give him wages for the Sabbath"!

[5]He was silent. He said to him: Did you hear anything about this?

[6]He said to him: Thus said Rav Sheshet: Where he acquired from his hand.

RASHI

בשקנו מידו – שאם יקלקל שמירתו, ישלם, הא ודאי שלם, שהרי הוריד עצמו לכך ושיעבד נכסיו.

TERMINOLOGY

אִשְׁתִּיק **He was silent.** Sometimes a scholar is "silent" in the face of an objection raised against his viewpoint, either because he does not have a satisfactory answer or because he thinks the answer is so obvious that there is no need to reply.

NOTES

בְּשֶׁקְּנוּ מִיָּדוֹ **Where he acquired from his hand.** According to the Halakhah, a person may obligate himself by symbolically transferring an object (usually a handkerchief) to another party. Thus the obligation referred to here is a form of *kinyan sudar*. This procedure, known as "acquiring from one's hand," proves that a person sincerely intends to carry out his promise.

The commentators ask, however, why the bailee must perform a *kinyan sudar* to render himself liable for the loss or theft of sacred property, since a bailee can ordinarily obligate himself without performing any formal procedure, simply by agreeing to undertake special liability (see *Bava Metzia* 94a). Indeed, *Ritva* is of the opinion that there is no need to perform *kinyan sudar*. According to his view, the

HALAKHAH

הֶפְסֵד שְׂכַר שׁוֹמֵר **When does a paid bailee lose his wages?** The laws laid down in the Torah regarding bailees do not apply for land, slaves or promissory notes. Thus a paid bailee is not responsible if these items were lost or stolen. He only receives pay for his services, however, if he takes an oath affirming that he cared properly for the deposit." (Ibid., *Ḥoshen Mishpat* 301:1.)

SAGES

רַבִּי יִצְחָק בַּר אַבָּא Rabbi Yitzḥak bar Abba. Rabbi Yitzḥak bar Abba was a fourth-generation Amora from Eretz Israel. He is cited together with Rabbi Zera, and apparently left Eretz Israel for Babylonia, where he eventually settled.

TRANSLATION AND COMMENTARY

וְכֵן אֲמַר [1]**And similarly Rabbi Yoḥanan said:** The Baraita is referring to a case **where** the bailee formally **obligated himself** to pay for loss or theft of the consecrated property entrusted to his care, even though he would ordinarily be exempt in such a case.

רַבִּי שִׁמְעוֹן אוֹמֵר [2]The Gemara now proceeds to comment on the next clause of our Mishnah, which states: **"Rabbi Shimon says: Sacrifices for which** a person **is responsible** (to replace them should they be lost or harmed, as explained in the commentary on the Mishnah, above, 56b) are **subject to** the laws of ***ona'ah***, [3]**but sacrifices for which** a person **is not responsible are not subject to** the laws of ***ona'ah***." [4]**A Tanna** (a reciter of Baraitot) **taught** a Baraita **before Rabbi Yitzḥak bar Abba** which dealt with the guilt-offering made by a bailee who confesses to having lied under oath when he claimed that the deposit was not in his possession (see Leviticus 3:21ff.). The question arose as to whether the guilt-offering is required of a bailee who falsely denies having consecrated property in his possession. [5]The Baraita dealt with the issue as follows: **"Concerning sacrifices for which the owner is responsible** and which were entrusted to a bailee, **if the bailee** falsely denies under oath that he received a sacrificial animal into his care and later admits his guilt, **he is liable** to bring a guilt-offering. [6]**For I apply** to him the verse in the Torah concerning a person who sins in connection with such items (Leviticus 5:21): 'If a soul sins and commits a trespass **against the Lord, and lies** to his neighbor ... he shall bring a guilt-offering.' In order to be liable, the guilty person must commit a trespass 'against the Lord.' If a bailee falsely denies receiving into his care a sacrifice for which the owner is responsible, such a denial is considered an offense 'against the Lord,' since the sacrifice belongs to God, rather than to the person who consecrated it, and therefore the bailee is liable for the guilt-offering. [7]**But concerning consecrated property for which** the owner **is not responsible, the bailee is exempt** from bringing a guilt-offering, [8]**for I apply** to him the same verse in the Torah concerning a person who sins in connection with such items, but with the order of words reversed: 'If a soul sins and commits a trespass **against his neighbor, and lies.'"** Such an offense is not considered an offense "against the Lord" but only "against his neighbor," for the consecrated property in this case belongs to the person who consecrated it, and therefore the bailee is exempt from bringing a guilt-offering.

[1]וְכֵן אֲמַר רַבִּי יוֹחָנָן: בְּשֶׁקָּנוּ מִיָּדוֹ.

[2]"רַבִּי שִׁמְעוֹן אוֹמֵר: קָדָשִׁים שֶׁחַיָּיב בְּאַחֲרָיוּתָן, יֵשׁ לָהֶן אוֹנָאָה. [3]וְשֶׁאֵינוֹ חַיָּיב בְּאַחֲרָיוּתָן, אֵין לָהֶן אוֹנָאָה".

[4]תָּנֵי תַּנָּא קַמֵּיהּ דְּרַבִּי יִצְחָק בַּר אַבָּא: [5]"קָדָשִׁים שֶׁחַיָּיב בְּאַחֲרָיוּתָן, חַיָּיב, [6]שֶׁאֲנִי קוֹרֵא בָּהֶן: 'בַּה' וְכִחֵשׁ'. [7]וְשֶׁאֵינוֹ חַיָּיב בְּאַחֲרָיוּתָן, פָּטוּר, [8]שֶׁאֲנִי קוֹרֵא בָּהֶן: 'בַּעֲמִיתוֹ וְכִחֵשׁ'".

LITERAL TRANSLATION

[1]And so did Rabbi Yoḥanan say: Where he acquired from his hand.

[2]"Rabbi Shimon says: [Concerning] sacrifices for which he is responsible, there is *ona'ah* for them. [3]But [concerning sacrifices] for which he is not responsible, there is no *ona'ah* for them."

[4]A Tanna taught before Rabbi Yitzḥak bar Abba: [5]"[Concerning] sacrifices for which he [the owner] is responsible, he [the bailee] is liable, [6]for I read concerning them: 'Against the Lord, and he lies.' [7]But [concerning sacrifices] for which he [the owner] is not responsible, he [the bailee] is exempt, [8]for I read concerning them: 'Against his neighbor, and he lies.'"

RASHI

תני תנא – לענין שבועת הפקדון אשם גזילות. **קדשים שהבעלים חייבין באחריותן** – כגון דאמר "הרי עלי" והפרישן והפקידן לזה, וכפר ונשבע והודה, חייב קרבן שבועה. **שאני קורא בהן בה' וכחש** – קא סלקא דעתך טעם דחיובא משום דהן של גבוה קרינן בהו "ומעלה מעל בה' וכחש". **ושאינן חייבין הבעלים באחריותן פטור** – הנשבע, שאני קורא בהן "בעמיתו וכחש" מפני שהם קרוין של עמיתו, ודעמיתו פטור, דבעינן "בה'".

NOTES

Gemara spoke of performing a symbolic act of acquisition because this is how people usually obligate themselves.

Rosh, however, explains that a verbal declaration only creates a binding obligation if the bailee agrees to guard a lay person's property. In such cases, a bailee renders himself liable through words alone, in exchange for the satisfaction and honor he receives from having the depositor entrust his property to him. However, since all people are trusted to guard Temple property, a bailee with whom such property has been deposited derives no special satisfaction. Hence, mere verbal declaration without an accompanying *kinyan sudar* cannot create a binding obligation on a bailee guarding Temple property.

HALAKHAH

שֶׁקָּנוּ מִיָּדוֹ Where he acquired from his hand. "If a bailee formally obligates himself to guard the deposit more carefully than is required by Torah law, he is bound by the agreement as stipulated." (*Shulḥan Arukh, Ḥoshen Mishpat* 301:4.)

[1]אֲמַר לֵיהּ: כְּלַפֵּי לַיָּיא?! [58B] [2]אִיפְּכָא מִסְתַּבְּרָא!
[3]אֲמַר לֵיהּ: אִיסְמֵיהּ?
[4]אֲמַר לֵיהּ: לָא. [5]הָכִי קָאָמַר: ״קָדָשִׁים שֶׁחַיָּיב בְּאַחֲרָיוּתָן, חַיָּיב, דְּאִיתְרַבּוּ מִ׳בַּה׳ וְכִחֵשׁ׳. [6]וְשֶׁאֵינוֹ חַיָּיב בְּאַחֲרָיוּתָן, פָּטוּר, דְּאִמְעִיט מִ׳בַּעֲמִיתוֹ וְכִחֵשׁ׳״.
[7]״רַבִּי יְהוּדָה אוֹמֵר: אַף הַמּוֹכֵר סֵפֶר תּוֹרָה, מַרְגָּלִית, וּבְהֵמָה, אֵין לָהֶם אוֹנָאָה״.

TRANSLATION AND COMMENTARY

אֲמַר לֵיהּ [1]This interpretation of the verse is problematic: Rabbi Yitzḥak **said to** the Tanna who recited the Baraita: **Just the opposite!** [58B] [2]Exactly **the opposite** is more reasonable! Consecrated property for which the donor remains responsible — where, for example, the donor pledged an animal as a sacrifice in the Temple — is regarded as remaining the donor's property until it is actually given to the Temple, and when the verse speaks of "one's neighbor's" property it is referring to property of this kind. Consecrated property for which the donor is not responsible — for example, if the donor pledged a specific animal as a sacrifice in the Temple — is regarded as the property of the Temple as soon as it is pledged, and when the verse speaks of "the Lord's" property it is referring to property of this kind. The Baraita's citation of the term "the Lord's" as referring to "consecrated property for which the owner is responsible" and the term "his neighbor's" as referring to "consecrated property for which the owner is not responsible" is inconsistent with this reasoning.

אֲמַר לֵיהּ אִיסְמֵיהּ [3]The Tanna **said to** Rabbi Yitzḥak bar Abba: **Shall I delete** this Baraita because it is incorrect, as you have demonstrated?

אֲמַר לֵיהּ לָא [4]Rabbi Yitzḥak bar Abba **said to him: No;** the Baraita should be understood in a different manner, according to which the bailee is liable for a guilt-offering if he falsely denied under oath that he had been entrusted with consecrated property for which the owner is responsible — not because such property is treated as "the Lord's," but *in spite* of the fact that it is so considered. [5]And the Baraita can be explained **as follows:** "In the case of **consecrated property for which** the owner **is responsible, the bailee is liable** to offer a guilt-offering, **as** such property **is included by** the expression **"against the Lord, and he lies."** One might have thought that even if the bailee denies receiving consecrated property for which the owner is responsible, he should be exempt from bringing a guilt-offering because he denied being entrusted with property which does not belong to "his neighbor." Therefore the verse teaches that even if the bailee denies under oath that he received such property, and thereby sins "against the Lord," he is nevertheless liable because the owner is liable for it. [6]**But** in the case of **consecrated property for which** the owner **is not responsible,** the bailee **is exempt, since** such items **are excluded by** the expression **"against his neighbor, and he lies."** The guilt-offering is only brought for offenses committed "against one's neighbor," whereas here the property did not belong to "one's neighbor," but to the Lord.

רַבִּי יְהוּדָה אוֹמֵר [7]The Gemara now proceeds to elucidate the final clause in the Mishnah, which stated: **"Rabbi Yehudah says: Even in the case of someone who sells a Torah scroll, an animal or a pearl, the laws of** *ona'ah* **do not apply."**

LITERAL TRANSLATION

[1]He said to him: Just the opposite (lit., "towards where are you facing?")! [58B] [2]The opposite is more reasonable!

[3]He said to him: Shall I delete it?

[4]He said to him: [5]No. It says thus: "[Concerning] sacrifices for which he [the owner] is responsible, he [the bailee] is liable, for they are included by 'Against the Lord, and lies.' [6]But [concerning sacrifices] for which he [the owner] is not responsible, he [the bailee] is exempt, for they are excluded by 'Against his neighbor, and he lies.'"

[7]"Rabbi Yehudah says: Even [in the case of] someone who sells a Torah scroll, a pearl or an animal, there is no *ona'ah* for them."

RASHI

כלפי לייא — כלפי היכן הדבר נוטה. לייא = היכא, כגון (ברכות נח,א): חלבי לנהרא כגני לייא. **איפכא מסתברא** — כל הדברים נראין הפך, דשאינו חייב באחריותן דה׳ נינהו טפי משחייב באחריותן. ואם באת לחייבו בשל גבוה ולפוטרו בשל הדיוט, כן היה לו לומר: קדשים שחייב באחריותן פטור, שאני קורא בהן ״בעמיתו וכחש״, שאינו חייב באחריותן חייב שאני קורא בהן ״בה׳ וכחש״. ועוד: דהדיוט הוה ליה לחיובי טפי, דהא שומרי הקדשות פטורין מן השבועה ומכל הבא על ידה. **איסמייה** — אסיר משנה זו מגירסתי. **הכי קאמר כו׳** — האי שאני קורא בהן ״בה׳ וכחש״. לא משמע בה׳ וכחש ולא בעמיתו, ולחיוביה משום שהן של הקדש. אלא הכי קאמר: קדשים שחייב באחריותן — חייב קרבן שבועה, לפי שהן של עמיתו. ואם באת לפוטרו לפי שהן של הקדש — להכי אתא ״בה׳ וכחש״ לרבויינהו, אף אם יש בהן לד גבוה. **ושאין חייב באחריותן פטור** — לפי שאני קורא בהן למעטן ״בעמיתו וכחש״ והכא ליכא עמיתו, ואימעט מ״בעמיתו וכחש״.

TERMINOLOGY

כְּלַפֵּי לַיָּיא Just the opposite! (Lit., "towards where are you facing?") This expression is used to show astonishment at a Halakhic ruling or interpretation which seems totally illogical: "Just the opposite" should be the case!

אִיפְּכָא מִסְתַּבְּרָא The opposite [of what was just stated] is more reasonable! An expression of astonishment concerning a statement, the opposite of which appears to be more reasonable.

אִיסְמֵיהּ "Shall I delete it?" The Mishnah and Baraita reciters, who knew numerous Baraitot by heart, did not always know whether these Baraitot were Halakhically reliable (or textually accurate). Therefore the Sages occasionally ordered them to "delete" such Baraitot (i.e., to refrain from citing them in the future).

LANGUAGE

אִיסְמֵיהּ "Shall I delete it?" This expression is derived from the root סמי, "to blind," from which it comes to mean "remove," or destroy."

BACKGROUND

בְּהֵמָה וּמַרְגָּלִית Animals, pearls, etc. Animals used for plowing were ordinarily paired, and when plowing animals matched each other perfectly, the quality and efficiency of their work were greatly enhanced. Hence people were willing, if necessary, to pay considerably more than the regular market price of an animal to find a perfect match for it. For the same reason, people were willing to pay substantially more than standard market prices to find perfect matches for the horses that drew their chariots. As for pearls and other precious stones, these were often strung together (or set in patterns) as jewelry, and jewelry made from perfectly matched stones was worth considerably more than that made from stones that did not match perfectly.

SAGES

רַבִּי יְהוּדָה בֶּן בְּתֵירָא Rabbi Yehudah ben Betera. The Bnei Betera family produced renowned Sages over a number of generations. Some members of the family served as Nasi during the time of Hillel, but transferred the position to him. The two most famous Sages of the family were Rabbis Yehudah and Yehoshua Bnei Betera.

It is almost certain that there were two Sages named Yehudah ben Betera. The second may have been the grandson of the first. Both lived in the city of Netzivin (Nisibis) in Babylonia — one while the Temple was still standing, and the second at the end of the Tannaitic period. The Yehudah ben Betera whose teaching is cited here is probably the second one. He was one of the greatest Torah scholars of his age, and organized the study of Torah throughout Babylonia before the great Yeshivot were establised. He was held in great veneration by the Sages of Eretz Israel.

BACKGROUND

סוּס בַּמִּלְחָמָה Horses in wartime. Horses were of critical importance in wartime, both to save individual lives and to help win the war, so potential buyers were willing to pay far more than the standard market price for a good horse.

LANGUAGE

חֲטִיטוֹם Helmets. This word is derived from the Greek καταῖτυξ, *kataitux*, meaning "leather helmet."

1 תַּנְיָא: ״רַבִּי יְהוּדָה אוֹמֵר: אַף הַמּוֹכֵר סֵפֶר תּוֹרָה, אֵין לָהּ אוֹנָאָה, 2 לְפִי שֶׁאֵין קֵץ לְדָמֶיהָ. 3 בְּהֵמָה וּמַרְגָּלִית, אֵין לָהֶם אוֹנָאָה, מִפְּנֵי שֶׁאָדָם רוֹצֶה לְזַוְּוגָן. 4 אָמְרוּ לוֹ: וַהֲלֹא הַכֹּל אָדָם רוֹצֶה לְזַוְּוגָן״!

5 וְרַבִּי יְהוּדָה?

6 הָנֵי חֲשִׁיבִי לֵיהּ, וְהָנֵי לָא חֲשִׁיבִי לֵיהּ.

7 וְעַד כַּמָּה?

8 אָמַר אַמֵימָר: עַד כְּדֵי דְמֵיהֶם.

9 תַּנְיָא: ״רַבִּי יְהוּדָה בֶּן בְּתֵירָא אוֹמֵר: אַף הַמּוֹכֵר סוּס, וְסַיִיף וַחֲטִיטוֹם בַּמִּלְחָמָה, אֵין לָהֶם

LITERAL TRANSLATION

1 It has been taught: "Rabbi Yehudah says: Even [in the case of] someone who sells a Torah scroll, there is no *ona'ah* for it, 2 because there is no limit to its value. 3 [Concerning] an animal and a pearl, there is no *ona'ah* for them because a man wishes to match them. 4 They said to him: But does not a man want to match everything?"

5 And Rabbi Yehudah?

6 These are important to him, and those are not important to him.

7 And up to how much?

8 Amemar said: Up to their value.

9 It has been taught: "Rabbi Yehudah ben Betera says: Even [in the case of] someone who sells a horse, or a sword, or a helmet in [time of] war, there is no

RASHI

לזווגן — מי שיש לו שור יפה לחרישה מחזר על אחר שכמותו לצמדו עמו בעול, שהמצמיד שור חלש עם הבריא מקלקל את הבריא. וכן מרגלית נאה (עם חבירתה) למלאות עם חבירתה בזהב מן היחידית. **חשיבי ליה** — וחביב לו זיווגן. **ועד כמה** — לא הוי אונאה. **כדי דמיהם** — כפליים. **חטיטום** = מגן. **במלחמה** — בתוך המלחמה.

TRANSLATION AND COMMENTARY

תַּנְיָא 1 The Gemara cites a Baraita which explains the reasoning behind Rabbi Yehudah's ruling: **It was taught** in a Baraita: **"Rabbi Yehudah says: Even in the case of someone who sells a Torah scroll, the laws of *ona'ah* do not apply to it 2 because there is no limit to its value.** Since the Torah is the word of God, it is priceless, and hence it is impossible to overcharge for a Torah scroll. 3 **An animal and a pearl are not subject to *ona'ah* because a person wishes to match them.** A person who already has a beast of burden may wish to buy another animal of the same size and strength, so that he can make efficient use of the pair for plowing (since it is difficult to plow with animals of different capacities). Likewise, a person who already has a pearl may wish to match it exactly, to prepare an attractive piece of jewelry. Hence people are willing to pay considerably more than the market value of the animal or pearl in order to secure the proper match, and do not begrudge paying the excessive price. Therefore, the ordinary laws of *ona'ah* do not apply in these cases. 4 The Sages questioned the second part of Rabbi Yehudah's ruling and **said to him: But do not people want to match** almost **everything!"** There is hardly anything that someone does not want to match with something else. Thus the laws of *ona'ah* should never apply, because it can always be claimed that the buyer was willing to pay more than the item's true value in order to get the right match! And since even Rabbi Yehudah agrees that ordinary merchandise is subject to the laws of *ona'ah*, animals and pearls should be treated no differently.

וְרַבִּי יְהוּדָה 5 The Baraita does not record Rabbi Yehudah's response to the Sages' objection, so the Gemara asks: **And** how would **Rabbi Yehudah** reply to the Sages' objection?

הָנֵי חֲשִׁיבִי לֵיהּ 6 The Gemara answers: **These** particular items — an animal and a pearl — **are** particularly **important** to the buyer to match, and hence he is willing to pay much more than their market value to ensure a perfect match. **But those** other items **are not** so **important to** a buyer to match, and a person is unwilling to spend extra money in order to obtain a perfect match. Therefore, according to Rabbi Yehudah, animals and pearls are excluded from the laws of *ona'ah*, but other merchandise is not.

וְעַד כַּמָּה 7 The Gemara continues to analyze Rabbi Yehudah's opinion: Granted that there are certain items — animals or pearls — for which a person is willing to pay more than their true value. **But up to how much** can the seller overcharge for these items? There must be some limit to the amount that a person would pay for them, and if the seller charges more than that amount, the laws of *ona'ah* should take effect!

אָמַר אַמֵימָר 8 **Amemar said** in reply: **Up to** double **their** market **value.** The seller is permitted to charge up to twice such an item's true value and the laws of *ona'ah* will still not apply. But if he charges more than double the value, the laws of *ona'ah* take effect.

תַּנְיָא 9 The Gemara ends its discussion of this Mishnah: The following **has been taught** in a Baraita: **"Rabbi Yehudah ben Betera said: Even in the case of someone who sells a horse, a sword or a helmet in time of war,**

NOTES

עַד כְּדֵי דְמֵיהֶם Up to their value. Thus the laws of *ona'ah* apply only if the seller charges more than double the price of pearls and animals. But since there is no limit to the value of a Torah scroll, it is impossible to overcharge for one (*Torat Ḥayyim*).

TRANSLATION AND COMMENTARY

the laws of ***ona'ah* do not apply to** such a transaction, [1]**because** during a war a person's very **life depends on these** items, and people are willing to pay considerably more than what they are really worth."

Thus Rabbi Yehudah ben Betera's opinion parallels Rabbi Yehudah's, as both Tannaim maintain that the laws of *ona'ah* do not apply if a buyer is willing to pay more than the ordinary market value of the merchandise.

LITERAL TRANSLATION

ona'ah for them, [1]because life depends on (lit., "is in") them."

MISHNAH [2]Just as there is *ona'ah* in buying and selling, so too there is *ona'ah* in words.

[3]One may not say to him [a merchant]: "How much is this object," if one does not wish to buy [it].

[4]If [someone] was a repentant [sinner], one may not say to him: "Remember your earlier deeds." [5]If he is the son of converts, one may not say to him: "Remember the deeds of your fathers," [6]for it is said: "You shall not wrong a stranger, nor shall you oppress him."

אוֹנָאָה, [1]מִפְּנֵי שֶׁיֵּשׁ בָּהֶן חַיֵּי נֶפֶשׁ".

משנה [2]כְּשֵׁם שֶׁאוֹנָאָה בְּמִקָּח וּמִמְכָּר, כָּךְ אוֹנָאָה בִּדְבָרִים.

[3]לֹא יֹאמַר לוֹ: "בְּכַמָּה חֵפֶץ זֶה"? וְהוּא אֵינוֹ רוֹצֶה לִיקַּח. [4]אִם הָיָה בַּעַל תְּשׁוּבָה לֹא יֹאמַר לוֹ: "זְכוֹר מַעֲשֶׂיךָ הָרִאשׁוֹנִים". [5]אִם הוּא בֶּן גֵּרִים לֹא יֹאמַר לוֹ: "זְכוֹר מַעֲשֵׂה אֲבוֹתֶיךָ", [6]שֶׁנֶּאֱמַר: "וְגֵר לֹא תוֹנֶה וְלֹא תִלְחָצֶנּוּ".

MISHNAH כְּשֵׁם שֶׁאוֹנָאָה בְּמִקָּח [2]Having completed its discussion of the laws of fraud, the Mishnah now turns to laws governing human relationships. The connection between these two topics is the Hebrew word *ona'ah* (אוֹנָאָה), which means not only fraud or overreaching but also the causing of anguish to others. The Mishnah declares: **Just as there is** a law prohibiting *ona'ah* — fraud **in buying and selling — so too there is** a law prohibiting verbal *ona'ah* (אוֹנָאַת דְּבָרִים), in which anguish is caused to other people by hurting their feelings.

לֹא יֹאמַר לוֹ [3]The Mishnah now shows how words may cause pain. The first example is related to the previous topic — buying and selling: A customer **may not say to a merchant:** "How **much is this** article" **if he does not** in fact **wish to buy it,** as this arouses false hopes in the seller, who will be upset if the questioner does not purchase the item.

אִם הָיָה בַּעַל תְּשׁוּבָה [4]The Mishnah now considers examples totally unrelated to the previous discussion: **If someone is a repentant sinner,** other people **must not** remind him of his past by **saying to him: "Remember your earlier deeds."** [5]Likewise, **if** someone is **the son of converts,** other people **must not** remind him of his origins by **saying to him: "Remember the deeds of your fathers."** In fact, there is a special prohibition against causing anguish to converts, [6]**for the verse** (Exodus 22:20) **says: "You shall not wrong** (*tonu*, from the same Hebrew root as *ona'ah)* **a stranger** (i.e., a convert) **nor shall you oppress him."**

NOTES

שֶׁיֵּשׁ בָּהֶן חַיֵּי נֶפֶשׁ Because life depends on them. It is not clear whether Rabbi Yehudah ben Betera's view is accepted or not. On the one hand, no one disputes this opinion, so it would appear that it should be accepted. On the other hand, the Gemara implies elsewhere (see, for example, *Yevamot* 106a and the commentators there) that a person who overcharges for objects or services necessary for survival is only entitled to the true value of the object or service he provided. Following this reasoning, it would appear that the prohibition against *ona'ah* should apply to military implements in wartime, contrary to the viewpoint of Rabbi Yehudah ben Betera (*Remakh*).

אוֹנָאַת דְּבָרִים Verbal *ona'ah*. Verbal *ona'ah* means insulting others, hurting their feelings, or putting them to shame (compare, for example, Isaiah 49:26, "I shall feed them that oppress you with their own flesh," where the same Hebrew root is used). *Meiri* suggests that two types of transgression are subsumed under the category of verbal *ona'ah*: (1) Causing a person financial loss through one's words, and (2) putting another person to shame. Indeed, both types of offense are discussed in the Mishnah. In the first case, the seller thinks the buyer did not buy the merchandise because he felt it was overpriced (and not because he did not want to buy it in the first place); hence the seller is likely to cut prices. Thus, the buyer's conduct is liable to cause the seller an unnecessary financial loss. And the next two cases in the Mishnah (where one reminds a penitent or descendant of proselytes of their origins) constitute verbal *ona'ah* because they involve putting others to shame.

כְּשֵׁם שֶׁאוֹנָאָה בְּמִקָּח Just as there is *ona'ah* in buying and selling, so too there is *ona'ah* in words. *Baḥ* explains that the Mishnah had to teach us that verbal *ona'ah* is prohibited, because we might not otherwise have inferred this from the Biblical text, which ostensibly refers to financial fraud and not to verbal wrongdoing.

לֹא יֹאמַר לוֹ בְּכַמָּה חֵפֶץ One may not say: "How much is this object?" This is forbidden because it causes the seller distress, since he mistakenly thinks that he will be able to conclude the sale. Moreover, such behavior may even cause the seller financial loss (see *Rashbam*, *Pesaḥim* 112b).

LANGUAGE

אוֹנָאָה Fraud, wrongdoing, overreaching. This word, generally translated "fraud" (i.e., overcharging and underpaying, financial dishonesty), is derived from the root ינה or אנה, whose basic meaning in Biblical Hebrew is "to cause distress." The primary meaning of this root also plays a part in Mishnaic Hebrew, as we see from our Mishnah where we read: "Just as there is *ona'ah* in buying and selling, so too there is *ona'ah* (i.e., causing distress, or hurting other people's feelings) in words."

BACKGROUND

אוֹנָאַת דְּבָרִים Verbal *ona'ah*. As the Mishnah indicates, verbal *ona'ah* includes a wide variety of activities, from intentionally disappointing others (by pretending that one wants to buy something when one in fact does not), to insulting them outright. Verbal *ona'ah* of this sort is not grounds for lawsuits to be adjudicated in court, although it is considered an extremely grave offense which is punishable at the hands of Heaven.

אִם הָיָה בַּעַל תְּשׁוּבָה If someone was a repentant sinner.... If a person sincerely and completely repents for his misdeeds, they are forgiven, and he must thereafter be treated as a righteous man. Hence, it is considered a gratuitous insult to remind a penitent of his past.

גמרא [1]תָּנוּ רַבָּנַן: ״׳לֹא תוֹנוּ אִישׁ אֶת עֲמִיתוֹ׳. בְּאוֹנָאַת דְּבָרִים הַכָּתוּב מְדַבֵּר. [2]אַתָּה אוֹמֵר בְּאוֹנָאַת דְּבָרִים, אוֹ אֵינוֹ אֶלָּא בְּאוֹנָאַת מָמוֹן? [3]כְּשֶׁהוּא אוֹמֵר: ׳וְכִי תִמְכְּרוּ מִמְכָּר לַעֲמִיתֶךָ, אוֹ קָנֹה מִיַּד עֲמִיתֶךָ׳, [4]הֲרֵי אוֹנָאַת מָמוֹן אָמוּר. [5]הָא מָה אֲנִי מְקַיֵּים ״לֹא תוֹנוּ אִישׁ אֶת עֲמִיתוֹ״? בְּאוֹנָאַת דְּבָרִים. [6]הָא כֵּיצַד? [7]אִם הָיָה בַּעַל תְּשׁוּבָה אַל יֹאמַר לוֹ: ׳זְכוֹר מַעֲשֶׂיךָ הָרִאשׁוֹנִים׳. [8]אִם הָיָה בֶּן גֵּרִים אַל יֹאמַר לוֹ: ׳זְכוֹר מַעֲשֵׂה אֲבוֹתֶיךָ׳. [9]אִם הָיָה גֵּר וּבָא לִלְמוֹד תּוֹרָה, אַל יֹאמַר לוֹ: [10]׳פֶּה שֶׁאָכַל נְבֵילוֹת וּטְרֵיפוֹת,

LITERAL TRANSLATION

GEMARA [1]Our Rabbis taught: "'You shall not wrong one another.' [2]The verse is speaking of verbal *ona'ah*. You say [it refers] to verbal *ona'ah*, but might it not be [referring] to monetary *ona'ah*? [3]When [the verse] says: 'And if you sell something to your neighbor, or buy something from your neighbor's hand,' [4]the case of monetary *ona'ah* has been stated. [5]How then do I interpret (lit., 'establish') 'You shall not wrong one another'? [It refers] to verbal *ona'ah*. [6]How so? [7]If [someone] was a repentant [sinner], one may not say to him: 'Remember your earlier deeds.' [8]If he was the son of converts, one may not say to him: 'Remember the deeds of your fathers.' [9]If he was a convert and he came to study Torah, one may not say to him: [10]'Shall the mouth that has eaten carrion and forbidden (literally, 'torn') animals,

TRANSLATION AND COMMENTARY

GEMARA תָּנוּ רַבָּנַן [1]**The Rabbis taught** the following Baraita, which discusses a verse in Leviticus (25:17): "The verse says: **'You shall not wrong** (*tonu*, from the same Hebrew root as *ona'ah*) **one another,** but you shall fear your God, for I am the Lord your God.' **The verse is speaking of verbal *ona'ah*.** It is prohibiting the use of words that cause other people anguish." [2]The Baraita defends its interpretation of the verse by asking a rhetorical question: **"You say** that the word *ona'ah* appearing in this verse **refers to verbal *ona'ah*. But might it not be referring to monetary *ona'ah*** overcharging and underpaying — and causing people anguish is thus not prohibited by the Torah?" [3]The Baraita explains: "The verse cannot be referring to monetary *ona'ah*, for there is an earlier **verse** (ibid., 25:14), **which says: 'And if you sell something to your neighbor, or buy something from your neighbor's hand,** do not oppress (*tonu*, from the same root as *ona'ah*) one another.' [4]Thus we see that **the case of monetary *ona'ah* has** already **been stated** explicitly. And since the Torah has already explicitly forbidden fraudulent business dealings in verse 14, the verse cited at the beginning of the Baraita (verse 17) must be intended to teach us something different. [5]**How then do I interpret** the expression **'You shall not wrong one another'** in verse 17? **This** verse must **be referring to verbal *ona'ah*."** [6]The Baraita now explains the law in detail: **"How so?** What constitutes verbal *ona'ah*?" [7]The Baraita explains: **"If someone is a repentant sinner,** other people **must not** remind him of his past by **saying to him: 'Remember your earlier deeds.'** [8]Likewise, **if** someone **is the son of converts,** other people **must not** remind him of his origins by **saying to him: 'Remember the deeds of your fathers.'"** [9]The Baraita now adds several examples not found in our Mishnah: **"If a convert came to study Torah,** other people **must not** insult him by **saying to him:** [10]**'Shall the mouth that** once **ate carrion and forbidden animals,**

BACKGROUND

פֶּה שֶׁאָכַל נְבֵילוֹת וכו׳ **Shall the mouth that has eaten carrion, etc.** The various types of food mentioned here are considered repulsive, and not just forbidden. Indeed, a non-Jew may eat such foods, and Jews are explicitly permitted to sell animal carcasses to non-Jews (see Deuteronomy 14:21). Thus reminding a convert that he once ate forbidden foods has emotional rather than Halakhic significance. Other Talmudic passages, too, indicate that eating non-kosher food (even unwittingly) exerts a deleterious influence on those who do so.

NOTES

אִם הָיָה גֵּר **If he was a convert.** The commentators ask why the Gemara does not speak of wronging converts by reminding them of their former deeds. *Maharsha* answers that this is not considered *ona'ah*. On the contrary, the fact that a convert was able to abandon his former ways and draw near to God demonstrates his spiritual greatness. *Pnei Yehoshua*, however, explains that the convert's deeds before he converted are not attributable to him, since a convert is Halakhically considered "like a newborn child" who has no connection with his past.

HALAKHAH

אוֹנָאַת דְּבָרִים **Verbal *ona'ah*.** "Just as it is prohibited to wrong other people in business by overcharging or underpaying, so too it is prohibited to wrong others verbally by hurting their feelings. Indeed, verbal *ona'ah* is a graver offense than fraud in business, since it is directed against the person himself rather than against his property. Moreover, someone who shames another person cannot rectify the wrong by paying money. Moreover, if the offended party demands Divine retribution from the person who humiliated him, his prayers are answered immediately." (*Shulḥan Arukh, Ḥoshen Mishpat* 228:1.)

כֵּיצַד אוֹנָאַת דְּבָרִים **What is considered verbal *ona'ah*?** "It is forbidden to ask how much something costs if one does not intend to buy it, or to send ass-drivers to someone who does not sell produce. It is forbidden to remind a repentant sinner of his past deeds, or to remind the son of proselytes of his ancestors' deeds. Similarly, it is forbidden to tell a person afflicted in any way that he deserves to suffer as punishment for his sins." (Ibid., 228:4.)

שְׁקָצִים וּרְמָשִׂים, בָּא לִלְמוֹד תּוֹרָה שֶׁנֶּאֶמְרָה מִפִּי הַגְּבוּרָה?׳ [1]אִם הָיוּ יִסּוּרִין בָּאִין עָלָיו, אִם הָיוּ חֳלָאִים בָּאִין עָלָיו, אוֹ שֶׁהָיָה מְקַבֵּר אֶת בָּנָיו, [2]אַל יֹאמַר לוֹ כְּדֶרֶךְ שֶׁאָמְרוּ לוֹ חֲבֵירָיו לְאִיּוֹב: ׳הֲלֹא יִרְאָתְךָ כִּסְלָתֶךָ, תִּקְוָתְךָ וְתֹם דְּרָכֶיךָ? [3]זְכָר נָא מִי הוּא נָקִי אָבָד?׳ [4]אִם הָיוּ חַמָּרִים מְבַקְּשִׁין תְּבוּאָה מִמֶּנּוּ, לֹא יֹאמַר לָהֶם: [5]׳לְכוּ אֵצֶל פְּלוֹנִי, שֶׁהוּא מוֹכֵר תְּבוּאָה׳, וְיוֹדֵעַ בּוֹ שֶׁלֹּא מָכַר מֵעוֹלָם. [6]רַבִּי יְהוּדָה אוֹמֵר: אַף לֹא יִתְלֶה עֵינָיו עַל הַמִּקָּח בְּשָׁעָה שֶׁאֵין לוֹ דָּמִים. [7]שֶׁהֲרֵי הַדָּבָר מָסוּר לַלֵּב, וְכָל דָּבָר הַמָּסוּר לַלֵּב נֶאֱמַר בּוֹ: ׳וְיָרֵאתָ מֵאֱלֹהֶיךָ׳״.

LITERAL TRANSLATION

abominations and creeping things, come to study Torah that was uttered by the mouth of the Almighty?' [1]If suffering befell someone, [or] if illness befell him, or if he was burying his sons, [2]one should not say to him in the way that [Job's] friends said to Job: 'Is not your fear [of God] your confidence, your hope and the uprightness of your ways? [3]Remember, I pray you, whoever perished, being innocent?' [4]If ass-drivers were seeking produce from someone, he may not say to them: [5]'Go to so-and-so, who is selling produce,' when he knows that he has never sold [produce]. [6]Rabbi Yehudah says: One may not even cast one's eyes on merchandise when one has no money. [7]For the matter is entrusted to the heart, and concerning any matter that is entrusted to the heart it was said: 'And you shall fear your God.'"

TRANSLATION AND COMMENTARY

abominations and creeping things (such as insects and rodents), all of which are types of non-kosher food, **come** now **to study Torah that was uttered by the mouth of the Almighty?'** [1]Also, **if** a person **is suffering, or has become ill, or if his children** have died and he **is burying** them, [2]it is wrong to suggest that the tragedy might have been averted had the person been more scrupulous, **in the manner of Job's friends** after tragedy befell him. The suffering person's friends **should not say to him: "Is not your fear of God your confidence, your hope and the uprightness of your ways? [3]Remember, I pray you, who ever perished being innocent?'** These words spoken to Job (Job 4:6-7) imply that God does not allow innocent people to come to harm. Speaking in this way to a bereaved or suffering person is forbidden as verbal *ona'ah*, since it is tantamount to accusing the sufferer or the deceased of being a sinner. [4]An example of another kind: **If ass-drivers are seeking** to buy **produce from** a person, and he does not have produce to sell them, **he must not say to them: [5]'Go to so-and-so who is selling produce,' when he knows that** the other person has **never sold produce,** for by speaking in this way, he is causing the ass-drivers (and the person to whom he sent them) needless distress. [6]**Rabbi Yehudah said:** A person **may not even cast his eyes on merchandise if he has no money** to purchase it. Even though he does not say anything, he arouses false hopes in the seller merely by staring at the merchandise." Having described a number of examples of verbal *ona'ah*, the Baraita concludes by explaining the last words of the verse in Leviticus (25:17) on which the Baraita is based: "And you shall fear your God, for I am the Lord your God." The Baraita points out that there is no objective definition of hurtful words: **"For** the same words may be helpful or destructive, depending on the circumstances, the tone of voice, and the speaker's intent. Thus, practically speaking, it is impossible to enforce this law, because the speaker can always claim that he really meant no harm. If he sent the ass-drivers to another merchant, he can pretend that he really thought that the other had produce to sell. If he stared at merchandise, he can claim that he was considering buying it, but decided not to. [7]**In cases** such as **these, the matter is entrusted to the** person's own **heart.** This law cannot be enforced by a human court, because no one can know another person's thoughts. However, the person himself knows whether his intentions were good or evil. **And concerning any matter that is entrusted to** a person's own **heart the verse says: 'And you shall fear your God.'** For He who knows a person's innermost thoughts and intentions will enforce His law." This concludes the Baraita.

RASHI

שהרי דבר המסור ללב – ולפיכך נאמר בו "ויראת מאלהיך". האי "שהרי" – ליתן טעם למה נאמר בו יראה נקט ליה, והכי קאמר: שהרי כל הדברים הללו אין טובתן ורעתן מסורה להכיר אלא ללבו של עושה, הוא יודע אם לעקל אם לעקלקלות, ויכול הוא לומר: לא עשיתי כי אם לטובה, הייתי סבור שיש לך תבואה למכור או הייתי חפץ לקנות מקח זה. **וכל דבר המסור ללב** – של אדם, נאמר בו הוי ירא מן היודע מחשבות, אם לטובה אם לאונאה.

BACKGROUND

אִם הָיוּ יִסּוּרִין בָּאִין עָלָיו If suffering befell someone. While many statements are found in Rabbinic literature to the effect that suffering is a punishment for sin (although the Rabbis admitted that there were exceptions to this rule), it is improper to accuse sufferers of wrongdoing, since only God knows what other people's merits and transgressions are.

לְכוּ אֵצֶל פְּלוֹנִי Go to so-and-so. From here we may infer that not only are outright insults forbidden, but so are remarks made facetiously, if they are likely to cause others distress.

אַף לֹא יִתְלֶה עֵינָיו עַל הַמִּקָּח One may not even cast one's eyes on merchandise. From here we learn that even actions that are likely to arouse false hopes in the seller (such as "casting one's eyes" on merchandise) are forbidden as verbal *ona'ah*.

NOTES

הֲלֹא יִרְאָתְךָ כִּסְלָתֶךָ "Is not your fear of God your confidence?" *Maharsha* explains that the word כִּסְלָתֶךָ — here rendered "your confidence" — means "your fortune." Thus, the verse as a whole would mean: "As long as you were blessed with good fortune you feared God, but in fact you are not a God-fearing person."

TRANSLATION AND COMMENTARY

אָמַר רַבִּי יוֹחָנָן [1]The Gemara now cites a number of other statements made by the Sages about the importance of not inflicting anguish. **Rabbi Yoḥanan said in the name of Rabbi Shimon ben Yoḥai: Verbal** *ona'ah* **is a greater sin than monetary** *ona'ah*. [2]**For concerning** the former **the verse** (ibid.) **says: "And you shall fear your God,"** [3]**and concerning** the latter **the verse** prohibiting monetary *ona'ah* (ibid., 25:14) **does not say: "And you shall fear your God."** This shows that the Torah considers causing people anguish a sign of disrespect for God, in a way that monetary *ona'ah* is not.

וְרַבִּי אֶלְעָזָר [4]**Rabbi Elazar** suggested a further reason why verbal wrongdoing is considered more heinous than monetary fraud, and **said: The former applies to the victim's person,** whereas **the latter** applies only **to his money.**

רַבִּי שְׁמוּאֵל בַּר נַחְמָנִי [5]**Rabbi Shmuel bar Naḥmani** added yet another reason and **said:** Monetary *ona'ah* is less severe because it **is subject to restitution.** If someone overcharges or underpays, he can recompense the victim by simply paying the difference. **But** verbal *ona'ah* **is not subject to restitution.** Even if the wrongdoer tries to atone for his sin by compensating the victim, the anguish he caused can never be completely undone.

תָּנֵי תַּנָּא [6]**A Tanna** (Baraita reciter) **taught** the following Baraita **before Rav Naḥman bar Yitzḥak: "Anyone who shames another person in public is as if he sheds his blood."** The Hebrew expression for shaming someone is *malbin panim* (מַלְבִּין פָּנִים), which literally means "whitening the face." The connection between shaming a person and shedding his blood is based on this literal meaning.

אֲמַר לֵיהּ [7]Rav Naḥman bar Yitzḥak **said to the Tanna: You say well.** The Baraita you cited expresses a profound truth. **For** when a person is publicly shamed, **we see that the red** color of his face as he blushes **disappears and whiteness takes its place** as he pales. In this sense it may truly be said that the shamed person's blood is being shed.

[1]אָמַר רַבִּי יוֹחָנָן מִשּׁוּם רַבִּי שִׁמְעוֹן בֶּן יוֹחַאי: גָּדוֹל אוֹנָאַת דְּבָרִים מֵאוֹנָאַת מָמוֹן, [2]שֶׁזֶּה נֶאֱמַר בּוֹ: ״וְיָרֵאתָ מֵאֱלֹהֶיךָ״, [3]וְזֶה לֹא נֶאֱמַר בּוֹ: ״וְיָרֵאתָ מֵאֱלֹהֶיךָ״. [4]וְרַבִּי אֶלְעָזָר אוֹמֵר: זֶה בְּגוּפוֹ, וְזֶה בְּמָמוֹנוֹ. [5]רַבִּי שְׁמוּאֵל בַּר נַחְמָנִי אָמַר: זֶה נִיתָּן לְהִישָּׁבוֹן, וְזֶה לֹא נִיתָּן לְהִישָּׁבוֹן. [6]תָּנֵי תַּנָּא קַמֵּיהּ דְּרַב נַחְמָן בַּר יִצְחָק: ״כָּל הַמַּלְבִּין פְּנֵי חֲבֵירוֹ בָּרַבִּים כְּאִילּוּ שׁוֹפֵךְ דָּמִים״. [7]אֲמַר לֵיהּ: שַׁפִּיר קָא אָמְרַתְּ, דְּחָזֵינָא לֵיהּ דְּאָזֵיל סוּמָּקָא וְאָתֵי חִוָּורָא.

LITERAL TRANSLATION

[1]Rabbi Yoḥanan said in the name of Rabbi Shimon ben Yoḥai: Verbal *ona'ah* is a greater [sin] than monetary *ona'ah*, [2]for concerning this one it was said: "And you shall fear your God," [3]but concerning that one it was not said: "And you shall fear your God."

[4]And Rabbi Elazar says: This [applies] to [the victim's] person, and that to his money.

[5]Rabbi Shmuel bar Naḥmani said: This can be restored, but that cannot be restored.

[6]A Tanna taught before Rav Naḥman bar Yitzḥak: "Anyone who shames (lit., 'whitens the face of') his fellow in public is as if he sheds blood."

[7]He said to him: You said well, for we see in him that redness goes out and whiteness comes.

BACKGROUND

כְּאִילּוּ שׁוֹפֵךְ דָּם **Is as if he sheds blood.** In a sense, putting another person to shame is tantamount to assassination, since it destroys his social status and personal honor.

NOTES

גָּדוֹל אוֹנָאַת דְּבָרִים מֵאוֹנָאַת מָמוֹן **Verbal** ***ona'ah*** **is more serious than monetary** ***ona'ah***. In addition to the reasons suggested by the Gemara, *Maharsha* explains that verbal *ona'ah* is particularly serious because it reflects an attitude of contempt towards God. Specifically, a person who commits verbal *ona'ah* attempts to convey the impression that he did not mean to hurt the victim's feelings. Thus such a person shows that he is attempting to deceive God, even though he is afraid to deceive other people. By contrast, if a person defrauds another person financially, other people realize that he has done so, and thus his conduct does not imply that he fears man more than God.

HALAKHAH

הַמַּלְבִּין פְּנֵי חֲבֵירוֹ **One who shames his fellow in public.** "A person who puts other people to shame in public, or calls other people derogatory names, has no share in the world to come unless he repents." (*Rambam, Sefer HaMada, Hilkhot De'ot* 6:8; ibid., *Hilkhot Teshuvah* 3:14.)

TRANSLATION AND COMMENTARY

אָמַר לֵיהּ [1]Abaye said to Rav Dimi: About what are people especially careful in Eretz Israel?

אָמַר לֵיהּ [2]Rav Dimi said to Abaye: About putting people to shame. [3]For Rabbi Ḥanina said: All descend to Gehinnom (hell) after death in punishment for their sins, except for three categories of people.

הַכֹּל סָלְקָא דַּעְתָּךְ [4]At first glance, this statement seems incredible, and the Gemara immediately objects: Can it enter your mind to think that "all descend"? Is it conceivable that all people, except for those falling into one of the three categories about to be specified, deserve to be punished in Gehinnom?

אֶלָּא אֵימָא [5]Rather, Rabbi Ḥanina's statement needs to be amended as follows: Say: Everyone who is punished and descends to Gehinnom will eventually, after due time for atonement, ascend and leave Gehinnom, except for three types of sinners who descend to Gehinnom and do not ascend, because their crimes are so heinous. [6]The following are the three sins: (1) Someone who cohabits with a married woman. (2) Someone who puts another person to shame in public. (3) Someone who calls another person by a derogatory name.

מְכַנֶּה הַיְינוּ מַלְבִּין [7]The Gemara objects: Calling a person by a derogatory name is the same as shaming him. Why then are they considered distinct categories?

אַף עַל גַּב [8]The Gemara answers: There are cases in which calling a person by a derogatory name does not put him to shame. Rabbi Ḥanina listed this sin separately to teach us that it is an exceedingly grave offense to call a person by a derogatory name even if he was used to this derogatory name being used in place of his name, and is no longer embarrassed by it. For the *intent* of the person who uses the derogatory name is to degrade another human being, and that intention is a crime in its own right, even if no one is actually hurt by it.

אָמַר רַבָּה בַּר בַּר חָנָה [9]The Gemara cites additional Rabbinic teachings which stress the gravity of putting other people to shame: Rabbah bar Bar Ḥanah said in the name of Rabbi Yoḥanan:

[1]אָמַר לֵיהּ אַבַּיֵי לְרַב דִּימִי: בְּמַעַרְבָא בְּמַאי זְהִירֵי?
[2]אָמַר לֵיהּ: בְּאַחְוורֵי אַפֵּי.
[3]דְּאָמַר רַבִּי חֲנִינָא: הַכֹּל יוֹרְדִין לַגֵּיהִנָּם, חוּץ מִשְּׁלֹשָׁה.
[4]הַכֹּל סָלְקָא דַּעְתָּךְ?
[5]אֶלָּא אֵימָא: כָּל הַיּוֹרְדִין לַגֵּיהִנָּם עוֹלִים, חוּץ מִשְּׁלֹשָׁה שֶׁיּוֹרְדִין וְאֵין עוֹלִין. [6]וְאֵלּוּ הֵן: הַבָּא עַל אֵשֶׁת אִישׁ, וְהַמַּלְבִּין פְּנֵי חֲבֵירוֹ בָּרַבִּים, וְהַמְכַנֶּה שֵׁם רַע לַחֲבֵירוֹ.
[7]מְכַנֶּה הַיְינוּ מַלְבִּין!
[8]אַף עַל גַּב דְּדָשׁ בֵּיהּ בִּשְׁמֵיהּ.
[9]אָמַר רַבָּה בַּר בַּר חָנָה אָמַר רַבִּי יוֹחָנָן:

LITERAL TRANSLATION

[1]Abaye said to Rav Dimi: About what are [people] careful in Eretz Israel (lit., "the west")?

[2]He said to him: About putting [people] to shame.

[3]For Rabbi Ḥanina said: All descend to Gehinnom, except for three.

[4]Can it enter your mind [that] "all [descend]"?

[5]Rather, say: All who descend to Gehinnom ascend, except for three who descend and do not ascend. [6]And they are these: Someone who cohabits with a married woman, someone who shames his fellow in public, and someone who calls his fellow by a bad name.

[7]Calling [a person by a bad name] is the same as shaming!

[8]Even though he is used to it as his name.

[9]Rabbah bar Bar Ḥanah said in the name of Rabbi Yoḥanan:

RASHI

הכל סלקא דעתך – וכי הכל יורדין. **הכי גרסינן: כל היורדין לגיהנם עולין.** **דדש ביה** – כבר הורגל בכך שמכנים אותו כן, ואין פניו מתלבנות ומכל מקום – זה להכלימו מתכוין.

BACKGROUND

הַכֹּל יוֹרְדִין לַגֵּיהִנָּם All who descend to Gehinnom. Elsewhere (*Rosh HaShanah* 17a) the Gemara states that "the wicked are judged in Gehinnom for twelve months," after which their sins are atoned for. However, certain sins are so heinous that they can never be expiated, and of such sinners we read in Isaiah (66:24): "Their worm shall not die, neither shall their fire be quenched."

הַבָּא עַל אֵשֶׁת אִישׁ Someone who cohabits with a married woman. The sin of adultery is extremely grave, and it is forbidden by the Ten Commandments. In other sources (see *Ḥagigah* 9b) the gravity of this prohibition is discussed. In addition to violating a severe prohibition and offending God, the adulterer also causes anguish and suffering to the woman's husband. Moreover, if the adultery comes to light, the woman is forbidden to her husband forever, so she too suffers not only for her sin but also by being separated from her husband.

NOTES

בְּמַעַרְבָא בְּמַאי זְהִירֵי About what are people careful in the West? The Gemara assumes that the residents of the "West" (i.e., Eretz Israel) were especially careful not to put others to shame, because doing so is tantamount to shedding blood, and the Torah explicitly exhorts us to avoid "defiling the land" (i.e., Eretz Israel) by committing murder (see Numbers 35:33 f; *Iyyun Ya'akov*).

חוּץ מִשְּׁלֹשָׁה שֶׁיּוֹרְדִין Except for three who descend. *Meiri* (following *Ramban*) explains that the penalty for these offenses is so severe because people who commit them generally do not realize that what they did is wrong, and hence do not repent.

HALAKHAH

הַמְכַנֶּה שֵׁם רַע לַחֲבֵירוֹ Someone who calls his fellow by a bad name. "It is forbidden to call other people by derogatory names in order to humiliate them, even if they are used to such names." (*Shulḥan Arukh, Ḥoshen Mishpat* 228:8.)

TRANSLATION AND COMMENTARY

[59A] [1]Putting another person to shame in public is so grievous a sin that **it would be** preferable **to cohabit with a woman whose marital status is unclear,** even though such relations carry the risk of committing the serious crime of adultery, rather than **shame anyone publicly.**

מְנָא לָן [2]The Gemara asks: **From where do we know this?** What is the Biblical source for this statement?

מִדְּדָרַשׁ רָבָא [3]The Gemara answers: Rabbi Yoḥanan's statement was based on an interpretation of a verse in Psalms (35:15), **as expounded by Rava.** According to Rava's interpretation, King David's critics publicly embarrassed David about his relationship with Bathsheba, the wife of Uriah the Hittite (II Samuel, Chapter 11), and their offense was more serious than the illicit relationship itself. **For Rava expounded** as follows: **What is the meaning of** the following verse (Psalms 35:15), in which King David declared: **"And when I stumbled** my enemies **rejoiced and gathered together...they tore me, and did not cease"**? In this verse, King David laments that his enemies are constantly seeking opportunities to persecute him, but Rava explains that it has a deeper meaning. The Hebrew word *tzal'i* (צַלְעִי) — literally "my stumbling" — can also mean "my rib," or metaphorically, "my wife," since Eve was created from Adam's rib. Furthermore, the Hebrew words *lo damu* (לֹא דָמוּ) — literally "did not cease" or "did not fall silent" — can also mean "there was no blood." According to Rava, the verse, which speaks of David's enemies in general, actually refers to one particular sort of persecutor — the rivals who publicly humiliated David after his adultery with Bathsheba became public knowledge. Thus, according to Rava's explanation, David's enemies "rejoiced and gathered together over the scandal involving my wife." [4]At this point **David said before the Holy One, Blessed be He: "Master of the Universe, it is revealed and known before You that** I have atoned for my sin. In fact, **if** my enemies **were to tear my flesh** to pieces, **my blood would not drip to the ground"** (translating "did not cease" as "there would be no blood"). David's enemies would not be able to draw any more blood from him, because it is as if he has already lost all his blood from fasting to atone for his sin. Thus we see that it is a great wrong to torment a repentant sinner — to tear his flesh and seek to draw his blood — by seeking to humiliate him over

[59A] [1]נוֹחַ לוֹ לְאָדָם שֶׁיָּבוֹא עַל סְפֵק אֵשֶׁת אִישׁ וְאַל יַלְבִּין פְּנֵי חֲבֵירוֹ בָּרַבִּים.

[2]מְנָא לָן?

[3]מִדְּדָרַשׁ רָבָא. דְּדָרַשׁ רָבָא: מַאי דִּכְתִיב: "וּבְצַלְעִי שָׂמְחוּ וְנֶאֱסָפוּ... קָרְעוּ וְלֹא דָמוּ". [4]אָמַר דָּוִד לִפְנֵי הַקָּדוֹשׁ בָּרוּךְ הוּא: "רִבּוֹנוֹ שֶׁל עוֹלָם, גָּלוּי וְיָדוּעַ לְפָנֶיךָ שֶׁאִם הָיוּ מְקָרְעִים בְּשָׂרִי, לֹא הָיָה דָּמִי שׁוֹתֵת לָאָרֶץ.

LITERAL TRANSLATION

[59A] [1]It is better (lit., "easier") for a man to cohabit with a woman about whom there is a doubt whether she is married and not to put his fellow to shame in public.

[2]From where do we [know this]?

[3]From what Rava expounded. For Rava expounded: What is [it] that is written: "And when I stumbled, they rejoiced and gathered themselves together...they tore me, and did not cease." [4]David said before the Holy One, blessed be He: "Master of the Universe, it is revealed and known before You that if they had torn my flesh, my blood would not have dripped to the ground.

RASHI

ובצלעי — בשביל אשתי זו, שמתחילה חטאתי בה, כמו (בראשית ב) "ויבן את הצלע", שמחו ונאספו. **קרעו ולא דמו** — אם קרעוני לא מצאו דם. **כדדרש רבא** — דטובה מעשה של דוד ובת שבע משלהם. וספק אשת איש היא. שהיוצא למלחמת בית דוד גט כריתות כותב לאשתו על מנת שאם ימות שתהא מגורשת מעכשיו, ולא תיזקק ליבם, וכל אותן הימים היא ספק מגורשת, אם מת — מגורשת מתחילה, ואם לא מת — לא נתגרשה.

NOTES

הַבָּא עַל סְפֵק אֵשֶׁת אִישׁ Cohabitation with a woman about whom there is a doubt whether she is married. The commentators (*Tosafot* and others) ask why the Gemara spoke of a woman whose marital status is doubtful rather than of one who is definitely married. Among the explanations offered is that of *Talmidei Rabbenu Yonah* (in *Berakhot*), who suggest that it is easier to atone for a sin which one has definitely committed than for an uncertain sin, since people tend to rationalize uncertain sins away, claiming that they never sinned in the first place.

Tosafot here explains that the reference is to David's sin with Bathsheba, the wife of Uriah the Hittite. According to a Rabbinic tradition, even at that early time it was common for soldiers to give their wives a conditional bill of divorce, so that if the soldiers did not return from battle the wives would be divorced from the date the bill of divorce was given. Accordingly, Bathsheba was merely a "doubtfully married woman" with respect to David.

HALAKHAH

אֵשֶׁת אִישׁ Cohabitation with a married woman. "One who wittingly has conjugal relations with a married woman other than his wife is subject to death by strangulation." (*Rambam, Sefer Kedushah, Hilkhot Issurei Bi'ah* 1:6.)

TRANSLATION AND COMMENTARY

his past misdeeds. [1]David continues: **"Not only** do my enemies rejoice over my stumbling, but also they constantly draw attention to the matter **even when they engage in** the study of areas of the Halakhah that have nothing to do with me or my sin, such as the study of **the laws of *Nega'im*** (ritual impurity conferred by leprosy; Leviticus, Chapter 13 ff.) **and** the laws of ***Ohalot*** (ritual impurity conferred by "tents" spread over a corpse; Numbers 19:14)." "For example," David continues, "they ask me a Halakhic question of law which sounds innocuous but is meant solely to humiliate me. [2]Thus **they will say to me: 'David, what is the death penalty for someone who cohabits with a married woman?'** — a transparent reference to Bathsheba." [3]David, however, replied to them in kind: **"And I say to them:** 'Someone who cohabits with a married woman is subject to **death by strangulation, but** despite the gravity of his sin, **he** still **has a share in the world to come.** [4]On the other hand, **someone** — like you — **who puts another person to shame in public, does not have a share in the world to come."** Thus, says Rava, it was on the basis of this Midrashic interpretation of the verse from Psalms that Rabbi Yoḥanan said that it is worse to put a repentant sinner to shame, than to cohabit with a woman whose marital status is in doubt. Bathsheba had received a bill of divorce from her husband before he went off to war, and the bill of divorce was to take effect retroactively in the event that he did not return alive. While her husband was away at war, Bathsheba was considered a woman who might be divorced but might also still be married. For if her husband died, she would be divorced retroactively, but if he returned from the war, she would still be married to him.

וְאָמַר מָר זוּטְרָא בַּר טוֹבִיָּה [5]The Gemara now cites additional Rabbinic statements about the gravity of putting a person to shame in public. **Mar Zutra bar Toviyyah said in the name of Rav, and some say:** [6]**Rav Ḥana bar Bizna said in the name of Rabbi Shimon Ḥasida, and some say: Rabbi Yoḥanan said in the name of Rabbi Shimon ben Yoḥai:** [7]**It is better for a man to cast himself into a fiery furnace than to put another person to shame in public.**

[1]וְלֹא עוֹד, אֶלָּא אֲפִילּוּ בְּשָׁעָה שֶׁעוֹסְקִין בִּנְגָעִים וָאֳהָלוֹת אוֹמְרִים לִי: [2]׳דָּוִד, הַבָּא עַל אֵשֶׁת אִישׁ מִיתָתוֹ בַּמֶּה׳? [3]וַאֲנִי אוֹמֵר לָהֶם: ׳מִיתָתוֹ בְּחֶנֶק, וְיֵשׁ לוֹ חֵלֶק לָעוֹלָם הַבָּא. [4]אֲבָל הַמַּלְבִּין אֶת פְּנֵי חֲבֵירוֹ בָּרַבִּים אֵין לוֹ חֵלֶק לָעוֹלָם הַבָּא׳״.
[5]וְאָמַר מָר זוּטְרָא בַּר טוֹבִיָּה אָמַר רַב; [6]וְאָמְרִי לָהּ: אָמַר רַב חָנָא בַּר בִּיזְנָא אָמַר רַבִּי שִׁמְעוֹן חֲסִידָא; וְאָמְרִי לָהּ אָמַר רַבִּי יוֹחָנָן מִשּׁוּם רַבִּי שִׁמְעוֹן בֶּן יוֹחַאי: [7]נוֹחַ לוֹ לְאָדָם שֶׁיַּפִּיל עַצְמוֹ לְכִבְשַׁן הָאֵשׁ וְאַל יַלְבִּין פְּנֵי חֲבֵירוֹ בָּרַבִּים.

LITERAL TRANSLATION

[1]And not only [this], but even when they engage in [the laws of] *Nega'im* ("Leprosies") and *Ohalot* ("Tents") they say to me: [2]'David, what is the death [penalty] for someone who cohabits with a married woman?' [3]And I say to them: 'His death is by strangulation, but he has a share in the world to come. [4]But someone who puts his fellow to shame in public does not have a share in the world to come.'"

[5]And Mar Zutra bar Toviyyah said in the name of Rav; [6]and some say: Rav Ḥana bar Bizna said in the name of Rabbi Shimon Ḥasida; and some say: Rabbi Yoḥanan said in the name of Rabbi Shimon ben Yoḥai: [7]It is better for a man to cast himself into a fiery furnace and not to put his fellow to shame in public.

NOTES

נְגָעִים וָאֳהָלוֹת The laws of *Neg'aim* and *Ohalot*. The commentators attempt to explain why David's opponents were studying these particular laws. *Tosafot* says that even though the laws of *Nega'im* and *Ohalot* have no connection with the laws of adultery, David's opponents nevertheless saw fit to digress from studying these Halakhot in order to discuss his sin.

Others suggest that these examples were given because the Sages said (*Pesaḥim* 50a) that, even though these laws are considered extremely complex in this world, they will be easy to master in the world to come. By contrast, putting other people to shame is generally considered a minor sin in this world, whereas it will be considered a major transgression in the world to come (*Iyyun Ya'akov*). Others explain that the Gemara spoke of *Nega'im* and *Ohalot* because leprous diseases befall people who speak ill of others — even if what they say is true, as in the case of King David. Thus the Gemara implies that David's opponents slandered him even though they should have known better, since they were studying the laws of *Nega'im* (*Riaf*).

מִיתָתוֹ בְּחֶנֶק, וְיֵשׁ לוֹ חֵלֶק לָעוֹלָם הַבָּא His death is by strangulation, but he has a share in the world to come. This statement seems to contradict the Gemara's previous statement (above, 58b), that adulterers "descend and do not ascend." *Rid* explains that the discussion here refers to a case in which the adulterer repented, in which case he indeed has a share in the world to come. *Ritva*, however, suggests that the death penalty atones for the adulterer's transgression, and he offers yet another explanation: An adulterer "descends and does not ascend" only if a *mamzer* was born from the illicit union. In such cases it is impossible to repent fully, since a palpable manifestation of the sin still exists (cf. Mishnah *Ḥagigah* 1:7).

SAGES

מָר זוּטְרָא בַּר טוֹבִיָּה Mar Zutra bar Toviyyah. A second-generation Babylonian Amora, Mar (or Rav) Zutra bar Toviyyah was an outstanding disciple of Rav, and in many Talmudic passages he transmits Rav's Halakhic and Aggadic teachings. After Rav's death, Mar Zutra studied in the yeshivah of Rav Yehudah, where he became a student-colleague of that scholar. His own teachings are also cited in a number of places.

רַב חָנָא בַּר בִּיזְנָא Rav Ḥana bar Bizna. A Babylonian Amora of the second and third generations, Rav Ḥana bar Bizna, who was a Rabbinical judge in Pumbedita, often transmitted the teachings of Rabbi Shimon Ḥasida. He was renowned among the scholars of his time both as an expert on Aggadah and as a Halakhic authority.

רַבִּי שִׁמְעוֹן חֲסִידָא Rabbi Shimon Ḥasida. A Palestinian Amora of the first and second generations, Rabbi Shimon Ḥasida must be distinguished from Rabbi Shimon HeḤasid, who was a Tanna and appears in several Baraitot.

BACKGROUND

בְּשָׁעָה שֶׁעוֹסְקִין בִּנְגָעִים וָאֳהָלוֹת When they engage in the laws of *Nega'im* and *Ohalot*. Many Aggadic passages depict King David as the head of a yeshivah engaged in intensive Torah study, much like the Mishnaic and Talmudic Sages. Such anachronistic descriptions did not disturb the Talmudic Sages, since their main interest was to illustrate moral lessons in a manner which their listeners would find meaningful, and anachronistic depictions of Biblical personalities certainly served this goal.

נוֹחַ לוֹ לְאָדָם שֶׁיַּפִּיל עַצְמוֹ לְכִבְשַׁן הָאֵשׁ It is better for a man to cast himself into a fiery furnace. *Tosafot* and *Rabbenu Yonah* seem to take this statement literally, and thus it follows that one should submit to death, if necessary, rather than put others to shame. Indeed, the Gemara relates elsewhere (*Ketubot* 67b) that the Amora Mar

Ukva entered a fiery furnace together with his wife in order to avoid putting someone to shame. However, *Rambam* and *Meiri* seem to maintain that Mar Zutra's statement was meant figuratively, and was only intended to emphasize the severity of the prohibition against publicly shaming others.

SAGES

רַב חִינְנָא בְּרֵיהּ דְּרַב אִידִי **Rav Ḥinena the son of Rav Idi.** A Babylonian Amora of the third generation, Rav Ḥinena the son of Rav Idi was apparently a student of Rav Adda bar Ahavah (the first), and various teachings (primarily Aggadic) are cited in his name.

BACKGROUND

עַם שֶׁאִתְּךָ בְּתוֹרָה וּבְמִצְוֹת **A people that is with you in observance of the Torah and the commandments.** This Halakhah, which applies to the laws of verbal *ona'ah*, has parallels among other Halakhot governing honorable behavior with others. The basic assumption in all these cases is that one only honors those who are worthy of honor. A father or a leader is worthy of honor by virtue of his elevated position, and one may not disgrace, curse, or embarrass a fellow-Jew even if he is not conspicuously worthy of honor. However, someone who deviates from Jewish laws and commits sins in public brings dishonor upon himself by his deeds, thus depriving himself of the right to be honored by others. Therefore, until he repents, the rules about honoring other people do not apply to him.

לְעוֹלָם יְהֵא אָדָם זָהִיר בְּאוֹנָאַת אִשְׁתּוֹ **A man should always be careful about distressing his wife.** Even though God punishes all sinners, He answers immediately the cries of those who demand Divine redress, such as women who are more sensitive to insult than men (see Exodus 22:21-22). In addition, people are more likely to quarrel with their wives than with other women. It should also be noted that people are more apt to treat their wives disrespectfully

TRANSLATION AND COMMENTARY

מְנָא לָן [1]The Gemara asks: **From where** in the Bible **do we know this?**

מִתָּמָר [2]It answers: **From** the case of **Tamar** (Genesis, Chapter 38). Tamar had been married to two of Judah's sons, each of whom had died without issue. Under the law of levirate marriage, she was required to marry another member of Judah's family. Judah seemed reluctant to allow her to marry his only remaining son, so Tamar disguised herself as a prostitute, seduced Judah himself, and persuaded him to give her his signet, cord, and staff. She became pregnant, and Judah accused her of adultery while already betrothed under the levirate-marriage law. The punishment for that crime was death by burning. Tamar's response **is written** in verse 25: **"When she was brought forth** to be executed, **she sent to her father-in-law** saying, I am pregnant by the man to whom this signet, cord, and staff belong." Tamar made no effort to clear herself by publicly declaring that Judah himself was the father of her unborn child. She waited until the last moment and left the matter to Judah's own conscience. Thus we see that she was willing to be burned to death, rather than publicly humiliate her father-in-law. Accordingly, we may infer that it is better to be cast into a fiery furnace than to put another person to shame in public.

אָמַר רַב חִינְנָא בְּרֵיהּ דְּרַב אִידִי [3]Continuing its discussion of the laws of verbal *ona'ah*, the Gemara notes: **Rav Ḥinena the son of Rav Idi said: What is the meaning of** the verse (Leviticus 25:17): **"And you shall not wrong each man his neighbor"?** Who is the "neighbor" to whom the verse refers? Rav Ḥinena the son of Rav Idi answers: [4]The verse means: **"Do not wrong a people that is with you in observance of the Torah and the commandments."** According to Rav Ḥinena, the word *amito* (עֲמִיתוֹ) — "his neighbor" — should be interpreted as if it were two words, *am ito* (עִם אִתּוֹ), meaning "the people with him," i.e., people who are "together with him" in that they are religiously observant. Accordingly, he infers that the prohibition against verbal *ona'ah* applies specifically among people who are themselves observant of the Torah and its commandments.

אָמַר רַב [5]The Gemara now considers another Rabbinic statement about the gravity of causing anguish to other people. **Rav said: A person should always be careful about distressing his wife.** Rav explains: There is a reason why it is an especially grave sin for a husband to hurt his wife. [6]**Since** a wife's **tears are close at hand** — she is apt to shed tears if her husband insults her — Divine **punishment for distressing her is** also **near** at hand and ready to befall her husband as soon as he insults her. For while it is reprehensible to cause people anguish, it is even more serious to drive them to tears.

LITERAL TRANSLATION

[1]From where do we [know this]?

[2]From Tamar, for it is written: "When she was brought forth, she sent to her father-in-law."

[3]Rav Ḥinena the son of Rav Idi said: What is [it] that is written: "And you shall not wrong each man his neighbor"?

[4]Do not wrong a people that is with you in [observance of] the Torah and the commandments.

[5]Rav said: A man should always be careful about distressing his wife, [6]for since her tears are close at hand, [the punishment for] distressing her is near.

[1]מְנָא לָן?

[2]מִתָּמָר, דִּכְתִיב: ״הִיא מוּצֵאת, וְהִיא שָׁלְחָה אֶל חָמִיהָ״.

[3]אָמַר רַב חִינְנָא בְּרֵיהּ דְּרַב אִידִי: מַאי דִּכְתִיב: ״וְלֹא תוֹנוּ אִישׁ אֶת עֲמִיתוֹ״? [4]עַם שֶׁאִתְּךָ בְּתוֹרָה וּבְמִצְוֹת אַל תּוֹנֵיהוּ.

[5]אָמַר רַב: לְעוֹלָם יְהֵא אָדָם זָהִיר בְּאוֹנָאַת אִשְׁתּוֹ, [6]שֶׁמִּתּוֹךְ שֶׁדִּמְעָתָהּ מְצוּיָה, אוֹנָאָתָהּ קְרוֹבָה.

RASHI

היא מוצאת והיא שלחה — אף על פי שהיו מוציאין אותה לשריפה לא אמרה להם: ליהודה נבעלתי, אלא שלחה לו: למי שאלה לו אנכי הרה, ואם יודה הוא מעצמו — יודה. **עמיתו** — עם אתו. **באונאת אשתו** — באונאת דברים, לצערה. **אונאתה קרובה לבא** — פורענות אונאתה ממהר לבא.

NOTES

עַם שֶׁאִתְּךָ עֲמִיתוֹ **"His neighbor" — one who is with you.** *Ritva* explains that this refers to a man's wife (rather than "a people that is with you," as explained in our commentary), since a man's wife is especially close to him (and hence "with him"). This explanation also accounts for the Gemara's association of the two seemingly independent themes of distressing people who are not observant and distressing one's wife.

אוֹנָאַת אִשְׁתּוֹ **Distressing one's wife.** Distressing any woman is a very serious offense, but the Gemara spoke specifically of distressing one's wife, because a man is required to honor his wife more than himself (*Iyyun Ya'akov*).

HALAKHAH

אוֹנָאַת אִשְׁתּוֹ **Wronging one's wife.** "A man must be especially careful not to hurt his wife's feelings, since she is easily hurt and liable to cry." (*Shulḥan Arukh, Ḥoshen Mishpat* 228:3.)

[1]אָמַר רַבִּי אֶלְעָזָר: מִיּוֹם שֶׁנֶּחֱרַב בֵּית הַמִּקְדָּשׁ נִנְעֲלוּ שַׁעֲרֵי תְפִילָּה, [2]שֶׁנֶּאֱמַר: "גַּם כִּי אֶזְעַק וַאֲשַׁוֵּעַ, שָׂתַם תְּפִלָּתִי". [3]וְאַף עַל פִּי שֶׁשַּׁעֲרֵי תְפִילָּה נִנְעֲלוּ, שַׁעֲרֵי דְמָעוֹת לֹא נִנְעֲלוּ, [4]שֶׁנֶּאֱמַר: "שִׁמְעָה תְפִלָּתִי ה', וְשַׁוְעָתִי הַאֲזִינָה. אֶל דִּמְעָתִי אַל תֶּחֱרַשׁ".

[5]וְאָמַר רַב: כָּל הַהוֹלֵךְ בַּעֲצַת אִשְׁתּוֹ נוֹפֵל בַּגֵּיהִנָּם, [6]שֶׁנֶּאֱמַר: "רַק לֹא הָיָה כְאַחְאָב, וגו'". [7]אֲמַר לֵיהּ רַב פַּפָּא לְאַבַּיֵי: וְהָא אָמְרִי אֱינָשֵׁי: "אִיתְּתָךְ גּוּצָא, גְּחֵין וְתִלְחוֹשׁ לָהּ"! [8]לָא קַשְׁיָא. הָא בְּמִילֵּי דְעָלְמָא, וְהָא בְּמִילֵּי דְבֵיתָא. [9]לִישָּׁנָא אַחֲרִינָא: הָא בְּמִילֵּי דִשְׁמַיָּא, וְהָא בְּמִילֵּי דְעָלְמָא.

LITERAL TRANSLATION

[1]Rabbi Elazar said: From the day the Temple was destroyed the gates of prayer have been locked, [2]as it is said: "Also when I cry and shout, He shuts out my prayer." [3]But even though the gates of prayer have been locked, the gates of tears have not been locked, [4]as it is said: "Hear my prayer, Lord, and give ear to my cry. You will not hold Your peace at my tears."

[5]And Rav said: Whoever follows his wife's counsel falls into Gehinnom, [6]as it is said: "But there was none like Ahab, etc." [7]Rav Pappa said to Abaye: But surely people say: "[If] your wife is short, bend down and whisper to her"! [8]There is no difficulty. This [applies] to worldly matters, and this to domestic matters. [9]Another version: This [applies] to heavenly matters, and this to worldly matters.

RASHI

שמעה תפלתי – אין לשונו מלשון בקשה, שמבקש מאת הקדוש ברוך הוא שישמע תפלתו. אבל "אל תחרש" יש לשונו מלשון בקשה, ולומר: בזו אני בוטח שאין דרכך לשתוק ולא להחריש. "אל תחרש", אל תעשה, אל תתן, משמשין לשון בקשה ומשמשין לשון עתיד. כגון (תהלים קכא) "אל יתן למוט", הרי לשון בקשה, "ויאמר יעקב לא תתן לי מאומה" (בראשית ל), הוא לשון עתיד. **רק לא היה כאחאב** – סיפיה דקרא "אשר הסתה אותו איזבל אשתו". [**אתתך גוצא** = אשתך קטנה – כפוף עצמך ושמע דבריה].

TRANSLATION AND COMMENTARY

אָמַר רַבִּי אֶלְעָזָר [1]The Gemara now introduces another Rabbinic statement regarding the power of tears. **Rabbi Elazar said: From the day the Temple was destroyed the gates of prayer have been locked.** Nowadays, prayers are not accepted as readily as they were before the destruction, [2]**as the verse** (Lamentations 3:8), describing the situation after the destruction, **says: "Also when I cry and shout, He shuts out my prayer."** [3]**But,** Rabbi Elazar continues, **even though the gates of prayer have been locked, the gates of tears are not locked.** Even today, anyone who cries for divine intervention can still expect to be answered, [4]**as the verse** (Psalms 39:13) **says: "Hear my prayer, Lord, and give ear to my cry. You will not hold your peace at my tears."** The Psalmist *asks* that his prayers be heard, but states unequivocally that God will not hold His peace at his tears." Thus it follows that one who sheds tears before God is guaranteed divine assistance, even when ordinary prayers might not suffice.

וְאָמַר רַב [5]**And Rav** further **said** that, although a husband must take care not to hurt his wife's feelings, he should not follow her advice — for **whoever follows his wife's counsel will** eventually **fall into Gehinnom,** as his wife is liable to persuade him to commit a transgression. Rav illustrates his point by citing the case of Ahab, the most wicked of the Kings of Israel. Ahab committed his most serious sins at his wife's instigation, [6]**as the verse says** (I Kings 21:25): **"But there was none like Ahab,** who gave himself over to do what was evil in the sight of the Lord, as Jezebel his wife had incited him." Thus we see that a person who follows his wife's advice is liable to be condemned to Gehinnom.

אֲמַר לֵיהּ רַב פַּפָּא לְאַבַּיֵי [7]**Rav Pappa** challenged Rav's directive to shun the advice offered by one's wife and **said to Abaye: But surely people say: "If your wife is short, bend down and whisper to her,"** which shows that a husband should seek his wife's counsel!

לָא קַשְׁיָא [8]The Gemara resolves the contradiction: **There is** really **no difficulty.** Rav's recommendation to avoid seeking one's wife's counsel **applies to general matters** which a woman would be unlikely to understand. Following her advice in such matters could be disastrous. The popular proverb, on the other hand, which urges husbands to go to extremes to seek their wives' counsel, applies **to domestic matters,** which are a woman's domain. [9]**Another version** of the Gemara's resolution of the contradiction was also suggested: According to this version, Rav's statement **applies** specifically **to religious matters.** The popular proverb, on the other hand, applies **to general matters**, to anything that is not religious in nature, whether it is domestic

than they would other women.

BACKGROUND

מִיּוֹם שֶׁנֶּחֱרַב בֵּית הַמִּקְדָּשׁ נִנְעֲלוּ שַׁעֲרֵי תְפִילָּה From the day the Temple was destroyed, the gates of prayer have been locked. Jewish philosophers explain that an especially close relationship obtained between God and the Jews as long as the Temple was standing, and hence prayer and repentance brought an immediate, tangible divine response during this period. By contrast, the destruction of the Temple brought an era of divine wrath in its wake; therefore, God's providence is not always fully manifest, and prayer is not as readily accepted.

שַׁעֲרֵי דְמָעוֹת לֹא נִנְעֲלוּ The gates of tears have not been locked. Even though divine providence is not always manifest since the destruction of the Temple, God nevertheless answers the prayers of sufferers on an individual basis; hence the Gemara's statement that "the gates of tears" are never locked. It is worth noting that numerous liturgical poems, some of which are recited during the closing service (*Ne'ilah*) on Yom Kippur, focus on this theme.

NOTES

מִיּוֹם שֶׁנֶּחֱרַב בֵּית הַמִּקְדָּשׁ From the day the Temple was destroyed. As long as the Temple was standing, people's prayers ascended to Heaven through the Temple gates (cf. I Kings 8:48 and *Rashi* on Genesis 28:17). Thus, after the Temple was destroyed, the gates of prayer were "locked" (*Maharsha*).

TRANSLATION AND COMMENTARY

or not. In all such questions, the wife's opinion is at least as good as the husband's, and her advice is invaluable.

אָמַר רַב חִסְדָּא [1]The Gemara now cites three additional Rabbinic statements dealing with the dire consequences of *ona'ah* — wronging one's fellow man — whether by fraud ("monetary *ona'ah*"; אוֹנָאַת מָמוֹן) or by causing him anguish ("verbal *ona'ah*"; אוֹנָאַת דְּבָרִים). All three statements make the same point, using different metaphors: that God takes a special interest in avenging the sins of fraud and verbal cruelty. The first metaphor is based on the image of prayers passing through the gates of Heaven on their way to God. On their way, they tend to be delayed or intercepted by the angels who guard the gates. **Rav Ḥisda said: All the** heavenly **gates are locked except for the gates** through which pass claims **of** redress for ***ona'ah.*** While other prayers may be intercepted and may not necessarily be answered, the prayers of a person who has been wronged and seeks divine intervention pass through the heavenly gates and go directly to God, who promptly answers them. In support of his statement, Rav Ḥisda quotes a verse which will also form the basis of the other two metaphors brought below. [2]**As the verse says** (Amos 7:7): **"Behold, the Lord stands by a wall** made by **a plumbline, and in His hand is a plumbline."** A plumbline is an instrument of measurement used to determine whether walls are vertical. From the image that God is holding a plumbline in His hand, we learn that He is particular about any deviation from correct measure. In other words, God pays direct attention to matters of *ona'ah* and does not allow them to be intercepted at the "gate in the wall."

אָמַר רַבִּי אֶלְעָזָר [3]The second metaphor is based on the idea that God normally punishes sin through messengers. In other words, God has built various mechanisms into the structure of the world, which right wrongs and punish evildoers. **Rabbi Elazar said: Every** sin **is punished by the hand of a messenger,** and not directly by the hand of God, **except for** the sin of *ona'ah*, for which God Himself exacts immediate punishment. [4]**As the verse says: "And in His hand is a plumbline."** The "plumbline" which determines whether *ona'ah* has been committed is held by God himself, implying that He personally attends to punishing those guilty of *ona'ah.*

אָמַר רַבִּי אַבָּהוּ [5]The third metaphor is based on the image of a heavenly curtain drawn between the Divine Presence and the rest of the world. In this image, God does not pay direct attention to events on the other side of the curtain, leaving them to be dealt with by His angels and messengers. **Rabbi Abbahu said: There are three sins before which the** heavenly **curtain is not closed.** Three offences remain within God's view and are

[1]אָמַר רַב חִסְדָּא: כָּל הַשְּׁעָרִים נִנְעָלִים חוּץ מִשַּׁעֲרֵי אוֹנָאָה, [2]שֶׁנֶּאֱמַר: "הִנֵּה ה׳ נִצָּב עַל חוֹמַת אֲנָךְ, וּבְיָדוֹ אֲנָךְ". [3]אָמַר רַבִּי אֶלְעָזָר: הַכֹּל נִפְרָע בִּידֵי שָׁלִיחַ חוּץ מֵאוֹנָאָה, [4]שֶׁנֶּאֱמַר: "וּבְיָדוֹ אֲנָךְ". [5]אָמַר רַבִּי אַבָּהוּ: שְׁלֹשָׁה אֵין הַפַּרְגּוֹד נִנְעָל בִּפְנֵיהֶם:

LITERAL TRANSLATION

[1]Rav Ḥisda said: All the gates are locked except for the gates of *ona'ah*, [2]as it is said: "Behold, the Lord stands by the wall of a plumbline, and in His hand is a plumbline."

[3]Rabbi Elazar said: Everything is punished by the hand of a messenger except for *ona'ah*, [4]as it is said: "And in His hand is a plumbline."

[5]Rabbi Abbahu said: [There are] three [sins] before which the curtain is not closed:

RASHI

כל השערים – של תפלה ננעלו. **חוץ משערי אונאה** – הלועק על אונאת דברים אין השער ננעל בפניו. **הכל על ידי שליח** – נפרעים על כל עבירות על ידי שליח. **ובידו** – לא מסרה לשליח. **פרגוד** – מחילה שבין שכינה לצבא מרום. **אינו ננעל** – להפסיד ראייתן מן המקום, אלא תמיד רואה אותם עד שיפרע.

NOTES

מִשַּׁעֲרֵי אוֹנָאָה **The gates of *ona'ah*.** This does not mean that other prayers are not answered. Rather, people who offer other petitions must wait longer to have their requests fulfilled. By contrast, the prayers of those who have been wronged are answered immediately (*Torat Ḥayyim*).

שֶׁנֶּאֱמַר הִנֵּה ה׳ נִצָּב עַל חוֹמַת אֲנָךְ **As it is said: "Behold, the Lord stands by a wall of a plumbline."** *Maharsha* explains the inference from the verse somewhat differently from our commentary. According to him, one who stands inside a city whose gates are locked cannot see what is happening outside the city, whereas God, who (as it were) "stands by the wall of a plumbline," can see what is happening outside. Thus the verse implies that God perceives all wrongdoing, and no wall can separate Him from those who are wronged.

בִּידֵי שָׁלִיחַ **By the hand of a messenger.** *Rabbenu Yehonatan* explains the difference between sins punished directly by God and those punished by messengers as follows: Since messengers — meaning divine messengers as well as the structure of causality in the natural world — are not always available, people who commit ordinary sins are not always punished immediately. By contrast, offenses punished directly by God receive immediate redress, since God is everywhere.

HALAKHAH

שַׁעֲרֵי אוֹנָאָה לֹא נִנְעָלוּ **The gates of *ona'ah* are not locked.** "The prayers of a person who was the object of verbal *ona'ah* are answered immediately." (*Shulḥan Arukh, Ḥoshen Mishpat* 228:1.)

[1] אוֹנָאָה, וְגֶזֶל, וַעֲבוֹדָה זָרָה. [2] אוֹנָאָה, דִּכְתִיב: ״וּבְיָדוֹ אֲנָךְ״. [3] גָּזֵל, דִּכְתִיב: ״חָמָס וָשֹׁד יִשָּׁמַע בָּהּ עַל פָּנַי תָּמִיד״. [4] עֲבוֹדָה זָרָה, דִּכְתִיב: ״הָעָם הַמַּכְעִיסִים אוֹתִי עַל פָּנַי תָּמִיד וגו׳״.

[5] אָמַר רַב יְהוּדָה: לְעוֹלָם יְהֵא אָדָם זָהִיר בִּתְבוּאָה בְּתוֹךְ בֵּיתוֹ, [6] שֶׁאֵין מְרִיבָה מְצוּיָה בְּתוֹךְ בֵּיתוֹ שֶׁל אָדָם אֶלָּא עַל עִסְקֵי תְבוּאָה, [7] שֶׁנֶּאֱמַר: ״הַשָּׂם גְּבוּלֵךְ שָׁלוֹם, חֵלֶב חִטִּים יַשְׂבִּיעֵךְ״. [8] אָמַר רַב פַּפָּא: הַיְינוּ דְּאָמְרִי אֱינָשֵׁי: ״כְּמִשְׁלַם שַׂעֲרֵי מִכַּדָּא, נָקִישׁ וְאָתֵי תִּגְרָא בְּבֵיתָא״. [9] וְאָמַר רַב חִינְנָא בַּר פַּפָּא: לְעוֹלָם יְהֵא אָדָם זָהִיר בִּתְבוּאָה בְּתוֹךְ בֵּיתוֹ, שֶׁלֹּא נִקְרְאוּ יִשְׂרָאֵל דַּלִּים אֶלָּא עַל עִסְקֵי תְבוּאָה, [10] שֶׁנֶּאֱמַר: ״וְהָיָה אִם זָרַע יִשְׂרָאֵל וגו׳״, [11] וּכְתִיב: ״וַיַּחֲנוּ

LITERAL TRANSLATION

[1] *Ona'ah*, and robbery, and idolatry. [2] *Ona'ah*, as it is written: "And in His hand is a plumbline." [3] Robbery, as it is written: "Violence and robbery is heard in her before Me continually." [4] Idolatry, as it is written: "The people that provoke Me to My face continually, etc."

[5] Rav Yehudah said: A man should always be careful that there is grain in his house, [6] for strife is found in a man's house only because of matters of grain, [7] as it is said: "He makes peace in your borders, and fills you with the finest of the wheat."

[8] Rav Pappa said: This is what people say: "When the barley is gone from the jar, strife knocks and comes into the house."

[9] And Rav Ḥinena bar Pappa said: A man should always be careful that there is grain in his house, for Israel were called poor only because of matters of grain, [10] as it is said: "And it was when Israel had sown, etc.," [11] and it is written: "And they encamped

TRANSLATION AND COMMENTARY

immediately redressed: [1] **Ona'ah, robbery, and idolatry.** [2] We know that *ona'ah* receives direct divine attention, **as the verse** (ibid.) **says: "And in His hand is a plumbline."** The "plumbline" is readily available in God's hand, and the "curtain" does not interfere with His punishment. [3] The same applies to **robbery, as the verse** (Jeremiah 6:7) **says: "Violence and robbery is heard in** Jerusalem; **they are before Me constantly."** Here, too, robbery is said to be constantly before God, implying that He is always available to attend to its retribution, and it does not remain on the other side of the "curtain" as do other sins. [4] The same applies to **idolatry, as the verse** (Isaiah 65:3) **says: "The people that provoke Me to My face continually,** that sacrifice in gardens, and burn incense upon altars of brick." These are idolatrous rites, and Rabbi Abbahu infers that, since idoltrous "provocations" are constantly before "God's face," idolatry receives God's immediate personal attention, without obstruction from the "curtain."

אָמַר רַב יְהוּדָה [5] The Gemara now returns to the question of how a husband should behave toward his wife. Since a husband must not cause his wife anguish, it is wise to avert the domestic problems that often lead to quarrels. **Rav Yehudah said: A man should always be careful to have** enough **grain in his house.** [6] **For strife only besets a man's house because of matters related to grain** — when there is not enough food to eat. [7] **As the verse says** (Psalms 147:14): **"He who makes peace in your borders** does so by **satisfying you with the finest of the wheat,"** implying that people who do not have "the finest of the wheat" (i.e., sufficient food to eat) will not have "peace in their borders."

אָמַר רַב פַּפָּא [8] **Rav Pappa said: This is what people say.** Rav Yehudah's Scriptural exposition corresponds to the following proverb: **"When barley is gone from the jar, strife knocks** at the door **and comes into the house."**

וְאָמַר רַב חִינְנָא בַּר פַּפָּא [9] **Rav Ḥinena bar Pappa** suggested a further reason for keeping one's house well stocked with food, and **said: A person should always be careful to have** enough **grain in his house, for Israel were only called "poor" because of matters related to grain,** when their food was destroyed. In other words, a person is not really poor until he has no food. [10] **As the verse says** (Judges 6:3): **"And so it was when Israel had sown** that the Midianites came up, and the Amalekites, and the children of the East came up against them." [11] **And it is written** in the next verse (ibid. 6:4), **"And they encamped against** the Israelites, and destroyed the

RASHI

ובידו אנך — משמע שהיא תמיד אצלו ומשמש בה. **על פני** — לפני, ואין מחיצה בינו לבין העבירה. **אימתי גבולך שלום** — כש״חלב חטים ישביעך״ הקדוש ברוך הוא. **מכדא** — כד שנותנים בו שעורים. **נקיש ואתי תגרא** — התגר מקשקש ובא. ואני שמעתי: הכד מקשקש, כדרך כלי ריקם שנשמע בו קול הברה כשמקשקשין עליו.

TERMINOLOGY

אָמְרִי אֱינָשֵׁי People say. A term used that introduces a popular proverb or saying.

BACKGROUND

כְּמִשְׁלַם שַׂעֲרֵי מִכַּדָּא When the barley is gone from the jar. This proverb comes to illustrate the Gemara's statement that financial problems are a principal cause of domestic strife. Indeed, poverty is likely to bring out and enhance other, family-related problems of a non-economic nature, which might not otherwise arise. The Gemara apparently stressed this point to discourage people from making investments which could cause severe financial difficulties in the short run, even though they might be potentially lucrative in the long run.

NOTES

כְּמִשְׁלַם שַׂעֲרֵי מִכַּדָּא When the barley is gone from the jar. Barley was generally used as animal fodder in Talmudic times. Thus the maxim cited here implies that strife only befalls a house if its occupants have become so poor that they do not even have barley to eat (*Ein Ya'akov*).

עֲלֵיהֶם וגו׳״, [1]וּכְתִיב: ״וַיִּדַּל יִשְׂרָאֵל מְאֹד מִפְּנֵי מִדְיָן״. [2]וְאָמַר רַבִּי חֶלְבּוֹ: לְעוֹלָם יְהֵא אָדָם זָהִיר בִּכְבוֹד אִשְׁתּוֹ, שֶׁאֵין בְּרָכָה מְצוּיָה בְּתוֹךְ בֵּיתוֹ שֶׁל אָדָם אֶלָּא בִּשְׁבִיל אִשְׁתּוֹ, [3]שֶׁנֶּאֱמַר: ״וּלְאַבְרָם הֵטִיב בַּעֲבוּרָהּ״. [4]וְהַיְינוּ דַּאֲמַר לְהוּ רָבָא לִבְנֵי מְחוֹזָא: ״אוֹקִירוּ לִנְשַׁיְיכוּ כִּי הֵיכִי דְּתִתְעַתְּרוּ״. [5]תְּנַן הָתָם: ״חֲתָכוֹ חוּלְיוֹת וְנָתַן חוֹל בֵּין חוּלְיָא לְחוּלְיָא,

TRANSLATION AND COMMENTARY

increase of the earth." [1]**And it is written** at the end of the passage (ibid., 6:6): **"And Israel became very poor because of Midian."** Thus we see that the Bible calls the Israelites "poor" after their grain was destroyed by their enemies.

וְאָמַר רַבִּי חֶלְבּוֹ [2]The Gemara continues its discussion of how a husband should conduct himself towards his wife. **Rabbi Ḥelbo said: A man should always be careful about his wife's honor, for blessing** (prosperity) **is only found in a man's house on account of his wife,** [3]**as the verse says** (Genesis 12:16): **"And** Pharaoh **treated Abram well for** his wife's **sake,** and he had sheep and oxen, etc." Accordingly, Rabbi Ḥelbo argues, the Torah is teaching us that in general a man's prosperity comes from his wife. [4]**And this is what Rava said to** his fellow townspeople, **the people of Meḥoza: Honor your wives so that you may become wealthy.**

תְּנַן הָתָם [5]The Gemara now relates a story connected with the issue of causing anguish to other people, although its theological significance far transcends this specific ethical concern. The story begins with a Mishnah from tractate *Kelim,* which deals with the susceptibility of utensils to ritual impurity. If a primary source of ritual impurity, such as a dead animal, comes into contact with a utensil, the utensil becomes ritually impure only if it is susceptible to ritual impurity. The susceptibility of a utensil to contracting ritual impurity depends on its construction and on the material from which it is made. **We learned in a Mishnah** taught **elsewhere** (*Kelim* 5:10) that there is a difference of opinion regarding an oven: **"If** someone **cut** an earthenware oven horizontally **into** ring-shaped **pieces, and** then reconstructed it and **put sand between the pieces,** afterwards spreading clay on the oven to join the pieces together,

LITERAL TRANSLATION

against them, etc.," [1]and it is written: "And Israel became very poor because of Midian."

[2]And Rabbi Ḥelbo said: A man should always be careful about his wife's honor, for blessing is found in a man's house only on account of his wife, [3]as it is said: "And he treated Abram well for her sake." [4]And this is what Rava said to the people of Meḥoza: "Honor your wives so that you may become wealthy." [5]We have learned there: "[If] he cut it [into] segments and put sand between segment and segment,

RASHI

וידל ישראל — לעיל מיניה כתיב ״ויחנו עליהם וישחיתו את יבול הארץ״. **אוקירו נשייכו** = כבדו נשותיכם. **מחוזא** — עיר שהיה רבא דר בתוכה כך שמה. **חתכו חוליות** — תנור העשוי חוליות מצרפו בכבשן כדרך כלי חרס, ואחר כך צירף החוליות, ונתן חול בין חוליא לחוליא.

NOTES

חֲתָכוֹ חוּלְיוֹת וְנָתַן חוֹל If he cut it into segments and put sand. Various explanations of the dispute between Rabbi Eliezer and the Sages have been suggested by the commentators. Some authorities explain that they disagreed as to whether an oven that was initially manufactured by cementing separate pieces of ceramic together can become ritually impure (i.e., if it later comes in contact with a dead body, etc.; thus *Rambam*, *Ra'avad* and others). Rabbi Eliezer maintains that the oven cannot contract ritual impurity, because the pieces do not fit together well, and hence the oven is considered broken, and the law is that broken utensils cannot contract ritual impurity (*Ra'avad*).

Others explain that the "oven of Akhnai" was a normal oven which had become ritually impure, after which the owner cut it into separate pieces which he later cemented together (*Rash*, *Ritva*, and others). According to this explanation, Rabbi Eliezer maintained that the oven becomes ritually pure, because cutting it into pieces is tantamount to breaking it, and even though it was later cemented together the pieces do not fit together well, because the sections of the oven remain separated from each other by layers of sand.

HALAKHAH

כְּבוֹד אִשְׁתּוֹ Honoring one's wife. "The Sages said that a man should love his wife like himself, and honor her more than himself." (*Rambam, Sefer Nashim, Hilkhot Ishut* 15:19.)

תַּנּוּר שֶׁחֲתָכוֹ חוּלְיוֹת An oven cut into segments. "An earthenware oven which was cut into pieces horizontally can become ritually impure, if it was overlaid with clay and the clay fired, even if there are layers of sand between the pieces," following the view of the Sages. (Ibid., *Sefer Tohorah, Hilkhot Kelim* 16:5.)

SAGES

רַבִּי חֶלְבּוֹ Rabbi Ḥelbo. A third-generation Babylonian Amora, Rabbi Ḥelbo was one of Rav Huna's outstanding students, and transmitted many of Rav Huna's Halakhic teachings. Later, Rabbi Ḥelbo immigrated to Eretz Israel (during Rav Huna's lifetime), apparently settling in Tiberias. There he met Rabbi Yoḥanan and studied Aggadah with Rabbi Shmuel bar Naḥmani, and Halakhah with the outstanding disciples of Rabbi Yoḥanan.

Rabbi Ḥelbo's Halakhic and Aggadic teachings are found in both the Babylonian and Jerusalem Talmuds, and many Amoraim of the next generation in Eretz Israel cite his teachings. He left no children.

BACKGROUND

כְּבוֹד אִשְׁתּוֹ His wife's honor. The honor referred to here is not merely respectful behavior and speech. It also has practical implications. Since people often honor each other because of their attire and jewelry, a husband is obligated to make certain that his wife is dressed in a way that does honor to him in public, and he must be more scrupulous of his wife's honor than of his own in this matter. This ruling explains the connection between honoring one's wife and earning a blessing. Anyone who honors his wife and buys her possessions, even above his economic status, is worthy of a blessing for that reason.

וְהַיְינוּ דַּאֲמַר לְהוּ רָבָא לִבְנֵי מְחוֹזָא And this is what Rava said to the people of Meḥoza. Rava lived in Meḥoza, and eventually moved the Pumbedita Yeshivah to that city, which was a major commercial center. Most of the Jews who lived there were apparently merchants who supported themselves solely through commerce, as opposed to most other Jews during that period, who engaged in agriculture. Accordingly, Rava phrased his remarks in a manner appropriate to the Meḥozans, since the residents of that city were very concerned about financial matters and were

TRANSLATION AND COMMENTARY

[1]**Rabbi Eliezer declares** the resulting oven **ritually pure** — i.e., not susceptible to ritual impurity — because in his opinion the oven is no longer regarded as a complete utensil and is therefore no longer susceptible to ritual impurity. While the pieces have indeed been joined together once more, the oven is nevertheless regarded as built of broken fragments, and such a structure is not susceptible to ritual impurity. **The Sages,** on the other hand, **declared it** to be sufficiently reconstructed to be **ritually impure** — i.e., subject to ritual impurity. In their opinion, although the oven was reconstructed from separate pieces, it is to be viewed as a repaired and whole vessel, because of the clay that has been spread over it on the outside. Notwithstanding the sand that separates its pieces, it is a single, whole unit, and is susceptible to ritual impurity like any other oven. [59B] And such an oven was called **'the oven of Akhnai.'"** (*Akhnai* means a type of snake.)

מַאי עַכְנַאי [2]The Gemara asks: **What is "Akhnai"?** Why was the oven named after a snake?

אָמַר רַב יְהוּדָה [3]The Gemara replies: **Rav Yehudah said in the name of Shmuel:** The Mishnah is hinting at the fierce argument between Rabbi Eliezer and the Sages, described in the Baraita below. The Rabbis who disputed Rabbi Eliezer's view **entwined** Rabbi Eliezer **with words, like a snake** wrapping itself around its prey, **and they** succeeded in having the oven **declared ritually impure.**

תָּנָא [4]The details of the dispute **were taught in** the following Baraita: **"On that day, Rabbi Eliezer used all the arguments in the world.** He produced powerful arguments to justify his position that the oven should be considered unreconstructed and not susceptible to ritual impurity. **But** the Sages **did not accept his** arguments, and insisted that the oven was susceptible to ritual impurity. [5]After Rabbi Eliezer saw that he was not able to persuade his colleagues with logical arguments, **he said to them: 'If the Halakhah is in accordance with me, let this carob tree prove it.'** [6]**The carob tree** immediately **uprooted** itself and moved **one hundred cubits — and some say four hundred cubits — from its** original **place.** [7]The Sages **said to him: 'Proof cannot be brought from a carob tree.'** [8]Rabbi Eliezer **then said to** the Sages: **'If the Halakhah is in accordance with me, let the channel of water prove it.' The channel of water** immediately **flowed backward,** against the direction in which it usually

[1]רַבִּי אֱלִיעֶזֶר מְטַהֵר וַחֲכָמִים מְטַמְּאִין. [59B] וְזֶה הוּא תַּנּוּר שֶׁל עַכְנַאי״.

[2]מַאי עַכְנַאי?

[3]אָמַר רַב יְהוּדָה אָמַר שְׁמוּאֵל: שֶׁהִקִּיפוּ דְּבָרִים כְּעַכְנָא זוֹ, וְטִמְּאוּהוּ.

[4]תָּנָא: ״בְּאוֹתוֹ הַיּוֹם הֵשִׁיב רַבִּי אֱלִיעֶזֶר כָּל תְּשׁוּבוֹת שֶׁבָּעוֹלָם וְלֹא קִיבְּלוּ הֵימֶנּוּ. [5]אָמַר לָהֶם: ׳אִם הֲלָכָה כְּמוֹתִי, חָרוּב זֶה יוֹכִיחַ׳. [6]נֶעֱקַר חָרוּב מִמְּקוֹמוֹ מֵאָה אַמָּה — וְאָמְרִי לָהּ אַרְבַּע מֵאוֹת אַמָּה. [7]אָמְרוּ לוֹ: ׳אֵין מְבִיאִין רְאָיָה מִן הֶחָרוּב׳. [8]חָזַר וְאָמַר לָהֶם: ׳אִם הֲלָכָה כְּמוֹתִי, אַמַּת הַמַּיִם יוֹכִיחוּ׳. חָזְרוּ אַמַּת

LITERAL TRANSLATION

[1]Rabbi Eliezer declares it ritually pure and the Sages declare it ritually impure. [59B] And this is the oven of Akhnai."

[2]What is Akhnai?

[3]Rav Yehudah said in the name of Shmuel: Because they encircled [him with] words like this snake, and declared it ritually impure.

[4]It has been taught: "On that day, Rabbi Eliezer used (lit., 'replied') all the arguments (lit., 'replies') in the world, but they did not accept [them] from him. [5]He said to them: 'If the Halakhah is in accordance with me, let this carob tree prove [it].' [6]The carob tree was uprooted from its place one hundred cubits — and some say four hundred cubits. [7]They said to him: 'One does not bring proof from a carob tree.' [8]He then said to them: 'If the Halakhah is in accordance with me, let the channel of water prove [it].' The channel of water turned

RASHI

רבי אליעזר מטהר — שאין זה כלי חרס אלא בנין, כעין כלי גללים וכלי אדמה שאין מקבלין טומאה. **וחכמים מטמאין** — דאזלי בתר סוליות. שאר תנורים שלהם היו עשוים כעין קדירות גדולות ופיו למעלה, ונורף בכבשן כשאר קדירות ומטלטלים. אלא שהיה מושיבו על הארץ או על הדף, ומדביק את טפילות הטיט סביב על כולו לעשותו עב שיקלוט ויחזיק את חומו. **עכנאי** — נחש. דרכו לעשות בעגולה להכניס זנבו אצל פיו.

therefore interested in any advice that might make them rich.

REALIA

תַּנּוּר שֶׁל עַכְנַאי **The oven of Akhnai.** An oven of Akhnai (based on an oven found in Masada). According to Rabbi Eliezer, if such an oven was cut into pieces horizontally (cf. the lines in the illustration), it could not become susceptible to ritual impurity even if the pieces were later cemented together.

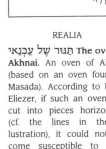

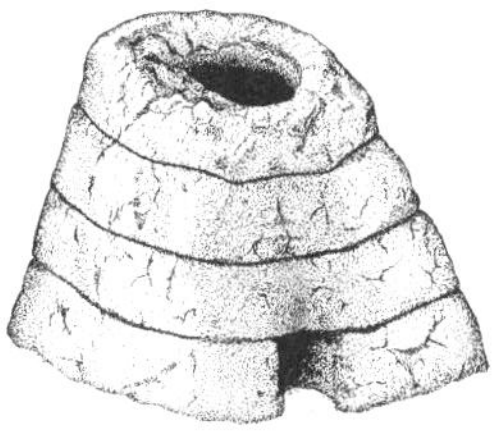

LANGUAGE

עַכְנָא **Snake.** This is the Aramaic form of the Greek word ἔχις, or ἔχιδνα, *echis* or *echidna*, meaning "snake," "viper." Some authorities believe that Akhnai was the name of the man who made the oven (*Tosafot* and others). Several people mentioned in the sources bear this name, especially in the form current in Eretz Israel, Ḥakhinai (חֲכִינַאי). According to this interpretation, the words of the Gemara here are a homiletic addition, indicating that the name of the oven was appropriate.

NOTES

שֶׁהִקִּיפוּ דְּבָרִים כְּעַכְנָא **Because they entwined him with words like a snake.** Just as a snake winds itself round its prey and does not permit it to escape, so too the Sages offered such cogent proof of their viewpoint that Rabbi Eliezer was unable to refute their objections (*Rabbenu Nissim Gaon*).

חָרוּב וְאַמַּת הַמַּיִם **The carob tree and the channel of water.** The commentators explain that God performs miracles for

SAGES

רַבִּי אֱלִיעֶזֶר Rabbi Eliezer. When the name "Rabbi Eliezer" occurs in the Talmud without a patronymic, it refers to Rabbi Eliezer ben Hyrcanus (also known as Rabbi Eliezer the Great), who was one of the leading scholars in the period after the destruction of the Second Temple.

Rabbi Eliezer was born to a wealthy family of Levites, which traced its descent back to Moses. Rabbi Eliezer began studying Torah late in life, but quickly became an outstanding and beloved disciple of Rabban Yoḥanan ben Zakkai. Indeed, Rabban Yoḥanan remarked that "if all the Sages of Israel were on one side of the scale and Eliezer ben Hyrcanus on the other, he would outweigh them all."

Rabbi Eliezer was known for his remarkable memory, and was famed for faithfully reporting and following the traditions of others without altering them. He himself leaned towards the views of Bet Shammai, even though he studied with Rabban Yoḥanan ben Zakkai, who was a follower of Bet Hillel. Rabbi Eliezer's principal opponent, Rabbi Yehoshua ben Ḥananyah, generally followed the views of Bet Hillel, and many basic Halakhic disputes between these scholars are reported in the Mishnah.

Because of his staunch and unflinching adherence to tradition, Rabbi Eliezer was unwilling to accede to the majority view where his own views were based on tradition. Indeed, Rabbi Eliezer's conduct generated so much tension among the Sages that his own brother-in-law, Rabban Gamliel, eventually excommunicated him, to prevent controversy from proliferating. This ban was lifted only after Rabbi Eliezer's death.

All the Sages of the next generation were Rabbi Eliezer's students. Most prominent among them was Rabbi Akiva. Rabbi Eliezer's son, Hyrcanus, was also a Sage.

TRANSLATION AND COMMENTARY

flowed. [1]The Sages **said to him: 'Proof cannot be brought from a channel of water** either.' [2]Rabbi Eliezer **then said to** the Sages: **'If the Halakhah is in accordance with me, let the walls of the House of Study prove it.' The walls of the House of Study** then **leaned** and were about **to fall.** [3]**Rabbi Yehoshua,** one of Rabbi Eliezer's chief opponents among the Sages, **rebuked** the falling walls, **saying to them: 'If Talmudic scholars argue with one another** in their discussions **about the Halakhah, what affair is it of yours?'** [4]The walls **did not fall** down, **out of respect for Rabbi Yehoshua, nor did they straighten, out of respect for Rabbi Eliezer, and** indeed those walls **still remain leaning** to this day. [5]Rabbi Eliezer **then said to** the Sages: **'If the Halakhah is in accordance with me, let it be proved** directly **from Heaven.'** [6]Suddenly **a heavenly voice went forth and said** to the Sages: **'Why are you disputing with Rabbi Eliezer? The Halakhah is in accordance with him in all circumstances!'** [7]**Rabbi Yehoshua rose to his feet and** quoted a portion of a verse (Deuteronomy 30:12), **saying:** 'The Torah **is not in heaven!'"**

הַמַּיִם לַאֲחוֹרֵיהֶם. [1]אָמְרוּ לוֹ: 'אֵין מְבִיאִין רְאָיָה מֵאַמַּת הַמַּיִם'. [2]חָזַר וְאָמַר לָהֶם: 'אִם הֲלָכָה כְּמוֹתִי, כּוֹתְלֵי בֵית הַמִּדְרָשׁ יוֹכִיחוּ'. הִטּוּ כּוֹתְלֵי בֵית הַמִּדְרָשׁ לִיפּוֹל. [3]גָּעַר בָּהֶם רַבִּי יְהוֹשֻׁעַ, אָמַר לָהֶם: 'אִם תַּלְמִידֵי חֲכָמִים מְנַצְּחִים זֶה אֶת זֶה בַּהֲלָכָה, אַתֶּם מַה טִּיבְכֶם'? [4]לֹא נָפְלוּ, מִפְּנֵי כְּבוֹדוֹ שֶׁל רַבִּי יְהוֹשֻׁעַ, וְלֹא זָקְפוּ, מִפְּנֵי כְּבוֹדוֹ שֶׁל רַבִּי אֱלִיעֶזֶר, וַעֲדַיִן מַטִּין וְעוֹמְדִין. [5]חָזַר וְאָמַר לָהֶם: 'אִם הֲלָכָה כְּמוֹתִי, מִן הַשָּׁמַיִם יוֹכִיחוּ'. [6]יָצְאתָה בַּת קוֹל וְאָמְרָה: 'מַה לָּכֶם אֵצֶל רַבִּי אֱלִיעֶזֶר שֶׁהֲלָכָה כְּמוֹתוֹ בְּכָל מָקוֹם'? [7]עָמַד רַבִּי יְהוֹשֻׁעַ עַל רַגְלָיו וְאָמַר: 'לֹא בַּשָּׁמַיִם הִיא'".

LITERAL TRANSLATION

backward. [1]They said to him: 'One does not bring proof from a channel of water.' [2]He then said to them: 'If the Halakhah is in accordance with me, let the walls of the House of Study prove [it].' The walls of the House of Study leaned to fall. [3]Rabbi Yehoshua rebuked them, [and] said to them: 'If Talmudic Sages argue with one another about the Halakhah, what affair is it of yours (lit., "what is your nature")?' [4]They did not fall, out of respect for Rabbi Yehoshua; but they did not straighten, out of respect for Rabbi Eliezer, and they still remain leaning. [5]He then said to them: 'If the Halakhah is in accordance with me, let it be proved from Heaven.' [6]A [heavenly] voice went forth and said: 'Why are you [disputing] with Rabbi Eliezer, for the Halakhah is in accordance with him everywhere?' [7]Rabbi Yehoshua rose to his feet and said: 'It is not in heaven.'"

NOTES

the righteous in every generation, just as He did in Biblical times for the Prophets. Accordingly, God demonstrated His agreement with Rabbi Eliezer's view by performing these wonders (see *Rabbenu Ḥananel* and *Rabbenu Nissim Gaon*). *Rabbenu Ḥananel*, however, maintains that these miracles did not actually occur. Rather, they took place in a dream witnessed by one of Rabbi Eliezer's contemporaries (which was nevertheless taken seriously by the Rabbis).

The commentators suggest various explanations as to why Rabbi Eliezer appealed to a carob tree, to a stream of water, and to the walls of the House of Study to prove that he was correct (see *Maharsha* and others). *Rabbi Shlomo Molkho* explains that these items symbolized the various elements of which the world is composed.

יָצְאתָה בַּת קוֹל A heavenly voice went forth. The commentators attempt to explain how the heavenly voice could be wrong (as shown by the fact that the Rabbis refused to accept it). *Rabbenu Nissim Gaon* suggests that, since the heavenly voice declared that "the Halakhah is in accordance with Rabbi Eliezer *everywhere*," without specifically mentioning the case of the "oven of Akhnai," the Sages felt that this case might be an exception. Moreover, the heavenly voice might have been a divine attempt to test the Rabbis, to see whether they could be induced to deviate from their original decision, which was binding (because it was arrived at by majority rule).

Rabbi Shlomo Molkho claims that the disputed oven was indeed ritually pure, as Rabbi Eliezer had said. But the Rabbis declared it impure, so as to prevent confusion with other types of ovens, which are susceptible to ritual impurity according to all opinions. The Sages' ruling thus constituted a "protective measure" intended to prevent inadvertent violation of the law.

HALAKHAH

לֹא בַּשָּׁמַיִם הִיא It is not in heaven. "The Torah states of itself: 'It is not in heaven,' and from here we learn that a prophet is not authorized to introduce new laws which do not appear in the Torah. Even if a prophet performed signs and wonders, declaring that God sent him to introduce new laws or cancel existing ones, or to suggest novel Halakhic interpretations, he is a false prophet." (*Rambam, Sefer HaMada, Hilkhot Yesodei HaTorah* 9:1.)

1 מַאי ״לֹא בַּשָּׁמַיִם הִיא״?
2 אָמַר רַבִּי יִרְמְיָה: שֶׁכְּבָר נִתְּנָה תּוֹרָה מֵהַר סִינַי, אֵין אָנוּ מַשְׁגִּיחִין בְּבַת קוֹל, שֶׁכְּבָר כָּתַבְתָּ בְּהַר סִינַי בַּתּוֹרָה: ״אַחֲרֵי רַבִּים לְהַטֹּת״.
3 אַשְׁכְּחֵיהּ רַבִּי נָתָן לְאֵלִיָּהוּ, אֲמַר לֵיהּ: ״מַאי עָבֵיד קוּדְשָׁא בְּרִיךְ הוּא בְּהַהִיא שַׁעְתָּא״?
4 אֲמַר לֵיהּ: ״קָא חָיֵיךְ וְאָמַר: ׳נִצְּחוּנִי בָּנַי, נִצְּחוּנִי בָּנַי׳״.
5 אָמְרוּ: ״אוֹתוֹ הַיּוֹם הֵבִיאוּ כָּל טְהָרוֹת שֶׁטִּיהֵר רַבִּי אֱלִיעֶזֶר וּשְׂרָפוּם בָּאֵשׁ, וְנִמְנוּ עָלָיו וּבֵרְכוּהוּ. 6 וְאָמְרוּ: ׳מִי יֵלֵךְ וְיוֹדִיעוֹ׳? 7 אָמַר לָהֶם רַבִּי עֲקִיבָא: ׳אֲנִי אֵלֵךְ, שֶׁמָּא

LITERAL TRANSLATION

[1] What does "it is not in heaven" [mean]? [2] Rabbi Yirmeyah said: That the Torah was already given on Mount Sinai, [and] we do not pay attention to a [heavenly] voice, for You already wrote in the Torah at Mount Sinai: "After the majority to incline." [3] Rabbi Natan met Elijah [and] said to him: "What did the Holy One, blessed be He, do at that time?" [4] He said to him: "He smiled and said: 'My sons have defeated Me, My sons have defeated Me.'" [5] They said: "That day they brought all the objects that Rabbi Eliezer had declared ritually pure and burned them in a fire, and they voted (lit., 'were counted') about him and they excommunicated (lit., 'blessed') him. [6] And they said: 'Who will go and inform him?' [7] Rabbi Akiva said to them: 'I will go, lest

TRANSLATION AND COMMENTARY

מַאי לֹא בַּשָּׁמַיִם הִיא [1] The Gemara interrupts the Baraita and asks for a clarification: **What** did Rabbi Yehoshua mean when he quoted the Scriptural verse that "the Torah **is not in heaven**"?

אָמַר רַבִּי יִרְמְיָה [2] **Rabbi Yirmeyah said** in reply: Since God **already gave the Torah** to the Jewish people **on Mount Sinai, we no** longer **pay attention to heavenly voices** that attempt to intervene in matters of Halakhah. **For You,** God, **already wrote in the Torah at Mount Sinai** (Exodus 23:2), **"After the majority to incline."** From this verse we learn that Halakhic disputes must be resolved by majority vote of the Rabbis. God could not contradict His own decision to allow Torah questions to be decided by free debate and majority vote.

אַשְׁכְּחֵיהּ רַבִּי נָתָן לְאֵלִיָּהוּ [3] The Gemara relates that generations later **Rabbi Natan met** the Prophet **Elijah.** (Several of the Talmudic Sages had visions of Elijah the Prophet, and discussed Halakhic questions with him.) Rabbi Natan asked Elijah about the debate between Rabbi Eliezer and Rabbi Yehoshua. **He said to him: "What did the Holy One, blessed be He, do at that time** when Rabbi Yehoshua refused to heed the heavenly voice?" [4] In reply, **Elijah said to** Rabbi Natan: "God **smiled and said: 'My sons have defeated Me, My sons have defeated Me!'"** God's sons "defeated Him" with their arguments. Rabbi Yehoshua was correct in his contention that a view confirmed by majority vote must be accepted, even where God Himself holds the opposite view.

אָמְרוּ [5] The Rabbis who related this story in the Baraita continued and **said: "That day,** Rabbi Eliezer would not accept the Sages' decision. They, therefore, decided to make a public demonstration of their decision. **They brought all the foodstuffs** that had been prepared in an Akhnai oven and **which Rabbi Eliezer had declared ritually pure, and burned them in a fire,** to show that Rabbi Eliezer's position was rejected by the Halakhah. Afterwards **they** met **and took a vote and excommunicated** Rabbi Eliezer ('blessed' here is a euphemism for 'excommunicated') for refusing to accept the majority view." The Baraita continues to describe the consequences of this momentous act. Even though the Sages thought they were justified, they could expect Rabbi Eliezer to be sorely offended. They wished to mitigate the anguish he would feel as much as possible, in view of the gravity of hurting the feelings of another person. (It is because of this section of the Baraita that this story is related here.) [6] "The Sages **said: 'Who will go and inform** Rabbi Eliezer that he has been excommunicated? [7] **Rabbi Akiva said to them: 'I will go,** since I am his student and I will inform him in the most tactful

RASHI

כל טהרות שטיהר רבי אליעזר — על ידי מעשה שאירע נשאלה הלכה זו בבית המדרש, שנפלה טומאה לאויר תנור זה, וחזרו ועשאו על גביו טהרות, וטיהרם רבי אליעזר. והביאום ושרפום לפניו.

BACKGROUND

בַּת קוֹל A heavenly voice. The Hebrew expression employed here (בַּת קוֹל) has two different meanings: (1) An echo (literally, בַּת קוֹל means "daughter of a voice"), and (2) a heavenly voice, i.e., a quasi-prophetic voice which a person hears within himself, although he perceives it as coming from outside himself. Hearing such a "heavenly voice" was regarded as a type of revelation, albeit of lesser clarity and force than actual prophecy. Hence the expression בַּת קוֹל, because such a voice is an "echo" of true prophecy.

לֹא בַּשָּׁמַיִם הִיא It is not in heaven. Even though it is explicitly forbidden to deviate from Torah law (and indeed, a prophet who advocates the abrogation of Torah law is punishable by death), the Torah itself recognized the outstanding Torah scholars of each generation as the authoritative interpreters of the law, and hence the Gemara's statement that the Torah is "not in heaven."

NOTES

נִצְּחוּנִי בָּנַי My sons have defeated Me. The commentators attempt to explain why God smiled when "His sons defeated Him." Some authorities explain that God was happy because the Sages, by refusing to accept the heavenly voice, affirmed their belief in the eternity of the Torah, demonstrating that even a prophet is not authorized to alter Torah laws (see *Rambam*'s introduction to *Mishneh Torah*).

וּבֵרְכוּהוּ They excommunicated him. *Rashi* explains that a ban of *niddui* — "ostracism" — was pronounced against Rabbi Eliezer, such ostracism being the standard penalty for people who treated other scholars disrespectfully. A person ostracized in this manner was not permitted to wear leather shoes or cut his hair, and other people were required to keep at least four cubits away from him.

Ramban and other commentators, however, explain that a more severe type of ban, *ḥerem* — "excommunication" — was pronounced against Rabbi Eliezer. Unlike *niddui*, *ḥerem* entails a prohibition against doing business with the

TRANSLATION AND COMMENTARY

manner possible, **lest someone** else **who is unsuitable will go and inform him** in a rude, insulting manner, **and as a result** Rabbi Eliezer **will** become so angry that he will cause **the entire world to be destroyed** in divine retribution for the anguish caused him.' [1]**What did Rabbi Akiva do** in order to inform Rabbi Eliezer? [2]**He dressed in black garments and wrapped himself in black, and sat before** Rabbi Eliezer **at a distance of four cubits,** since it is prohibited to stand or sit within four cubits of a person who has been excommunicated. [3]**Rabbi Eliezer said to** Rabbi Akiva: **'Akiva, what is the difference between today and yesterday?** Why are you acting so strangely today, dressing in black and sitting at a distance from me?' [4]Rabbi Akiva **said to** Rabbi Eliezer: **'My teacher, it seems to me that your colleagues are staying away from you.'** In this way Rabbi Akiva delicately informed Rabbi Eliezer that he had been excommunicated. [5]Rabbi Eliezer understood the message, so **he too rent his garments and took off his shoes** as a sign of mourning, **and he slipped down** from his chair **and sat on the ground** like a mourner. [6]Rabbi Eliezer's **eyes streamed with tears** of shame and anguish. [7]Rabbi Eliezer's anguish had immediate consequences. **The world was smitten: One-third of the olives, one-third of the wheat, and one-third of the barley** were destroyed. [8]Indeed, **some say that even the dough in women's hands swelled** and spoiled."

ילֵךְ אָדָם שֶׁאֵינוֹ הָגוּן וְיוֹדִיעוֹ, וְנִמְצָא מַחֲרִיב אֶת כָּל הָעוֹלָם כּוּלּוֹ׳. [1]מֶה עָשָׂה רַבִּי עֲקִיבָא? [2]לָבַשׁ שְׁחוֹרִים, וְנִתְעַטֵּף שְׁחוֹרִים, וְיָשַׁב לְפָנָיו בְּרִיחוּק אַרְבַּע אַמּוֹת. [3]אָמַר לוֹ רַבִּי אֱלִיעֶזֶר: ׳עֲקִיבָא, מַה יּוֹם מִיּוֹמַיִם׳? [4]אָמַר לוֹ: ׳רַבִּי, כִּמְדוּמֶה לִי שֶׁחֲבֵירִים בְּדֵילִים מִמְּךָ׳. [5]אַף הוּא קָרַע בְּגָדָיו וְחָלַץ מִנְעָלָיו, וְנִשְׁמַט וְיָשַׁב עַל גַּבֵּי קַרְקַע. [6]זָלְגוּ עֵינָיו דְּמָעוֹת. [7]לָקָה הָעוֹלָם: שְׁלִישׁ בְּזֵיתִים, וּשְׁלִישׁ בְּחִטִּים, וּשְׁלִישׁ בִּשְׂעוֹרִים. [8]וְיֵשׁ אוֹמְרִים: אַף בָּצֵק שֶׁבִּידֵי אִשָּׁה טָפַח״.

[9]תָּנָא: ״אַךְ גָּדוֹל הָיָה בְּאוֹתוֹ הַיּוֹם, שֶׁבְּכָל מָקוֹם שֶׁנָּתַן בּוֹ עֵינָיו רַבִּי אֱלִיעֶזֶר נִשְׂרַף. [10]וְאַף רַבָּן גַּמְלִיאֵל הָיָה בָּא בִּסְפִינָה, עָמַד עָלָיו נַחְשׁוֹל לְטַבְּעוֹ. [11]אָמַר: ׳כִּמְדוּמֶה לִי שֶׁאֵין זֶה אֶלָּא בִּשְׁבִיל רַבִּי אֱלִיעֶזֶר בֶּן הוּרְקָנוֹס׳. [12]עָמַד עַל רַגְלָיו

LITERAL TRANSLATION

someone who is unsuitable will go and inform him, and as a result he will destroy the entire world.' [1]What did Rabbi Akiva do? [2]He dressed in black [garments] and wrapped himself in black, and sat before him at a distance of four cubits. [3]Rabbi Eliezer said to him: 'Akiva, what is [the difference between] today and any other day (lit., 'what is one day from two days')?' [4]He said to him: 'Rabbi, it seems to me that [your] colleagues are staying away from you.' [5]He, too, rent his garments and took off his shoes, and he slipped down and sat on the ground. [6]His eyes streamed with tears. [7]The world was smitten: one-third of the olives, and one-third of the wheat, and one-third of the barley. [8]And some say [that] even the dough in a woman's hands swelled."

[9][A Tanna] taught: "There was a great calamity on that day, for every place upon which Rabbi Eliezer laid his eyes was burnt. [10]And Rabban Gamliel, too, was coming on a ship, [and] a wave rose up against him to drown him. [11]He said: 'It seems to me that this is only because of Rabbi Eliezer ben Hyrcanus.' [12]He rose to his feet

RASHI

לבש שחורים — ענין צער ואבל. **אף הוא קרע בגדיו** — שהמנודה חייב בקריעה. **חלץ מנעליו** — שהמנודה אסור בנעילת הסנדל, במועד קטן (טו,ב). **ונשמט** — מן הכסא. **טפח** — נתקלקל. **אך גדול** = מכה גדולה. **רבן גמליאל** — נשיא היה, ועל פיו נעשה.

תָּנָא [9]The Gemara now quotes another Baraita that describes the consequences of Rabbi Eliezer's excommunication: **A Tanna taught: "There was great** divine wrath on **the day** Rabbi Eliezer was excommunicated and a great **calamity** befell the world, **for whatever Rabbi Eliezer laid his eyes upon was burnt.** [10]**Rabban Gamliel, too,** was affected; he **was traveling on a ship, and a** huge **wave rose over him to drown him.** As Nasi and head of the central yeshivah at Yavneh, Rabban Gamliel was the leading Sage of the period. Therefore he was personally responsible for the measures taken against Rabbi Eliezer. [11]When Rabban Gamliel realized that he was about to drown, **he said** to himself: **'It seems to me that this can only be** happening to me **because of** the anguish caused to **Rabbi Eliezer ben Hyrcanus.'** [12]Rabban Gamliel **rose to his feet**

NOTES

excommunicated person. To be sure, people were ordinarily not put into *ḥerem* unless repeated *niddui* proved ineffective. But Rabbi Eliezer was treated especially strictly, since his defiant attitude bordered on outright rebellion against the Sages.

לָבַשׁ שְׁחוֹרִים He dressed in black garments. *Maharsha* explains that Rabbi Akiva did this out of respect for Rabbi Eliezer, acting as if he, Rabbi Akiva, had been excommunicated, rather than his teacher. For the same reason, Rabbi Akiva euphemistically said that "it seems to me that your colleagues are staying away from you," rather than "have excommunicated you."

TRANSLATION AND COMMENTARY

and said: 'Master of the Universe, You know full well that I did not excommunicate Rabbi Eliezer **for my own** personal **honor, nor for the honor of my father's house. Rather,** Rabbi Eliezer was excommunicated **for Your honor,** because it is essential that no individual, great as he may be, should reject a decision reached by the majority, **so that controversies will not multiply in Israel.'** [1]Swayed by Rabban Gamliel's explanation, **the sea** then **rested from its wrath.**

אִימָּא שָׁלוֹם [2]The Gemara continues with one final story in relation to Rabbi Eliezer's excommunication, which connects the incident to the prohibition against verbal *ona'ah*: **Imma Shalom, Rabbi Eliezer's wife, was** also **Rabban Gamliel's sister.** [3]**From this incident** — Rabbi Eliezer's excommunication — **onward, she would not let Rabbi Eliezer fall on his face** when he recited his prayers. On weekdays, it is customary to recite supplicatory prayers, called "falling on one's face." Imma Shalom did not allow her husband to recite these prayers, lest he pray for divine assistance to overcome the tragedy that had befallen him, and Rabban Gamliel, her brother, might be punished. [4]**One day,** Imma Shalom thought that **it was** the day of **the New Moon** (*Rosh Ḥodesh*), the first day of the month according to the lunar calendar, when these supplicatory prayers are not recited. Imma Shalom therefore assumed that her husband would not recite this prayer on that day, and did not take care to keep him from "falling on his face." But in fact Imma Shalom had erred in her calculations, and she mistook **a full month for a short one.** The moon takes about twenty-nine-and-a-half days to revolve around the earth. Accordingly, some months (called "short" or "defective" months) are twenty-nine days long, while others (called "full" months) are thirty days long. Imma Shalom thought that the preceding month had been short (i.e., only twenty-nine days long), when in fact it was "full" (thirty days long). Thus, the day that she thought was Rosh Ḥodesh was really the last day of the previous month, when it was customary to offer special supplications. [5]**Some say** that the incident happened in a slightly different manner: **A poor person came and stood at the door, and** Imma Shalom **brought out bread for him,** as a result of which she was temporarily distracted. [6]For whichever reason, she was distracted and **she found** Rabbi Eliezer **fallen on his face** in prayer. **She said to him: "Rise! You have killed my brother."** She was certain that Rabban Gamliel had died, since she assumed that Rabbi Eliezer had given expression to the pain he felt because of his excommunication, and that this had led to divine retribution against Rabban Gamliel. [7]**Meanwhile,** as Imma Shalom was talking to her husband, **the sound of a horn came from Rabban Gamliel's house** and an announcement was made confirming the fact **that he had died.** [8]Rabbi Eliezer **said to** Imma Shalom: **"How did you know** that Rabban Gamliel had died?" [9]**She said to him: "I have the following**

וְאָמַר: ׳רִבּוֹנוֹ שֶׁל עוֹלָם, גָּלוּי וְיָדוּעַ לְפָנֶיךָ שֶׁלֹּא לִכְבוֹדִי עָשִׂיתִי, וְלֹא לִכְבוֹד בֵּית אַבָּא עָשִׂיתִי, אֶלָּא לִכְבוֹדְךָ, שֶׁלֹּא יִרְבּוּ מַחֲלוֹקוֹת בְּיִשְׂרָאֵל׳. [1]נָח הַיָּם מִזַּעְפּוֹ״.

[2]אִימָּא שָׁלוֹם, דְּבֵיתְהוּ דְּרַבִּי אֱלִיעֶזֶר, אַחְתֵּיהּ דְּרַבָּן גַּמְלִיאֵל הֲוַאי. [3]מֵהַהוּא מַעֲשֶׂה וְאֵילָךְ לָא הֲוָה שָׁבְקָה לֵיהּ לְרַבִּי אֱלִיעֶזֶר לְמֵיפַל עַל אַפֵּיהּ. [4]הַהוּא יוֹמָא רֵישׁ יַרְחָא הֲוָה, וְאִיחֲלַף לָהּ בֵּין מָלֵא לְחָסֵר. [5]אִיכָּא דְּאָמְרִי: אֲתָא עַנְיָא וְקָאֵי אַבָּבָא, אַפִּיקָא לֵיהּ רִיפְתָּא. [6]אַשְׁכַּחְתֵּיהּ דְּנָפַל עַל אַנְפֵּיהּ, אֲמַרָה לֵיהּ: ״קוּם! קְטַלִית לְאָחִי״. [7]אַדְּהָכִי, נְפַק שִׁיפּוּרָא מִבֵּית רַבָּן גַּמְלִיאֵל דְּשְׁכִיב. [8]אֲמַר לָהּ: ״מְנָא יָדַעַתְּ״? [9]אֲמַרָה לֵיהּ: ״כָּךְ

LITERAL TRANSLATION

and said: 'Master of the Universe, it is revealed and known before You that I did not do [this] for my [own] honor, nor did I do [it] for the honor of my father's house, but for Your honor, so that controversies will not multiply in Israel.' [1]The sea rested from its wrath."

[2]Imma Shalom, Rabbi Eliezer's wife, was Rabban Gamliel's sister. [3]From that incident onward she did not let Rabbi Eliezer fall on his face. [4]One day it was the New Moon, and she mistook a full [month] for a short one. [5]Some say: A poor person came and stood at the door, [and] she brought out bread for him. [6]She found him fallen on his face, [and] she said to him: "Rise! You have killed my brother." [7]Meanwhile the sound of a horn came from Rabban Gamliel's house that he had died. [8]He said to her: "From where did you know?" [9]She said to him: "I have

RASHI

שלא ירבו מחלוקות — שלא ירגיל היחיד לחלוק על המרובין. **אימא שלום** — כך שמה. **בין מלא לחסר** — סבורה היתה שיהא החדש חסר וקבוע ביום שלשים, ולא יפול ביום החדש על פניו. והיה מלא, ולא נקבע עד יום שלשים ואחד, ולא נזהרה בו ביום שלשים ונפל על פניו.

BACKGROUND

אִימָּא שָׁלוֹם Imma Shalom (lit., "Mother Shalom"). "Imma" is apparently an honorific title applied to distinguished women, either because of their age or their personal status. Like other women from important families, Imma Shalom was learned; and in other places as well she reports the teachings of her brother and traditions from her father's house.

לְמֵיפַל עַל אַפֵּיהּ To fall on his face. "Falling on one's face" is an act of private prayer consisting of supplications and requests recited following the Eighteen Benedictions in the synagogue, and it is also part of the service on fast days. During Talmudic times people actually used to prostrate themselves — "to fall on their faces" — on the floor. Afterwards it became the practice to perform this action symbolically, by placing one's head on one's hand. Today this prayer is known as *Taḥanun* (תַּחֲנוּן — "supplication") and has a standard form, the main portion of which is a passage from Psalms.

נְפַק שִׁיפּוּרָא The sound of a horn came. In Talmudic times a person's death was announced by a blast of the shofar, so that everyone would be informed in advance of the funeral. It was particularly necessary to announce the death of the Nasi, because of the great honor with which he was regarded, and everyone had to take part in mourning for him.

BACKGROUND

הַמְאַנֶּה אֶת הַגֵּר **Someone who wrongs a convert.** As the Gemara indicates here, a special prohibition applies to wronging and oppressing converts (in addition to the more general prohibition against oppressing any Jew). Even though converts are considered full-fledged Jews, special laws apply to them: Since converts cannot look to their families for support (and are fully dependent upon God instead), they are more sensitive to insult, and hence they need special protection. Moreover, converts are entitled to special privileges since they willingly chose to leave their non-Jewish background to join the Jewish people.

TRANSLATION AND COMMENTARY

tradition from my grandfather's house: All the heavenly **gates are locked except for the gates** through which prayers concerning ***ona'ah*** pass." And since Rabbi Eliezer had been the victim of verbal *ona'ah,* his wife was certain that his prayers would be answered.

תָּנוּ רַבָּנַן [1]The Gemara now presents another Baraita which elaborates on the prohibition against verbal *ona'ah*: **Our Rabbis taught: "Someone who wrongs a convert** by verbal *ona'ah* **violates three prohibitions, and someone who oppresses him** in financial matters **violates two** prohibitions."

מַאי שְׁנָא מְאַנֶּה [2]The Gemara challenges the distinction made in this Baraita: **Why is someone who** verbally **wrongs a convert** treated **differently** — more severely — than someone who oppresses him financially? [3]**Is it because three prohibitions were written** in connection with someone who verbally wrongs a stranger (understood in this context as a convert), namely: (1) **"And a stranger you shall not wrong"** (Exodus 2:2). (2) **"And if a stranger dwells with you in your land, you shall not wrong him"** (Leviticus 19:33). **And** (3) **"You shall not wrong, each man his fellow"** (Leviticus 25:17) — the verse quoted at the beginning of the discussion, above 58b, which prohibits causing anguish to any fellow Jew. [4]Now, **a convert is included in** the category of **a fellow** Jew, therefore, this verse also prohibits causing anguish to converts. [5]But, argues the Gemara, the same should also apply to a person who **oppresses** a convert financially! Here, too, **three prohibitions** are violated. For there **are also** three prohibitions **written** about oppressing a convert, namely: (1) **"And you shall not oppress him"** (Exodus 22:2), the continuation of the first verse cited above, which prohibits causing anguish. (2) **"And a stranger you shall not oppress"** (Exodus 23:9). **And** (3) **"You shall not be to him as a usurer"** (Exodus 22:24), which prohibits forcing a Jew to take desperate measures to repay a debt that he is not in a position to repay. [6]Now, **a convert is included** in this prohibition which, once again, applies to all Jews! Thus, it would appear that a person who oppresses a convert financially violates three prohibitions, and not just two, as stated in the Baraita!

מְקוּבְּלָנִי מִבֵּית אֲבִי אַבָּא: כָּל הַשְּׁעָרִים נִנְעָלִים חוּץ מִשַּׁעֲרֵי אוֹנָאָה״.

[1]תָּנוּ רַבָּנַן: ״הַמְאַנֶּה אֶת הַגֵּר עוֹבֵר בִּשְׁלֹשָׁה לָאוִין, וְהַלּוֹחֲצוֹ עוֹבֵר בִּשְׁנַיִם״.

[2]מַאי שְׁנָא מְאַנֶּה? [3]דִּכְתִיבִי שְׁלֹשָׁה לָאוִין: ״וְגֵר לֹא תוֹנֶה״, ״וְכִי יָגוּר אִתְּךָ גֵּר בְּאַרְצְכֶם, לֹא תוֹנוּ אֹתוֹ״, וְ״לֹא תוֹנוּ אִישׁ אֶת עֲמִיתוֹ״, [4]וְגֵר בִּכְלַל ״עֲמִיתוֹ״ הוּא? [5]לוֹחֲצוֹ נַמִי, שְׁלֹשָׁה כְּתִיבִי: ״וְלֹא תִלְחָצֶנּוּ״, ״וְגֵר לֹא תִלְחָץ״, וְ״לֹא תִהְיֶה לוֹ כְּנֹשֶׁה״, [6]וְגֵר בִּכְלָל הוּא!

LITERAL TRANSLATION

this tradition from my grandfather's house: All the gates are locked except for the gates of *ona'ah*."

[1]Our Rabbis taught: "Someone who wrongs a convert violates three prohibitions, and someone who oppresses him violates two."

[2]Why is someone who wrongs [a convert] different? [3][Is it] because three prohibitions are written: "And a stranger you shall not wrong," "And if the stranger dwells with you in your land, you shall not wrong him," and "You shall not wrong each man his fellow," [4]and a convert is included in "his fellow." [5][If] he oppresses him, too, three [prohibitions] are written: "And you shall not oppress him," "And a stranger you shall not oppress," and "You shall not be to him as a usurer," [6]and a convert is included!

RASHI

מבית אבי אבא — מבית אבי המשפחה, שבת נשיאים היתה, והם מבית דוד. **חוץ משערי אונאה** — לפי שצער הלב הוא, וקרוב להוריד דמעות. **המאנה את הגר** — אונאת דברים. **הלוחצו** = דוחקו. **לא תהיה לו כנושה** — לחץ הוא, שדוחקו לתבוע חובו. **הכי גרסינן: מאי שנא מאנה דכתיב ביה תלתא: ״וגר לא תונה״, ״לא תונו אותו״, ״ולא תונו איש את עמיתו״** — וגר בכלל עמיתו הוא. **לוחצו נמי תלתא כתיב ביה** — ״וגר לא תלחץ״, ״ולא תלחצנו״, ו״לא תהיה לו כנושה״.

NOTES

מִבֵּית אֲבִי אַבָּא **From my grandfather's house.** *Rashi* and *Tosafot* explain that Imma Shalom was referring to her descent from the royal House of David. *Ritva* observes that the reference may be to Rabban Shimon ben Gamliel the first, whose teachings were not so well known as those of other members of the dynasty.

חוּץ מִשַּׁעֲרֵי אוֹנָאָה **Except for the gates of *ona'ah*.** Even though the Sages who excommunicated Rabbi Eliezer were apparently justified in doing so, they were punished because they hurt his feelings and caused him unnecessary distress (*Rabbi Ya'akov Emden*).

HALAKHAH

אוֹנָאַת הַגֵּר **Wronging a convert.** "One must be especially careful not to hurt a convert either by wounding him with unkind words or by defrauding him financially, since the Torah explicitly forbids this on many occasions." (*Shulḥan Arukh, Ḥoshen Mishpat* 228:2.)

TRANSLATION AND COMMENTARY

אֶלָּא [1]In the light of this objection, the Gemara amends the Baraita and concludes: **Rather, the law is the same** for a person who wrongs a convert verbally and one who oppresses him financially. In both cases, the offender **violates three prohibitions.**

תַּנְיָא [2]Continuing the discussion about wronging a convert, the Gemara notes: **It was taught in a Baraita: "Rabbi Eliezer the Great** (Rabbi Eliezer ben Hyrcanus) **says: Why did the Torah warn us about converts in thirty-six places — and some say in forty-six places?** Why did the Torah consider it necessary so frequently to stress the importance of protecting the interests of converts?" [3]Rabbi Eliezer answers: **"Because the inclination** of converts **is bad,** and insulting or mistreating them may cause them to return to their former ways."

מַאי דִּכְתִיב [4]The Gemara concludes its discussion about showing sensitivity to converts by commenting on the verse cited in the previous discussion: **What is the meaning of** the verse (Exodus 22:2): **"And a stranger you shall not wrong and you shall not oppress him, for you were strangers in the land of Egypt"?** Converts are similar to new immigrants in a strange land. Why does the fact that the Jewish people, too, were once strangers in Egypt give them greater insight into the prohibition against causing converts anguish?

תָּנֵינָא [5]The Gemara answers: **We have learned** in a Baraita: **"Rabbi Natan said:** This verse teaches us: **Do not point out your own defect in another person."** A Jew should not wrong a convert by reminding him that he is a newcomer living among a people that was not always his own, for the Jews themselves were once in the same situation. [6]**And this is what people say:** Rabbi Natan's exposition of the verse is corroborated by the following proverb: **Someone who had a relative who was hanged, should not say to another person, "Hang** up this **fish,"** because any mention of hanging recalls his family's shame.

MISHNAH אֵין מְעָרְבִין פֵּירוֹת [7]Having considered the monetary *ona'ah* involved in overcharging or underpaying, and the verbal *ona'ah* involved in putting other people to shame, the Mishnah now turns to another type of *ona'ah*. Certain business practices are forbidden because they involve deception, even though it is not possible to quantify the fraud in financial terms. In general, a merchant may not tell a customer that his product has some intangible advantage that it in fact does not have. For example, if a merchant claims that he is selling the produce of a particular field, he **may not mix produce** from another field

LITERAL TRANSLATION

[1]Rather, both in this case and in that [he violates] three [prohibitions].

[2]It has been taught: "Rabbi Eliezer the Great says: Why did the Torah warn [us] in thirty-six places — and some say in forty-six places — concerning a convert? [3]Because his inclination is bad.

[4]What is [the meaning of] that which is written: "And a stranger you shall not wrong and you shall not oppress him, for you were strangers in the land of Egypt?"

[5]We have learned: "Rabbi Natan said: A defect that is in you do not say to your fellow." [6]And this is what people say: Someone who had a person who was hanged in his family, should not say to his fellow, "Hang a fish."

MISHNAH [7]One may not mix produce (lit., "fruit")

[1]אֶלָּא, אֶחָד זֶה וְאֶחָד זֶה בִּשְׁלֹשָׁה.

[2]תַּנְיָא: "רַבִּי אֱלִיעֶזֶר הַגָּדוֹל אוֹמֵר: מִפְּנֵי מַה הִזְהִירָה תּוֹרָה בִּשְׁלֹשִׁים וְשִׁשָּׁה מְקוֹמוֹת — וְאָמְרִי לָהּ בְּאַרְבָּעִים וְשִׁשָּׁה מְקוֹמוֹת — בְּגֵר? [3]מִפְּנֵי שֶׁסּוּרוֹ רַע".

[4]מַאי דִּכְתִיב: "וְגֵר לֹא תוֹנֶה וְלֹא תִלְחָצֶנּוּ, כִּי גֵרִים הֱיִיתֶם בְּאֶרֶץ מִצְרָיִם"?

[5]תָּנֵינָא: "רַבִּי נָתָן אוֹמֵר: מוּם שֶׁבְּךָ אַל תֹּאמַר לַחֲבֵרְךָ". [6]וְהַיְינוּ דְּאָמְרִי אֱינָשֵׁי: דִּזְקִיף לֵיהּ זְקִיפָא בִּדְיוֹתְקֵיהּ, לָא נֵימָא לֵיהּ לְחַבְרֵיהּ "זְקֵיף בִּינִיתָא".

מִשְׁנָה [7]אֵין מְעָרְבִין פֵּירוֹת

RASHI

מום שבך אל תאמר לחברך — כיון דגרים הייתם, גנאי הוא לכם להזכיר שם גירות. **מאן דאית ליה זקיפא בדיותקיה לא נימא לחבריה זקיף ביניתא** — מי שיש לו תלוי במשפחתו לא יאמר לעבדו או בן ביתו: תלה לי דג זה, שכל שם תלייה גנאי הוא לו.

משנה אין מערבין פירות בפירות — בעל הבית שאומר: פירות שדה פלוני אני מוכר לך כך וכך סאין, לא יערבנו בפירות שדה אחרת.

LANGUAGE

סוּרוֹ His inclination. According to some authorities this word derives from a Biblical word meaning something which has spoiled, as in Psalms, 14:3, where the related verb means "became filthy." Others claim that it is a short form of סֵיאוּר, something which has turned sour, in the figurative sense of moral corruption.

בִּדְיוֹתְקֵיהּ In his family. This word is derived from the Middle Persian *dutak*, which means "family."

BACKGROUND

סוּרוֹ רַע His inclination is bad. The phrase סוּרוֹ רַע mainly refers to bad habits. A convert, who did not grow up as a Jew, was educated and habituated to a different way of life, and if he is insulted he may easily return to his previous ways.

מוּם שֶׁבְּךָ אַל תֹּאמַר לַחֲבֵרְךָ A defect that is in you do not say to your fellow. As the Torah itself states, Jews must be sensitive to the suffering of strangers, since they too were strangers in Egypt, as it is written (Exodus 23:9): "For you know the heart of a stranger, since you were strangers in the land of Egypt." Rabbi Natan adds another dimension to the reasoning: Since the Jews themselves were strangers, they should not taunt others for this flaw. They, too, wandered through foreign countries, and did not always have a country of their own.

REALIA

בִּינִיתָא Fish.

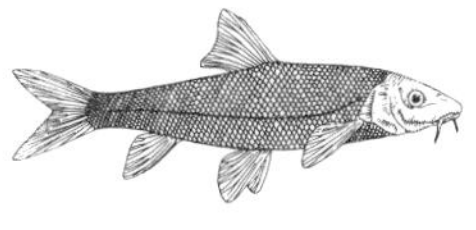

A type of fish called *binita* in both Aramaic and Arabic. Approximately 200 types of fish from the carp family, which are found throughout the world, are considered *binita*. Some of these fish are small, while others are very large. Two types of *binita* are found in Eretz Israel (primarily in the Sea of Galilee), and to this day are considered exceptionally choice (among other things, because of their high nutritional value). The

NOTES

שְׁלֹשִׁים וְשִׁשָּׁה — אַרְבָּעִים וְשִׁשָּׁה Thirty-six places ... forty-six places. Midrash Tanḥuma states that there are fifty-eight such places. It would seem, therefore, that the thirty-six or forty-six "warnings" mentioned here include all the other Biblical verses that speak of strangers, e.g., "You were strangers in Egypt" (Exodus 22:20, etc.). *Ra'avad* explains that the difference of opinion regarding how many "warnings" there are depends on which verses are included — all verses which refer to strangers, or only those that do not mention strangers together with widows and orphans.

סוּרוֹ רַע Because his inclination is bad. *Rashi* (*Horayot* 13a, and see *Rashash*, ibid.) explains: Because his natural inclination is evil.

binita found in Syria and Babylonia are even larger. *Binita* were baked and cooked. From the reference in the Gemara to hanging such fish, we may infer that it was also customary to dry them.

TERMINOLOGY

בֶּאֱמֶת אָמְרוּ In truth they said. This expression usually introduces an authoritive and uncontested Halakhah — a Halakhah handed down to Moses on Mount Sinai (הֲלָכָה לְמֹשֶׁה מִסִּינַי).

BACKGROUND

לְעָרֵב קָשֶׁה בְּרַךְ To mix strong wine with mild wine. By "strong wine" the Mishnah means wine with a high alcohol content, whereas "mild wine" has a low alcohol concentration. Nowadays, too, grapes grown in different areas produce wines with different alcohol concentrations. The Mishnah assumes that buyers generally preferred wine with a higher alcohol content, both because it tasted better and because such wine lasted longer and was less likely to spoil.

TRANSLATION AND COMMENTARY

with this produce, as the buyer may have a personal preference for produce from that particular field. **Even** where the quality of the produce of the two fields is the same — for example, where both fields have new produce — it is forbidden to mix **new** produce **with** other **new** produce. [60A] [1]**And it goes without saying** that it is prohibited to deceive the buyer by combining produce of different qualities, such as **new produce with old produce.** The word "produce" in this context refers primarily to grain. Since older grain makes a better flour, older produce is worth more. By adding inferior produce to it, the seller reduces the value of the merchandise, which the buyer mistakenly thinks consists entirely of old produce.

בֶּאֱמֶת אָמְרוּ [2]**In truth** the Sages **said** that even though it is ordinarily prohibited to combine different grades of produce, it is permitted to do so if the quality of the produce added is indisputably superior to that which the buyer intends to acquire. Thus, in the previous example, it would be permitted to add old grain to new grain; and **in the case of wine, it is permitted to mix strong wine with mild wine, since** the strong wine **improves** the taste of the mild one.

אֵין מְעָרְבִין [3]Similarly, a wine merchant **may not mix the wine sediment** found in one barrel of wine **with wine** from another barrel. Even though, as the Mishnah will explain, the merchant is entitled to include a certain percentage of sediment in the wine he sells, he may not add sediment from another barrel, if the wine in this barrel happens to be unusually clear, for the sediment from the other barrel may cause the wine to spoil. **But** when the seller transfers wine from his barrel into the buyer's container, **he may give** the buyer the wine with **its** own **sediment**, and he need not strain out the sediment that is already there.

מִי שֶׁנִּתְעָרֵב [4]If **someone's wine was** diluted by being **mixed with water, he may not sell it in a shop, unless he informs** the buyer that it has been diluted. The normal practice was to dilute wine with water immediately before serving it, but not beforehand. Thus, if the merchant sold diluted wine without informing his customer, he would be likely to deceive him as to its true value. [5]Moreover, the owner of the diluted wine may **not** sell it **to a** wine **merchant** at all, **even if he informed** the merchant that the wine was diluted. **Since it was** not customary to sell diluted wine in shops, the reason the merchant was willing to buy this unsalable wine could **only have been to deceive** potential customers by selling it as undiluted wine.

בְּפֵירוֹת, אֲפִילּוּ חֲדָשִׁים בַּחֲדָשִׁים. [60A] [1]וְאֵין צָרִיךְ לוֹמַר חֲדָשִׁים בִּישָׁנִים.
[2]בֶּאֱמֶת אָמְרוּ: בַּיַּיִן, הִתִּירוּ לְעָרֵב קָשֶׁה בְּרַךְ, מִפְּנֵי שֶׁהוּא מַשְׁבִּיחוֹ.
[3]אֵין מְעָרְבִין שִׁמְרֵי יַיִן בְּיַיִן, אֲבָל נוֹתֵן לוֹ אֶת שְׁמָרָיו.
[4]מִי שֶׁנִּתְעָרֵב מַיִם בְּיֵינוֹ לֹא יִמְכְּרֶנּוּ בַּחֲנוּת אֶלָּא אִם כֵּן הוֹדִיעוֹ. [5]וְלֹא לַתַּגָּר אַף עַל פִּי שֶׁהוֹדִיעוֹ, שֶׁאֵינוֹ אֶלָּא לְרַמּוֹת בּוֹ.

LITERAL TRANSLATION

with produce, [not] even new with new. [60A] [1]And it is not necessary to say new [produce] with old [produce].

[2]In truth they said: In [the case of] wine, they permitted to mix strong (lit., "hard") [wine] with mild [wine], since it improves it.

[3]One may not mix wine sediment with wine, but he may give him its sediment.

[4]Someone whose wine was mixed with water may not sell it in a shop unless he informed him. [5]And he may not [sell it] to a merchant even if he informed him, for he only [takes it] to defraud with it.

RASHI

ואין צריך לומר חדשים בישנים — פסק למכור לו ישנים לא יערב בהן חדשים, שהישנים יבישים ועושין קמח יותר מן החדשים. **מפני שמשביחו** — קשה משביח את הרך. לפיכך, פסק עמו רך — מערב בו קשה. ודוקא קתני קשה ברך ולא רך בקשה. פסק עמו קשה — לא יערב בו את הרך. וכן אין צריך לומר חדשים בישנים, דוקא, אבל ישנים בחדשים, שפיר דמי. **אין מערבין שמרי יין ביין** — בגמרא מפרש לה. **ימכרנו בחנות** — פרוטה פרוטה. **אלא אם כן הודיעו** — לכל אחד ואחד מהן שמים מעורבין בו. **ולא לתגר** — ימכרנו ביחד, ואף על פי שמודיעו. **לפי שאינו לוקחו אלא לרמות** — ולמכרו בחנות.

NOTES

שֶׁאֵינוֹ אֶלָּא לְרַמּוֹת בּוֹ For he only takes it to defraud with it. It is forbidden to sell diluted wine to merchants because they are likely to resell it to shopkeepers without telling them that it has been diluted, particularly since they themselves did not dilute it (*Sma*).

HALAKHAH

בַּיַּיִן הִתִּירוּ לְעָרֵב In the case of wine they permitted to mix. "It is permitted to mix strong wine with milder wine (and vice versa [*Rema*]) if it is still in the winepresses, since doing so improves the taste of the mixture. However, if people ordinarily taste wine before they buy it, it is permitted to mix strong wine with milder wine (and vice versa), even if the wine has been removed from the winepresses, provided that the mixture tastes adulterated." (Ibid., 228:11.)

מִי שֶׁנִּתְעָרֵב מַיִם בְּיֵינוֹ Someone whose wine was mixed with water. "It is prohibited to dilute wine with water before selling it. However, if wine was accidentally mixed with water, the mixture may be sold in a shop, provided that the

TRANSLATION AND COMMENTARY

[1]On the other hand, **in places where it is customary** for merchants **to add water to wine** before selling it, **it is permitted** for them **to add** water and then sell the wine without warning their customers, for the customers naturally assume that the wine has been diluted.

הַתַּגָּר נוֹטֵל מֵחָמֵשׁ גְּרָנוֹת [2]The Mishnah concludes by noting that, even though a private person who claims he is selling the produce of a particular field may not mix produce from a different field with it, **a merchant may take grain from five** different **granaries and put it into one** single **container, or** wine **from five** different **winepresses and put it into one cask.** Even though a buyer who sees the merchant collecting grain at a particular granary may believe that he is selling grain from that field alone, it is still permitted, because this is normal business practice. [3]In general, the merchant is permitted to mix produce in the customary fashion, **as long as he does not intend to combine** produce of inferior quality with superior produce, and represent the mixture as produce of superior quality.

GEMARA תָּנוּ רַבָּנַן [4]The Mishnah ruled that it is forbidden to add inferior produce, but it is permitted to add superior produce. However, the added produce must be indisputably superior in every way. **Our Rabbis taught** the following Baraita: **"It goes without saying that** if new produce is cheaper than older produce — for example, **where the new** produce **sells for four** se'ahs of produce per sela, **and the old for three** se'ahs of produce per sela — then the old produce is indisputably superior to the new, and **it is not permitted to mix** the new produce with the older produce and then charge a higher price for the entire mixture, for this is outright deception. On the other hand, in such a case it would be permitted to add old produce to a supply of new produce. [5]**But** the prohibition against mixing applies **even** in less straightforward cases, such as **when** the new produce costs more than the older produce — for example, when the **new** produce **sells for three** se'ahs of produce per sela **and the older** produce **sells for four** se'ahs of produce per sela. Even though this

[1]מָקוֹם שֶׁנָּהֲגוּ לְהַטִּיל מַיִם בַּיַּיִן, יַטִּילוּ.

[2]הַתַּגָּר נוֹטֵל מֵחָמֵשׁ גְּרָנוֹת וְנוֹתֵן לְתוֹךְ מְגוּרָה אַחַת, מֵחָמֵשׁ גִּתּוֹת וְנוֹתֵן לְתוֹךְ פִּיטוֹם אֶחָד, [3]וּבִלְבַד שֶׁלֹּא יְהֵא מִתְכַּוֵּין לְעָרֵב.

גמרא [4]תָּנוּ רַבָּנַן: "אֵין צָרִיךְ לוֹמַר חֲדָשׁוֹת מֵאַרְבַּע וִישָׁנוֹת מִשָּׁלֹשׁ דְּאֵין מְעָרְבִין. [5]אֶלָּא אֲפִילּוּ חֲדָשׁוֹת מִשָּׁלֹשׁ וִישָׁנוֹת

LITERAL TRANSLATION

[1][In a] place where they are accustomed to add water to wine, they may add.

[2]A merchant may take [grain] from five granaries and put [it] into one container, [or] from five winepresses and put [it] into one cask, [3]as long as he does not intend to mix [them].

GEMARA [4]Our Rabbis taught: "It is not necessary to say that [where] new [sells] for four and old for three, one may not mix. [5]But even [where] new [sells] for three and old

RASHI

מקום שנהגו להטיל מים ביין יטילו — דכיון שנהגו — אין כאן טעות, שכל היינות בחזקת כן. **התגר נוטל מחמש גרנות וכו'** — שהכל יודעין בו שלא גדלו בשדותיו, ומבני אדם הרבה לוקח, ובחזקת כן לוקחין. **מגורה** — אוצר שאוצרין בו תבואה. גורן — הוא שדשין וזורין בו את התבואה, ודרך התגר לקנות מבעלי בתים בשעת הגורן, ולהכניס למגורה שלו. **שלא יתכוין לערב** — ולהוציא קול לקנות הרוב ממקום משובח, לערב בו ממקום אחר, ושכיניו סבורין שכל הפירות מאותו מקום.

גמרא תנו רבנן אין צריך לומר חדשות מארבע — סאין בסלע. **וישנות משלש** — סאין בסלע. **דאין מערבין** — חדשות בישנות, דהואיל ובחזקת ישנות מוכרן, נמצא מאנהו ומוכר לו זולות בתורת יקרות.

BACKGROUND

מָקוֹם שֶׁנָּהֲגוּ לְהַטִּיל מַיִם בַּיַּיִן In a place where they are accustomed to add water to wine. Wine was almost always diluted before being drunk. Indeed, some of the Rabbis maintained that undiluted wine was unfit for consumption, and hence no blessing was to be recited over it. Precisely by how much wine was diluted varied from place to place, both because of variations in local drinking habits and because grapes cultivated in different areas produced vintages of different strengths. However, wine was usually diluted by mixing one part of wine with two parts of water. Nevertheless, wine was generally sold undiluted, and only mixed with water by the buyer (unless it was sold for immediate consumption).

LANGUAGE

פִּיטוֹם Cask. The Hebrew word should be read פִּיטוֹס, from the Greek πίθος, *pithos*, which means a large earthenware jar.

REALIA

פִּיטוֹם (more correctly פִּיטוֹס) **Cask.**

A **פִּיטוֹס** was a very large earthenware jar. Its height was the height of a man, and it contained hundreds of liters of liquid.

NOTES

תַּעֲרוֹבֶת פֵּירוֹת Mixing produce. *Rashi* explains that it is prohibited to mix produce grown in different fields, because the buyer may want produce from a particular field. *Ra'avad* and *Rosh*, however, explain that it is only prohibited to mix inferior produce with superior produce.

HALAKHAH

buyer is informed that the wine is diluted. However, such a mixture may not be sold to a merchant (even if he is told that the wine is diluted), lest he deceive potential buyers by selling the mixture to them without informing them that it is diluted." (Ibid., 228:12.)

מָקוֹם שֶׁנָּהֲגוּ לְהַטִּיל מַיִם בַּיַּיִן In a place where they are accustomed to add water to wine. "In places where it is customary to dilute wine with water, this is permitted while the wine is still in the winepresses," following the Mishnah's ruling and Rav's explanation in the Gemara. (Ibid., 228:13.)

הַתַּגָּר מְעָרֵב מִכַּמָּה מְקוֹמוֹת Merchants may mix produce from different sources. "Merchants may buy wine prepared in different winepresses, or grain stored in different granaries, and mix them together, since everyone knows that such food was obtained from different sources, unless the merchant did so with the express intention of deceiving his customers," following the Mishnah. (Ibid., 228:16.)

עֵירוּב פֵּירוֹת בְּפֵירוֹת Mixing different kinds of produce. "It is forbidden to mix a small amount of inferior produce with a large quantity of superior produce and sell the mixture as if it were superior produce. It is even forbidden to mix new produce with other new produce, and it goes without saying that it is forbidden to mix old produce, which is worth more than new produce, with new produce. In addition, it is

LANGUAGE

עֲדָא אָמְרָה This says. This expression is Galilean Aramaic, the dialect spoken in Eretz Israel, as opposed to Babylonian Aramaic, the dialect used in the Babylonian Talmud. Indeed, this term appears frequently in the Jerusalem Talmud, where it is spelled הָדָא אָמְרָה, ע and ה interchanging because people did not distinguish between guttural letters at that time.

TRANSLATION AND COMMENTARY

particular supply of new produce is superior, the merchant **may** still **not mix** the new produce with the older produce and sell the mixture as old produce, even if he charges the lower price for the entire mixture. The reason is as follows: It is possible that **a person** may be willing to pay more for new produce **because he wants to age it** — i.e., to store it for a long time — and new produce stores better than old. But a customer who specifies that he wishes to purchase old produce is clearly not interested in storing it. Hence, for him, the new produce is inferior and the seller is guilty of deception if he sells it to him as old."

בֶּאֱמֶת אָמְרוּ [1]The Gemara now analyzes the next clause of the Mishnah: **"In truth** the Sages **said: In the case of wine, it is permitted to mix strong wine with mild wine, since this improves it, etc."** [2]Without reference to the ruling itself, the Gemara comments on an unusual expression it contains: **Rabbi Elazar said: This** Mishnah **implies** that **every** time we find the expression **"in truth they said"** in a Mishnah, the statement so introduced **is** accepted as an authoritative **Halakhic** ruling. Rabbi Elazar states that our Mishnah is the classic example of this phrase, since the ruling in question is clearly authoritative, because the reasoning behind it is explicit ("because doing so improves it") and indisputable. Accordingly, we may infer from here that wherever the expression "in truth they said" appears, the ruling so introduced is authoritative, even if the reasoning behind the ruling is not as obvious as it is here.

אָמַר רַב נַחְמָן [3]**Rav Naḥman said:** The Sages **taught this Mishnah** — that it is permitted to mix strong wine with milder wine — only when the wines are still **in the winepresses**. Only in the early stages of production, before the wines have completed the process of fermentation, does blending the different kinds improve the quality. However, after each type of wine has already acquired its own distinct flavor and aroma, blending may spoil the resulting mixture, and is prohibited.

וְהָאִידָּנָא [4]**But,** the Gemara asks, why do merchants **nowadays mix** different kinds of wine, even though **the wines are not in the winepresses** any more, and each type of wine has already acquired its distinctive flavor and aroma?

מֵאַרְבַּע אֵין מְעָרְבִין, מִפְּנֵי שֶׁאָדָם רוֹצֶה לְיַשְּׁנָן".
[1]"בֶּאֱמֶת אָמְרוּ: בַּיַּיִן, הִתִּירוּ לְעָרֵב קָשֶׁה בְּרַךְ מִפְּנֵי שֶׁהוּא מַשְׁבִּיחוֹ וכו'". [2]אָמַר רַבִּי אֶלְעָזָר: עֲדָא אָמְרָה: כָּל "בֶּאֱמֶת אָמְרוּ" הֲלָכָה הִיא.
[3]אָמַר רַב נַחְמָן: וּבֵין הַגִּיתּוֹת שָׁנוּ.
[4]וְהָאִידָּנָא דְּקָא מְעָרְבִי שֶׁלֹּא בֵּין הַגִּיתּוֹת?

LITERAL TRANSLATION

for four one may not mix, since a man may wish to age them."

[1]"In truth they said: In [the case of] wine, they permitted to mix strong [wine] with mild [wine], since it improves it, etc." [2]Rabbi Elazar said: This says: Every "in truth they said" is the Halakhah.

[3]Rav Naḥman said: And they taught [this] in (lit., "between") the winepresses.

[4]And nowadays, when they mix [when the wine] is not in the winepresses?

RASHI

אלא אפילו חדשות משלש וישנות מארבע אין מערבין – ואף על פי שהחדשות יקרות מהן. **מפני שאדם רוצה לישנן** – מפני שעילוי דמיהן של חדשות אינן מפני שהן טובות כישנות, אלא שאדם רוצה לישנן. וזה שפסק עמו על הישנות, אינו רוצה לישנן, לפיכך אסור לערב בהו חדשות ואפילו מעולות בדמים. **עדא אמרה** = זאת אומרת. כל עדא כמו הדא. **באמת הלכה** – מדיהב טעם למילתיה "מפני שמשביחו", ואין לגמגם בדבר, ונקט בה למתניתין "באמת" – שמע מינה כל היכא דתני "באמת" הלכה, ואין לחסם ולגמגם בדבר. **ובין הגיתות שנו** – דמשביחו, שתוססין זה עם זה ונעשים טעם אחד, אבל לאחר הגיתות, שכבר קלט כל אחד ריחו וטעמו, אין משביחו אלא פוגמו.

NOTES

כָּל בֶּאֱמֶת אָמְרוּ Every "in truth they said." According to *Rashi*, followed by our commentary, since the Mishnah set forth the reasoning for its ruling, we may infer that this decision is binding, and thus the same presumably applies in all cases in which the expression "in truth they said" is used.

Rabbenu Yehonatan, however, maintains that "in truth they said" is tantamount to a formula used in an oath, and hence we may infer that any statement so introduced is binding. *Rav Hai Gaon* had a slightly different reading in the Gemara here, namely: "Every statement introduced by the expression 'in truth they said' is a Halakhah transmitted to Moses at Sinai," i.e., a law given orally to Moses by God. However, *Ri* (cited by *Rosh* in *Hilkhot Mikva'ot*) observes that certain laws introduced by the expression "in truth they said" are of Rabbinic origin. Thus the Gemara must mean that these rulings are as clear-cut and decisive as those transmitted to Moses at Sinai.

בֵּין הַגִּיתּוֹת In the winepresses. When different kinds of wine are mixed while still in the winepresses, the resulting mixture retains its flavor for a long time. However, if they are mixed later, the mixture retains its flavor for only a short time, after which it spoils. Hence this is forbidden, since the buyer will think that the mixture will retain its flavor for a long time (*Ḥiddushim HaMeyuḥasim LeRitva* and *Meiri*).

HALAKHAH

forbidden to mix new produce with old produce even if the old produce is worth more," following the Mishnah and the Gemara's interpretation. (*Shulḥan Arukh, Ḥoshen Mishpat* 228:10.)

TRANSLATION AND COMMENTARY

אָמַר רַב פַּפָּא [1]In reply, **Rav Pappa said: Since people are aware** that the custom nowadays is to mix different kinds of wine, **and** they are nevertheless willing to **waive** their right to unadulterated wine, there is no objection to mixing different types of wine, even after the wines have left the winepresses.

רַב אַחָא בְּרֵיהּ דְּרַב אִיקָא [2]**Rav Aḥa the son of Rav Ika** suggested an alternative explanation for the common practice. He **said: Whose view does this** practice reflect? [3]**It is Rabbi Aḥa's, as was taught in** the following Baraita: **"Rabbi Aḥa permits** merchants to mix different kinds of food **in the case of something which is** ordinarily **tasted** before it is purchased." Thus, according to Rabbi Aḥa, it is permitted to mix different types of wine, because people ordinarily taste wine before they buy it, and can therefore easily detect that it has been mixed.

וְאֵין מְעָרְבִין שְׁמָרֵי יַיִן [4]The Gemara proceeds to analyze the next clause of the Mishnah: **"And he may not mix wine sediment with wine, but he may give him its sediment, etc."** [5]**But surely,** the Gemara argues, this clause is self-contradictory! How can the Mishnah state that "the merchant may give the buyer its sediment," when it **said in the first clause** of the statement **that "he may not mix"** wine sediment with wine **at all?** [6]**Now you may say** that this contradiction can be resolved by interpreting the second clause of the statement as follows: To **what** case **does** the Mishnah's permission **"to give** the buyer **its sediment"** apply? [7]Only **when** the seller **informed** the buyer that he was giving him wine containing sediment, and obtained the buyer's consent. Conversely, the Mishnah's prohibition against mixing sediment with wine applies only where he did not inform him. Thus the Mishnah would be referring to two different cases, and would not contradict itself. [8]But this interpretation is unacceptable, as the Gemara now explains: **Surely the latter clause of the Mishnah** explicitly mentions informing the buyer, as it **teaches: "He may not sell** diluted wine **in a shop unless he informs** the buyer that it was diluted; **nor** may he sell it **to** a wine **merchant, even if he informed him** that it was diluted." Thus we see that when the Mishnah wishes to make this point, it does so explicitly. [9]**This implies that the first clause**, which permits giving the buyer sediment and does not stipulate that the buyer should be informed, **applies even if** the seller **did not inform** the buyer that the wine contained sediment! Since the clause of the Mishnah which permits giving the buyer sediment does not specify that the buyer must be told that the wine contains sediment, it would appear that this is permitted even if the buyer was not told that the wine contains sediment! Thus the internal contradiction in the Mishnah stands: Is one allowed to mix sediment with the wine or not?

אָמַר רַב יְהוּדָה [10]**Rav Yehudah** suggested a solution, **saying:** In fact, the Mishnah does not contradict itself.

[1]אָמַר רַב פַּפָּא: דְּיָדְעִי וְקָא מָחֲלִי.

[2]רַב אַחָא בְּרֵיהּ דְּרַב אִיקָא אָמַר: הָא מַנִּי? [3]רַבִּי אַחָא הִיא. דְּתַנְיָא: "רַבִּי אַחָא מַתִּיר בְּדָבָר הַנִּטְעָם".

[4]"וְאֵין מְעָרְבִין שְׁמָרֵי יַיִן בְּיַיִן, אֲבָל נוֹתֵן לוֹ אֶת שְׁמָרָיו וכו'". [5]וְהָא אָמַרְתְּ רֵישָׁא אֵין מְעָרְבִין כְּלָל! [6]וְכִי תֵּימָא: מַאי "נוֹתֵן לוֹ אֶת שְׁמָרָיו"? [7]דְּקָא מוֹדַע לֵיהּ? [8]הָא, מִדְּקָתָנֵי סֵיפָא: "לֹא יִמְכְּרֶנּוּ בַּחֲנוּת אֶלָּא אִם כֵּן מוֹדִיעוֹ, וְלֹא לַתַּגָּר אַף עַל פִּי שֶׁמּוֹדִיעוֹ", [9]מִכְּלָל דְּרֵישָׁא אַף עַל גַּב דְּלָא מוֹדַע לֵיהּ!

[10]אָמַר רַב יְהוּדָה: הָכִי קָאָמַר:

LITERAL TRANSLATION

[1]Rav Pappa said: Since [people] know and forgive.

[2]Rav Aḥa the son of Rav Ika said: Whose [opinion] is this? [3]It is [that of] Rabbi Aḥa. For it was taught: "Rabbi Aḥa permits in [the case of] something which is tasted."

[4]"And one may not mix wine sediment with wine, but he may give him its sediment, etc." [5]But surely you said [in] the first clause [that] one may not mix at all! [6]And if you say: What is "he may give him its sediment"? [7]That he informs him? [8]Surely, since the last clause teaches: "He may not sell it in a shop unless he informs him, and he may not [sell it] to a merchant even if he informs him," [9]this implies that the first clause [applies] even if he did not inform him!

[10]Rav Yehudah said: He says thus:

RASHI

דידעי — הכל יודעים שהוחזקו לערב. **בדבר הנטעם** — שאדם טועם קודם שלקחו, ויכול להבחין שנתערב בו. **והא מדקתני סיפא** — ומפליג בין הודיעו ללא הודיעו — **מכלל דרישא דקתני "אבל נותן לו את שמריו"** — אף על גב דלא אודעיה.

SAGES

רַב אַחָא בְּרֵיהּ דְּרַב אִיקָא Rav Aḥa the son of Rav Ika. A fifth-generation Babylonian Amora, Rav Aḥa the son of Rav Ika was the nephew of Rav Aḥa bar Ya'akov (both scholars apparently lived in the same city, Papunya). Rav Aḥa the son of Rav Ika studied with many fourth- and fifth-generation Amoraim, and engaged in Halakhic discussions with Rav Pappa, and later with Rav Ashi. His teachings — some of which were transmitted by his student, Rav Huna bar Manoaḥ — are cited in various places in the Talmud.

רַבִּי אַחָא Rabbi Aḥa. A Tanna of the last generation. Rabbi Aḥa's teachings appear only in Baraitot, but not in the Mishnah. Rabbi Aḥa cites the dicta of other fifth-generation Tannaim; and many of the last Tannaim, in turn, cite his teachings.

HALAKHAH

עֵירוּב בְּדָבָר הַנִּטְעָם Mixing foods where people taste the food first. "In places where it is customary to taste food before buying it, it is permitted to mix ingredients of varying quality, provided that everyone can ascertain this by tasting the mixture," following Rava and Rabbi Aḥa, whose views seem to be accepted by the Talmud. (Ibid., 228:14.)

BACKGROUND

שָׁמְרִים שֶׁל אֶמֶשׁ **Yesterday's sediment.** Wine sediment is used to expedite the fermentation of the grape juice, transforming it into wine. Such sediment was also used to produce wine at home. In addition, wine sediment was used as a food supplement for animals, since it is rich in protein. However, people generally avoided mixing sediment of different types, since they taste different from one another, and hence are apt to spoil the taste of the grapes used for wine production.

מִזְגָּא דִּידִי מֵידַע יְדִיעַ **My mixing is well known.** Rava was of the opinion that each part of wine should be diluted with three parts of water (rather than two, as done by most people). Indeed, the Gemara relates elsewhere (see *Nedarim* 55a) that Rav Yosef, who was blind, was able to ascertain through taste that a particular mixture of wine had been prepared by Rava.

TERMINOLOGY

תַּנְיָא נַמִי הָכִי **It was also taught thus.** A term used to introduce a Baraita which supports the previous statement by the Gemara or by an individual Amora.

TRANSLATION AND COMMENTARY

This is what the Mishnah **is saying:** The merchant **may not mix** wine and sediment from two different barrels. For example, he may not take the **sediment** from **yesterday's** barrel of wine and mix it with **today's** wine, **nor** may he mix sediment from **today's** wine **with yesterday's** wine. (The Gemara's use of "yesterday" and "today" is merely an illustration. The same rule would apply to two barrels opened on the same day.) [1] **But he may give** the buyer the barrel of wine with **its own** sediment, and need not strain the wine before selling it.

תַּנְיָא נַמִי הָכִי [2] The Gemara now cites a Baraita which supports Rav Yehudah's interpretation of the Mishnah: The following Baraita **also taught this:** "Rabbi Yehudah says: When the seller **pours out wine for another person,** transferring the wine from his own barrel into the other person's container, **he may not mix** sediment from **yesterday's** barrel **with** wine from **today's** barrel, **nor** may he mix sediment from **today's** barrel **with** wine from **yesterday's** barrel, [3] **but he may mix yesterday's** sediment **with** wine from **yesterday's** barrel, **or today's** sediment **with** wine from **today's** barrel."

מִי שֶׁנִּתְעָרֵב [4] The Gemara proceeds to discuss the next clause of the Mishnah: "If **someone's wine was mixed with water, he may not sell it in a shop unless he informs** the buyer that it has been diluted, **etc.**" [5] The Gemara relates that **Rava was** once **brought wine from a shop,** after which **he mixed it with water and tasted it.** [6] The wine Rava bought, however, **was not tasty,** so **he sent it back to the shop.**

אֲמַר לֵיהּ אַבַּיֵי [7] **Abaye** then **said to Rava: But surely we have learned** in our Mishnah: "**One may not** sell wine diluted with water **to a merchant, even if one informed him** that it was diluted." How, then, could Rava have sent diluted wine back to the shop? Why was he not concerned lest the merchant pass it off as undiluted wine?

אֲמַר לֵיהּ [8] In reply, Rava **said to** Abaye: **My mixture is** easily **recognizable,** for I add more water to my wine

LITERAL TRANSLATION

One may not mix yesterday's sediment with today's, nor today's with yesterday's, [1] but he may give him its sediment.

[2] It was also taught thus: "Rabbi Yehudah says: Someone who pours off wine for his fellow, he should not mix yesterday's with today's, nor today's with yesterday's, [3] but he may mix yesterday's with yesterday's, or today's with today's."

[4] "Someone whose wine was mixed with water may not sell it in a shop, unless he informs him, etc." [5] Rava was brought wine from a shop, he mixed it [with water, and] tasted it, [and] it was not tasty. [6] He sent it [back] to the shop.

[7] Abaye said to him: But surely we have learned: "And he may not [sell it] to a merchant, even if he informed him"! [8] He said to him: My mixing is

אֵין מְעָרְבִין שְׁמָרִים שֶׁל אֶמֶשׁ בְּשֶׁל יוֹם, וְלֹא שֶׁל יוֹם בְּשֶׁל אֶמֶשׁ, [1] אֲבָל נוֹתֵן לוֹ אֶת שְׁמָרָיו. [2] תַּנְיָא נַמִי הָכִי: "רַבִּי יְהוּדָה אוֹמֵר: הַשּׁוֹפֶה יַיִן לַחֲבֵירוֹ, הֲרֵי זֶה לֹא יְעָרֵב שֶׁל אֶמֶשׁ בְּשֶׁל יוֹם, וְלֹא שֶׁל יוֹם בְּשֶׁל אֶמֶשׁ, [3] אֲבָל מְעָרֵב שֶׁל אֶמֶשׁ בְּשֶׁל אֶמֶשׁ, וְשֶׁל יוֹם בְּשֶׁל יוֹם".

[4] "מִי שֶׁנִּתְעָרֵב מַיִם בְּיֵינוֹ הֲרֵי זֶה לֹא יִמְכְּרֶנּוּ בַּחֲנוּת אֶלָּא אִם כֵּן מוֹדִיעוֹ וְכוּ'". [5] רָבָא אַיְיתוּ לֵיהּ חַמְרָא מֵחֲנוּתָא, מְזַגֵיהּ, טַעֲמֵיהּ, לָא הֲוָה בָּסִים. [6] שַׁדְּרֵיהּ לַחֲנוּתָא. [7] אֲמַר לֵיהּ אַבַּיֵי: וְהָא אֲנַן תְּנַן: "וְלֹא לַתַּגָּר אַף עַל פִּי שֶׁהוֹדִיעוֹ"! [8] אֲמַר לֵיהּ: מִזְגָּא דִּידִי מֵידַע

RASHI

שֶׁל אֶמֶשׁ – מֵיִין שֶׁשָּׁפָה אֶמֶשׁ, וְנִשְׁאֲרוּ הַשְּׁמָרִים, אֵין מְעָרְבִין אוֹתוֹ בֵּין שְׁמָרֵי הַיּוֹם, שֶׁשְּׁמָרֵי יַיִן זֶה מְקַלְקְלִין יַיִן אַחֵר. אֲבָל נוֹתֵן הוּא לוֹ אֶת שְׁמָרָיו – שֶׁל יַיִן עַצְמוֹ. וְיַיִן וּמַעֲשֶׂה לָאו דַּוְקָא, וְהוּא הַדִּין לְיוֹם וְיוֹם מִשְׁתֵּי חָבִיּוֹת, אֶלָּא אוֹרְחָא דְּמִילְּתָא נָקַט, דִּסְתָם יוֹם וְאֶמֶשׁ מִשְׁתֵּי חָבִיּוֹת. הַשּׁוֹפֶה יַיִן – כָּל דָּבָר הַצָּלוּל הַנִּזְרָק בְּנַחַת מִכְּלִי אֶל כְּלִי שֶׁלֹּא יְּעַרְבוּ בּוֹ שְׁמָרִים קָרוּי לֵיהּ שְׁפִיָּה. מְזַגֵיהּ – נָתַן בּוֹ מַיִם שֶׁכֵּן דַּרְכּוֹ. בָּסִים – מְבוּסָס וְטוֹב. וְהָא אֲנַן תְּנַן וְלֹא לַתַּגָּר שֶׁאֵינוֹ אֶלָּא לְרַמּוֹת כו' – וְתַגְוֵוֵי הַיְינוּ תַגָּר, וִיחֲזוֹר חֲנוֹוֵי זֶה וִימְכְּרֶנּוּ בִּמְקַח יַיִן בַּחֲנוּת. וַהֲרֵי הַמַּיִם מְעוּרָבִין בּוֹ וְאָתָה מַכְרַת לוֹ, וְאָכֵל "לִפְנֵי עוֵר" (וַיִּקְרָא יט). מִזְגָּא דִּידִי מֵידַע יְדִיעַ – שֶׁאֲנִי נוֹתֵן בּוֹ מַיִם הַרְבֵּה.

NOTES

מִזְגָּא דִּידִי **My mixing.** Wine had to be diluted in Talmudic times because it was so strong. Rava's mixture was known to be especially weak: While most people diluted one part of wine with two parts of water, Rava diluted each part of wine with three parts of water.

HALAKHAH

תַּעֲרוֹבֶת שְׁמָרִים **Mixing sediments.** "It is forbidden to mix sediment from one container of wine with wine from another container. However, one may mix sediment from a particular container of wine when selling wine from that container (*Rosh*)." (*Shulḥan Arukh, Ḥoshen Mishpat* 228:15, and *Sma* ad loc.)

יְדִיעַ. [1]וְכִי תֵּימָא דְּטָפֵי וּמְחַיְּילֵיהּ וּמְזַבֵּין לֵיהּ, [2]אִם כֵּן אֵין לְדָבָר סוֹף.

[3]״מָקוֹם שֶׁנָּהֲגוּ לְהַטִּיל מַיִם בַּיַּיִן, יַטִּילוּ וכו׳״. [4]תָּנָא: ״לְמֶחֱצָה לִשְׁלִישׁ וְלִרְבִיעַ״.

[5]אָמַר רַב: וּבֵין הַגִּיתּוֹת שָׁנוּ.

משנה [6]רַבִּי יְהוּדָה אוֹמֵר: לֹא יְחַלֵּק הַחֶנְוָנִי קְלָיוֹת וֶאֱגוֹזִין לַתִּינוֹקוֹת, מִפְּנֵי שֶׁהוּא מַרְגִּילָן לָבֹא אֶצְלוֹ, וַחֲכָמִים מַתִּירִין.

LITERAL TRANSLATION

well known. [1]And if you say that he may add [wine] and make it stronger and sell it, [2]if so, there is no end to the matter.

[3]"[In a] place where they are accustomed to add water to wine, they may add, etc." [4][A Tanna] taught: "By half, by one-third, or by one-fourth."

[5]Rav said: And they taught [this] in the winepresses.

MISHNAH [6]Rabbi Yehudah says: A shopkeeper must not distribute parched grain or nuts to children, since he accustoms them to come to him, but the Sages permit [this].

TRANSLATION AND COMMENTARY

than do most people. Therefore, I am permitted to return the wine to the merchant, for he will be unable to sell my wine as undiluted wine and there is no possibility that potential buyers will be deceived. [1]**And if you say that** it is still forbidden to return the diluted wine to the merchant, because the merchant, if he is dishonest, **may add** undiluted **wine** to the mixture **to make it stronger, and** then **sell it** as ordinary wine — in which case potential buyers may be misled into thinking that the wine has not been diluted at all and buy it at the full price, making me an accessory to fraud — such reasoning is invalid. [2]For **if so, there is no end to the matter.** Such reasoning would lead to the absurd conclusion that it is forbidden to sell *any* wine to a merchant, since he may then dilute it and resell it as ordinary wine! The prohibition applies only to items that readily lend themselves to deceptive practices. Accordingly, the Gemara concludes that diluted wine may be resold to a merchant if the seller is reasonably certain that the merchant will be unable to pass it off as undiluted.

מָקוֹם שֶׁנָּהֲגוּ [3]The Gemara now turns to the next clause of our Mishnah: **"In a place where** merchants **are accustomed to add water to wine, they may add** water, **etc."** [4]Commenting on this Mishnah, a **Tanna taught:** "The amount of water which may be added in such places is **half** the amount of the wine, or **one-third, or one-fourth,** depending on the local custom."

אָמַר רַב [5]**Rav said: This Mishnah,** which permits the diluting of wine with water, **was taught** only with regard to wine still **in the winepresses** and which had not yet begun to ferment. At that point adding water to the unfermented grape juice does not cause it to spoil. However, once the juice ferments, it is prohibited to add water. Hence, if the merchant failed to dilute the wine in time, he may not do so later.

MISHNAH רַבִּי יְהוּדָה אוֹמֵר [6]The Mishnah now considers other business practices that border on deceit. **Rabbi Yehudah says: A shopkeeper must not distribute parched grain or nuts** or any other treat **to children** free of charge, **since he** thereby **accustoms them to come to him** and buy from him, and this is unfair competition. Competition between merchants should be based only on quality and price. Attracting customers by manipulating the minds of children is the same as defrauding the other merchants. **But the Sages permit this** practice.

BACKGROUND

קְלָיוֹת **Parched grain.** This refers to grains of wheat or barley roasted while the ears were not completely ripe. The roasting process transforms some of the starch in the grain into sugar, and the grain becomes sweet. Such parched grain was sometimes processed into sweet flour for the baking of cakes. Usually, however, the parched grain was eaten as a sweet and was a natural choice for a shopkeeper who wanted to attract young children to buy his wares.

RASHI

וכי תימא מייתי חמרא חייא ומערב ביה – עד שלא יהא ניכר טעם המים.

אם כן – דלכולי האי חיישינן. **אין לדבר סוף** – שאף המים לבדם אסור למכור לחנווני, שמא יערבם ביין. ולא חשו אלא בזמן שאני מוכר לו דבר העשוי לרמות בו כמות שהוא עכשיו. **למחצה לשליש ולרביע** – הכל כמנהג המדינה יטיל מים, אם מחצה, מחצה, אם שליש, שליש.

NOTES

אֵין לְדָבָר סוֹף **There is no end to the matter.** I.e., if we are so concerned that the wine may be adulterated, it should even be forbidden to sell *water* to a merchant, since he may use it to dilute wine (*Rashi*). *Ritva* explains the text to mean that if we are concerned that the wine will be tampered with, we should not be permitted to sell wine to a merchant under any circumstances.

לֹא יְחַלֵּק... וְלֹא יְפַחוֹת **Distributing parched grain and lowering prices.** The Mishnah did not combine these cases into a single sentence, i.e., "Rabbi Yehudah forbids distributing parched grain and lowering prices, while the Sages permit this," because they are different. According to the Sages, distributing parched grain is permitted, whereas lowering prices is praiseworthy (*Ein Yehosef*).

HALAKHAH

הַחֶנְוָנִי הַמְחַלֵּק קְלָיוֹת וֶאֱגוֹזִין **A shopkeeper who distributes parched grain or nuts.** "A shopkeeper is permitted to distribute without charge parched grain, nuts, etc., to children, in order to encourage them to buy from him. Similarly, he may charge less than other shopkeepers do," following the view of the Sages. See also *Arukh HaShulḥan*, who suggests that it is only permitted to sell food at a discount, but not other merchandise. (Ibid., 228:18.)

[1] וְלֹא יְפַחוֹת אֶת הַשַּׁעַר, וַחֲכָמִים אוֹמְרִים: זָכוּר לַטּוֹב. [2] לֹא יָבוֹר אֶת הַגְּרִיסִין. דִּבְרֵי אַבָּא שָׁאוּל. [3] וַחֲכָמִים מַתִּירִין. [4] וּמוֹדִים שֶׁלֹּא יָבוֹר מֵעַל פִּי מְגוּרָה, שֶׁאֵינוֹ אֶלָּא כְּגוֹנֵב אֶת הָעַיִן.

[5] אֵין מְפַרְכְּסִין לֹא אֶת הָאָדָם, וְלֹא אֶת הַבְּהֵמָה, וְלֹא אֶת הַכֵּלִים.

גמרא [6] מַאי טַעֲמַיְיהוּ דְּרַבָּנַן?

LITERAL TRANSLATION

[1] And he may not lower the price, but the Sages say: He is remembered for good.
[2] He must not sift pounded beans. [These are] the words of Abba Shaul. [3] But the Sages permit [this].
[4] But they agree that he must not sift from the top of a bin, for it is only [done] to deceive the eye.
[5] One may not paint a man, or an animal, or utensils.
GEMARA [6] What is the reasoning of the Sages?

TRANSLATION AND COMMENTARY

[1] Likewise, according to Rabbi Yehudah, a shopkeeper **should not lower his prices** below the fair market value of his merchandise, since this too is considered unfair competition. It is unethical to try to drive one's competitors out of business by engaging in a price war. **But the Sages say** that if a shopkeeper lowers his prices, **he is remembered for good.** Thus, not only is it permitted to lower prices, but this is even considered praiseworthy, as the Gemara will explain.

לֹא יָבוֹר אֶת הַגְּרִיסִין [2] Likewise, a merchant **should not sift pounded beans** and then charge more for the beans than usual. **These are the words of Abba Shaul.** Abba Shaul forbids sifting pounded beans because the seller may then charge more for them than they are really worth, and the buyer, impressed by their appearance, may overestimate their value. [3] But in this case as well **the Sages permit this** practice. [4] However, even the Sages **agree that** a merchant **should not sift the top of** a pile of produce **in a bin** and leave the rest unsifted, **since this is only done to deceive.** Once the inferior produce at the top has been removed, the customers see only the superior produce, and they might be deceived into believing that the bin is filled with produce of the same superior quality.

אֵין מְפַרְכְּסִין [5] Similarly, a merchant **may not paint a person** (i.e., a slave), **an animal, or utensils** that he is selling, to deceive the buyer by improving their appearance.

GEMARA מַאי טַעֲמַיְיהוּ [6] The Gemara considers the first clause of the Mishnah, in which the Sages disagree with Rabbi Yehudah and permit distributing free treats to children. The Gemara asks: **What is the Sages' reasoning?** Why do they not agree with Rabbi Yehudah that competition should be based on quality and price alone?

RASHI

משנה ולא יפחות את השער – למכור בזול, מפני שמרגיל לבא אצלו ומקפח מזונות חבירו. זכור לטוב – שמתוך כך אוצרי פירות מוכרין בזול. גריסין – פולין גרוסות בריחים אחת לשתים. לא יבור את הפסולת – לפי שמתוך שנראות יפות הוא מעלה על דמיהם הרבה מדמי הפסולת שנטל מהם. וחכמים מתירין – טעמא מפרש בגמרא. ומודים שלא יבור מעל פי המגורה – למעלה, להראות יפות, ואת הפסולת שבתוכו לא בירר. לפי שאינו אלא כגונב את העין – בברירה זו. ואין מפרכסין – מפרש בגמרא. לא את האדם – עבד כנעני העומד לימכר.

גמרא שיסקי – *פרונ"ש. מאי טעמא – נקט "זכור לטוב", לשון ברכה.

BACKGROUND

גְּרִיסִים **Pounded beans.** Pounded beans were usually crushed with special instruments, after which other types of foods were prepared from them. Indeed, foods prepared from legumes of this sort were very popular among the general public.

SAGES

אַבָּא שָׁאוּל **Abba Shaul.** A Tanna of the third and fourth generations, Abba Shaul was a younger contemporary of Rabbi Akiva. The name "Abba" was an honorific title given to Sages of early generations. He is described as being "the tallest of his generation" — a description accurately reflecting both his physical appearance and the high regard in which he was held. Many of his Halakhic rulings — even when expressed as a minority opinion — became the basis for later Halakhic practice.

LANGUAGE (RASHI)

פרונ"ש* From the old French *prunes*, meaning "plums."

NOTES

דִּבְרֵי אַבָּא שָׁאוּל **These are the words of Abba Shaul.** *Ḥiddushim HaMeyuḥasim LeRitva* had a slightly different reading here, namely: "This *follows* the words [i.e., opinion] of Abba Shaul" (כְּדִבְרֵי אַבָּא שָׁאוּל). The commentator observes that Abba Shaul was himself a merchant, and exceptionally strict about deceiving others, as we learn from other passages in the Talmud. Thus the Mishnah means that sifting pounded beans is forbidden "according to Abba Shaul's opinion," i.e., in accordance with his own personal practice.

פִּרְכּוּס אָדָם **It is forbidden to paint a person.** A woman may beautify herself in order to appear more attractive than she really is (and find a husband). However, she may not conceal visible physical defects, as this is outright deception (*Rabbi Ya'akov Emden*).

HALAKHAH

לָבוֹר מֵעַל הַמְּגוּרָה **Sifting from the top of a bin.** "A merchant may remove inferior produce from the top of a bin, so the rest of the produce will look better and the merchant will be able to charge more for it, so long as he also removes all the inferior produce below the surface of the bin." (Ibid., 228:17.)

יִפּוּי סְחוֹרָה **Improving the appearance of merchandise.** "It is forbidden to alter the appearance of merchandise (animals, utensils, or people) to make it look better than it really is. Thus it is prohibited to dye a slave's beard so that he will look younger, or to feed an animal with broth made from bran to make it look fatter (or to scrape it so that it will look better), or to dye old clothing so that it will seem new. However, it is permitted to dye or otherwise improve the appearance of new merchandise, since doing so does not mislead potential buyers (because the merchandise really is new — *Sma*). Likewise, it is forbidden to soak meat or to inflate an animal's entrails to make it look better (unless all merchants ordinarily do so — *Sma*)." (Ibid., 228:9,15.)

[1]דְּאָמַר לֵיהּ: ״אֲנָא מְפַלֵּיגְנָא אַמְגוּזֵי, וְאַתְּ פָּלֵיג שִׁיסְקֵי״. [2]״וְלֹא יִפְחוֹת אֶת הַשַּׁעַר, וַחֲכָמִים אוֹמְרִים: זָכוּר לַטּוֹב וכו׳״. [3]מַאי טַעְמָא דְּרַבָּנַן? [60B] [4]מִשּׁוּם דְּקָא מַרְוַוח לְתַרְעָא.

[5]״וְלֹא יָבוֹר אֶת הַגְּרִיסִין. דִּבְרֵי אַבָּא שָׁאוּל. וַחֲכָמִים מַתִּירִין, וכו׳״. [6]מַאן חֲכָמִים?

[7]רַבִּי אַחָא, דְּתַנְיָא: ״רַבִּי אַחָא מַתִּיר בְּדָבָר הַנִּרְאֶה״.

[8]״אֵין מְפַרְכְּסִין לֹא אֶת הָאָדָם וכו׳ וְלֹא אֶת הַכֵּלִים״. [9]תָּנוּ רַבָּנַן: ״אֵין מְשַׁרְבְּטִין אֶת הַבְּהֵמָה, וְאֵין נוֹפְחִין בַּקְּרָבַיִים, וְאֵין שׁוֹרִין אֶת הַבָּשָׂר בַּמַּיִם״. [10]מַאי ״אֵין מְשַׁרְבְּטִין״?

LITERAL TRANSLATION

[1]Because he can say to him: "I am distributing nuts, and you may distribute plums."

[2]"And he may not lower the price, but the Sages say: He is remembered for good, etc." [3]What is the reasoning of the Sages?

[60B] [4]Because he eases the market price.

[5]"And he must not sift pounded beans. [These are] the words of Abba Shaul. But the Sages permit, etc." [6]Who are the Sages?

[7]Rabbi Aḥa, for it was taught: "Rabbi Aḥa permits in [the case of] something which is visible."

[8]"One may not paint a person ... nor utensils." [9]Our Rabbis taught: "One may not stiffen an animal, and one may not inflate the entrails, and one may not soak meat in water."

[10]What is "one may not stiffen"?

TRANSLATION AND COMMENTARY

דְּאָמַר לֵיהּ [1]The Gemara answers: **Because** the seller **can say to** any merchant who accuses him of unfair competition: **"I am distributing nuts** in order to attract customers, **and you can distribute plums!** No one is preventing you from doing the same or better."

וְלֹא יִפְחוֹת אֶת הַשַּׁעַר [2]The Gemara proceeds to analyze the next clause in the Mishnah: "Likewise, according to Rabbi Yehudah, **he may not lower his prices** below the fair market value of his merchandise, **but the Sages say:** A merchant who lowers his prices is **remembered for good, etc."** [3]The Gemara asks: **What is the Sages' reasoning?** Why do the Sages maintain that a merchant who lowers his prices is to be "remembered for good"?

[60B] מִשּׁוּם דְּקָא מַרְוַוח לְתַרְעָא [4]The Gemara answers: **Because** a merchant who lowers his own prices also **brings down the** general market **price.** If one merchant lowers his prices, others will follow, leading to a general reduction in prices. According to the Sages, competitive prices are not only ethical, but they also benefit consumers.

וְלֹא יָבוֹר אֶת הַגְּרִיסִין [5]The Gemara now takes up the next clause of the Mishnah: **"And he** must **not sift pounded beans** and then charge more for the beans than usual, because customers may be misled into paying more than the beans are actually worth. **These are the words of Abba Shaul. But the Sages permit** this, **etc."** [6]The Gemara asks: **Who are the Sages** who disagree with Abba Shaul here? Whose opinion are they following and what is the basis of their argument?

רַבִּי אַחָא [7]The Gemara answers: The Sages follow the opinion of **Rabbi Aḥa, as was taught in** the following Baraita: **"Rabbi Aḥa permits** improving the appearance of merchandise in the hope of attracting customers **in a case where** the change **is visible."** Rabbi Aḥa is of the opinion that it is permitted to attract customers by improving the appearance of merchandise, provided that the buyer sees what he is paying for. Thus, in the case of pounded beans, if the customer is willing to pay extra for sifted beans, it can only be to save himself the trouble of sifting them. Therefore, it is not considered unethical for the seller to sift them, even when he charges extra for this service.

אֵין מְפַרְכְּסִין [8]The Gemara proceeds to discuss the next clause of the Mishnah: "A merchant **may not paint a person ... or utensils** to make them look better than they really are, thereby deceiving the buyer." [9]The Gemara cites a Baraita which presents other rulings in a similar vein: **Our Rabbis taught: "A person** selling live animals **may not stiffen** the hair of **an animal** to make it look sleeker before presenting it for sale, **nor** may a butcher selling **entrails inflate** them to make them look bigger, **nor** may a butcher selling **meat soak it in water** to improve its appearance. These practices are forbidden because their purpose is to deceive.

מַאי אֵין מְשַׁרְבְּטִין [10]The Gemara asks: Precisely **what** did the Baraita mean when it said: "One **may not stiffen** an animal's hair"?

RASHI

גמרא שיסקי — *פרונ״ש. **מאי טעמא** — נקט ״זכור לטוב״, לשון ברכה. **משום דמרווח תרעא** — ואוצרי פירות יראו שהוזלו וימכרו בזול. **מתיר בדבר הנראה** — הלא יכול הלוקח לראות ולהבין מה דמי הפסולת הנברר מאלו, שישנו באחרים. וטוב לו להעלות בדמיהן של אלו יתר על כן מפני הטורח. **משרבטין** — לשון שרביט, כדמפרש לקמיה. שזוקף שער הבהמה כשרביט שתראה שמינה. **ואין נופחין בקרביים** — בני מעיים הנמכרים בבית הטבח שיראו רחבים וגדולים. **ואין שורין בשר במים** — שמלבין, והכחוש נראה שמן.

LANGUAGE

שִׁיסְקֵי Plums. Various explanations of the etymology of this word have been offered. Perhaps the most convincing is that this is an Aramaic form of the Hebrew שֵׁיזָף — jujube, *zyzziphus vulgaris.*

LANGUAGE (RASHI)

פרונ״ש* From the old French *prunes,* meaning "plums."

REALIA

שִׁיסְקֵי Plums. שִׁיסְקֵי, more properly translated as "jujube," are from the buckthorn family (*Rhamnaceae*). Jujube trees are deciduous, and they have fine, thorny branches with serrated leaves. These trees are common in various parts of Asia; certain types of jujube are grown in Eretz Israel as well. The fruits of this tree are small and red and have a bittersweet taste. They were usually dried and eaten as candies.

TERMINOLOGY

מַאן חֲכָמִים רַבִּי פְּלוֹנִי Who are the Sages? Rabbi X. Sometimes, when a Tannaitic source ascribes a particular viewpoint to "the Sages" (חֲכָמִים), the Talmud may use this expression to prove that this is in fact the view of an individual Sage.

TRANSLATION AND COMMENTARY

הָכָא תַּרְגְּמוּ [1]The Gemara answers: **Here** in Babylonia, the Rabbis **explained** that a merchant may not feed animals **broth made of bran,** since this causes the animal's stomach to swell and its hair to stand up.

זְעֵירִי אָמַר רַב כָּהֲנָא [2]**Ze'iri said in the name of Rav Kahana:** The Baraita is referring to **brushing an animal's hair** to stiffen it and make the animal appear bigger than it really is.

שְׁמוּאֵל שְׁרָא לְמִרְמָא תּוּמֵי לְסַרְבְּלָא [3]Continuing its discussion of what constitutes prohibited misrepresentation of merchandise, the Gemara relates that **Shmuel permitted putting fringes on a cloak** to make it look more attractive. Similarly, **Rav Yehudah permitted scouring fine cloth,** to present it at its best. [4]Likewise, **Rabbah permitted beating rough cloth** — linen or canvas — to make it appear finer. **Rava permitted drawing** decorative designs on cloth, in the shape of little **arrows,** for example. [5]**Rav Pappa bar Shmuel permitted the drawing** of decorations **on baskets.**

וְהָא אֲנַן תְּנַן [6]Having cited the rulings of all these Amoraim, the Gemara objects that such conduct seems to contradict our Mishnah: **But surely we** have **learned** in our Mishnah: "One **may not paint a person or an animal or a utensil** to make it look better than it is, so as not to deceive potential buyers"!

לָא קַשְׁיָא [7]The Gemara answers: **There is no difficulty** resolving this contradiction between the Mishnah's ruling and that of the various Amoraim cited here. [8]The permissive rulings of the Amoraim only **apply to new** merchandise, whereas the Mishnah's prohibition applies **to old** merchandise. The Mishnah does not object to making merchandise look more attractive, provided no deception is involved. What the Mishnah forbids is misleading customers by painting old merchandise to make it look new. But if the merchant is not hiding anything, and the buyer is ready to pay more for a more attractive article, the merchant is permitted to enhance the appearance of his merchandise.

פִּרְכּוּס דְּאָדָם מַאי הִיא [9]The Gemara continues its discussion of the Mishnah by asking: **What** did the Mishnah mean by a seller **"painting a person"?**

[1]הָכָא תַּרְגְּמוּ: מַיָּא דְּחִיזְרָא. [2]זְעֵירִי אֲמַר רַב כָּהֲנָא: מִזְקַפְתָּא. [3]שְׁמוּאֵל שְׁרָא לְמִרְמָא תּוּמֵי לְסַרְבְּלָא. רַב יְהוּדָה שְׁרָא לְכַסְכּוּסֵי קְרָמֵי. [4]רַבָּה שְׁרָא לְמֵידַק צְרָדֵי. רָבָא שְׁרָא לְצַלּוּמֵי גִּירֵי. [5]רַב פַּפָּא בַּר שְׁמוּאֵל שְׁרָא לְצַלּוּמֵי דִּיקוּלֵי.

[6]וְהָא אֲנַן תְּנַן: "אֵין מְפַרְכְּסִין לֹא אֶת הָאָדָם, וְלֹא אֶת הַבְּהֵמָה, וְלֹא אֶת הַכֵּלִים"!

[7]לָא קַשְׁיָא. [8]הָא בַּחֲדַתֵּי, הָא בְּעַתִּיקֵי.

[9]פִּרְכּוּס דְּאָדָם מַאי הִיא?

LITERAL TRANSLATION

[1]Here they explained: Broth [made] of bran.

[2]Ze'iri said in the name of Rav Kahana: Brushing up [the animal's hair].

[3]Shmuel permitted putting fringes on a cloak. Rav Yehudah permitted scouring fine cloth. [4]Rabbah permitted beating rough cloth. Rava permitted painting arrows. [5]Rav Pappa bar Shmuel permitted painting baskets.

[6]But surely we have learned: "One may not paint a man, nor an animal, nor utensils"!

[7]There is no difficulty. [8]This [applies] to new ones, this to old ones.

[9]What is painting a man?

RASHI

מיא דחיזרא — משקין אותה מי סובין, והם נופחין מעיה ושערה נזקף. **מזקפתא** = קירצוף, *אשטליי״ר בלעז. **למירמא תומי לסרבלא** — **פרנזי״ש, לייפותו עושין לו תלאי מחוטי משי סביב. **לכסכוסי** = ***אנפריי״ש בלעז, במי סובין. **קרמי** = בגדים המצויירים, ****אוברי״ץ בלעז. **למידק צרדי** — להדק בגדי קנבוס במקבות עץ, שיראה חוטן דק. **לצלומי גירי** — לצייר חיצים. **דיקולי** = סלים. **בחדתי** — מותר, שאינו אלא ליפות. והרוצה להוסיף על דמיהם בשביל יופיים, מוחל הוא. **בעתיקי** — אסור, שגונב את העין שנראים כחדשים.

LANGUAGE

סַרְבְּלָא **Cloak.** This word, which also appears in the Bible (Daniel 3:21, 27), refers to a certain type of trousers worn in Persia (the word is derived from the Persian *salvar,* "trousers"). It seems that the same root is used here, even though it apparently means "mantle," or "cloak" in the present context.

פִּרְכּוּס **Painting.** The origin of this word is uncertain. Some scholars are of the opinion that it come from the Greek root περκάζω, *perkazo,* meaning to darken, in the sense of a beard becoming darker.

REALIA

צַלּוּמֵי גִּירֵי **Painting arrows.** A decoration embroidered on the hem of a Greek garment.

BACKGROUND

לְכַסְכּוּסֵי קְרָמֵי **Scouring fine cloth.** *Rashi* interprets קְרָמֵי as "colored garments," while *Arukh* explains that it means "thin, expensive clothes."

LANGUAGE (RASHI)

אשטלי״ר* From the Old French *estrelier,* "to comb, to brush animal hair."

פרנזי״ש** From the Old French *frenjes,* which means "fringes hanging from the corner of a garment."

אנפריי״ש*** From the Old French *enpeser,* "wash, launder."

אוברי״ץ**** From the Old French *ovres,* which means "cloth with decorations and embroidery."

SAGES

זְעֵירִי **Ze'iri.** A second generation Babylonian Amora, Ze'iri was a student of Rav. After his teacher's death, Ze'iri apparently immigrated to

NOTES

לְמִרְמָא תּוּמֵי לְסַרְבְּלָא **Putting fringes on a cloak.** *Ra'avad* explains that this refers to tying fringes which hang from the garment in pairs (the word תּוּמֵי being equivalent to the word תְּאוֹמֵי, meaning "pairs"), to make the garment stronger and more attractive.

צַלּוּמֵי דִּיקוּלֵי **Painting on baskets.** The word צַלּוּמֵי is cognate to the Hebrew צֶלֶם — "image" — and means "to draw" (patterns), while דִּיקוּלֵי — "baskets" — are woven baskets, which were usually made from palm leaves, but occasionally from willow branches and the like. The common denominator in all these cases is that the Rabbis permitted improving the appearance of merchandise even if potential buyers would not necessarily realize that such improvements had been made, as long as they were not deceived into thinking that they were buying top-quality merchandise.

בַּחֲדַתֵּי וּבְעַתִּיקֵי **New ones and old ones.** Cosmetic improvements on new merchandise are permitted, because they cause only a slight increase in price. In fact, the price rises only because of the labor invested in improving the item, as a result of which it is more likely to attract potential buyers. However, it is forbidden to improve the appearance of old merchandise, because the improvements conceal existing flaws and make the merchandise look new, which

TRANSLATION AND COMMENTARY

כִּי הָא דְּהַהוּא עַבְדָּא סָבָא [1]The Gemara explains that this refers to **cases like** that described in the following story. There was **a certain old slave** whose hair had turned white, and **who went and dyed his head and his beard** black, to make himself look younger. [2]The slave then **came before Rava and said to him: "Buy me** as your slave." [3]In reply Rava **said to** the slave: **"Let the poor be members of your household"** (*Avot* 1:5), meaning that he preferred to employ poor Jews as domestic servants for wages, because the livelihood of paupers takes priority over that of slaves. [4]Seeing that Rava was not interested in buying him, the slave **came before Rav Pappa bar Shmuel, who bought him.** [5]**One day** Rav Pappa bar Shmuel **said to** his new slave: **"Give me** some **water to drink."** [6]Rather than perform this simple task, the slave **went and whitened his head and beard** by washing off the dye. [7]The slave then **said to** Rav Pappa bar Shmuel, his master: "You can now **see that I am older than your father!** It is not proper for you to make me perform menial tasks." [8]When Rav Pappa bar Shmuel heard this, **he said of himself,** paraphrasing a Biblical verse (Proverbs 11:8), **"The righteous is delivered out of trouble, and another** (the original text reads: "the wicked," but Rav Pappa did not wish to call himself wicked) **comes in his stead."** Thus Rava — the "righteous" of the verse — preferred to employ the poor and was saved from trouble, while Rav Pappa bar Shmuel — the "other" who "came in Rava's stead" — was punished by buying a worthless slave.

[1]כִּי הָא דְּהַהוּא עַבְדָּא סָבָא דַּאֲזַל צְבַעֵיהּ לְרֵישֵׁיהּ וּלְדִיקְנֵיהּ. [2]אֲתָא לְקַמֵּיהּ דְּרָבָא, אֲמַר לֵיהּ: ״זִיבְנָן״. [3]אֲמַר לֵיהּ: ״יִהְיוּ עֲנִיִּים בְּנֵי בֵיתְךָ״. [4]אֲתָא לְקַמֵּיהּ דְּרַב פַּפָּא בַּר שְׁמוּאֵל, זְבַנֵיהּ. [5]יוֹמָא חַד אֲמַר לֵיהּ: ״אַשְׁקְיַין מַיָּא״. [6]אֲזַל חַוְּורֵיהּ לְרֵישֵׁיהּ וּלְדִיקְנֵיהּ. [7]אֲמַר לֵיהּ: ״חֲזִי דַּאֲנָא קַשִּׁישׁ מֵאֲבוּךְ״. [8]קָרֵי אַנַּפְשֵׁיהּ: ״צַדִּיק מִצָּרָה נֶחֱלָץ, וַיָּבֹא אַחֵר תַּחְתָּיו״.

הדרן עלך הזהב

LITERAL TRANSLATION

[1]Like that [case] of a certain old slave who went [and] dyed his head and his beard. [2]He came before Rava [and] said to him: "Buy me." [3]He said to him: "Let the poor be members of your household." [4]He came before Rav Pappa bar Shmuel, [and] he bought him. [5]One day he said to him: "Give me water to drink." [6]He went [and] whitened his head and his beard. [7]He said to him: "See that I am older than your father." [8]He said (lit., "read") of himself: "The righteous is delivered out of trouble, and another comes in his stead."

RASHI

צבעיה — שהיה זקנו לבן וצבעו שחור, ונראה כבחור. **זיבנן** — קנה אותי לעבד. ונכרי היה, דעבד עברי אסור לאחר חורבן, שאין היובל נוהג. **ויהיו עניים בני ביתך** — משנה היא (אבות פרק א משנה ה). טוב לי לפרנס עניי ישראל וישמשוני. **דיקניה** — זקנו. **צדיק מצרה נחלץ** — זה רבא.

הדרן עלך הזהב

Eretz Israel, where he became an outstanding student of Rabbi Yoḥanan. Despite his youth, Ze'iri was honored by Rabbi Yoḥanan and Resh Lakish as a great man (indeed, Rava remarked that any Mishnah which Ze'iri did not explain was not explained properly). Ze'iri may have returned later to Babylonia, and his Halakhic teachings were transmitted by the students of Rav Huna.

Some scholars hold that there were two Ze'iris, one of whom was a colleague of Rav. At any rate, Ze'iri is definitely not identical with the later Amora Rabbi Zera (or Ze'ira, as he is sometimes known in the Jerusalem Talmud).

רַב פַּפָּא בַּר שְׁמוּאֵל Rav Pappa bar Shmuel. A Babylonian Amora of the third and fourth generations, Rav Pappa bar Shmuel studied with Rav Ḥisda and Rav Sheshet, and later engaged in Halakhic discussions with Abaye and Rava. Rav Pappa bar Shmuel lived in Pumbedita, where he was a Rabbinical judge. Indeed, the Gemara states elsewhere (*Sanhedrin* 17b) that Talmudic references to "the judges of Pumbedita" refer to Rav Pappa bar Shmuel. The Gemara also relates that Rav Pappa bar Shmuel instituted a new unit of measurement, which was used in the city of Papunya.

NOTES

it is not. Indeed, this is forbidden even if the buyer is informed that the merchandise is old; otherwise, it is obvious that deceiving people this way is forbidden (see *Ḥiddushim HaMeyuḥasim LeRitva*).

הַהוּא עַבְדָּא סָבָא A certain old slave. *Rashi* explains that the old man was a non-Jew who sold himself to a Jewish master. *Rashi* argues that the Gemara could not have been referring to a Jewish slave (i.e., a Jew who sold himself into slavery because of poverty; see Leviticus 25:39), because Jews were not sold into slavery after the destruction of the Temple. (Jewish slavery was only practiced while the Jubilee Year was observed, and observance of the Jubilee Year ceased with the destruction of the Temple.)

Rashba, however, claims that *Rashi*'s interpretation is impossible: If the old man was a non-Jewish slave, he could not have sold himself to a new master, since he still belonged to his previous master. Nor could the old man have been a non-Jewish slave who had already been emancipated, since such a person would be treated like any other Jew (according to the Halakhah, a non-Jewish slave automatically becomes a Jew once he is freed). Accordingly, *Rashba* explains that the old man was an ordinary non-Jew who wanted to sell himself to work for Rava or Rav Pappa bar Shmuel.

Ra'avad offers yet another explanation. According to him, the old man was a Jew. However, when he said, "Buy me," he did not mean "Buy me as a slave," but rather "Hire me for a long period of time" (i.e., three years or more), since being hired for such a long period is tantamount to being sold.

דַּאֲנָא קַשִּׁישׁ מֵאֲבוּךְ That I am older than your father. When Rav Pappa bar Shmuel heard this, he realized that it was inappropriate to ask the slave for a drink, since all elderly people deserve honor and respect (*Maharsha*).

צַדִּיק מִצָּרָה נֶחֱלָץ The righteous is delivered out of trouble. *Iyyun Ya'akov* explains that Rav Pappa bar Shmuel considered Rava "righteous" because he followed the Mishnah's teaching that "paupers should be members of one's household," and hence Rava was "delivered out of trouble."

HALAKHAH

יִהְיוּ עֲנִיִּים בְּנֵי בֵיתְךָ Let the poor be members of your household. "It is better to invite orphans and poor persons to join one's household, to avail oneself of their services and to support them, rather than to buy slaves for this purpose." (Ibid., *Yoreh De'ah* 251:6; see *Shakh* and *Taz* ad loc.)

Conclusion to Chapter Four

This chapter examines many of the fundamental principles governing the acquisition of movable property. According to the accepted view (that of Rabbi Yoḥanan), movables can be acquired by Torah law by paying for them. By Rabbinic decree, however, monetary payment cannot serve as an instrument of acquisition; consequently, even after payment is made, the object still belongs to the seller, and both parties may still retract. Movables can be acquired by drawing them into one's possession (*meshikhah*), after which neither party may retract and the buyer is obligated to pay for his purchase. Even though payment by itself cannot effect a binding sale, if one of the parties wishes to retract after payment has been made, the other party may demand that the courts pronounce a curse upon him. Moreover, there are times when even the violation of a mere verbal agreement is prohibited, so that one who reneges on such an agreement is labeled dishonest.

For a sale to be binding, *meshikhah* must be performed on the merchandise being bought, and not on the money used as payment. When two parties exchange coins, "money" is defined in relative terms, so that one type of coin is treated as the merchandise and the other as the money used as payment. Thus, coins minted from metals other than silver are considered "merchandise" in relation to silver coins, even though such coins are considered "money" vis-à-vis other objects.

This chapter also presents many of the laws regarding *ḥalifin* — the exchange of one article for another. According to the accepted view, coins cannot effect *ḥalifin*, nor can they be acquired through *ḥalifin*. Produce cannot effect *ḥalifin*, but can be acquired through *ḥalifin*. *Ḥalifin* can only be effected with a utensil that belongs to the buyer, even if the utensil is not worth a *perutah*.

The chapter continues with the laws pertaining to *ona'ah* — overcharging and underpaying. These laws apply to most types of property, but not to land, slaves, promissory notes or property consecrated to the Temple. If one overcharged or underpaid by less than one-sixth, the difference between the market price of the article and the price charged is waived. However, if one overcharged or underpaid by exactly one-sixth of what the merchandise is worth, the surcharge must be refunded, though the sale is not canceled. If one overcharged or underpaid by more than one-sixth, the sale is canceled completely if one of the parties so wishes. Likewise, if one overcharged or underpaid by even the slightest amount for something sold by weight, measure or number, the sale is canceled. Just as a seller is forbidden to overcharge for merchandise, so too is a buyer forbidden to underpay. However, the amount of time given to each party to cancel the sale varies, depending on which of the two parties was defrauded. The *ona'ah* laws apply not only to ordinary people, but even to professional merchants, despite the fact that they presumably know the worth of the merchandise they sell.

The last part of the chapter discusses "verbal wrongdoing," i.e., hurting other people's feelings, which is deemed a graver offense than monetary fraud, both because it cannot be rectified by monetary means, and because it is directed against one's person rather than one's property. Anyone who puts his fellow to shame is subject to divine retribution, and not to court-administered penalties. Anything that causes the listener distress is considered "verbal wrongdoing," whether it be an outright insult or rebuke, or merely a joke or facetious comment. While it is prohibited to insult anyone, this offense is particularly serious if the person offended was a convert, since the Torah added a special prohibition against wronging such a person. The chapter concludes by teaching that it is forbidden to mislead potential buyers by touching up the merchandise one sells, or otherwise misrepresenting it.

List of Sources

Agudah, Halakhic work by Rabbi Alexander Zuslin HaKohen, Germany (d. 1349).

Aḥaronim, lit., "the last," meaning Rabbinical authorities from the time of the publication of Rabbi Yosef Caro's code of Halakhah, the *Shulḥan Arukh* (1555).

Arukh HaShalem, Aramaic dictionary edited by Alexander Kohut (1894) on the basis of the *Arukh* by Rabbi Natan of Rome (11th century).

Arukh HaShulḥan, commentary on *Shulḥan Arukh* by Rabbi Yeḥiel Mikhel Epstein, Byelorussia (1829–1908).

Ba'al HaMa'or, Rabbi Zeraḥyah ben Yitzḥak HaLevi, Spain, 12th century. *HaMa'or*, Halakhic commentary on *Hilkhot HaRif.*

Baḥ (Bayit Ḥadash), commentary on *Tur* by Rabbi Yoel Sirkes, Poland (1561–1640).

Bertinoro, Ovadyah 15th-century Italian commentator on the Mishnah.

Birkat Shmuel, novellae on *Bava Metzia* by Rabbi Baruch Ber Leibowitz, Lithuania (1866–1939).

Ein Ya'akov, collection of Aggadot from the Babylonian Talmud by Rabbi Ya'akov ben Shlomo Ḥabib, Spain and Salonika (c. 1445–1515).

Ein Yehosef, novellae on *Bava Metzia* by Rabbi Yosef Ḥazan, Turkey (c. 1615–1700).

Ein Yitzḥak, Responsa by Rabbi Yitzḥak Elḥanan Spector, Lithuania (1817–1896).

Even HaEzer, section of *Shulḥan Arukh* dealing with marriage, divorce, and related topics.

Gra, Rabbi Eliyahu ben Shlomo Zalman (1720–1797), the Gaon of Vilna. Novellae on the Talmud and *Shulḥan Arukh.*

Ha'amek She'elah, commentary by Rabbi Naphtali Tzvi Yehudah Berlin, Volozhin, Lithuania (1817–1893) on *She'iltot* (by Rav Ahai Gaon, Babylonia, 8th century).

Halakhah LeMoshe, commentary by Rabbi Ḥayyim Moshe Amarilio on the fourth book of *Mishneh Torah, Sefer Nashim,* Salonika (1695–1748).

Ḥatam Sofer, responsa and novellae on the Talmud by Rabbi Moshe Sofer (Schreiber), Pressburg (1763–1839).

Ḥiddushim HaMeyuḥasim LeRitva, novellae on the Talmud by a Narbonnese pupil of Rabbi Shlomo of Montpellier, France, 13th century.

Ḥoshen Mishpat, section of *Shulḥan Arukh* dealing with civil and criminal law.

Imrei Zutrei, novellae on *Bava Metzia* by Rabbi Shmuel Shmelke of Przedborz, Poland, 19th century.

Kesef Mishneh, commentary on *Mishneh Torah* by Rabbi Yosef Caro, author of the *Shulḥan Arukh.*

Leḥem Abirim, novellae on the Talmud by Rabbi Avraham ben Azuz, Morocco, 16th century.

Magen Gibborim, novellae on the Talmud by Rabbi Eliezer DiAvilah, Morocco (1714–1761).

Maḥaneh Efraim, Responsa and novellae on *Mishneh Torah* by Rabbi Efraim ben Aharon Navon, Constantinople (1677–1735).

Maharam, Rabbi Meir of Lublin (1558–1616). Novellae on the Talmud.

Maharsha, Rabbi Shmuel Eliezer ben Yehudah HaLevi Edels, Poland (1555–1631). Novellae on the Talmud.

Maharshal, Rabbi Shlomo ben Yeḥiel Luria, Poland (1510–1573). Novellae on the Talmud.

Meiri, commentary on the Talmud (called *Bet HaBeḥirah*) by Rabbi Menaḥem ben Shlomo, Provence (1249–1316).

Mishḥat Aharon, novellae on the Talmud by Rabbi Aharon Zelig of Ostrog, Poland, 17th century.

Mordekhai, compendium of Halakhic decisions by Rabbi Mordekhai ben Hillel HaKohen, Germany (1240?–1298).

Nefesh Ḥayyah, novellae on *Bava Metzia* by Rabbi Moshe Betzalel Luria, Poland, 19th century.

Nimmukei Yosef, commentary on *Hilkhot HaRif* by Rabbi Yosef Ḥaviva, Spain, early 15th century.

Nishmat Adam, Halakhic decisions based on *Shulḥan Arukh, Ḥoshen Mishpat*, by Rabbi Avraham ben Yeḥiel Mikhel Danzig, Danzig and Vilna (1748–1820).

Pnei Moshe, commentary on the Jerusalem Talmud by Rabbi Moshe ben Shimon Margoliyot, Lithuania (c. 1710–1781).

Pnei Yehoshua, novellae on the Talmud by Rabbi Ya'akov Yehoshua Falk, Poland and Germany (1680–1756).

Ra'avad, Rabbi Avraham ben David, commentator and Halakhic authority. Wrote comments on the *Mishneh Torah*. Provence (c. 1125–1198?).

Rabbenu Ḥananel (ben Ḥushiel), commentator on the Talmud, North Africa (990–1055).

Rabbenu Nissim Gaon, Egypt, first half of 11th century. Talmudist.

Rabbenu Shlomo ben HaYatom, Italy, 11th–12th century. Commentator on the Talmud.

Rabbenu Tam, commentator on the Talmud, Tosafist, France (1100–1171).

Rabbenu Yehonatan, Yehonatan ben David HaKohen of Lunel, Provence, Talmudic scholar (c. 1135–after 1210).

Rabbi Aharon HaLevi, Spain, 13th century. Novellae on the Talmud.

Rabbi Ḥayyim of Brisk, Rabbi Ḥayyim Soloveichik of Brisk (1853–1918). Novellae on *Mishneh Torah*.

Rabbi Shlomo Molkho, Portugal and Eretz Israel (c. 1500–1532). Author of *Sefer HaMefo'ar*.

Rabbi Ya'akov Emden, Talmudist and Halakhic authority, Germany (1697–1776).

Rabbi Zvi Ḥayyot (Chajes), Galician Rabbi, 19th century.

Ramakh, Rabbi Meir HaKohen of Rothenburg, Germany (14th century). Author of *Hagahot Maimoniyot* (commentary on *Mishneh Torah*).

Rambam, Rabbi Moshe ben Maimon, Rabbi and philosopher, known also as Maimonides. Author of *Mishneh Torah*, Spain and Egypt (1135–1204).

Ramban, Rabbi Moshe ben Naḥman, commentator on Bible and Talmud, known also as Naḥmanides, Spain and Eretz Israel (1194–1270).

Ran, Rabbi Nissim ben Reuven Gerondi, Spanish Talmudist (1310?–1375?).

Rashash, Rabbi Shmuel ben Yosef Shtrashun, Lithuanian Talmud scholar (1794–1872).

Rashba, Rabbi Shlomo ben Avraham Adret, Spanish Rabbi famous for his commentaries on the Talmud and his responsa (c. 1235–c. 1314).

Rashbam, Rabbi Shmuel ben Meir, commentator on the Talmud (1085–1158).

Rashi, Rabbi Shlomo b. Yitzḥak, the paramount commentator on the Bible and the Talmud, France (1040–1105).

Rav Hai Gaon, Babylonian Rabbi, head of Pumbedita Yeshivah, 10th century.

Razah, Rabbi Zeraḥyah HaLevi, see *Ba'al HaMa'or*.

Rema, Rabbi Moshe ben Yisrael Isserles, Halakhic authority, Poland (1525 or 1530–1572).

Remah, novellae on the Talmud by Rabbi Meir HaLevi Abulafya, Spain (c. 1170–1244).

Ri, Rabbi Yitzḥak ben Shmuel of Dampierre, Tosafist, France (died c. 1185).

Ri Migash, Rabbi Yosef ben Migash, commentator on the Talmud, Spain (1077–1141).

Riaf, Rabbi Yoshiyah ben Yosef Pinto, Eretz Israel and Syria (1565–1648). Commentary on *Ein Ya'akov*.

Rid, see *Tosefot Rid*.

Rif, Rabbi Yitzḥak Alfasi, Halakhist, author of *Hilkhot HaRif*, North Africa (1013–1103).

Rishonim, lit., "the first," meaning Rabbinical authorities active between the end of the Geonic period (mid-11th century) and the publication of the *Shulḥan Arukh* (1555).

Ritva, novellae and commentary on the Talmud by Rabbi Yom Tov ben Avraham Ishbili, Spain (c. 1250–1330).

Ritzbash, Rabbi Tzemaḥ ben Sheshet, Algeria, 15th century. Responsa.

Rivan, Rabbi Yehudah ben Natan, French Tosafist, 11th–12th centuries.

Rosh, Rabbi Asher ben Yeḥiel, also known as Asheri, commentator and Halakhist, Germany and Spain (c. 1250–1327).

Sefer HaḤinnukh, anonymous work on the 613 Biblical precepts, 14th century.

Sefer Mikkaḥ U'Mimkar by *Rav Hai Gaon*. Treatise on the laws of commerce.

Shakh (Siftei Kohen), commentary on *Shulḥan Arukh* by Rabbi Shabbetai ben Meir HaKohen, Lithuania (1621–1662).

Shittah Mekubbetzet, a collection of commentaries on the Talmud by Rabbi Betzalel ben Avraham Ashkenazi of Safed (c. 1520–1591).

Shulḥan Arukh, code of Halakhah by Rabbi Yosef Caro, b. Spain, active in Eretz Israel (1488–1575).

Sma (Sefer Meirat Einayim), commentary on *Shulḥan Arukh, Ḥoshen Mishpat*, by Rabbi Yehoshua Falk Katz, Poland (c. 1550–1614).

Talmid Rabbenu Peretz, commentary on *Bava Metzia* by the school of the Tosafist Rabbi Peretz of Corbeil, France (13th century).

Talmidei Rabbenu Yonah, commentary on *Hilkhot HaRif*, by the school of Rabbi Yonah of Gerondi, Spain (c. 1190–1263).

Taz, abbreviation for *Turei Zahav*. See below, *Turei Zahav*.

Terumat HaDeshen, responsa and Halakhic decisions by Rabbi Yisrael Isserlin, Germany (15th century).

Torat Ḥayyim, novellae on the Talmud by Rabbi Avraham Ḥayyim Shor, Galicia (d. 1632).

Tosafot, a collection of commentaries and novellae on the Talmud, expanding on Rashi's commentary, by the French-German Tosafists (12th–13th centuries).

Tosefot Rid, commentary on the Talmud by Rabbi Yeshayahu ben Mali di Trani, Italian Halakhist (c. 1200–before 1260).

Tosefot Yom Tov, commentary on the Mishnah by Rabbi Yom Tov Lipman HaLevi Heller, Prague and Poland (1579–1654).

Tur, abbreviation of *Arba'ah Turim*, Halakhic code by Rabbi Ya'akov ben Asher, b. Germany, active in Spain (c. 1270–1343).

Turei Zahav, commentary on *Shulḥan Arukh*, by Rabbi David ben Shmuel HaLevi, Poland, (c.1586–1667).

Yoreh De'ah, section of *Shulḥan Arukh* dealing with dietary laws, interest, ritual purity, and mourning.